Interdisciplinary Perspectives on E–Collaboration:
Emerging Trends and Applications

Ned Kock
Texas A&M International University, USA

Information Science REFERENCE

INFORMATION SCIENCE REFERENCE

Hershey · New York

Director of Editorial Content:	Kristin Klinger
Director of Book Publications:	Julia Mosemann
Acquisitions Editor:	Lindsay Johnston
Development Editor:	Julia Mosemann
Publishing Assistant:	Sean Woznicki
Typesetter:	Deanna Zombro
Quality control:	Jamie Snavely
Cover Design:	Lisa Tosheff
Printed at:	Yurchak Printing Inc.

Published in the United States of America by
Information Science Reference (an imprint of IGI Global)
701 E. Chocolate Avenue
Hershey PA 17033
Tel: 717-533-8845
Fax: 717-533-8661
E-mail: cust@igi-global.com
Web site: http://www.igi-global.com/reference

Library of Congress Cataloging-in-Publication Data

Interdisciplinary perspectives on e-collaboration : emerging trends and applications / Ned Kock, editor.
    p. cm.

  Includes bibliographical references and index.
  Summary: "This book focuses on e-collaboration technologies that enable group-based interaction, and the impact that those technologies have on group work"--Provided by publisher.

  ISBN 978-1-61520-676-6 (hardcover) -- ISBN 978-1-61520-677-3 (ebook) 1.
Teams in the workplace. 2. Internet. I. Kock, Ned F., 1964-
  HD66.I56 2010
  658.4'02202854678--dc22
                    2009047177

British Cataloguing in Publication Data
A Cataloguing in Publication record for this book is available from the British Library.

Table of Contents

Section 2
Adaptation and Creativity in E-Collaboration

Detailed Table of Contents

Section 1
Emerging Issues and Debate

Can e-collaboration technologies help achieve world peace by supporting international trade? At first glance, this seems like an unusual and somewhat nonsensical question. The variables involved, particularly international trade and world peace, may appear to be too broad and socially complex to be meaningfully influenced by e-collaboration technologies. Also, the connection between these variables, if it exists, seems at best counterintuitive. Yet, there is empirical evidence that humans might have evolved what could be called a trading instinct, with the fitness-enhancing goal of either reducing or eliminating the likelihood of violent conflict between trading groups. This would explain why so many people seem compelled to engage in trade interactions, even when they do not need the goods or services that are being traded. This chapter argues that such trading instinct might have evolved, and if it did, that the evolution of the trading instinct happened in the context of face-to-face interactions. Therefore, the same instinct in modern humans would require e-collaboration media of high naturalness (i.e., high face-to-face similarity) to properly play its conflict reduction role. In this sense, e-collaboration media naturalness may act as a moderator of the effect that trade may have on the trading parties' predispositions to later engage in or support violent conflict, either with each other or with members of the trading parties' national groups.

The increasing availability of mobile devices in today's business contexts raises the demand to shift the focus of groupware framework design. Instead of solely focusing on functional requirements of specific application domains or device characteristics, non-functional requirements need to be taken into account as well. Flexibility concerning the integration of devices and tailorability of the framework according to different usage contexts is essential for addressing device heterogeneity. Besides flexibility, in order to support the development of real-world applications involving heterogeneous devices, robustness and scalability concerns have to be addressed explicitly by the framework.

Tharrenos Bratitsis, University of Western Macedonia, Greece
Angelique Dimitracopoulou, University of the Aegean, Greece

This chapter focuses on the explanatory and interpretation issues that arise when the integrated Interaction Analysis (IA) features are used by teachers – moderators. The importance of applying additional interpretative value to seemingly simple quantitative measurements is highlighted through several implemented case studies. The core objective of this chapter is to outline the importance of appropriate Interpretation of the IA indicators, thus enhancing collaboration in multiple levels.

Adriana S. Vivacqua, Federal University of Rio de Janeiro, Brazil
Jano Moreira de Souza, Federal University of Rio de Janeiro, Brazil

With the increase in information available, systems must be sensitive to users' attention foci, minimizing interruptions, helping focus and providing information according to current tasks. The authors of this chapter investigate ways to determine awareness foci through email-based user interaction analysis. The goal is to be able to draw inferences as to with whom and about what a user is collaborating, enabling a system to automatically distribute awareness information and adapt itself according to users' needs without much configuration.

Jesus Camacho, CICESE, Mexico
Leonardo Galicia, CICESE, Mexico
Victor M. Gonzalez, University of Manchester, UK
Jesus Favela, CICESE, Mexico

Many modern working environments are characterized by the need to manage multiple activities simultaneously. This is the case of hospital work, which also demands a high degree of mobility and collaboration among specialists. These working conditions have motivated the authors to design and implement mobileSJ, a mobile information management tool based on the concept of working spheres.

The tool allows users to gather information related to a working sphere, including documents, contacts and pending tasks. The tool assists users when switching between tasks, facilitates the sharing of activity related information with colleagues, as well as the synchronization of information among multiple devices, including handheld computers and public displays.

Section 2
Adaptation and Creativity in E-Collaboration

Athanasios Nikas, Athens University of Economics and Business, Greece
Angeliki Poulymenakou, Athens University of Economics and Business, Greece

This research applies contributions from the social sciences to examine how organisations adapt information systems in a project team setting. Its main concern is to study the set of events and actions implicated in the institutionalisation of an information system. The motivation for this research has been to address the following questions: why well designed information systems are so often not successfully adapted or used by organisations? How the adaptation process affects and is affected by work context characteristics? This research focuses on analyzing the adaptation process of a collaborative platform in a project team, in the context of the construction industry by applying adaptive structuration theory.

Eiko Yamamoto, National Institute of Information and Communications Technology, Japan
Hitoshi Isahara, National Institute of Information and Communications Technology, Japan

Creativity is required in many fields of endeavor — especially industry and scientific research. Creative tasks considered in this chapter include not only creative tasks by single individual or multiple individuals, but also collaborative tasks accomplished by a group of individuals with support of e-collaboration technologies. The difficulty of formulating new ideas calls for the development of an environment that supports creativity. Moreover, it is known that people tend to become more creative when they use words that are related thematically rather than taxonomically. In light of this, the authors sought to extract lists of words having a thematic relation. In this chapter, the authors propose a method of extracting such word lists and verify through Web retrieval that word lists with a thematic relation can support creativity.

Jane Fedorowicz, Bentley University, USA
Isidro Laso-Ballesteros, European Commission, Belgium
Antonio Padilla-Meléndez, University of Málaga, Spain

This chapter describes the challenges of supporting creativity and innovation through e-collaboration technologies and tools and proposes how future technologies and tools can help to mitigate issues arising from working virtually. The authors discuss how future advancements in communications and information sharing technologies will help to make virtual team location transparent, while improving access to common work processes and information repositories.

Chapter 9

Umer Farooq, Pennsylvania State University, USA
John M. Carroll, Pennsylvania State University, USA
Craig H. Ganoe, Pennsylvania State University, USA

This chapter investigates the design of tools to support everyday scientific creativity in distributed collaboration. Based on an exegesis of theoretical and empirical literature on creativity and group dynamics, the authors present and justify three requirements for supporting creativity: support for divergent and convergent thinking, development of shared objectives, and reflexivity.

Chapter 10

Pierre Hadaya, Université du Québec à Montréal, Canada
Robert Pellerin, École Polytechnique de Montréal, Canada

Based on the literature on the diffusion of innovations and on information systems, and building on emerging concepts in electronic collaboration (e-collaboration), this chapter analyses the influence of various determinants on manufacturing firms' intent to use Web-based interorganizational information systems (IOISs) to share inventory information with their key suppliers. This theoretical model is tested on data collected from 498 senior managers of Canadian manufacturing firms. The findings indicate that a manufacturing firm's organizational readiness, its past experience with e-commerce and its business relationships all affect its future use of Web-based IOISs to share inventory information with its key suppliers.

Chapter 11

Luc Cassivi, Université du Québec à Montréal, Canada
Pierre Hadaya, Université du Québec à Montréal, Canada
Elisabeth Lefebvre, École Polytechnique de Montréal, Canada
Louis A. Lefebvre, École Polytechnique de Montréal, Canada

This chapter focuses on the impact of strategic and tactical collaborative actions as well as e-collaboration tools efficiency on process and relational innovations which in turn should influence product innovations. The results of this study show that tactical collaborative actions are more geared to lead firms to innovate rather than strategic actions. Findings also suggest that relational innovation has an effect on product innovation for the upstream perspective, whilst process innovation influences product innovation for the downstream perspective.

    Angel L. Meroño-Cerdan, University of Murcia, Spain
    Pedro Soto-Acosta, University of Murcia, Spain
    Carolina Lopez-Nicolas, University of Murcia, Spain

This study seeks to assess the impact of collaborative technologies on innovation at the firm level. Collaborative technologies' influence on innovation is considered here as a multi-stage process that starts at adoption and extends to use. Thus, the effect of collaborative technologies on innovation is examined not only directly, the simple presence of collaborative technologies, but also based on actual collaborative technologies' use. Given the fact that firms can use this technology for different purposes, collaborative technologies' use is measured according to three orientations: e-information, e-communication and e-workflow. To achieve these objectives, a research model is developed for assessing, on the one hand, the impact of the adoption and use of collaborative technologies on innovation and, on the other hand, the relationship between adoption and use of collaborative technologies.

    Irma Becerra-Fernandez, Florida International University, USA
    Matha Del Alto, NASA Ames Research Center, USA
    Helen Stewart, NASA Ames Research Center, USA

Today, organizations rely on decision-makers to produce "mission critical" decisions that are based on inputs from multiple domains. The ideal decision-maker has a profound understanding of specific domains coupled with the experience that allows them to act quickly and decisively on the information. Daily they face problems and failures that are too difficult for any individual person to solve; therefore teams are now required who share their knowledge in spontaneous collaborations. Since requisite expertise may not all reside in the same organization, nor be geographically co-located, virtual networked teams are needed. This chapter presents a case study describing the development and use of Postdoc, the first Web-based collaborative and knowledge management platform deployed at NASA.

    Vicki L. Sauter, University of Missouri - St. Louis, USA

Today's technologies can support joint, but physically disparate work efforts. Some groups of professionals that could benefit from using these technologies do not adopt them, while others use the technologies frequently. This study provides an in-depth examination of how and when one organization accepted technology in their decision making efforts. The research examines actual usage of the technology rather than the less strong, but more common measure, intention to use technology. As a result, the chapter has helped bridge the gap between what people intend to do and what they actually do, thereby providing both a stronger theoretical basis for the TAM model and some insights into the evolution of the TAM model.

This chapter presents the results of an empirical study to examine the effectiveness of a computerized
negotiation support system (NSS) in supporting bargaining carried out in a dispersed, but synchronous
setting. In the study, pairs of college students, using the NSS, participated in a simulated industrial
bargaining scenario that tested the impact of communication media employed and level of conflict on
contract outcomes and negotiator attitudes. The subjects, located in separate rooms, played the roles
of buyer and seller engaged in negotiations either by telephone (audio-conferencing) or Lotus Notes
(computer conferencing). In both low and high conflict, the efficiency aspects of audio-conferencing
– a richer medium in which more communication can take place more quickly – overshadowed any
negative social cues transmitted.

Chapter 16

Using a case study approach to compare and contrast the cultures and knowledge management approaches of two organizations, the study suggests the ways in which organizational culture influences
knowledge management initiatives as well as the evolution of knowledge management in organizations.
Whereas in one organization, the KM effort became little more than an information repository, in the
second organization, the KM effort evolved into a highly collaborative system fostering the formation
of electronic communities.

Section 3
Advanced Conceptual and Theoretical Issues

Recent years have seen the growing use of virtual worlds such as Second Life and World of Warcraft
for entertainment and business purposes, and a rising interest from researchers in the impact that virtual
worlds can have on patterns of e-collaboration behavior and collaborative task outcomes. This chapter
looks into whether actual work can be accomplished in virtual worlds, whether virtual worlds can provide
the basis for trade (B2C and C2C e-commerce), and whether they can serve as a platform for credible

studies of e-collaboration behavior and related outcomes. The conclusion reached at is that virtual worlds hold great potential in each of these three areas, even though there are certainly pitfalls ahead.

This research examines the impact of computer-mediated communication, distributed communication, and knowledge of prior baseline behavior on an individual's propensity to make veracity judgments. Subjects were motivated to detect deception by participating in a Prisoner's Dilemma game with monetary rewards. Methodologies of other deception detection studies are compared and existing theoretical models are extended. This study found that more detection confidence can come from knowledge of a person's prior baseline behavior, being proximally located, the type of communication media used, and perceived relational closeness. These factors indirectly lead to less deception detection through more detection confidence and reliance on the truth bias, a fundamental belief in the truthfulness of others, even in a computer mediated environment.

Chapter 19

The Web's global reach provides evolutionary behavioral scientists unique opportunities to investigate human universals steeped in a common and evolved human nature. This chapter argues that many forms of online sexual communication are indicative of our evolved mating minds including the manner by which female escorts are "advertised" online. It is demonstrated that online advertisers provide a restricted set of morphological cues whilst advertising female escorts, these being congruent with men's evolved aesthetic preferences. Specifically, it is shown that irrespective of cultural setting, online escorts advertise waist-to-hip ratios (WHR) that are in line with the near-universal male preference for women that possess WHRs of 0.70.

Chapter 20

Central to the design of successful virtual learning initiatives is the matching of technology to the needs of the training environment. The difficulty is that while the technology may be designed to complement and support the learning process, not all users of these systems find the technology supportive. Instead, some users' conceptions of learning, or epistemological beliefs may be in conflict with their perceptions of what the technology supports. Using data from 307 individuals, this research study investigated the process and outcome losses that occur when friction exists between individuals' epistemological beliefs and their perceptions of how the technology supports learning. Specifically, the results indicated that when there was friction between the technology support of learning and an individual's epistemological beliefs course communication, course satisfaction, and course performance were reduced. Implications for design of virtual learning environments and future research are discussed.

Chapter 21

This chapter reports on a study that investigates the knowledge transfer between an information systems/technology (IT) department and non-IT departments during information technology projects. More specifically, the authors look into the link between the knowledge management capabilities of the IT department and the effectiveness and efficiency of the knowledge transfer to a client department. Knowledge management capabilities are defined by Gold et al. (2001) as the combination of knowledge infrastructure capabilities (structural, technical, and cultural) and knowledge processes capabilities (acquisition, conversion, application, and protection). Data collected through a web-based survey result in 127 usable questionnaires completed by managers in large Canadian organizations. Data analysis performed using PLS indicates that knowledge infrastructure capabilities are related to the knowledge transfer success, and more specifically to its effectiveness whereas knowledge processes capabilities are only related to the efficiency of such transfer.

Preface

This book focuses on e-collaboration technologies that enable group-based interaction, and the impact that those e-collaboration technologies have on groups. The term e-collaboration is being used here as an umbrella term that comprises several other closely related fields, commonly known as computer-mediated communication, computer-supported cooperative work, groupware, group support systems, and collaboration technologies. Within this scope, this book addresses a range of e-collaboration topics, with emphasis on two broad areas: (a) interdisciplinary perspectives on e-collaboration, a theme that permeates the entire book; and (b) adaptation and creativity in e-collaboration, which is addressed in a targeted fashion by several of the chapters.

The explosion in the use of e-collaboration technologies in organizations and society in general is a relatively recent phenomenon. The idea that successful group collaboration is important for organizational performance was quite well established already in the mid 1900s, during the post World War II period. Technologies were indeed available to support e-collaboration in that period, mostly in the form of mainframe-based systems. However, the use of e-collaboration tools to support group work in organizations was slow to catch up, mainly because the cost of computer technologies was too high for those technologies to be used by anyone other than specialized personnel (often called the "computer folks") working in central information processing departments.

This situation has of course changed substantially over time, especially after the 1980s, when there was an explosion in the use of computer networks, and when computer equipment became relatively cheap. This allowed for the provision in organizations of increasingly decentralized access to computer and information resources. Central information processing departments gradually lost their monopoly on computer and information resources, and many central information processing departments were dissolved and replaced by information technology support departments.

Loss of monopoly on information by centralized departments was soon followed by another business trend. This new trend was the increasing involvement of computer experts in highly successful entrepreneurial endeavors, which led many of the previously called nerdy types to become extremely wealthy and assume different organizational titles, such as president and chief executive officer (CEO). Two examples are Steve Jobs at Apple, and Bill Gates at Microsoft. Many others exist.

With the explosive growth of the Internet and the Web in the 1990s, most computers became interconnected, which led some to see the computer as less of an autonomous processing unit than an entry point to a vast pool of network-based resources. The increasing use of e-collaboration technologies that this enabled led to many possibilities, of which one of the most exciting has been the ability to conduct collaborative tasks with individuals interacting at different times (i.e., in an asynchronous manner) and from different places (e.g., different cities or countries).

E-collaboration's success attracted attention from researchers, and an increasing number of them shifted their attention to the study of e-collaboration phenomena. New publication outlets for research on e-collaboration were started, including the *International Journal of e-Collaboration* and the Book Series that comprises this volume.

This book, the fourth in the Advances in E-Collaboration Book Series, is organized in three main sections – Section I: Emerging Issues and Debate; Section II: Adaptation and Creativity in E-Collaboration; and Section III: Advanced Conceptual and Theoretical Issues. Each section contains several chapters written by experts. In Section I a range of emerging e-collaboration topics are discussed, setting the stage for the next section, which is the core section of the book. That core section then explores in more detail the topics of adaptation and creativity in e-collaboration; that is, how individuals and groups adapt their behavior in order to improve their e-collaboration performance, and how individuals and groups explore creative ideas employing e-collaboration technologies. The third and final section discusses advanced conceptual and theoretical issues related to the topics covered in the previous sections.

Most of the chapters in this book are original or revised versions of selected articles published in the *International Journal of e-Collaboration*. I have had the pleasure and honor of serving as Founding Editor-in-Chief of that Journal since its first issue was published in 2005.

The contributing authors are among the most accomplished researchers in the world today in the areas of interdisciplinary e-collaboration research, and adaptation and creativity in e-collaboration. I am most grateful for their contributions to the *International Journal of e-Collaboration* and to this book, which has been a great pleasure to edit together my colleagues at IGI Global.

One attractive aspect of this book is the nice blend of conceptual, theoretical and applied chapters found here. This blend makes me confident that the book will serve both academics and practitioners very well. I hope that this book will stimulate further research interdisciplinary e-collaboration research, adaptation and creativity in e-collaboration, and related topics. It is also my hope that this book will serve as a valuable source of ideas for managers involved in projects that rely heavily on e-collaboration technologies.

Ned Kock, Editor
Texas A&M International University

Acknowledgment

No book project can be completed successfully without the support of a dedicated editorial team. I would like to thank the team at IGI Global for that. Special thanks go to Mehdi Khosrow-Pour, Jan Travers, and Kristin Klinger. Many thanks are also due to Heather Probst, Julia Bonner, and their journal editorial team for their support in the development of several issues of the *International Journal of e-Collaboration*. Since most of the chapters in this book are revised versions of articles previously published in that journal, many of the chapters published here would not exist without Heather's and Julia's excellent support.

I thank Texas A&M International University for their institution support. Special recognition in that respect is due to Ray Keck, the University's President; and Pablo Arenaz, our new Provost. Many thanks go to the Sanchez Family Foundation for its unwavering support of the University and its A.R. Sanchez, Jr. School of Business. Thanks are also due to the great group of colleagues with whom I have been sharing the third floor of Pellegrino Hall on the University's beautiful campus. They make up the Division of International Business and Technology Studies, which I have had the pleasure to serve in the capacity of Founding Chair. My special thanks go to Cindy Martinez, for her excellent support of the Division.

Last, but most important of all, I would like to thank my family for their love and support. This book is dedicated to them.

Ned Kock

Section 1
Emerging Issues and Debate

Chapter 1
Achieving World Peace through International Trade:
Can E-Collaboration Technologies Help Make this Happen?

Ned Kock
Texas A&M International University, USA

ABSTRACT

Can e-collaboration technologies help achieve world peace by supporting international trade? At first glance, this seems like an unusual and somewhat nonsensical question. The variables involved, particularly international trade and world peace, may appear to be too broad and socially complex to be meaningfully influenced by e-collaboration technologies. Also, the connection between these variables, if it exists, seems at best counterintuitive. Yet, there is empirical evidence that humans might have evolved what could be called a trading instinct, with the fitness-enhancing goal of either reducing or eliminating the likelihood of violent conflict between trading groups. This would explain why so many people seem compelled to engage in trade interactions, even when they do not need the goods or services that are being traded. This chapter argues that such trading instinct might have evolved, and if it did, that the evolution of the trading instinct happened in the context of face-to-face interactions. Therefore, the same instinct in modern humans would require e-collaboration media of high naturalness (i.e., high face-to-face similarity) to properly play its conflict reduction role. In this sense, e-collaboration media naturalness may act as a moderator of the effect that trade may have on the trading parties' predispositions to later engage in or support violent conflict, either with each other or with members of the trading parties' national groups.

INTRODUCTION

Anthropological evidence suggests that the human species has evolved what could be called a "trading

instinct" over many of years of Darwinian adaptation, where trade acts as a social catalyst and thus as a suppressor of violent conflict among trading groups. Yet, the geographical and cultural separation between modern groups engaged in international trade makes it difficult for the trading instinct to

DOI: 10.4018/978-1-61520-676-6.ch001

achieve its evolutionarily adaptive goal. The trading instinct notion implies that trade has social as well as utilitarian purposes. The social purposes include building alliances and curbing violence among trading groups.

Without enough natural, or face-to-face-like, human interaction it is unlikely that the trading instinct will achieve its conflict reduction and other social purposes; even though it may achieve its main utilitarian purpose, namely the economically beneficial international exchange of needed goods or services. The more face-to-face-like a communication medium is the higher is its degree of naturalness. Therefore non-face-to-face international trade interactions may benefit the least from its potential social benefits.

This is arguably a problematic state of affairs, since it appears that the greatest potential for conflict in modern society is between groups that are located in different countries and that have markedly different cultures. It is argued in this chapter that e-collaboration tools that increase the naturalness of electronic trade interactions can play the role of enablers of international trade. As such they can go some way toward solving this problem, and perhaps contribute to world peace. In other words, the argument made here is that individuals who trade through natural electronic media (perhaps media that allow them to interact in a face-to-face-like manner), may be less inclined to engage in violent conflict with one another. As more and more individuals participated in this type of interactions, a national climate would be created that would be less conducive to support for wars between countries. If individual members of a nation A have a favorable predisposition toward individuals in another nation B, it is likely that they will not be inclined to support belligerent actions by the government of nation A (or groups that represent nation A) against nation B.

THE UTILITARIAN VIEW OF INTERNATIONAL TRADE

International trade is more often than not viewed from a utilitarian perspective. One group of individuals, who make up a nation, owns a good or service that is either needed or desired by some other group of individuals in a different nation. The result is trade between the two national groups in one of its many forms, including: the exchange of goods or services for other goods or services, known as bartering; and the more typical exchange of goods or services for cash or a promise of future cash payment, which is the most typical instance of trade.

The utilitarian view of international trade essentially is that trade is necessary so that individuals or groups can acquire goods and services that they are not capable of efficiently producing themselves. This view is indeed consistent with the historic view of trade among nations, and the tremendous growth in international trade that occurred since the 19th century. Arguably that growth has been largely motivated by the notion that certain nations are more efficient producers of specific goods than others. When a nation is a more efficient producer of a certain class of goods (e.g., a type of metal used in manufacturing) than another nation, then trade of that class of goods benefits both nations.

Several theoretical models of international trade have been proposed that are closely related to the utilitarian view. One of these theoretical models is the Ricardian model of international trade, named after the English stockbroker and economist David Ricardo (see Figure 1). Ricardo is seen by many as the creator of the first conceptual frameworks for the systematic study of economics. Along with notable classical economics scholars such as Adam Smith and Thomas Malthus, he was one of the most influential thinkers during the phase that was marked by a major shift in the understanding of economics. The shift was from the ruler's (e.g., the king's) interests to

Figure 1. David Ricardo

class-based interests. This new way of thinking about economics saw the wealth of a country as more strongly tied to the sum of all individual incomes in the country, and less so to the king's personal wealth.

Ricardo's trade ideas were strongly influenced by the work of several predecessors, notably Adam Smith's treatise on the wealth of nations (Smith, 1776). Ricardo hypothesized that countries would fully specialize in the production of certain goods, instead of producing a wide array of goods, and that their areas of specialization would depend on factor endowments (e.g., abundance of certain minerals, rich agricultural soil). For example, countries rich in certain metals would specialize in the production of goods that rely on those metals.

Yet, there are many instances in which international trade happens regardless of need, or in a non-utilitarian manner. Nowhere does this seem more evident than in the modern electronic marketplaces. Good examples here are the electronic marketplaces created by companies such as eBay, which allow individuals and organizations to buy goods and services around the world. eBay was founded in 1995 by Pierre Omidyar and is undoubtedly one of the most successful electronic trading companies in the world.

The following story has become part of eBay's lore, and illustrates the above point. The first item sold on eBay through an electronic auction was a broken laser pointer, for a little less than $15. Surprised, eBay's founder Omidyar contacted the buyer and asked why someone would want to buy a laser pointer that was broken. The answer provided by the buyer was that someone may want to collect broken laser pointers.

Perhaps there are other, deeper reasons why people trade goods and services. This may sound counterintuitive, but there is some evidence from the field of evolutionary psychology that human beings may have what we could call a "trading instinct." That is, human beings in general may have an innate compulsion to engage in trade; a compulsion that is influenced by our genetic makeup and that has been endowed on us by evolution through natural selection.

The field of evolutionary psychology is concerned with the study of genetically influenced instincts that were adaptive in our evolutionary past (Barkow et al., 1992; Buss, 1999). Those instincts may or may not play a positive role in our lives today. For example, our craving for foods with high calorie content today is believed to be an instinct motivated by the scarcity of those foods in our ancestral past.

EVOLUTIONARY PSYCHOLOGICAL EXPLANATIONS OF BEHAVIOR

Before we proceed further with the argument that modern humans posses an evolved trading instinct, let us take a look at how evolutionary psychological explanations of behavior can be developed. These types of explanations can address a wide range of behavioral patterns found in modern humans, including behavior toward technology.

Evolutionary psychology builds on the modern synthesis of Charles Darwin's (1859; 1871) theory of evolution of species by selection; which comprises evolution by natural (or environmental) selection in general (Darwin, 1859), as well as in response to the more specific evolutionary force of sexual selection (Darwin, 1871). Evolutionary psychology applies notions from the modern synthesis to the understanding of the evolution of the human brain and the complex set of brain modules that regulate human behavior.

Renewed interest in evolutionary explanations of human behavior, particularly since the mid-1990s, may suggest that Darwin's theory has been somehow rediscovered by modern researchers. This is incorrect. Researchers interested in evolutionary theories that can be used for information systems theorizing should be aware that there has been steady progress over the years in the expansion and refinement of the original theory of evolution. Much of that progress has been made by researchers who resorted to mathematical formalizations of evolutionary phenomena building on fundamentals of genetics (Hartl & Clark, 2007), and who published their conclusions primarily in peer-reviewed academic journals. By and large those conclusions have been hidden from the popular literature for many years, and have been partially disseminated through the efforts of bestselling authors such as Dawkins (1990), Miller (2000) and Pinker (2002).

Past research has rarely employed evolutionary psychological explanations and predictions regarding human behavior for the understanding of human-technology interaction phenomena. Interest in this line of research has been increasing since the early 2000s. There have been few studies building on human evolution ideas, and to some extent on evolutionary psychological ideas, in the areas of electronic consumer behavior (Hantula et al., 2008; Rajala and Hantula, 2000; Smith and Hantula, 2003), computer-mediated communication (Kock, 2004; 2005; Kock et al., 2008), virtual team leadership (DeRosa et al., 2004), electronic user interface design (Hubona and Shirah, 2006), online mate selection (Saad, 2008), and information search and use behavior (Spink and Cole, 2006).

A simple example can be used to illustrate how a psychological trait could have evolved in our evolutionary past by natural selection. First the trait in question would have to be associated with a genotype, which was a set of interrelated genes (Boaz & Almquist, 2001; Hartl & Clark, 2007; Maynard Smith, 1998) that influenced the formation of the psychological trait. An example of psychological trait would be "attention to colors". Individuals possessing this trait would have an instinctive response to objects displaying colors other than black and white, paying more attention to them. Individuals not possessing this trait would pay no particular attention to those objects.

Like most gene-trait relationships, the relationship between genotype and psychological trait was moderated by the ancient development environment. The term "environment" is used here broadly; generally meaning all factors that were not genetic in nature, such as social, nutritional, climatic, and other related factors. The ancient development environment was the environment surrounding our hominid ancestors in their formative years; that is, while they developed from fertilized egg stage to reproductive maturity. For example, if a mother's milk was very low in certain nutrients proper development of color vision could have been impaired. Even in the presence of the required genotype, that impairment could make attention to colors impossible due to color blindness.

The psychological trait related to heightened attention to colors influenced the performance of an individual that possessed the trait in an ancient task such as hunting or foraging. For example, let us assume performance associated with the task of foraging for nutritious fruits. In this case, individuals who paid special attention to colors would generally have higher performance than individuals who did not, because colors are indicative of the presence of important nutrients in fruits (Boaz & Almquist, 2001; Cartwright, 2000).

Individuals who were more successful at the task of foraging for nutritious fruits would also be more resistant to disease, and thus would survive in higher quantities. Since one must be alive to procreate and care for offspring, those individuals would also have higher "fitness". In population genetics (Hartl & Clark, 2007; Maynard Smith, 1998), the term fitness (usually indicated as W) generally refers to the success with which an individual's genes are passed on to successive generations. It is usually measured through the number of surviving offspring or grand-offspring of an individual.

The process above, repeated generation after generation, would lead the genotype and the related psychological trait to spread from one single individual to the vast majority of our ancestors. This process is what is generally referred to as evolution by natural selection.

The same genotype and related psychological trait that evolved in our evolutionary past can have an impact in the context of modern behavior toward technology, often affecting modern task performance in tasks where technology is used. However, that would not normally be related to survival success or fitness among modern humans, because modern humans are no longer subject to the same selection pressures that our ancestors faced in our evolutionary past.

For example, the psychological trait "attention to colors" could affect the performance of individuals in information search tasks using computer interfaces that employ various colors, compared with interfaces that used no colors other than black and white. In a modern task such as searching for information using a computer interface, individuals who possess this evolved psychological trait would have better performance with a color-enabled computer interface than with a computer interface that displays only black and white objects. Yet, this psychological trait would have no impact on the survival success or fitness of modern humans.

THE EVOLUTIONARY VIEW OF TRADE

Meg Whitman, the longtime Chief Executive Officer of eBay, has said many times that trading is in the human DNA. This statement has been often given in response to questions related to the utilitarian view of trade. According to the utilitarian view of trade, there is always the possibility that trade may reach a saturation point or even go down, as people acquire everything that they possibly need for utilitarian purposes.

However, if trade is at least in part genetically induced, then human beings will keep on trading regardless of their need for certain goods of services. This assumption, if correct, certainly bodes well for companies that earn revenue by intermediating trades. And eBay is one of the world leaders in this area.

If the propensity to trade is an instinct that is somehow genetically influenced, one would expect it to be a human universal. That is, one would expect trade to occur in all cultures, not only in one or two. If a variety of different cultures engage in trade, then it is less likely that trade is a cultural artifact, which opens the door for the conclusion that trade is indeed influenced by an instinct related to an evolved genotype.

A look at different cultures today allows us to reach the same conclusion that Murdock (1958) reached almost 50 years ago in a compilation of 67 human universals, which is that trade is found in every culture in the world. This is true regardless of the apparent level of development of the culture. Trade is present in cultures perceived as primitive as well as in cultures perceived as highly advanced.

So, if we have a trading instinct, why is it that such instinct evolved and became part of our genetic inheritance? Or, in other worlds, why has the evolution of a trading instinct been adaptive in our evolutionary past? Since the fossil record provides limited evidence to answer these questions, one must resort to the study of so-called primitive cultures to understand the possible advantage of trade from a reproductive fitness perspective.

Cultures that are perceived as primitive, such as hunter-gatherer indigenous cultures in the Amazon, are likely to have a lifestyle that is in certain aspects similar to that of our hominid ancestors. So, if trade enhances the reproductive fitness of the individuals that engage in it – that is, their ability to pass on their genes to the next generation – than a study of such hunter-gatherer cultures should shed some light on why this should be so.

One of the most compelling and enlightening long-term studies of non-urban cultures is that conducted by Napoleon A. Chagnon (see Figure 2) of the Yanomami (a.k.a. the Yanomamo), a native group inhabiting a portion of the Amazonian jungle on the border of Venezuela and Brazil. Chagnon's (1977) portrayal of the Yanomami as a fierce and violent people contradicted the view of the noble savage that was popular among anthropologists at the time. While that portrayal led to much criticism from established contemporary anthropologists, it is now widely accepted, especially among evolutionary psychologists, as a major contribution to the understanding of human nature.

Even at the time it was published, Chagnon's portrayal was consistent with the early work of several evolutionary biologists, paleo-anthropologists and primatologists. It is remarkably consistently with the more recent work by evolutionary psychologists, suggesting that human beings are likely to be violent by nature. The following quote illustrates Chagnon's portrayal of the Yanomami.

The thing that impressed me most was the importance of aggression in their culture. I had the opportunity to witness a good many incidents that expressed individual vindictiveness on the one hand and collective bellicosity on the other. These ranged in seriousness from the ordinary incidents of wife beating and chest pounding to dueling and organized raiding by parties that set out with

Figure 2. Napoleon Chagnon with the Yanomami

the intention of ambushing and killing men from enemy villages (Chagnon; 1977, p. 2).

The Yanomami's propensity toward violence against members of different villages provides the basis on which we can understand the role of trade from an evolutionary perspective. Violence generally leads to a decrease in reproductive fitness among those involved. For example, violent interactions would likely lead to a certain percentage of deaths among those involved (both winners and losers), and thus a decrease in the probability that the individuals involved would pass on their genes to the next generation. Here Chagnon's insightful ethnographic study of the Yanomami highlights the role that trade likely had in reducing violence among members of trading villages.

Each village has one of more special products that it provides to its allies. These include such items as dogs, hallucinogenic drugs (both cultivated and collected), arrow points, arrow shafts, bows, cotton yarn, cotton and vine hammocks, baskets of several varieties, clay pots, and, in the case of several contacted villages, steel tools and aluminum pots. This specialization in production cannot be explained in terms of the distribution of natural resources ... The explanation of specialization must be sought, rather, in the sociological aspects of alliance formation. Trade functions as a social catalyst ... (Chagnon, 1977, p. 100).

The most interesting part of the quote above, for the purposes of the discussion presented here, is that "... [the] specialization in production cannot be explained in terms of the distribution of natural resources ..." That is, trade among the Yanomami was not carried out for utilitarian reasons, as villages that were self-sufficient still engaged in trade to acquire goods that they could produce themselves. Yet, trade seemed to lead to alliances and thus a decrease in the likelihood that trading partners would commit violence against one other. It also seemed to increase the likelihood that trading partners would support each other in case of potential violent conflict with third parties, which could act as a deterrent to violent conflict.

A simple set of predictions that follow from the discussion above can be summarized in this way. Our hominid ancestors developed an instinct that fostered a propensity to engage in trade. Trade among groups of hominids fostered the creation of alliances and therefore decreased the likelihood of fitness-impairing violence. This type of violence decreases one's reproductive capacity, even among the members of the group that is perceived as being the winner. One example is group violence that results in the death of one of more individuals among winners and losers. The genes that influenced the trading instinct have spread throughout the entire species, and can be observed today in the behavior of buyers and sellers. Examples of such behavior are non-utilitarian trades through electronic marketplaces like eBay.

INTERNATIONAL TRADE AND E-COLLABORATION

The discussion above suggests that a trading instinct might well have been evolved through Darwinian evolutionary processes as catalysts for social interactions. Those social interactions ultimately increased the reproductive fitness of the participants, thus spreading the genes that influenced the trading instinct throughout the human species.

Yet, the social interactions of our hominid ancestors were mostly face-to-face. In fact, there is evidence that during over 99 percent of our hominid evolution cycle, we have communicated primarily face-to-face (Kock, 2005; Kock & Hantula, 2005). Therefore, one can expect that some disruption of the beneficial effects of the trading instinct, such as those leading to alliance formation and reduction in the propensity toward violence, will result from trade exchanges being carried out without any face-to-face interaction.

Of course, the above may not affect most people's propensity to trade, since the trading instinct will still exist. Nevertheless, lack of face-to-face interaction may prevent some of the social interaction benefits from being experienced in international trade situations. The large geographical distances between international trading partners typically prevent face-to-face interaction from happening. Without face-to-face interaction, trade may still take place, but with diminished social interaction benefits.

Here is where e-collaboration tools can potentially play an important role by supporting quasi-natural interaction among buyers and sellers located in different countries. This is especially true of e-collaboration tools that enable face-to-face-like interaction, such as the widely publicized virtual reality environment called Second Life, developed by the San Francisco-based company Linden Research, Inc. In Second Life, individuals can create virtual versions of themselves (called avatars; see Figure 3), interact and collaborate with each other, and trade in virtual dollars. The virtual dollars are exchangeable for actual currency; U.S. dollars only, at the time of writing.

The above discussion suggests that trade may be a form of social grooming (see, e.g., Dunbar, 1996). Therefore media naturalness theory (Kock, 2005), which essentially argues that human beings have a brain designed to communicate primarily face-to-face, leads to the conclusion that the use of communication media with a high degree of naturalness may contribute to the social grooming effect of trade.

According to media naturalness theory different media present different levels of an attribute called naturalness. The level of naturalness of an electronic communication medium is presented as correlated with the degree of similarity between the electronic medium and the face-to-face medium. Key elements inherent in face-to-face communication are synchronicity (i.e., same-time interaction), physical co-location, the ability to convey and listen to speech, the ability to employ and observe facial expressions, and the ability to employ and observe body language during communication interactions (Kock, 2005).

An electronic trade web site that supported text-based chat-like interaction between sellers and buyers would be preferable, in that respect, to a site that enabled only asynchronous e-mail-like interaction. A site supporting audio-conferencing interaction would be preferable to one supporting only text-based chat-like interaction. A site supporting video-conferencing interaction would be preferable to one supporting only audio-conferencing interaction, and so on.

ACHIEVING WORLD PEACE THROUGH TRADE AND E-COLLABORATION

The argument put forth here is made up of four main parts. The first is that human beings have evolved a trading instinct through Darwinian processes, with

Figure 3. A journalist and his avatar in Second Life

trade operating as a social interaction catalyst that decreased the chance of conflict between trading groups. The second part of the argument is that the naturalness of the communication medium through which trade takes place is related to the degree of effectiveness of the trading instinct to operate as a social catalyst. That is, trade is more likely to be a social catalyst and conflict suppressor if it is carried out through a communication medium of high naturalness.

In the absence of a medium of high naturalness, trade may effectively fulfill a utilitarian role. However, it may not play the desirable social catalyst and conflict suppression roles that it has been originally designed by human evolution to play. This sets the stage for the third part of the argument put forth here, which is that international trade is more likely to rely on media of low naturalness to take place than local trade. This is primarily because of the geographic distance separating buyers and sellers engaged in international trade interactions, and the fact that currently most of these interactions rely on text-based asynchronous electronic communication tools. Examples of those tools are e-mail, text-based interaction media provided by trade intermediaries, and electronic data interchange systems; the latter are also known as EDI.

Low medium naturalness is not the only obstacle to the fulfillment of the trading instinct's social goals. The widespread use of wholesale trade can also create similar obstacles. This is especially the case in wholesale trade conducted by profit-seeking organizations on behalf of individuals, instead of retail trade conducted by the individuals themselves. The reason is that wholesale sale requires significantly less one-on-one human interaction to be accomplished than retail trade. Incidentally, wholesale trade is significantly more common in international trade than is retail trade, with the possible exception of trade in border towns.

Arguably the above situation is a problematic one, especially when we look at recent news in connection with international conflict. Judging from recent events, it seems that the greatest potential for conflict in modern society is between groups that are raised and educated in different countries, civil wars notwithstanding. Not only are groups raised and educated in different countries normally geographically apart, but also often separated by deep cultural disparities. This opens the door for the fourth and final part of the argument advanced here, which is that e-collaboration tools with high levels of naturalness can support the type of rich trade interaction that enable the trading instinct to have its evolutionarily adaptive positive social impact.

Theoretical propositions can be developed incorporating the predictions of each of the four parts of the argument discussed above. Those theoretical propositions could be depicted as a causal model. In its simplest form, the model would contain two causal propositions, or propositions that connect pairs of independent and dependent variables (see Figure 4). Proposition P1 predicts that the degree of international trade will be positively related to the degree of world peace observed. Proposition P2 is that the degree of e-collaboration media naturalness through which international trade takes place positively moderates the relationship between international trade and world peace.

As pointed out by Popper (1992), no theoretical model is of much value if it cannot be falsified.

Figure 4. Key theoretical propositions

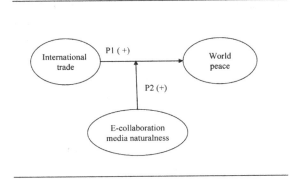

And how can the model depicted in Figure 4 be tested and thus falsified? At first glance, the wide encompassing nature of the model makes it virtually impossible to falsify. However, that assumption proves to be wrong when we look into the testability of the fundamental predictions of the model. Those fundamental predictions can be tested in field investigations of countries that engage in different levels of trade using various e-collaboration media, and even in semi-controlled experimental studies.

One possible and realistic test of the model would entail the following. Several countries could set up shop in two virtual reality environments, one with a high degree of naturalness and one with a low degree of naturalness, and let their virtual citizens engage in actual retail trade. The virtual reality environment with a high degree of naturalness could be Second Life. The virtual reality environment with a low degree of naturalness could be one in which buyers and sellers would interact primarily electronically through text and in an asynchronous manner.

Data would then be collected from the citizens of the various countries that actually traded among themselves, before and after the trading interactions occurred. The data would be primarily about the citizens' propensity to engage in conflict with those citizens of other countries with which they traded. If propensity to engage in conflict were significantly higher for before trade than for after trade data, then one could conclude that the data supported proposition P1. If that was not the case, the data would be seen as contradicting P1, and thus falsifying the theoretical model.

If propensity to engage in conflict were significantly higher in the high degree of naturalness than in the low degree of naturalness environment, for after trade data, then one could conclude that the data supported proposition P2. That is, proposition P2 would be tested as an interaction effect between degree of e-collaboration media naturalness and international trade, where the degree of naturalness is expected to positively moderate the effect of international trade on world peace.

As can be inferred from the discussion above, the type of research that would validate the theoretical model proposed here would be probably costly and difficult to implement. Nevertheless, given the high stakes associated with the underlying phenomenon, conducting research on this issue is arguably a must. World peace is not only desirable; the alternative is likely to be disastrous for the human species as a whole. Perhaps we can use knowledge about survival in our ancient past to save lives today, even though the environments that our hominid ancestors were much different than the ones created by modern societies.

ACKNOWLEDGMENT

This chapter is adapted from an article previously published in the *International Journal of e-Collaboration*. The author would like to thank the following individuals for comments and suggestions on a previous version of this chapter: Napoleon Chagnon, Vanessa Garza, Jaime Ortiz, and Ronaldo Parente. Publicly available images from the following Web sites have been used as a basis for this chapter: www.eumed.net, news. boisestate.edu, www.gawker.com, as well as the Web sites maintained by Google and Wikipedia.

All errors and omissions are the sole responsibility of the author.

REFERENCES

Barkow, J. H., Cosmides, L., & Tooby, J. (Eds.). (1992). *The adapted mind: Evolutionary psychology and the generation of culture*. New York: Oxford University Press.

Boaz, N. T., & Almquist, A. J. (2001). *Biological anthropology: A synthetic approach to human evolution*. Upper Saddle River, NJ: Prentice Hall.

Buss, D. M. (1999). *Evolutionary psychology: The new science of the mind*. Needham Heights, MA: Allyn & Bacon.

Cartwright, J. (2000). *Evolution and human behavior: Darwinian perspectives on human nature*. Cambridge, MA: The MIT Press.

Chagnon, N. A. (1977). *Yanomamo: The fierce people*. New York: Holt, Rinehart and Winston.

Darwin, C. R. (1859). On the origin of species by means of natural selection. Cambridge, MA: Harvard University Press. (Facsimile of the first edition, reprinted in 1966).

Darwin, C. R. (1871). *The descent of man, and selection in relation to sex*. London, England: John Murray.

Dawkins, R. (1990). *The selfish gene*. Oxford, UK: Oxford University Press.

DeRosa, D. M., Hantula, D. A., Kock, N., & D'Arcy, J. P. (2004). Communication, trust, and leadership in virtual teams: A media naturalness perspective. *Human Resource Management Journal, 34*(2), 219–232.

Dunbar, R. I. M. (1996). *Grooming, gossip and the evolution of language*. London, England: Faber & Faber.

Hantula, D. A., Brockman, D. D., & Smith, C. L. (2008). Online shopping as foraging: The effects of increasing delays on purchasing and patch residence. *IEEE Transactions on Professional Communication, 51*(2), 147–154. doi:10.1109/TPC.2008.2000340

Hartl, D. L., & Clark, A. G. (2007). *Principles of population genetics*. Sunderland, MA: Sinauer Associates.

Hubona, G. S., & Shirah, G. W. (2006). The Paleolithic Stone Age effect? Gender differences performing specific computer-generated spatial tasks. *International Journal of Technology and Human Interaction, 2*(2), 24–46.

Kock, N. (2004). The psychobiological model: Towards a new theory of computer-mediated communication based on Darwinian evolution. *Organization Science, 15*(3), 327–348. doi:10.1287/orsc.1040.0071

Kock, N. (2005). Media richness or media naturalness? The evolution of our biological communication apparatus and its influence on our behavior toward e-communication tools. *IEEE Transactions on Professional Communication, 48*(2), 117–130. doi:10.1109/TPC.2005.849649

Kock, N., Chatelain-Jardón, R., & Carmona, J. (2008). An experimental study of simulated Web-based threats and their impact on knowledge communication effectiveness. *IEEE Transactions on Professional Communication, 51*(2), 183–197. doi:10.1109/TPC.2008.2000345

Kock, N., & Hantula, D. A. (2005). Do we have e-collaboration genes? *International Journal of e-Collaboration, 1*(2), i–ix.

Maynard Smith, J. (1998). *Evolutionary genetics*. New York: Oxford University Press.

Miller, G. F. (2000). *The mating mind: How sexual choice shaped the evolution of human nature*. New York: Doubleday.

Murdock, G. P. (1958). Outline of world cultures. New Haven, CN: Human Relations Area Files Press.

Pinker, S. (2002). *The blank slate: The modern denial of human nature*. New York: Penguin Putnam.

Popper, K. R. (1992). *Logic of scientific discovery*. New York: Routledge.

Rajala, A. K., & Hantula, D. A. (2000). Towards a behavioral ecology of consumption: Delay-reduction effects on foraging in a simulated Internet mall. *Managerial and Decision Economics, 21*(1), 145–158. doi:10.1002/mde.979

Saad, G. (2008). Advertised waist-to-hip ratios of online female escorts: An evolutionary perspective. *International Journal of e-Collaboration, 4*(3), 40–50.

Smith, A. (1776). The wealth of nations. Vols. I and II. J.M. London, England: Dent & Sons.

Smith, C. L., & Hantula, D. A. (2003). Pricing effects on foraging in a simulated Internet shopping mall. *Journal of Economic Psychology, 24*(5), 653–674. doi:10.1016/S0167-4870(03)00007-2

Spink, A., & Cole, C. (2006). Human information behavior: Integrating diverse approaches and information use. *Journal of the American Society for Information Science and Technology, 57*(1), 25–35. doi:10.1002/asi.20249

Chapter 2
Supporting Synchronous Collaboration with Heterogeneous Devices[1]

Axel Guicking
Fraunhofer Integrated Publication and Information Systems Institute (IPSI), Germany

Peter Tandler
Fraunhofer Institute for Computer Graphics (IGD), Germany

Thomas Grasse
Jeppesen GmbH, Germany

ABSTRACT

The increasing availability of mobile devices in today's business contexts raises the demand to shift the focus of groupware framework design. Instead of solely focusing on functional requirements of specific application domains or device characteristics, nonfunctional requirements need to be taken into account as well. Flexibility concerning the integration of devices and tailorability of the framework according to different usage contexts is essential for addressing device heterogeneity. Besides flexibility, in order to support the development of real-world applications involving heterogeneous devices, robustness and scalability concerns have to be addressed explicitly by the framework. This article presents Agilo, a groupware framework for synchronous collaboration. The framework incorporates approaches addressing flexibility, robustness, and scalability issues. The combination of these concerns makes it suitable for development of collaborative applications involving up to hundreds of users. As an example application, a commercial electronic meeting system is presented by illustrating typical usage scenarios, explaining application-specific requirements and describing the system design.

INTRODUCTION

During the last decade, the use of mobile devices in daily work scenarios has massively increased. Although mobile devices have found their way into business work settings, the application areas are still most often limited to individual services like synchronizing personal calendars, note-taking, and browsing the Web. The research on the integration and use of mobile devices in collaborative settings is constantly growing. It has been pointed out that the use of application frameworks is an adequate way to simplify the design and development of applications in general and groupware in particular (Fayad & Schmidt, 1997; Schuckmann, Kirchner, Schümmer, & Haake, 1996). Following the increasing trend of mobility in CSCW (Computer-Supported Collaborative Work) scenarios, new groupware application frameworks have been developed or existing groupware frameworks have been extended in order to support mobile devices.

While there exist several groupware frameworks addressing mobile devices of one particular type, others take into account the diversity of devices to be supported in the same runtime environment. The devices constituting such heterogeneous environments exhibit diverse characteristics (Raatikainen, Christensen, & Nakajima, 2002; Weiser, 1991). Most notably these are (a) limitations of processing and battery power, memory, and user interface (UI) capabilities, (b) diverse input/output techniques, (c) unreliable network conditions, and (d) a highly dynamic environment including specific context information, for example, changing user and device locations. While some of these characteristics are immanently present in any heterogeneous environment, others depend on the specific domain and usage scenario. For example, wireless devices nearly always exhibit unreliable network connectivity due to interferences and dead spots. However, specific context information like device locations might not be relevant for particular applications.

The increasing availability of different devices—mainly mobile devices—in everyday life[2] puts new demands not only on addressing device characteristics and functional requirements of specific application domains but also on nonfunctional requirements. Nonfunctional requirements, as they exist for real-world or even commercial applications, usually encompass (among others) robustness and scalability/performance (Robinson, Pawlowski, & Volkov, 2003). These observations can be phrased as three requirements that a framework for real-world groupware applications in heterogeneous environments needs to fulfill.

First, the framework has to provide *flexibility* with respect to the integration of new and different devices. In order to implement and execute applications using different devices, the framework must put as few constraints as possible on device and network characteristics. In fact, it might well be necessary to tailor and extend the behavior of the framework itself. For example, depending on characteristics of particular devices, available framework services such as data distribution mechanisms or messaging protocols might need to be adapted or new ones have to be implemented. Second, the framework must provide *robustness* (reliability) with respect to network and device failures. For example, short-term interruptions of network connections should be handled (ideally) transparently by the framework while more severe failures, for example, device failures or long-term network interruptions, usually should trigger a notification to the end user. Third, the framework needs to provide *scalability* with respect to the number of devices in a single runtime environment. Although the number of collaborating users mainly depends on the application domain and usage scenario, the increasing availability of devices allows considering large-scale groupware environments with even hundreds of users and devices.

This article presents Agilo, a groupware framework for building applications for synchronous collaboration in heterogeneous environments (Guicking & Grasse, 2006; Guicking, Tandler, & Avgeriou, 2005). Agilo addresses applications that are "user-driven": In contrast to "streaming" application scenarios that consist of (more or less) continuous data streams (e.g., video-conferencing systems), Agilo supports the development of applications which consist of user actions that are distributed to other devices as needed. Agilo moves the application development support for heterogeneous environments one step further into the direction of real world and even commercial application areas. This article focuses on how Agilo meets the three requirements identified above.

This article is structured as follows: First, existing groupware frameworks supporting the integration of heterogeneous devices are presented and analyzed according to the three requirements. Then, the main concepts of the Agilo framework are explained and discussed with respect to flexibility, robustness, and scalability. As an extensive sample application using Agilo, a commercial electronic meeting system, called "Digital Moderation", is presented. It addresses facilitated meetings with support for heterogeneous devices in large-scale, face-to-face, and virtual meetings. Experiences gathered during application development are described and preliminary experimental studies of the framework performance under varying conditions are presented afterwards. The article concludes with a few open research questions.

STATE OF THE ART

There exists a wide variety of frameworks that provide comprehensive support for the development of groupware applications. However, the support of heterogeneous devices often has been added belatedly to existing frameworks that originally have been designed to support the application development for desktop and PC-based groupware applications, for example, Pocket DreamTeam (Roth, 2003) or Manifold (Marsic, 2001). During the last few years, frameworks have been proposed to support the development of groupware applications using either mobile devices exclusively or using heterogeneous devices. Here, we focus on the discussion of the more related groupware frameworks for heterogeneous environments. The systems presented here are analyzed by means of the aspects flexibility, robustness, and scalability.

The DOORS system has been designed for asynchronous collaboration in heterogeneous environments which has been extended to support synchronous collaboration as well (Preguiça, Martins, Domingos, & Duarte, 2005). It provides partially replicated data objects in order to allow working on shared data while disconnected (so-called co-objects). DOORS offers flexibility regarding data synchronization and concurrency control aspects. However, since applications have to make use of co-objects for accessing shared data, other communication mechanisms such as more low-level message-passing with a tailorable messaging protocol (which might be more feasible for some domains and limited devices) need to be implemented by extending the co-object notion. Thus, DOORS provides only limited flexibility. DOORS explicitly addresses "large-scale environments" (Preguiça, Martins, Domingos, & Duarte, 2000) by maximizing data availability and providing replicated servers. This allows handling intermittent network disconnections. However, to our knowledge, only a few prototypical applications have been implemented. No concrete information about handling device failures and no empirical data about framework scalability are available.

The Manifold framework (Marsic, 2001) is an extension of the DISCIPLE framework (Marsic, 1999) supporting heterogeneous devices. It uses a data-centric approach for data sharing: while data is shared among all collaborators using XML (Extensible Markup Language), it is presented and adapted according to device-specific capabilities using XSL (Extensible Stylesheet Language). Manifold uses a multitier architecture by separating concerns in a presentation layer, domain logic, and collaboration functionality. While DISCIPLE already provides support for heterogeneity on the networking level, Manifold makes use of Java Beans in order to provide support for heterogeneous devices on the application and interaction level.

Although applications built using Manifold focus on the domain of Virtual Reality, the framework itself provides a highly flexible approach— especially because XML is used as generic format for data exchange. However, Manifold does not allow replacing the XML-based data transfer with other messaging protocols. XML may lead to higher network load than using a more concise data representation. DISCIPLE provides appropriate mechanisms in order to recover from network or device failures, so both frameworks provide a robust communication infrastructure. Performance studies of DISCIPLE reveal update times for a single PDA communicating with a PC in the range of more than 3 seconds (Krebs, Ionescu, Dorohonceanu, & Marsic, 2003). To our knowledge, no data concerning scalability with respect to the number of devices is available.

Pocket DreamTeam (Roth, 2003) is an extension of the Java-based DreamTeam platform (Roth, 2000) in order to support mobile collaboration. DreamTeam is a Peer-to-Peer (P2P) based platform for synchronous collaborative applications using so-called "resources" which form the basis for collaborative applications, for example, shared texts or shared Web pages. Each resource can communicate with their corresponding peer resources using synchronous remote method calls. Pocket DreamTeam handles the restrictions of wireless connections by using remote proxies that mediate state changes between peer resources. These proxies are located on stationary parts of the network and therefore provide reliable network connectivity to other peers that

may act as proxies themselves. As described in Roth (2003), a DreamTeam application has to be ported to C++ for use in Pocket DreamTeam. The flexibility provided by Pocket DreamTeam is limited because wired devices are necessary for reliable data access. The remote proxies together with an optimistic replication approach provide robustness concerning intermittent network and device failures. To our knowledge, no data about performance and scalability of the Pocket DreamTeam platform has been published.

QuickStep is a toolkit designed to support data-centered collaborative applications for handheld devices based on record-based shared data such as to-do lists and calendars (Roth & Unger, 2001). In order to avoid conflicts, only the creator of a record is allowed to modify it which in turn allows fast synchronization of replicated objects. However, it does not provide typical groupware services like session management (all users connected to a central server implicitly join a session). Furthermore, QuickStep primarily addresses collaboration of co-located users, for example, meeting scenarios to synchronize personal calendars. Due to these limitations, QuickStep does not support the development of more complex groupware applications that would need more sophisticated groupware services such as concurrency control or session management. Since QuickStep explicitly addresses mobile devices, temporary disconnections are handled using a mirroring/caching approach. However, no information about handling server failures and data about system performance and scalability is available.

The BEACH environment has been designed to support synchronous collaboration using heterogeneous devices (Tandler, 2004). As an example application for asynchronous brainstormings using limited devices (in this case Palm Pilot V), PalmBeach has been implemented (Tandler, 2004). However, PalmBeach is a separate application that has been implemented from scratch using a proprietary messaging protocol in order to allow for communication with more capable devices running the BEACH platform. The BEACH platform itself focuses on more capable devices such as notebooks integrated in physical artifacts such as tables and chairs. The integration of memory- and processor-constrained devices in BEACH environments is very limited. According to Tandler (2004), robustness concerns regarding device failures as well as intermittent network failures are open issues. Although scalability is implicitly addressed, no empiricial data about system performance with respect to the number of devices has been published.

Summary

All presented systems provide at least moderate flexibility and (except BEACH) partial robustness. To the best of our knowledge, no empirical data about scalability and system performance is available for most systems. None of the systems provides the desired level of flexibility in a robust and scalable way (cf. Table 1). This result is not surprising because all systems presented are systems to implement new concepts for supporting collaboration in heterogeneous environments focusing on novel approaches and methodologies. The other "extreme" are commercial platforms

Table 1. Summary of the described frameworks with respect to their support of flexibility, robustness, and scalability; + denotes full support, ○ denotes partial, and – denotes no or very limited support; ? indicates that no empirical data has been found in the literature

System	Flexibility	Robustness	Scalability
DOORS	○	○	?
Manifold	+	+	–
Pocket DreamTeam	○	+	?
QuickStep	○	○	?
BEACH	○	–	?

like Lotus Notes (Kawell, Beckhardt, Halvorsen, Ozzie, & Greif, 1988) or Sametime[3] that are highly scalable and robust but do not provide appropriate framework capabilities to implement more complex groupware applications.

The Agilo framework presented in this article tries to fill this gap. It provides flexibility on the one hand and explicitly addresses robustness and scalability concerns on the other hand.

FRAMEWORK DESIGN

The Agilo framework is based on a client-server distribution model. This approach provides several advantages: Depending on the application domain or usage scenario, other distribution models like P2P or hybrid approaches (Roth & Unger, 2000) can be built on top of the client-server model (by deploying server-specific components on some or all client devices) much easier than the other way round. In addition, the system becomes more scalable with respect to keeping shared data consistent throughout the system—in a "full" P2P setting, each device needs to connect to each other device which reduces the possibilities to use memory-constrained devices. However, the well-known limitation of a client-server distribution model is the central point of failure (Phillips, 1999). Therefore, the system must provide appropriate robustness mechanisms concerning failures of server software and hardware.

The framework architecture is composed of three layers (see Figure 1). The bottom or *network abstraction layer* provides a high-level abstraction of network *connections* that allows the implementation of applications independent of underlying network and transport characteristics. Typical connection implementations use TCP (Transmission Control Protocol) sockets or—to support nodes secured by firewalls—HTTP (Hypertext Transfer Protocol) request/response pairs, where clients constantly poll the server to send and receive accumulated data.

Figure 1. Architectural layers of the Agilo framework

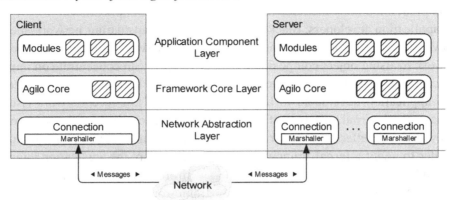

As basic communication abstraction, Agilo provides asynchronous *messages* to send data between clients and the server. Synchronous messages are realized on top of asynchronous messages that can be used by clients to send a request to the server and block until a response from the server arrives. Messages can have an explicit priority in order to be able to process more important messages earlier than other messages (e.g., logout messages). A *marshaller* associated with each connection is responsible for converting messages into byte sequences before they are transmitted and bytes back into messages after they have been received by the client or server.

The middle or *framework core layer* consists of mandatory framework components. On the server side, a client registry manages client connections and their individual connectivity states. A message handler component on client- and server-side is responsible for handling incoming messages and forwarding them to interested application *modules*.

These modules, located on the upper or *application component layer*, are domain-specific components containing the application logic. Thus, application developers usually are faced with this layer by assembling and implementing appropriate components to be executed on clients or server. Modules are registered at the message

handler component to get notified about incoming messages using a *message filter* which defines a boolean expression to accept or ignore specific messages. By using this approach, a single module can listen to different kinds of messages, and different modules can get notified about the same incoming message. Modules are registered at a local registry that allows retrieving local module instances using nodewide unique lookup names in order to access application logic of other local modules by direct method calls.

More technical details of the architectural design can be found in Guicking and Grasse (2006). The next section explains how the framework design addresses flexibility, robustness, and scalability.

Support for Flexibility

Most of the framework parts located at the framework core layer are implemented analogously to the module abstraction (indicated by the hatched squares in Figure 1). This way, most of framework internal parts can be tailored, adapted or even exchanged depending on the needs of the application domain or depending on specific device characteristics. This approach can be seen as a mixed approach of a whitebox and blackbox framework (Fayad & Schmidt, 1997): Whitebox frameworks support extensibility by providing base classes to be inherited and predefined hook methods to be over-ridden by application developers. Blackbox frameworks provide interfaces to plug components into the framework by using object composition and delegation. While whitebox frameworks usually require application developers to have close knowledge of the internal structure of the framework, they provide better support for the developer in order to adapt internal framework functionality than blackbox frameworks. Blackbox frameworks, on the other hand, are generally easier to use and extend but hide most of the framework functionality. Agilo provides both template methods and framework base classes to be extended on the one hand, as well as interfaces in order to plug in modules on the other hand. The blackbox parts of the framework are fully sufficient to build less complex applications that can be easily accomplished by less-experienced developers. However, the whitebox parts allow fine-tuning of framework behavior and internal structures by more experienced developers in order to meet domain or application-specific needs and requirements.

Agilo provides asynchronous messages as basic means for communication between clients and server. Based on this communication abstraction, synchronous messages, which are conceptually similar to Remote Procedure Calls (RPC), are provided by the core framework. However, more high-level abstractions are provided as optional framework modules. For example, a generic data replication mechanism provides a service for transactional data replication where objects are replicated to interested clients. Using a publish/subscribe approach, clients can subscribe to individual objects or types of objects in order to get notified about object changes. Since all three communication approaches make use of the same "communication stream" (they all use asynchronous messages), it is possible to seamlessly integrate the different data distribution concepts

in the same application which also supports the evolution of applications.

By encapsulating network-specific behavior in the network abstraction layer, application developers can concentrate on implementing the application logic and user interfaces without taking care of low-level network issues. Moreover, this approach allows tailoring or exchanging the network connection implementations without the need to adapt the application logic.

In order to maximize applicability of the Agilo framework, the framework is implemented using Java. For many of the more capable devices on the market today, Java Virtual Machines (JVM) based on the Java Micro Edition (JavaME) are available. Devices for when no JVM is available or that do not provide enough resources to execute JavaME-based applications; client applications based on other programming languages can be integrated into Agilo applications by using customized messaging protocols allowing more interactive applications than purely Web-based applications. Since the messaging protocol details are encapsulated in the marshaller, the conversion of messages into byte sequences and back into messages can be implemented independent of the network protocol being used. In fact, this separation of concerns allows the seamless integration of diverse devices into a single application environment.

Support for Robustness

Robustness concerns address the following three areas: network failures, hardware failures, and software failures. In order to provide robustness concerning network connectivity, three different requirements have to be met: (a) messages cannot get lost, (b) messages are delivered in total order with respect to a single connection, and (c) messages cannot get corrupted. Depending on the underlying network protocol being used by a specific connection implementation, one or more requirements might be already ensured (e.g., the total ordering of messages is guaranteed for TCP-based connections). In addition to these requirements, short-term harmless network failures should be handled transparently in order to minimize distraction of the application end user.

In case of a short-term network failure, the client-side connection implementation continuously tries to reconnect to the server, and—upon successful reconnection—any accumulated messages on client- and server-side are transmitted. In this case, the reconnection is handled transparently and the end user usually does not recognize any massive delay. However, if a client cannot reconnect within a few seconds, client-side modules are notified in order to provide some kind of end-user feedback or to perform a module restart. This behavior seems appropriate since a failing reconnect may also indicate that the server has been shut down or crashed—a situation of which the end user usually should be informed.

In case messages get lost (req. a) or messages are received in the wrong order (req. b), the receiving node explicitly requests the missing messages (for this reason, outgoing messages are enumerated and buffered on the sender side; Figure 2). Depending on the network protocol, the receiver occasionally submits the number of the last message received in order to allow the sender to remove buffered outgoing messages. Compared to an explicit acknowledgment of every message, this "optimized ACK" approach obviously reduces network traffic and idle times of the sender.

Detecting message corruptions is the responsibility of the marshaller since corruptions affect the unmarshalling of messages (Figure 2). Whether the end user should get notified about message corruptions mainly depends on the security requirements of the domain and usage scenario. Therefore, a module can get notified by the marshaller in case of failing unmarshalling.

Robustness concerning hardware failures is currently supported only in a limited way for server failures using an optional message logging module. Incoming messages are stored persistently and, in case of a server device failure, the server

Figure 2. Unmarshalling and robustness requirements

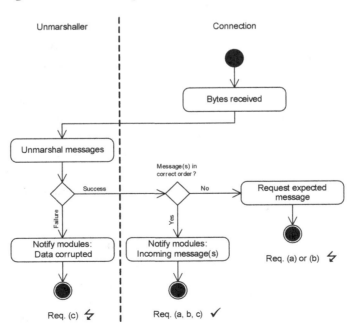

can be restarted and its status is automatically recovered by replaying the stored messages. The logging can be tailored by specifying filter rules defining which messages should be logged. Since clients automatically try to reconnect in case the connection to the server is broken, this is a simple yet powerful way to allow restarting the server during runtime. In case the device of the server is exchanged, it must be manually configured analogously to the previously used server device (e.g., the IP address needs to be identical). Besides this limitation, the message-logging approach obviously does not scale well with respect to the number of stored messages. In order to avoid these limitations, other approaches are currently being evaluated.

Regarding software failures, the same approach as for hardware failures exists. While the framework core catches nonserious exceptions and notifies application-specific exception handlers, severe software failures (e.g., deadlocks in application or framework modules) are not yet detected by the framework. In case of severe software failures, the server has to be restarted, thus applying the recovery approach described above. More intelligent and autonomous approaches to improve the fault-tolerance of the server are currently designed and evaluated.

Support for Scalability

For client-server based systems, the scalability and performance of the server and the reduction of network traffic are the most crucial factors (Phillips, 1999).

The modular design of the framework allows the deployment of the server as part of an application server that provides load-balancing mechanisms such as dynamic component distribution among several server instances. However, the general scalability of the server can only be determined empirically. For this reason, preliminary studies examining the performance of the Agilo server under varying environmental conditions

were conducted. The studies and their results are described later on.

APPLICATIONS

Based on Agilo, two applications for heterogeneous environments from different domains have been implemented: First, the OPUS system for public safety organizations that use mobile devices for communication between and coordination of relief units. Second, a commercial meeting support system called Digital Moderation[4] that supports the use of heterogeneous devices. An overview of both systems can be found in Guicking and Grasse (2006); detailed information about the design and implementation of OPUS can be found in Grasse (2005).

In this article, we present the Digital Moderation system: first, several usage scenarios and application-specific requirements are illustrated before the overall system design is described.

Digital Moderation

The Digital Moderation system is a commercial meeting support system for facilitated meetings providing conceptual as well as technical scalability with respect to the number of meeting participants (meetings with up to several hundreds of users supported). The main characteristics of the Digital Moderation system are easy tailorability and extensibility to accommodate different facilitation methods, sophisticated facilitation services in order to increase meeting performance and the integration of heterogeneous devices.

Digital Moderation supports different meeting scenarios. Here, three scenarios will be illustrated in more detail. Co-located meetings are typically either small workshops with 10-20 participants, or large events with up to several hundreds of users. If participants are distributed, they can use Digital Moderation for virtual workshops over the Internet. These scenarios have been selected to cover different aspects how the system can be applied. Figure 3 illustrates the general setup of a co-located meeting.

Scenario 1: Large Event for Enterprise Strategy Development

After a merger, two companies face the challenge to form a common enterprise strategy. Therefore, the management board decides to bring top and middle management together to agree on the new company's strategy and to ensure support and participation to implement it. Altogether, 250 participants are invited. In the meeting, five people are grouped per table, sharing one notebook. The meeting is run by a professional facilitator, supported by a team of two technical directors who monitor progress and navigate through the meeting agenda. Additionally, two

technicians help the meeting participants when technical problems occur. Their PDAs inform them about temporarily disconnected devices and requests for assistance by participants, which automatically show up on the user interface of the technicians' PDAs. This way, technical issues can be handled more efficiently and less disruptingly. The smooth integration of the technicians and their responsibilities into the meeting context leads to improved user satisfaction.

Scenario 2: Co-Located Crisis Workshop of a Project Team

In a project team, coordination problems and increasingly strained situations lead to massively delayed deadlines. In order to solve these problems, it has been decided to perform a "crisis workshop." An external facilitator is invited

Figure 3. Sketch of a co-located digital moderation meeting scenario. Application-specific Agilo modules on the different nodes are denoted by hatched boxes.

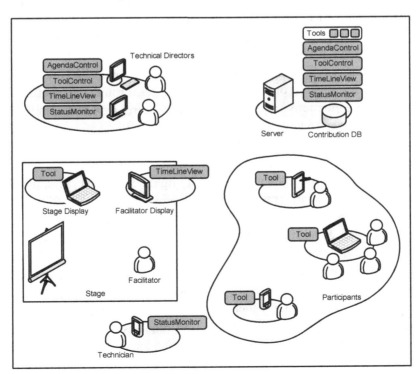

who has long experience performing this kind of workshops. For the workshop, laptops owned by the company are used. Three participants share a laptop, so that during some phases of the workshop, they are engaged in discussion as they must agree on a common result. In other phases when each participant's opinion is important, they take turns and hand over the laptop to the others at the table. As some participants have brought their PDAs, they quickly log in to the meeting during these parallel phases and use their personal devices for input. The user interface is adapted to their pen-based devices. The ideas they generate during brainstorming sessions also keep their original handwriting attached to the ideas stored on the server.

At some point during the workshop, the facilitator recognizes that the prepared script is not optimal. Therefore, the facilitator quickly adapts the agenda and inserts a sequence of new tools to explore the additional aspect just discovered. Immediately after the meeting, the meeting notes are uploaded to the team's collaboration server.

Scenario 3: Virtual Project Meeting

In order to solve a tricky design problem, Digital Moderation is used for a creative session involving users from different company sites. At one site, a meeting room with two large interactive displays is used for the meeting. The project members from the other sites participate in the meeting using their desktop PCs. As two participating designers do a lot of sketching, they use their tablet PCs while a usability consultant is currently traveling and joins the meeting with a Smartphone from a train. Depending on the devices used, the users get an adapted UI so that ideas can be entered using keyboard, pen, or voice. The tablet PCs are also used to generate sketches of different design alternatives during the meeting which are attached to the submitted ideas. The project manager receives awareness information for both co-located and remote participants, seeing how many contributions already have been made and whether someone is still engaged in the current phase. When the connection to the Smartphone is lost, he is informed immediately. However, as soon as the phone can be reached again, the connection is automatically restored and the device is synchronized.

Requirements

From these usage scenarios, several requirements related to the application environment and implementation can be directly derived. These requirements can be grouped into the two categories facilitation support and support for heterogeneous devices.

Facilitation Support

In order to prepare a meeting, the facilitator needs to perform several actions before the meeting starts (Bostrom, Anson, & Clawson, 1993; Hayne, 1999), for example, preparing the meeting agenda and select and tailor appropriate tools for particular meeting tasks. However, here we concentrate on actions during and after the meeting as these actions are affected by the device heterogeneity.

During a meeting, the facilitator (or director) navigates through the meeting agenda and monitors the progress of the individual participants. Therefore, the system has to provide monitoring and control components (these are also necessary for the technicians in scenario 1). Furthermore, it might be necessary to spontaneously adapt the meeting process by inserting and tailoring new tools in the agenda. Therefore, the system must provide data modification and synchronization mechanisms in order to dynamically synchronize all devices in the meeting and provide appropriate displays for the participant devices.

Generating a meeting report after the meeting requires a persistency backend storing the participants' individual—and potentially device-specific—contributions. Since the data from the meeting might be integrated into a company IT infrastructure (cf. scenario 2), the output format of the report must be tailorable.

Support for Heterogeneous Devices

It has been shown that the IT infrastructure used in meetings may have a negative impact on participant satisfaction and quality of meeting results if not designed to "stay in the background" as much as possible (Wiberg, 2001). Obviously, this requires that the system operates in a fairly autonomous way in order to reduce manual device (re)configurations during the meeting. This is even more important if different devices should be supported. Because of the heterogeneity of UI and input/output characteristics, the system has to provide support for device-specific tailoring of user interfaces for the various tools and software components (cf. scenarios 1 and 2). In order to enable the automatic generation of comprehensive meeting reports, the system must handle and store data provided in different formats.

The requirements concerning facilitation support have already been analyzed extensively in the according literature (e.g., Hayne, 1999; Nunamaker, Briggs, Mittleman, Vogel, & Balthaz-

ard, 1997). However, integrating heterogeneous devices in facilitated meeting scenarios in a way that diverse scenarios are covered has not yet been examined extensively. Focusing on the integration of devices, the next section sketches the overall design and implementation aspects of the Digital Moderation system.

Design Overview of the Digital Moderation System

The Digital Moderation system is based on the concepts of meetings, tools, and contributions (see Figure 4). A *meeting* is a session where users with different roles (such as facilitator, participant, or technician) come together (either face-to-face or in a virtual meeting room). A *tool* implements a specific task performed by participants during a meeting, such as a brainstorming, voting or a clustering task. A tool is realized as a client-side and server-side Agilo module. One important part of a meeting is the meeting agenda which consists of a sequence of tools. A *contribution* is information entered by participants using a client device during the meeting, for example, an idea or visual sketch during a brainstorming or a single vote during a voting task. Each task consists of

Figure 4. The domain objects of the digital moderation system

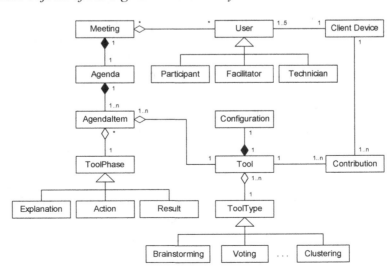

usually three phases: during the *explanation phase*, the facilitator explains to the participants the UI of the specific tool and how to use it. During the *action phase*, the UI of the current tool is displayed on the participants' devices (adapted to the device characteristics) and participants enter their contributions (as described in the scenarios above, several users may share a single client). During the *result phase*, the facilitator presents the contributions collected during the action phase at a shared visual screen.

During the meeting, the facilitator (or a technical director) uses a control client to centrally coordinate the meeting process by moving to the next agenda item. Besides the ability to coordinate the meeting process, other facilitation services are available as separate Agilo modules on this client as well (such as a status monitor, a timeline view, and the ability to adapt the meeting agenda; cf. Figure 3). The deployment of client modules is dynamically tailored according to the meeting scenario and specific device. For example, in large events, the technicians' PDAs get a specific UI for the status monitor, and, in distributed meetings, participants have access to the result display since a shared visual screen is not available.

In order to increase code reuse, modules are implemented using the Model-View-Controller pattern; that is, a module consists of the application logic and one or more views (UI components). The server selects and configures UI components for specific client modules: after connecting, the client sends device information (UI dimensions, available UI libraries, and client module names) to the server which in turn selects the best-matching UI components for the requested modules and sends the according class information back to the client.

GENERAL EXPERIENCES

Up to now, the Agilo framework has been used by some 20 application developers whose expertise ranges from less-experienced Java developers to expert Java developers with comprehensive experience in developing distributed systems. Compared to Agilo, other groupware frameworks, for example, COAST (Schuckmann et al., 1996) and DyCE (Tietze, 2001), provide more functionality as part of the nondividable framework core which leads to two immanent limitations. First, larger frameworks put more constraints on how to use and extend the framework which massively increases the learning time of application developers. Second, these frameworks require more system resources which limit the applicability for heterogeneous environments. The experiences gained during the development of the two applications confirm these conclusions. The modularity and flexibility of Agilo substantially supports the evolution of applications. New functionality can be implemented by introducing new kinds of messages and developing additional modules. This way, new functionality can be easily added without affecting stability and correctness of existing application logic.

So far, three applications have been implemented using Agilo. Besides the OPUS system mentioned above and the Digital Moderation system, the chat framework "ConcertChat" uses Agilo as communication backend. ConcertChat provides sophisticated support to tightly integrate chats with different kinds of workspaces (Mühlpfordt & Stahl, 2007).

The Digital Moderation system has already been used successfully in meetings with up to 220 participants involving more than 50 devices, about 40 of them connected using Wi-Fi (Figure 5 shows a photograph of one of these events). During some of these events, access points failed or had to be reconfigured (e.g., changing the Wi-Fi channel). Although the client devices connected to these access points were temporarily disconnected, the participants using these devices did not notice the short interruptions and could follow the meeting without getting distracted.

Figure 5. Photograph of a meeting with the Digital Moderation System in December 2006 (courtesy of RWE Rhein-Ruhr AG)

Performance of the Agilo Server

In order to analyze empirically the performance and scalability of the Agilo Server, we recently started conducting experiments using the Digital Moderation system. Our initial studies exclusively measure the message throughput (i.e., processing speed) of the central server. The preliminary results achieved by these studies give a first impression of the server performance.

Setup

The studies were conducted during March 2007 in one of the student labs at Fraunhofer IPSI using 21 notebooks and PCs (at least Pentium 3 with 600 MHz, running Java 1.4.2 on Windows XP Professional, and connected via cable or Wi-Fi). The server was running on a Pentium 4-PC (with Hyper-Threading support), 2 GB RAM and a maximum JVM heap size of 1 GB. The server was configured for a production setting (i.e., no logging output was generated). The other machines were used as participant devices. All machines were connected using TCP connections.

The server performance was measured using a brainstorming tool where all participant contributions are broadcasted to all clients. The submission of contributions was triggered by a special remote control client. Pretests had shown that executing multiple Java applications concurrently on the same device may lead to unrealistic pauses due to process and thread scheduling of the operating system. Thus, only scenarios with up to 20 participants have been examined.

Two experiments with different message sizes have been conducted: (a) Message size was approximately 1200 bytes and (b) approximately 12000 bytes. Both experiments were composed of three settings with 5, 10, and 20 clients, respectively. For each of these settings, several test runs with a varying "activity level" (i.e., the message sending frequency of the individual clients) have been performed. The data of all test runs was averaged over a period of one minute.

Results

The results of the experiments are shown in Figure 6. *Messages Sent* specifies the number of all messages being sent from all clients. The *Server Process Rate* (SPR) specifies the amount of incoming messages that are immediately processed

Figure 6. Results of the performance experiments. The ovals indicate areas of realistic message sending scenarios for the digital moderation system (further explanation in the text)

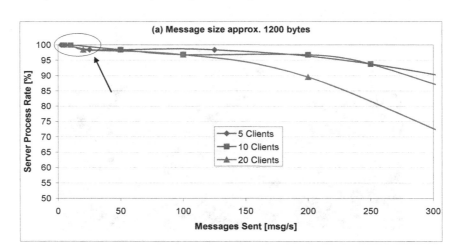

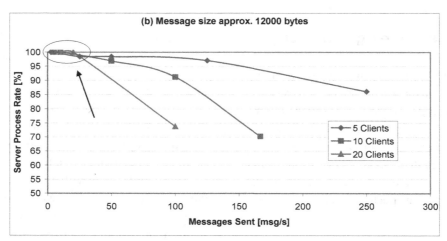

by the server (unprocessed messages are buffered until they are processed).

In experiment (a), the overheads caused by connection handling (I/O) and message marshalling increasingly affect the setting with 10 clients at about 250 messages sent (i.e., the client message sending rate per second (CMSR) is 25 messages). As expected, the overheads are higher for larger numbers of clients: for 20 clients, the SPR is dropping down at a CMSR of 10 messages. For settings with five clients, the SPR is decreasing moderately.

In experiment (b), the SPR is dropping down more rapidly compared to experiment (a). Especially, in the setting with 20 clients, the SPR is dropping off noticeably between 20 and 100 messages per second (CMSR of 1 and 5, respectively). Due to a software bug, in experiment (b) the server crashed quite often with a memory overflow exception for higher message sending rates. However, the available results of the experiments show the expected behavior—the SPR is decreasing if I/O handling and message marshalling overheads are increasing (either by more connections, more messages, or larger messages).

Discussion

As stated above, the Agilo framework addresses groupware applications that are based on explicit messages. In contrast to streaming-based approaches, messages are usually created and caused by some kind of user action. Therefore, the number of messages created by a single user rarely exceeds one message per second. Analyzing log files of the Digital Moderation session shown in Figure 5 revealed that user input was in fact much less: During a brainstorming, a single participant entered five contributions or less (during a period of at least 5 minutes)—even with five participants sharing one device, these are approximately five contributions per minute. Contributions were sent as messages of about 1200 bytes in size. Taking this into account when considering the performance results shows that real-world settings have a SPR between 97% and 100%—even independent of the examined message sizes. The ovals in Figure 6 mark these realistic settings.

Although not empirically tested, the results provide some indications of the server behavior for larger numbers of devices. If the CMSR equals one, the X-axis could be interpreted as number of devices. Although more I/O and marshalling overhead needs to be taken into account, the Agilo server performance is expected to be tolerable as it is currently implemented.

In order to increase the SPR for settings with larger message sizes and higher numbers of devices, the Digital Moderation system is currently being extended to replace the naïve approach of broadcasting contributions by an intelligent contribution delivery service. This service delivers contributions only partially to clients, depending on the current tool, tool phase, and specific client device. Since these are orthogonal dimensions, a two-step approach is used to forward contributions to clients: first, contributions are filtered according to the current tool, its configuration, and the current phase in order to identify the clients that need to get notified of the new contribution. Sec-

ond, contributions are filtered and manipulated using a device-specific preprocessor. For example, a drawing created by a user using a tablet PC is transformed on server-side into a thumbnail before it is delivered to a device with small UI dimensions. Since the preprocessing step might be time-consuming, the dynamically generated "data views" are cached and reused for similar devices. If necessary, users can individually query the server for the original contents.

This optimization obviously requires server-side computation time. However, we expect that it will outweigh the marshalling and connection handling overheads of the naïve approach and therefore will increase the SPR for settings with larger messages. In fact, we already expect better results by adding caching mechanisms to the currently used naïve approach. Instead of marshalling the connection-specific message for each connection individually, a message delivered to several clients that use the same marshaller should be marshalled only once. The connection-specific message ID then becomes part of the messaging protocol as additional header field.

Although extending the contribution delivery is still ongoing, these initial studies have shown that the performance of the Agilo server suits very well for real-world scenarios.

CONCLUSION AND FUTURE WORK

This article presented Agilo, a client-server-based framework for synchronous groupware in heterogeneous environments. Three requirements that are essential for implementing real-world applications—flexibility, robustness, and scalability—are explicitly addressed by the framework. Following a mixed whitebox/blackbox approach, the framework provides a highly modular architecture allowing even tailoring framework-internal behavior as needed for specific application domains and devices. Agilo offers a high degree of flexibility by encapsulating independent system aspects and by providing different communication abstraction that can be intermixed in a single application. In its current state, the framework addresses robustness concerns mainly by handling network failures and various resulting error conditions. Performance issues are addressed by the modular design which allows flexible deployment and component distribution. As sample application, the commercial electronic meeting system Digital Moderation was presented that has been built using Agilo. System scalability and performance in its current implementation have been measured empirically in different initial experimental settings using the Digital Moderation system.

Although the framework is already in a "stable" state, there are three aspects that require further research. First, as already mentioned above, more intelligent robustness-ensuring mechanisms are necessary addressing device and software failures. Second, further experiments are necessary in order to understand the effects of other parameters (network bandwidth, large numbers of different devices, etc.) on overall system performance. Third, in order to address performance limitations of the current implementation, server-side marshalling and connection handling overheads need to be reduced—especially for handling large messages. One approach to address the latter aspect has already been sketched above for the Digital Moderation system. Other approaches that should be examined are autonomous load-balancing mechanisms, message aggregation, and compression in order to reduce connection handling and intelligent caching strategies in order to reduce the marshalling overhead.

REFERENCES

Bostrom, R., Anson, R., & Clawson, R. (1993). Group facilitation and group support systems. In L.M. Jessup & J.S. Valacich (Eds.), *Group support systems: New perspectives* (pp. 146-168). New York: Macmillan Publishing Company.

Fayad, M., & Schmidt, D.C. (1997). Object-oriented application frameworks. *Communications of the ACM, 40*(10), 32-38.

Grasse, T. (2005). *Eine Systemarchitektur zur effizienten Steuerung von mobilen Einsatzkräften* [in German]. Diploma thesis, FernUniversität Hagen, Germany.

Guicking, A., & Grasse, T. (2006). A framework designed for synchronous groupware applications in heterogeneous environments. In Y.A. Dimitriadis, I. Zigurs, & E. Gómez-Sánchez (Eds.), *Proceedings of the 12th International Workshop on Groupware* (pp. 203-218). Berlin: Springer-Verlag.

Guicking, A., Tandler, P., & Avgeriou, P. (2005). Agilo: A highly flexible groupware framework. In H. Fuks, S. Lukosch, & A.C. Salgado (Eds.), *Proceedings of the 11th International Workshop on Groupware* (pp. 49-56). Berlin: Springer-Verlag.

Hayne, S.C. (1999). The facilitators perspective on meetings and implications for group support systems design. *ACM SIGMIS Database*, 30(3-4), 72-91.

Kawell, L., Jr., Beckhardt, S., Halvorsen, T., Ozzie, R., & Greif, I. (1988). Replicated document management in a group communication system. In *Proceedings of the 1988 ACM Conference on CSCW* (pp. 395-404). New York: ACM Press.

Krebs, A.M., Ionescu, M., Dorohonceanu, B., & Marsic, I. (2003). The DISCIPLE system for collaboration over the heterogeneous Web. In *Proceedings of the 36th Annual Hawaii International Conference on System Sciences*. Washington, DC: IEEE Computer Society Press.

Marsic, I. (1999). DISCIPLE: A framework for multimodal collaboration in heterogeneous environments. *ACM Computing Surveys, 31*(2).

Marsic, I. (2001). An architecture for heterogeneous groupware applications. In *Proceedings of the International Conference on Software Engineering* (pp. 475-484). Washington, DC: IEEE Computer Society Press.

Mühlpfordt, M., & Stahl, G. (2007). The integration of synchronous communication across dual interaction spaces. In *Proceedings of Computer Supported Collaborative Learning.*

Nunamaker, J.F., Briggs, R.O., Mittleman, D.D., Vogel, D.R., & Balthazard, P.A. (1997). Lessons from a dozen years of group support systems research: A discussion of lab and field findings. *Journal of Management Information Systems, 13*(3), 163-207.

Phillips, W.G. (1999). *Architectures for synchronous groupware* (Tech. Rep. No. 1999-425). Kingston, Canada: Queen's University.

Preguiça, N., Martins, J.L., Domingos, H.J.L., & Duarte, S. (2000). Data management support for asynchronous groupware. In *Proceedings of the 2000 ACM Conference on CSCW* (pp. 69-78). New York: ACM Press.

Preguiça, N., Martins, J.L., Domingos, H.J.L., & Duarte, S. (2005). Integrating synchronous and asynchronous interactions in groupware applications. In H. Fuks, S. Lukosch, & A.C. Salgado (Eds.), *Proceedings of the 11th International Workshop on Groupware* (pp. 89-104). Berlin: Springer-Verlag.

Raatikainen, K.E., Christensen, H.B., & Nakajima, T. (2002). Application requirements for middleware for mobile and pervasive systems. *ACM Mobile Computing and Communications Review, 6*(4), 16-24.

Robinson, W.N., Pawlowski, S.D., & Volkov, V. (2003). Requirements interaction management. *ACM Computing Surveys, 35*(2), 132-190.

Roth, J. (2000). DreamTeam: A platform for synchronous collaborative applications. *AI & Society, 14*(1), 98-119.

Roth, J. (2003). The resource framework for mobile applications: Enabling collaboration between mobile users. In *Proceedings of the 2003 International Conference on Enterprise Information Systems* (pp. 87-94).

Roth, J., & Unger, C. (2000). An extensible classification model for distribution architectures of synchronous groupware. In R. Dieng-Kuntz, A. Giboin, L. Karsenty, & G. De Michelis (Eds.), *Proceedings of the 4th International Conference on the Design of Cooperative Systems* (pp. 113-127). Amsterdam: IOS Press.

Roth, J., & Unger, C. (2001). Using handheld devices in synchronous collaborative scenarios. *Personal and Ubiquitous Computing, 5*(4), 243-252.

Schuckmann, C., Kirchner, L., Schümmer, J., & Haake, J.M. (1996). Designing object-oriented synchronous groupware with COAST. In M.S. Ackerman (Ed.), *Proceedings of the 1996 ACM Conference on CSCW* (pp. 30-38). New York: ACM Press.

Tandler, P. (2004). *Synchronous collaboration in ubiquitous computing environments.* Doctoral thesis, Darmstadt University of Technology, Darmstadt, Germany.

Tietze, D. (2001). *A framework for developing component-based cooperative applications.* Doctoral thesis, Darmstadt University of Technology, Darmstadt, Germany.

Weiser, M. (1991, September). The computer for the 21st century. *Scientific American*, pp. 94-104.

Wiberg, M. (2001). RoamWare: An integrated architecture for seamless interaction in between mobile meetings. In *Proceedings of the International ACM SIGGROUP Conference on Supporting Group Work* (pp. 288-297). New York: ACM Press.

ENDNOTES

[1]   An earlier version of this article was published in the *Proceedings of the 12th Inter-national Workshop on Groupware: Design, Implementation, and Use*, CRIWG 2006, held at Medina del Campo, Spain.

[2]   http://www.windowsfordevices.com/news/NS6794614763.html

[3]   http://www-142.ibm.com/software/sw-lotus/sametime

[4]   http://www.digital-moderation.com

This work was previously published in the International Journal of e-Collaboration, Vol. 4, Issue 1, edited by N. Kock, pp. 1-19, copyright 2008 by IGI Publishing (an imprint of IGI Global).

Chapter 3
Interpretation of Computer Based Interaction Analysis Indicators:
A Significant Issue for Enhancing Collaboration in Technology Based Learning

Tharrenos Bratitsis
University of Western Macedonia, Greece

Angelique Dimitracopoulou
University of the Aegean, Greece

ABSTRACT

DIAS is an Asynchronous Discussion Forum Platform, mainly developed in order to offer extended monitoring and interaction analysis support, by providing a wide range of indicators jointly used in various situations, to all discussion forae users (individual students, groups, moderators/teachers or even researchers/observers), appropriate for their various roles in different activities. This chapter focuses on the explanatory and interpretation issues that arise when the integrated Interaction Analysis (IA) features are used by teachers – moderators. The importance of applying additional interpretative value to seemingly simple quantitative measurements is highlighted through several implemented case studies. This research indicates that the teachers' tasks can be supported using such approaches. More complex diagrams, with potentially increased underlying interpretation power, provide a more insightful examination of the status and evolvement of a discussion, as well as the contribution and performance of the participants (as individuals or as groups). Students cooperate more fruitfully, by utilizing IA indicators for assessing and selfregulating their actions, thus facilitating the moderator's tasks. It relies upon the moderator to manage this aspect of such tools to his/her benefit. Core objective of this chapter is to

DOI: 10.4018/978-1-61520-676-6.ch003

outline the importance of appropriate Interpretation of the IA indicators, thus enhancing collaboration in multiple levels. The notion of Interpretative Schemas is deployed and their potential exploitation is thoroughly explored, using examples from real teaching settings. In fact, the significance of interpreting visualization data in a combined way and from different perspectives is designated, leading to the conclusion that this issue needs to be further researched.

INTRODUCTION

The past few years we witness increased research mobility concerning tools for analyzing and supporting technology based collaborative learning activities, by distance in particular. Recent developments in learning theory have emphasized the importance of context and social interaction (Stahl, 2006). In this vein, Computer Mediated Communication tools (CMC) and in particular asynchronous discussion forae are widely used in formal or informal educational contexts, applying principles of constructivism, emphasizing in social interaction during learning activities (Gunawardena et al, 1997).

Actually, an asynchronous discussion forum is a characteristic example of a computer supported tool, used collaboratively in multiple ways. In general, intense research has been conducted over the years in order to support, improve and enhance collaboration in various areas (e.g. CSCW, CSCL, etc). Computer-based Interaction Analysis (IA) is an emerging field of research within the academic community, focusing in the analysis, in an automated way, of interactions among users, in various collaborative situations (Dimitracopoulou et al, 2005). Apart from selecting the raw data and designing the appropriate analysis algorithm, the results' visualized presentations, as well as the interpretation of the produced depictions are very important issues for consideration. In this chapter, we discuss these issues using examples from research conducted by implementing IA tools in order to support the participants of asynchronous discussion learning activities.

The chapter is structured as follows. First an overview of the IA research field is presented. Then the implemented research approach is described, including: a) the theoretical background, b) an overview of the existing Forum Type software and the corresponding support tools, c) a description of the system (DIAS) which was designed and implemented specifically for the presented research approach and the integrated IA indicators, d) an extended discussion of the *Interpretation* issue be presenting the notion of an *Interpretative Schema*, e) results from the implemented research, and f) conclusions. Finally, the chapter is summarized with a concluding discussion, in which the research trends of the IA research field are presented focusing on the positive outcomes for the e-Collaboration area in general.

INTERACTION ANALYSIS

Computer-based Interaction Analysis (IA) is defined as the automatic or semi-automatic process aiming at understanding the computer mediated activity, drawing on data obtained from the participants' activities. This understanding can be utilized for supporting the human or artificial actors in order to undertake part of the activity's control, by contributing to awareness, self-assessment or even regulation and selfregulation (Dimitracopoulou, 2009).

Research Field Overview

The Interaction Analysis process consists in recording, filtering and processing data regarding system's usage and user activity variables, in order to produce the analysis indicators. These indicators may concern: a) the mode, the process or the 'quality' of the considered 'cognitive system' learning activity; b) the features or the quality of the interaction product; or c) the mode, the process or the quality of the collaboration, when acting in the frame of a social context forming via the technology based learning environment (Dimitracopoulou et al, 2005).

The Interaction Analysis results are presented to the learning activities' participants (students, teachers or moderators) in an appropriate format (graphical, numerical, literal), interpretable by them. The corresponding information provide an insight of their own or overall current or previous activity allowing them to reflect on a cognitive or metacognitive level, and thus act in order to self-regulate their activities and behavior, either as individuals or as cognitive groups. Additionally, IA provides information to the activity observers (teachers, administrators or researchers), in order to analyze the complex cognitive and social phenomena that may occur. The expected outcome is the optimization of the activity through: a) better activity design, regulation, coordination and evaluation by the forum moderator, and b) refined participation and learning outcome for the students through reflection, self-assessment and self-regulation.

Nowadays, the automated analysis of participants' interactions is actually following two divergent, but at the same time complementary, directions. The first regards systems which based on interaction analysis results and taking into account the profiles and cognitive processes of individuals or collaborating groups, adapt the learning environment to their own needs and preferences. They even provide appropriate supporting or guiding messages. The second direction consists in providing information directly to human actors, based on the interaction analysis results, so as to assist them selfregulate their actions, behavior or decisions, supporting them on the level of awareness and metacognition (Dimitracopoulou & Bruillard, 2006). In the first direction, decisions are made by the system (leading eventually to Adap-

tive or Intelligent Tutoring Systems), while in the second, it is the human actors that take control of the activity (Dimitracopoulou, 2009).

The need to support participants in such manner derives from the intensive use of technology based environments in every day educational practice, especially under the scope of collaborative learning approaches, and the complex cognitive or social interactions that take place within their boundaries. On one hand, students seem to need information on their own as well as their collaborators' actions that could support awareness, metacognition and subsequently selfregulation within the learning activity. On the other hand, teachers (acting mostly as moderators), especially in real class contexts, need structured information on the ongoing activity, allowing them to intervene in a more appropriate manner and take actions upon the quality of the activity outcome or the quality of the actual collaboration. Moreover, teachers need support in order to perform formative evaluation of their educational action.

Most of the existing learning systems appear to have limitations when used by students, mainly due to the difficulties the students have in developing and applying metacognitive skills, related to their own actions and processes. Additionally they often fail to properly participate in collaborative settings, interacting with their partners appropriately. On the other hand, teachers who are in charge of several students, acting as advisors or moderators, often fail to interpret the hug number of complex interactions that may take place simultaneously, and act accordingly. The result is that they are often unable to detect collaboration breakdowns and bottleneck phenomena that could lead to frustrating experiences or even abandonment of new learning experiences, in favor of traditional teaching methods.

The need to address these problems has lead to the emergence of a new research field, during the past few years, that of Computer-base Interaction Analysis. It is related to the design of technology based learning environments, with the core aim of this field being the study of participants' interactions and implementation of tools in order to support regulation, when addressed to the teacher or the moderator, and selfregulation, when addressed directly to the students (Dillenbourg et al. 2002; Reimann 2003; Petrou & Dimitracopoulou, 2003; Fesakis et al. 2004; Jermann 2004; Vassileva et al. 2004; Gerosa et al. 2005; Michozuki et al. 2005, Nakahara et al. 2005, Reyes & Tchounikine 2005; Bratitsis & Dimitracopoulou 2006a, Hlapanis & Dimitracopoulou, 2007; Teplovs et al. 2007; Kay et al. 2007).

Interaction Analysis Tools

An IA indicator depicts variables indicating "something'" related to the mode or the quality of individual activity (e.g. modeling approach, quality of hypothesis testing, etc.), the mode or the quality of the collaboration (e.g. division of labor, categories of specific contributions), the process or the quality of the collaborative product.

A distinction between low level and high level indicators can be made. The low level indicators do not usually have an autonomous interpretative value and are inferred directly from the raw interaction data. They mostly contain information similar to that described by the workspace awareness concept. High level indicators usually have an inherent interpretative value and are inferred by complex process from the interaction data. They are often produced by calculations involving several low level indicators and provide information related to the group awareness and other complex concepts. Many of the IA indicators, produced in visual form come under the Information Visualization filed, presenting abstract information, providing insights and new perspectives of interactions among participants (Bratitsis & Dimitracopoulou, 2007b).

An IA tool produces one or more IA indicators. It can be a distinct tool that collects, aggregates and analyzes data for that matter or it can be integrated, as an internal module or part of the overall code,

into a learning environment. The main features of an IA tool are (Dimitracopoulou, 2009):

1. The *intended users*, according to its designers. They can be participants of the learning activity (students, teachers, moderators, tutors, etc), observers (teachers, moderators not directly involved in the activity, system administrators, etc) or the system itself (when it takes into account analysis data in order to produce guiding or supporting messages or to adapt to the participants needs)
2. The attributed *status*, regarding the relation of the IA tool to the learning environment. The IA tool can be integrated into the learning environment as an internal component, link to the learning environment as an external component or an independent tool which can exchange data with the learning environment.
3. The *model of interaction produced* by the IA tool. This feature relates to the depiction of the actual interaction by the IA tool. The result can be more or less complete and detailed, distinguishing the produced IA indicators into low and high level indicators.

In general, reviewing the literature we can distinguish the following applied uses of IA tools:

*   *Supporting students in decision making.* Students may utilize IA tools in order to decide on how to proceed within the learning activity. Several researchers have reported alterations in participation ratio, quality and overall behavior of the students, when they reviewed IA indicators (e.g. Bratitsis & Dimitracopoulou 2007a, 2008; Nakahara et al, 2005; Cheng & Vassileva, 2004; Zumbach et al, 2005). Moreover, studies reported regulation in the orientation of an activity, based on the analysis of both participants' interactions and activity content (Michozuki et al, 2005).

- *Assist students regulate the process of the activity.* When learning activities are divided into distinct phases, IA tools have been found to assist students comply with the activity setting (e.g. Bratitsis & Dimitracopoulou, 2006b)
- *Support teachers make moderating decisions, such as interventions to students.* Single or sets of IA indicators may assist moderators detect problematic situations which they need to attend to (Bratitsis & Dimitracopoulou, 2006b, 2008; Chen & Vassileva, 2004), or they simply relieve the moderating task by visualizing related data in a concentrated form (Gerosa et al, 2005).
- *Assist teachers evaluate their students.* Although summative individual evaluation is not yet supported completely, several researchers have presented IA tools which partially assist teachers in their evaluating tasks (Gerosa et al, 2004; Baros & Verdejo, 2000).
- *Support teachers' selfregulation of teaching strategies.* A teacher may access IA data in order to alter the applied teaching strategy or tactic during the evolvement of the learning activity (e.g. Petrou, 2005) or evaluate the applied strategy after the completion of the learning activity. The latter may assist the teacher in improving the design of subsequent, similar activities.

ASYNCHRONOUS DISCUSSIONS: APPLIED RESEARCH APPROACH

In the previous section, a brief overview of the Interaction Analysis research field, mainly for supporting selfregulation was presented. In this section, a tangible application of original applied research, under the scope of the IA field is presented, providing the opportunity to further discuss upon the significance of properly inter-preting the produced IA indicators for further utilization. Following a general overview of the research approach and the interpretation issues that arise is presented, focusing on the teacher's perspective. Since a teacher, using asynchronous discussions as a learning activity, operates as a moderator too, the terms teacher and moderator will be used as synonyms henceforth.

The rest of this section is structured as follows: the theoretical background of the research is initially deployed, where analysis approaches in order to measure quality aspects of asynchronous discussions are examined. The importance of intense interaction among discussions' participants, as a prerequisite for the development of *Critical Thinking* and *Knowledge Construction*, at extension, is highlighted. The significance of the moderating tasks, along with the emerging difficulties is cited, underlining the necessity for the construction of corresponding supporting tools. Then an overview of the existing Forum Type software, implementing supporting tools is presented, along with emerging drawbacks. The DIAS system and the integrated supporting tools, in the form of IA indicators, are described afterwards. The *Interpretation* issue is thoroughly addressed, by providing an example of an *Interpretative Schema*, while trying to demonstrate how the analysis point of view may differentiate the conclusions deriving from the system's diagrams. Subsequently, the implemented research studies are described and the emerging results are presented in the final section.

Computer Mediated Communication (CMC)

Computer Mediated Communication (CMC) tools, allowing communication among users by means of networked computers, for the purpose of discussing topics of mutual interest, are actually used in educational, working, or everyday life contexts. In particular asynchronous discussion forae are nowadays widely used in formal or informal educational contexts, applying principles of constructivism, emphasizing in social interaction during learning activities (Gunawardena et al, 1997; Collins & Berge, 2001; Corich et al, 2004). Recently, research is focusing towards finding methods for the evolvement and support of critical thinking through interactions, taking place within asynchronous discussions, in order to achieve high quality learning (Stahl, 2006). Such a goal requires tools, frameworks and methods for the facilitation of monitoring, and/or self-reflection and therefore selfregulation that could be supported by the automated analysis of the complex interactions that occur.

The presented research approach tries to meet these goals by applying Computer based Interaction Analysis techniques, taking into account quantitative data. A discussion forum platform with integrated IA tools called D.I.A.S. (Discussion Interaction Analysis System) has been developed (Bratitsis, 2007). The core aim is to support all users (moderators, learners, researchers, etc) and facilitate discussion learning activities (Bratitsis & Dimitracopoulou, 2005; 2006a; 2006b, 2007a), by implementing a wide range of IA indicators. The system was built mainly for use within a learning context, but can also be used for other purposes, such as open-audience discussions forae within corporative networks, scientific networks, etc (mainly in the CSCW spectrum).

Theoretical Background

Critical Thinking is a process that allows learners to gain new knowledge through problem solving and collaboration. It focuses on the process of learning than just attaining information, involving discovering how to analyze, synthesize, judge and create-apply new knowledge to real-world situations (Walker, 2005). While implementing discourse activities by means of asynchronous discussion forae, higher levels of interaction are needed to encourage learners to think critically. Since Mason described her model of qualitative

discussion analysis and the five dimensions introduced by Henri (1992) up to the approach of Gunawardena et al (1997) and the *Community of Inquiry* model developed by Garisson et al (2001), the importance of the interactions of a person within a community is underlined, in order to achieve critical, high order thinking along with internal reflection. As pointed out by Dillenbourg (1999) it is necessary for the learner to externalize his/her thoughts and ideas in order to achieve proper reflection, thus promoting writing messages as discussion forae to an ideal reflective process. Literature points out that intensive discussion and social interaction may lead to multiple knowledge construction phases (Schellens & Valcke, 2005).

Several categories have been proposed for differentiating approaches, addressed to a teacher – moderator attempting to detect and evaluate quality aspects of online discussions (Corich et al, 2004). We distinguish two major categories: a) surface analysis through activity reports and quantitative measurements which indicate the possibility of quality within a discussion, and b) in depth, quality analysis approaches (Stahl, 2006). The first category approaches, propose measuring dimensions that indicate the extent of collaboration in a discussion (and therefore the quality), such as the amount of messages in a thread (Harasim, 1993), thread depth for distinguishing important threads (Hewitt, 2005) or mean number of words (Benbunan-Fich & Hiltz, 1999). On the other hand, one may find approaches for measuring argumentation quality, knowledge building through critical thinking and collaboration level in asynchronous discussions. Most of them consist in analyzing the message content by applying proper coding schemes. They introduce certain analysis dimensions, including user participation, cognitive, metacognitive and interactive behavior, but they are considered to be time consuming (Henri, 1992; Gunawardena et al, 1997; Garisson et al, 2001). A review of the literature also reveals important work on the design of collaborative learning activities, asynchronous discussions in particular, which emphasizes on the importance of the moderator's role and the teaching strategy to be followed (Palloff & Pratt, 1999; Reimann, 2003).

During discourse activities, several issues need to be attended in order to sustain discussions and facilitate knowledge construction, such as reduced user participation, off topic argumentation, untimely confrontation of arising difficulties and problematic user behaviors. It is the moderator (Salmon, 2000; Hewitt, 2005; Walker, 2005) who designs the activity pattern, assigns roles, divides labor, monitors, advises and takes all the necessary actions, in order to ensure proper conditions for high order thinking and learning. All these tasks result in a huge work load (Gerosa et al, 2005), which increases exponentially to the participants' group size. Brace-Govan (2003) gives an example of discussion forum activity in the context of a university course, with a group of 20 students contributing with half a page messages, twice a week. This results to a total of 200 pages of written material, which is increased significantly, in the case of two or three parallel courses and groups. Besides, building the communication medium and providing initial instructions is not adequate (Hiltz, 1997). Proper design and constant effort is required in order to sustain an adequate level of collaboration (Jerman et al, 2001; Barros & Verdejo, 2000). Good moderating is popularly viewed as one way to improve quantity, quality and depth in online discussions (Hewitt, 2005). This includes decisions based on monitoring users' interactions and estimating the current status, using proper tools. For that matter we can distinguish: a) Mirroring/Awareness tools, b) Metacognitive tools, and c) Advising/Moderating tools (Jermann et al, 2001; Reimann, 2003).

Summarizing, the importance and difficulty of the moderator's tasks are widely accepted and evinced in literature, highlighting the need for corresponding supporting tools. On the other hand, Reimann (2003) states that even the most successful community requires a system to monitor and sanction members' behavior, but this works best when the monitoring is carried out by the members themselves rather than by an external authority. Thus part of the monitoring and regulating process should be carried out by the participants themselves, undertaking a portion of the moderator's work load. Action based collaboration analysis (Muehlenbrock & Hoppe, 1999) has been proposed as a framework for applying meaning to quantitative interaction information, thus supporting collaboration management.

At extension, the axis of the current research is peer support in asynchronous discussion learning activities in order to trigger metacognition, leading to selfregulation, as well as to facilitate the moderator's tasks. Our intention is to build tools, applying IA techniques in discussions' activity data, visualizing quantitative information.

Related Work

While examining Forum and Forum type software, we find that commercial or open source products, such as WebCT, WebWiz and PhpBB provide minimum analysis information. Most of them present simple usage indicators, such as activity information (number of messages posted and read), a few statistical indicators (most and least busy day, etc), online users, number of messages per day, number of unread messages, etc. We consider this minimal information available at the moderator's service, which supports forum usage only as a subsidiary tool of a Learning System (Bratitsis & Dimitracopoulou, 2005).

Several new and promising approaches implementing graphical representations of asynchronous discussions' features and parameters can be found while reviewing recent literature. For example, the i-Bee system visualizes relationships between users (appearing as bees) and keywords (appearing as flowers) in online messages, in real time. It also provides snapshots of past discussions and animations. The distance between flowers and bees, their status (e.g. flying/sleeping bee, blossomed/closed flower) and their orientation depend on discussion parameters, such as keyword usage frequency and recent user activity (Mochizuki et al, 2005). According to empirical studies, using video recording, the researchers argue that their system helps students to orient in a discussion. It is addressed mostly to the learners' selfregulatory processes. Moderators may use this system in order to acquire an overview of the learners' orientation within discussions and detect messages containing selected keywords. Researchers state that the system needs additional development, in order to further assist teachers – moderators.

Another example of using powerful visualizations via metaphors is the i-Tree system which visualizes the discussion status on mobile phones using a tree representation. The tree corresponds to a single user, whose activities designate its appearance. Thereby the tree's log and branches are related to the number of messages, the leaves' range and color correlate to message reading, the fruits depend on the answers the user has received and the appearance of the sky is designated by the whole discussion status (Nakahara et al, 2005). Using an experimental and a control group, along with evaluative questionnaires, the researchers reported increase in the users' tendency to only read messages and replies. On the other hand, they seemed to lack attention to the learning goal of the activity, by being more interested in the appearance of their individual tree. Understanding of the metaphor decoding was not completely examined, failing to explain why students missed some functionalities of the representation. Finally, this system was not intended to be utilized by a teacher – moderator.

Mailgroup is a Forum Type Tool with integrated analysis tools emerging from the Social Network Analysis (SNA) field. It implements an alternative method for representing message sequence in asynchronous discussions, taking into account both chronological and logical constituents (Reyes & Tchounikine, 2005). SNA was used to

examine the effect of this method in the actual communication, concluding that the approach was encouraging.

Other approaches also exist, integrating Fuzzy Logic techniques in order to assess and evaluate the collaboration level in a discussion based on several parameters (Degree system) (Barros & Verdejo, 2000) or providing a variety of visualized statistical information (add-on for the AulaNet platform) in order to help the teacher coordinate discussions and obviate undesirable situations or progress of the discussion (Gerosa et al, 2005). The latter approach is not interested mainly in the learning occurring within a discussion forum. The researchers aimed at providing a set of visualized tools for improving coordination issues related to the moderator. They imply that it is up to the moderators to rely on the system's dynamics and introduce discussion proper based activities to ensure learning outcomes.

Finally, researchers have been developing analysis tools that function complementally with well known discussion platforms. For example a set of tools has been implemented for the Knowledge Forum system (Teplovs et al, 2007), visualizing simple (participation tool), as well as complex data (semantic and writing tool). The description of the approach implies that although the visualized indicators can be viewed by all types of users, even students, it is mostly the teachers and moderator that benefit from the proposed tools while performing evaluating tasks (during or after the discussion activities).

All the approaches presented in this section, are based on quantitative analysis of activity data. They include tools addressed to students and/or moderators, facilitating their tasks during the learning activities, as opposed to in depth analyses, mentioned in the previous section, which are applied after the completion of the learning activity. The Degree system proposes indicators, attempting to evaluate a single student's performance, as well as the collaboration of a group. Nevertheless, the evaluative method is not transparent. On the

Table 1. Discussion forum software characteristics

Software	Functionalities	Disadvantages	Addressed to
WebCT, phpBB, WebWiz	Simple statistical awareness information	No real IA indicators	All users
i-Bee	Visualized representation of user – keyword relation	Not enough facilitation addressed to moderators	Students mostly
i-Tree	Visualized representation of user activity on mobile phones	Considers few activity characteristics. Addressed only to students.	Students only
MailGroup	SNA indicators, Structure Awareness	Indicators addressed to the moderator. Adequate number of messages is required	Analysis tools, only to the Moderator
Degree	Various collaboration quality indicators & advising mechanisms	Closed system, not easy to customize, with non-transparent indicator calculation.	All users
AulaNet add-on	Visualized statistical information drawn from log files	Various diagrams, addressed only to the moderator, poor empirical research	Moderator only
Knowledge Forum Tool set	Visualized tools for participation, collaboration, content and semantic analysis	Small set of indicators. They are not yet utilized in favor of the students. Not much empirical research yet	All users

other hand, the other systems evaluate the individual performance. The visualization in the i-Tree system is based on the individual performance, but it focuses on the motivation of the student, rather than attempting to evaluate his/her performance. Even for that matter, not all the constituents of a student's activity are considered during the conducted analysis. A similar approach is used in the i-Bee system, which mainly addresses the motivation issue in order to help students orientate within a discussion. Finally, not much empirical research has been conducted with the tools suite for the Knowledge Forum system in order to reach to concrete conclusions. Concluding, several systems integrating IA methods exist, but almost none addresses the issue of individual assessment and evaluation. Only the Degree system tries to meet this goal, but the analysis method is rather non-transparent.

The DIAS System

The DIAS system (Discussion Interaction Analysis System) has been developed by the LTEE labora-

tory of the University of the Aegean (Bratitsis, 2007). It is a fully functional discussion forum platform, with an underlying database management system for data recording. Several functionalities are implemented for facilitating user participation and the moderators' alternative discussion strategy planning. Additionally about sixty five (65) visualized indicators (including all possible variations) are produced, varying from simple statistical awareness information to complex cognitive and metacognitive indicators. Different sets are addressed to the teacher or moderator and the students - users, along with the corresponding interpretative schema for various discussion strategies or usage scenarios.

Our main goal is to offer direct assistance to users, supporting them in the level of awareness of their actions, as well as their collaborators, in order to activate their metacognitive processes, thus allowing them to self-regulate their activities. In parallel, we aim in supporting the discussion moderators (e.g. teachers) in order to 'identify' problematic situations and difficulties that require regulative interventions. More information about

Figure 1. Screenshots from the DIAS system

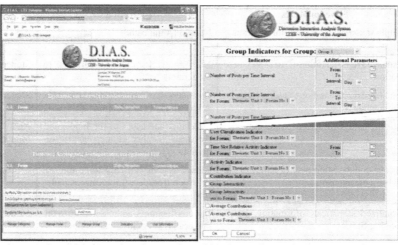

a) DIAS Discussions & Tools main Interface   b) Group Indicators' Selection Interface

the implementation of DIAS can be reviewed in (Bratitsis & Dimitracopoulou, 2005; 2006a; 2006b).

The main screen of the system is shown in figure 1a. Some useful information (time and length of the previous connection, date time and user-id) for the logged in user is displayed on top of the screen, under the logo image. The ongoing discussions are listed bellow (blue area) and some awareness information (unread and new messages, currently online users). Several buttons are available, on the bottom part of the screen, used for manipulation of user groups, access rights, message types, discussions and discussion categories. One of them, labeled Indicators, leads to indicator selection forms, such as the one displayed in figure 1b, which contains a list of all the group related indicators. A user has to select the desired indicators by clicking on the corresponding check box and fill in the appropriate additional parameters (e.g. starting and ending date). Followingly, by pressing the Ok button, the requested indicators are dynamically calculated and displayed. Especially for the implemented case studies, the indicators displayed to the participating students were pre-selected, depending on the instructional design.

DIAS Interaction Analysis Indicators

The indicators produced by the DIAS system may reveal different information to different types of users or roles. They can be divided into 4 main categories, depending on the perspective they describe. *Individual point of view* indicators present information related to the actions or the product by an individual user (figure 2a, 2b). For example, bar-charts showing number and/or types of messages per selected time slot and period and pie-charts showing activity distribution among various forae. Indicators presenting information regarding the actions or the product by a group of users, without distinction of the individual activity of each member, constitute the *Undifferentiated Group point of view* category. Such indicators are mainly activity diagrams in bar-chart format. On the other hand, in *Differentiated Group point of view* indicators, the individual's activity can be distinguished. This category includes indicators showing comparative information regarding the actions of all the members of a group, such as the ones presented in figures 3a, 3b and 3c. Finally, indicators presenting information regarding total user and group activity within the discussion forum

Figure 2. Indicators addressed to individual users

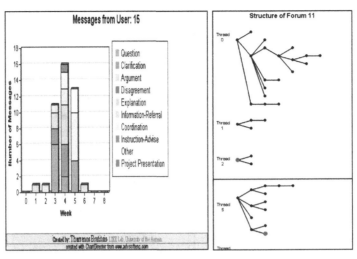

a) User Type Messages per week   b) Tree Structure

constitute the *Community point of view* category (e.g. *Community Type Messages* indicator, a bar chart exactly as the one displayed in figure 2a, but presenting the number of messages produced by all the system's participants).

All the indicators are produced by measuring quantitative activity data, such as number and size of messages written and read, by whom, etc. Their plethora results in having charts varying from low (presenting very simple and understandable information) to high interpretative value (providing several aspects of information, which can be different, depending on the type of user who is reading the indicator). Some of them are addressed to individual users (e.g. individual activity reports), some others to groups. Teachers–moderators or researchers–observers have increased information needs, due to higher complexity of responsibilities within a discussion forum (they want to monitor, assess and evaluate). Thus, several indicators are addressed only to them (figures 2a and 2b).

The indicator in figure 2a is an example containing low level information, easy to interpret. It shows the number of messages written by the corresponding user per week, in a stacked bar format. The colors constituting the bars represent the number of each type of message, the user has used during the corresponding time period. An example also addressed to a single user, but bearing a higher interpretative value is the *Tree Structure* indicator (figure 1b). It presents the threads constituting a discussion forum, in a tree-structure format. Messages are represented by vortices, and line segments depict their relations (which message is written as an answer to another). All the messages written by the corresponding user are colored red, giving a quick overview of his/her participation within the discussion forum. Applying a higher explanatory level, this diagram indicates the user's general attitude, by depicting whether he/she takes initiative, starting conversations, or acts more passively by joining conversations on latter phases. Finally the user's participation ratio (threads per forum) can also be calculated, thus giving an overall image of the user's behavior.

In figure 3, three indicators addressed to different types of users are shown. Students, as well as moderators – observers may review these indicators, drawing different conclusions. The *Activity*

Figure 3. Indicators addressed to various user profiles

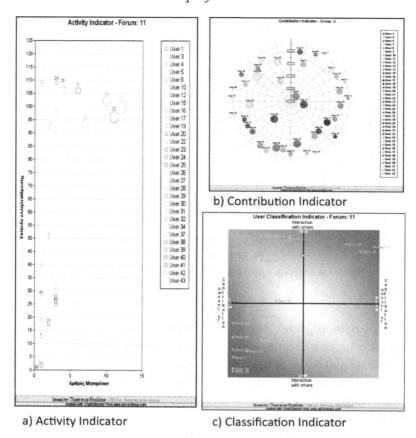

a) Activity Indicator
b) Contribution Indicator
c) Classification Indicator

Indicator, shown in figure 3a, is a XY scattered chart, with the X-Axis representing the number of messages written and the Y-Axis representing the number of messages read by a user. A circle corresponds to each user, growing proportionally to the number of types of messages used and the number of forae, the designated user participates in. The *Contribution Indicator*, shown in figure 3b, is a polar chart, in which each user is represented by a circle. The distance of the circle from the circumference of the diagram is proportional to the activity of the corresponding user, as a percentage of the total number of messages. Discussion initiations are subsidized. The size of the circle depends on the number of message types used. Finally, the *User Classification Indicator*, shown in figure 3c is a XY scattered chart with

the X-Axis representing the amount of contribution (messages written as a percentage of the total number of messages) and the Y-Axis representing the amount of Interaction (messages read as a percentage of the available number of messages) by a user. Both Axes are scaled from Low to High. By inspecting each one of the aforementioned indicators, a user may examine his/her activity in comparison with the collaborating users and thus obtaining a picture of the overall activity and his/her individual progress accordingly.

On the other hand, a moderator may also see if all users have extreme or balanced behavior (Arrogant users: write many messages but don't read other users' messages. Passive: read many messages, but don't write enough). All three indicators present similar information, but with significant differences. Comparative overview is easier using the *Classification Indicator*, with the mean values for each activity constituent viewable (corresponding to the axes). *Activity Indicator* presents the absolute values, thus depicting the actual gap between the users. *Contribution Indicator*, on the other hand contains activity information only about message writing, with even easier comparison among the users, due to the appearance of the chart. Depending on the teaching strategy followed and the activity design, important information may be drawn from these indicators, regarding user behavior meeting the expected goals.

Interpretative Schemas for the DIAS System

Apart from reviewing diagrams with significant explanatory power, one may combine information from several indicators using an *Interpretative Schema*, in order to extract more concrete and precise conclusions. An *Interpretative Schema* is a set of instructions, explaining the manner and order of combining information from different indicators, in order to extract additional, qualitative information. In the remainder of this section, we will examine a set of indicators addressed to the teacher-moderator, which may help him/her evaluate the quality of a student's participation (henceforth called User X). These indicators are: *Classification Indicator* which has already been presented, *SNA Answers Indicator*, *SNA Reads Indicator*, *User Time Reads Indicator* and several statistical Bar Charts.

By inspecting the *Classification Indicator*, the moderator may see how active (writing and reading messages) User X is, in comparison with the other users and the mean values of each activity constituent (represented by the two Axes' position). The first conclusion is whether User X has extreme or balanced behavior. The second conclusion is whether User X's performance is far ahead from the mean values in any of the two

activity constituents. Similar information may be extracted using the *Activity Indicator*, but the comparisons, especially with the mean activity values would harder, due to the appearance of the diagrams. Only absolute values may be additionally examined using the *Activity Indicator*, if desired.

The next step would be to examine the two SNA diagrams shown in figures 4. For the *SNA Answers Indicator* (figure 4a), the system produces a social matrix, according to Ucinet DL format and Agna matrix format for further processing. For N users, the Answers social matrix is an NxN matrix. The number placed in the cell designated by line A and column B is equal to the number of messages written by user A as answers to messages of user B. If the value of the cell is a positive integer, an arrow connects the vortices corresponding to User A and User B in the SNA diagram, pointing to User B. By quickly inspecting the SNA diagram deriving from the social matrix, the moderator can see whether User X is isolated or holds a central position within the discussion. Furthermore, if User X seems active in message writing (conclusion drawn from the Classification Indicator), this diagram can show if he/she is exchanging information with other users or not, by posting answers to and receiving answers from them. The number of users collaborating with User X can be detected, revealing interesting information. For example a very active user (Classification Indicator) may be isolated in this diagram, thus not contributing to the quality of the discussion and the overall collaboration (no one is posting answers to him/her). This could indicate low argumentative value of this user's messages, off topic writing, arrogant behavior or lack of knowledge regarding the topic. In any of these cases, the moderator may diagnose a problematic situation and act accordingly.

For the *SNA Reads Indicator* (figure 4b), the numeric value in the cell of the corresponding social matrix designates the number of messages written by user B, that user A has read, corre-

Figure 4. Indicators combined to produce an interpretative schema

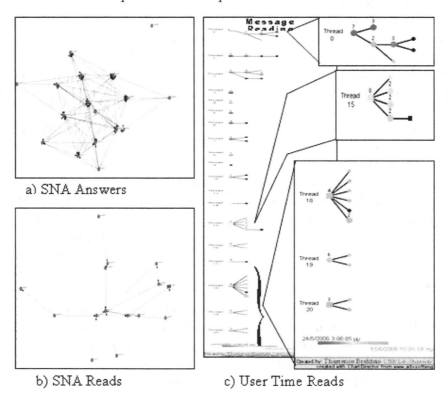

a) SNA Answers

b) SNA Reads

c) User Time Reads

spondingly. This diagram indicates the amount of other students whose messages User X reads and consequently his/her involvement in the collaborative discussion activity. While the Classification Indicator shows the amount of messages read, this diagram additionally shows the dissemination of these messages to the according amount of authors. In combination with the Answers SNA diagrams, the moderator can see whether User X is participating in a closed user group, interacting heavily inter se and lightly with the rest of the users. This may designate undesired behavior regarding the collaborative activity. Furthermore, this diagram reveals the amount of users who have read messages posted by User X. If he/she holds a relatively central position within this diagram but appears to be isolated or obscure in the Answers SNA diagram, then he/she writes messages which are read by many other users, but not answered to. Consequently User X could

be a discussion coordinator or possibly face a participation problem that needs further attention by the discussion moderator.

Finally, a more sophisticated version of the previously presented *Tree Structure Indicator* (figure 2b) which is addressed only to the moderator, called *User Time Reads Indicator* (figure 4c) should be examined. Here, the vortices representing messages are colored, according to the time User X has read the corresponding message. Unread messages are colored black, whereas messages written by User X are represented by small rectangles. If User X has read a message more than once, then the corresponding vortex or rectangle is bigger, with the number of readings adjacent to it (on the top side). On the lower end of the diagram, a gradient color line shows the time period correspondence. This indicator shows in detail a user's extend of embroilment with the discussion forum and whether User X

Figure 5. Interpretative schema for individual student's performance evaluation

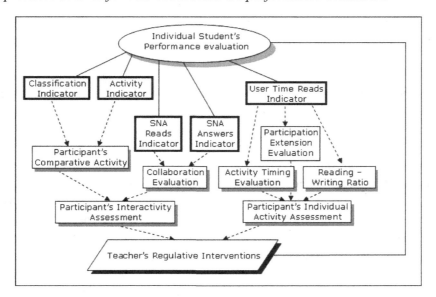

is active mostly in earlier or later phases of the discussion activity. This could be the case of a user who simply agrees or disagrees with other users' arguments but doesn't contribute with new information and ideas, which may be confirmed by further inspecting his/her messages.

More detailed information may be extracted by reviewing simple statistical indicators in bar chart format, such as the one shown in figure 2a. Many variations are available, giving the moderator the opportunity to retrieve the exact requested information. This indicator set constitutes an example of indicator information utilization and is graphically represented in figure 5. Many combinations may be formed with various indicators, forming various interpretative schemas.

Summarizing, we may distinguish two levels of interpretation, regarding the IA indicators. The first level includes single diagrams and is further resolved into two categories, one being the decoding of quantitative information from a diagram and the other being the further utilization of this information in behalf of the learning process, based on the activity settings. This results in adding explanatory value to the indicators. For

example, the *Tree Structure* indicator does not only indicate the amount of messages written by a user and their placement within a discussion forum, but may reveal aspects of the user's overall behavior, designating his/her initiative status (does the user initiate discussions or participates more passively, in latter phases?). Another example is simple bar charts, showing the number of every type of messages per day. Apart from their statistical, awareness value, they can also be used to monitor users' productivity (as individuals or in groups), thus comparing it with the expected values, deriving from the activity planning. The second level consists in applying *Interpretative Schemas*, combining information from different indicators, in order to reach more insightful and concrete conclusions. The terms *"explanatory"* and *"interpretative"* will be used for the first and second level of interpretation accordingly, throughout this chapter.

Research Methodology

Four case studies implementing a different learning approach (discussion plans and strategies) have been designed *in situ*, constituting the main teaching method for the corresponding semester courses. In the initial pilot study, the three moderators' intervention was reduced only to the definition of sub-discussion topics, whenever that seemed to be necessary. Students, forming one group, discussed topics related to the course material and their semester assignments. Indicators were revealed to them gradually, during the duration of the discussion; from simple indicators after the first week, to more complex ones towards the end. In the second case study, the teacher introduced the topic for each discussion, along with some initial studying references. Two groups were formed, working in parallel discussions, one of which (experimental group) was able to review indicators, as opposed to the other (control group). For the remaining of the discussion, he tried to monitor the activity and remind the students of the time schedule and the final goal, whenever needed. In the third study, the teacher presented an initial text, containing keywords, which were assigned to students for further studying and concepts' clarification through literature research and were presented - discussed through the forum for a few days. The teacher intervened in order to help dissolve concepts' confusions, remind the time schedule, trigger discussion using appropriate comments or questions, offer assistance when requested. Finally he summarized the ongoing discussion, linking the results with the next phase's text. During six consecutive phases, students presented theoretical backgrounds, summarized research papers and presented their own case study ideas involving asynchronous discussions applied in collaborative learning context. Two groups were formed and working in parallel in this case too, acting as experimental and control groups in matters of being able to review indicators. Finally groups joined in a concluding discussion, where all the students were able to review indicators, in an attempt to monitor any possible changes in student behavior. In the fourth and last case study, the teacher presented a problem with two

possible solutions for the students to choose, thus forming two groups. Each group argued in favor of their choice, designating the other choice's disadvantages. Reports were exchanged and discussed further in a joined discussion. The teacher's interventions were limited to reminding the time schedule, triggering activity in order to fulfill the goals. In this case too, one of the groups was the experimental and the other the control group.

As aforementioned, in this chapter we are mainly focusing in the teacher's perspective. Following each study, semi-structured interviews took place with the teachers. Especially in the initial study, we used a participatory design approach, in order to receive valuable feedback from the users (especially the teachers) in a very early stage of the system's implementation. For that matter, they were asked to *evaluate the system and assess their overall experience*. While intending to *examine the transparency of the produced indicators and the proposed interpretative schemas* (or even construct new ones), *evaluate the indicators' contribution to the facilitation of the moderator's, coordinator's or observer's work*, we reviewed all the corresponding information and discussed it with the teachers, during the interviews. Additionally, we intended to identify *ways of evaluation and assessment of a discussion* bypassing the need of thoroughly reading all the messages or using time-consuming methods, such as content analysis, by examining message content and analyzing user participation and behavior data, using the actual IA indicators of the system. Finally, utilizing the fact that all the postgraduate students in case studies 2 and 3 were school teachers, we asked them to fill a questionnaire (both as teachers and as learners), grading the usefulness of the indicators for each one of the presented teaching strategies, two months after the conclusion of the course.

Summarizing, our objectives through these studies were to initially investigate the effect of the IA indicators to the students' behavior and the learning process at extension. We aimed at researching the potentiality of sustaining col-

Table 2. Implemented case studies

Study	Population	Duration
1 *(pilot)*	40 postgraduate students in one group – 3 teachers	6 weeks
2 *(experimental)*	14 postgraduate students in two groups – 1 teacher	7 weeks
3 *(experimental)*	14 postgraduate students in two groups – 1 teacher	7 weeks
4 *(experimental)*	30 undergraduate students in two groups – 1 teacher	7 weeks

laboration by triggering the students' metacognitive skills, leading them to selfregulation of their activities. From the teacher's perspective, especially as a moderator, *this could result to the facilitation of his/her tasks, by transferring part of the collaboration management and the learning locus of control to the students, relieving the moderating work/load.* Additionally, we wanted to study *whether these indicators can assist the moderator's monitoring and decision making tasks.* Finally, *using the IA indicators as an evaluation and assessment tool was part of our objectives.* Underlying steps towards these objectives were first of all to explore the transparency of the proposed IA indicators, substantiating the intentions of the system's design and then to identify and record the emerging needs of the teachers as well as their preferences in order to detect any unsatisfied requests and improve the system.

In fact, in the research findings presented in the current chapter we focus mainly on the teacher's−moderator's perspective, attempting to *investigate the various ways of facilitating his/her tasks* and *the impact of appropriate IA Indicators' Interpretation to this process.*

Results

As aforementioned, the intention throughout this chapter is to examine the significance of proper interpretation when reviewing IA indicators, in order to support the designated tasks of all the actors involved in collaborative activities, using asynchronous discussions as an example of such activities. In this section research results will be

presented in three subsections, depending on their origin: *Interviews, Examination of Discussion Activity Data using IA indicators* and *Questionnaires.* In the first part, we present information extracted from the semi-structured interviews attempting to address the questions of:

1. evaluating the system while trying to address all the participants' (students and teachers) requests
2. examining the transparency of the produced indicators
3. recording further information needs expressed by the teachers
4. investigating the teachers' appreciation of the notion of Interpretative Schemas, and
5. examining if the IA indicators can support the moderator's tasks and in what way.

The goal is to highlight the fact that interpretation of complex diagrams in order to extract important, high level information should not be expected to occur always. People tend to immediately understand the obvious information and not further examine such diagrams, thus failing to "read between the lines". Consequently they often miss to observe important, implicit information which actually are more important for their ongoing tasks.

Following, in the second part, we apply a specific Interpretative Schema and thoroughly examine the behavior of an individual student, in order to substantiate our claim that such Schemas may facilitate the teacher's moderating tasks, as well as his/her evaluating tasks. Furthermore, by pointing out observed attempts of indicators' manipulation by some students, while trying to appear more productive and effective, this example shows how the monitoring and decision taking tasks of the teacher can be facilitated. While students interpreted IA indicators in a way that suited their pursuit of appearing as "better students in the teacher's eyes" and thus regulate their actions towards that, the application of a different interpretation approach on the same indicators reveals more interesting information to the teacher. We mainly focus on the interpretation of distinct or sets of IA indicators, in the form of Interpretative Schemas, in order to underline the significance of "proper reading" of the produced diagrams.

Finally, in the third part, we present the results of a questionnaire addressed to the students of case studies 2 and 3. As aforementioned, all of them were educators (mostly secondary level teachers), participating as student in postgraduate level courses. Thus they were asked to evaluate the indicators' usability as teachers and as students, having experience in both perspectives. We present the results focusing mostly on the teachers' perspective.

Part A: Interviews

Regarding the *system's evaluation*, comments made by the teachers were acknowledged, in order to improve the functionality of the system. We claim that our main intension, of building an independent, flexible and customizable platform for asynchronous discussions was fulfilled, after some minor adjustments in the process (Bratitsis & Dimitracopoulou 2005; 2006a). All the users were asked (teachers and students) to report any unsatisfied needs in matters of system functionality, during the interviews, but they did not request any additional elements. Overall, teachers *assessed their experience* positively, even though half of them had no significant prior experience, using asynchronous discussions for teaching purposes. They did not face any major problems

while using the DIAS system or adjusting their teaching strategy, in order to include dialogic learning activities. Moreover, they were very interested in studying the provided information through the IA indicators.

While examining the *transparency of the proposed indicators*, explanatory discussions with the teachers occurred, before and after the case studies' implementation. All the comments related to the appearance of the diagrams were carefully considered, in order to improve the indicators. The first concrete conclusion is that although the indicators are considered to be generally transparent (all the diagrams were understandable and clear), interpretation instructions, should have been provided in advance. These instructions should not only include information for reading the indicators, but also ways of utilizing the presented information to the teachers' benefit, in various manners. This ensures that information deriving from the system's indicators will not be accidentally disregarded. For example, it is relatively easy for someone to understand that the *Tree Structure* indicator (figure 2b) distinguishes the messages written by an individual user and their propagation throughout the discussion threads. Additionally, it designates the general attitude of the user, by depicting whether he/she takes initiative, starting conversations, or acts more passively by joining conversations on latter phases. This refined information seems to lack many users' attention when reviewing this indicator for the first time and should be underlined in advance in order to be better utilized. Likewise, *Interpretative Schemas* should have also been provided in advance, as it is difficult for everybody to individually imagine such ways of combining information, thus drawing more concrete conclusions. Once validated and correlated with real teaching settings, these *Schemas* can be considered valuable aids for the teacher (see next subsection).

Furthermore, some of the teachers' comments related to their specific needs for IA information. An example of data indicated as missing, during the initial study, is the size of messages in matters of words. It was requested, because it was considered to provide a quality aspect of a user's participatory behavior, as also indicated in the literature (Benbunan-Fich & Hiltz, 1999), in combination with simple quantitative information (such as number of messages). This process of ideas' exchange and needs' recording, led us to the design of various, new indicators such as the *User Time Reads* indicator shown in figure 2c, which presents user activity more insightfully.

The initial study was designed mainly for researching the students' reactions to the use of the IA indicators. As aforementioned, we chose to implement an open discussion, where students could voluntarily exchange ideas, resources and comments. Teachers introduced the initial topic, dividing it further in order to facilitate discussions and monitored the process. Having no hard moderating tasks to perform, *Interpretative Schemas* were not introduced to them. While examining all the IA indicators, during the interviews, their need for such schemas arose. It was justified by the plethora of indicators and the details of the discussion depicted by them. As one teacher stated, "*it is the quantity of information provided that makes me hesitate to even attempt to distinguish the most useful indicators for my needs. You should provide instructions for combining the diagrams according to the desired task, such as evaluating an individual user's performance*". This validated our initial intention to create and test Interpretative Schemas, which we tested during the following three studies. Such an example is analyzed in the next section.

Part B: Examining Discussion Activity Data by Applying an Interpretative Schema

As stated in the "research methodology" section, the *support of the moderator's task, using the IA indicators* was an important objective of our research. In general, throughout all the interviews

with the teachers, we found that some of the indicators are more helpful than others, but the overall impression is rather positive (as stated in the previous subsection). To give a representative example, we will use a part of the Interpretative Schema presented earlier in this chapter (see figure 5) to examine the activity of an individual student.

Simple Activity Analysis

The designated student participated in study No 1, with 39 more postgraduate students. All of them wrote 533 messages in total. Examining the *Contribution Indicator* (figure 3b), this student was the most active one, having written almost 10% (52 out of 533) of the total messages and having used all the available message types (size of the corresponding circle). This can be validated by the *Classification Indicator*, in which she appears on the right edge of the diagram, with a significant distance from the following students. Examining her vertical position on the chart, she was found to be right above the horizontal axis, which corresponds to a value slightly above the mean value of the amount of messages read. Up to this point, by examining simple quantitative information, this student's participation seems exceptional. This impression is validated by the *Activity Indicator*, where she appears to be on the right edge of the chart. Furthermore, 18 out of 40 students appear in a higher vertical position on the diagram, having read more messages than her. The vertical gaps between them were not big, enhancing the "ideal" participating image of this student. Examining this student's interactions with her collaborators, we found that she posted answers to 14 (35%) of them, which can be considered a satisfying ratio. She answered to all the students, whose messages she had read, thus appearing to highly contribute to the evolvement of the discussion.

Up to this point, the activity analysis implies that the contribution of this student is very good. Her participation ratio and her collaboration with her fellow students are both high. All the data examined for this matter are mainly simple activity data. To put it in simpler words, the numbers show that this student is performing very well. In the next subsection we apply the Interpretative Schema in order to take a different perspective of the "numbers", so as to confirm (or not) her good performance.

Interpretative Schema Application

Interesting information is revealed, when examining the time factor in the activity of the designated student. The duration of the discussion activity was 6 weeks. Out of 52 total messages, this student wrote 24 (46%) during the last week and totally 43 (83%) during the last 2 weeks. Considering that closer to the end the overall activity was normally decreasing, we decided to examine the amount of students who read these last messages. We found that 31% (8 out of 26) were read by 4 or less of her collaborators, indicating that the content of her last messages was not properly distributed within the collaborating team. Additionally, she read 332 messages, of which 51% (170) during the last 2 weeks. Having written most of her messages during the same period, we may conclude that her contribution to the overall discussion is not as highly qualitative as it initially appeared to be, due to the timing of her activity. This could have been noticed by inspecting the *User Time Reads Indicator* (figure 4c), in combination with the rest of the Interpretative Schema's indicators. It is important to notice that this correlation does not have to be applied for every student, since the latter indicator (User Time Reads) will not provide significant information for students who seem to perform badly through the inspection of the simpler indicators (e.g. Classification indicator or Contribution indicator).

Confirmation of Observations

For further analysis, we decided to examine this student's messages further. Careful reading revealed that surprisingly, the content of the messages was rather interesting, well written and documented. Later on, during her interview, she was asked to comment this delayed activation of hers. She stated that "*it was mostly due to lack of time during the early stages of the discussion activity, in order to fully commit to it*". On the other hand, she admitted that the indicators motivated her highly, in order to work harder. She characterized her initial motivation as "contemptible", trying to precede a certain student, who happened to have an outstanding performance. Nevertheless, the results proved that her potential in contributing to the discussion was very high. Consequently this student could have contributed much more in the discussion, if she had participated in a more timely fashion. Close *monitoring* of the activity, *using the indicators* during the forum-based discussion process, could have revealed this student's low performance during the first half of the activity, thus giving the moderator the chance to intervene accordingly. This would have resulted in behalf of the overall learning activity.

Additional Testimonies

The student in the previously presented example had very good potential in contributing to the asynchronous discussion activity, but failed to do so due to the timing of her activation. Furthermore the teacher failed to notice this issue, thus missing the opportunity to intervene and support the student, in favor of the overall collaborative activity. On the other hand, a small minority of the other students tried to improve their status by writing some small, insignificant messages towards the end. This could have made them appear as more efficient and active, if only activity diagrams were examined, such as the *Activity* (figure 3a) and the *Contribution* (figure 3b) indicators. For that matter, several students admitted trying to interpret the relevance of the size of the corresponding circles in these indicators, in order to act accordingly. Erroneous interpretation of the circle size could lead them to faulty regulative decisions upon their activity.

Even in the *Classification* indicator (figure 3c), their attempts (writing more messages at the end) would improve only their horizontal positioning on the diagram. Thus an asymmetry in their behavior (writing many and reading fewer messages) would have been noticed. Even if they tried to further game the system by faking the reading of messages, adding the time dimension in a statistical chart (e.g. figure 2a), students appearing passive during most parts of the discussion and showing an unusual increase of their productivity towards the end can be easily detected. Graphically, this can be easily observed using the *Tree Structure* indicator. Finally, other indicators measuring the message sizes in words are available, showing the distribution of words in all the messages written by a user. Nevertheless, students admitted that they were able to detect their "cheating" collaborators, although they were not able to review word counting indicators. A review of the available indicators and simple collation with the actual activity within the discussions was enough for them, thus indicating which contributions they should pay attention to. Concluding, it is rather unlikely for a student to game the system by manipulating all the measured variables at the same time. Besides, users' attempt to falsify and manipulate system's reports in order to improve their status is a well known issue in collaborative settings (Sun & Vassileva, 2006).

Related Conclusions

The above examples show how IA indicators can be utilized in a combined way by applying an *Interpretative Schema*, for supporting the monitoring and evaluative tasks of the moderator. It is obvious that by combining indicators, the conclusions are

significantly different than the ones extracted by each indicator individually. Thus, interpretation of the indicators is a very important factor when applying IA techniques to monitor user activity. This also designates the need for more complex indicators, which can present significant aspects of users' action in a more compact form. One example is the *User Time Reads Indicator* (figure 4c), which contains information regarding the amount of messages written and read, as well as the time factor of an individual users' actions, at a glance.

More indicators have been implemented in order to facilitate moderating tasks, such as the *Thread Propagation* and *Thread Propagation Word* indicators (figure 6), presented in Bratitsis & Dimitracopoulou (2006a). They distinguish the most important threads within a forum, for the moderator or an observer to review. Additionally, under specific teaching settings these two indicators provide a more *qualitative assessment* of a discussion. As described in Bratitsis & Dimitracopoulou (2007b), examination of the indicators' values ratio leads to conclusions regarding the discussion content. Specifically, it is proportional to the quantity of unique ideas negotiated in a discussion thread, in the context of collaboratively building justification arguments, in order to support a selected viewpoint. Thus the required effort to assess a discussion decreases, which is very convenient when large groups are interacting. The previously described example demonstrates how the moderator can evaluate the students' individual activity, distinguishing the assiduous from the negligent ones, by applying the proposed *Interpretative Schema*. Similarly, this example demonstrates that preliminary assessment of individual or even group activity and/ or performance can occur, by applying the proper interpretation approach to the seemingly simple statistical indicator depicted in figure 6.

Additional, very interesting ideas were mentioned by the actual users during the interviews, adding interpretative value to existing indicators

Figure 6. Thread propagation and thread propagation word indicators (DIAS system)

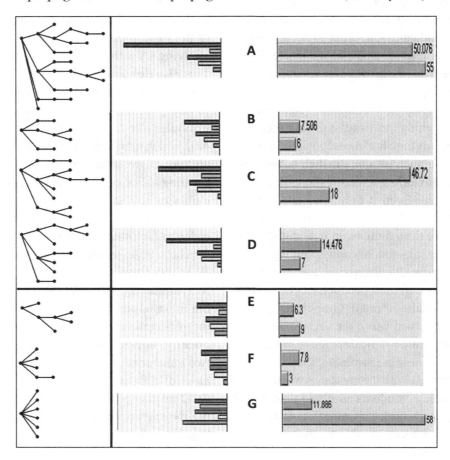

in relation to discussion scenarios or phases. For example, in a discussion activity with a summarizing phase, the moderator can review the *Classification Indicator*, in order to assign the task to the appropriate user. This could be the most active user, who probably has a better image of the overall discussion or one of the less active users, thus motivating him/her to participate more. During a coordinative phase, the *Tree Structure Indicator* may be used to quickly inspect the number of answers posted to a coordinating message, designating the appropriate time for advancing to the next phase of the activity.

Part C: Questionnaires

Having discussed these explanatory and interpretation issues and ideas with the students in case studies 2 and 3, we asked them to fill a questionnaire, two months after the conclusion of the course. This time period was considered adequate for them to better assimilate the application of IA techniques in asynchronous discussions, designed for learning purposes. Eight possible discussion collaboration scripts which could be applied to discourse activities were presented and explained to them. An example of such a discussion script is the one used in Case Study 4, incorporating opinion conflict and negotiation of meanings and arguments in the context of a learning discourse activity. Being experienced high school teachers and having participated in a discussion learning activity as students, they were asked to answer both from the teachers' and the students' perspective. The questionnaire included two tables, with the available indicators as rows and the collaboration scripts as columns, one for each perspective. They had to fill the cells with the appropriate grade, providing their opinion for using the corresponding indicator with the corresponding collaboration script. The grading scale was from 1 (Not Useful) to 5 (Necessary).

Focusing on the teachers' perspective, the results revealed a preference to complex indicators with high explanatory value. We calculated the mean value of all the grades, for all the discussion scripts. The designated as more useful indicators were *Tread Propagation* (grade 4.21) and *Tread Propagation Word* (grade 4.16) indicators (Bratitsis & Dimitracopoulou, 2006b). Three more indicators assigned a mean grade over 4 (very useful). These were the *User Performance Indicator* (grade 4.14), which presents comparative information regarding the amount of messages written by all the users and their sizes in matters of words, the *Activity Indicator* (grade 4.07) shown in figure 3a and the *User Time Reads Indicator* (grade 4.05), shown in figure 4c. All the indicators were graded over 3 (useful), whereas the lowest grades were assigned to indicators with low explanatory value. The latter were statistical bar charts, showing the number of answers to a single user's messages (grade 3.29), the number of messages by a group per time interval (grade 3.33), the number of users posting answers to an individual user (grade 3.37) and the number of users receiving answers from an individual user (grade 3.37).

Discussion

Through our studies with the DIAS system in real settings, we concluded that *IA tools can significantly facilitate the tasks of a teacher*, a moderator or even an observer, external to the activity. The importance of such quantitative information has been highlighted in the literature (Gerosa et al, 2005; Mazza & Milani, 2003; Reffay & Chanier, 2003). The element differentiating our approach is our attempt to go one step further from just presenting statistical information, by adding explanatory values and applying Interpretative Schemas.

Our experience showed that this can be a perpetual process. New needs constantly arise, leading to the design of new, more complex indicators. Of course the production rate of new indicators decreases over time, but we were surprised to hear some new ideas after conducting four studies and implementing more than 65 indicators. Consequently, it would be legitimate to say that providing a set of explanatory values or a few Interpretative Schemas is not enough. A repository of ideas for indicators' utilization should be built, which will be enriched in the future. It is not very easy to estimate the number of case studies needed to reach a saturation level for that matter, due to the variety of discussion scripts, educational settings and learning contexts.

Overall, the IA approach was positively accepted by all the participants. This conclusion is further validated by the final questionnaire's answers, in which all the indicators were graded from useful (grade 3) to necessary (grade 5). Users preferred more, indicators containing complex information, which may be interpreted in various ways. One explanation for this is that simpler information can be more or less monitored subconsciously, during participation (for example number of messages written by an individual user). Consequently, simple statistical indicators function more as confirmatory tools for the users' obtained impressions. On the contrary, more complex indicators represent information in an automated manner, which would demand considerable effort and time to extract manually.

Considering *users' selfregulation within a learning activity as an additional facilitation to the moderating tasks of a teacher*, we intended to also examine the influence of the IA indicators to the discussion activity evolvement, focusing on students' behavior. The main conclusion is that the indicators act as an additional motive for user's activity, thus providing means for increased interaction between the students (Bratitsis & Dimitracopoulou, 2006b). Evidence of improvement in the students' behavior during dialogic activities has also been collected (Bratitsis & Dimitracopoulou, 2007a; 2009). It relies upon the teacher to manage this aspect of the tool to his/her benefit, by providing an appropriate set of indicators to forum participants so as to selfregulate their own activity. We have found that different indicators affect users' behavior in a different way. We are working towards the definition of sets of indicators, appropriate for different discourse learning activities. This, of course, demands many case studies to be implemented, in order to further research the effects of the indicators on the users' behavior, as individuals and as groups. Thus, the moderator would have the opportunity to select the indicators more suitable to the designed activity, further decreasing his/her work load, by transferring a portion of the regulative tasks to the users.

Moreover, the moderator can utilize *Interpretative Schemas*, in order to make decisions and then motivate students in an appropriate way to improve their participation quality. As explained in the example presented in the previous section, the corresponding student was cognitively capable of contributing more to the discussion's quality. It was the timing of her actions that reduced the effectiveness of her messages. Hence, closer monitoring of her activity through the indicators, could lead the moderator to intervene, in order to trigger her motivation status at an earlier stage of the discussion. Consequently, this student, her collaborators and the dialogic activity overall could have gained more, through this process, at a cognitive level.

Basic student monitoring is possible using only a small set of indicators. For example the *Activity*, *Contribution* and *Classification* indica-

tors, in combination with the two SNA diagrams, presented in this paper are enough in most of the cases, provided that they are reviewed in regular basis, in order to provide an overview of the status shifting through time. They depict the current situation for all the students at the same time, whereas individual indicators, such as the *Tree Structure* or the *User Time Reads* indicator could be examined rarely, when needed. In fact, a challenging idea for future work would be to combine the metrics from these indicators in a much more complex algorithm, in order to produce alerts for the moderator, designating undesired student behavior (cheaters, delayed participants etc). Consequently the moderator should be able to thorough examine the problem, by reviewing more detailed information, by various indicators.

The core objective of this chapter was to explore the impact of proper *Interpretation* in the overall learning process, using an example from research implemented in asynchronous discussions; the facilitation of the teacher's - moderator's tasks in particular. The first step for that matter would be to explore the transparency of the proposed IA indicators, substantiating the intentions of the system's design. At a next level, recording of the emerging needs of the teachers was attempted, in order to detect any unsatisfied requests, which led to the implementation of additional, more complex indicators (Bratitsis & Dimitracopoulou, 2006b), thus implementing a more complete system. Overall, the results were promising, with the users appearing very enthusiastic in using such tools. Correlating the produced information and the constructed *Interpretative Schemas* with the actual evolvement and outcome of the discussions, interesting conclusions were drawn. As presented in the "results" section, applying a different angle in the indicators' examination, underlying information may emerge, such as the exposure of the actual intentions of a user. The example of the individual student, or even the detection of students trying to manipulate the participation variables, proves this point. After all, as the *Information Visualization* theory supports, the goal is to combine raw data in visual forms, providing different perspectives of them (Card et al, 1999). An additional conclusion is that detailed instructions are better provided in advance, in order to further utilize the produced information.

FUTURE WORK: RESEARCH TRENDS

Concluding, we claim that *Interpretation* is a very important issue in visualizing information, which needs to be further researched. A simple reorganization of the structure of a raw data set, collected within a collaborative working environment, may reveal new meaning and interpretation opportunities for the involved actors (Bratitsis & Dimitracopoulou, 2007b). The power of visualized indicators has been outlined in the literature (Mazza & Milani, 2005). Especially the research area of implementing supporting, evaluating and assessment tools for Collaborative (learning) systems in order to enhance the actual process and/or the learning outcome has a lot to gain by such approaches.

Furthermore, we explore the needs of moderators, in asynchronous discussion forae other than for learning purposes (e.g. in the CSCW spectrum: such as open-audience discussions forae within corporative networks, scientific networks, etc). A complementary, overall goal is to associate activities and identifiable user action patterns, easily inspected through the visualized IA indicators. Thus models of the expected participants' (user modeling) behavior may be constructed, which in time can lead to the implementation of adaptable collaborative tools.

The core statement of this chapter is that the design of technology based learning environments should not only concern the functionalities which facilitate acting, but also provide support to manage activity and interactions. After all, high interaction capabilities of any learning environment do not ensure adequate utilization (Hiltz, 1997). Thus such environments should ideally be linked to an IA tool component, integrated or external (Dimitracopoulou, 2009).

The IA research field is relatively new. Especially the investigation of the effect of IA tools on actors' selfregulation is still at an early development phase. Nevertheless it grows intensively and presents interesting and important results. Its potential is justified by the fact that even the simplest IA tools can be effective, provided they are interpreted properly. Such examples have been presented within this chapter. Much research is still needed in order to further examine proper utilization of IA tools and the potential benefits for collaborative learning (and not only limited to this) environments and activity design. Ideally, IA tools will eventually be addressed to both human and artificial users (the actual systems), servicing their corresponding needs (Dimitracopoulou, 2009).

The overall conclusion is that e-Collaboration of any type can benefit from the achievements of the Computer-based Interaction Analysis research field, in multiple ways.

REFERENCES

Barros, B., & Verdejo, F. (2000). Analyzing student interaction processes in order to improve collaboration. The DEGREE approach. *International Journal of AIED, 11*, 221–241.

Benbunan-Fich, R., & Hiltz, R. (1999). Impacts of asynchronous learning networks on individual and group problem solving: A field experiment. *Group Decision and Negotiation, 8*(5), 409–426. doi:10.1023/A:1008669710763

Brace-Govan, J. (2003). A method to track discussion forum activity: The Moderators' Assessment Matrix. *The Internet and Higher Education, 6*, 303–325. doi:10.1016/j.iheduc.2003.08.003

Bratitsis, T. (2007). *Development of flexible supporting tools for asynchronous discussions, by analyzing interactions among participants, for technology supported learning.* Unpublished doctoral thesis, School of Humanities, University of the Aegean, Rhodes, Greece.

Bratitsis, T., & Dimitracopoulou, A. (2005). Data Recording and Usage Interaction Analysis in Asynchronous Discussions: The D.I.A.S. System. In C. Choquet, V. Luengo, & K. Yacef (organizers), *Workshop on Usage Analysis in Learning Systems, The 12th International Conference on Artificial Intelligence in Education AIED 2005,* Amsterdam.

Bratitsis, T., & Dimitracopoulou, A. (2006a). Monitoring and Analyzing Group Interactions in Asynchronous Discussions with the DIAS system. *The 12th Int. Workshop on Groupware, CRIWG 2006, Spain* (pp. 54-61). Springer Verlag.

Bratitsis, T., & Dimitracopoulou, A. (2006b). Indicators for measuring quality in asynchronous discussion forae. *International Conference, Cognition and Exploratory Learning in the Digital Age,* CELDA 2006, 8-10 December 2006, Barcelona, Spain.

Bratitsis, T., & Dimitracopoulou, A. (2007a). Interaction Analysis n Asynchronous Discussions: Lessons learned on the learners' perspective, using the DIAS system. *Int. Conference CSCL 2007,* New Jersey, USA

Bratitsis, T., & Dimitracopoulou, A. (2007b). Collecting and analyzing interaction data in computer-based group learning discussions: An overview. *Workshop on Personalization in E-Learning Environments at Individual and Group Level, 11th International conference on User Modeling,* Corfu, Greece, 25-29 June 2007

Bratitsis, T., & Dimitracopoulou, A. (2008). Monitoring and Analysing Group Interactions in Asynchronous Discussions with DIAS system. *International Journal of e-Collaboration,* 4(1), 20–40.

Bratitsis, T., & Dimitracopoulou, A. (2009). Studying the effect of Interaction Analysis indicators on students' Selfregulation during asynchronous discussion learning activities. In A. Dimitracopoulou, C., O'Malley, D. Suthers, P. Reimann (eds) Computer Supported Collaborative Learning Practices - CSCL 2009 Community Events Proceedings, ISLS, Volume I, pp 601-605

Card, S., Mackinlay, D., & Shneiderman, B. (1999). *Readings in Information Visualization, using vision to think.* Morgan Kaufmann.

Cheng, R., & Vassileva, J. (2004). Adaptive rewarding mechanism for sustainable online learning community . In Looi, C.-K. (Eds.), *Artificial Intelligence in Education.* IOS Press.

Collins, M., & Berge, Z. (2001). *Resources for moderators and facilitators of online discussion.* Retrieved from http://www.emoderators.com/moderators.html

Corich, S., Kinshuk, Hunt L. (2004). Assessing Discussion Forum Participation: In Search of Quality. *Int. Journal of Instructional Technology and Distance Learning,* 1(12), 3–12.

Dillenbourg, P. (1999). Introduction: What do you mean by collaborative learning? In Dillenbourg, P. (Ed.), *Collaborative learning: Cognitive and computational approaches* (pp. 1–19). Elsevier.

Dillenbourg, P., Ott, D., Wehrle, T., Bourquin, Y., Jermann, P., Corti, D., & Salo, P. (2002). The socio-cognitive functions of community mirrors. In F. Fluckiger, C. Jutz, P. Schulz & L. Cantoni (Eds.), *Proceedings of the 4th International Conference on New Educational Environments.* Lugano, May 8-11, 2002.

Dimitracopoulou, A. (2009). Computer based Interaction Analysis Supporting Self-regulation: Achievements and Prospects of an Emerging Research Direction. In M. Spector, D. Sampson, Kinshuk, P. Isaias (Guest Eds.), Special Issue: Cognition and Exploratory Learning in Digital Age, Technology, Instruction, Cognition and Learning (TICL). Vol 6(4), pp 291-314.

Dimitracopoulou, A., et al. (2005). State of the art of interaction analysis for Metacognitive Support & Diagnosis. *IA JEIRP Deliverable D.31.1.1.* Kaleidoscope NoE, December 2005. Retrieved from www.noe-kaleidoscope.org

Dimitracopoulou, A., & Bruillard, É. (2006). Enrichir les interfaces de forums par la visualisation d'analyses automatiques des interactions et du contenu. *Revue STICEF, 13.*

Fesakis, G., Petrou, A., & Dimitracopoulou, A. (2004). Collaboration Activity Function: An interaction analysis tool for Computer Supported Collaborative Learning activities. In *4th IEEE International Conference on Advanced Learning Technologies* (ICALT 2004), August 30-Sept 1, 2004, Joensuu, Finland.

Garisson, D. R., Anderson, T., & Archer, W. (2001). Critical thinking, cognitive presence and computer conferencing in distance education. *American Journal of Distance Education, 15*(1), 7–23. doi:10.1080/08923640109527071

Gerosa, M. A., Pimentel, G. P., Fuks, H., & Lucena, C. (2005). No need to read messages right now: helping mediators to steer educational forums using statistical and visual information. In T. Koschmann, T. Chan, D. Suthers (Eds.), Proceedings of Computer Supported Collaborative Learning 2005: The Next Ten Years! (pp. 160-169). Taipei, May 30-June 4, 2005, Taiwan, ISLS, LEA editions.

Gerosa, M. A., Pimentel, M. G., Fuks, H., & Lucena, C. (2004). Analyzing Discourse Structure to Coordinate Educational Forums. Intelligent Tutoring Systems. *7th International Conference, ITS 2004* (pp. 262-272). Berlin: Springer.

Gunawardena, C., Lowe, C., & Anderson, T. (1997). Analysis of global online debate and development of interaction analysis model for examining social construction of knowledge in computer conferencing. *Educational Computing Research, 17*(4), 397–431.

Harasim, L. (1993). *Global Networks: Computers and International Communication.* London, Cambridge: MIT Press.

Henri, F. (1992). Computer conferencing and content analysis . In Kaye, A. R. (Ed.), *Collaborative learning through computer conferencing: The Najaden papers* (pp. 117–136). Berlin: Springer-Verlag.

Hewitt, J. (2005). Towards an Understanding of How Threads Die in Asynchronous Computer Conferences. *Journal of the Learning Sciences, 14*(4), 567–589. doi:10.1207/s15327809jls1404_4

Hiltz, S. R. (1997). Impacts of college level courses via asynchronous learning networks: Some preliminary results. *Journal of Asynchronous Learning Networks, 1*(2).

Hlapanis, G., & Dimitracopoulou, A. (2007). A School-Teachers' Learning Community: Matters of Communication Analysis . In Kirschner, P., & Lai, K.-W. (Eds.), *Journal of Technology, Pedagogy, and Education, 16(1).*

Jermann, P. (2004). *Computer Support for Interaction Regulation in Collaborative Problem Solving,* PhD Thesis, University of Geneva.

Jermann, P., Soller, A., & Muehlenbrock, M. (2001). From Mirroring to Guiding: A Review of State of the Art Technology for Supporting Collaborative Learning. In Dillenbourg, P., Eurelings, A., & Hakkarainen, K. (Eds.), *Proceedings of EuroCSCL* (pp. 324–331). Maastricht.

Kay, J., Yacef, K., & Reimann, P. (2007). Visualisations for Team Learning: Small Teams Working on Long-term Projects. In C. Chinn, G. Erkens, S. Puntambekar, (Eds). *Proceedings of the International Congress CSCL 2007: Computer Supported Collaborative Learning, Mice, Minds and Society* (pp. 351-353), July 21-26, 2007, Rutgers, The State University of New Jersey, USA. ISLS Inc.

Mazza, R., & Milani, C. (2005). Exploring Usage Analysis in Learning Systems: Gaining Insights from Visualizations. In C. Choquet, V. Luengo & K. Yacef (organizers), *Workshop on Usage Analysis in Learning Systems, The 12th International Conference on Artificial Intelligence in Education AIED 2005*, Amsterdam.

Mochizuki, T., Kato, H., Hisamatsu, S., Yaegashi, K., Fujitani, S., Nagata, T., et al. (2005). Promotion of Self-Assessment for Learners in Online Discussion Using the Visualization Software. In T. Koschmann, T. Chan, & D. Suthers (Eds.), Proceedings of Computer Supported Collaborative Learning 2005: The Next Ten Years! (pp. 440-449). Taipei, May 30-June 4, 2005, Taiwan, ISLS, LEA editions, USA.

Muehlenbrock, M., & Hoppe, H. U. (1999). Computer-supported interaction analysis of group problem solving. In C. Hoadley & J. Roschelle (eds.), *Proceedings of the conference on Computer-supported Collaborative Learning, CSCL-99*, (pp. 398-405). Mahwah, NJ: Erlbaum

Nakahara, J., Kazaru, Y., Shinichi, H., & Yamauchi, Y. (2005). iTree. Does the mobile phone encourage learners to be more involved in collaborative learning? In T. Koschmann, T. Chan, & D. Suthers (Eds.), Proceedings of Computer Supported Collaborative Learning 2005: The Next Ten Years! (pp. 470-478). Taipei, May 30-June 4, 2005, Taiwan, ISLS, LEA editions, USA.

Palloff, R. M., & Pratt, K. (1999). *Building Learning Communities in Cyberspace: Effective strategies for the online classroom*. San Francisco: Jossey-Bass Publishers.

Petrou, A. (2005). *Teachers' roles and strategies during educational exploitation of collaborative learning, being supported by appropriate computational environments*. PhD Thesis, School of Humanities, University of the Aegean, Greece.

Petrou, A., & Dimitracopoulou, A. (2003). Is synchronous computer mediated collaborative problem solving 'justified' only when by distance? Teachers' point of views and interventions with co-located groups during every day class activities. In Wasson, B., Ludvigsen, S., & Hoppe, U. (Eds.), *Proceedings of Computer Supported Collaborative Learning 2003: Designing for Change in Networked Learning Environments*. Kluwer Academic Publishers.

Reffay, C., & Chanier, T. (2003). How social network analysis can help to measure cohesion in collaborative distance-learning. In B. Wasson, S. Ludvigsen, & U. Hoppe (Eds.), *Designing for Change in Networked Learning Environments (Proceedings of the CSCL 2003 Conference)* (pp. 343-352). Bergen, Norway: Kluwer AP

Reimann, P. (2003). How to support groups in learning: More than problem solving. In V. Aleven, et al (Eds.), *Artificial Intelligence in Education (AIED 2003)*. Supplementary Proceedings. University of Sydney.

Reyes, P., & Tchounikine, P. (2005). Mining learning groups' activities in Forum-type tools. In T. Koschmann, T. Chan, & D. Suthers (Eds.), Proceedings of Computer Supported Collaborative Learning 2005: The Next Ten Years! (pp. 509-513). Taipei, May 30-June 4, 2005, Taiwan, ISLS, LEA editions, USA.

Salmon, G. (2000). *E-moderating: the key to teaching and learning online*. London: Kogan Page.

Schellens, T., & Valcke, M. (2005). Collaborative learning in asynchronous discussion groups: What about the impact on cognitive processing? *Computers in Human Behavior*, *21*, 957–975. doi:10.1016/j.chb.2004.02.025

Stahl, G. (2006). *Group Cognition: Computer Support for Building Collaborative Knowledge*. Acting with Technology Series. MIT Press.

Sun, L., & Vassileva, J. (2006). Social Visualization Encouraging Participation in Online Communities. *The 12th International Workshop on Groupware* (pp. 349-363). CRIWG 2006, Spain: Springer Verlag

Teplovs, C., Donoahue, Z., Scardamalia, M., & Philip, D. (2007). Tools for Concurrent, Embedded, and Transformative Assessment of Knowledge Building Processes and Progress In C. Chinn, G. Erkens, & S. Puntambekar (Eds.), *Proceedings of the International Congress CSCL 2007: Computer Supported Collaborative Learning, Mice, Minds and Society* (pp. 720-722). July 21-26, 2007, Rutgers, The State University of New Jersey, USA. ISLS Inc.

Vassileva, J., Cheng, R., Sun, L., & Han, W. (2004). Designing Mechanisms to Stimulate Contributions in Collaborative Systems for Sharing Course-Related Materials. *ITS 2004, Workshop on Computational Models of Collaborative Learning*. Maceio, Alagoas, Brazil, August 30 - September 3, 2004

Walker, G. (2005). Critical Thinking in Asynchronous Discussions. *Int. Journal of Instructional Technology & Distance Learning*, *2*(6), 15–21.

Zumbach, J., Schonemann, J., & Reimann, P. (2005). Analyzing and Supporting Collaboration in Cooperative Computer-Mediated Communication . In Koschmann, T., Suthers, D., & Chan, T. W. (Eds.), *Computer Supported Collaborative Learning 2005: The Next 10 Years!* (pp. 758–767). Mahwah, NJ: Lawrence Erlbaum.

Chapter 4
The Vineyard Approach:
A Computational Model for Determination of Awareness Foci in E–Mail–Based Collaboration[1]

Adriana S. Vivacqua
Federal University of Rio de Janeiro, Brazil

Jano Moreira de Souza
Federal University of Rio de Janeiro, Brazil

ABSTRACT

Recent research has noted that individuals engage in multiple collaborations simultaneously and have difficulties managing these different contexts. Studies indicate that awareness of others' activities plays an important part in collaboration. Proximity also has a strong effect on collaboration, as maintaining awareness of peers becomes harder in distributed environments. Many awareness systems have been proposed to deliver information on peers' activities or status, which usually either require extensive configuration by the user or disseminate information regardless of users' interests. With the increase in information available, systems must be sensitive to users' attention foci, minimizing interruptions, and helping focus and providing information according to current tasks. We have been investigating ways to determine awareness foci through e-mail-based user interaction analysis. Our goal is to be able to draw inferences as to whom and about what a user is collaborating, enabling a system to automatically distribute awareness information and adapt itself according to users' needs without much configuration.

INTRODUCTION

People often participate in several projects at the same time, dividing their time and attention accordingly (Moran, 2005). Recent studies have shown that individuals organize themselves and their work to accomplish different tasks, very often with different collaborators multitasking among these different groups (Gonzalés & Mark, 2005). Participation in multiple groups usually means that, depending on the situation, an individual might have distinct roles and obligations, perform different activities, and work towards different goals, all of which must be managed so they do not conflict with each other. When individuals collaborate, they often shift back and forth between individual and shared work (Gutwin, Greenberg, Blum, & Dyck, 2005): to a large extent, collaborative work is performed individually and periodically synchronized with others. This means that individual activities must be supported and tied to their group context as appropriate (Pinelle & Gutwin, 2005). In these conditions, individuals need tools that enable them to quickly switch into closer interaction when necessary and to easily relate their work to that of others.

The dissemination of network technology and adoption of distributed work teams by organizations has led to a move towards remote work: individuals that used to be collocated might now be spread throughout the world. In virtual work teams, members are geographically dispersed and communicate and coordinate via electronic tools (Hertel, Geister, & Konradt, 2005). In collocated environments, individuals can observe others and accompany their activities, thereby gathering awareness information (Gutwin & Greenberg, 2004). In virtual environments, opportunities for collaboration, interaction, and information exchange are compromised, as are casual interactions and observation of others. The focus of our research is on improving awareness of the work environment in order to facilitate group work. We present a method to automatically distribute task awareness information among group members, based on the discovery of collaborative partnerships through interaction analysis. The Vineyard system has been conceived as a means of integrating individual work with its group context, with the goal of improving cohesion and reducing fragmentation. We expect such a system will promote informal interaction and facilitate opportunistic collaboration when deployed.

The remainder of this article is organized as follows: in the next section, we briefly present the theoretical underpinnings of our research, followed by a presentation of related systems in the third section. The Vineyard approach is presented in the fourth section, followed by a preliminary analysis in the fifth section and a discussion in last section.

THEORETICAL BACKGROUND

Recent observations have brought to light the networked nature of work. Castells (1996) has argued extensively that network technology has led to structural changes in organizations and personal relations, transforming them into networks of interconnected elements. This networked form leads to higher adaptability and flexibility, as it is well suited to handle the highly dynamic environment within which organizations must now operate (Bernoux, 1999). In a similar vein, Wellman and Gulia (1999) have long pointed to the existence of personal networks, through which individuals relate to each other, form communities, and get work done, and Granovetter (1973, 1983) showed how individuals navigate these networks to achieve objectives such as finding jobs, stressing the importance of having several ties to different people. More recently, Nardi, Whittaker, and Schwarz (2002) described how people work within "intensional networks", and the amount of work that goes into creating and maintaining these networks. With the dissemination of networking technology, this type of configuration should become more frequent, as individuals will find it easier to form networks to achieve goals.

In day-to-day situations, groups of actors have control over job allocation, production planning, and control (Carstensen & Schmidt, 2002). This enables a group to quickly adapt to new demands generated by the environment or unexpected events. Many of these decisions are the result of arrangements between peers, which reflect on the work that finally gets done (Bernoux, 1999). Individuals engaged in these networked teams have an increasingly hard job keeping track of the different ongoing collaborations and configurations within which they are enmeshed (Gonzalés & Mark, 2005). Awareness of current and past efforts becomes necessary, since one individual might work on a shared artifact for a while and another may pick it up later (Edwards & Mynatt, 1997). In this section, we introduce some of the concepts associated with our research, namely awareness, attention, and locales.

Awareness

Situation awareness involves perception and interpretation of relevant elements of the environment. Awareness is knowledge about the environment that must be maintained as it changes. Staying aware of others is taken for granted in everyday interactions but becomes hard in distributed systems, where communication and interaction resources are poor (Gutwin & Greenberg, 2004). Awareness facilitates collaboration by simplifying communication and coordination, allowing better management of coupling and determination of the need to collaborate: prior research has established that awareness of others is important in integrating a group (Narine, Leganchuk, Mantei, & Buxton, 1997), creating and maintaining shared context (Gutwin & Greenberg, 2004), and establishing contact (Greenberg & Johnson, 1997).

The Focus and Nimbus model of awareness (Rodden, 1996) considers that a set of objects in space interact based on their levels of awareness. This awareness is manipulated through the overlap of subspaces within which an object directs its presence (nimbus) or attention (focus), where:

- Nimbus is the information given out by each object in the space, which can be perceived by others, and
- Focus describes the objects at which a user directs his or her attention.

In computational settings, users give out information via the applications they interact with and the operating system, and this information is normally not relayed to others. However, some of it might be useful to help the group coordinate and conduct its work: users should be able to pick up part of the information generated by others, depending on their focus. We determine users' focus through an analysis of their ongoing interactions.

Social Worlds and the Locales Framework

The Locales Framework (Fitzpatrick, 1998) provides a set of abstractions to support the design and analysis of collaborative work. It is based on the notion of continually evolving action and of *Social Worlds*. A Social World is a group of people who share a commitment to collective action, and it forms the prime structuring mechanism for interaction (Fitzpatrick, Tolone, & Kaplan, 1995). Individuals are usually involved in multiple social worlds at a time and typically engage in multiple tasks or activities that span more than one social world. This is in accordance with recent observations by Gonzalés and Mark (2005), who describe individuals multitasking between several collaborations and the effort that goes into managing these multiple relationships.

A *Locale* arises from the use of space and resources by a group. It maps the relationship between a Social World (and its interaction needs) and the *sites* and *means* its members use to meet those needs. Sites are the spaces (e.g., shared file systems) and means are objects contained in these spaces (e.g., the files and documents stored in this file system) (Fitzpatrick, Kaplan, & Mansfield, 1998). Collaboration support systems should take into account the emergent and situated nature of work and the fact that individuals constantly reorganize to perform their tasks. In Vineyard, the *sites* are e-mail systems, and the *means* are messages and attachments sent between collaborators. An analysis of these *Locales* should elicit the social worlds that use them.

Attention Allocation and Interaction Analysis

Attention is focused mental engagement on a particular item of information (Davenport & Beck, 2001). It is a selective, cognitive process, through which individuals absorb information. Information consumes attention, and the increase in the available information creates a demand for attention that is hard to meet. Each individual functions as an information provider, trying to attract attention to documents, memos, e-mails, or projects (Davenport & Beck, 2001). Controlling one's attention has become an important part of everyday life and appropriate attention allocation is fundamental, as work needs to be attended to in order to get done. Individuals prioritize their allocation of attention according to their goals and to the arrangements they have made with others, and this is usually reflected in their patterns of interactions.

Electronic interactions, such as e-mail, fora, or messenger logs, usually leave traces which can be analyzed. These interactions display certain rhythms that correspond to each individual's work patterns (Perer, Shneiderman, & Oard, 2005) and can be used to study the evolution of an individual's interests (as the individual relates to others in different domains) or collaborative endeavors: intense message exchange usually accompanies cooperative work. Additionally, individual patterns of e-mail exchange can also indicate hierarchy and positioning in a group (Fisher & Dourish, 2004).

Social network analysis concerns the study of social entities and their relationships, such as co-authorship or communication between people. Individuals and the relations between them are often represented as graphs (sociograms) or matrices (Wasserman & Faust, 1994), upon which network analysis can be performed. Social

network analysts look at the world in terms of patterns or regularities in relationships between actors: Sociocentric analysis looks at relationship structures from a global perspective, while ego-centric analysis focuses on the individual (*ego*) and the individual's interactions with a set of others (*alters*) (Scott, 1991). An egocentric network, where ties are constructed based on the analysis of interactions through electronic communication, can be searched to discover ongoing collaboration and positioning within the group.

The distribution of attention among users' contacts and projects is reflected in their behavior. Therefore, interaction and social network analysis should elicit the user's priorities and enable a system to maintain an updated collaboration profile. The allocation of attention between acquaintances provides a user's priorities regarding ongoing collaboration. If each e-mail received is a demand for attention, each e-mail responded to is a clear action on the information contained therein. This send-receive dynamic lasts as long as there is a common focus of attention.

RELATED SYSTEMS

Most awareness systems fall into one of two categories: channel-based information dissemination or event subscription notification systems. In channel-based distribution, users select a certain channel and all that goes through this channel is shown to the user. In event notification approaches, the user subscribes to certain events and is informed when these happen (usually through a text message or alert). Perhaps the simplest example of awareness information provision, messengers in general have been widely adopted and have become a frequent means of communication. Most provide ways for a user to express whether the user is available, busy, or "out for lunch", passing that information on to the user's peers through icons in a graphical interface.

Early awareness work was heavily geared towards the use of video to support personal awareness and informal interactions. CRUISER (Root, 1988) and Portholes (Dourish & Bly, 1992) are two examples: these systems provided video interfaces to display images of other individuals in the office. Experiments with these systems revealed that the possibility of easily engaging peers generated a number of new, spontaneous interactions. This added awareness of their peers and strengthened the sense of community between group members. Along a similar vein, MultiVNC (Gutwin et al., 2005) displays miniatures of peers' desktops in order to improve awareness in a working group and increase collaboration. It does not filter or verify what may be of interest to the user, and the user interface was found to be quite busy, taking up a lot of screen space.

CommunityBar (McEwan & Greenberg, 2005) is a configurable interface that enables users to keep abreast of group members' activities through media items (e.g., Webcams, sticky notes, chat windows) providing identity, presence, and some activity information. Users tell the system which peers they want to keep track of and through what media, and the system provides information through the selected channels. The user is left to sift through the information contained therein and decide what is valuable. Users liked the ability to configure their focus and nimbus, but it was considered an overhead by the authors, who stated that automatic determination of focus and nimbus should be looked into. A later study (Romero, McEwan, & Greenberg, 2006) showed that CommunityBar worked best for small cohesive groups, but was not a useful tool to support ad hoc groups, which formed outside the explicit structure provided by the system. Users complained about the lack of historical information and the added effort necessary to explicitly define focus. Feedback on the appropriateness of information was mixed, with many users indicating that CommunityBar information was sometimes a distraction they did not want. These channel-based systems provide information regardless of their content, sometimes distracting their users from their objectives. With Vineyard, we aim to perform content based matching, filter information down to that with is more important to the user, and reinforce ongoing collaborations.

On a slightly different vein, Muller, Geyer, Brownholtz, Wilcox, and Millen (2004) describe a collaboration support system that uses shared objects as the basic element: an object defines a list of people who have access to its content and generates notifications to its users of any ongoing activity on it. This provides fine grained awareness of who is working on what, which may serve as a trigger for opportunistic collaboration. The CSCW3 system (Gross, 1999) works in a similar way, but the shared object in this case is the Web page: it enables users to view who is currently browsing the same page or has done it previously and move into interaction (via chat) when desired, besides exchanging bookmarks or history lists. This means users can be total strangers, as their only link is the fact that they are browsing the same Web page. Shared artifacts are a powerful means of tying users together and discovering opportunities for interaction. However, systems based on these artifacts are intrinsically limited to already shared resources and do not bring in new elements that may enrich the group context. The Vineyard approach does not limit itself to shared artifacts, as it can also identify activity in nonshared artifacts related to the ongoing joint project.

Many awareness technologies are implemented as notification servers, where users subscribe to certain events and are informed when those happen (Ramduny, Dix, & Rodden, 1998). This usually means that some effort must go into configuring the system, telling it what events to observe and send notifications. For instance, awareness in the PIÑAS (Morán, Favela, Martínez-Enríquez, & Decouchant, 2002) system is controlled via subscriptions to users and artifacts, which generate notifications whenever an element a user has subscribed to is activated. Thus, users were notified when they were working on the same document. Given that needs change according to the situation, configurations need to be constantly revised to keep in step with users' needs. PIÑAS was used to construct Doc2U (Morán et al., 2002), a shared editing environment where information about who is editing which parts of a shared document is distributed among peers logged into the shared editing environment.

Elvin (Fitzpatrick, Kaplan, Mansfield, David, & Segall 2002) is an event-based notification system developed to support different information distribution applications. Among the client applications developed, Tickertape displays event information in a small scrolling window and lets users know when events they have subscribed to happen. Information is distributed according to users' explicit event subscription configurations, which indicate the producers they want to focus on. Certain rules can be created to filter message contents (e.g., time of occurrence). Another event based system, Nessie (Prinz, 1999), enables users to construct interest profiles and provides information about other users who are logged on and about events that have happened since their last login that match their interest profiles. These profiles are lists of events each user desires to be notified about, manually specified by the user. Similarly, the DIVA system (Sohlenkamp & Chwelos, 1994) adopts an office space metaphor and allows users to specify rooms where they collaborate with others, insert objects, and so forth. and users are notified when resources within these rooms change. This organizational metaphor makes it easier for users to understand the subscription procedure. The TeamSpace system (Geyer, Richter, Fuchs, Frauenhofer, Daijavad, & Poltrock, 2001) is a Web-based system that enables teams to create shared spaces and organize their work. Changes in these spaces generate notifications to users involved. The greatest shortcoming of these types of systems is that they have to be explicitly configured by the user and demand reconfiguration when users'

needs change. In fast paced environments, where groups and projects come and go, this can become an issue. With Vineyard, we aim to construct a system that can reconfigure itself in accordance with the user's activities, adapting to new needs and configurations of work.

A more flexible proposal, Piazza (Isaacs, Tang, & Morris, 1996), allowed a user, while working on assignments, to see what other users (who are working on similar tasks) are doing. Their measure of similarity is based on three dimensions: data being manipulated, moment of manipulation, and by what application. In this manner, people using the same data through different applications are considered to be close, and information is shared between them. This is similar to the approach used by the Navigator system (Vivacqua et al., 2007b), where information is distributed to users working on similar tasks. Similarity is calculated based on the occurrence of keywords in documents: the more keywords the documents have in common, the greater their similarity. While very similar to our approach, these systems look for new peers and opportunities for collaboration. Vineyard restricts the information to those peers with whom the user is collaborating, in order to reduce disruption levels and support ongoing collaboration.

Some systems were built based on social networks, but most have the goal of finding experts. ReferralWeb (Kautz, Selman, & Shah, 1997) was a prototype to locate expertise within a company. It was based on references provided by users about who they might call regarding certain topics. Agents would follow these recommendation chains to find users that could help with given problems. The system would process users' files, extracting keywords from messages exchanged with others, to build the user's view of each of the user's contacts. McArthur and Bruza (2003) present a method to construct networks of people and keywords from e-mail data. These networks can later be used to determine who has knowledge on what topics, enabling the discovery of people with similar interests. Another approach for social network use is presented by Groth (2003), where the author uses networks to locate individuals with a certain expertise and availability through an analysis of their activities and tasks. In the aforementioned approaches, the emphasis is on finding experts and navigating the social network to create awareness of who knows what. Unlike these systems, we aim to identify working groups and to provide activity awareness information only for these individuals, while tasks are under way. It is meant as a system to assist coordination and collective action. Social Networks are used as means for active inferencing, monitoring, and influencing collaboration, as suggested in Martinez, Dimitriadis, Tardajos, Velloso, and Villacorta (2003). The emphasis is not in the display and visualization of the networks but in detecting and using patterns within these networks.

THE VINEYARD APPROACH TO AWARENESS INFORMATION DISTRIBUTION

The Vineyard system is based on two previous designs: CUMBIA (Vivacqua, Moreno, & Souza, 2005), an agent based peer-to-peer architecture to support opportunistic interaction, and Navigator (Vivacqua et al., 2007b), a messenger system that also provides task awareness information based on user profiles. The CUMBIA framework defines an agent-based architecture for the capture and distribution of information, where users are supported by groups of agents. CUMBIA agents have individual tasks (capturing and organizing information, searching for other users, reasoning about and distributing information to other users in the network, interacting with the user) and exchange information to support their users. Navigator was an implementation of the CUMBIA architecture with agents providing introductions to promote the discovery of new collaborators. Initial tests with CUMBIA and Navigator quickly led to the realization that filtering mechanisms were necessary to reduce the amount of information gathered and distributed. Vineyard also implements the CUMBIA architecture, with the goal of helping users manage their ties to others and assist ongoing collaboration, by focusing on current collaborators and providing information related to joint tasks.

Vineyard is a distributed peer to peer system to provide awareness information relating to ongoing tasks. Users are assisted by groups of agents that reason about their users' interactions and activities and exchange information with other peers, keeping their users informed of others' activities. Thus, each group's goal is to *maintain awareness between peers by displaying information about the activities of its user's acquaintances*. To reach this goal, the agents:

1. collect information generated by the user while working on his or her computer;
2. exchange information with other users' collectives; and
3. provide information to the user about his or her alters' activities.

Given the large amount of information available, a filtering agent must filter the information down to that which might be of interest to its user. This agent determines awareness foci through an analysis of its users' ongoing interactions. Agents perform three main tasks: data collection, which gathers data from system resources; analysis, which reasons with this data and incoming data to decide what to show to the user; and display, which displays results to the user. The basic architecture is shown in Figure 1. The analysis process is explained in the following paragraphs.

To reason about its user's needs, agents gather information about ongoing interactions from e-mail logs. This information is organized to represent ongoing relationships and interest foci. Figure 2 shows the concepts involved and their relationships: the *user* is an individual who

Figure 1. Vineyard architecture

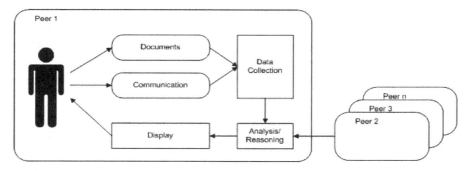

Figure 2. User interaction model

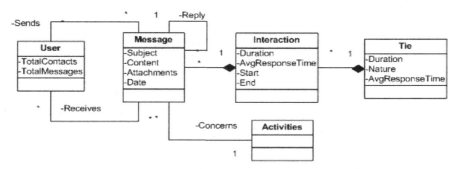

performs his or her own work in a computational environment and interacts with others through e-mail or other computer-based media, and is the center of analysis. A *tie* is a relationship between two users. These relationships are built over time, through a series of *interactions*, which may be work related or personal. An interaction involves a series of *message exchanges* between two users. These could potentially happen over e-mail, messenger, discussion fora, in person, or on the telephone. At this time, Vineyard analyzes only e-mail-based interactions. Each message contains a sender and a recipient, date, subject, content, and attachments. When a message is a reply to another message, the response time is also calculated.

The full set of user acquaintances is extracted from the logs (all contacts who have sent or received messages to the user), and an egocentric network is built linking the user to his or her many contacts. This network can be viewed as a tree with ego (the user) at the root and his or her alters (the acquaintances) at the first level, to which the information generated by each user (the list of tasks he or she is currently performing) is then added as a second level. Selecting the appropriate information is a question of determining which leaves in this tree are of interest to the user and pruning the answer space accordingly. That which is relevant to the user we call the *focus of interest*, and its determination is a two-step process:

1. discovering which peers the user might be interested in (selecting nodes at the first level); and
2. figuring out which of their activities the user would want to know about (selecting the leaves).

In the user's network, *Ego* is the user (normally determined by looking at the *From* field of outgoing e-mails) and other e-mail senders and recipients (taken from the *From, To, CC*, and *BCC* fields) form the user's list of acquaintances (the *Alters*). The system groups e-mail messages and their replies (determined via *Subject, Message-ID*, and *Reference-To* tags) into interactions and qualifies each reply by the time it took the user to respond (extracted from the *Date* field). An interaction contains several messages and is qualified by length (number of e-mails) and duration (time from first to last message).

A tie is characterized by the frequency of interaction between alters, that is, how often they exchange mail. For ego, average frequency of interaction and average response time are also calculated as a whole (how quickly does ego respond to any e-mail or how often he or she sends/receives e-mail) and per alter (how often ego sends e-mail to alter A and how quickly ego replies to messages from alter B). To reduce the search space, this network is pruned before adding the set of activities each alter is performing.

For the second level selection, the system performs content analysis on the messages sent to and received from the remaining peers, to determine their topics as well as sender-recipient groups. This enables the system to establish interaction themes and define the shared context for ego and each alter, which can then be used for matching the group context to individual tasks being performed by each team member.

First Level Search: Determining Current Collaborators

The first level prune tries to answer the following question: given the universe of user acquaintances, which ones are the user collaborating with and would be interested in keeping track of? The emphasis is on finding current collaborators, in order to seek information on activities that relate to joint work.

A list of alters is built using the values of the *From, To, CC*, and *BCC* fields from each user's e-mail logs. Tyler and Tang (2003) suggest that contents of the Outbox are more important than the contents of the Inbox in this type of analysis, as they reflect interactions the user has actually decided to engage in. Thus, the initial list is pruned by removing those alters to whom the user has not sent any messages. These are individuals who have sought the user's attention (and thus figure in the acquaintance list) but have gotten none, so there is most likely little interest in the user's part in keeping track of these peers' activities.

Co-occurrence in messages (i.e., multiple recipients) indicates the social groups a user is part of. There are certain rhythms to work, and activity within a group changes according to the need. Thus, a group may be very active for a period of time and slow down after a certain point (e.g., project completion or reaching a milestone). This means the system must constantly check for the formation of new groups and changes in activity patterns. This activity is reflected in the levels of interaction among group members. To determine which groups are capturing the user's attention, the system looks for discrepancies between the user's current behavior and the user's normal behavior. Variables that currently characterize e-mail exchanges are the number of messages exchanged (*Message Quantity*) and response time (*Response Time*). For each alter, we compare the current behavior to the normal behavior (the previously calculated average).

Alters and groups receiving more attention than usual are the ones a user is interested in. A series of replies in a period of time shorter than the average, or an intensification of exchanges (i.e., more messages exchanged than usual), indicate ongoing collaboration. Groups in which the user is very active are of more interest, with activity providing an indication of the focus of attention.

It should be noted that a user's social worlds are not defined only by a group of individuals but also by the shared context that brings them together. This means that content analysis is needed to disambiguate interactions, defining the social worlds as a set of individuals with a shared theme, goal, or project. It can thus be used to determine what activities relate to each social world.

Second Level Prune: Determining Collaboration Themes and Related Activities

The determination of which activities are related to the user is done through content analysis and matching of interactions to ongoing activities. The initial implementation uses standard keyword extraction and indexing techniques to elicit message and activity themes. Ongoing activities with contents that match the contents of ongoing interactions (determined in the previous step) are shown to the user. For this step, the agent must keep track of its user's activities, periodically extracting ongoing activity lists from the operating system, with application and file names. Textual files (pdfs, Word documents, Web pages) are processed for keywords in the same manner as messages and compared to ongoing interactions, yielding a relation between individual tasks and the social worlds a user is inserted in.

For textual analysis and matching, keyword vectors are built to represent interactions and tasks. These are constructed using the TFiDF algorithm (Salton, 1988), which generates weighed keyword vectors given textual documents, compared using the vector space model (Baeza-Yates & Ribeiro-Neto, 1999), where documents are matched using the cosine measure of proximity. Given that most of the activities under consideration are information processing tasks that involve a large amount of textual information (word processing, Web site surfing and searching, chat, etc.), this is a feasible approach, which should elicit activities that are related to previous conversations. As established methods for information retrieval and matching, TFiDF and cosine measures (Baeza-Yates

& Ribeiro-Neto, 1999) have been extensively applied and tested, with good results. However, other indexing and retrieval techniques exist, such as Latent Semantic Analysis (LSA) (Deerwester, Dumais, Furnas, Landauer, & Harshman, 1999), ontology based retrieval (e.g., Jun-feng, Wei-ming, Wei-dong, Guo-hui, & Zhen-ning, 2005; Paralic & Kostial, 2003), or the use of speech act theory to classify messages (Cohen, Carvalho, & Mitchell, 2004) to improve indexing and retrieval. The current approach could be substituted for any of these, and further research is necessary to determine the one which would yield the best results in this particular case.

At this stage, granularity is coarse, and only high level tasks are displayed (e.g., editing a file, but not which paragraph). More fine grained control, analysis, and display would enable the user to "drill down" to obtain more information.

Usage Scenario

In its final form, the system will behave in a manner similar to a messenger system: the user has a display which shows peers and their activities. The user interface is shown in Figure 3. This interface enables the user to visualize his or her peers' activities, which relate to joint work.

As an illustration, picture user Eduardo who starts to collaborate with peers Adriana and Jonice (see Figure 3). Agents process Eduardo's e-mail logs, as well as personal logs for each of the users in the system (Adriana, Jonice, Xexeo, Diogo, etc.) and detect levels of interaction indicative of collaboration, with a rise in message exchange. From their usual couple of messages a month, they rose to two to three messages a week and are now up to two messages a day, thus warranting the selection of Adriana and Jonice as collaborators by the system. An analysis of these interactions elicits the most relevant keywords to be "mobile", "collaboration", "computing", "context", "paper", "APA", "style", "formatting", as their discussions regard a paper under construction that concerned

Figure 3. Vineyard user interface

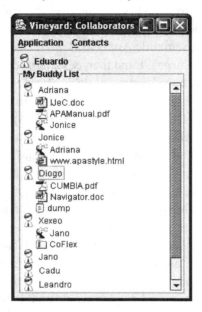

context in mobile computing and collaboration that should be formatted using APA style.

Eduardo is editing the paper while Jonice is accessing a Web page with formatting instructions, discussing formatting details with Adriana, and checking an unrelated reference, and Adriana is reading the formatting style manual, formatting the paper, chatting with Jonice, and searching the Web for movie times. Agents process these documents and Web pages, extracting keywords and comparing these to the keywords extracted from their e-mail interactions, finding a match between their conversations and the document being edited by Eduardo, the document being formatted and the style manual being read by Adriana, the formatting pages being accessed by Jonice and Adriana and Jonice's ongoing conversation.

As the keywords match certain resources in use by Adriana and Jonice, these are shown to Eduardo as relevant to their collaboration. Jonice and Adriana's other activities are discarded, as they do not concern Eduardo. The information is sent to Eduardo, so he will know what other activities are underway. With it, he realizes that

others are editing the same document concurrently, which could cause a conflict, and he decides to engage them in conversation about their joint paper. Similarly, Adriana and Jonice will receive information on Eduardo's activity editing the report and may decide to take action on it.

A similar scenario has Eduardo and Diogo working together on a class project, so Eduardo can see that Diogo is editing their project report and reading the architectural specification. Should the user so desire, it is possible to start a chat session, engaging the peer in work related interaction. We anticipate this additional knowledge will make users aware of opportunities for interaction and stimulate project related discussion.

PRELIMINARY ANALYSIS

An intermediary version of the system was built to enable verification of some of the assumptions involved and to obtain user feedback. This version performs structural e-mail parsing, extracting senders and recipients, and builds sociograms. Ties between users are qualified in terms of message count (messages sent and received), and no content analysis is performed. An interface displays the sociograms, with the possibility of exploration by slicing the data into different temporal intervals and sources, as seen in Figure 4. It implements a spring-embedded graph layout, using the Fruchterman-Rheingold force model (Fruchterman & Rheingold, 1991). This algorithm treats a graph as a set of nodes that repel each other, but are connected by springs which attract the nodes. It generates a mapping that reflects node proximity while attempting to minimize line crossings. The visualization was built using the Java language and the JUNG library for graph construction and display. It should be noted that this is an analysis interface and not the intended interface for the final system. This was used to interview users regarding their social worlds and how they relate to ongoing work and awareness needs, to obtain a

Figure 4. Visualization screenshot, several cliques are visible

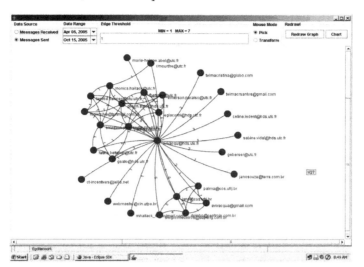

preliminary analysis and get user feedback before proceeding with system implementation.

To perform an initial verification of the first-level prune (determination of collaborators), we worked with three assumptions: (1) that social worlds are reflected in e-mail; (2) that participation in a social world indicates interest; and (3) that activity levels for a social world change over time. Four users' e-mail logs were processed, and these users were interviewed with their respective sociograms at hand for inspection. Our users are all heavy e-mail users with several thousand e-mail messages in their mailboxes. One is a university professor, and the three others are students at the same university. They often communicate with students and colleagues via e-mail, frequently exchanging files with their collaborators and recommendations in their messages. The majority of their activities consists of writing documents (papers, reports, grant proposals), studying (reading documents of Web pages), or coding. We explored their sociograms with them, slicing the data in different ways. We asked users if:

1. the cliques they identified in their sociograms were related to projects or other collaborations going on at the time;

2. different cliques became active when the temporal range was changed;

3. patterns of message exchange reflected projects;

4. the social worlds in which the user had not participated (other than as an "observer") were of interest as far as peer task awareness.

When asked, our users were capable of relating existing social worlds with the cliques that showed up in their sociograms. However, not all of these social worlds were related to ongoing work. In certain situations, cliques represented groups with nonwork-related shared context (e.g., students in the same department), who were not in direct collaboration. This observation confirms that social worlds do map to cliques, but it does not follow that all these represent joint work. While further investigation is necessary to determine how to differentiate between work and nonwork messaging, it should be noted that it is hard to dissociate the personal from the work aspects when dealing with interpersonal relationships. Many relationships have a dual nature, being partially work related and partially personal, and these two facets have an effect on each other. That

Figure 5. Time based interaction graph

should be taken into account when analyzing ties to assist the user.

Changes in time slots brought different groups to the forefront, displaying changes in activity levels. Social worlds became more or less active according to group needs, and the user's participation in them also varied in intensity, indicating interest. Slicing the data into shorter time periods considerably reduced the number of messages and the corresponding visualization, making it easier to identify subgroups. This confirmed that social worlds' activity levels are reflected on e-mail. Inspecting the temporal graph (seen in Figure 5), where time is sliced into daily e-mail exchanges, one could easily see changes in the interaction pattern. A dormant relationship suddenly springs to life, with e-mails being exchanged daily (sometimes several messages a day, depending on the urgency), and then dies out as abruptly when deadlines are reached. This confirms the assumption that temporal patterns are detectable through e-mail, even when working with considerably shorter periods than those presented by Perer et al. (2005). Changes were often quite abrupt, going from no interaction to four messages a day overnight. While this was expected, we had also hoped to see softer patterns, where interactions would gradually increase with time.

Users confirmed that social worlds in which they did not actively participate were not of much interest to them as far as activity awareness. An analysis of available data revealed that most were announcements or mailing lists that were not related to any projects. Project-based mailing lists

usually had users' interest, and they engaged in active participation. Users wanted to be aware of their closer, more immediate collaborators and activities related to pressing projects, where there was a lot of coordination to be done, and had no desire to be aware of everybody's work, although in some cases they would like to remain superficially aware of what was going on in a group. This indicates that, for task awareness purposes, incoming threads in which the user has not participated can be left out. In computational terms, this significantly reduces graph size and, consequently, memory needed and processing time. As an illustration, in one case, this meant well over 70% of the total contacts found in the mailbox. Large amounts of spam and announcement mailing lists account for most of the e-mails left out in this particular case.

Within the e-mails, there were several instances of project-related social worlds, usually qualified by intense interaction in a shorter period of time (weeks or a few months). This suggests a way of more effectively picking activity-related groups. Further data inspection showed that structure alone was sometimes not sufficient to tease activity apart, especially when there were overlapping social worlds. These needed to be qualified according to the interaction themes, so that they could be effectively differentiated. There were a few overlapping social worlds, where a group worked together on more than one project at the same time. Within our data sets, there were also a few social worlds embedded in other social worlds. While a user will probably not be interested in keeping close track of the activities of members of larger groups with whom he or she has little in common, he or she may want to receive periodic summaries or reports on how work has been progressing within the group. Thus, awareness can be seen as a continuum, with needs tied to users' levels of participation in groups. The user might desire to have more or less information (regarding both depth and frequency) about others, depending on the level of involvement. Further research is needed into this topic to better determine depth and level of detail of the information desired.

Number of messages sent by ego proved to be a reasonable qualifier for ties, unlike the number of messages sent by an alter. Some alters sent over 200 messages over a 6-month period and were neither collaborators nor of any interest to the user. A user's outgoing messages reflected user's participation and interest in social worlds more accurately. Engaging in conversations involves an investment of time and effort that indicates a certain level of commitment to the group. Accordingly, the algorithms process a user's outgoing messages first, determining the relevant alters and then fits incoming messages in with these.

To verify the value of message content analysis, we performed an initial analysis on one set of interactions related to a large scale 3-year project involving 15 parties in 6 different countries (where 6 were technical collaborators). Messages were posted on a closed forum, which constituted the main form of communication for the group. Messages were manually coded into several categories (among which, administrative, scheduling, and technical discussion) and threads were tagged according to their general objective. Interactions containing technical discussion about the project at hand and possible alternatives comprised about 20% of the total interactions, and the remainder constituted organizational threads (e.g., meeting scheduling, checkpoint reports, etc.) (Vivacqua et al., 2007a).

Terms selected by the coder as distinguishing terms in messages could also be found in documents, which indicates that technical discussions are related to the individual work participants were performing, especially documents they were composing or reading. This fact leads us to believe that textual content based matching would be successful in this situation. We also hypothesize that attachments and links included in messages would contain highly relevant content, possibly providing a better content source than message content, as they can be interpreted as personal "recommendations": their content has been deemed relevant to the work at hand by a participant. In this case, their content could be added to those of messages when performing the match to ongoing tasks. An experiment to verify this correlation using the information retrieval techniques suggested here is underway, where messages and documents will be automatically indexed and searched based on key terms selected according to their frequency. Our test will include verifying the value of attachments and links in this process.

DISCUSSION AND FUTURE WORK

The system is currently under implementation, as the analysis algorithms are integrated with the actual messenger interface. This approach seems promising, as it provides a way to explore awareness needs of individuals in relation to their ongoing collaborations. E-mail-based analysis can elicit interaction patterns that denote role attribution or the organization of a team (Fisher & Dourish, 2004). We expect different roles and organizational patterns will have different information needs (e.g., core vs. periphery members differ in terms of nature, quantity, and depth of the information desired), but further research is needed to clarify this point.

The system is being constructed in Java, using a number of additional libraries: JUNG for graph construction and display, JFreeChart for time charts, MStor to access local e-mail logs, PDFBox to access PDF files, JACOB to interface with Windows applications (Office), and Lucene for textual indexing.[2] E-mails are extracted and stored in an Access database.

Our approach works best for distributed groups, which interact, coordinate, and exchange ideas using text based media through the computer (e.g., e-mail, messenger, or discussion fora). Arguably, it does not work with video, audio, or other media, where other methods of analysis would be necessary. It provides matches for activities such as document composition, reading, or browsing the Web, where textual documents are manipulated and can be correlated to discussion. Again, other media are left out. Additionally, we expect it will not provide good matches for activities such as coding, despite the fact that it involves document manipulation. This is because coding involves a different language, which is usually not present in discussion (save for situations when specific coding problems are being discussed, and there were none present in our sample message set). In fact, a difficulty we did encounter when attempting to perform content analysis was language: in our initial message sets, all of the discussion was undertaken in Portuguese, whereas documents were written in English. This language difference may prove to be a great barrier for the system. Vineyard also suffers from a bootstrap problem: to establish interaction patterns, it needs prior records of interaction; otherwise it will take time to learn new the user's work patterns.

Nardi et al. (2002) state that two processes are fundamental in networked work: remembering (people, their interests, ongoing collaborations, etc.) and communicating (with the peers, whether involved in collaboration or not). Vineyard aims to assist users in remembering their ongoing projects by relating individual and group work. Gonzalés and Mark (2005) also state that a common problem when multitasking among several collaborations is remembering arrangements made and not letting anything "fall through the cracks". Provision of information relating the individual with the groups and ongoing projects helps the user keep in step with the different projects, while also keeping track of others' work and discovering opportunities for interaction and discussion. Additionally, by analyzing interactions, it may be possible to find resources that would interest a peer and can be volunteered in order to reinforce a relationship, something that constantly happens in networked work (Nardi et al., 2002)

Thus, we will continue to explore the interplay between interaction and awareness needs, as we believe this is a relevant issue. Even though our preliminary analysis was small, with only a few subjects, it indicates some directions for further research: to develop a more complete mapping between interaction levels and awareness needs, other variables need to be taken into account, such as response time and content. New experiments need to be designed, with more users and different emphasis, so that other information can be gleaned from the data. One of our next activities will be a controlled experiment to check on the effects of different types of information at different moments.

Further work needs to go into mechanisms to accumulate activity information in order to present it asynchronously (e.g., one user comes in after a while and receives information on what the others did since he or she was last logged in, regardless of whether they are logged in or not). This generates issues such as how long to keep certain information, when to discard it, and how to distribute it.

Privacy Issues

Whenever information is automatically collected or distributed, privacy becomes an issue. The automatic management of a user's nimbus is an open issue at this point. For the time being, we leave the choice of what to make available to the user. We are adopting a three-tiered privacy scheme, where a user can define whether a task is public (anyone can see it), protected (selected peers can see it), or private (nobody can see). The user will be able to select which alters, keywords, or resources fall within each of the tiers, and who has access to what in the protected level. When a task is found that should be propagated to other peers, it is checked against the specified restrictions to see if it falls within a specific privacy tier and whether it can be sent to the requesting agent.

Currently, users' activities fall into one of the following categories: manipulation of shared objects, manipulation of nonshared objects, and chat between members. We are working with the assumption that all shared objects and interactions within a social world can be made public to members of that social world. For instance, editing or forwarding a file that has been sent around as an attachment, or chat related to the project between members of the social world. Manipulation of nonshared objects is a more complex case. For our initial prototypes, we prefer to err on the side of caution and block all nonshared material. These simple heuristics should help us decide on whether to send information around until a better privacy scheme is in place. Upon reflection, this transparency might compromise the capability of political articulation within a group, so we expect some reaction from users.

Modern organizations are composed of networks of interacting actors, where relations between them are subject to constant renegotiation (Bernoux, 1999). More often than not, knowledge is exchanged and work is undertaken through these informal relations between workers, in networks that cut across departmental, functional, and organizational boundaries. Thus, modern organizations require coordination and integration of activities across these boundaries, and information systems should provide support for distributed coordination and decision making, while helping the individual user manage the many collaborations he or she is inserted in.

In this article, we have presented an approach to the determination of awareness foci based on egocentric e-mail-based interaction analysis. This is a promising line of research that holds many possibilities for further work. Many studies have applied social network analysis to uncover relations between people and patterns of interaction, but few have used these patterns as a basis for a system to actively assist the user. With Vineyard, we build on the Focus and Nimbus theory, adding methods to automatically determine a user's focus.

ACKNOWLEDGMENT

This work was partially supported by CAPES and CNPq.

REFERENCES

Baeza-Yates, R., & Ribeiro-Neto, B. (1999). *Modern information retrieval*. Addison-Wesley.

Bernoux, P. (1999). *La sociologie des entreprises*. Paris: Éditions du Seuil.

Carstensen, P., & Schmidt, K. (2002). Self governing production groups: Towards requirements for IT support. In *Proceedings of the 5th IFIP International Conference on Information Technology in Manufacturing and Services (BASYS'02)* (pp. 49-60). Netherlands: Kluwer Academic Publishers.

Castells, M. (1996). *A sociedade em rede* (8th ed.) [portuguese translation of The Rise of the Network Society]. São Paulo, Paz e Terra.

Cohen, W.W., Carvalho, V.R., & Mitchell, T.M. (2004). Learning to classify email into speech acts. In *Proceedings of the 2004 Conference on Empirical Methods in Natural Language Processing*, Barcelona, Spain.

Davenport, T.H., & Beck, J.C. (2001). *The attention economy: Understanding the new currency of business.* Boston: Harvard Business School.

Deerwester, S., Dumais, S., Furnas, G.W., Landauer, T.K., & Harshman, R. (1990). Indexing by latent semantic analysis. *Journal of the Society for Information Science, 41*(6), 391-407. John Wiley & Sons.

Dourish, P., & Bly, S. (1992). Portholes: Supporting awareness in distributed work group. In P. Bauersfeld, J. Bennett, & G. Lynch (Eds.), *Proceedings of the 1992 ACM Conference on Human Factors in Computing Systems (CHI'92)* (pp. 541-547). New York: ACM Press.

Edwards, K., & Mynatt, E. (1997). Timewarp: Techniques for autonomous collaboration. In *Proceedings of the 1997 Conference on Human Factors in Computing Systems (CHI 1997).* New York: ACM Press. Retrieved July 19, 2007, from http://acm.org/sigchi/chi97/proceedings/paper/wke.htm

Fisher, D., & Dourish, P. (2004). Social and temporal structures in everyday collaboration. In *Proceedings of the 2004 Conference on Human Factors in Computing Systems (CHI 2004)* (pp. 551-558). New York: ACM Press.

Fitzpatrick, G. (1998). *The locales framework: Understanding and designing for cooperative work.* Unpublished doctoral thesis, University of Queensland, Australia.

Fitzpatrick, G., Kaplan, S., & Mansfield, T. (1998). Applying the locales framework to understanding and designing. In *Proceedings of the 1998 Australasian Computer Human Interaction Conference (OzCHI 1998)* (pp. 122-129). IEEE Computer Society.

Fitzpatrick, G., Kaplan, S., Mansfield, T., David, A., & Segall, B. (2002). Supporting public availability and accessibility with Elvin: Experiences and reflections. *Computer Supported Coopera-* *tive Work, 11*(3), 447-474. Norwell, MA: Kluwer Academic Publishers.

Fitzpatrick, G., Tolone, W., & Kaplan, S. (1995). Work, locales and distributed social worlds. In *Proceedings of the 1995 European Conference on Computer Supported Cooperative Work (ECSCW 1995)* (pp. 1-16). Berlin: Springer.

Fruchterman, T., & Rheingold, E. (1991). Graph drawing by force-directed placement. *Software: Practice and Experience, 21*(11), 1129-1164. John Wiley & Sons.

Geyer, W., Richter, H., Fuchs, L., Frauenhofer, T., Daijavad, S., & Poltrock, S. (2001). A team collaboration space supporting capture and access of virtual meetings. In *Proceedings of the 2001 International ACM SIGGROUP Conference on Supporting Group Work (GROUP'01)* (pp. 188-196). New York: ACM Press.

Gonzalés, V.M., & Mark, G. (2005). Managing currents of work: Multi-tasking among multiple collaborations. In H. Gellersen et al. (Eds.), *ECSCW 2005: Proceedings of the 9th European Conference on Computer-Supported Cooperative Work* (pp. 143-162). Netherlands: Springer.

Granovetter, M. (1973). The strength of weak ties. *The American Journal of Sociology, 78*(6), 1360-1380.

Granovetter, M. (1983). The strength of weak ties: A network theory revisited. *Sociological Theory, 1*, 201-233. American Sociological Association.

Greenberg, S., & Johnson, B. (1997). *Studying awareness in contact facilitation.* Paper presented at the Workshop on Awareness and Collaborative Systems at the 1997 Conference on Human Factors in Computing Systems, Atlanta, Georgia.

Gross, T. (1999, May 16-17). Supporting awareness and cooperation in digital information environments. In *Proceedings of the Basic Research Symposium at the Conference on Human Fac-*

tors in Computing Systems (CHI'99), Pittsburgh, Pennsylvania.

Groth, K. (2003). *Using social networks for knowledge management.* Paper presented at the Workshop on Moving From Analysis to Design: Social Networks in the CSCW Context at the 2003 European Conference on Computer Supported Cooperative Work (ECSCW 2003), Helsinki, Finland.

Gutwin, C., & Greenberg, S. (2002). A descriptive framework of workspace awareness for real-time groupware. *Computer Supported Cooperative Work, 11*, 411-446. Kluwer Academic Publishers.

Gutwin, C., & Greenberg, S. (2004). The importance of awareness for team cognition in distributed collaboration. In E. Salas & M. Fiore (Eds.), *Team cognition: Understanding the factors that drive process and performance* (pp. 177-201). APA Press.

Gutwin, C., Greenberg, S., Blum, R., & Dyck, J. (2005). *Supporting informal collaboration in shared-workspace groupware* (Interaction Lab Tech. Rep. No. HCI-TR-2005-01). University of Saskatchewan, Canada.

Hertel, G., Geister, S., & Konradt, U. (2005). Managing virtual teams: A review of current empirical research. *Human Resource Management Review, 15*, 69-95. Elsevier.

Isaacs, E.A., Tang, J.C., & Morris, T. (1996). Piazza: A desktop environment supporting impromtu and planned interactions. In M. Ackerman (Ed.), *Proceedings of the 1996 ACM Conference on Computer Supported Cooperative Work (CSCW'96)* (pp. 315-324). New York: ACM Press.

Jun-feng, S., Wei-ming, Z., Wei-dong, X., Guo-hui, L., & Zhen-ning, X. (2005). Ontology-based information retrieval model for the semantic Web. In *Proceedings of the 2005 IEEE International Conference on e-Technology, e-Commerce and e-Service (EEE'05)* (pp. 152-155).

Kautz, H., Selman, B., & Shah, M. (1997). ReferralWeb: Combining social netwroks and collaborative filtering. *Communications of the ACM, 40*(3), 63-65. New York: ACM Press.

Martinez, A., Dimitriadis, Y., Tardajos, J., Velloso, O., & Villacorta, M. (2003). *Integration of SNA in a mixed evaluation approach for the study of participatory aspects of collaboration.* Paper presented at the Workshop on Moving From Analysis to Design: Social Networks in the CSCW Context at the 2003 European Conference on Computer Supported Cooperative Work (ECSCW 2003), Helsinki, Finland.

McArthur, R., & Bruza, P. (2003). *Discovery of social networks and knowledge in social networks by analysis of email utterances.* Paper presented at the Workshop on Moving From Analysis to Design: Social Networks in the CSCW Context at the 2003 European Conference on Computer Supported Cooperative Work (ECSCW 2003), Helsinki, Finland.

McEwan, G., & Greenberg, S. (2005). *Community bar: Designing for awareness and interaction.* Paper presented at the Workshop on Awareness Systems: Known Results, Theory, Concepts and Future Challenges at the 2005 Conference on Human Factors in Computing Systems (CHI 2005), Portland, Oregon.

Moran, T.P. (2005). Unified activity management: Explicitly representing activity in work support systems. Paper presented at the Workshop on Activity: From a Theoretical to a Computational Construct at the 2005 European Conference on Computer Supported Cooperative Work (ECSCW 2005), Paris, France.

Morán, A.L., Favela, J., Martínez-Enríquez, A.M., & Decouchant, D. (2002). Before getting there: Potential and actual collaboration. In *Proceedings of the 2002 International Workshop in Groupware (CRIWG 2002)*. Berlin: Springer-Verlag.

Muller, M.J., Geyer, W., Brownholtz, B., Wilcox, E., & Millen, D.R. (2004). One-hundred days in an activity-centric collaboration environment based on shared objects. In *Proceedings of the SIGCHI Conference on Human Factors in Computing Systems* (pp. 375-382). New York: ACM Press

Nardi, B., Whittaker, S., & Schwarz, H. (2002). NetWORKers and their activity in intensional networks. *Computer Supported Cooperative Work, 11*, 205-242. Kluwer Academic Publishers.

Narine, T., Leganchuk, A., Mantei, M., & Buxton, W. (1997). Collaboration awareness and its use to consolidate a disperse group. In *Proceedings of TC13 International Conference on Human-Computer Interaction (Interact 1997)*. Chapman & Hall.

Paralic, J., & Kostial, I. (2003, September). Ontology-based information retrieval. In *Proceedings of the 14th International Conference on Information and Intelligent Systems (IIS 2003)*, Varazdin, Croatia (pp. 23-28).

Perer, A., Shneiderman, B., & Oard, D.W. (2005). *Using rhythms of relationships to understand email archives* (Tech. Rep. No. TR 2005-82). Institute for Systems Research, University of Maryland. Retrieved July 19, 2007, from http://techreports.isr.umd.edu/ARCHIVE/dsp_details.php?isrNum=82&year=2005&type=TR&center=ISR

Pinelle, D., & Gutwin, C.A. (2005). Groupware design framework for loosely coupled groups. In *Proceedings of the 2005 European Conference on Computer Supported Cooperative Work (ECSCW 2005)*. Berlin: Springer.

Prinz, W. (1999). NESSIE: An awareness environment for cooperative settings. In S. Bødker, M. Kyng, & K. Schmidt (Eds.), *Proceedings of the 6th European Conference on Computer Supported Cooperative Work (ECSCW'99)* (pp. 391-410). Kluwer Academic Publishers.

Ramduny, D., Dix, A., & Rodden, T. (1998). Exploring the design space for notification servers. In S. Poltrock & J. Grudin (Eds.), *Proceedings of the 2002 ACM Conference on Computer Supported Cooperative Work (CSCW'98)* (pp. 227-235). New York: ACM Press.

Rodden, T. (1996). Populating the application: A model of awareness for cooperative applications. In *Proceedings of the 1996 Conference on Computer Supported Cooperative Work (CSCW 1996)* (pp. 87-96). New York: ACM Press.

Romero, N., McEwan, G., & Greenberg, S. (2006). A field study of community bar: (mis)-matches between theory and practice (Rep. No. 2006-826-19). Department of Computer Science, University of Calgary, Alberta, Canada. T2N 1N4.

Root, R. (1988). Design of a multi-media vehicle for social browsing. In I. Greif (Ed.), *Proceedings of the 1988 ACM Conference on Computer Supported Cooperative Work (CSCW'88)* (pp. 25-38). New York: ACM Press.

Salton, G. (1988). *Automatic text processing: The transformation, analysis and retrieval of information by computer*. Addison-Wesley Publishing.

Scott, J. (1991). *Social network analysis: A handbook*. London: Sage Publication.

Sohlenkamp, M., & Chwelos, G. (1994). Integrating communication, cooperation, and awareness: The DIVA virtual office environment. In *Proceedings of the 1994 Conference on Computer Supported Cooperative Work (CSCW '94)* (pp. 331-343). New York: ACM Press.

Tyler, J., & Tang, J. (2003). When can I expect an email response? A study of rhythms in email usage. In *Proceedings of the 2003 European Conference on Computer Supported Cooperative Work (ECSCW 2003)*. Berlin: Springer.

Vivacqua, A.S., Barthès, J.P., & Souza, J.M. (2007a). Supporting self governing software design groups. In *Proceedings of the Computer Supported Cooperative Work in Design III 10th International Conference (CSCWD 2006)*. Berlin: Springer-Verlag. Lecture Notes in Computer Science, 4402.

Vivacqua, A.S., Mello, C.R., Souza, D.K., Menezes, J.A., Marques, L.C., Ferreira, M.S., & Souza, J.M. (2007b). Time based activity profiles to recommend partnership in a P2P network. In *Proceedings of the 11th Conference on Computer Supported Cooperative Work in Design (CSCWD'07)*, Melbourne, Australia.

Vivacqua, A.S., Moreno, M., & Souza, J.M. (2005). Using agents to detect opportunities for collaboration. In *Proceedings of the Computer Supported Cooperative Work in Design II 9th International Conference (CSCWD 2005)*. Berlin: Springer-Verlag. Lecture Notes in Computer Science, 3865.

Wasserman, S., & Faust, K. (1994). *Social network analysis: Methods and applications*. Cambridge: Cambridge University Press.

Wellman, B., & Gulia, M. (1999). Netsurfers don't ride alone: Virtual communities as communities. In B. Wellman (Ed.), *Networks in the global village* (pp. 331-366). Boulder, CO: Westview Press.

ENDNOTES

[1] An earlier version of this article was published in the Proceedings of the 12th International Workshop on Groupware: Design Implementation and Use, CRIWG 2006, held in Medina del Campo, Spain.

[2] http://jung.sourcefourge.net/; http://www.jfree.org/jfreechart/; http://mstor.sourceforge.net/; http://www.pdfbox.org/; http://danadler.com/jacob/; http://lucene.apache.org/java/docs/index.html

This work was previously published in the International Journal of e-Collaboration, Vol. 4, Issue 1, edited by N. Kock, pp. 41-59, copyright 2008 by IGI Publishing (an imprint of IGI Global).

Chapter 5
mobileSJ:
Managing Multiple Activities in Mobile Collaborative Working Environments[1]

Jesus Camacho
CICESE, Mexico

Leonardo Galicia
CICESE, Mexico

Victor M. Gonzalez
University of Manchester, UK

Jesus Favela
CICESE, Mexico

ABSTRACT

Many modern working environments are characterized by the need to manage multiple activities simultaneously. This is the case of hospital work, which also demands a high degree of mobility and collaboration among specialists. These working conditions have motivated us to design and implement mobileSJ, a mobile information management tool based on the concept of working spheres. The tool allows users to gather information related to a working sphere, including documents, contacts, and pending tasks. The tool assists users when switching between tasks, facilitates the sharing of activity related information with colleagues, as well as the synchronization of information among multiple devices, including handheld computers and public displays. We conducted a usability test and a focus group to inform the design of a new version of the tool and to know how the tool could support the work of medical interns by facilitating the management and sharing of resources, providing more efficient means of communication with colleagues and increasing their personal productivity.

INTRODUCTION

Modern work environments require professionals to constantly switch among different activities. Within the context of office work, previous studies have shown that the engagement in each activity can be rather brief, averaging just a few minutes (Czerwinski, Horvitz, & Wilhite, 2004; Gonzalez & Mark, 2004). Professionals can switch between different activities because they are interrupted (unexpected visit, a call phone, etc.) or because, by their own initiative, they decide to focus on another task. Studies have shown that people interrupt themselves as much as they are externally interrupted (Sproull, 1984) and that immediate resumption of an interrupted activity is not always likely to happen, occurring just two-thirds of the time (Gonzalez & Mark, 2004). Commonly the transition between activities is not simple because it requires important context switching, not just of mental states but also switching at the level of retrieving physical or digital representations of resources. In order to preserve the status of an activity and facilitate context retrieval, people often organize their workspaces or seed "marks" on it (Kirsh, 2001; Malone, 1983; Rouncefield, Hughes, Rodden, & Viller, 1994). For instance, it has been noticed that many professional have clutter over their desks and usually they are disrupted by changes made to this apparent "muddle", because this apparent clutter includes landmarks of the actions and activities that they need to do (Kidd, 1994). Furthermore, organizing workspaces can be complex when multiple activities are managed simultaneously, and when multiple resources are associated to each activity. This is because performing an activity usually implies the use of a diversity of information resources such as documents, notes, agendas, calendars, or diagrams. Consequently, the need to remember the location and gather all the information resources related to an activity is likely to involve certain effort and sometimes results on cognitive overload for the user, which can be even more challenging in the digital realm, as current computer operating systems make the invocation of such resources a complex and time consuming task (Kaptelinin, 2003; Voida, Mynatt, MacIntyre, & Corso, 2002).

Although handling resources and managing multiple activities can be problematic for many types of information work contexts, a particularly challenging context is the one experienced by medical workers. Hospitals are dynamic and intensive work environments where people have multiple activities and responsibilities, and cope with frequent contingencies that require them to constantly adjust and readjust their actions (Bardram & Bossen, 2003). In addition, hospital workers are highly mobile and experience a high degree of collaboration and coordination with colleagues. The activities of most hospital workers clearly are not tied to a desktop or a specific location because they need to move to locate colleagues, take care of patients, and access information and other resources distributed in space (Bardram & Bossen, 2003; Muñoz, Rodriguez, Favela, Gonzalez, & Martinez-Garcia, 2003). This phenomenon identified as local mobility (Belloti & Bly, 1996) requires the user to change "workplace" constantly and even suddenly. Besides, the specialized nature of medical work makes the treatment and care of patients an inherently collaborative effort among specialized medical workers who have to be in constant communication with each other to be able to perform their activities.

In this article, we describe the design of an application to support mobile workers in managing their multiple activities and collaborations. Based on the concept of working sphere proposed by Gonzalez and Mark (2005), we defined an application to support medical interns while carrying out their activities. The rest of this article is organized in the following way. In the second section, we briefly explain our approach to the concept of working sphere and its instantiation in the application named "Sphere Juggler", which served as the basis for the tool mobileSJ presented here. In the third section, we discuss mobile worker's need to manage multiple activities by focusing on the work of a particular kind of medical workers: medical interns. In the fourth section, we describe the application mobileSJ, its functionality, and architecture. The fifth section presents the results of a usability test and a focus group conducted with potential users, as well as a discussion of the findings. Finally, in the last section, we present conclusions and directions for future work.

WORKING SPHERES

The concept of "working spheres" (Gonzalez & Mark, 2004) was introduced as a proposal to conceive the way in which people organize and execute their work activities. A working sphere has been defined as "a set of interrelated tasks, which share a common motive, involve the interaction with a particular constellation of people, use ensembles of resources and have their own individual time framework" (Gonzalez & Mark, 2004). As a concept, a working sphere refers to a particular way to abstract human work from the perspective of those executing it and, more important, as a way to represent those efforts that transcend mere actions (e.g., a phone call). From a system perspective, a working sphere could be supported by implementing a repository where the resources and the applications concerning each sphere can be stored and easily recovered whenever necessary. The application "Sphere Juggler" (Morteo, Gonzalez, Favela, & Mark, 2004) implements the concept of working sphere and creates its computational representation: an e-sphere. This application allows the user to manage multiple activities and information and contextual resources in a centralized way. The user can define e-spheres for each activity and associate to them information resources, contacts relevant to the activity, e-mails related to the activity, and pending issues to help the user's prospective memory.

When a user switches between e-spheres, each e-sphere is enabled to quickly gather and retrieve its own workspace state (windows positions, status, and overlay order) and context information, such as opened documents, idle time, and so forth in a silent manner. Thus, the application hides the resources and state of the previous sphere and shows the ones related to the recently restored activity. This provides the user with the necessary context when changing activities.

MOBILE WORKERS WITH MULTIPLE ACTIVITIES: THE CASE OF MEDICAL INTERNS

To illustrate the need to support the management of multiple activities in a mobile and intensively collaborative working environment such as a hospital, we consider the work of a medical intern. We base our analysis on the results of a workplace study conducted in the internal medicine area of a midsize teaching hospital (Moran, Tentori, Gonzalez, Favela, & Martinez, 2006). The daily routine and typical duties of an intern can be summarized as follows: Medical interns meet at 7 a.m. with the physician in charge of the area at the internal medicine office, where they briefly discuss the night's events described by the intern who worked the night shift. After the discussion, the interns gather information related to the patients assigned to them and place it in each of the patients' bedrooms. They walk down to the laboratory to gather laboratory results of the patients and attach them to the medical record. Later, the interns meet at the internal medicine office, and, for one or two hours, they listen to a colleague's assessment of a particular medical issue or interesting clinical case. After that, they go to the bed wards where, along with the physician, they conduct the ward round. During the round, they discuss each patient's clinical case consulting the patient's medical record and laboratory tests. Finally, once the medical interns finish the round, the rest of the shift is spent mostly doing paperwork in the internal medicine office. Medical interns are considered physicians in training; they provide the most hours of patient care in the unit and are constantly moving throughout the hospital. Interns are responsible for the care of five or six patients. One of their main responsibilities is to create clinical histories whenever a new patient arrives in the hospital. They are also responsible for providing care and follow-up on patients during their stay in the hospital. Other tasks for which medical interns are responsible have a more collaborative nature; for instance, they participate in ward rounds with attending physicians and in meetings where clinical cases are discussed. Finally, since they are still students, they have to prepare presentations and reports for their courses. The following subsections describe in more detail how the demands of medical intern's work shape the requirements for a system supporting the management of their multiple working spheres.

Management of Multiple Activities and Resources

Given that medical interns have to cope with multiple activities, which are often fragmented by interruptions and which require them to gather and consult a great amount of information resources, the application must provide users with mechanisms to easily manage their activities and their associated resources. Most of the medical intern's activities are centered on their patients and their courses, which can be considered their main working spheres. These working spheres might not be exclusively their own; they are often shared, as is the case of a patient whose care is the responsibility of the intern, but also of the attending physician and responsible nurse. In addition, the responsibility is transferred to other interns as they change shifts. When the intern returns the next day, the intern needs to get updated on the current state and main events related to the patients for which the intern is responsible.

User Mobility

Although medical interns use computers, a system based solely on a desktop application will not provide interns with adequate support since they are constantly moving around the hospital. A previous study revealed that medical interns spend at least 40% of their work shift away from a base location, such as an office or medical station (Moran et al., 2006). Thus, the application should be designed to be used in both desktop computers and mobile devices such as Personal Digital Assistants (PDAs) or SmartPhones. The desktop based version and the mobile version have to be independent but must have the ability to synchronize their contents. Thus, the application should provide mechanisms for the synchronization of activities and resources, taking into account the differences in the capacities of the devices, both in terms of memory as well as screen size.

High Degree of Collaboration and Communication

Because of its complex nature, hospital work demands close coordination and collaboration among different specialists. In order to support these collaborative interactions, the application must include mechanisms for the users to share activities and information resources among heterogeneous devices, such as between two PDAs when two colleagues encounter each other in a hallway. The application should also allow the visualization of spheres and resources in semipublic displays to facilitate the collaboration among colleagues. Besides, the application must provide users with simple mechanisms to communicate with colleagues while the user is on the move.

THE mobileSJ APPLICATION

mobileSJ was designed and implemented to assist mobile users in the management of their multiple activities and collaborations. The application has its origin in a previous design called Sphere Juggler that runs on desktop computers and does not support shared activities and collaborations (Morteo et al., 2004). In contrast, mobileSJ runs on PDAs and SmartPhones and includes a set of capabilities not present in Sphere Juggler, like sharing of activities and resources, as well as ways to communicate with colleagues on the move through either SMS messages or phone calls. This application is completely independent but at the same time offers the ability to communicate and synchronize with the desktop Sphere Juggler. We illustrate the functionality offered by mobileSJ by considering a typical work shift of a medical intern, as described in the third section.

Support for the Management of Activities

The medical intern has several patients, as well as a few school projects. The intern uses Sphere Juggler in his or her Personal Computer (PC) and mobileSJ in his or her PDA. Over time, the intern has created an e-sphere for each activity and associated information resources, contact information, and pending issues. He might also search specialized medical digital libraries for information relevant to the intern's activities and associate this new information (URLs, PDF documents, etc.) to the corresponding e-spheres. When the intern has to go to the hospital, the intern connects the PDA to the PC, which launches a synchronization application. The application automatically transfers the new resources created in the PDA to the PC. The interface of the synchronization application shown on Figure 1a allows the user to select those files that the intern wants copied from the PC to the PDA or deleted from it. This is done in consideration of the limited storage capacity of the PDA. To assist the user in deciding which files to transfer, the size of each file is indicated, as well as the remaining space in the PDA. Alternatively, the user can synchronize spheres over the Internet through a Web service application called SincroServer, thus making his or her spheres and resources available wherever he or she has Internet access (his or her workplace or school). When the intern arrives at the hospital, he or she no longer needs to locate and gather documents related to each of his or her patients. He can access those documents directly from the e-spheres in mobileSJ.

Support for Mobility

During the ward round, when the group arrives with a patient assigned to the medical intern,

Figure 1. (a) Synchronization application; (b) e-spheres and their associated resources; (c) adding a new resource to an e-sphere

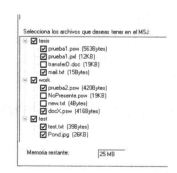  

the intern uses mobileSJ to select the sphere that represents that patient, and the application displays the information resources, contacts, and reminders of pending issues associated to the patient (Figure 1b). If the intern needs to consult any of these resources, he or she just selects it and the resource is opened in the appropriate application (i.e., Web browser, PDF reader, etc.). This is done without the need for the user to specify the resource location or the application required to open it. The application shows all the information resources contained in each sphere either if they are physically in the PDA or not (indicating the latter with a special icon). When the user needs a resource that is not in the PDA, he or she can download it easily from the SincroServer application, or if the intern does not want the resource to be copied to the PDA or the PDA does not have an application capable to handle the resource, the intern can visualize the resource remotely from his PDA through the remote access capability. Furthermore, through SincroServer, the user can synchronize any specific sphere he or she needs (or all of them) with the server while he or she is moving around the hospital, selecting the information resources he or she wants to download (through a wireless Internet connection). During the ward round, the intern might create additional resources related to his or her activities (personal or medical notes, photos, link to a Web page, etc.), and automatically associate them to the current activity (Figure 1c). When the medical intern finishes the round, he or she moves to the physicians' office to write the medical notes. The intern connects his PDA to the PC and the synchronization application merges his or her e-spheres and transfers the new resources he or she has created or changed to the desktop computer. Once in the desktop computer, the intern can comfortably edit the notes he or she took in the PDA to complete the medical note, consulting information resources related to the patient from Sphere Juggler when required.

Support for Collaboration

As the intern moves around the hospital to work, the medical intern needs to consult with the attending physician, nurses, and other interns. To discuss a clinical case, the intern can use mobileSJ either by sharing a working sphere with a colleague or by using the application to navigate the resources related to a working sphere on a public display. To work with a colleague on a shared sphere, the intern selects the e-sphere and then the resources that the user wants to transfer to either a public display or the PDA of the co-worker (Figure 2a). This is done to ensure that the application will not transfer resources considered as private by the user. When the public display receives the sphere and its resources, it automatically displays its information resources. In this way, the colleagues can comfortably review the case on the public display. When they finish the interaction, the medical intern can transfer the updated sphere to his colleague's PDA. When the mobileSJ running in the PDA detects the sphere, it transfers it automatically and inserts the received sphere/resources in the sphere tree, making it immediately available to the intern from his or her own mobileSJ client. In addition to these collaborative services, mobileSJ allows users to send e-mail or SMS messages and, when working in a SmartPhone, initiate a telephone call. Contacts can be associated to e-spheres like any other resource. When working on an e-sphere, the user can select the contact he or she wants to communicate with, and the system shows the intern the various mechanisms available to establish the communication (Figure 2b). This is done directly from the mobileSJ interface without the need to introduce a telephone number or open external applications. The user just needs to select the contact and the communication option, and the system does the rest.

Figure 2. (a) User selection of resources to be shared or transferred; (b) communication options

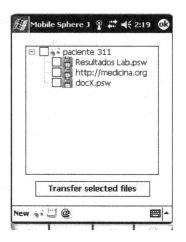 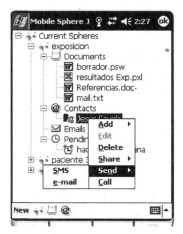

Implementation of mobileSJ

mobileSJ runs on PDAs and SmartPhones with the WindowsCE operating system. The application is implemented in five modules on the PDA and two more modules implemented to handle the synchronization between the PDA and a desktop computer or a server (Figure 3).

mSJ Module

The mSJ module is the interface through which the user interacts with the system, allowing the user to create and manipulate e-spheres and their associated resources. This module handles the invocation of resources in the appropriate applications and also monitors the resource, registering changes in order to inform the synchronization process which resources have been modified in the device. mSJ uses all the other PDA modules to perform all the functionalities the mobile Sphere Juggler is capable of doing, like communication or collaboration capabilities. This module also interacts with the modules in the desktop computer (sincroSJ) and the Web server (SincroServer) to synchronize the spheres.

Synchronization Modules

The sincroSJ and SincroServer modules have the same functionality, the synchronization of spheres and resources between two devices. The sincroSJ module is actually an independent application which runs in a desktop computer. It is used to synchronize spheres between the desktop computer and a mobile device through an ActiveSync connection when the user connects his or her PDA to the PC, a mechanism commonly used to synchronize data with mobile devices. However, this approach forces the user to keep his or her PDA connected while synchronizing spheres. To add flexibility to the synchronization process, SincroServer can be used to synchronize the spheres of a device (desktop computer or mobile device) with the spheres of a server through the Internet (the module is implemented through a set of Web services). In this way, the user can access his or her spheres and resources wherever he or she has Internet access. Further, to add more flexibility, the SincroServer was implemented as an on-demand function: the user can indicate the application to synchronize just a specific sphere or resource with the server.

Figure 3. mobileSJ architecture, showing the modules deployed in the PDA, PC, and Web server

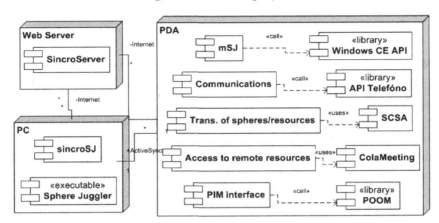

Transfer Module

This module allows users to transfer spheres and resources between different devices like PCs, PDAs, and public displays. This module detects all registered devices in the proximity and presents them as options for the user to decide to which device the user wants to transfer the sphere/resource. To actually transfer the resources, this module uses the application SCSA (Software Components for Salsa Agents) (Rodríguez & Favela, 2003). For the desktop computer side, this functionality is implemented through the SALSA framework (Rodríguez & Favela, 2003). This framework allows the implementation of autonomous agents which react to certain events and perform actions according to the events raised. All the event notification process is done through an agent broker. The implementation in the mobile device uses a framework version called mSALSA which is specifically designed to be used in mobile devices.

Communication Module

The Communication module is responsible for handling communication with contacts associated to the user's activities. This includes the ability to send e-mails, SMS messages, and phone calls. To make all those communication operations faster and more flexible, they are performed directly from this module without the need of third party applications. This module interacts directly with the phone API of the device and implements its own messaging and e-mail clients.

Remote Access Module

This module allows the user to remotely visualize on the mobile device files stored in the desktop computer. This is convenient for large files that the user does not want stored in the PDA, or those for which there is no corresponding application in the PDA. The user can remotely manipulate the application from the PDA.

PIM Module

Finally, the application includes a module that handles associations between contacts and pending issues in the PIM (personal information management) tool of the PDA and mobileSJ, allowing the user to seamlessly and consistently work with both applications. The user can add contacts to a sphere that were previously defined in the PIM tool, or add new elements to the PIM tool database directly from the mobileSJ interface and, at the same time, associate them to a sphere.

EVALUATION

With the purpose of evaluating the application mobileSJ and exploring its potential to support the activities of medical interns, we conducted a usability test and a focus group. Each evaluation focused on one of the two main factors influencing technology adoption, namely ease of use and perceived usefulness (Davis & Venkatesh, 1996). The usability evaluation required users to perform specific tasks with little previous knowledge of the system to determine if the system is easy to use. The focus group was conducted with medical interns and was aimed at understanding how well mobileSJ supports their main activities. We aimed at testing and improving our design by focusing on the way in which medical interns conceptualize their activities, the level of support required in four of their main daily routines, and the challenges they face when managing multiple activities.

Usability Test

We conducted a usability test with 16 participants divided into 2 groups of 8. One was the control group which used the regular tools (file manager, contacts manager, mail client, etc.) included in a SmartPhone with Windows CE to perform the test, and the other group used mobileSJ's features to complete the same tasks. All participants had previous experience with the use of PDAs and touch screens. The purpose of the test was to explore the features of mobileSJ in a simulated environment which forced the users to constantly switch between tasks and to manage the resources associated to them. We prepared an evaluation room were the experiment was conducted, which included a digital whiteboard (SmartBoard), two

computers, and two SmartPhones, one of them running mobileSJ. The usability test was carried out in the following way: The participants were asked to complete questions related to three main topics. Each topic represented a different area of interest and required different information resources. An application on the SmartBoard showed participants the questions, changing the topic from time to time, so that they could interact with each topic several times, switching between topics and forcing them to manage the different resources necessary to answer each question. Participants read the question displayed on the SmartBoard and then used their SmartPhone to search and consult the information resources needed to answer that question by selecting one of four possible answers.

Results

Participants were instructed on the test (5 min.) and then were trained on the use of the technology, particularly the use of the SmartBoard and mobileSJ (10 min.). Once they were familiar with the technology, they performed the tasks assigned showing no significant differences in time ($t = 0.75$). After completing the test, each participant filled out a questionnaire about the perception of comfort with the tool (with or without mobileSJ). The questionnaire had a Likert scale to qualify the feeling of comfort while they performed the task required during the test. The Likert scale was divided between 1 (strongly disagree) to 7 (strongly agree) where 4 was neutral. The difference was statistically significant ($t < 0.05$, for 95% confidence interval), with an average result for the control group of 5.89 ($sd = 0.45$) and 6.33 ($sd = 0.29$) for the group that used mobileSJ. We found, on the other hand, no significant difference between the groups in the number of tasks completed. During the experiment, the mobileSJ tool worked without error and users were able to work with it with limited training.

Focus Group

The focus group was conducted in a room with a meeting table, blackboard, display, and projector. We installed a video camera and voice recorders in the room to capture all events during the session. We invited five medical interns from the public local hospital in Ensenada, Mexico; all of them had recently finished their one year internship and consequently were very familiar with hospital work and its routines. Three of the five attended the session. The session was conducted by one moderator; three other people worked controlling the equipment or distributing information; one more worked as observer and note-taker. The moderator and the observer sat with the medical interns at the table. Information was presented using a projector and slide presentation software running in a personal computer. The session lasted approximately one and half hours and it was divided into two parts.

The first part started with an explanation of the concept of actions and activities and how activities are composed by actions and resources; after that, the medical interns participated in an exercise where they were asked to write and describe their main activities during a typical shift in the hospital. They were asked to indicate the resources used to complete those activities. After this, we asked them questions about their activities with the purpose of clarifying their nature. When this part was finished, we presented to them the concept of working spheres and showed them examples of the actions and resources associated to them. By presenting the concept of working spheres at the end, we were aiming at finding how well the activities described by the medical interns matched the way we conceptualized the working spheres for the implementation of mobileSJ. During the second part of the focus group, we presented a demo of mobileSJ running in a SmartPhone. We used the screen to project the operations performed on the device, with the purpose of facilitating the understanding of the

functionality of the application. Using the SmartPhone, the moderator showed how mobileSJ can support tasks performed by medical interns at their workplace. During the session we presented four main routines for which we foresaw that the application can be particularly useful:

- **Patient Visits Round:** Medical interns are responsible for the care of about five or six patients including the creation and maintenance of their clinical histories. These histories consisted of resources such as x-rays, laboratory result, notes, medical records, and so forth.
- **Medical Note Elaboration:** After visiting their patients, medical interns need to elaborate the medical note of all of them using a personal computer. The information for this process comes from the personal notes taken during the visit.
- **Preparation of Presentations:** Medical interns are still students, and consequently they have to prepare some presentations and reports for their courses. With this activity, they need to manage several resources including pictures, medical information, patient data, and so forth.
- **Collaboration with Colleagues:** We emphasized the collaborative nature of their work, by highlighting their participation in ward rounds with attending physicians and in meetings where clinical cases are discussed.

After this demo, we conducted a session of questions and open discussion about the features, advantages, and limitations of mobileSJ.

Results

The results from the analysis of the session indicate that the activities conceptualized by medical interns are likely to be supported by the actual implementation of mobileSJ. We found that examples of activities indicated by medical interns match with the previous conceptions and scenarios that we identified to guide the design and implementation of mobileSJ. Interestingly, in spite that they work in different areas of the hospital, many of their activities are similar in nature. During this part, we also found that some of them explicitly pointed out their PDAs as resources to perform some activities (e.g., patient visits round, medical note elaboration, and ward round). From the second part of the session, we were able to identify the reactions towards the main features of mobileSJ as well as obtain information about functionality that we were not supporting at the time and that were considered in the final design of the application. In the following subsections, we discuss some of these findings.

Sharing of Resources

Due to the fast pace and mobile environment where medical interns are immersed, many interactions with other medical personnel are needed to carry out their activities. These interactions involve sharing different resources and information. Consequently mobileSJ was designed to allow users to transfer and share a particular e-sphere with a colleague. Users can select the e-sphere, and then select the resources that they want to transfer to the PDA of the co-worker. This feature in the mobileSJ was considered useful by all medical interns in the focus group. The participants found the functionality particularly useful in cases when they need to consult a clinical case with others, and also when they shift their turn or even when they shift to another area in the hospital, as the following comment indicates:

Typically, during shifting we share all events and pending issues via Bluetooth with co-workers that receive the new ward ... but it's better this way, we could save a lot of time, and it could avoid forgetting to pass something to others. Often with a lot of events and pending issues, usually we forget to mention some of them.

The medical interns in the focus group pointed out that nowadays most medical interns in the hospital use some kind of electronic device to support their activities; these devices are cell phones, PDAs, iPods, USB drives, and laptops. Consequently, most of them are familiar with this kind of technology, and with the fact that with all these devices is relatively easy to share information with others. However, they said that unfortunately all the resources in these devices are not organized by activities or patients, and they spend a lot of time when trying to share electronic documents (notes, images, reminders, etc.) with colleagues at the end of the shift. Medical interns in the focus group judged very positively the feature of mobileSJ that let the user control the sharing of resources by specifying which ones can be shared and which ones should be considered private resources.

Communications

The mobileSJ running in a SmartPhone allows users to send e-mail, SMS, and initiate a telephone call. Similar to other resources, contacts can be associated to e-spheres. Thus, the user can select and call the contact they want to communicate with, directly from the mobileSJ interface. Medical interns in the focus group pointed out that it is very common for them to use mobile phones to communicate with each other while in the hospital. Consequently, they foresaw great value with the integration of functionality. This was particularly relevant with regards to the transferring of pending issues as the following comment from one of the participants indicates:

Often we forget to attend a pending issue related to one patient. When we are out the hospital and we remember it, we send a SMS to a colleague to ask about the pending issue ... and with this tool it's easier ... or occasionally we don't have enough time to search information in the web and we ask a colleague to search that information for us and he does it ... and sends it by email to us.

Because mobileSJ runs in a SmartPhone, it can receive all incoming SMS, calls, and e-mail messages anywhere. Medical interns can move around the hospital performing their activities and, while covered by wireless connection (GMS or WiFi), they can be notified about these events being able of managing and organizing them promptly.

The medical interns were pleased to have enhanced functionality in a single tool. They pointed out that they usually carry a cell phone, PDAs, and USB drive; they noticed that with mobileSJ they would need just one device.

One of the medical interns in the focus group was concerned with the organization of contacts in mobileSJ. He was confused by the way in which contacts are associated to e-spheres.

Personal Productivity

Because medical interns have several patients assigned to them, as well as a few school projects, we proposed that they could use mobileSJ to create an e-sphere for each of their activities associating information resources, contact information, and pending issues to them. With regards to this, all medical interns in the focus group were pleased with mobileSJ's features and how the tool could help them manage their multiple activities. All agreed on the potential of the tool to be used on a daily basis in the hospital. Also, they perceived that this tool could save them some time by helping them to be more productive. One of them expressed this in the following way:

... the organization of pending issues, the organizations of patients ... because it's true, we have a lot of them, maybe twenty and we don't know where to start ... I think this tool can help me organize myself ....

Similarly, another medical intern commented on how mobileSJ could speed up the administrative part of their work:

Right ... organizing and saving time, because when I am in the patient visit round, I take notes for each patient, and when I finish the round I spend about fifteen minutes reorganizing all the notes and rewriting them in the computer ... with this tool you can do it on the fly and associate them directly to each patient ...

Discussion

With the purpose of identifying future improvements to mobileSJ's features, we asked the medical interns what features they would consider adding or eliminating from the application. In general, the participants were happy with the actual features and stated that the systems has the potential for supporting their activities by improving the way in which they organize and use documents while with the patients, manage pending issues, and communicate with others. However, as it was mentioned before, one area of concern was with regards to the manner in which contacts are organized, indicating that they would need practice to adjust to this form or organization. Participants perceived that the application was easy to use given that (1) the interface of the system was similar to the one they use while operating their personal computers and (2) they are already familiar with mobile devices (PDAs and mobile phones) and integrating them as part of their normal work practices. Some comments pointed out that users would prefer to have some level of flexibility with regards to the different ways they can visualize and organize the resources. Two medical interns commented that despite the adequacy of the proposed organization scheme, they would like it better if the resources could be organized showing patients (e-spheres) and pending issues by area of speciality or by shift turn. These observations agree with the findings emerging from the exercise of identification and characterization of activities as we noticed that at a general level activities among interns are similar; however, at a higher level of abstraction, their description coincides with the particular areas in which the hospital is organized. Medical interns expressed the need to manage and organize their activities at both levels.

CONCLUSION

Working environments, such as hospitals, are characterized by the need to manage multiple activities simultaneously, constant local mobility, frequent interruptions, and intense collaboration and communication. These conditions impose important demands on users that need to frequently switch between tasks, contributing to a decrease in efficiency and becoming a source of errors and mishaps. We have designed an implemented a mobile task management tool called mobileSJ, which allows users to associate digital resources to a working sphere, navigate through them, share spheres and resources with colleagues, and communicate with them through various means. We conducted a usability test with 16 participants and a focus group with three medical interns with the purpose of evaluating the mobileSJ application and exploring its potential to support their activities. We aimed to test and improve our design by focusing on the way medical interns conceptualize their activities and the challenges around managing multiple activities. The results from the analysis of the session indicate that the activities conceptualized by medical interns can be adequately supported by the actual implementation of mobileSJ. We found that written activities by medical interns match with the previous scenarios identified to guide the design of actual implementation of mobileSJ; therefore, theses activities can be technologically supported with this tool. Our future work will focus on providing new ways to present and organize e-spheres and its resources. We perceive that some degree of flexibility should be provided in order for people to establish their own organizational schemes following their preferences with regards to the conceptualization of work. From the findings, we conclude that at least one higher level of functional organization beyond the concept of working sphere would be required to make the system more flexible. This will allow people to organize e-spheres, for instance, by the medical area.

ACKNOWLEDGMENT

We would like to thank all medical interns that participated in the focus group and Gilberto Borrego and Issac Noe Garcia for their help with defining and running the focus group session.

REFERENCES

Bardram, J.E., & Bossen, C. (2003). Moving to get aHead: Local mobility and collaborative work. In *Proceedings of the European Conference on Computer-Supported Cooperative Work (ECSCW)*, Helsinki, Finland (pp. 355-374). ACM Press.

Belloti, V., & Bly, S. (1996). Walking away from the desktop computer: Distributed collaboration and mobility in a product design team. In *Proceedings of the Conference on Computer-Supported Cooperative Work (CSCW)*, Boston, Massachusetts (pp. 209-218). ACM Press.

Czerwinski, M., Horvitz, E., & Wilhite, S. (2004). A diary study of task switching and interruptions. In *Proceeding of the Conference on Human Factors in Computing Systems (CHI)*, Vienna, Austria (pp. 175-182). ACM Press.

Davis, F.D., & Venkatesh, V. (1996). A critical assessment of potential measurement biases in the technology acceptance model: Three experiments. *International Journal of Human Computer Studies, 45*(1), 19-45.

González, V., & Mark, G. (2004). Constant, constant, multi-tasking craziness: Managing multiple working spheres. In *Proceedings of the Conference on Human Factors in Computing Systems (CHI)*, Vienna, Austria (pp. 113-120). ACM Press.

González, V. and G. Mark (2005): 'Managing currents of work: Multi-tasking among multiple collaborations' in European Conference in Computer Supported Cooperative Work, Spring Verlang, September 18-22, Paris, France.

Kaptelinin, V. (2003). UMEA: Translating interaction histories into project context. In *Proceedings of the Conference on Human Factors in Computing Systems (CHI)*, Fort Lauderdale, Florida (pp. 353-360). ACM Press.

Kidd, A. (1994). The marks are on the knowledge worker. In *Proceedings of the Conference on Human Factors in Computing Systems (CHI)*, Boston, Massachusetts (pp. 186-191). ACM Press.

Kirsh, D. (2001). The context of work. In *Proceedings of the Conference on Human Factors in Computing Systems (CHI)* (pp. 305-322). ACM Press.

Malone, T. (1983). How do people organize their desks? Implications for the design of office information systems. *ACM Transactions on Office Information Systems, 1*(1), 99-112.

Moran, E.B., Tentori, M., Gonzalez, V., Favela, J., & Martinez, A. (2006). Mobility in hospital work: Towards a pervasive computing hospital environment. *International Journal of Electronic Healthcare, 3*(1), 72-89.

Morteo, R., Gonzalez, V., Favela, J., & Mark, G. (2004). Sphere Juggler: Fast context retrieval in support of working spheres. In *Proceedings of the 5th Mexican International Conference in Computer Science (ENC)*, Colima, Mexico (pp. 361-367). IEEE Press.

Munoz, M., Rodriguez, M., Favela, J., Gonzalez, V., & Martinez-Garcia, A. (2003). Context-aware mobile communication in hospitals. *IEEE Computer, 36*(8), 60-67.

Rodríguez, M., & Favela, J. (2003). Autonomous agents to support interoperability and physical integration in pervasive environments. In *Proceedings of the International Atlantic Web Intelligence Conference (AWIC)* (pp. 278-287). Springer-Verlag.

Rouncefield, M., Hughes, J.A., Rodden, T., & Viller, S. (1994). Working with constant interruption: CSCW and the small office. In *Proceedings of the Conference on Computer-Supported Cooperative Work (CSCW)*, Chapel Hill, North Carolina (pp. 275-286). ACM Press.

Sproull, L.S. (1984). The nature of managerial attention. *Advances in Information Processing in Organizations, 1*, 9-27.

Voida, S., Mynatt, E.D., MacIntyre, B., & Corso, G.M. (2002). Integrating virtual and physical context to support knowledge workers. *IEEE Pervasive Computing, 1*(3), 73-79.

ENDNOTE

[1] An earlier version of this article was published in the Proceedings of the 12th International Workshop on Groupware: Design, Implementation, and Use, CRIWG 2006, held in Medina del Campo, Spain.

This work was previously published in the International Journal of e-Collaboration, Vol. 4, Issue 1, edited by N. Kock, pp. 60-73, copyright 2008 by IGI Publishing (an imprint of IGI Global).

Section 2
Adaptation and Creativity
in E–Collaboration

Chapter 6
Capturing the Appropriation Dynamics of Web–Based Collaboration Support in Project Team's Work Context

Athanasios Nikas
Athens University of Economics and Business, Greece

Angeliki Poulymenakou
Athens University of Economics and Business, Greece

ABSTRACT

This research applies contributions from the social sciences to examine how organizations adapt information systems in a project team setting. Its main concern is to study the set of events and actions implicated in the institutionalization of an information system. The motivation for this research has been to address the following questions: why well designed information systems are so often not successfully adapted or used by organizations? How the adaptation process affects and is affected by work context characteristics? In our research we are focusing on analyzing the adaptation process of a collaborative platform in a project team, in the context of the construction industry by applying adaptive structuration theory.

INTRODUCTION

Technological adoption has been researched from various perspectives within Information Systems research comprising a pervasive topic in IS research (Lin et al. 2005). Core frameworks exploring the topic as an innovation adoption or innovation diffusion phenomenon, featuring in the literature are: the Diffusion of Innovations (Rogers 1983), the Theory of Reasoned Action (Ajzen & Fishbein, 1975) and the Theory of Planned Behavior (Ajzen, 1985; Taylor & Todd, 1995) which provide the theoretical basis for the Technology Acceptance Model (Davis, Bagozzi & Warshaw, 1989). However, increasing evidence suggests that these "rational" frameworks neglect the realities of implementing technology innovations within organizations, especially when adoption decisions are made at the organizational, division, or workgroup levels (Fichman & Kemerer, 1997;

DOI: 10.4018/978-1-61520-676-6.ch006

Orlikowski, 1993; Wynekoop, 1992). Thus rather than fitting the conditions under which traditional models of innovation diffusion (Rogers, 1983) or technology acceptance (Davis et al 1989) were created, the reality of IT innovation adoption and implementation within organizational settings may require alternative views to examine how people adapt advanced information technologies in the context of their work place (Orlikowski, 2000).

Feldman and March (1981) note that technology plays a distinctive and interpersonal role in organizations. Susman et al. (2003) contend that the introduction of collaborative technology in the work place does not necessarily enhance intensive collaboration among project participants. In this line of reasoning it is important to investigate the changes that the introduction of collaborative technologies brings to the work place and how these technologies are actually used by people. Social theory has a substantial part to play in the development of the discipline of IS, in helping to understand and interact with the societal, organizational and personal contexts without which the technology is meaningless. Anthony Giddens has made a substantial contribution to that theory, and his work has been taken up by a number of IS researchers. Sahay (1997) suggests that the increasing use of structuration theory results from two evolutionary and convergent trends in IS. On one hand, there is an emphasis toward the use of more integrative approaches in which understanding how IT gets integrated into work and organizational systems is key. Nevertheless, we adopt structurational theoretical concepts in order to reveal the technology-organization relationship and to better understand how the social structures embedded within the collaboration technology affect and are getting affected by work context characteristics. Several authors note that teamwork cannot be understood apart from the organizational context in which it is embedded (Ancona 1990; Mohran et al 1995). For this purpose we need to understand how humans act, view, reflect, accept or neglect the entrance of a new technology in the social context of their work place.

By adopting a structuration approach it is assumed that the adoption and use of a novel technology are not deterministic; technologies are structured by users in their context of use (Contractor & Eisenberg, 1990; DeSanctis & Poole, 1994; Orlikowski, 1992). In our research the context of use is distributed project teams which are defined as groups of people who interact through independent tasks guided by a common purpose, and who collaborate across space, time and organizational boundaries primarily through electronic means (Maznevski & Chudoba, 2000). In line with other authors (Ekstedt et al 1999; Clark et al 1997) we define project teams as structures of independently managed individuals, often geographically distributed, that possess complementary capabilities and who cooperate temporarily to meet predefined objectives within predetermined deadlines through a non-repetitious string of complex activities.

Specifically, we aim to investigate how the contextual dimensions of the collaborative context of a project team influence the adaptation process of a collaborative technology. In this context we apply adaptive structuration theory as proposed by DeSanctis and Poole (1994), which expounds the nature of social structures within advanced information technologies and the key interaction processes that feature in their use.

A STRUCTURATIONAL APPROACH IN IS CONTEXT

Giddens suggests that structuration theory is dealing with the science dilemma between deterministic and voluntaristic approaches of human action, concerned with the following issues: a) the nature of human action and the acting self, b) how interpretations should be conceptualized in relation to institutions, and c) with grasping the social connotations of social analysis. Specifically, Giddens (1979) incorporates three main notions of the interpretative approach to research in social sciences: the need to classify actions vis a vis intentions, reasons and motives; to associate the analysis of social action with the analysis of institutions; the need to include a logic for a scientific method. Structures are regarded as rules and resources recursively implicated in social reproduction (Giddens, 1984). Rules are the normative elements and codes of signification and resources are divided in two types: a) the authoritative resources which derive from the coordination of the activity of human agents and b) the allocative resources, which stem from control material products or of aspect of the material world. According to structuration theory the moment of production of action is also the moment of its reproduction in the context of day-to-day enactment of social life.

Structuration theory has been applied as a framework for doing research in information systems. The most representative works are those of Orlikowski (1991), Walsham (1993), DeSanctis and Poole (1994) and more recently Majchrzak (2000). Orlikowski (1991) contends that technology does not determine human actions; it only conditions social practice in various levels of the organisation i.e. inter-organizational, individual and group. Her research contributes to our thinking of technology as having a dialectical relationship with organizations. Walsham (1993) proposes structuration theory to investigate how context influences process. DeSanctis and Poole (1994) propose *adaptive structuration theory* as a framework for studying variations in organizational change that occur as advanced technologies are used. Structuration theory has drawn criticism from several social scientists (Clegg, 1979; Gregson, 1989; Sica 1986). While structuration theory has been characterized as a meta-theory difficult to apply in empirical research, the theory's central preoccupation with explaining human action offers considerable merits in helping us understand

the complexities of adopting novel technologies in the workplace.

Several models in the literature describe how the adaptation process unfolds. Tyre and Orlikowski (1994) note that the adaptation process evolves over time in response to interruptions or misalignments and is constrained by pre-existing structures (Giddens, 1984; Barley, 1986) of the social context, i.e. the organization. Tyre and Orlikowski (1994) focus mainly on the significance of discrepant events which unfold during the adaptation process until the discrepancies among the technology and the performance criteria are aligned, i.e. improved collaboration and quality of work. However, they argue that technological adaptations are not gradual, but initially steep with only brief windows of opportunity in which technology can be modified. Similarly, Leonard-Barton (1988) proposes that the technology adaptation process can be seen as cycles of misalignments, followed by alignments, followed by more but smaller-scale misalignments, slowly evolving to a point in which the delivery system meets the established performance criteria. Sarker and Sahay (2003) apply structuration theory as a meta-framework to help link the microlevel communication patterns with the more macro-structures representing the environmental context as well as the characteristics of virtual teams over time. DeSanctis and Poole (1994) suggest that within the implementation context of the new technology the adaptation process unfolds in processes by which technologies are adapted.

Introducing Adaptive Structuration Theory

Adaptive structuration theory (AST) extends current structurational models of technology-trigerred change to consider the mutual influence of technology and social processes (DeSanctis and Poole 1994). Adaptive structuration theory provides a framework that describes the interplay among advanced information technologies, social

Figure 1. Adaptive structuration model (DeSanctis and Poole, 1994)

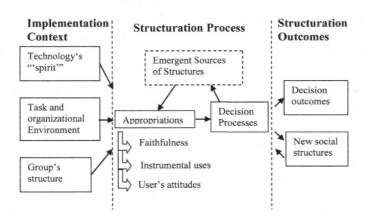

structures and human interaction (DeSanctis & Poole 1994). In this study we apply adaptive structuration theory as a framework for studying the adaptation process that unfolds following the introduction of an advanced information technology in the work context of a distributed team. This theory combines two theoretical concepts: *structuration*, which is the act of bringing the rules and resources from an advanced technology or other social structure into action as the process by which social structures are produced and reproduced in social life (Giddens, 1979); and *appropriations* (Ollman, 1971) which provide an illustrative picture of the process by which people use advanced information technologies, and describe the interplay between people and the technology. This model is represented in figure 1 and is the one that we espouse as a roadmap to analyze the case presented in our study.

The DeSanctis and Poole (1994) model describes the implementation context and the process by which technologies are adapted as consisting of structures, appropriations, and decision outcomes. Technology structure, organizational environment and group's structure constitute the implementation context in which the technology is introduced, and as such, affect appropriations, which in turn affect decision outcomes. Appropriations are defined as the immediate, visible actions that are

assessed by documenting exactly how technology structures are being invoked for, or constrained in use within a specific context (Majchrzak et al. 2000). DeSanctis and Poole propose that appropriations can be analyzed for their *faithfulness* (the extent to which appropriations are in line with the technology's 'spirit'), their *instrumental uses*, or the *users' attitude*. The social structures within the technology includes the structural features of the technology (e.g specific rules and resources, or capabilities offered by the system) as well as the technology's 'spirit', the initial goals and values embedded in the technology's design and specifying how people ought to act when using the system. Other sources of social structures within groups are the content and constraints of individuals' work tasks (McGrath 1984) including roles and actions of team members, the modes of interaction among group members and the organizational environment, which include the nature of the organizational environmental variables, such as culture and structure. One hypothesis proposed by DeSanctis and Poole is that at least one structure – technology 'spirit'- does not change during the adaptation process and poses a constraint on adaptation (Majchrzak et al 2000). DeSanctis and Poole contend that this hypothesis is necessary to understand how technology structures trigger organizational change. However, during the initial stages of the adaptation process even technology 'spirit' is sensitive to some changes. Majchrzak et al. (2000) suggest, that any structure is candidate for constraining the adaptation process not by virtue of what it is (e.g. technology, politics, status), but by the simple reality of not being malleable.

Finally, an interesting issue for many researchers is the nature of *continuity* of the adaptation process (Majchrzak et al. 2000). Tyre and Orlikowski suggest that the adaptation process occur discontinuously, with discontinuities occurring during brief windows of opportunity. Leonard-Barton characterize adaptation as a highly continuous process in response to the emerging misalignments. In our study we found similar to Majchrzak et al (2000) that the adaptation process may be neither inherently discontinuous nor continuous but rather responsive to changes in structural malleability, whenever such changes occur.

RESEARCH QUESTIONS

In summary, the theoretical approaches discussed above posit technology as embodying structures (built by designers during technology development), which are then appropriated by users during the use of the technology. Regarding these models Orlikowski (2000) highlights human action or the actions associated with embedding structures within a technology during its development as a central aspect of these models. Several authors have urged for further theoretical development of a structurational perspective on technology in explaining the consequences associated with the use of new and reconfigurable information technologies to further understand human action during the use of such technologies (Sproull & Goodman 1990; Weick, 1990). In this study we adopt this research perspective to investigate how social structures are being modified as people interact recurrently with the properties of the collaborative technology, whether these were built in, added on,

modified or emergent during its use. Our aim is a deeper of understanding of the complexity of organization-technology relationship and a better comprehension of the intricacies and afflictions raised by the implementation of collaboration technologies within the context of their use.

Due to the diversity of the models discussed above regarding the adaptation process, Majchrzak et al (2000) describe as the ideal research site the one in which all structures would be as malleable as possible, yet occurring in a real-world context so that external validity is obtained. In this context the following research question is addressed:

How the adoption of a CT affects and is getting affected by work context characteristics and to identify specific work context characteristics that affect the adaptation process.

The answer to the general research question will be given through the investigation of the subsequent research issues by:

(1) investigating the types of appropriations that occur during the adaptation process.
(2) examining the role of pre-existing group structures and organizational environment during the adaptation process.

RESEARCH CONTEXT: A DISTRIBUTED PROJECT TEAM AND THE COLLABORATIVE TECHNOLOGY

The empirical setting involves a newly constituted and geographically distributed team involved in the construction of a new hospital wing. For this specific project, the group was directed to use a web-based collaboration platform to improve project communication and coordination activities, management and control. An extremely interesting attribute met in construction projects as noted by Danwood et al. (2002) is the uniqueness of the production processes and the products themselves, which add to malleability of existing structures in construction organizations. In construction projects, a variety of organizations temporarily join together to create a 'temporary multiorganization' (Cherns & Bryant 1984), to exchange complex data and various types of information within the duration of project. Thus, an information lattice (network) is created, where actors diffuse and exchange various categories of information; this grid is built on virtual and malleable structures.

The empirical setting is particularly conducive to address our research questions as the temporary nature of work and the uniqueness of enacted processes offer us the opportunity to observe the malleability of structures and the reconfigurability of the technology and the technology 'spirit' itself. At this point it is essential to note that the particular collaboration technology adopted was further developed and customized for this particular project. This means that in the early implementation stages the technology 'spirit' can be characterized as incoherent, since new features were added and the technology began to be used consistent with its later coherent 'spirit', almost 3 months after its initial implementation. This study is concerned with collaborative technology mediation of complex processes (task allocation, time scheduling, coordination of the building process), and coordination among the multiple organizations (prime contractor, contractors and their various sub-contractors) for improving collaboration, project management and control. The distributed team is constituted by members of a variety of collaborating organizations, bringing together complementary (or cumulative) skills, competencies, technology know-how regarding the various aspects of the project under way. Townsend et al. (1998) notes that distributed teams are temporary and thus adaptive to organizational and environmental changes. The combination of geographic dispersion of team members with the plurality and diversity of participant's expertise, impose disciplinary heterogeneity, different or-

ganizational affiliations, and lack of pre-existing cooperative relationships due to the uniqueness of the project, which all of require the team to establish new structures that will serve information sharing and collaboration activities (Grudin 1994; Javerpnaa & Leidner, 1998; Majchrzak, 2000).

Collaboration technologies include, at a minimum, a virtual workplace that provides a repository recording of the process of the group, electronic information-sharing (such as though file sharing, e-mail, and electronic whiteboards), meta-information on the entries in the repository (such as date, sequence, and author of each contribution), and easy access and retrieval from the repository (Romano et al. 1998). Such systems facilitate the access, creation, processing, storage, retrieval, distribution and analysis of information across positional, physical and temporal boundaries and allow the incorporation of members from other units and organizations with specific, otherwise difficult-to obtain expertise (Lipnack & Stamps, 1997)

In our case, DIMER a medium sized Greek construction company, is the prime contractor of a construction consortium, formed especially for accomplishing the goals of a specific project. The general director of DIMER decided the introduction of a web-based collaboration platform in order to improve coordination of project work (in this case the project concerns the construction of a new hospital wing), monitoring and reporting the progress of the construction project. Armstrong and Priola (2001) note that in order to understand group processes, it is necessary to investigate how team members interact within the group. The distributed team is consisted of five geographically dispersed teams bound by contractual agreements (Technical and Financial Annexes of the description of project work):

- The senior manager of DIMER, who was the prime contractor of the project and responsible for delivering it on time to the client (the Greek Ministry of Health).

- The project manager who was responsible for controlling and monitoring the overall construction processes of the project (employed by DIMER).
- The procurement manager who was responsible for supplying the construction site with materials and equipment (employed by DIMER).
- The construction workflow supervisor who was responsible for consulting the construction site manager on implementing the instructions carried by the designs (employed by DIMER).
- The construction site manager who is responsible for managing the construction work at the construction site (an independent company).

The use of the platform lasted for 8 months while the project budget reached almost 6 million Euros. The construction site was located in an agricultural area 300 km away from the head offices of the prime contractor and the other parties. The collaboration technology under investigation was tailored to support the following services:

- project progress monitoring
- coordination of project activities
- project record keeping
- information sharing and exchange within the construction consortium

The system comprised a management platform available through the Internet, addressing the specific needs of the construction project. As an integrated management information system it offered instant access project data related to daily operations and project administration by providing a construction site diary and communication logs (create/update project plan, timesheets), collaboration and communication (online meetings, video conferencing, chatting, redlining), document workflow and task assignments to project members (permissions, authoring, logs, redlining).

There were 12 types of information objects being exchanged among the distributed team such as the Request for Information forms, transmittal and memorandum forms, proposal requests, architect's supplementary instructions, change order forms, construction change directives, revision forms and logs, project progress reports, photographs, shop drawings and various check lists. The introduction of the new Information System posits new management challenges to be addressed in terms of coordination, communication and control as the basic elements affecting virtual project management (Khazanchi & Zigurs 2006). A prerequisite for efficient and effective collaboration with the system was the accurate and timely handling and monitoring of the exchanged information between the construction consortium and the management of the emerging information lattice.

RESEARCH APPROACH AND METHOD OF ANALYSIS

The study was set up to understand the process whereby the project team was adapting the technology over 8 month life span, and for this purpose a descriptive case study was used (Walsham, 1993). Several authors note that case study is a well-accepted approach to study the complex phenomena of technology implementation in an organizational setting (Orlikowski and Baroudi, 1991; Yin, 1994). The researchers were asked to contribute to the solution of a real business problem. In this context, one of the business participants of the project, the IT vendor, asked researcher's consultation regarding the implementation of the collaboration platform in the construction project. As the primary source of data we conducted more than 25 interviews with the IT consultant who was responsible for the system's implementation and documentary materials, which is a widely accepted effort for data collection (Myers, 1997). We also interviewed the system's IT developer at several points during the implementation process to determine his original intentions regarding the use of the technology and to understand how the technology had been finally used. Furthermore, we investigated documentation material i.e. construction coding, industrial process standards (Royal Institute of British Architects), and interviewed several professionals in the industry in order to understand the role and the structural properties of each actor participating in the project. At this point it is worth mentioning that one of the researchers of this study already had work experience in a medium size construction company, which familiarized him with the construction projects' work flow. In addition to the interviews, we also examined the 693 entries to the system to examine how the system was actually used since we had full access rights from the first day of its installation. The IT vendor created an on-line account for the researchers, and we were observing the enrolment

of the system for 3 months. We spent one hour per day observing how information was diffused, collaboration evolved and team members' used the system. The research approach is illustrated in figure 2.

As a first step, we traced the "implementation context". We studied technical reports regarding the construction industry to explicitly understand the roles of the experts which participate in the construction phase of a project in general, and understand how and with what means they cooperate with each other. Thereafter, we interviewed the IT consultant to identify pre-existing roles and responsibilities for each team member for that particular project, i.e., how the team members would typically communicate a drawing's amendment. Structures were grouped according to the DeSanctis and Poole (1994) classification of technology, group, and organi-

Figure 2. Research approach

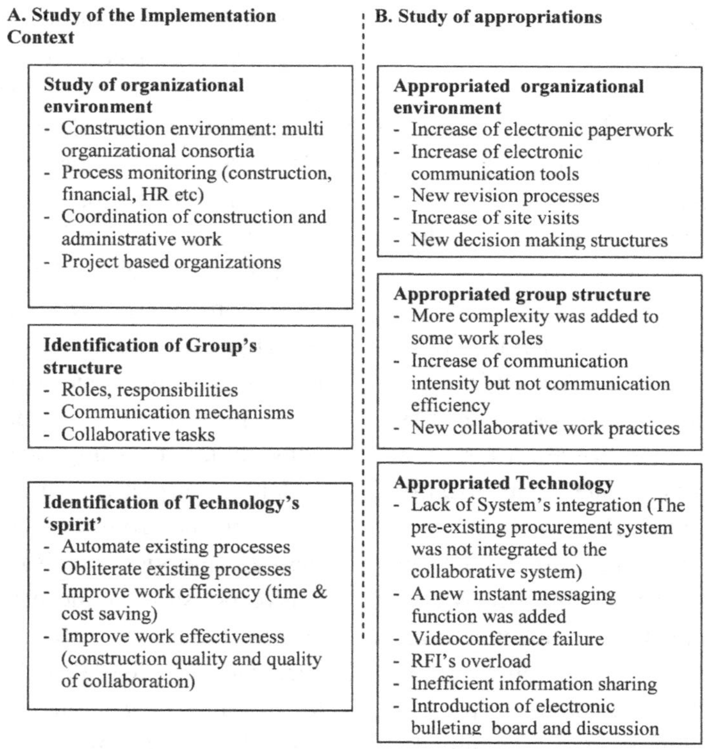

A. Study of the Implementation Context

Study of organizational environment
- Construction environment: multi organizational consortia
- Process monitoring (construction, financial, HR etc)
- Coordination of construction and administrative work
- Project based organizations

Identification of Group's structure
- Roles, responsibilities
- Communication mechanisms
- Collaborative tasks

Identification of Technology's 'spirit'
- Automate existing processes
- Obliterate existing processes
- Improve work efficiency (time & cost saving)
- Improve work effectiveness (construction quality and quality of collaboration)

B. Study of appropriations

Appropriated organizational environment
- Increase of electronic paperwork
- Increase of electronic communication tools
- New revision processes
- Increase of site visits
- New decision making structures

Appropriated group structure
- More complexity was added to some work roles
- Increase of communication intensity but not communication efficiency
- New collaborative work practices

Appropriated Technology
- Lack of System's integration (The pre-existing procurement system was not integrated to the collaborative system)
- A new instant messaging function was added
- Videoconference failure
- RFI's overload
- Inefficient information sharing
- Introduction of electronic bulleting board and discussion

zational environment. Furthermore, we tried to identify and understand pre-existing structures before the introduction of the system in order to understand the new emerging structures among the distributed team. Since the essential nature of the task—new project construction—did not change throughout the project, the task structure was not examined (Majchrzak et al. 2000). In our case the prime contractor (DIMER) provided the organisational environment by maintaining organizational culture, protecting the project from risk, and preserving control in the face of an inherently unpredictable creative process by assigning to the project manager the control of the project. In this line the technology 'spirit' is described from the view of the prime contractor and its designer. Hence, we follow DeSanctis and Poole (1994) suggestions in order to eliminate contradictions regarding the interpretation of the 'spirit' of the technology when using multiple sources of evidence.

In the second step of the analysis we identified the technology appropriations that occurred. Appropriations are defined by DeSanctis and Poole (1994) as "immediate, visible actions that evidence deeper structuration processes" (p. 128). This means that misalignments to the initial 'spirit' of the technology were exemplary documented by specifically focusing on the dialectic relationship between the users of the technology (i.e. their reactions) and the social structures embedded within the technology (i.e. the structure of communication, collaboration and the new work practices introduced).

THE IMPLEMENTATION CONTEXT: PRE-EXISTING STRUCTURES

The study of the implementation context is organized by the following procedure: a) identification of pre-existing structures and b) misalignments and appropriated structures during project's lifespan. In this section the nature (content) of construction project work is discussed in order to understand tasks, roles, timelines, managerial processes and control, information exchange (types and their uses) and communication patterns involved in the context collaboration. This section ends with analyzing the technology's spirit which was introduced to our case, and was considered in the beginning as the one structure that did not significantly change (DeSanctis & Poole, 1994). However, it is important to note that the technology spirit in the early stages of the implementation is in flux and later on as it is used in routine ways becomes more stable.

Organizational Environment

DIMER is the construction company responsible for completing the objectives of the construction phase of the project, which is to safely build a hospital wing as specified in the contract documents within the budget and schedule approved by the Greek Ministry of Health. DIMER is tasked with completing the buy-out of all components in the construction contract (typically a Guaranteed Maximum Price or GMP), coordinating their delivery and installation, and facilitating the inspection process up to actual building occupancy. Throughout the usual course of construction, DIMER's project manager meets weekly with other sub-contractors (such as the construction site manager, the procurement manager and the construction site supervisor), receives progress reports, tracks submittal status, budget and schedule, and resolves field conflicts and drawing discrepancies. DIMER's project manager leads each meeting, sets the agenda and documents the decisions and outcomes taken, and subsequently reports back to the senior manager of DIMER. However, it is very tedious from the prime contractor's view, to monitor all the processes and the coordination activities that take place during the construction process. Decision-making and conflict resolution demand a highly structured information environment, where the prime contractor can easily retrieve the information needed to reach a decision. An unstructured information environment might lead to erroneous decisions due to an incomplete representation of a situation.

Collaboration within construction consortia and hence among project team members deals with producing, issuing and circulating reports/ documents and having frequent meetings to agree on scheduling, method, and sometimes project strategy issues. Thus, there is a need for the related information to be instantly available. The collaboration among the diverse participants in this project relies on effective use of communication channels in conjunction with the exchange of valid and updated information among project participants. Effective communication is also important to monitor and control the project's activities according to the project's detailed work plan. In terms of appropriation topics, the existing organizational environment consisted of engineers who made little use of electronic communication tools, preferring to discuss issues in face-to-face encounters. This collaboration process was characterized by a hierarchical notion of information sharing as only those who needed to be aware of particular pieces of information were receiving it.

Group Structures

The typical group structure in a construction project is for all organizations to have a lead engineer known as project manager. Management, in this case project management in a distributed project team, is required to meet tangible goals related directly to project performance (such as monitoring costs, assuring quality, meeting time schedules) as well as intangible goals such as establishing mutual trust and sharing a common vision. During the construction phase, efficient and effective collaboration among the project participants is critical. The construction phase is comprised of a group of either multiple sub-processes, or various phases such as: feasibility study, architectural and conceptual design, design development, bidding, construction, and facilities management. Specific pieces of information such as shop drawings, approvals, change orders, inspection reports, and reviews augment the actual construction work. Each individual process requires close collaboration with other team members that contribute to the fulfillment of particular processes. As is typical in construction projects of this kind, in our case the civil engineer, mechanical engineer, electrical engineer, and experts of other specialized faculties cooperate for the successful completion of a building's blueprint. The construction site manager communicated on a daily basis with the construction workflow supervisor and on a regular basis with the raw materials supplier. The various engineers and specialists rarely interacted with each other and the project manager acts as a communication hub among the participants. Team members discussed common tasks and exchanged documents with any assumptions, interpretations and comments explained verbally. The project manager maintained a paper based project binder for his personal use, in which he placed copies of all types of documents exchanged in the project. The project's binder contained drawings, plans, invoices and orders according to project work. Meeting minutes were the only conversations documented of the entire project. The project manager, who reported back to the senior manager of the prime contractor, was the only team member who was aware of the complete 'picture' of the project in its full detail.

Within, the existing group structure engineers and other specialists use their personal IT tools (e.g. AutoCad, MS Word/Excel) to store information by keeping it in personalized formats and in their personal systems; the project manager shared his knowledge on a need-to-know basis; and the management structure in which team members functioned was characterized as hierarchical since the team members communicated often via the project manager, while he, in turn reported progress and changes to plans and blueprints back to the senior manager of the prime contractor.

Technology's 'Spirit'

The social structures within the collaborative technology can be described in two ways as prompted by DeSanctis and Poole (1994): the structural features, which are the specific types of rules and resources, or capabilities offered by the system; and the 'spirit' of the technology, which is the general intent of the technology with regard to values and goals underlying a given set of structural features. In this context the structural features of the technology included the creation of a shared information repository, which would contain in electronic formats the full amount of information exchanged in the project. Team members initially claimed that by using this technological application they would be able to post all drawings, conversations, schedules, meeting minutes, technical requirements, assumptions, design rationales and decisions, and, by the same token, they would easily access and retrieve the information stored by them and other team members. Furthermore, the creation of an information repository served one of the basic goals for implementing the system regarding the prime contractor's need for better coordination and project monitoring. The system, sponsored by the prime contractor, was supposed to serve the project manager's needs in tracking, retrieving, sharing and monitoring project information. It was also expected to reduce time wasted in finding people to supply the necessary information required, and in having face-to-face meetings. Time taken on critical project management tasks such as reviewing and estimating project progress was also expected to be reduced. A particular system feature, the Request for Information (RFI) message was designed to 'link' and index communications regarding specific project design features requiring clarification and/or more detailed information. An RFI typically originates from the construction site manager; suppliers or other subcontractors; who submit their requests for information to the Project manager. Once the question has been answered, the process reverses itself as the response makes its way back to the originator.

In order to identify the technology 'spirit' we followed DeSanctis and Poole (1994- p.126) directions by analyzing: a) the design metaphor underlying the system; b) the features it incorporates; c) the user interface; and d) the training material. Furthermore, to avoid the danger of arising contradictions during the identification of the 'spirit', as suggested by DeSanctis and Poole (1994), we interviewed both the designer of the system and the prime contractor, who decided to buy the system. The technology 'spirit' can be articulated as follows: every organization which participated in the consortium could use the technology asynchronously, everyone would contribute actively in storing project information (formal and informal), all of the stored information would be shared by everyone and accompanied with powerful search tools that would make the retrieval of information a straightforward task by overcoming the difficulties arising from the geographic dispersion of the team. The technology enhanced functions for integrating the work of multiple parties that were expected to reduce the need for face-to-face meetings and thus reduce the cost of travel. In sum the overall goal was to coordinate activities, monitor project work, and provide the prime contractor with relevant information to make decisions. In this sense the collaborative technology had a great potential to influence the social aspects of work. Table 1 illustrates the tools and the application areas of the collaboration platform.

APPROPRIATIONS AND MISALIGNMENTS

In this section we investigate how the collaborative technology has been appropriated by the distributed work team in the construction project. We document **adaptations** made to the technology and we discuss how the organizational environ-

Table 1. System tools and application areas

Tool	Application areas
Workflow management	Development/production, storage and sharing of information concerning the specific project work, its functions and other administrative processes. It supports the automation of work processes by routing information among the different actors according to a predefined (or ad hoc) sequence representing the process.
Document management	Development, storage, sharing, retrieving of information organized in electronic archives, RFIs.
Data conferencing	Exchanging of text messages and application sharing (e.g AutoCAD)
News and bulletin boards	Storage, sharing and retrieving of information (news and announcements) among the project participants
Discussion forum	Development/production, storage and sharing of information in specific discussion groups corresponding to subject relevance
Project calendar	Scheduling of project work for individual and group coordination
Video conferencing	Inter-personal and group communication

ment, the group structure and the 'spirit' of the technology were being affected. According to DeSanctis and Poole (1994) while appropriation 'moves' the group may: a) directly adapt and use the new social structures, or b) relate them to other structures (e.g. the task environment), or c) be constrained by the new structures and/or d) make judgments. The appropriations can be described as: a) faithful or unfaithful to the 'spirit' of the technology; b) instrumental uses with regards to accomplishment of task activities or managing communication; c) attitudes with regards to how the group perceive the technology features; and d) decision processes including group's idea generation process, task interdependence and /or conflicts. However, the collaboration technology was developed and customized to meet the requirements of this particular project. This assumes that the project group structures were relatively consistent during the early adaptation stages, and the technology was being appropriated in order to fit existing structures. In this line of reasoning the faithfulness of the appropriations to the 'spirit' of the technology is subject to the interpretation of technology's incoherent or coherent 'spirit' as the adaptation process evolves over time. This is an alternative view of looking appropriations since the collaborative system was not at the time of the implementation a 'steadfast' application ready for installation in any construction project. Thus,

the study of appropriations is not only an issue of judging an appropriation as faithful or unfaithful, but also whether or not the technology's 'spirit' is coherent enough to judge the nature of appropriation during the adaptation process.

Appropriated Organizational Environment

The first misalignment of the 'spirit' of the technology was that the system was not used by all actors as the prime means for collaboration and information exchange. For example, the construction site manager turned to traditional means of communication (such as the telephone) in situations where his need for orders and directions was immediate during the work day. This type of appropriation created a first 'negative attitude' towards the 'instrumental use' of the system in situations where the need for collaboration can be characterized as intensive.

The social structures of collaboration among the project team were transformed since the electronic paperwork of composing electronic reports was increased, and face-to-face meetings were reduced. Thus, in terms of appropriation topics, the existing organizational environment was transformed from engineers who made little use of electronic communication tools to engineers who made extensive use of electronic communication tools. The way that engineers would typically communicate was misaligned. These misalignments are related to differences between how they previously communicated with others (face-to-face meetings), when they communicated with team members (with the system they communicated asynchronously regardless time and space limitations), and what they communicated (with the system they communicated project information in electronic and written formats). A good example is provided by looking at the communication processes involved in blueprint decisions.

Previous to the introduction of the system, information exchange was a really complicated process, because the interested parties had to save drawings in CDs and then courier them to specific recipients. Through system functionalities, they were aiming at storing specific plans and drawings to specific folders, which would then be accessible through the web. A second goal to achieve was to reduce resources spent on resolving disputes and travelling. The system promised to create a full audit trail containing all the meeting minutes, actions, comments requests, approvals and notifications generated during the project lifespan. The important benefit for the project manager and the prime contractor was that they would be aware instantly of who had published what, when and by whom it was reviewed. Thus far the nature of appropriation is faithful to the technology 'spirit' since the prime contractor would benefit from the improvement in project monitoring.

In the process of revising the implementation study/plans, for example, the construction workflow supervisor was responsible for monitoring the tasks and the processes of the construction project in correspondence with the feasibility, architectural, electric and mechanical studies. The system allowed some redlining and videoconference facilities. The project manager's testimonial proves that the revision process of the implementation study/plans was unfaithful to the 'spirit' of the technology:

"Our purpose for introducing the system to the consortium was to reduce paperwork and bureaucracy. Previously, the usual procedure to exchange high capacity files was to save them in CDs and courier them to the interested parties. This meant that we needed at least one day to deliver a drawing to a recipient. We estimated that we were going to exchange at least 10 CDs full of drawings, plans and other types of documents during the construction phase, which could be translated to the loss of 10 very valuable work days. We had great expectations from the system because it would facilitate a web-based document inventory, accessible at any time. However, established procedures in the construction are very difficult to overcome. For example, when a drawing had to be amended, the revised version of the drawing as well as with the instructions following it, needed to be in hard copy form in order to be confirmed with the architect's signature. The receipt of the drawing had also to be acknowledged to both the project manager and the prime contractor in writing. Therefore, sending these documents electronically failed to complete these endorsement procedures. The mixing of hard and electronic copies in the participant organizations made it extremely difficult to process the right information whenever it was necessary."

This resulted in further mistakes and misinterpretation of information almost on a daily basis since drawings and documents have not been up-to-date and instantly available. Thus, since this 'instrumental' use of the system was questioned, team members turned to blame the system. Team members confronted daily the risk on acting on information that was out-of date, or incomplete resulting in negative 'attitudes' towards the system. Furthermore, this resulted in the augmentation of site visits and travelling time for arranging face-to-face meetings to resolve misunderstandings, all these were rather unfaithful to the system's 'spirit'.

Appropriated Group Structure

As mentioned earlier one of the primary goals of the system was to create a common information repository accessible by the team members. Before the introduction of the system the project manager was acting as an information gatekeeper. The technology's 'spirit' was to discharge the project manager from this task and to actually bypass him as an 'information hub'. By the same token he was acting as the one who was responsible to resolve issues and conflicts related to problems that were arising in the execution of work. With the system undertaking the information provision role, it was felt that work issues could now be resolved directly among concerned actors. Thus a new social structure emerged regarding specific work tasks as provided by the technology 'spirit'. An instant messaging function was added to the system's functionalities for this purpose. This resulted in the appropriation of the decision making process since the project manager was not being kept informed on direct communications between other actors and in some cases he got bypassed. For example, during the second month of the project, the construction site manager indicated that he had a private conversation and agreement with the construction work flow supervisor regarding specifications of the material to be used for the brackets which would brace the 2nd floor of the hospital wing which happened to be slightly different to that originally specified. The project manager's authorization was not sought out in this case. Therefore, group communication and collaboration structures were appropriated faithfully to the technology's 'spirit' of decentralization, but the control part of the project manager's role was misaligned.

At the onset of adopting the collaborative platform, group members were keen to align their work with the 'spirit' of the technology, because they expected to reap high benefits from their new modes of work. Time would be saved from avoiding face-to-face meetings, working remotely would be facilitated through the access to project information via the web, and coordination of work would be enabled both by the system's electronic collaboration features and by the information supplied on the progress of work. Team members agreed to use the system to record all of their project related communications. In this sense, faithful appropriation of technology's 'spirit' comprised a source of generating a new social structure of collaboration within the project team. This appropriation, however, introduced complex work processes for some actors. For example, besides overseeing the actual construction of the hospital wing the construction site manager had to fill in forms, send orders and maintain a daily project activity log electronically. He also had to distribute RFIs when he needed information to complete a task instead of resolving such issues by means of communication such as telephone or fax. However, the lack of standardized information paths, tasks and procedures resulted in great hesitations and increased uncertainty for the construction site manager regarding the system's use and its competences. Specifically, he was uncertain as to whether he was actually sending the right information to the right party, especially when the silence effect occurred. The silence effect (Crampton, 2001), i.e. delays in getting replies to sent messages (e.g. RFIs), led him to believe that other team members actually agreed with his proposals or where indifferent to his requests. Often, when he didn't get immediate replies to his RFIs, he was sending them again to multiple recipients in order to ensure that they would reach the right recipient. Gradually, this person lost his self-confidence regarding his ability to use the system and lead him to consider it as a hindrance to his work. For other team members also, the high level of detail at which information was recorded in the system was often creating problems as a high volume of amendments to project data needed to be acknowledged, authorized, or otherwise processed, a fact that was affecting negatively their work productivity and their attitudes towards the use of the system.

Part of this problematic situation may be attributed to the content of the training courses provided to the group members, which did not touch upon issues related to anticipated changes in the design of work. Indicatively, the IT consultant testified regarding the training of construction site manager:

"...the construction site manager participated to the training courses provided to all team members simultaneously and not individually due to time restrictions. There was a great hurry for starting the construction work and the training courses were being based on an earlier version of the platform than the one which was finally released for actual use. However, we noted to the prime contractor that the construction site manager had a low IT literacy level, and that he would need some extra courses to attend in order to be ready with the release of the system. But the prime contractor claimed that we have no time for that and that the construction site manager has been doing this job for almost two decades and he knows his work better than everybody else..."

The compilation of periodic and progress reports using the system comprised a very complex and difficult process, requiring high accuracy levels which the construction site manager failed to obtain. The system design featured information on the complete set of action plans for the project and required a constant supply of updated information on what was being done in the construction site, in accordance to the planned level of resource usage for each task, work package and work unit in the project.

The new social structures provided by the appropriation of the pre-existing work tasks constrained the rules and the resources of various actors resulting in negative attitudes towards the use of the system. For example, the construction site manager dealt with new complex tasks to fulfill; the project manager lost part of his ability to control information and its flow; and for other team members the system reduced their perceived benefits premised from its use.

Appropriated Technology

During the initial stages of the implementation of the system several appropriations occurred to the technology until before became stabilized. The instrumental use of the system was premised to support the following activities: material ordering, purchasing, and invoicing. Misalignments occurred during the integration of the various functionalities regarding project plans and schedules with the existing materials procurement system of the prime contractor. This resulted in problems with stock control of the materials and an inability to make accurate predictions of the resource requirements for the project.

Such incidents caused several appropriations to the technology and new social structures emerged in terms of new tasks and collaborative processes. Specifically, during the course of the project the system was modified in various ways. For example, team members requested and received a feature that enabled instant and personal messaging to the other members, which were on-line. The project manager initially objected to this feature claiming that it would limit the transparency of the transactions between members, as he would not be able to regularly monitor those conversations. Furthermore, one month into the use the collaboration platform by the distributed team, we observed that the amount of clarifications and requests for information regarding some particular tasks increased rapidly, which rendered the navigation and searching for information almost impossible. It is worth mentioning that almost 108 entries have been registered regarding a technical detail about the type and the dimensions of the windows that were going to be fit in the 1st floor of the building. These RFIs also constituted information relevant to project monitoring, albeit 'buried' among vast amounts of unnecessary detail, and thus overloaded with irrelevant information the project manager.

Information sharing was also another function of the technology which was finally unfaithfully appropriated compared to the initial "spirit". For example, three months after the release of the system the archive file contained almost 150 different headings of RFIs, which made the navigation among them an extremely complicated process. To this end the team requested and received the extra technical functionality of an information tree that first would enable the categorization of RFIs according to specific project tasks and dates, and would also allow reference links to the entries. The problem was that someone had to put in all the entries to the information tree in order for the reference links to be functional. The IT consultant suggested that the project manager should be responsible for this task. However, he was unable to perform this task due to time constraints and the system was reverted to its previous state of use. In this context the 'spirit' of the technology was appropriated unfaithfully since the opportunity to create a knowledge repository regarding project work did not occur. The actual use of the system was limited to servicing communication and monitoring purposes. With inefficient information sharing structures, the adoption of the system ended up increasing rather than decreasing the amount of questions asked by team members regarding drawings, plans and supplies.

Table 2 summarizes the research findings mentioned above. In the first column the pre-existing structures are identified, the second column illustrates how the structures have been appropriated and changed due to the existence of the discrepant events. Finally, the last column presents the structuration outcomes, which include decision outcomes and emerging structures as the outcome of the appropriated structures.

DISCUSSION

The analysis of the case illustrates how the distributed team initially tried to adapt the 'spirit' of the technology 'as is'. The first adaptation concerned the appropriation of the 'organizational environment' itself. However, over time, as the consortium confronted unintended events it found impossible to leave the technology intact if their performance goals were to be achieved. Problems occurred particularly when specific work practices had to be adjusted and transformed to meet the tangible goals of the emerging team social structures. Specifically, we refer to the roles of the project manager and particularly the construction site manager, who comprised two actors of team's social context. These new tasks, emerging from the introduction of the technology, resulted in these two members to become more individually active. However, group identification requires individuals to act from a group perspective (Whitworth et al. 2001).

Case analysis illustrates the complexity of the construction practice, the lack of established standards and protocols, the increased group functional diversity and the intensive collaboration activities among team members. However, misalignment appeared mostly when the team came in touch with the new technology, since, as noted earlier the essential nature of the task – management of construction work – did not change. To this end, group functional diversity appears responsible not only for misalignments in technology structures, but also to the group and organisational structures. The misalignments and misinterpretations observed in our case were mostly the outcome of group functional diversity. In this respect we concur with Susman et al. (2003) who contend that functional diversity within the team not only leads to misinterpretations and misunderstandings, but may also make it more difficult for team members to reconcile these misinterpretations. Finally, technology should be designed in a manner that makes its use beneficial to people who intensively

Table 2. Summary of the research findings

Pre-existing structures	Appropriations	Discrepant events	Structuration outcomes
Technology - Office automation systems (MS Office, word processor and excel) - CAD/CAM design applications - Telephone/Fax - Project binder **Organisational environment** - Centralised decision making process - Temporary organisational network - Geographically dispersed organisations - Diversity of organisational cultures and expertise - Hard copy information records **Group structures** - Face to face meetings - Need to know basis information sharing - Hierarchical collaboration between team and management - Diverse professional backgrounds	**Technology** - Electronic communication of information asynchronously - Team uses a common tool to collaborate - Electronic formats and repositories of information - Use of electronic bulletin board and discussion forum - Use of powerful search tools and search based on keywords **Organisational environment** - Cross functional project team - Participative decision making - Electronic documentation of information - Reduction of project meetings - One common information repository - Transparent processes and information diffusion - Electronic project diary **Group structure** - Reduction of face to face meetings - Electronic collaboration and communication - Creation of a common information repository for past construction procedures followed consultation and project solving sessions	**Technology** - Information overload - Problems in stock control - Videoconference failure - Bandwidth bottlenecks - Use of telephone or fax instead of the functions of the collaborative technology. - Informal type of electronic documents - Use of personal email of electronic bulletin board and discussion forum - Difficult to find old information entries due to duplicates **Organisational Environment** - Lack of standardised processes - Project manager can't make sense of project reports - Organisations insisted on keeping information on two level (organisational and inter-organisational) **Group Structure** - Increase of communication time and site visits for demarcations and misunderstandings solving - Team confronts problems to use communication features - The construction site manager finds very time consuming process to put entries to the system, his nature of work changes dramatically - Increase of conflicts - Decrease of trust - Increase of task rework - Retrieving of information through the system was more time consuming that people connections	**Technology** - Collaboration platform abandonment - Use of traditional communication means **Organisational environment** - Loss of the vision of accomplishing a common goal and focusing on performing individual tasks. - Loss of project monitoring and control - Project delays - Time constraints to accomplish project goals **Group structure** - Decrease of trust during the execution of collaborative tasks - Lack of transparency - Low level employees blame the technology for reworking and felt threaten by its use - Information overload - New management structures are emerging since the construction site manager communicates directly with the project manager and bypasses other participants.

collaborate to perform complementary tasks and therefore to increase its use in distributed teams. To this respect further research is needed to explore how task interdependence affects the use of collaborative technologies in project teams.

Each organization in construction preserves its own internal processes and procedures described by different information standards, hence, it is somehow encouraging for construction organizations to use such systems to store and retrieve information on activities associated with past projects in order to create an information repository for internal use. In this vein Vaidyanathan (2006)

suggests, that the generation and dissipation of knowledge and information needs to be embedded in subsequent project processes, instantly available to the project members. For example, the tasks involved in the construction process of building floors can be characterized as a repeated process in construction projects, thus standard definitions for this particular construction task can be found by analyzing previous construction projects. However, the construction industry lacks procedural standards and each organization keeps its own standards of working. The establishment of information and procedural standards is essential in order to contribute to the design and the adoption of such systems at an industry level that will finally permit these technologies to meet their intended 'spirit'. At this point further investigation is needed in order to explore the malleability of existing organizational processes and structures and whether they act as a barrier or enable the adaptation of new processes implied by the introduction of collaborative technologies.

Over more, the Tyre and Orlikowski (1994) model of discontinuous adaptations responding to windows of opportunities does not fit well in our case. These discrepant events occurred sporadically and individually throughout the project's lifespan. They were perceived as unwelcome problems and not as opportunities. Furthermore, problems such as the stance of the construction site manager, had a long duration in time and they cannot be characterized as short time windows of opportunity.

This study premises the primacy of organizing practices in organizational change (Orlikowski, 1996). For this reason we invoke Orlikowski to question the beliefs that organizational change must be planned, that technology is the primary cause of technology-based organizational transformation, and that radical changes always occur rapidly and discontinuously. Organizational transformation, implied by the implementation of a challenging information system should be seen as *"an ongoing improvisation enacted by organizational actors trying to make sense of and act coherently in the world."* (Orlikowski, 1996). In this line we propose, that there is an apparent need for users to "make an individual sense" of the collaborative context in which they work and the real challenge for managers is to promulgate actors with the 'new' context of collaboration. Our study reveals that the emerging context of collaboration was not communicated or explained in detail to the team members. The importance of collective sense making for successful distributed team work is noted by Crampton (2001).

Open Research Issues

Future research could explore how particular contextual variables, extracted from this exploratory case study affect the adoption process of collaborative technologies in project teams.

The organizational setting investigated is a temporary organizational setting constituted of project based organizations. In this regard, a great research challenge is to explore the integration of non-routine collaborative tasks and processes in a collaborative technology. Our study reveals that these systems (platforms) necessitate the formulation of new formal and informal work procedures (i.e. roles, tasks, co-ordination activities) that need to be continuously embedded into existing 'compulsory' processes as well as in informal norms. Therefore, further investigation is needed to shift the focus of adoption efforts from ensuring system utilization to rethinking and re-designing emerging collaborative tasks implied by the introduction of the collaborative technology. However, the definition of appropriate work tasks during the construction phase can be a laborious and tedious process and need to be classified in categories that reflect basic group processes. This is due to the unique nature of construction projects in general, which involve too many individual and different work tasks and make their definition an expensive and time consuming process. Fortunately, a real optimistic fact is that many tasks in the construction may be repeated and used as general models for new projects. But before these tasks become routine tasks, it is purposeful to consider how to treat them when they are at a non-routine level. For tasks that actors perceived as non-routine it was observed that actors started to communicate by traditional communication mediums and an increase of face-to-face meetings was observed, when the first misalignments with the 'spirit' of the technology occurred. This is in line with both the task-technology theories and virtual team literature that argue for the importance of face-to-face meetings (e.g. Maznevski & Chudoba 2000; Crampton

2001; Hinds & Bailley 2003). Hence, the richness of the communication medium was not comprised a supporting mechanism to overcome non-routine tasks difficulties. These findings make us to join other researchers that question the value of media richness for explaining how individuals perform effectively in distributed teams (Saunders 2000; Majchrzak 2005).

Often instant communication was important to resolve issues and reach interim decisions to be made. This mode of intense collaboration was achieved only by actors turning to traditional communication means instead of using electronic communication. Furthermore, a high degree of unstructured information exchange among the actors was observed. This resulted in misunderstandings which finally resulted in increased requests for face-to-face meetings. The use of the system as a communication medium lowered trust levels and hindered the establishment of social relationships while (construction) work was at the same time characterized by low transparency. In such situations the cultivation of team relationships found to be prominent. The importance of mechanism providing easy and instant communication processes comprised an essential component that the collaboration must provide to the team members in order to serve their intensely collaboration needs. All these issues found to describe the collaboration context of the specific project team and affected significantly the adaptation process of the collaboration technology. Future research may explore the dimensions of the nature of collaboration extracted from this exploratory case study in order to search for appropriate constructs that will empirically measure their influence to the adoption process of collaborative technologies.

ACKNOWLEDGMENT

This research is funded from the Greek Ministry of Education (25%) and the European commission (75%) under the Operational Programme "Education and Primary Vocational Training" (EPEAEK II - http://www.epeaek.gr/).

REFERENCES

Ajzen, I. (1985). From Intentions to Action: A Theory of Planned Behavior . In Kuhl, J., & Beckmann, J. (Eds.), *Action Control From Cognition to Behavior* (pp. 11–39). New York: Springer-Verlag.

Ajzen, I., & Fishbein, M. (1980). *Understanding Attitudes and Predicting Behavior*. Englewood Cliffs, NJ: Prentice-Hall.

Ancona, D. G. (1990). Outward Bound: Strategies for Team Survival in an Organisation. *Academy of Management Journal*, *33*, 334–365. doi:10.2307/256328

Armstrong, S., J., & Priola, V. (2001). Individual differences in cognitive style and their effects in task and social orientations of self-managed work teams. *Small Group Research*, *32*(3), 283–312. doi:10.1177/104649640103200302

Barley, S. R. (1986). Technology as an Occasion for Structuring: Evidence from Observations of CT Scanners and the Social Order of Radiology Departments. *Administrative Science Quarterly*, *31*, 78–108. doi:10.2307/2392767

Cherns, A. B., & Bryant, D. T. (1984). Studying the client's role in construction management. *Construction Management and Economics*, *2*, 177–184.

Clark, K. B., & Wheelwright, S. C. (1997). Organizing and Leading "Heavyweight" Development Teams . In Tushman, M. L., & Anderson, P. (Eds.), *Managing Strategic Innovation and Change* (pp. 419–432). New York: Oxford University Press.

Contractor, N., & Eisenberg, E.Communication Networks and New Media in Organizations . In Fulk, J., & Steinfield, C. (Eds.), *Organizations and Communication Technology* (pp. 143–172). Newbury Park, CA: Sage.

Crampton, C. D. (2001). The mutual knowledge problem and its consequences for dispersed collaboration. *Organization Science*, *12*, 346–371. doi:10.1287/orsc.12.3.346.10098

Crampton, C. D. (2002). Attribution in distributed work groups . In Hinds, P., & Keisler, S. (Eds.), *Distributed work: new ways of working across distance using technology*. Cambridge, MA: The MIT Press.

Danwood, N., Akinsola, A., & Hobbs, B. (2002). Development of automated communication of system for managing site information using internet technology. *Automation in Construction*, *11*(5), 557–572. doi:10.1016/S0926-5805(01)00066-8

Davis, R. D., Bagozzi, R. R., & Warshaw, P. R. (1989). User Acceptance of Computer Technology: Comparison of Two Theoretical Models. *Management Science*, *35*(8), 982–1003. doi:10.1287/mnsc.35.8.982

DeSanctis, G., & Poole, M. (1994). Capturing the Complexity in Advanced Technology Use: Adaptive Structuration Theory. *Organization Science*, *5*(2), 121–147. doi:10.1287/orsc.5.2.121

Ekstedt, E., Lundin, R. A., Söderholm, A., & Wirdenius, H. (1999). *Neo-Industrial Organising, Renewal by action and knowledge formation in a project-intensive economy*. London: Routledge.

Feldman, M. S., & March, J. G. (1981). Information in Organisations as Signal and Symbol. *Administrative Science Quarterly*, *26*(2), 171–186. doi:10.2307/2392467

Fichman, R. G., & Kemerer, C. F. (1997). The Assimilation of Software Process Innovations: An Organizational Learning Perspective. *Management Science*, *43*(10), 1345–1363. doi:10.1287/mnsc.43.10.1345

Giddens, A. (1979). *Central problems in social theory*. Berkeley, CA: University of California Press.

Giddens, A. (1984). *The Constitution of Society: Outline of the Theory of Structuration*. Berkeley, CA: University of California Press.

Grudin, J. (1994). Groupware and social Dynamics: Eight Challenges for Developers. *Communications of the ACM*, *37*(1), 93–105. doi:10.1145/175222.175230

Hayne, S. C., & Smith, C. A. P. (2005). The Relationship Between e-Collaboration and Cognition . *International Journal of e-Collaboration*, *1*(3), 17–34.

Hinds, P. J., & Bailey, D. E. (2003). Out of sight, out of sync: Understanding conflict in distributed teams. *Organization Science*, *14*(6), 615–632. doi:10.1287/orsc.14.6.615.24872

Jarvenpaa, S. L., & Leidner, D. E. (1998). Communication and Trust in Global Virtual Teams. [online journal]. *Journal of Computer-Mediated Communication*, *3*(4).

Khazanchi, D., & Zigurs, I. (2006). Patterns for Effective Management of Virtual Projects: Theory and Evidence. *International Journal of e-Collaboration*, *2*(3), 25–49.

Leonard-Barton, D. (1988). Implementation as Mutual Adaptation of Technology and Organization. *Research Policy*, *17*, 251–267. doi:10.1016/0048-7333(88)90006-6

Lin, A., & Silva, L. (2005). The social and political construction of technological frames. *European Journal of Information Systems*, *14*, 49–59. doi:10.1057/palgrave.ejis.3000521

Lipnack, J., & Stamps, J. (1997). *Virtual Teams*. New York: Wiley.

Majchrzak, A. Rice, R. E. Malhotra & King, N. (2000). Technology adaptation: The case of a computer-supported inter-organisational virtual team. *Management Information Systems Quarterly*, *24*(4), 569–600. doi:10.2307/3250948

Majchrzak, A., Malhotra, A., & John, R. (2005). Perceived Individual Collaboration Know-How Development through Information Technology – Enabled Contextualisation: Evidence from distributed teams. *Information Systems Research*, *16*(1), 9–27. doi:10.1287/isre.1050.0044

Maznevski, M. L., & Chudoba, K. M. (2000). Bridging space over time: Global virtual team dynamics and effectiveness. *Organisational Science*, *11*(5), 473–492. doi:10.1287/orsc.11.5.473.15200

Mohrman, S. A., Cohen, S. G., & Mohrman, A. M. Jr. (1995). *Designing Team-Based Organizations: New Forms for Knowledge Work*. San Francisco, CA: Jossey-Bass Publishers.

Myers, M. D. (1997) Qualitative Research in Information Systems. Retrieved from http://www.misq.org/misqd961/isworld

Ollman, B. (1971). *Alliennation: Marx's Conception of Man in Capitalist society*. Cambridge University Press.

Orlikowski, W. J. (1992). The Duality of Technology: Rethinking The Concept of Technology in Organizations. *Organization Science*, *3*(3), 398–427. doi:10.1287/orsc.3.3.398

Orlikowski, W. J. (1993). CASE Tools as Organizational Change: Investigating Incremental and Radical Changes in Systems Development. *Management Information Systems Quarterly*, *17*(3), 309–340. doi:10.2307/249774

Orlikowski, W. J., & Baroudi, J. J. (1991). Studying Information Technology in Organizations: Research Approaches and Assumptions. *Information Systems Research*, *2*, 1–28. doi:10.1287/isre.2.1.1

Orlikowski, W. L. (1996). Improvising Organisational Transformation Over Time: A situated change perspective. *Information Systems Research*, *7*(1), 63–92. doi:10.1287/isre.7.1.63

Orlikowski, W. L. (2000). Using technology and constituting structures: A Practice Lens for Studying Technology in Organisations . *Organization Science*, *11*(4), 404–428. doi:10.1287/orsc.11.4.404.14600

Pinsonneault, A., & Caya, O. (2005). Virtual Teams: What We Know, What We Don't Know. *International Journal of e-Collaboration*, *1*(3), 1–16.

Rogers, E. M. (1983). *Diffusion of Innovations* (3rd ed.). New York: The Free Press.

Romano, N. Jr, Nunamaker, J., Briggs, R., & Vogel, D. (1998). Architecture, Design, and Development of An HTML/Javascript Web-Based Group Support System. *Journal of the American Society for Information Science American Society for Information Science*, *49*(7), 649–667. doi:10.1002/(SICI)1097-4571(19980515)49:7<649::AID-ASI6>3.0.CO;2-1

Sahay, S. (1997). Implementation of information technology: A time-space perspective. *Organization Studies*, *18*(2), 229–260. doi:10.1177/017084069701800203

Sarker, S., & Sahay, S. (2003). Understanding virtual team development: An interpretive study. *Journal of the Association for Information Systems*, *4*(1), 1–38.

Scanlin, J. (1998) The Internet as an enabler of the Bell Atlantic project office. *Project Management Journal*, June 6-7

Sproull, L. S., & Goodman, P. S. (1990). Technology and organisation: Integration and opportunities . In Sproull, L. S., & Goodman, P. S. (Eds.), *Technology and Organiations* (pp. 254–265). San Francisco: Jossey-Bass.

Susman, G., Gray, B. L., Perry, J., & Blair, C. E. (2003). Recognition and reconciliation of differences in interpretation of misalignments when collaborative technologies are introduced into new product development teams. *Journal of Engineering and Technology Management, 20*, 141–159. doi:10.1016/S0923-4748(03)00008-0

Taylor, S., & Todd, R. A. (1995). Understanding IT Usage: A Test of Competing Models. *Information Systems Research, 6*(2), 144–176. doi:10.1287/isre.6.2.144

Townsend, A., DeMarie, S., & Hendrickson, A. (1998). Virtual Teams: Technology and the Workplace of the Future. *The Academy of Management Executive, 12*(3), 17–29.

Tyre, M. J., & Orlikowski, W. J. (1994). Windows of Opportunity: Temporal Patterns of Technological Adaptation In Organizations. *Organization Science, 5*(1), 98–118. doi:10.1287/orsc.5.1.98

Vaidyanathan, G. (2006). Networked Knowledge Management Dimensions in Distributed Projects. *International Journal of e-Collaboration, 2*(4), 19–36.

Walsham, G. (1993). Interpretive Case Studies in IS research: Nature and Method. *European Journal of Information Systems, 4*, 74–81. doi:10.1057/ejis.1995.9

Weick, K. (1990) Technology as equivoque. P. S. Goodman, L. S. Sproull and Associates, eds. Technology and Organisation (pp. 1-44). San Francisco: Jossey-Bass.

Whitworth, B., Gallupe, B., & McQueen, R. (2001). Generating agreement in computer-mediated groups . *Small Group Research, 32*(5), 625–665. doi:10.1177/104649640103200506

Wynekoop, J. L. (1992). Strategies for Implementation Research: Combining Research Methods. In J.l. DeGross, J.D. Becker & J.J. Elam (Eds.), *Proceedings of the 13th International Conference on Information Systems* (pp. 195-206).

Yin, R. K. (1994). *Case Study Research, Design and Methods* (2nd ed.). Newbury Park, CA: Sage.

Chapter 7
Creativity Support via Terms in Thematic Relations

Eiko Yamamoto
National Institute of Information and Communications Technology, Japan

Hitoshi Isahara
National Institute of Information and Communications Technology, Japan

ABSTRACT

Creativity is required in many fields of endeavor—especially industry and scientific research. Creative tasks we consider in this article include not only creative tasks by single individual or multiple individuals, but also collaborative tasks accomplished by a group of individuals with support of e-collaboration technologies. The difficulty of formulating new ideas calls for the development of an environment that supports creativity. Moreover, it is known that people tend to become more creative when they use words that are related thematically rather than taxonomically. In light of this, we sought to extract lists of words having a thematic relation. In this article, we propose a method of extracting such word lists and verify, through Web retrieval, that word lists with a thematic relation can support creativity. The verification method is based on the belief that we can acquire certain knowledge if a word list directs us to informative Web pages and the knowledge included in such pages is useful and can itself stimulate creativity. As a result of our experiment, we report that our methodology can extract word lists available to support creativity.

INTRODUCTION

Expansion of imagination is crucial for lively creativity. However, expanding one's imagination can be difficult because of complex/complicated inferences and deductions are required. Also,

putting multiple individuals' imaginations together in the collaborative task would be difficult; therefore, the development of an environment that supports creativity is required.

One simple method of supporting creativity is to provide users with words that tend to spark the imagination. Moreover, as for collaborative task, such words can put scattered imaginations together because they can be shared information in the group. However, words presented randomly are unlikely to be useful at promoting creativity, at least when one collects their thoughts, because they tend to trigger divergent ideas. Words must be chosen carefully, and only pertinent words should be provided. There are at least two kinds of relations between two words: a taxonomical relation and a thematic relation (Wisniewski & Bassok, 1999). It has been reported that both the taxonomical relation and the thematic relation between two objects are important to the recognition of the relations between them. The former is a relation that represents the physical resemblance between two objects such as "cow" and "horse" or "horse" and "animal"; the latter is a relation of two concepts in a thematic scene, such as "milk" and "cow" as recollected in the scene "milking a cow." This division also applies to the relation between the concepts represented by words.

Previous research on creative design has reported that a word pair with a thematic relation sparks the imagination more than does a pair with a taxonomical relation. Such a sparking of the imagination is necessary in product development (Harakawa et al., 2005; Taura & Nagai, 2005; Nagai et al., 2006). Also, thematic relation must be very effective for creativity in an environment with support of e-collaboration technologies, although observing a thematic relation among words from resources shared among individuals for a collaborative task is very difficult.

In light of the above, we tried to extract from large-scale domain-specific documents useful word lists in which a thematic relation exists among the words. In this article, we propose a method for extracting such related word lists, and we verify their capability to support creativity.

In order to extract related word lists, we utilize inclusive relations between words based on a modifiee/modifier relationship between words in documents, which is an application of a method

developed for automatically constructing a semantic hierarchy (a type of taxonomical relation) from a corpus (Yamamoto et al., 2005). Inclusive relations are evaluated by the complementary similarity measure (CSM), which was developed to recognize degraded machine-printed text (Hagita & Sawaki, 1995).

For verification, we examined whether the extracted word lists directed us to informative pages on the Web. To some extent, the capability to retrieve informative pages corresponds to the capability to support creativity. This arises from the idea that we can acquire specific knowledge if a word list directs us to informative Web pages. The knowledge contained in such pages might include useful products and should at least serve to stimulate creativity.

CREATIVITY IN E-COLLABORATION

Electronic collaboration (e-collaboration) is defined as collaboration using electronic technologies among different individuals to accomplish a common task. It includes fields such as computer-mediated communication, computer-supported cooperative work, and group support systems (Kock, 2005). So far, there is much research which discuss processes reaching agreement in e-collaboration context, such as decision making (Fjermestad, 2005), requirements determination (Evaristo & Watson-Manheim, 2005) and sensemaking support (Nosek, 2005). However, there is little research which treats creativity support in e-collaboration context. There is research on electronic brainstorming (Dennis et al., 2005; Dennis & Williams, 2005), but there is no research which proposed concrete method to extract information useful in creativity support from huge amount of Web data.

Research on supporting creativity has recently become popular with the growing recognition that creativity is crucial to solving problems in industry, academia, and many other spheres of endeavor. In this article, we introduce a method of automatically extracting related word lists from documents, and discuss the possibility of applying our methodology to the creativity support.

Creative tasks we consider include collaborative tasks with support of e-collaboration technologies. To support creativity in an e-collaboration environment—that is, to support collaboration in accomplishing a creative task among multiple individuals—participants should be guided commonly by some directional clues for solving problems related to the task. However, it is difficult to derive such clues from general-purpose knowledge and resources, even if their resources are shared and managed properly.

The word lists extracted by our proposed method can be used as a kind of directional clues which can support a collaborative task for creativity because the clues can be used to put multiple individuals' imaginations together and to spark each individual's imagination leading a direction. Putting scattered imaginations together is an effective way for decision support.

As for the area of creative design, because concept-synthesis—that is, sparking the imagination with two different concepts (words)—is the most important process, providing effective word pairs can be a powerful means of stimulating creativity. Previous research has reported that a word pair with a thematic relation sparks the imagination more than a word pair with a taxonomical relation does. Such a sparking of the imagination is necessary in product development (Harakawa et al., 2005; Taura & Nagai, 2005; Nagai et al., 2006). In design, it is necessary to carefully consider not only a product's attributes but also its functions and interface; in other words, the human factor must also be considered. Among semantic relations between words, the taxonomical relation is a semantic hierarchical relation and it is useful to understand the meaning of a word. However, from the viewpoint of creativity, a word pair having a taxonomical relation can directly give clues to the association between the attributes of the product,

but it cannot give clues for associating the function and interface of the product. Therefore, the taxonomical relation is limited in its ability to spark the imagination toward original products. On the other hand, a word pair having a thematic relation tends to spark the imagination widely because it gives clues for associating not only a product's attributes but also its functions and interface. Recognizing objects via a thematic relation is to recognize them from a human perspective. Consequently, the thematic relation is expected to be closely related to creativity in design.

As mentioned, the thematic relation is a powerful clue in supporting creativity. Finding word lists with thematic relations from resources shared by different individuals or different topics is very difficult; therefore, using a statistical method, we tried to extract word lists having a thematic relation from documents as an effective means of supporting creativity. Moreover, we used domain-specific documents as a knowledge source in our experiment. These documents correspond to resources stored for a common task in e-collaboration.

In the domain of psychology, creativity has been studied from a variety of viewpoints. In social psychology, Amabile (1996) has proposed that there exist three important components for creativity: domain-relevant skills, creativity-relevant skills, and task motivation. She then argued that high-quality creativity is possible if the level of each of these components is above average and the relationship between the components and creativity can be modeled. Also proposed are the chance-configuration model (Simonton, 1988) and system model (Csikszentmihalyi, 1999). In cognitive psychology, the investment model is the typical approach (Sternberg & Lubart, 1991). However, since a standard for creativity has yet to be defined, no evaluation method has been established, although Amabile (1996) has described the possibility that we can evaluate the quality of creativity through the quantitative difference in the components she has mentioned.

We undertook a computational experiment to verify the ability of our extracted word lists to stimulate (or contribute to) creativity. We clearly demonstrated that our word lists lead to informative Web pages; that is, that they can provide knowledge as clues for creative inspiration.

ACQUISTION OF WORD LISTS

We applied a method of automatically constructing semantic hierarchies from corpora proposed by Yamamoto et al. (2005) in order to acquire word lists that can direct users to new information and can be directly used to boost creativity. The method is based on the Complementary Similarity Measure (CSM).

Complementary Similarity Measure

CSM was developed as a means of recognizing degraded machine-printed text. It was designed to accommodate heavy noise or graphical designs (Hagita & Sawaki, 1995). An appearance pattern is expressed as an n-dimensional binary feature vector. When $V_i = (v_{i1}, ..., v_{in})$ is a vector for word w_i and $V_j = (v_{j1}, ..., v_{jn})$ is a vector for word w_j, $CSM(V_i, V_j)$ is defined as follows:

$$CSM(V_i, V_j) = \frac{ad - bc}{\sqrt{(a+c)(b+d)}},$$

$$a = \sum_{k=1}^{n} v_{ik} \cdot v_{jk}, \qquad b = \sum_{k=1}^{n} v_{ik} \cdot (1 - v_{jk}),$$

$$c = \sum_{k=1}^{n} (1 - v_{ik}) \cdot v_{jk}, \quad d = \sum_{k=1}^{n} (1 - v_{ik}) \cdot (1 - v_{jk}),$$

$$n = a + b + c + d.$$

Because the denominator is asymmetric, CSM is an asymmetric measure. Therefore, $CSM(V_i, V_j)$ usually differs from $CSM(V_j, V_i)$ switched V_i and V_j. For example, when V_i is 1110010111 and V_j is 1000110110, parameters are $a = 4$, $b = 3$, $c = 1$, and $d = 2$ and $CSM(V_i, V_j)$ is higher than $CSM(V_j, V_i)$. According to the asymmetric feature, we can estimate that the appearance pattern of w_i includes one of w_j.

Previous research has reported being able to determine a hierarchical relation between two words, based on the inclusive relation between word appearance patterns estimated by CSM value (Yamamoto et al., 2005; Kanzaki et al., 2004). If w_i is "animal" and w_j is "tiger," CSM can determine that "animal" is a hypernym of "tiger."

CSM-Based Word List Extraction

We used an extension of the CSM-based method proposed by Yamamoto et al. (2005) to extract word lists having a relation that is not limited to a hierarchical relation from domain-specific documents. In order to extract hierarchies among abstract nouns, they used the appearance pattern of abstract nouns for co-occurring words. However, they limited co-occurring words to adjectives defined as hyponyms of abstract nouns. Under the condition that co-occurring words are hyponyms of target words, we can extract only a semantic hierarchical structure. Therefore, by utilizing inclusive relations between words based on a modifiee/modifier relationship in documents, we tried to extract not only word lists with hierarchical relations (i.e., taxonomical relations) but also word lists with various other relations.

We first extracted word pairs having an inclusive relation between the words by calculating the CSM value in both directions. The word pairs we extracted are expressed by a tuple $<w_i, w_j>$, where $CSM(V_i, V_j)$ has higher value than $CSM(V_j, V_i)$ when word w_i has the appearance pattern V_i and word w_j has the appearance pattern V_j. We call w_i the "left word" and w_j the "right word."

This method uses CSM to compute the similarity between word appearance patterns, extracts tuples according to their CSM value, and connects words based on their relation, where the CSM value is normalized between 1.0 and 0.0. We construct word lists from tuples with CSM values higher than a certain threshold (TH). Suppose we have <A, B>, <B, C>, <Z, B>, <C, D>, <C, E>, and

<C, F> in the order of their CSM values, which are above TH. Let <B, C> be an initial word list {B, C}. We create a word list as follows.

1. We find the tuple with the highest CSM value among the tuples in which the word at the tail of the current word list—for example, word "C" in {B, C}—is a left word, and connect the right word of the tuple to the tail of the current word list.

2. In this example, word "D" is connected to {B, C} because <C, D> has the highest CSM value among the three tuples <C, D>, <C, E>, and <C, F>, making the current word list {B, C, D}.

3. This process is repeated until no tuples can be chosen.

4. We find the tuple with the highest CSM value among the tuples in which the word B at the head of the current word list—for example, word "B" in {B, C, D}—is the right word, and connect the left word of the tuple to the head of the current word list.

5. Similarly, word "A" is connected to the head of {B, C, D} because <A, B> has a CSM value higher than that of <Z, B>, making the current word list {A, B, C, D}.

6. This process is repeated until no tuples can be chosen.

In this example, we obtained the word list {A, B, C, D}. In this way, we construct all word lists by beginning with each tuple, using tuples whose CSM values are higher than TH. Finally, from the word lists obtained, we remove word lists that are embedded in other word lists.

If we set TH to a low value, it is possible to obtain lengthy word lists. When the TH is too low, the number of tuples that must be considered becomes overwhelming and the reliability of the measurement decreases. Consequently, we experimentally set TH.

EXPERIMENTAL DATA

In our experiment, we used domain-specific documents in Japanese from the medical domain gathered from the Web pages of a medical school. We did this to show that the CSM-based method can be applied to the extraction of useful word sets. The Japanese documents we used totaled 37 Mbytes (10,144 pages). The total number of sentences in the documents was 225,402. We used neither medical dictionaries nor any other technical dictionaries.

As mentioned, we extracted word lists by utilizing inclusive relations of the appearance pattern between words based on a modifiee/modifier relationship in documents. Fortunately, the Japanese language has case-marking particles that provide semantic relations between two elements in a dependency relation, which is a kind of modifiee/modifier relationship. For our experiment, we used such particles and extracted the data from the documents we gathered.

First, we parsed sentences with the KNP[1]. From the results, we collected dependency relations matching one of the following five patterns of case-marking particles. With A, B, P, Q, R, and S as nouns (including compound words), V as a verb, and <*X*> as a case-marking particle, the five patterns are as follows:

- A <*no* (of)> B
- P <*wo* (object)> V
- Q <*ga* (subject)> V
- R <*ni* (dative)> V
- S <*ha* (topic)> V

We used five case-marking particles in the above patterns: <*no*>, <*wo*>, <*ga*>, <*ni*>, and <*ha*>. Suppose we have the following sentence:

Taro <ha> Mitsuko <kara> Jiro <ga> Hanako <ni> daiya <no> yubiwa <wo> ageta <to> kiita.

This sentence means "Taro heard from Mitsuko that Jiro had given Hanako a diamond ring." From this sentence, we can extract five dependency relations between words as follows:

- *daiya* (diamond) *<no> yubiwa* (ring)
- *yubiwa <wo> ageta* (had given)
- *Jiro <ga> ageta*
- *Hanako <ni> ageta*
- *Taro <ha> kiita* (heard)

From this set of dependency relations, we compiled the following types of experimental data items:

- **NN-data** based on co-occurrence between nouns. For each sentence in our document collection, we gathered nouns followed by all five of the case-marking particles we used and nouns proceeded by <no>; that is, A, B, P, Q, R, and S. For the above sentence, we can gather Taro, Mitsuko, Jiro, Hanako, daiya, and yubiwa. The number of data items equals the number of sentences in the documents.
- *NV-data based on a dependency relation between noun and verb.* We gathered nouns P, Q, R, and S followed by each of the case-marking particles *<wo>*, *<ga>*, *<ni>*, and *<ha>* for each verb V. We named them **Wo-data** (the number of gathered relations was 20,234), **Ga-data** (15,924), **Ni-data** (14,215), and **Ha-data** (15,896), respectively. For the verb *ageta* in the above sentence, the Wo-data is *yubiwa*, Ga-data is *Jiro*, and so on. The number of data items equals the number of kinds of verbs.
- **SO-data** *based on a collocation between subject and object.* We gathered subject Q followed by the case-marking particle *<ga>* that depends on the same verb V as the object P for each object followed by the case-marking particle *<wo>*. The number of gathered relations was 4,437. For the

above example, we can gather the subject *Jiro* for the object *yubiwa* because we have the dependency relations *Jiro <ga> ageta* and *yubiwa <wo> ageta*. The number of data items equals the number of kinds of objects.

When we represent experimental data with a binary vector, the vector corresponds to the appearance pattern of a noun. Parameters for calculating the CSM-value correspond to the number of dimensions in each situation. Figure 1 shows images of the appearance pattern expressed by the binary vector for each data item. The number of dimensions equals the number of data items for each experimental data. For NN-data, each dimension corresponds to a sentence. The element of the vector is 1 if the noun appears in the sentence and 0 if it does not. Similarly, for NV-data, each dimension corresponds to a verb. For SO-data, we represent the appearance pattern for each subject with a binary vector where each dimension corresponds to an object.

EXPERIMENT

In applying the CSM-based method, we represented experimental data for medical terms with a binary vector. We used descriptors in the 2005 Medical Subject Headings (MeSH) thesaurus[2] and translated them into Japanese. The number of terms in Japanese which appear in this experiment was 2,557. In our experiment, we thus extract word lists consisting of those 2,557 medical terms.

To avoid an upsurge in the number of word lists extracted, we carefully set the threshold (TH) and chose tuples that exceeded the TH to extract word lists. We chose word lists consisting of three or more terms from the extracted word lists and used them for verification.

We show examples of word lists extracted by the CSM-based method in Figures 2 and 3.

Figure 1. Appearance patterns of a binary vector for each experimental data item

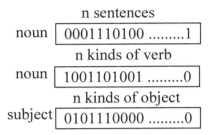

Figure 2. Examples of word lists obtained from NN-data

> data - causation - depression - reduction
>   - platelet count - bone marrow examination
>
> neonate - patent ductus arteriosus - necrotizing enterocolitis
>
> secretion - gastric acid - gastric mucosa - duodenal ulcer
>
> skin - atopic dermatitis - herpes viruses - antiviral drugs
>
> fatigue - uterine muscle - pregnancy toxemia
>
> water - oxygen - hydrogen - hydrogen ion
>
> person - nicotiana - smoke - oxygen deficiencies

Figure 3. Examples of word lists obtained from SO-data

> latency period - erythrocyte - hepatic cell
>
> snow - school - gas
>
> variation - death - limb
>
> hospitalist - corneal opacities - triazolam
>
> cross reaction - apoptoses - injuries
>
> research - survey - altered taste - rice
>
> environment - state interest - water - meat - diarrhea
>
> rights - energy generating resources - cordia - education - deforestation

Note that we extracted word lists consisting of the Japanese medical terms, which 2,557 terms found in the medical documents we used. English words and sentences in the following part of this article were obtained from the MeSH thesaurus for the sake of explanation.

RESULTS

Comparison with the Baseline Method

First, we show the capability of the CSM-based method in selecting informative tuples by comparing it with the typical method using co-occurrence as a baseline method. To do this, we compiled a list of tuples that co-occurred at least twice in the NN-data, and sorted it according to the co-occurrence frequency. We show the top ten tuples for each method in Table 1.

For example, both methods gave the highest score to the tuple <administration, treatment> in the first row of Table 1. This indicates that, if the frequency of the tuple is high, the CSM value of the tuple is also high. Because general terms have a tendency to appear more frequently than technical terms in the documents, we can see many tuples of general terms near the top of the baseline list.

On the other hand, the tuple <iron, transferrin> in the fourth row has a high CSM value, though it does not appear near the top of the list sorted by frequency because the frequency is low. We used the two words in this tuple as key words for retrieving information on the Web and were able to find a page in a medical dictionary that includes the sentence "Iron is taken into the body

Table 1. The top 10 tuples extracted from NN-data by each method

CSM-based	Baseline
<administration, treatment>	<administration, treatment>
<daughter, nursery school>	<attention, referral>
<attention, referral>	<daughter, nursery school>
<iron, transferrin>	<environment, variation>
<woods, orangutan>	<humans, environment>
<daughter, son>	<daughter, son>
<role, cytokine>	<nature, rights>
<stroke, epilepsy>	<mail, laboratories>
<secretion, glucocorticoid>	<person, cordia>
<nature, rights>	<humans, societies>

with the molecule transferrin." This shows that we can obtain meaningful information about "iron" as it appears in the medical domain by using this word pair as keywords in an online search. This suggests that CSM can extract informative word pairs that can be useful for information retrieval. This leads us to guess that word lists consisting of such word pairs are informative. Even these simple tuples can direct us toward available information capable of sparking our imaginations; moreover, simply providing them could support creativity.

Another feature of the CSM-based method is that it can calculate the inclusive relations between two words and the results can be merged. That is, once we obtain two tuples <A, B> and <B, C>, even though they are tuples extracted from different sentences, we can obtain the word list {A, B, C}. On the other hand, the co-occurrence frequency extracts only the co-occurrence relations and two tuples extracted from different sentences cannot be merged easily. This feature of CSM is not limited to within a sentence. Therefore, the CSM-based method can use not only information within a sentence, but also information from a wider context.

Comparison with the MeSH Thesaurus

We compared the CSM-based word lists with the MeSH trees in the 2005 MeSH thesaurus. Because the MeSH trees are hierarchical representations of words in the MeSH thesaurus, the word lists that agree with the MeSH trees represent taxonomical relations among words. Other word lists represent thematic relations among words. As the former would not do much to inspire the imagination, we will use the latter word lists—which can spark the imagination to a greater degree—in the next section to verify the capability to support creativity.

The MeSH trees are hierarchical arrangements of headings with their associated tree numbers. We gathered synonyms or closely related heading terms stored as cross-references in the MeSH thesaurus and added them to the MeSH trees. The tree number includes information about the category. The MeSH headings are organized into 15 categories, which are represented by an alphabetic character at the head of the identifier for each term. The hierarchical structure of terms can be seen by tracing their identifiers (Figure

Figure 4. Segments of a MeSH tree

A01	body region
:	
A01.378	limb
A01.378.610	lower limb
A01.378.610.250	foot
A01.378.610.250.149	ankle
:	
A01.378.800	upper limb
A01.378.800.075	arm
A01.378.800.420	elbow
A01.378.800.667	hand
A01.378.800.667.430	finger
A01.378.800.667.430.705	thumb
:	

Table 2. Distribution of words composing each CSM-based word list in MeSH categories

Data		No. of Word Lists	Distribution in Category	
			One (%)	Two (%)
NN		594	24 (4)	169 (28)
NV	Wo	199	35 (18)	42 (21)
	Ga	62	12 (19)	19 (31)
	Ni	37	3 (08)	14 (38)
	Ha	85	6 (07)	26 (31)

4.) Notice that some headings are classified into more than one category.

If a word list extracted by the CSM-based method demonstrates a hierarchical relation among words, the words in the CSM-based word list are classified into one category in the MeSH trees. That is, if an extracted word list agrees with the MeSH thesaurus, we can conclude that a taxonomical relation exists among the words. We examined the distribution of words in the MeSH categories for each type of experimental data except SO-data (Table 2).

In Table 2 we found that, for NN-data and NV-data, the percentage of CSM-based word lists whose words were distributed within one MeSH category was between 4% and 19% and the cumulative percentage of the CSM-based word lists whose terms were distributed within one or two categories was between 32% (4 + 28) and 50% (19 + 31). Of the CSM-based word lists, Ga-data provided the highest agreement ratio. The reason for this seems to be that the subject case represented by the case-marking particle <*ga*> restricts nouns more stringently than do the others. Also, comparing the results of NN-data and NV-data, we found that the word lists extracted from NV-data agreed with the MeSH thesaurus to a greater degree than did those extracted from NN-data.

This suggests that we obtained more word lists having taxonomical relations among words from NV-data than from NN-data. SO-data is based on a collocation between subject and object; that is, the word lists obtained comprise subjects followed by the case-marking particle <*ga*> that depend on the same verb as the object for each object followed by the case-marking particle <*wo*>. For example, when we have "*ningen* (person) <*ga*> *hon* (book) <*wo*> *yomu* (read)," which means "a person reads a book," and "*nezumi* (mouse) <*ga*> *hon* (book) <*wo*> *kajiru* (gnaw)," which means "a mouse gnaws a book," we estimate the relation between the words *ningen* and *nezumi* with CSM. Therefore, we can surmise that the information we obtain from this data will not agree with a general thesaurus because we do not limit the verbs that subjects and objects depend on. Actually, the word lists we obtained from SO-data agreed little with the MeSH trees. This suggests that word lists extracted from SO-data would be most effective at sparking creativity.

Figure 5 shows examples in which all the terms in a word list are classified into one category, and Figure 6 shows examples in which terms are classified into two categories. The data from which we obtained each word list is given in parenthesis. The underlined terms in Figure 6 are those classified in a different category.

For verification in the next section, we used word lists whose words are distributed in two or more MeSH categories. However, we found that

Figure 5. Examples in which all terms are classified into one category

Figure 5. Examples in which all terms are classified into one category

```
skin - abdomen - cervix - cavitas oris - chest (NN)
cardiovascular disease - coronary artery disease
    - bronchitis - thrombophlebitides - flatulence
    - hyperuricemia - lower back pain
    - ulnar nerve palsies - brain hemorrhage
    - obstructive jaundice (Wo)
extrasystole - bronchospasm - acute renal failure
    - colitides - diabetic coma - pancreatitides (Ga)
hand - mouth - ear - finger (Ni)
snake - praying mantis - scorpion (Ha)
```

Figure 6. Examples in which terms are classified into two categories

```
ice cream - chocolate - wine (Ni)
ovary - spleen - palpation (NN)
bleeding - pyrexia - hematuria - consciousness disorder
    - vertigo - high blood pressure (Ga)
variation - cross reactions - outbreaks - secretion (Wo)
cough - fetus
    - bronchiolitis obliterans organizing pneumonia (Ha)
```

in some of those word lists, all words could be classified into one category. For example, we were able to extract "ice cream - chocolate - wine," shown in the first word list of Figure 6. This is obviously correct from the viewpoint of language processing because all items are edible. However, "ice cream" and "wine" are categorized as foods and "chocolate" is categorized as a material in the MeSH thesaurus. Such word lists were extracted mainly from NV-data. Thus, we found that the CSM-based method can extract better semantic relations from corpora, even from the viewpoint of taxonomical relations. We removed such word lists from the set of word lists to be verified.

VERIFICATION

By using the extracted word lists to retrieve Web pages, we examined the capability of our extracted word lists to expand knowledge. The keywords that directed us toward informative pages on the Web can be considered keys to acquiring knowledge related to such informative pages.

We used the extracted word lists to retrieve Web pages in Japanese. We explain here some of the interesting results obtained from the 30 word lists used.

Using "ovary - spleen - palpation," the second word list shown in Figure 6, Google retrieved Web pages that include the information "Diseases of the ovary and spleen can be diagnosed by palpa-

tion." This indicates that this word list precisely directed us toward informative pages; that is, we were able to acquire knowledge. Similarly, using "bleeding - pyrexia - hematuria - consciousness disorder - vertigo - high blood pressure," shown in the third word list, we obtained Web pages that include the information that all of the words in the list are bad reactions to a certain medicine.

As another example, we retrieved informative Web pages using "data - causation - depression - reduction - platelet count - bone marrow examination," the first word list in Figure 2. This list was extracted from NN-data and is an example in which the terms are classified into three or more categories. This means that this word list contains relations that are not taxonomical relations (such as hierarchical relations). Therefore, we can infer that this word list will provide certain knowledge. Actually, this word list retrieved Web pages that included the sentence "Bone marrow examination is necessary because bone marrow illnesses can cause depression and reduced platelet count."

Next, we verified the capability of extracted word lists to support information retrieval. If a word list's capability is high in this regard, we would be able to use that word list to obtain high-quality knowledge from informative pages. We used "neonate - patent ductus arteriosus - necrotizing enterocolitis," the second word list in Figure 2, as an example. Using the single search term "necrotizing enterocolitis," Google retrieved 13,500 pages in Japanese that include the information "Necrotizing enterocolitis is a neonatal disease." Even when "neonate" is added as a search term, Google still retrieves 872 pages related to information about "prophylaxis of necrotizing enterocolitis and cure for this disease." On the other hand, if we input only "patent ductus arteriosus," we obtained 28,500 pages that include the information that "Patent ductus arteriosus is a neonatal disease." However, using all terms in the word list that our method extracted, that is, "neonate," "patent ductus arteriosus," and "necrotizing enterocolitis," Google retrieves just 182 pages and the top five pages among them are related to "neonate's patent ductus arteriosus and mefenamic acid," although these five pages are ranked beneath pages related to "the prophylaxis and the cure" that are listed at the top of the 872 pages extracted without "patent ductus arteriosus." These five pages include the following important information: "When mefenamic acid is used to treat patent ductus arteriosus, necrotizing enterocolitis may react badly to this medicine."

Similarly, among the word lists obtained from SO-data, "latency period - erythrocyte - hepatic cell," the first word list in Figure 3, retrieved pages related to "malaria." If we input "latency period" and "hepatic cell," Google retrieves many pages related to "hepatic trouble" in the 385 pages of retrieval results. By using this word list extracted with our method, that is, adding "erythrocyte," users can retrieve only the relevant and necessary pages, similar to the approach of a professional who knows that patients experience hepatic trouble during the latency period for malaria. The number of retrieval results is 181 pages. In the results, the page related to malaria is the seventh, though it does not appear within the top 100 of the results without "erythrocyte."

As for the second word list in Figure 3, it is originally a list of Japanese words obtained from SO-data, such as "*yuki* (snow) - *gakko* (school) - *gasu* (gas)." We translated the term "gas" in MeSH thesaurus into Japanese using existing machine translation system and obtained *gasu* in Japanese.

The Japanese word *gasu* is ambiguous: it can mean either "gas" or "fog" in English. Because the Web pages of the medical school we used for the experiment included pages on general issues as well as medical matters, our method extracted word lists which represent general knowledge, such as "*yuki* (snow) - *gakko* (school) - *gasu* (gas/ fog)." However, the word *gasu* means not "gas" but "fog" in the Japanese Web pages we retrieved with this word list of Japanese, as in "We cannot leave for school because a fog lay over the city on the snow day." This means that this kind of word list is useful knowledge for word-sense disambiguation; that is, the presence of the words *yuki* (snow) and *gakko* (school) disambiguates the meaning of *gasu* into "fog."

As the above examples show, the extracted word lists can direct us toward informative pages. We used experimental data from Web documents within the medical domain to show that the CSM-based method can be used to extract useful word lists for our purposes. We can determine whether these word lists are useful by using them to retrieve information on the Web. That is, if a word list can direct us to informative pages, we would be able to obtain knowledge from those pages. The capability to provide knowledge would correspond to the one to support creativity, because creativity becomes active as knowledge expands. Therefore, we can conclude that the CSM-based method can extract word lists available to support creativity.

In collaborative creative task, it is important for participants to take a common bearing from current stage of the task. In e-collaboration, this is based on the shared resources. That is, participants should be guided commonly by some directional clues inferred from the resources. In our experiment, we extracted word lists from medical documents which correspond with resources stored for a common task. We obtained word lists from such resources, and retrieved Web pages with those word lists. Knowledge, including in the retrieved pages, was surely directional clues which support active creativity for accomplishing their common task. Thus, we consider our methodology can be applied to e-collaboration environment.

CONCLUSION

In this article, we proposed a method for extracting from domain-specific document word lists with thematic relations available to support creative tasks including collaborative tasks accomplishing by a group of individuals with support of e-collaboration technologies, and verified the capability of the extracted word lists having a thematic relation to support creativity by retrieving information from the Web.

We used experimental data from medical documents to show that the CSM-based method can be used to extract useful word lists. We retrieved information from the Web using the extracted word lists and examined the retrieval results by way of verification. The verification method is based on the belief that we can acquire certain knowledge if a word list directs us to informative Web pages. The knowledge included in such pages is useful and can itself stimulate creativity.

As a result of our experiment, we found that the extracted word lists can direct us toward informative Web pages. Therefore, these word lists have the capability to stimulate creativity. This suggests our methodology can extract word lists available to support creativity.

REFERENCES

Amabile, T. (1996). *Creativity in context: Update to the social psychology of creativity.* Westview Press.

Csikszentmihalyi, M. (1999). Implications of a systems perspective for the study of creativity. In R. Sternberg (Ed.), *Handbook of Creativity* (pp. 313-335). Cambridge University Press.

Dennis, A., Pinsonneault, A., Hilmer, K., Barki, H., Galupe, B., Huber, M., & Bellavance, F. (2005). Pattern in electronic brainstorming. *International Journal of e-Collaboration, 1*(4), 38-57.

Dennis, A., & Williams, M. (2005). A meta-analysis of group size effects in electronic brainstorming. *International Journal of e-Collaboration, 1*(1), 24-42.

Evaristo, R., & Watson-Manheim, M. (2005). E-collaboration in distributed requirements determination. *International Journal of e-Collaboration, 1*(2), 40-56.

Fjermestad, J. (2005).Virtual group strategic decision making using structured conflict and consensus approaches. *International Journal of e-Collaboration, 1*(1), 43-61.

Hagita, N., & Sawaki, M. (1995). Robust recognition of degraded machine-printed characters using complementary similarity measure and error-correction learning. *Proceedings of the SPIE – The International Society for Optical Engineering, 2442*, (pp. 236-244).

Harakawa, J., Nagai, Y., & Taura, T. (2005). Study on Conceptual Synthesis in Design Creation— Role of Thematic Relation in Creativity— *2005 IDC International Design Congress IASDR,* on CD-ROM.

Kanzaki, K., Yamamoto, E., Ma, Q., & Isahara, H. (2004). Construction of an objective hierarchy of abstract concepts via directional similarity. *Proceedings of the 20th International Conference on Computational Linguistics, 2*, (pp. 1147-1153).

Kock, N. (2005). What is e-collaboration? *International Journal of e-Collaboration, 1*(1), i-vii.

Nagai, Y., & Taura, T. (2006). Formal Description of Concept-Synthesizing Process for Creative Design. In J. Gero (Ed.), *Design, Computing and Cognition 06* (pp. 443-460). Springer.

Nosek, J. (2005). Collaborative sensemaling support: Progressing from portals and tools to collaboration envelopes. *International Journal of e-Collaboration, 1*(2), 25-39.

Simonton, D. (1988). *Scientific genius: A psychology of science*. Cambridge University Press.

Sternberg, R., & Lubart, T. (1991). An investment theory of creativity and its development. *Human Development, 34*, 1-31.

Taura, T., & Nagai, Y. (2005). Primitives and principles of synthetic process for creative design—Taxonomical relation and thematic relation. In J. Gero & M. Maher (Eds.), *Computational and Cognitive Models of Creative Design VI* (pp. 177-194). Key Centre of Design Computing and Cognition University of Sydney.

Wisniewski, E., & Bassok. M. (1999). What makes a man similar to a tie? *Cognitive Psychology, 39*, 208-238.

Yamamoto, E., Kanzaki, K., & Isahara, H. (2005). Extraction of hierarchies based on inclusion of co-occurring words with frequency information. In *Proceedings of the 19th International Joint Conference on Artificial Intelligence*, (pp. 1166-1172).

ENDNOTES

[1]   A Japanese parser developed at Kyoto University.

[2]   The U.S. National Library of Medicine created, maintains, and provides the Medical Subject Headings (MeSH®) thesaurus.

This work was previously published in the International Journal of e-Collaboration, Vol. 4, Issue 2, edited by N. Kock, pp. 55-76, copyright 2008 by IGI Publishing (an imprint of IGI Global).

Chapter 8
E–Collaboration Tools and Technologies for Creativity and Innovation Enhancement[1]

Jane Fedorowicz
Bentley University, USA

Isidro Laso-Ballesteros[2]
European Commission, Belgium

Antonio Padilla-Meléndez
University of Málaga, Spain

ABSTRACT

IT–endowed collaboration within and between groups will catalyze creativity that, in turn, will facilitate organizational innovation and reduce barriers and inefficiencies amongst people working together. This chapter describes the challenges of supporting creativity and innovation through e-collaboration technologies and tools and proposes how future technologies and tools can help to mitigate issues arising from working virtually. The authors discuss how future advancements in communications and information sharing technologies will help to make virtual team location transparent, while improving access to common work processes and information repositories. They call for technology design researchers to include evaluation of how collaboration environments will be used by virtual teams in extant individual, team, organizational and cultural contexts. In this way, the implications of a technological advance on the creativity and innovation resulting from virtual teamwork can be assessed and understood, and generalized to appropriate settings.

INTRODUCTION

The use of technology to enhance individual or team creativity and innovation has become a popular topic among business practitioners and academic researchers. Discussions of creativity and innovation usually take on one of two flavors: either they develop out of a need to "improve" the work processes or output of a team or organization, or they reflect a new technological advance whose designers purport will change the way individuals or organizations operate. Attempts to connect the

DOI: 10.4018/978-1-61520-676-6.ch008

two are rare: designers are more likely to assume than evaluate how a technology or tool might effectively address the way things are, or could, or should, be accomplished in organizations.

These new technologies are endemic to virtual teams, whether because of the demands of the global economy or because new technologies enable them to work at higher levels of efficiency and effectiveness. In this chapter, we reflect on the nature of creativity and innovation in today's organizations, and focus on how collaboration technologies could and should be developed to assist virtual teams in their work.

CREATIVITY AND INNOVATION

Incremental change and adaptation are no longer sufficient for achieving growth in today's world, nor are they good enough to ensure a company's survival. Product, process and relational innovation are necessary for companies wishing to compete in the global economy. Organizational innovation depends on a company's ability to produce creative ideas that lead to breakthroughs in what they sell or how they sell. Successful innovation is hard, and companies invest heavily in training, technology and other means to support working arrangements that encourage and reward creative and innovative employees (Ford and Gioa, 1995). Researchers and practitioners still struggle to better understand how to enable, manage and measure creativity and innovation, even though both creativity and innovation have been the subject of organizational study for decades (Amabile, 1982; Burns and Stalker, 1961; Isaksen, et al., 1993).

Reacting to the need for better technology-based resources to support organizational innovation, information systems researchers have also explored how to design software for influencing creativity. The importance of creativity support systems is evident in the fact that the lead article in the first issue of *Information Systems Research*

proposed and tested design guidelines for systems to support user creativity (Elam and Mead, 1990). More recent work on how collaborative environments support creativity and innovation marries elements of organization theory with information systems design (Laudel, 2001).

Both creativity and innovation are difficult concepts to define. Innovation can result from creativity, but the two are not interchangeable. Many organizational researchers agree that creative ideas must be novel, and they must produce value (Ford, 1995). An innovation results from creativity plus successful implementation of the creative idea (von Stamm, 2003). Creativity can be seen as the first step in an innovation process (West, Sacramento and Fay, 2006) and can be considered a precondition linked to human talent (Yusuf, 2009). Innovation may pertain to new products, services, relationships with partners, or production and administrative processes, or it may enable a company to reach the marketplace more quickly than its competition (Damanpour, 1995; Moore, 1998). In simple terms, creativity is a necessary but not sufficient condition for innovation.

Organizations innovate; individuals create. In modern organizations, individuals rarely produce creative ideas in seclusion (Yusuf, 2009). Instead, individuals contribute to work groups or teams. The modern organization is challenged to provide a supportive working environment and reward structure to work groups so that they are more likely to produce ideas leading to competitive innovations. Individual success becomes measured by the success of the projects worked on, and employees soon learn the value of their own intellectual capital as a key component of career success (Ford and Gioa, 1995). It is up to the organization to determine the best team makeup and supporting infrastructure that will lead to both creative ideas and successful innovations.

In many cases, the most creative or innovative ideas are generated when a mix of internal and external team members combine their complementary skills and perspectives in new ways (Dougherty, 1992; West et al, 2006). These virtual teams, formed from a mix of in-house and contractual employees and external vendors, frequently will comprise members from globally distributed sites. The success of the virtual team will depend upon its ability to collaborate effectively across physical and cultural distances (Levina and Vaast, 2008). According to West (1995), support for innovation (including time, resources and managerial cooperation) is the single best predictor of the creativity and innovation of teams. One of the key resources used by today's teams is the collaborative technological infrastructure that permits communication, information sharing, process management, and decision making among scattered members. Today, with the increasing reliance on boundary-crossing processes and operational outsourcers, companies assemble more virtual teams, with geographically and/or organizationally distributed membership. As a result, there is increased demand for effective technologies to bridge the geographic, organizational and cultural gaps with which these teams must contend (Monalisa et al., 2008).

E-COLLABORATION TECHNOLOGY

In the global economy, collaboration within groups of geographically dispersed knowledge workers is quickly becoming the locus of creativity and innovation (Zhang and Lowry, 2008; Thomas and Bostrom, 2008). Advanced information and communication technologies (ICT) that can enable e-collaboration enhance group work, especially when teams must share information and make decisions across business and national boundaries. The potential for appointing global teams of people with different educational backgrounds, from different cultures, expands the necessary human capital for being creative and innovative, developing what is call *wikicapital* or the capital arising from networks (Yusuf, 2009).

E-collaboration technologies can supply seamless connectivity to allow work anywhere and anytime. Other technologies can ensure access to contextualized services (such as shared digital images or documents) and will permit easy interaction among team members. Moreover, they can help to manage the complexity derived from the diversity of workers, knowledge and other resources that must coordinate effort on a collective creative task. Link (2007) provides a good review of the various organizational roles of e-collaborators.

Many types of e-collaboration technologies are used to assist virtual teams. At the team level, proper use of these technologies are thought to lessen misunderstandings among distributed members, increase re-use of shared information and knowledge, and enable more efficient task management and allocation through competence networks. The intent of these improvements is to enhance the efficiency or effectiveness of the team's work. Carefully executed research is needed to assess whether improvements in these mediating task improvement factors caused by technology adoption lead to better team outcomes with respect to efficiency and effectiveness of decision making or project completion.

As a demonstration of how e-collaboration technology use affects team outcomes through its influence on intermediating activity, McNamara et al. (2008) showed how use of an e-collaboration technology increased a virtual team's information processing activity, which in turn led to better decisions by the team. Theirs is a good demonstration of how researchers should test the impact of a tool design feature on the eventual outcome of the team's work. Successful application of e-collaboration technology should not only be measured in terms of how the technology affects work activities or worker satisfaction, it should also be assessed in terms of the impact on the outcomes of those processes at the team or organizational level.

E-COLLABORATION, CREATIVITY AND INNOVATION

E-collaboration can play an important role in a company's quest for creativity and innovation. At the organizational level, new collaboration tools can enable innovations that produce a faster time to market, increase business model innovation, impose better consistency in cross-domain processes, and improve flexibility and reduce lead time in global product development. At the individual level, e-collaboration tools and technologies boost creativity through the reduction of routine work, decrease idle time through pervasive collaboration services and allow natural human interactions within a dispersed group. E-collaboration can facilitate work processes, and it can also improve the outcomes of these processes by enhancing a team's ability to play off of the ideas, processes and experiences of its members.

The e-collaboration technologies within interorganizational, multidisciplinary and/or technologically complex work groups pave the way towards collaborative environments involving both human and artificial artifacts. Collaborative environments will orchestrate interaction within networks of workers, partners and customers to boost creativity and innovation. Nanda and Singh (2009) present the key factors that interact to influence organizational creativity, and enhance creativity and innovation in the workplace: organizational culture and climate, individual characteristics and the support system. It is this support system that incorporates e-collaboration technologies.

Many technologies are proffered to support individual, group, organizational or interorganizational creativity. As seen in Table 1, these include a wide range of visualization tools, simulations, multimedia presentation and editing,

Table. 1. Samples of classes of creativity support tools and examples of products (from Schneiderman, 2007, p. 22)

INDIVIDUAL AND GROUP CREATIVITY SUPPORT TOOLS	
Information visualization tools	Spotfire, SAS JMP, DataDesk, ManyEyes, Digg
Specialized visualization tools: GIS	Google Maps, ArcInfo
Specialized visualization tools: gene expression analysis	GeneSpring, DNASTAR
Mathematical manipulation	MatLab, Mathematica
Engineering, architectural, industrial, product design	Autocad Inventor, DataCAD, SolidWorks
Simulation	SPICE, Tierra
New media development environments	Max/MSP, Pd, processing
Animation and interaction	Flash, FLEX, OpenLaszlo
Music	Cinescore, Cakewalk Sonar
Video editing	Premier, Final Cut Pro, Lightworks, iMovie, Windows MovieMaker
Concept Mapping	Inspiration, MindMapper, MindManager, Axon
GROUP AND SOCIAL CREATIVITY SUPPORT TOOLS	
Software Development	Eclipse, JDeveloper, Visual Studio
Wikis	Wikipedia, Wikia
Citizen Journalism	Blogger, Ohmynews, Slashdot
Media sharing	Flickr, YouTube
Music	Garageband, Macjams

cooperative software development, and Web-enabled publishing and meetings (Schneiderman, 2007). For example, Helander and Emami (2008) introduce the concept of an eLaboratory, which is a convergence of remote access technologies and collaboration-based eLearning. They propose an architecture for implementing a web portal to establish seamless integration of content-delivery, collaboration tools, and direct access to hardware resources as well as software applications. Tests of this architecture in use are essential for better understanding of the eLaboratory's value.

Environments endowed by e-collaboration technologies can provide access to expanded, shared experience and knowledge, and facilitate meetings among team members to deliver ideas that are more creative. More participants can be involved in the innovation process, qualified by knowledge and not by proximity. User-friendly "physual" (i.e., combining physical and virtual) collaborative environments can support the participation of previously unavailable expertise (e.g., from the elderly) into the creation of new innovative products. Given the restrictions and complexity introduced by geographically dispersed teams, uneven organizational resources and support, and diverse individual team member skill sets and decision making styles, there is ample opportunity to study how virtual teams select, use and evaluate e-collaboration tools.

E-collaboration tools cannot succeed without consideration of the context in which they are to be used. They must be matched to a set of needs, skills, and cultural and organizational settings, as well as the task at hand. Not all technologies work in all situations. For example, Cassivi, Hadaya, Lefebvre & Lefebvre (2008) analyzed the impact of strategic and tactical collaborative actions as well as e-collaboration tools' efficiency on process and relational innovations from both the upstream (i.e. order processing) and downstream (i.e. demand management, customer service) perspectives. They noted that tactical collaborative actions are more likely to lead firms to innovate

with both suppliers and customers than strategic actions. They also show the influence process and relational innovations have on product innovation.

Similarly, Meroño-Cerdan, Soto-Acosta, and Lopez-Nicolas (2008) studied the impact of collaborative technologies on innovation at the firm level. They categorize collaborative technologies' use as e-information, e-communication or e-workflow, and show how only e-information (i.e., supported by teamwork systems, such as shared databases and document management systems/workflow) has a significant impact on innovation. The article also suggests other indirect effects on innovation that flow through the influence of e-information.

Taking a broader perspective, Farooq, Craig, and Carroll (2008) derive a set of design requirements for creativity support tools through an extensive review of the literature on individual, dyadic and group creativity. The requirements include support for divergent and convergent thinking, development of shared objectives, and reflexivity (which encompasses reflection, planning and action by group members). They then describe a working prototype to illustrate design requirements for supporting scientific creativity and discuss the feasibility, effectiveness, and consequences of its use in distributed scientific collaboration. The article underscores the importance of tying in technology requirements with the underlying individual and interpersonal characteristics of the team members (West et al., 2006) and the techniques they use to achieve a collective goal (Markus, 2005).

As a research community, we do not yet know enough about how the use of these shared technologies can best aid in enhancing creativity and innovation. Designers of e-collaboration technologies must also measure the costs and benefits of use of their products to ensure that expected value is achieved (Hevner et al., 2004). We call on e-collaboration researchers to partner with colleagues in the social and behavioral sciences to shed light on this important area. In this way, we will be able to "walk the walk and talk the talk" of collaboration and creativity in a truly innovative and productive program of research.

THE FUTURE OF E-COLLABORATION TECHNOLOGIES

E-collaboration technologies, as a class, reflect a fairly recent advance in electronic support systems. New technologies are introduced faster than their value can be assessed. In this section, we discuss emerging trends in tools and technologies for supporting e-collaboration, and discuss how these might fit in with the tools and technologies virtual teams already employ.

Additional research is needed to understand the scope and value of new types of group-centric collaboration technologies, tools and methods. Challenges abound about how best to motivate people through group-friendly collaboration tools. Will supporting synchronous and asynchronous teamwork free employees from routine work to focus on creativity? Do these technologies enable the effective application of distributed knowledge and competencies? Explicit challenges arise from the need to empower people to work both on un-structured teams and in well-defined and stable set-tings through collaborative environments. We need new reference models for seamlessly integrated activity-oriented, context-aware collaboration services that provide enhanced knowledge sharing mechanisms, better decision-making processes and less burdensome group process support.

There are many unanswered questions remain-ing about how best to employ e-collaboration technologies in the pursuit of team-based creativity and organizational innovation. The following list contains research areas related to the design of collaborative environments, which would prove especially useful to those groups for whom creativ-ity and innovation are valued outcomes.

- "Cooperativity" of a Collaborative Environment. Cooperativity denotes the usability of a collaborative environment for a group and a collaborative process. The challenge would be to both promote cooperativity in regards to existing tool use, and to embed cooperativity-support-ing features in future collaborative tools.
- Modeling of collaborative context. From a user-oriented view this will result in a reduction of information and cooperation overload to reduce stress. This requires re-search on how to present information with multiple methods and representations, and to create audience-specific views based on the different roles and intellectual property rights interests involved in a collaboration process.
- Activity-oriented context-aware collabo-ration services supporting human interac-tions. Today's work is characterized by multi-tasking and many interruptions. This requires systems that allow users to de-velop and enhance their own collaborative environments, thus blurring the boundary between designing and using, and enable rapid context switching and provide imme-diate awareness of the status of a collab-orative process.
- Proactive collaboration-aware artifacts and objects are needed to transform static data so that the entire life cycle of shared arti-facts is supported.
- Support of pervasive collaboration. This requires research in other media than the PC-based computer: ePaper, augmented and mixed realities, ubiquitous and ambi-ent technologies. Special emphasis should be given to the use of these technologies in a collaborative setting and their integration in a collaborative environment.
- Integration between synchronous and asynchronous work. Current tools do not integrate both working patterns, but focus

on one or the other. Therefore, research is needed in environments allowing synchronous and asynchronous cross-domain communication/collaboration.

- Support for virtual communities of practice and of interest. Communities have emerged as one of the primary collaborative environments within which creative and innovative activities are framed and enabled within and across organizational social boundaries. Specific methods and tools are needed for their creation and persistence, and support for effective action within communities.

These design-related research challenges were informed by the drive towards increasing the scope and outreach of research efforts in collaborative environments. For example, attention is needed to make collaborative environments suitable for non-technical users, making sure that people who are not ICT specialists can easily relate to and control the ways in which software and hardware support group collaboration.

In terms of granularity of context, there would also be significant value to investigating differences between the global and regional context in terms of collaboration support needs and the context of using collaborative tools in different creative environments, as called for by Zhang and Lowry (2008) and von Stamm (2003).

On the other end of the IT competence spectrum, we should extend the reach of collaborative environments to the research and advanced technical development community itself, thus bringing the outcomes of using tools and environments closer to the researchers who conceptualize and design ("create"), implement ("innovate") and document these tools and environments.

FUTURE INTERNET AND IMMERSIVE COLLABORATIVE ENVIRONMENTS

Looking further out, collaboration technology and tools will become more and more invisible as they blend into the daily fabric of technology usage. At some point, e-collaboration technology will no longer pose an impediment to virtual team interaction, as it will evolve into a transparent alternative to face-to-face synchronous meetings.

Immersive collaboration environments are expected to be a cornerstone in the evolution of the Internet in the long term. While the previous section focuses on the incremental research needed on e-Collaboration technologies, this section focuses on long-term research endeavors to be undertaken by multidisciplinary research teams, including those supported under the auspices of the European Union Information Society Technologies (IST) Framework Programmes[3]. The final goal is to develop fully immersive collaborative environments that are used intensively as an intrinsic part of the Future internet[4] of 2030-50.

This section starts with a description of the likely outcomes of the Future internet that are expected to be tackled within upcoming research programs worldwide. The section ends with a list of targeted research directions needed to reach the desired outcomes.

Expected Outcome

Collaboration systems are already well established in the current Internet at the level of asynchronous shared workspaces (slow-time) and Internet messaging applications (near real-time). Voice over Internet Protocol and low quality face to face video communications are also available if reliability, video frame rate and ease of call setup are not considered critical issues. However, high quality, high reliability and easy to use Telepresence systems are still the preserve of dedicated network connections. This is a result of the lack of end-to-end Quality of Service (QoS) provision and high bandwidth in the general Internet.

Moreover, as audio and speech are important for face-to-face communications, spatial audio systems will form an essential part of 3D immersive environments in the Future Media Internet[5]. People will be able to hold virtual meetings with anyone, anywhere and anytime. The virtual acoustic environment will accompany the virtual visual environment to improve realism with perfectly matching sound source positions and acoustics. The compatibility issues between various recording techniques and reproduction systems will be overcome. Audio recording and reproduction systems will become ubiquitous and high-quality spatial audio will become the norm. In addition to reproduction, recorded audio will be used in analysis for automatic transcription of speech and other audio events that will help maintain a record of interactions between people.

Another important issue in face-to-face communication concerns the remote rendering of the appropriate auditory and visual cues responsible for expressive communication of the empathy, the resonance and synchronization that characterize physical face-to-face situations. The "embodiment" in the communication process is an important issue that the future internet is expected to support and exploit.

Furthermore, user acceptance of social community models based on technological intermediation strictly depends on the capability of creating realistic and immersive virtual worlds, able to mimic reality, while providing richer experiences and wider accessibility. This includes the possibility of communicating and interacting in a natural and intuitive way with the rest of the world, in a multi-cultural, multi-lingual, multimodal, multi-sensorial environment. The Quality of Experience (QoE) should be as much as possible independent of physical location, time, user characteristics (age, skills, etc.), available technological resources, and is closely related to

the support of non-verbal components including embodiment, affection, and empathy.

Targeted Research Directions

In order to achieve these goals, programmatic research funding is being targeted at improving the transparency of future internet-enabled communications for a wide variety of applications, users and purposes. Some of these tools and technologies will affect the ability of virtual teams to interact in ways close to or better than face-to-face groups might. These anticipated improvements are outlined in this section.

Whilst telecommunications have made it possible to shrink distances and allow people to communicate from afar, any future internet should seek to enable much more. The goal should not be just real time communication but the capability to enable shared experiences which are as compelling and as rich in their communication as are real world interactions. This section looks at a number of key challenges that we believe are critical to enabling such experiences. They include the challenge of designing user interfaces that are more natural for users, the challenge of spatialized and immersive audio, the challenge of higher fidelity visual images and the challenge of representing and framing experiences to meet users' social needs.

Natural Interfaces

Most contemporary applications are designed and built in logical tiers that separate the functions of presentation, of business logic and of storage. The top-most tier, presentation, is what the user sees. Application interfaces, as the cornerstone of that tier, affect the usability and user satisfaction of using a product and its commercial success. Providing products featuring a more human interface contributes to their market potential and success. Multi-modal interfaces approach this paradigm. Current state-of-the-art of multi-modal interfaces has moved from dialogue systems to multi-modal interaction frameworks, where the processes for conversational systems based on natural language are augmented with semantic-level content, such as that provided from visual input modalities. Existing research results and experience gained from the FET European programs in Presence will considerably boost the European progress and expertise in multimodal interfaces.

Spatial Interactive Immersive Audio

The perceived quality of multi-layered representation and composition of rich media experiences is significantly affected by the quality of the audio reproduction for each user. Social interaction between two or more individuals relies heavily upon them being able to hear each other's speech clearly and consistently. A future audio interface should allow for natural interaction between all group members in a high fidelity surround sound environment.

Supporting Social Communication and Interaction

Numerous approaches for collaboration and interaction currently exist, and the challenges facing each are different. The traditional technology-led view relates to the massive deployment of collaborative and participative 3D worlds within which people can interact through their avatars. An alternative view is to use Internet-based technologies to support real world social activities. The two approaches are not mutually exclusive, but each investigates solutions to the problem of effective collaboration and interactivity from different perspectives. From a human-centered perspective, a major problem concerns the design choices to be taken into account before presenting some parts of the system as virtual ones, and some others – as real ones. Another major question concerns the interaction means and devices to be used in order to effectively and pleasantly navigate in mixed environments. Yet another issue is the accessibility of current and future interaction devices as they will be used by a very large number of users.

Why and how do people collaborate and interact? In a work context, collaboration and interaction is necessary to achieve goals. Mehrabian (1981) observed that in communicating with people, especially about feelings or thoughts, non verbal cues such as body language and tone of voice were important as, where a conflict existed between what was said verbally and non-verbally, people most often believed the non-verbal communication.

In order for any future internet to take a significant role in such activities, it is clear that the technology should be able to become part of a framing event that is attractive to the participant and it must also support communication at verbal, vocal and visual levels.

CONCLUDING REMARKS

In summary, there are both behavioral and technological challenges to supporting real time collaboration and interaction within immersive environments. On the technology side, many of these can be considered to be extensions to established video and audio communications capabilities, including multimedia composition and coding standards, audiovisual orchestration and multimedia interpretation, while others are particular to the individual, team, organizational, and cultural settings in which a group faces the challenges of being creative and innovative in an increasingly complex world.

In particular, technologists need to be constantly reminded about the nature of human interaction so that technology investment can be focused on activities that are likely to meet the needs of more than the inquisitive nature of an engineer's mind. One cannot study creativity-supporting design features in a vacuum. Collaborative environment features, like all other technology used to support a work task, must match their purported use (Goodhue and Thompson, 1995). Thus, we urge design oriented researchers to consider the context in which each collaborative tool will be employed (Hevner et al., 2004). In particular, since so many virtual teams are involved in creative processes intended to lead to organizational innovations, it is imperative that tools for supporting virtual team communication, information sharing and decision making are tested in true collaborative settings.

REFERENCES

Amabile, T. M. (1982). *The Social Psychology of Creativity*. New York: Springer.

Burns, T., & Stalker, G. M. (1961). *The Management of Innovation*. London: Tavistock.

Cassivi, L., Hadaya, P., Lefebvre, E., & Lefebvre, L.A. (2008). The Role of Collaboration on Process, Relational, and Product Innovations in a Supply Chain. *International Journal of e-Collaboration*, *4*(4), 11–32.

Damanpour, F. (1995). Is Your Creative Organization innovative? In Ford, C. M., & Gioia, D. A. (Eds.), *Creative Action in Organizations: Ivory Tower Visions and Real World Voices* (pp. 125–130). Thousand Oaks, CA: Sage.

Dougherty, D. (1992). Interpretive Barriers to Successful Product Innovation in Large Firms. *Organization Science*, *3*, 179–202. doi:10.1287/orsc.3.2.179

Elam, J. J., & Mead, M. (1990). Can Software Influence Creativity? *Information Systems Research*, *1*(1), 1–22. doi:10.1287/isre.1.1.1

Farooq, U., Carroll, J. M., & Canoe, C. H. (2008). Designing for Creativity in Computer-Supported Cooperative Work. *International Journal of e-Collaboration*, *4*(4), 51–75.

Ford, C. M. (1995). Creativity is a Mystery: Clues for the Investigators' Notebooks . In Ford, C. M., & Gioia, D. A. (Eds.), *Creative Action in Organizations: Ivory Tower Visions and Real World Voices* (pp. 12–51). Thousand Oaks, CA: Sage.

Ford, C. M., & Gioia, D. A. (1995). Multiple Visions and Multiple Voices: Academic and Practitioner Conceptions of Creativity in Organizations . In *C.M. Ford & D.A. Gioia, Creative Action in Organizations: Ivory Tower Visions and Real World Voices* (pp. 3–11). Thousand Oaks, CA: Sage.

Goodhue, D. L., & Thompson, R. L. (1995). Task Technology Fit and Individual Performance. *Management Information Systems Quarterly*, *19*(2), 213–236. doi:10.2307/249689

Helander, M. G., & Emami, M. R. (2008). Engineering eLaboratories: Integration of remote access and eCollaboration. *International Journal of Engineering Education*, *24*(3), 466–479.

Hevner, A. R., March, S. T., & Park, J. (2004). Design Science in Information Systems Research. *Management Information Systems Quarterly*, *28*(1), 75–105.

Isaksen, S. G., Murdock, M. C., Firestien, R. L., & Treffinger, D. J. (Eds.). (1993). *Understanding and Recognizing Creativity: The Emergence of a Discipline*. Norwood, NJ: Ablex.

Laudel, G. (2001). Collaboration, creativity and rewards: why and how scientists collaborate. *International Journal of Technology Management*, *22*(7-8), 762–781. doi:10.1504/IJTM.2001.002990

Levina, N., & Vaast, E. (2008). Innovating or Doing as Told? Status Differences and Overlapping Boundaries in Offshore Collaboration. *Management Information Systems Quarterly*, *32*(2), 307–332.

Link, F. (2007). Coordination, Learning, and Innovation: the organizational roles of e-collaboration and their Impacts. *International Journal of e-Collaboration*, *33*, 53–70.

Markus, M. L. (2005). The Technology Shaping Effects of e-Collaboration Technologies: Bugs and Features. *International Journal of e-Collaboration*, *1*(1), 1–23.

McNamara, K., Dennis, A. R., & Carte, T. A. (2008). It's the Thought that Counts: The Mediating Effect of Information Processing in Virtual Team Decision Making. *Information Systems Management*, *25*(1), 20–32. doi:10.1080/10580530701777123

Mehrabian, A. (1981). *Silent Messages: Implicit Communication of Emotions and Attitudes* (pp. 75–80). Wadsworth Publishing Co.

Meroño-Cerdán, A. L., Soto-Acosta, P., & López-Nicolás, C. (2008). How do Collaborative Technologies Affect Innovation in SMEs? *International Journal of e-Collaboration*, *44*, 33–50.

Monalisa, M., Daim, T., Mirani, F., Dash, P., Khamis, R. & Bhusari, V. (2008). Managing Global Design Teams. *Research Technology Management*, July-August, 48-59.

Moore, K. R. (1998). Trust and Relationship Commitment in Logistics Alliances: A Buyer Perspective. *International Journal of Purchasing and Materials Management*, *34*(1), 24–37.

Nanda, T., & Singh, T. P. (2009). Determinants of creativity and innovation in the workplace: a comprehensive review. *International Journal of Technology . Policy and Management*, *9*(1), 84–106.

Schneiderman, B. (2007). Creativity Support Tools: Accelerating Discovery and Innovation. *Communications of the ACM*, *50*(12), 20–32. doi:10.1145/1323688.1323689

Thomas, D., & Bostrom, R. (2008). Building Trust and Cooperation through Technology Adaptation in Virtual Teams: Empirical Field Evidence. *Information Systems Management*, *25*(1), 45–56. doi:10.1080/10580530701777149

Thompson, L., & Choi, H. S. (Eds.). (2006). *Creativity and Innovation in Organizational Teams*. Mahweh, NJ: Erlbaum.

Von Stamm, B. (2003). *Managing Innovation, Design and Creativity*. West Sussex, England: Wiley.

West, M. A. (1995). Creative Values and Creative Visions in Teams at Work . In *C. M. Ford & D. A. Gioia (1995), Creative Action in Organizations: Ivory Tower Visions and Real World Voices* (pp. 71–77). Thousand Oaks, CA: Sage.

West, M. A., Sacramento, C. A., & Fay, D. (2006). Creativity and Innovation Implementation in Work Groups: The Paradoxical Role of Demands . In Thompson, L., & Choi, H. S. (Eds.), *Creativity and Innovation in Organizational Teams* (pp. 137–159). Mahweh, NJ: Erlbaum.

Yusuf, S. (2009). From Creativity to Innovation. *Technology in Society*, *31*(1), 1–8. doi:10.1016/j.techsoc.2008.10.007

Zhang, D., & Lowry, P. B. (2008). Issues, Limitations and Opportunities in Cross-cultural Research on Collaborative Software in Information Systems. *Journal of Global Information Management*, *16*(1), 61–84.

ENDNOTES

[1] This article builds upon the ideas first presented in Fedorowicz, J., Laso-Ballesteros, I., Padilla-Meléndez, A. (2008). Creativity, Innovation, and E-Collaboration. *International Journal of e-Collaboration*. Vol. 4, No. 4, pp. 1-10.

2   "Disclaimer: The views expressed in this document are those of the author and do not necessarily reflect the official position of the European Commission".

3   See http://cordis.europa.eu/ist/about/about.htm for information about these Programmes.

4   www.future-internet.eu

5   www.futuremediainternet.eu

Chapter 9
Designing for Creativity in Computer–Supported Cooperative Work

Umer Farooq
Pennsylvania State University, USA

John M. Carroll
Pennsylvania State University, USA

Craig H. Ganoe
Pennsylvania State University, USA

ABSTRACT

We are investigating the design of tools to support everyday scientific creativity in distributed collaboration. Based on an exegesis of theoretical and empirical literature on creativity and group dynamics, we present and justify three requirements for supporting creativity: support for divergent and convergent thinking, development of shared objectives, and reflexivity. We elaborate on these requirements by describing three implications for design to support creativity in context of computer supported cooperative work (CSCW): integrate support for individual, dyadic, and group brainstorming; leverage cognitive conflict by preserving and reflecting on minority dissent; and support flexibility in granularity of planning. We conclude by outlining a future research trajectory for designing and evaluating creativity support tools in the context of collaboratories.

INTRODUCTION

The social and collaborative nature of science has been emphasized by historians and philosophers of science, and sociologists interested in knowledge creation and diffusion (Crane, 1972; Thagard, 1998). To this end, history has documented numerous examples (Pycior, Slack, & Abir-Am, 1996; Watson, 1968).

A central aspect of and reason for scientific collaboration is creativity. Scientific creativity can be characterized as a process toward achieving an outcome recognized as innovative by the relevant community (Csikszentmihalyi, 1996). Creativity does not happen inside one person's head, but in the interaction between a person's thoughts and a socio-cultural context (Csikszentmihalyi, 1996).

Creativity has been a traditional focus of study in psychology. More recently, it has gained momentum as a research area in Human Computer Interaction (HCI) and Computer Supported Cooperative Work (CSCW). In context of these domains, we are interested in supporting—that is, evoking, enhancing, and sustaining—scientific creativity in distributed collaboration through socio-technical interventions. Requirements for such interventions have not been systematically investigated.

In this article, our goal is to articulate design requirements for supporting scientific creativity, drawing on diverse socio-psychological literature on creativity and group dynamics. Although our article does not present new empirical data, our integrated analysis marshals empirical findings from existing literature. We describe a working prototype to support the suggested design requirements and discuss the feasibility, effectiveness, and consequences of supporting creativity in distributed scientific collaboration with technology. We conclude by describing how our contribution fits into a broader research program for investigating creativity in CSCW.

RESEARCH SCOPE AND MOTIVATION

Creativity is critical to invention, innovation, and social progress at both the individual and societal levels (Candy & Hori, 2003; Florida, 2002, 2005; Sternberg & Lubart, 1999). Individuals are able to refine and improve their own performance, and groups, organizations, and societal institutions are able to sustain their existence and grow if and only if they can adapt and solve problems creatively in ever-changing circumstances (Feist, 1999).

The modern era of creativity research can be traced to Guilford's 1950 presidential address to the American Psychological Association (APA). Creativity in psychological and social sciences continues to be studied and written about in professional books (Boden, 2004; Sternberg, 1999) and journals (e.g., The Journal of Creative Behavior, since 1967; Creativity Research Journal, since 1988).

Since the early 1990's, computer and information science researchers have studied creativity in the context of technology. The first symposium on *Creativity and Cognition* (C&C) was held in 1993. Since then, five more C&C conferences have been held, with *ACM SIGCHI* sponsoring the conferences in 1999, 2002, 2005, and 2007. A special issue of *Communications of the ACM* was published in 2002 on *Creativity and Interface*. A special issue of *International Journal of Human Computer Studies* on creativity was also published in 2005. In order to articulate a research agenda on creativity in HCI, the U.S. National Science Foundation (NSF) organized a summer workshop in 2005 on creativity support tools (http://www.cs.umd.edu/hcil/CST/).

Creativity is an important focus of study in HCI and CSCW (Candy, 1997; Edmonds, 1994). There are assertions that today's knowledge workers can benefit from the use of software tools to enhance their creative strategies (Candy & Hori, 2003). For example, workflow support tools in organizations can encourage creativity for articulating innovative business solutions. Studying creativity in HCI and CSCW is different than in engineering or business management domains. This is because different research questions are the focus of study. For instance, existing tools for individual and collaborative work often contain interface elements that stymie creative efforts

(Burleson & Selker, 2002). HCI and CSCW specifically seek to address such questions.

In this article, we are driven by our impetus to support distributed scientists in working more creatively and thus effectively with their peers around the world through CSCW tools. We focus on scientific collaboration that involves *everyday* creativity, or "little C" creativity (Gardner, 1993), the sort that all of us evince in our daily lives— this involves everyday problem-solving and routinized scientific work. Although analyzing outstanding creative people (e.g., collaboration between Watson and his colleagues to discover the structure of DNA (Watson, 1968)) contributes toward establishing a framework for creativity (Gardner, 1993), understanding creativity in the context of everyday activities is equally important for letting people become more productive and create better work products (Fischer, 1999).

Although we are investigating how to support creativity in context of CSCW, it is important to mention how our research fits in the larger scope of e-collaboration. E-collaboration is broadly defined as collaboration using "electronic" and not just "computer" technologies among different individuals to accomplish a common task (Kock & D'Arey, 2002). Therefore, CSCW research—an interdisciplinary field that studies the way people work in groups and computer-supported solutions to support their dynamics—falls under the umbrella of e-collaboration (Kock, 2005).

RELATED WORK ON CREATIVITY SUPPORT TOOLS

Many collaborative tools for supporting the social creative process have been developed. For example, EVIDII allows designers to associate effective words and images, and then shows several visual representations of the relationships among designers, images, and words (Nakakoji, Yamamoto, & Ohira, 1999). Showing different representations evokes the individual designer's creativity by us-

ing design knowledge or representations created by other designers in the community, thereby supporting collective creativity.

Fischer (2005) argued that distances (across physical, temporal, and technological dimensions) and diversity (across different cultures) are important sources for social creativity. He discussed several examples of collaborative environments to support creative processes. For example, in the Envisionment and Discovery Collaboratory (Arias, Eden, Fischer, Gorman, & Scharff, 2000), participants collaboratively solve design problems of mutual interest such as urban transportation planning. The assumption is that complex design is a social creative process, and the integration of individual and social creativity takes place through face-to-face discussions in a shared construction space such as an electronic whiteboard.

The Caretta system (Sugimoto, Hosoi, & Hashizume, 2004) supports face-to-face collaboration by integrating personal (for individual reflections) and shared spaces (for group discussions) to support intuitivism. Interactive art (Giaccardi, 2004) is based on the premise that computational media enable people to operate at the source of the creative process by creating a pool of pixema, meaning individual pieces produced by different artists, which can be exchanged to synthesize new paintings. CodeBroker (Ye, 2001) monitors software developers' programming activities, infers their immediate task by analyzing semantic and syntactic information contained in their working products, and actively delivers task-relevant and personalized usable parts (Fischer, Nakakoji, Ostwald, Stahl, & Sumner, 1998) from a repository created by decomposing existing software systems. This ensures awareness of each other's work so that efforts are not duplicated and, therefore, developers can be more creative.

The aforementioned tools broadly support activities that are characteristic of creative HCI and CSCW endeavor (Shneiderman, 2000): (1) searching and browsing digital libraries; (2) consulting with peers; (3) visualizing data and processes;

(4) thinking by free associations; (5) exploring solutions—what-if tools; (6) composing artifacts and performances; (7) reviewing and replaying session histories; and (8) disseminating results.

However, design requirements for creativity support tools have been cursory in nature, not systematically grounded in the vast creativity literature that exists. For example, the eight design requirements elicited above from the Genex framework (Shneiderman, 2000), although useful as a precursory research agenda for user interface design for creativity, are rooted largely in one theory, the Theory of Flow (Csikszentmihalyi, 1996). The framework certainly provided a foundation for investigating creativity support tools in HCI and CSCW, but the time is right to revisit and enhance it in context of broader literature on collaborative scientific creativity.

Other HCI and CSCW research on creativity has attempted to carry the baton forward by extending the Genex design requirements. For example, Greene (2002) asserts the need to support smooth exploration and experimentation in creativity tools. This implies that there should be an easy way to undo and redo all or part of one's work, there should be no big penalties for mistakes, and there should be meaningful rewards for success. Another study discusses the need for devising a shared language and developing a common understanding in interdisciplinary collaboration (Mamykina, Candy, & Edmonds, 2002).

Because creativity research is a fledgling enterprise in CSCW, we wish to develop systematic methods for exploring the design space of supporting scientific creativity in distributed collaboration. We actualize this by developing *first-order approximations* (Ackerman, 2000), in the form of requirements to support creativity, emerging from theoretical extensions. Developing such approximations will attempt to bridge the gap between what is required socially and what we can do technically to support creativity. If CSCW merely contributes "cool toys" without fully understanding and leveraging the theoreti-

cal underpinnings of how people really work in groups to be creative, it will have failed its intellectual mission, resulting in unusable systems (Ackerman, 2000).

REQUIREMENTS FOR CREATIVITY

In this section, we present three requirements for creativity with associated *design rationale* (Moran & Carroll, 1996). The design rationale derives from an exegesis of diverse theoretical and empirical investigations in socio-psychological literature on creativity and group dynamics.

Support Divergent and Convergent Thinking

Creativity in science, as in most other domains, involves both divergent and convergent thinking (Guilford, 1983; Levine & Moreland, 2004). Thus, we propose that creativity tools in distributed collaboration should support both these forms of thinking.

Divergent thinking is the ability to generate a set of possible responses, ideas, options, or alternatives in response to an open-ended question, task, or challenge. Convergent thinking involves narrowing this set to one alternative, and then implementing this alternative by empirically testing and communicating it to the scientific community. Because the process of creativity involves a continuous interplay of and achieving a dynamic balance between divergent and convergent thinking (Isaksen, 1995), we do not treat them separately. Instead, from literature, we illustrate different ways that both divergent and convergent thinking can be facilitated, and eventually supported through technology.

In his study of collaborative circles—a group of peers who share similar occupational goals and who, through long periods of dialogue and collaboration, negotiate a common vision that guides their work—Farrell (2001) argues that the bulk of a circle's creative work (during divergent and convergent thinking) occurs within dyads that have developed close relationships. This result is different from traditional theories of creativity, which assert that creative work is most likely to be done by highly-autonomous individuals working alone (Kohut, 1985). It is also important to note that Farrell's result applies to everyday creativity, and not just to extraordinary dyads such as creative couples in science that are often cited as prime examples of creativity (e.g., Pierre and Marie Curie, Carl and Gerty Cori, etc. (Pycior, Slack, & Abir-Am, 1996)).

Farrell says that dyad members engage in instrumental intimacy, characterized by trust, uninhibited exchange of ideas, and mutual support. New ideas, even though they may be experienced as coming from a third source, are more likely to emerge in creative dyads for several reasons (Farrell, 2001). First, creativity is a form of deviance— doing something that authorities do not approve. A "partner in crime" enables a dyad member to neutralize the guilt and anxiety inherent in the creative process. Second, as a consequence of the mirroring and the identification with one another, each dyad member feels more cohesive, invests more in the self, and takes his/her own ideas more seriously. Third, the open exchange in free, often playful interactions between dyad members allows the linking of conscious and unconscious thoughts from both minds. Each member consequently uses the mind of the other as if it were an extension of his/her own. Finally, as each plays the role of critic for the other, the ideas are reworked into useful components for the emerging shared vision.

Given that larger groups are less likely to elicit the levels of trust and support found in collaborative pairs (Levine & Moreland, 2004), how can divergent and convergent thinking be facilitated in such groups? One well-established technique to support divergent thinking is group brainstorming. Brainstorming can compensate for motivation losses (Steiner, 1972), which tend to

increase in larger groups because there are fewer opportunities to participate productively, there is a sense that one's contributions are not critical or identifiable, and there is greater depersonalization (Arrow, McGrath, & Berdahl, 2000).

An interesting observation is that the process of brainstorming involving a group of scientists (who often use brainstorming effectively) differs significantly from a group of students (who typically do not) (Dunbar, 1997). For example, contrary to traditional brainstorming discourse in which group members are discouraged from criticizing others' ideas, evidence suggests that cognitive conflict within a scientific group can facilitate divergent thinking during brainstorming (Levine & Moreland, 2004). Group members often furnish new ideas that challenge group orthodoxy. Such challenges can facilitate learning, problem-solving at the individual level, and decision-making at the group level (Jehn, 1997). Evidence suggests that scientists are particularly likely to undergo conceptual change during laboratory meetings when they obtain surprising findings. This is not attributed to error discoveries, but rather to colleagues disagreeing with their interpretation (Dunbar, 1995) and a result of evolutionary "tinkering" (Dunbar, 1997), a series of small changes that produce major changes in a concept. Therefore, it follows that cognitive conflict, or "oppositional complementarity" (John-Steiner, 2000), has the potential to stimulate thoughtful consideration of new and creative ideas during brainstorming in scientific collaboration.

As noted previously, for group creativity to occur, groups must reach consensus on which idea is best, that is, convergent thinking. When it comes to creativity, available literature repeatedly demonstrates that groups rarely achieve the level of the sum of the individuals (McGrath, 1984). Part of the reason for the suboptimal performance of groups is that members strongly desire consensus, even straining for consensus, as argued by Janis (Janis, 1982), under the rubric of groupthink. The general phenomenon is as follows.

During consensus building, there is considerable evidence that discussion in a group of mostly like-minded members can extremize their views and enhance their confidence in those views, a phenomenon known as polarization (Fraser, 1971; Moscovici & Zavalloni, 1969). This results in premature movement to consensus (Hackman & Morris, 1975), thereby reducing the likelihood of creativity. There is evidence that majorities stimulate less novel or original thinking (Nemeth & Nemeth-Brown, 2003).

Given the problems associated with homogeneity, consensus, and majority views for both the quality of group decision-making and creative idea generation, one antidote appears to be *dissent* (Nemeth & Nemeth-Brown, 2003) rooted in minority influence theory. Based on such literature, it has been shown that dissent is a stimulus to divergent, convergent, and thus, creative thinking.

Minority dissent stimulates divergent thought, manifested in the search for information, the use of strategies, thoughts about the issue, detection of novel solutions, and creativity of solutions (Nemeth, 1995). Studies have invariably validated this basic theoretical premise (De Dreu & De Vries, 1993; Volpato, Maass, Mucchi-Faina, & Vitti, 1990). Some studies have even shown that minority dissent, even when wrong, stimulates a search for information on all sides of the issue (Nemeth & Rogers, 1996), and thus, thought is directed at more alternatives (Martin & Noyes, 1996; Nemeth, Rogers, & Brown, 2001).

We also argue that dissent can facilitate convergent thinking. Studies have demonstrated that minority dissent stimulates a reappraisal of a situation (Nemeth & Nemeth-Brown, 2003). In general, people do not assume that the minority view is correct. However, during convergent thinking, when a group is narrowing a set of alternatives to a single idea, the minority's consistency of maintaining his or her dissenting view raises doubt about the majority position (Nemeth & Nemeth-Brown, 2003). Such an interaction evinces more complexity of thought, reevaluation of the majority position, and subsequently leads the group to make better decisions (Van Dyne & Saavedra, 1996).

In general, studies (e.g., Van Dyne & Saavedra, 1996; Volpato et al., 1990) have consistently shown that minority dissent can stimulate creative solutions to problems. For example, Nemeth et al. (2001) ran a simulated study of a work setting with two groups, one that was exposed to a dissenting opinion and the other that was not. When asked to generate solutions, the group exposed to minority dissent came up with more creative solutions than the other control group (no dissent). Another study by De Dreu and West (2001) on existing organizations shows that dissent increases innovation in work teams but primarily when individuals participate in decision-making.

Support Development of Shared Objectives

One condition for creativity flow is having clarity of goals (Csikszentmihalyi, 1996). We propose that creativity tools in distributed collaboration should support development of shared objectives that engender clarity of goals. Shared objectives imply a group vision of the goals of its work that members wish to achieve.

In context of group innovation, clarity of group objectives is likely to facilitate innovation by enabling focused development of new ideas, which can be filtered with greater precision than if group objectives are unclear (West, 2003). When group objectives are shared or distributed, it is critical that all members hold the same understanding of the goals, and that they are also aware of how others in the group perceive the situation (Hutchins, 1995).

Developing shared objectives involves group members to leverage their domain-specific knowledge, which does not always lead to creativity but does appear to be a relatively necessary condition for it (see discussion in Nickerson, 1999, pp. 409-

410). This process also involves pooling information effectively (Stasser & Birchmeier, 2003) with high levels of interaction among group members. This can lead to cross-fertilization of perspectives that can spawn creativity and innovation (Mumford & Gustafson, 1988; Pearce & Ravlin, 1987). In general, high participation in decision-making (such as when group objectives are being formulated) means less resistance to change and therefore greater likelihood of innovations being implemented (Coch & French, 1948; Lawler & Hackman, 1969).

Theoretically, development of shared and clear objectives will facilitate innovation only if members are committed to the goals of the group (West, 2003). This is because strong goal commitment is necessary to maintain group member persistence for implementation in the face of resistance among other organizational members. For example, in a study of 418 project teams (Pinto & Prescott, 1987), it was found that a clearly-stated mission was the only factor that predicted success at all stages of the innovation process. Not having a shared commitment to common group objectives can result in breakdowns within local, global, and contextual group dynamics (Arrow et al., 2000). For example, lack of coordination between members (breakdown within local dynamics), greater disparity between a member's commitment to a group and the group's commitment to that particular member (breakdown within global dynamics), and/or lack of safety in the work environment (breakdown within contextual dynamics) can lead to dissolution of a group. Thus, due to a lack of shared vision of the group goals, such forces of group disintegration are likely to emerge (or become more apparent) and subsequently inhibit creativity (West, 2003).

An interesting finding from creativity literature is that even the intention to develop shared objectives is critical for creative endeavor. Henle (1962), for example, argues that we cannot find creative ideas by intentionally looking for them. She also argues, however, that if we are not re-ceptive to them, they will not come—that their occurrence requires an appropriate attitude on our part. This attitude is typically manifested in the intention to be creative, which is important for creative activity.

Nickerson (1999) also argues that purpose is essential to creative expression, and that a prerequisite for purpose is intention. He broadly defines purpose as a deep and abiding intention to develop one's creative potential—a long-term interest, on cognitive and emotional levels, in some form of creative expression. Studies have corroborated the importance of purpose in this long-term sense (e.g., Dedek & Cote, 1994; Perkins, 1981).

Support Reflexivity

Knowing how well one is doing is essential to being creative (Csikszentmihalyi, 1996). In the context of groups, this means the extent to which members collectively reflect on the group's objectives, strategies, and processes as well as their wider organizations and environments, and adapt them accordingly. This is known as reflexivity (West, 1996), a process that creativity tools should support in distributed collaboration.

Group reflexivity consists of three elements: reflection, planning, and action (adaptation) (West, 2003). Reflection, in general, consists of attention, awareness, monitoring, and evaluation of the object of reflection (West, 2003), with evaluation particularly being stressed as an important constituent in creative thinking (Runco & Chand, 1994).

Specifically, reflection is a process to ruminate over the object of reflection deeply in more detail. It is about critical thinking, which is thinking that is focused, disciplined, logical, and constrained (Nickerson, 1999). In some sense, reflection is a form of convergent thinking—it evaluates what divergent thinking offers, subjects the possibilities to criteria of acceptability, and selects some among them for further consideration (Nickerson, 1999).

Planning is one of the potential consequences of the indeterminacy of reflection, because during this indeterminacy, courses of action can be contemplated, intentions formed, and plans developed, and the potential for carrying them out is built up (West, 2003). Collaborative planning, as conceptualized by Rogoff (1995), involves foresight and improvisation, and is inherently a creative process. Planning typically involves top-down goal decomposition with development and ordering of plan fragments (Sacerdoti, 1974), interleaving with the other two elements of reflexivity (reflection and action) (Miller, Galanter, & Pribam, 1960), and opportunistic plan revision (Suchman, 1986).

High reflexivity exists when planning is characterized by greater detail, inclusiveness of potential problems, hierarchical ordering, and long- as well as short-range planning (West, 2003). More detailed intentions or plans are more likely to lead to innovative implementations (Frese & Zapf, 1994). For example, Gollwitzer's work (1996) suggests that goal-directed behavior or innovation will be initiated when the group has articulated implementation intentions. This is because planning creates conceptual readiness for, and guides group members' attention toward, relevant opportunities for action and means to accomplish the group's goal.

Action, the third element of reflexivity, refers to goal-directed behaviors relevant to achieving the desired changes in group objectives, strategies, processes, organizations, or environments identified by the group during the stage of reflection (West, 2003). Overall, as a result of reflexivity, a group's reality is continually renegotiated during interactions between group members (West, 2003). Understandings negotiated in one exchange among group members may be drawn on a variety of ways to inform subsequent discussions, and offer the possibility of helpful and creative transformations and meanings (Bouwen & Fry, 1996). For example, research with BBC television program production groups, whose work fundamentally requires creativity and innovation, provides support for these propositions (Carter & West, 1998).

WORKING PROTOTYPE TO SUPPORT CREATIVITY

Integrating seamless access to tools, collaborators, and their activities are desirable requirements to facilitate creativity in collaborative environments to effectively support human-to-human communication (Candy, 1997; Shneiderman, 2000). Here, we describe our working prototype to support creativity.

Infrastructure and System

Our prototype is known as BRIDGE (Basic Resources for Integrated Distributed Group Environments; http://bridgetools.sourceforge.net) (Ganoe, Somervell, Neale, Isenhour, Carroll, Rosson, & McCrickard, 2003). The BRIDGE infrastructure is seamlessly integrated with browser-based wiki-style asynchronous editing and also supports synchronous shared editing of complex documents through replicated objects (Isenhour, Rosson, & Carroll, 2001). Replicated objects are objects that are retrieved by multiple collaborating sessions and whose state is kept synchronized when any replica is changed. The underlying code base is implemented in Java using software design patterns and components.

For accessibility and familiarity, BRIDGE client systems look and behave like a normal Web site, with all content rendered as HTML and images. Simple forms of authoring are supported. Each page has an "Edit" link which supports editing and new page creation using a simple shorthand notation that requires no external authoring tools or knowledge of HTML. This is designed to present the kind of easy transition from browsing to authoring, and from authoring to collaborative authoring, which is supported in similar wiki-based systems.

Each BRIDGE Web page also has a "Full Editor" link that launches an interactive Java-based client. The Java client supports interactive authoring functionality that is not possible or practical using HTML-based forms. Further, this client supports synchronous, distributed collaboration between users on shared artifacts, such as drawings, documents, data tables and charts, and interactive maps.

Suite of Tools

Text chat is a fundamental communication tool that, in the context of long-term collaboration, has both synchronous and asynchronous interaction modes. The chat is persistent, and so collaborators who join a shared session late or have missed the session completely can benefit from reviewing the content. For those who participated in the chat synchronously, a persistent copy will be valuable as a transcript, perhaps serving as a record of task decomposition or other negotiation between group members. Finally, groups may decide to use the chat tool as a message board for fully asynchronous conversations.

There is multitude support for graphical content generation. This includes drawing tools like a collaborative concept map, paintbrush-like editor for shared construction of drawings, and functionality for creating interactive maps (panning and zooming features) that can be jointly annotated. BRIDGE also provides table and charting tools, supporting basic data management and information visualization capabilities. Account management tools allow users to manage custom sets of restricted accounts with desired scope and privileges.

One notable characteristic of BRIDGE is its support for awareness. Social awareness (Erickson & Kellogg, 2000) is provided through a user list that indicates their activity (active vs. inactive). Workspace awareness (Gutwin & Greenberg,

2002) is supported by viewing synchronous changes to shared artifacts. For example, two group members could collaboratively co-construct a shared document and see each other's changes synchronously. Changes to shared artifacts can also be seen asynchronously through version histories.

To be creative in a social setting, a collaborator needs to be aware of others and their work (Nakakoji et al., 1999) to establish and maintain a shared background of understanding. BRIDGE supports coordination and planning with activity awareness (Carroll, Neale, Isenhour, Rosson, & McCrickard, 2003): awareness of project work that supports group performance in complex tasks over long-term endeavors directed at major goals. A timeline interface provides a document history for a project along with a means for overlaying projects events like deadlines. As a user starts work on a shared document, a copy of the previous version is automatically stored for future reference. Figure 1 is a screenshot that illustrates many of these features.

Among many tools available in BRIDGE, the ones illustrated above generally support creativity in context of collaboratively accessing peers and their activities, planning, reflection on work, and idea generation.

DISCUSSION: IMPLICATIONS FOR DESIGN

The three requirements to support creativity with their design rationale (fourth section) suggest broader strategies to support scientific creative endeavors in distributed, computer-supported collaboration. At the most general level, the approach we are pursuing has three design heuristics. First, we are trying to *integrate support for individual, dyadic, and group brainstorming*. This approach contrasts with the strategy of just supporting *group* brainstorming. Second, we are trying to *leverage cognitive conflict for generating*

Figure 1. The BRIDGE workspace provides integrated timeline (top) and concept map (middle left) views of documents along with chat and a list of workgroup users logged (bottom). The selected note "Scientific Principles" (A) has the associated document displayed in the editor (middle right). The current version is also available from the timeline (B) as well as previous versions (C).

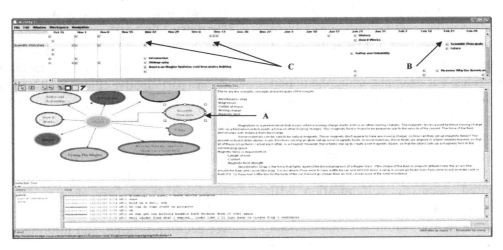

creative ideas by preserving and subsequently reflecting on minority dissent. This is different from existing approaches of typically supporting majority-driven consensus. Third, we are trying to *support flexibility in the granularity of planning,* instead of constraining planning to some specific level of detail.

Integrate Support for Individual, Dyadic, and Group Brainstorming

During the creative work stage, group members alternate between times when they work alone, in pairs, and times when they meet as a group (Farrell, 2001). Therefore, supporting these different brainstorming modalities and the alterations between them seems feasible. In BRIDGE, a user can provide privileges to others for sharing (viewing and/or editing) an artifact such as a concept map. These privileges can be issued to individuals or groups (e.g., members of a research lab). In this way, the concept map, for instance, can be made accessible to individuals, dyads, or a group comprising any number of individuals.

A brainstorming tool should also allow switching modalities while maintaining the content of the previous and forthcoming brainstorming sessions. For instance, switching from a group brainstorming session to an individual session should preserve the collaborative group work, and then create a newer version for individual brainstorming session. Maintaining history of brainstorming sessions, which would be bookmarked at the times of modality switching, would allow users to refer back to previous versions, assess changes temporally, and keep track of who did what. Such session histories would facilitate the metacognitive process of reflection and self-awareness (Shneiderman, 2000), and establishment of a reward structure for making work visible (Suchman, 1995).

Brainstorming techniques—such as drawing concept maps, affinity diagrams, or storyboarding—are often codified as graphical visualizations of knowledge. One way to integrate support for individual, dyadic, and group brainstorming is to use role-specific multiple view visualizations (Convertino, Ganoe, Schafer, Yost, & Carroll,

2005). Given that breaking problems down into components and looking at problems from different angles facilitates effective brainstorming and thus creativity (Levine & Moreland, 2004), multiple view visualizations could then possibly represent different perspectives on how a problem should be broken down, not just from the role of a group but also the perspectives of individual and dyadic roles. For example, using the notion of public and private spaces (Greenberg, Boyle, & Laberge, 1999), an individual could add ideas to the group brainstorming view privately, and later propagate these ideas to the group through the shared view.

Distributed scientific collaboration will typically involve long-term creative endeavors, manifesting more asynchronous collaborations than synchronous. In face-to-face brainstorming, empirical evidence suggests that the specific mental activity in which a brainstormer is engaged during breaks is important (Mitchell, 1998). Contents of short-term memory during a brainstorming break affect an individual's post-break brainstorming performance. If the activity performed during the break does not allow the task-relevant ideas and concepts to remain active in short-term memory, then the relevant categories will have to be reactivated following the break. For long-term and distributed scientific collaboration, which involves all three modalities of brainstorming (individual, dyadic, and group), supporting the process of ideation continuously is especially critical. One way to address this is to use notification systems to inform individuals, dyads, and groups of relevant changes to a shared artifact during the breaks between asynchronous interactions. These notifications would alert users via email or other action-evoking stimuli such as an awareness feature (e.g., popup alerts in a MOO; see Farooq, Rodi, Carroll, & Isenhour, 2003). As a result, users would possibly react to the changes or at least think about the history of previous interactions, which would provide some

level of cognitively preserving and tinkering prior brainstorming sessions.

Leverage Cognitive Conflict by Preserving and Reflecting on Minority Dissent

Moderate task-related conflict and minority dissent in a participative climate will lead to innovation by encouraging debate and to consideration of alternative interpretations of information available, leading to integrated and creative solutions. It seems that the social processes in groups necessary for minority dissent to influence the innovation process are characterized by high levels of team member interaction, influence over decision-making, and information sharing (West, 2003).

Preserving cognitive conflict and reflecting on minority dissent consists of two broad support mechanisms: documenting dissenting views and then finding these views during later consideration. A design feature that allows coding or flagging with an evocative, visual representation (e.g., user's avatar, color code) could be used to tag a dissenting opinion in a shared workspace. The shared workspace could represent a structured asynchronous discourse (Carroll, 1995) where group members can annotate discussion items. This scheme is somewhat similar to ones implemented in Issue-Based Information Systems (IBIS) developed by Horst Rittel (Rittel & Webber, 1973), where opinions could be tagged. Part of the difficulty with IBIS was the severe cognitive overhead dictated by the high degree of structure. User-directed annotations with open coding or flagging can alleviate such problems.

Annotations on a shared information repository, in addition to just tagging dissenting opinions, reinforce the idea of personal perspectives in the group context (Stahl & Herrmann, 1999). Stahl and Herrmann (1999) assert that during negotiation in computer-supported collaborations, it should always be possible for users to react to each other, at least by commenting. This maintains at least a partial overlap of their contents (both minority and majority views) that is key to reaching successful mutual understanding and coordination.

As mentioned before, part of the advantage of preserving dissenting opinions is to reappraise a specific situation at some later point in the long-term, asynchronous activity of distributed scientific collaboration. Viewing these cognitive conflicts temporally, say using a timeline view as in BRIDGE, can help to reevaluate orthodoxy especially at later stages of the group project when members tend to lose objectivity. Even the consideration of minority dissent, without implementation, can help strengthen the *autotelic* experience (Csikszentmihalyi, 1996).

Support Flexibility in the Granularity of Planning

Although more detailed plans can lead to creativity, imposing such constraints in collaborative systems can be problematic. For example, one of the classical findings in CSCW is that workflow systems for planning tasks are successful in supporting structured activity (Grudin, 1994), but otherwise may be too rigid, can potentially stymie creativity, and users often find ways to work around them.

We argue that a flexible, more opportunistic, and less imposing planning tool with different levels of detail would facilitate creativity. Planning can be conceptualized as strategic and operational (McGrath & Tschan, 2004). Strategic planning refers to a macro or purpose level of planning. It is knowledge- and intention-based: that is, it is driven by members' intentions, preferences, and information.

Operational planning involves hierarchical, temporal, referential, and technical structuring. "What will be done" (hierarchical) specifies the consequence of having intentions in strategic planning to develop shared objectives for col-

lection action. "When" (temporal) refers to the sequence of tasks. "By whom" (referential) is about leveraging social resources in the coordination network, within and outside of the group. Finally, "how" (technical) refers to the division of labor and allocation of roles in the network to fulfill group objectives.

Separating and supporting different levels of planning can allow flexibility in planning tools. Instead of a Gantt chart supporting all planning activities, different representations for different levels of planning seems more plausible. For example, in our BRIDGE system, the timeline provides a temporal representation of plans, whereas the concept map supports a hierarchical way of structuring plans. The technical structuring of plans is supported through a shared workspace that corresponds to the planning milestones. Each milestone in the timeline can be specified in detail within the workspace, which supports collaborative discussion and writing among group members.

Not all planning is explicit (McGrath & Tschan, 2004) because structuring of actions (i.e., planning) often has a basis in traditions and history, either of that group or of groups to which its members have previously belonged. One design feature to support the referential level of operational planning is to incorporate a social network as part of the planning workflow system.

Our argumentation for incorporating a social network is based on two phenomena. First, scientists use digital library sources (e.g., ACM digital library) to access and use scientific artifacts in their own endeavors. Second, these scientific artifacts are not just tangible and passive resources. They embody social and active intellectual entities with respect to the scientists who created these artifacts. Thus, social relationships and interactions among scientists in a community of interest or practice (Wenger, McDermott, & Snyder, 2002), at the very least, influence the development and operationalization of plans. This is because plans continuously change, along with the situation

(Suchman, 1986), and in scientific collaboration, an essential part of the situation are scientific peers and the knowledge they generate. It is then reasonable to expect that during scientific collaboration and specifically planning, collaborators not only want to leverage strong ties in their group (members of the group), but also weak ties outside of the group (larger scientific community) (Granovetter, 1973). Referential planning should not be narrowly construed as "who does what in the group", but more broadly as "who can be leveraged as a social resource within and outside of the group". Thus, social networks can enhance the depth of planning and articulation of work by facilitating horizontal informational flow across formal, recognized boundaries (Wellman, Salaff, Dimitrova, Garton, Gulia, & Haythornthwaite, 1996).

CONCLUSION AND FUTURE WORK

With the proliferation of advanced information and communication technologies, creative scientific work is increasingly being accomplished through collaboration between geographically-distributed peers. Our goal is to enhance such e-collaboration by designing CSCW tools to support scientific creativity in distributed computer-supported collaboration. Based on an exegesis of diverse literature on creativity, group dynamics, and their associated domains of study (e.g., organizational theory, collaborative problem solving, etc.), we presented three requirements to support creativity. These requirements appropriately update and enhance existing work in HCI and CSCW to support creativity because of their theory-based and empirical-rooted design rationale. These requirements are by no means exhaustive, but do represent a systematic effort toward developing first-order approximations for supporting creativity in context of CSCW. We chose these specific requirements among others because of their potential to be mediated by and supported through collaborative technology. We also proposed three

implications for design as discussion items based on our earlier requirements for creativity. More broadly, these implications manifest technical challenges for the CSCW community for exploring the design space in supporting creativity.

Building on our requirements and implications for design, we briefly outline here a future research trajectory for designing and evaluating creativity support tools in context of collaboratories. A collaboratory can be defined as a "center without walls, in which the nation's researchers can perform their research without regard to geographical location—interacting with colleagues, accessing instrumentation, sharing data and computational resource, and accessing information in digital libraries" (Wulf, 1993). The vision of collaboratories is that access to special equipment (e.g., a supercomputer or a one-of-a-kind telescope) or special research sites (such as polar regions and the upper atmosphere) could be shared through the Internet, creating centers for geographically-distributed scientists to collaborate.

The logical connection between collaboratories and creativity is an obvious and important one; collaboratories are systems that can support creativity between geographically-distributed scientists. However, this connection has been understudied (Carroll & Farooq, 2006). This is because the original justification for collaboratories was more a matter of resource access and logistics than of enhancing creativity. We believe it is plausible that having better access to instruments, research sites, datasets, and critical mass of one's professional colleagues *ipso facto* facilitates opportunities for greater scientific creativity. It would be useful to directly design and evaluate creativity support tools for collaboratories.

Our research group is currently exploring the enhancement of CiteSeer (http://citeseer.ist.psu.edu) as a collaboratory to support creative work between distributed scientists in the computer and information science community. CiteSeer (Giles, Bollacker, & Lawrence, 1998) is a search engine and digital library of literature in the computer and information science disciplines that is a free resource providing access to the full-text of nearly 700,000 academic papers, and over 10 million citations. CiteSeer currently receives over 1.5 million hits a day and is accessed by 150 countries and over a million unique machines monthly.

We recently concluded the first requirements phase of enhancing CiteSeer as a collaboratory. Based on a survey of CiteSeer users and follow-up interviews (Farooq, Ganoe, Carroll, & Giles, 2007), results suggest that participants want support for upstream stages of distributed collaboration. These upstream stages were identified as creative and divergent activities of scientific work. For example, participants expressed the need to support brainstorming to collaboratively discuss and interpret research ideas and papers with others in the scientific community.

We think it is a worthwhile research pursuit and contribution to explore the design of creativity support tools in the CiteSeer collaboratory. Combining our results from this article with our parallel design effort to enhance CiteSeer as a collaboratory, we are currently implementing proof-of-concept prototypes of creativity support tools to be integrated with CiteSeer. For instance, we are integrating some of the existing creativity support tools that our BRIDGE system provides with CiteSeer. In addition to designing creativity support tools, there is also a need to formulate and codify measures for evaluating creativity in computer-supported collaborations. To this end, a promising direction that we are contemplating is to develop multi-method measurement approaches, grounded in theories of collaborative activity *and* creativity (for analogous argumentation with respect to usability evaluation issues in CSCW, see Neale, Carroll, & Rosson, 2004).

ACKNOWLEDGMENT

This article extends an earlier, shorter version presented at the ACM International GROUP Conference on supporting group work in 2005 (Farooq, Carroll, & Ganoe, 2005). This work was partially supported by NSF grant CRI-0454052.

REFERENCES

Ackerman, M. (2000). The intellectual challenge of CSCW: The gap between social requirements and technical feasibility. *Human-Computer Interaction, 15*(2-3), 181-205.

Arias, E. G., Eden, H., Fischer, G., Gorman, A., & Scharff, E. (2000). Transcending the individual human mind - Creating shared understanding through collaborative design. *ACM Transactions on Computer-Human Interaction, 7*(1), 84-113.

Arrow, H., McGrath, J. E., & Berdahl, J. (2000). *Small groups as complex systems: Formation, coordination, development, and adaptation.* Thousand Oaks, CA: Sage.

Bly, S. (1998). Special section on collaboratories. *ACM Interactions, 5*(3), 31.

Boden, M. A. (2004). *The creative mind: Myths and mechanisms.* London: Routledge.

Bouwen, R., & Fry, R. (1996). Facilitating group development: Interventions for a relational and contextual construction. In M. A. West (Ed.), *The handbook of work group psychology* (pp. 531-552). Chichester, UK: Wiley.

Burleson, W., & Selker, T. (2002). Creativity and interface. *Communications of the ACM, 45*(10), 89-90.

Candy, L. (1997). Computers and creativity support: Knowledge, visualization, and collaboration. *Knowledge-Based Systems, 9*(6), 3-13.

Candy, L., & Hori, K. (2003). The digital muse: HCI in support of creativity: "Creativity and cognition" come of age: Towards a new discipline. *ACM Interactions, 10*(4), 44-54.

Carroll, J. M. (1995). How to avoid designing digital libraries: A scenario-based approach. *SIGOIS Bulletin, 16*(2), 5-7.

Carroll, J. M., & Farooq, U. (2006). Enhancing digital libraries to support creativity in distributed scientific communities: Making CiteSeer collaborative. *Designing for Usability in e-Science: An International Workshop on Interrogating Usability Issues in New Scientific Practice, within the Lab and within Society, Edinburgh, Scotland, January 26-27, 2006.*

Carroll, J. M., Neale, D. C., Isenhour, P. L., Rosson, M. B., & McCrickard, D. S. (2003). Notification and awareness: Synchronizing task-oriented collaborative activity. *International Journal of Human-Computer Studies, 58*, 605-632.

Carter, S. M., & West, M. A. (1998). Reflexivity, effectiveness, and mental health in BBC-TV production teams. *Small Group Research, 5*, 583-601.

Casper, T. A., Meyer, W. M., Moller, J. M., Henline, P., Keith, K., McHarg, B., Davis, S., & Greenwood, D. (1998). Collaboratory operations in magnetic fusion scientific research. *ACM Interactions, 5*(3), 56-65.

Chin, G., Jr., & Lansing, C. S. (2004). Capturing and supporting contexts for scientific data sharing via the biological sciences collaboratory. *Proceedings of the ACM Conference on Computer Supported Cooperative Work* (pp. 409-418).

Coch, L., & French, J. R. (1948). Overcoming resistance to change. *Human Relations, 1*, 512-532.

Convertino, G., Ganoe, C. H., Schafer, W. A., Yost, B., & Carroll, J. M. (2005). A multiple view approach to support common ground. *Proceedings of the 3rd International Conference on Coordinated and Multiple Views in Exploratory Visualization, London.*

Crane, D. (1972). *Invisible colleges: Diffusion of knowledge in scientific communities*. Chicago: University of Chicago Press.

Csikszentmihalyi, M. (1996). *Creativity: Flow and the psychology of discovery and invention.* New York: HarperCollins.

De Dreu, C. K. W., & De Vries, N. K. (1993). Numerical support, information processing, and attitude change. *European Journal of Social Psychology, 23*, 647-662.

De Dreu, C. K. W., & West, M. A. (2001). Minority dissent and team innovation: The importance of participation in decision-making. *Journal of Applied Psychology, 86*, 1191-1201.

Dudek, S. Z., & Cote, R. (1994). Problem finding revisited. In M.A. Runco (Ed.), *Problem finding, problem solving, and creativity* (pp. 130-150). Norwood, NJ: Ablex.

Dunbar, K. (1995). How scientists really reason: Scientific reasoning in real-world laboratories. In R. J. Sternberg & J. E. Davidson (Eds.), *The nature of insight*. Cambridge, MA: MIT Press.

Dunbar, K. (1997). How scientists think: Online creativity and conceptual change in science. In T. B. Ward, S. M. Smith, & S. Vaid (Eds.), *Conceptual structures and processes: Emergence, discovery, and change*. Washington, DC: APA Press.

Edmonds, E. A. (1994). Introduction: Computer-based systems that support creativity. In T. Dartnall (Ed.), *Artificial intelligence and creativity* (pp. 327-334). Dordrecht, Netherlands: Kluwer Academic.

Erickson, T., & Kellogg, W. A. (2000). Social translucence: An approach to designing systems that mesh with social processes. *ACM Transactions on Computer Human Interaction, 7*(1), 59-83.

Farooq, U., Carroll, J. M., & Ganoe, C. H. (2005). Supporting creativity in distributed scientific communities. *Proceedings of the International*

GROUP Conference on Supporting Group Work, Sanibel Island, Florida, November 6-9, 2005 (pp. 217-226). New York: ACM Press.

Farooq, U., Ganoe, C. H., Carroll, J. M., & Giles, C. L. (2007). Supporting distributed scientific collaboration: Implications for designing the CiteSeer collaboratory. *Proceedings of the Hawaii International Conference on System Sciences, Waikoloa, Hawaii, January 3-6, 2007* (p. 26c). Washington, DC: IEEE Computer Society.

Farooq, U., Rodi, C., Carroll, J. M., & Isenhour, P. L. (2003). Avatar proxies: Configurable informants of collaborative activities. *Proceedings of the ACM Conference on CHI* (pp. 792-793).

Farrell, M. P. (2001). *Collaborative circles: Friendship dynamics and creative work.* Chicago: University of Chicago Press.

Feist, G. J. (1999). The influence of personality on artistic and scientific creativity. In R. J. Sternberg (Ed.), *Handbook of creativity* (pp. 273-296). New York: Cambridge University Press.

Finholt, T. A., & Olson, G. M. (1997). From laboratories to collaboratories: A new organizational form for scientific collaboration. *Psychological Science, 8*(1), 28-36.

Fischer, G. (1999). Symmetry of ignorance, social creativity, and meta-design. *Proceedings of the 3rd Conference on Creativity and Cognition* (pp. 116-123). New York: ACM Press..

Fischer, G. (2005). Distances and diversity: Sources for social creativity. *Proceedings of the 5th Conference on Creativity and Cognition* (pp. 128-136). New York: ACM Press.

Fischer, G., Nakakoji, K., Ostwald, J., Stahl, G., & Sumner, T. (1998). Embedding critics in design environments. In M. T. Maybury & W. Wahlster (Eds.), *Readings in intelligent user interfaces* (pp. 537-559). San Francisco, CA: Morgan Kaufmann.

Florida, R. (2002). *The rise of the creative class: And how it's transforming work, leisure, community, and everyday life.* New York: Basic Books.

Florida, R. (2005). *The flight of the creative class: The new global competition talent.* New York: HarperCollins.

Fraser, C. (1971). Group risk taking and group polarization. *European Journal of Social Psychology, 1,* 493-510.

Frese, M., & Zapf, D. (1994). Action as the core of work psychology: A German approach. In H. C. Triandis, M. D. Dunnette, & L. M. Hough (Eds.), *Handbook of industrial and organizational psychology, 2nd ed.: Vol. 4* (pp. 271-340). Palo Alto, CA: Consulting Psychologists Press.

Ganoe, C. H., Somervell, J. P., Neale, D. C., Isenhour, P. L., Carroll, J. M., Rosson, M. B., & McCrickard, D. S. (2003). Classroom BRIDGE: Using collaborative public and desktop timelines to support activity awareness. *Proceedings of ACM UIST, Vancouver* (pp. 21-30).

Gardner, H. (1993). Seven creators of the modern era. In J. Brockman (Ed.), *Creativity* (pp. 28-47). New York: Simon & Schuster.

Giaccardi, E. (2004). *Principles of metadesign: Processes and levels of co-creation in the new design space.* Doctoral dissertation, CAiiA-STAR, School of Computing, Plymouth, UK.

Giles, C. L., Bollacker, K., & Lawrence, S. (1998). CiteSeer: An automatic citation indexing system. *Proceedings of the Conference on Digital Libraries, Pittsburgh, PA, June 23-26, 1998* (pp. 89-98). New York: ACM Press.

Gollwitzer, P. M. (1996). The volitional benefits of planning. In P. M. Gollwitzer & J. A. Bargh (Eds.), *The psychology of action: Linking cognition and motivation to behaviour* (pp. 287-312). New York: Guilford.

Granovetter, M. (1973). The strength of weak ties. *American Journal of Sociology, 78*(6), 1360-1380.

Greenberg, S., Boyle, M., & Laberge, J. (1999). PDAs and shared public displays: Making personal information public, and public information personal. *Personal Technologies, 3*(1), 54-64.

Greene, S. L. (2002). Characteristics of applications that support creativity. *Communications of the ACM, 45*(10), 100-104.

Grudin, J. (1994). Groupware and social dynamics: Eight challenges for developers. *Communications of the ACM, 37*(1), 92-105.

Guilford, J. P. (1983). Transformation: Abilities or functions. *Journal of Creative Behavior, 17*, 75-86.

Gutwin, C., & Greenberg, S. A. (2002). Descriptive framework for workspace awareness for real-time groupware. *Computer Supported Cooperative Work, 11*(3-4), 411-446.

Hackman, J. R., & Morris, C. G. (1975). Group tasks, group interaction processes, and group performance effectiveness: A review and proposed integration. In L. Berkowitz (Ed.), *Advances in experimental social psychology: Vol. 8* (pp. 45-99). New York: Academic Press.

Henle, M. (1962). The birth and death of ideas. In H. Gruber, G. Terrell, & M. Wertheimer (Eds.), *Contemporary approaches to creative thinking* (pp. 31-62). New York: Atherton.

Hutchins, E. (1995). *Cognition in the wild*. Cambridge, MA: MIT.

Isaksen, S. G. (1995). CPS: Linking creativity and problem solving. In G. Kaufmann, T. Helstrup, & K. H. Teigen, (Eds.), *Problem solving and cognitive processes: A festschrift in honour of Kjell Raaheim* (pp. 145-181). Bergen-Sandviken, Norway: Fagbokforlaget Vigmostad & Bjørke AS.

Isenhour, P. L., Rosson, M. B., & Carroll, J. M. (2001). Supporting interactive collaboration on the Web with CORK. *Interacting with Computers, 13*, 655-676.

Janis, I. L. (1982). *Groupthink: Psychological studies of policy decisions and fiascoes, 2nd ed.* Boston: Houghton Mifflin.

Jehn, K. A. (1997). Affective and cognitive conflict in work groups: Increasing performance through value-based intragroup conflict. In C. K. W. De Deru & E. Van de Vliert (Eds.), *Using conflict in organizations* (pp. 87-100). Thousand Oaks, CA: Sage.

John-Steiner, V. (2000). *Creative collaboration*. New York: Oxford University Press.

Kibrick, R., Conrad, A., & Perala, A. (1998). Through the far looking glass: Collaborative remote observing with the W. M. Keck Observatory. *ACM Interactions, 5*(3), 32-39.

Kock, N. (2005). What is e-collaboration? *International Journal of e-Collaboration, 1*(1), i-vii.

Kock, N., & D'Arcy, J. (2002). Resolving the e-collaboration paradox: The competing influences of media naturalness and compensatory adaptation. *Information Management and Consulting* (Special Issue on Electronic Collaboration), *17*(4), 72-78.

Kohut, H. (1985). *Self psychology and the humanities*. New York: W. W. Norton.

Kouzes, R. T., Myers, J. D., & Wulf, W. A. (1996). Collaboratories: Doing science on the Internet. *IEEE Computer, 29*(8), 40-46.

Lawler, E. E., III, & Hackman, J. R. (1969). Impact of employee participation in the development of pay incentive plans: A field experiment. *Journal of Applied Psychology, 53*, 467-471.

Levine, J. M., & Moreland, R. L. (2004). Collaboration: The social context of theory development.

Personality and Social Psychology Review, 8(2), 164-172.

Mamykina, L., Candy, L., & Edmonds, E. (2002). Collaborative creativity. *Communications of the ACM, 45*(10), 96-99.

Martin, R., & Noyes, C. (1996). Minority influence and argument generation. In C. J. Nemeth (Ed.), *British Journal of Social Psychology: Special Issue on Minority Influence, 35*, 91-103.

McDaniel, S. E., Olson, G. M., & Olson, J. S. (1994). Methods in search of methodology—Combining HCI and object orientation. *Proceedings of the ACM Conference on CHI* (pp. 145-151).

McGrath, J. E. (1984). *Groups: Interaction and performance.* Englewood Cliffs, NJ: Prentice Hall.

McGrath, J. E., & Tschan, F. (2004). *Temporal matters in social psychology: Examining the role of time in the lives of groups and individuals.* Washington, DC: APA.

Miller, G. A., Galanter, E., & Pribam, K. (1960). *Plans and the structure of behavior.* New York: Rinehart & Winston/Holt.

Mitchell, K. A. C. (1998). *The effect of break task on performance during a second session of brainstorming.* Unpublished master's thesis, University of Texas, Arlington.

Moran, T. P. (1983). Getting into a system: External-internal task mapping analysis. *Proceedings of the ACM Conference on CHI* (pp. 45-49).

Moran, T. P., & Carroll, J. M. (Eds.). (1996). *Design rationale: Concepts, techniques, and use.* Hillsdale, NJ: Lawrence Erlbaum.

Moscovici, S., & Zavalloni, M. (1969). The group as a polarizer of attitudes. *Journal of Personality and Social Psychology, 12*, 124-135.

Mumford, M. D., & Gustafson, S. B. (1988). Creativity syndrome: Integration, application, and innovation. *Psychological Bulletin, 103*, 27-43.

Nakakoji, K., Yamamoto, Y., & Ohira, M. (1999). A framework that supports collective creativity in design using visual images. *Proceedings of the 3rd Conference on Creativity and Cognition* (pp. 166-173). New York: ACM Press.

Neale, D. C., Carroll, J. M., & Rosson, M. B. (2004). Evaluating computer-supported cooperative work: Models and frameworks. *Proceedings of the ACM Conference on CSCW*, 112-121.

Nemeth, C. (1995). Dissent as driving cognition, attitudes, and judgments. *Social Cognition, 13*, 273-291.

Nemeth, C., & Nemeth-Brown, B. (2003). Better than individuals? The potential benefits of dissent and diversity. In P. B. Paulus & B. A. Nijstad (Eds.), *Group creativity: Innovation through collaboration* (pp. 63-84). New York: Oxford University Press.

Nemeth, C., & Rogers, J. (1996). Dissent and the search for information. *British Journal of Social Psychology, 35*, 67-76.

Nemeth, C., Rogers, J. D., & Brown, K. S. (2001). Devil's advocate vs. authentic dissent: Stimulating quantity and quality. *European Journal of Social Psychology, 31*, 707-729.

Nickerson, R. S. (1999). Enhancing creativity. In R. J. Sternberg (Ed.), *Handbook of creativity* (pp. 392-430). New York: Cambridge University Press.

Olson, G. M., Atkins, D. E., Clauer, R., Finholt, T. A., Jahanian, F., Killeen, T. L., Prakash, A., & Weymouth, T. (1998). The upper atmospheric research collaboratory (UARC). *ACM Interactions, 5*(3), 48-55.

Pearce, J. A., & Ravlin, E. C. (1987). The design and activation of self-regulating work groups. *Human Relations, 40*, 751-782.

Perkins, D. N. (1981). *The mind's best work.* Cambridge, MA: Harvard University Press.

Pinto, J. K., & Prescott, J. E. (1987). Changes in critical success factor importance over the life of a project. *Academy of Management Proceedings* (pp. 328-332).

Pycior, H. M., Slack, N. G., & Abir-Am, P. G. (Eds.). (1996). *Creative couples in the sciences.* New Brunswick, NJ: Rutgers Press.

Rittel, H., & Webber, M. (1973). Dilemmas in a general theory of planning. *Policy Sciences, 4,* 155-169.

Rogoff, B. (1995). Observing sociocultural activity on three planes: Participatory appropriation, guided participation, and apprenticeship. In J. V. Wertsch, P. del Rio, & A. Alvarez (Eds.), *Sociocultural studies of mind* (pp. 139-164). New York: Cambridge University Press.

Runco, M. A., & Chand, I. (1994). Problem finding, evaluative thinking, and creativity. In M. A. Runco (Ed.), *Problem finding, problem solving, and creativity* (pp. 40-76). Norwood, NJ: Ablex.

Sacerdoti, E. D. (1974). Planning in a hierarchy of abstraction spaces. *Artificial Intelligence, 5,* 115-135.

Schur, A., Keating, K. A., Payne, D. A., Valdez, T., Yates, K. R., & Myers, J. D. (1998). Collaborative suites for experiment-oriented scientific research. *ACM Interactions, 5*(3), 40-47.

Shneiderman, B. (2000). Creating creativity: User interfaces for supporting innovation. *ACM TOCHI, 7*(1), 114-138.

Sonnenwald, D. H., Whitton, M. C., & Maglaughlin, K. L. (2003). Evaluating a scientific collaboratory: Results of a controlled experiment. *ACM TOCHI, 10*(2), 150-176.

Stahl, G., & Herrmann, T. (1999). Intertwining perspectives and negotiation. *Proceedings of ACM GROUP* (pp. 316-325).

Stasser, G., & Birchmeier, Z. (2003). Group creativity and collective choice. In P. B. Paulus &

B. A. Nijstad (Eds.), *Group creativity: Innovation through collaboration* (pp. 85-109). New York: Oxford University Press.

Steiner, I. D. (1972). *Group process and productivity.* New York: Academic Press.

Sternberg, R. J. (Ed.). (1999). *Handbook of creativity.* New York: Cambridge University Press.

Sternberg, R. J. & Lubart, T. I. (1999). The concept of creativity: Prospects and paradigms. In R. J. Sternberg (Ed.), *Handbook of creativity* (pp. 3-15). New York: Cambridge University Press.

Suchman, L. A. (1986). *Plans and situated actions.* New York: Cambridge University Press.

Suchman, L. A. (1995). Making work visible. *Communications of the ACM, 38*(9), 56-64.

Sugimoto, M., Hosoi, K., & Hashizume, H. (2004). Caretta: A system for supporting face-to-face collaboration by integrating personal and shared spaces. *Proceedings of the ACM Conference on Computer-Human Interaction* (pp. 41-48).

Thagard, P. (1998). Ulcers and bacteria II: Instruments, experiments, and social interactions. *Studies in History and Philosophy of Biological and Biomedical Sciences, 29,* 317-342.

Van Dyne, L., & Saavedra, R. (1996). A naturalistic minority influence experiment: Effects on divergent thinking, conflict, and originality in work groups. *British Journal of Social Psychology, 35,* 151-168.

Volpato, C., Maass, A., Mucchi-Faina, A., & Vitti, E. (1990). Minority influence and social categorization. *European Journal of Social Psychology, 20,* 119-132.

Watson, J. D. (1968). *The double helix.* New York: Signet.

Wellman, B., Salaff, J., Dimitrova,, D., Garton, L., Gulia, M., & Haythornthwaite, C. (1996). Computer networks as social networks: Collaborative work, telework, and virtual community. *Annual Review of Sociology, 22*, 213-238.

Wenger, E., McDermott, R., & Snyder, W. (2002). *Cultivating communities of practice: A guide to managing knowledge*. Harvard Business School Press.

West, M. A. (1996). Reflexivity and work group effectiveness: A conceptual integration. In M. A. West (Ed.), *Handbook of work group psychology* (pp. 555-579). Chichester, UK: Wiley.

West, M. A. (2003). Innovation implementation in work teams. In P. B. Paulus & B. A. Nijstad (Eds.), *Group creativity: Innovation through collaboration* (pp. 245-276). New York: Oxford Press.

Wulf, W. (1993). The collaboratory opportunity. *Science, 261*, 854-855.

Ye, Y. (2001). *Supporting component-based software development with active component repository systems*. Doctoral dissertation, University of Colorado at Boulder.

This work was previously published in the International Journal of e-Collaboration, Vol. 4, Issue 4, edited by N. Kock, pp. 51-75, copyright 2008 by IGI Publishing (an imprint of IGI Global).

Chapter 10

Determinants of Manufacturing Firms' Use of Web–Based IOISs to Share Inventory Information with Key Partners:
Comparing the Supplier and Customer Perspectives

Pierre Hadaya
Université du Québec à Montréal, Canada

Robert Pellerin
École Polytechnique de Montréal, Canada

ABSTRACT

Based on the literature on the diffusion of innovations and on information systems, and building on emerging concepts in electronic collaboration (e-collaboration), this chapter analyses the influence of various determinants on manufacturing firms' intent to use Web-based interorganizational information systems (IOISs) to share inventory information with their key suppliers. This theoretical model is tested on data collected from 498 senior managers of Canadian manufacturing firms. Findings indicate that a manufacturing firm's organizational readiness, its past experience with e-commerce and its business relationships all affect its future use of Web-based IOISs to share inventory information with its key suppliers. The results of Tobit regressions also provide supporting evidence that firm size moderates the impact of the present use of e-commerce with suppliers on manufacturing firms' intent to use Web-based IOISs to share inventory information with key suppliers. Finally, subsequent analyses also demonstrate that the determinants of manufacturing firms' intent to use Web-based IOISs to exchange inventory information with key partners are the same whether the intended e-collaboration is to support relationships with key suppliers or key customers.

DOI: 10.4018/978-1-61520-676-6.ch010

INTRODUCTION

In today's highly global and competitive environment, firms' competitive advantage highly rests on their IT and supply chain management (SCM) capabilities (Pant *et al.*, 2003; Wade and Hulland, 2004). Supply chain management strategies and techniques are as varied as the disciplines from which they originate and the customers they are to serve (Boone *et al.*, 2007). Nonetheless, within the context of today's economy, where customer requirements are no longer limited to traditional issues such as higher quality and lower cost but also include speed of delivery and product variability, the adoption of **electronic collaboration (e-collaboration)** tools and practices is particularly critical to the success of supply chains (Kemppainen and Vepsäläinen, 2003; Sebastian and Lambert, 2003).

The present study aims to extend the body of knowledge in this research stream by identifying and measuring the influence of various **determinants** on manufacturing firms' intent to use **Web-based Interorganizational information systems (IOISs)** to share inventory information with their key suppliers. The second objective of this research is to assess the extent to which the determinants of manufacturing firms' intent to use Web-based IOISs to exchange inventory information with key partners will vary whether the intended e-collaboration is to support relationships with key suppliers or key customers. This line of inquiry is particularly relevant for two reasons. First, information sharing is one of the key dimensions of supply chain collaboration (Simatupang & Sridharan, 2004) and represents a good measure of collaboration, as realistic, informed, and detailed information sharing can improve partners' decision-making processes while encouraging people to act proactively to prevent problems and capitalize on new business opportunities (Min et al., 2005). Secondly,

Inventory information, one of the three types of information that can be shared between supply chain partners is especially interesting from a collaboration point of view as it seems to be more sensitive than product information and customer information and renders trading partners less willing to share it (Ovalle & Marquez, 2003).

Our decision to measure intended use (within the next 12 months) rather than current use of **Web-based IOISs** was made for three reasons: (1) As yet, few firms have capitalized on the full potential of **e-collaboration** (Barratt, 2003; Crum & Palmatier, 2004), and most of the ones that have still rely on EDI systems, not on the Internet, to do so because these proprietary networks were so costly to implement initially. (2) Some authors have already used this approach in studying the adoption of radical technological innovations (Lefebvre, Lefebvre, & Harvey, 1996). (3) The study of "trigger mechanisms" or stimuli to innovativeness represents a definite interest in both theory and practice, particularly in the development of public policies governing small and medium-sized enterprises (SMEs) (Damsgaard & Lyytinen, 1996).

The remainder of this chapter is organized as follows. The next section exposes the relevant theoretical background tied to the adoption of Web-based IOISs to exchange inventory information between supply chain partners. Next, the research model and hypotheses are presented, followed by a description of the research methodology. Research results are then presented and discussed. Next, subsequent analyses are conducted to assess whether the **determinants** of manufacturing firms' intent to use Web-based IOISs to exchange inventory information with key partners will vary whether the intended e-collaboration is to support relationships with key suppliers or key customers. The chapter concludes with the research limitations and the prospects for future research.

THEORETICAL BACKGROUND: WEB-BASED IOISs TO EXCHANGE INVENTORY INFORMATION BETWEEN SUPPLY CHAIN PARTNERS

"Collaboration" is a very broad and all-encompassing term. Within the SCM context, Anthony (2000 pp. 41–44) defines collaboration as two or more companies sharing the responsibility for exchanging common planning, management, execution, and performance measurement information. The fundamental rationale behind the concept is that by pooling their resources, collaborative supply chain partners can perform better than they could if each firm operated individually (Lambert, Emmelhainz, & Gardner, 1999). Inventory and cost savings (Sabath & Fontanella, 2002; Stank, Daugherty, & Autry, 1999), better demand planning (McCarthy & Golicic, 2002), increased operational flexibility to cope with uncertain demand (Fisher, 1997; Lee, Padmanabhan, & Whang, 1997), increased customer loyalty (Sabath & Fontanella, 2002), and the development of new skills and competencies (Verespej, 2005) are just some of the benefits firms expect from SCM collaboration.

Given that business-to-business interactions are often facilitated by Web-based tools and other **interorganizational information systems (IOISs),** the term **"electronic collaboration" (e-collaboration)** is generally used to describe relationships that go beyond simple buy-and-sell transactions (Johnson & Whang, 2002). E-collaboration is operationally defined as collaboration using electronic technologies to accomplish a common task (Kock, 2005) whereas the term "IOIS" refers to information and communications technology that transcends legal enterprise boundaries (Applegate, McFarlan, & McKenney, 1996; Cash & Konsynski, 1985; Kumar & van Dissel, 1996). Electronic data interchange (EDI) is probably the most commonly used technology allowing the exchange of information between business partners. However, in today's digital economy, more and more firms are turning to Web-based approaches to support their interorganizational activities. As highlighted by Elgarah et al. (2005, p. 8), "this migration reflects a movement away from a dyadic approach in data exchange, to more flexible cost-effective approaches that capitalize on many-to-many relationships." Today, SCM systems, e-collaboration tools and other Web-based IOISs play a crucial role in the evolution of supply chain relationships as they are able to support a number of collaboration processes ranging from direct procurement, replenishment, and delivery and design, to more strategic processes such as capacity planning (Cassivi, 2006).

Three **IOIS**-based methods can be adopted by neighboring partners in a supply chain to share inventory information: Continuous Replenishment Programs (CRP), Vendor-Managed Inventory (VMI) and Collaborative Planning, Forecasting and Replenishment (CPFR). The first two methods, CRP and VMI, exchange critical information on short-term activities (procurement and production schedule, demand forecasts, etc.). Suppliers merely react to real-time information provided by their downstream supply chain partners (e.g., manufacturers, distributors, and retailers) and often find it difficult to plan long-term demand. CRP facilitates the exchange of real-time inventory data between customers and suppliers and ensures continuous replenishment of inventory by suppliers (Raghunathan & Yeh, 2001). VMI improves customer-specific forecasting for manufacturers by making them responsible for managing inventories at their customers' storage locations (Cetinkaya & Lee, 2000; Waller, Johnson, & Davis, 1999). The CPFR method is broader in nature, as it plans all actions and measures that will affect supply chain partners in the future, for all supply chain activities (Holmström, Framling, Kaipia, & Saranen, 2002; Steermann, 2003). CPFR, a registered trademark of the Voluntary Interindustry Commerce Solutions (VICS) Association, is defined as a set of business processes that entities in a supply chain can use for collaboration on a number of retailer/manufacturer functions with the aim of improving the overall efficiency of the supply chain. CPFR is forecast-oriented and based on joint business plans in an inter-enterprise environment. It is segmented into three stages. The first stage, planning, involves two critical steps: front-end agreement and joint business plan. The second stage includes two forecast-oriented steps: sales-forecast collaboration and order-forecast collaboration. The final stage, replenishment, comprises one major step: order generation (VICS, 1998).

CONCEPTUAL FRAMEWORK AND RESEARCH HYPOTHESES

A number of authors have attempted to define **e-collaboration** and identify the related benefits for supply chain members (Jap & Mohr, 2002; Johnson, Klassen, Leenders, & Fearon, 2002; Ovalle & Marquez, 2003). However, as mentioned above, no empirical study has yet attempted to measure the influence of various **determinants** on manufacturing firms' intent to use **Web-based IOISs** to share inventory information with their key suppliers.

Previous studies have identified numerous variables as possible determinants of a firm's adoption of information technology. According to (2000 pp. 105-128), these determinants can be grouped into three categories: (1) those pertaining to the technologies and their diffusion contexts, including Rogers' (1995) attributes of innovations and the innovation characteristics identified by Tornatzky and Klein (1982) and others; (2) those pertaining to organizations and their adoption contexts, including firms' structural characteristics such as centralization and formalization (Zmud, 1982); and (3) those pertaining to the combination of technology and organization, including several process models used to guide innovation implementation (Brynjolfsson, Renshaw, & van Alstyne, 1997). However, since some authors ar-

gue that a unifying theory might be inappropriate due to the fundamental differences between the different types of innovations (Downs & Mohr, 1976; Fichman & Kemerer, 1993), we have limited our study to the following five groups of variables (see figure 1).

Determinant Related to Technology: Organizational Readiness

Organizational readiness is a measure of the technical and financial resources that are prerequisites for the adoption of **IOISs** (Swatman & Swatman, 1991). Studies have demonstrated that technological characteristics (e.g., IT infrastructure and IT capabilities) can encourage or hinder the adoption of IOISs (Premkumar & Ramamurthy, 1995). Organizational readiness, in the form of IS capabilities, is also required to support CPFR initiatives (Stank et al., 1999) or other methods adopted by neighboring partners in a supply chain that share inventory information. Other studies have also shown that adequate financial resources increase the success of IOIS adoption (Saunders & Clark, 1992). Some researchers have also found that organizational readiness positively affects firms' adoption of different types of IOISs, such as EDI (Iacovou, Benbasat, & Dexter, 1995), **Web-based IOISs** (Chang & Chen, 2005) and the Internet in general (Mehrtens, Cragg, & Mills, 2001).

The influence of a firm's readiness is of even greater importance in the case of SMEs, since the small number of employees in such enterprises often results in a lack of knowledge and expertise as far as information technologies are concerned (Julien, 1995; Thong, 2001).

Hence, based on the information provided above, we formulated Hypothesis 1:

Hypothesis 1: A manufacturing firm's organizational readiness will be positively related to its intent to use Web-based IOISs to share inventory information with its key suppliers.

Figure 1. Conceptual model

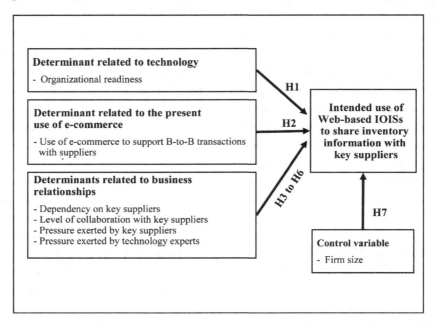

Determinant Related to the Present Use of Electronic Commerce

A firm's past experience with a variety of technologies may have a considerable influence on its future decisions regarding the adoption of similar technologies (Burgelman & Rosenbloom, 1989; Lefebvre, Harvey, & Lefebvre, 1991; Zogut & Zander, 1992). Likewise, a firm's current use of **Web-based IOIS** to support Business-to-Business (B-to-B) transactions may have a crucial impact on its future use of Web-based IOISs to collaborate with its trading partners. This statement arises from the fact that if a business acquires the necessary technological knowledge to make good use of an innovation it already has in its possession, it will be disposed to increase the use of that innovation in the future.

The literature on **IOISs** has already demonstrated, in the form of trajectory models, that firms generally start using e-commerce to support their B-to-B transactions with counterparts before they use it to support more complex processes such as sharing inventory information with their collabora-

tive partners (Johnson & Whang, 2002; Lefebvre, Lefebvre, Elia, & Boeck, 2005; Rao, Metts, & Mora Monge, 2003). For example, according to Lefebvre and Lefebvre (2002), the transition from the traditional to the virtual enterprise can be seen as a succession of technological waves where each wave is more complex than the one before it. According to these authors, a firm in the first wave starts using e-commerce to conduct B-to-B transactions with counterparts, whereas it adopts IOISs to collaborate with its supply chain partners further along in the transition process, at the fourth wave.

These statements led to our second hypothesis:

Hypothesis 2: A manufacturing firm's current use of e-commerce to support B-to-B transactions with its suppliers will be positively related to its intent to use Web-based IOISs to share information with its key suppliers.

Determinants Related to Business Relationships

The **determinants** related to **business relationships** seem to be the ones that exert the most powerful influence on the adoption of innovations that impact both a firm and its business partners (Fichman, 2000 pp. 105-128; Prescott & Conger, 1995), as is the case for collaborative **Web-based IOISs**. Four determinants corresponding to the characteristics of a manufacturing firm's business relationships may influence its intent to use Web-based IOISs to share inventory information with its key suppliers: its dependency on its key suppliers, its level of collaboration with its key suppliers, the pressure it undergoes from its key suppliers, and the pressure exerted by technology experts.

Dependency can be defined as a firm's need to maintain an exchange relationship with another company in order to fulfill some of its objectives (Frazier & Rody, 1991; Ganesan, 1994). There is a positive relationship between a firm's dependency on another firm and its level of coordination with the latter (Lonsdale, 2001; Malone & Crowston, 1994; Williamson, 1975). Some authors have demonstrated that a firm's level of vertical coordination with its business partners is positively linked to the adoption of information technologies (Gatignon & Robertson, 1989).

Other researchers have also demonstrated that dependency on suppliers may force manufacturing firms to adopt methods such as CRP to support their collaborative efforts with their upstream partners (Bagchi & Skjoett-Larsen, 2002). A firm that is dependent on a supplier is often pressured to use **IOISs** to collaborate with the latter in order to safeguard against opportunistic behaviors that might undermine this key relationship (Christy & Grout, 1994; Kersten, Schroeder, & Schulte-Bisping, 2004; Léger, Cassivi, Hadaya, & Caya, 2006).

Based on these arguments, we formulated Hypothesis 3:

Hypothesis 3: A manufacturing firm's dependency on its key suppliers will be positively related to its intent to use Web-based IOISs to share inventory information with those key suppliers.

Information sharing is at the heart of supply chain collaboration (Min et al., 2005). And, according to Marquez, Bianchi, and Gupta (2004), there is a broad consensus that information systems integration is a must if information is to be shared efficiently between supply chain partners. Moreover, **IOISs** are essential to efficiently support the CRP, VMI and CPFR methods of exchanging inventory information and improve supply chain performance (Chen, 1999; Towill, Naim, & Wikner, 1992; Wikner, Towill, & Naim, 1991). These arguments gave rise to our fourth hypothesis:

Hypothesis 4: A manufacturing firm's level of collaboration with its key suppliers will be positively related to its intent to use Web-based IOISs to share inventory information with those key suppliers.

A firm that is pressured by its business partners – such as customers, suppliers, investors, and technology providers – may be compelled to initiate and implement certain practices (Christensen & Bower, 1996; Foster, 1986; Pfeffer & Salancik, 1978). For example, Lefebvre et al. (1996) showed that the influence of customers and technology suppliers are two of the strongest **determinants** of the future adoption of advanced manufacturing technologies. The pressure exerted by a firm's external partners is all the more critical if the innovation is an interdependent technology, such as an **IOIS** (Bensaou & Venkatraman, 1996; Grover, 1993; Iacovou et al., 1995; Premkumar & Ramamurthy, 1995; Raymond, 1985; Reekers & Smithson, 1994; Riggins & Mukhopadyay, 1994), including Internet-based tools and SCM systems that support the exchange of inventory information among supply chain partners (Disney

& Towill, 2003; Saeed, Malhotra, & Grover, 2005). Moreover, several studies have demonstrated that external pressures greatly influence SMEs' adoption of information technologies (Hart & Saunders, 1997; Iacovou et al., 1995).

Two variables are included in our research model to assess the pressure exerted by key suppliers and technology experts on manufacturing firms. Based on the arguments provided above, we formulated Hypotheses 5 and 6:

Hypothesis 5: The pressure a manufacturing firm experiences from its key suppliers will be positively related to its intent to use Web-based IOISs to share inventory information with those key suppliers.

Hypothesis 6: The pressure a manufacturing firm experiences from technology experts will be positively related to its intent to use Web-based IOISs to share inventory information with its key suppliers.

Control Variable

The size of a company may influence its innovativeness (Chen & Fu, 2001; Lehman, 1985). Larger firms can afford to take the risk of adopting new technologies (Palvia, Means, & Jackson, 1994), whereas smaller companies are known for their flexibility and open-mindedness towards new ideas (Premkumar, Ramamurthy, & Crum, 1997). Thus, empirical findings concerning the influence of firm size on innovativeness are divided. Yet, on the basis of recent studies dealing with the adoption of B-to-B e-business (Charles, Ivis, & Leduc, 2002; Zhu & Kraemer, 2005), we are inclined to believe that the size of a manufacturing firm will be positively related to its intent to use **Web-based IOISs** to share inventory information with its key suppliers. Hence, we formulated our seventh hypothesis:

Hypothesis 7: The size of a manufacturing firm will be positively related to its intent to use Web-

based IOISs to share inventory information with its key suppliers.

RESEARCH METHODOLOGY

The description of the research methodology is divided into three complementary sections. The first highlights the procedure used to gather the data. The second presents and justifies the operationalization of the variables. Finally, the last section justifies the choice of the Tobit model to test the research hypotheses.

Data Collection and Responding Firms

All data were collected by means of an electronic questionnaire. Although this method may limit our panel and lower our response rate, it offers numerous advantages compared to traditional questionnaires, such as saving time and money (Dillman, 2000; Weible & Wallace, 1998) and ensuring data integrity (Mann & Stewart, 2000).

A systematic sample was derived from an up-to-date list of manufacturing firms obtained from a firm that specializes in Internet-based direct marketing. An e-mail was sent to the top executives or senior managers of approximately 4,000 Canadian manufacturing firms, describing the research topic and providing a hyperlink so they could easily access the electronic survey.

In order to obtain the highest possible response rate and encourage respondents to complete the whole survey, a personalized benchmark report was provided to those who took the time to participate in the electronic survey. We received 669 questionnaires, 171 of which were incomplete, probably due to participants' time constraints. The data analyzed in this study therefore originate from a sample of 498 Canadian firms. No significant differences (goodness of fit tests) were found between respondents and non-respondents with respect to firm size.

Table 1. Construct reliability

	Number of items	Cronbach's α (α)
Organizational readiness	7	0.91
Level of collaboration with key suppliers	2	0.73
Pressure exerted by technology experts	3	0.87

Research Variables

The survey instrument (presented in Appendix A) comprised both observable variables (e.g., size of the firm, present use of e-commerce to support B-to-B transactions with suppliers, firm's dependency on its key suppliers) and latent variables (e.g., organizational readiness, level of collaboration with key suppliers). Reliability of latent variables (Cronbach's alphas) ranged from 0.73 to 0.91 (Table 1).

The *organizational readiness* construct measures the extent to which manufacturing firms have the necessary predisposition to implement and use **Web-based IOISs**. This variable measures, on a 7-point Likert scale where 1 = "completely disagree" and 7 = "completely agree," the extent to which manufacturing firms have (1) the necessary management support (Grandon & Pearson, 2004); (2) the necessary financial resources (Grandon & Pearson, 2004); (3) staff members willing to change the way they work; (4) knowledgeable IT staff (Mehrtens et al., 2001); (5) knowledgeable non-IT staff (Mehrtens et al., 2001); (6) adequate IT infrastructure (Premkumar & Roberts, 1999); and (7) a level of systems integration with existing IS that is adequate for the use of Web-based IOISs (Grandon & Pearson, 2004; Premkumar & Ramamurthy, 1995).

The use of *e-commerce to support B-to-B transactions with suppliers* is measured by the percentage of procurement carried out via e-commerce.

Sheppard and Sherman's (1998) operationalization is used to measure manufacturing firms' dependency on key suppliers: the nature of the relationship is dependent (unilateral) and the intensity is deep. Hence, a firm with a limited number of suppliers that represent 75 percent or more of its procurement is categorized as dependent.

The *level of collaboration with key suppliers* construct measures the extent to which manufacturing firms participate in collaborative planning and take joint actions with their key suppliers. These two items are measured on a 7-point Likert scale where 1 = "not at all" and 7 = "to a great extent."

The *pressure exerted by technology experts* construct gauges the extent to which manufacturing firms' adoption of **IOISs** is influenced by (1) electronic intermediaries (i.e., electronic marketplaces); (2) consultants and integrators; and (3) technological vendors. These three items are measured on a 7-point Likert scale where 1 = "not at all" and 7 = "to a great extent."

Finally, the last two variables, *pressure exerted by key suppliers* and *intended use of Web-based IOISs to share inventory information with key suppliers* measure respectively the extent to which manufacturing firms' adoption of IOISs is influenced by their key suppliers and the extent to which they expect to use Web-based IOISs within 12 months to share inventory information with their key suppliers.

A pre-test was conducted with 20 senior managers of Canadian manufacturing firms in order to assess their understanding of the survey instrument. Based on their comments, some items were eliminated and minor modifications were made to improve the questionnaire.

Data Analyses with the Tobit Model

In order to assess the contribution and relative influence of the various **determinants** on manufacturing firms' intent to use **Web-based IOISs** to share inventory information with key suppliers, multivariate data analyses were conducted. And, since a significant number of firms - 212 to be precise – indicated that they did not intend to use Web-based IOISs to share inventory information with key suppliers, and thus gave a zero value to the dependent variable, the Tobit model was deemed more appropriate than the conventional regression model, given that it takes into account the truncated distribution of the dependent variable (Damsgaard & Lyytinen, 1996; Greene, 1997). Indeed, the Tobit model, devised by Tobin (1958), assumes that the dependent variable has a number of its values clustered at a limiting value, usually zero. The stochastic model underlying Tobit may be expressed by the following relationship (McDonald & Moffit, 1980):

$$y_t = X_t \beta + u_t \text{ if } X_t \beta + u_t > 0$$

$$= 0 \text{ if } X_t \beta + u_t \leq 0$$

$$t = 1,2,3,\ldots,N,$$

Where N is the number of observations;

y_t is the dependent variable,
β is a vector of unknown coefficients
u_t is an independently distributed error term assumed to be normal with zero mean and constant variance σ^2

RESEARCH FINDINGS AND DISCUSSION

Determinants of the Intended Use of Web-Based IOIS to Share Inventory Information with Key Suppliers

The data collected from the 498 companies were compiled and analyzed with SAS v. 8.2 (TS2M0). Prior to the regression test, we investigated potential multicollinearity. As the Pearson correlation values summarized in Table 2 indicate, there was no significantly large correlation between the variables that would indicate the need for concern over multicollinearity (Hair, Anderson, Tatham, & Black, 1998). We also conducted a confirmatory factor analysis (CFA) with the three latent variables to make sure that these variables displayed good convergent and discriminant validity.

The results of the Tobit regression are presented in Table 3. The **determinants** and the control variable explained 44.23% of the variance of the dependent variable (p = .0000). *Pressure exerted by technology experts* is by far the most significant variable. These people seem to play the role of opinion leaders and change agents by providing manufacturing firms with information and advice regarding **Web-based IOISs** and offering them strong technical support during the implementation process.

Two other determinants that relate to **business relationships** have an important impact on a manufacturing firm's intended use of Web-based IOISs to share inventory information with its key suppliers: the *level of collaboration with its key suppliers* and the *pressure exerted by its key suppliers*. However, a manufacturing firm's *dependency on key suppliers* does not influence its intended use of Web-based IOISs to share inventory information with its upstream partners. This result may be explained by the fact that, unlike most of the surveys conducted previously to assess **e-collaboration** use within tight supply chains headed by major prime contractors, this study investigated a large number of manufacturing firms – many of which are SMEs – that are active in various sectors and are not necessarily members of dependent networks. Indeed, descriptive statistics indicated that the manufacturing firms questioned were active in various sectors and less than 20% of them were dependent on key suppliers.

As expected, a manufacturing firm's *organizational readiness* is positively and significantly related to its intent to use **Web-based IOISs** to share inventory information with its key suppliers. Moreover, a firm's current *use of e-commerce*

Table 2. Pearson correlation matrix

Variables	(1)	(2)	(3)	(4)	(5)	(6)	(7)	(8)
(1) Firm size	1.000							
(2) Organizational readiness	−0.195****	1.000						
(3) Use of e-commerce to support B-to-B transactions with suppliers	−0.066	−0.0820*	1.000					
(4) Dependency on key suppliers	−0.2540****	−0.004	−0.011	1.000				
(5) Level of collaboration with key suppliers	0.169****	−0.237****	−0.018	−0.007	1.000			
(6) Pressure exerted by key suppliers	0.033	−0.361****	0.167****	0.056	0.229****	1.000		
(7) Pressure exerted by technology experts	0.163****	−0.456****	0.130***	0.055	0.270****	0.342****	1.000	
(8) Intended use of Web-based IOISs to share inventory information with key suppliers	0.174****	−0.285****	0.209****	0.002	0.265****	0.360****	0.428****	1.000

[a] p = level of two-tailed significance based on a chi-square distribution

* $p < .10$, ** $p < .05$, *** $p < .01$, **** $p < .001$

to support B-to-B transactions with its suppliers ultimately affects its intended use of **Web-based IOISs** for this purpose. This self-reinforcing phenomenon has also been observed in the case of various types of innovations unrelated to e-commerce (Burgelman & Rosenbloom, 1989; Lefebvre et al., 1996). Finally, the size of the firm strongly influences the future level of use of e-collaboration.

Based on the above discussion, Hypotheses 1, 2, 4, 5, 6 and 7 are confirmed whereas hypothesis 3 is not (see Table 4).

Relative Influence of the Determinants According to Firm Size

This section completes our investigation of the **determinants** of the intended use of **Web-based IOISs** by manufacturing firms to share inventory information with their key suppliers by verifying whether the role of the determinants differs depending on the size of the firm. To do so, the sample of 498 companies was divided into two groups – the bottom 1/3 (companies with fewer than 8 employees) and the top 1/3 (companies with more than 37 employees) of our sample – in order to assess, for each group, how the explanatory variables affect the dependent variable (see Table 5).

The percentage of the explained variance of the intended use of **Web-based IOISs** to share inventory information with key suppliers is a little higher within the top group than in the bottom group ($R^2 = 42.98\%$ versus $R^2 = 40.51\%$). Our results also highlight many similarities between the two groups since three **determinants** (*level of collaboration with key suppliers, pressure exerted by key suppliers* and *pressure exerted by technol-*

Table 3. Determinants of the intended use of IOISs to exchange inventory information with key suppliers (Tobit) (n = 498)

Variables	Estimate/ Standard error	p^a
Control variables		
Firm size (number of employees)[b]	2.7386	.0031***
Determinant related to technology		
Organizational readiness	1.3342	.0923*
Determinant related to the present use of e-commerce		
Use of e-commerce to support B-to-B transactions with suppliers[b]	3.2772	.0006****
Determinants related to business relationships		
Dependency on key suppliers	0.7141	.4743
Level of collaboration with key suppliers	3.6469	.0002****
Pressure exerted by key suppliers	3.7630	.0001****
Pressure exerted by technology experts	4.8590	<.001****
Pseudo R² [c]	44.23%	
Level of significance	0.0000***	

[a] p = level of one-tailed significance based on a chi-square distribution

* p < .10, ** p < .05, *** p < .01, **** p < .001

[b] Expressed as a natural logarithm in order to normalize the variables

[c] Pseudo $R^2 = 1 + (L_\omega/L_\Omega)^{2/n}$ where L_ω is the maximum likelihood function with all of the parameters ($\beta_0, \beta_1, ..., \beta_p$), L_Ω is the maximum likelihood function with only the parameter β_0, and n is the size of the sample

Table 4. Summary of the findings

Number	Hypotheses	Finding
1	A manufacturing firm's organizational readiness will be positively related to its intent to use Web-based IOISs to share inventory information with its key suppliers.	Confirmed
2	A manufacturing firm's current use of e-commerce to support B-to-B transactions with its suppliers will be positively related to its intent to use Web-based IOISs to share information with its key suppliers.	Confirmed
3	A manufacturing firm's dependency on its key suppliers will be positively related to its intent to use Web-based IOISs to share inventory information with those key suppliers.	Not supported
4	A manufacturing firm's level of collaboration with its key suppliers will be positively related to its intent to use Web-based IOISs to share inventory information with those key suppliers.	Confirmed
5	The pressure a manufacturing firm experiences from its key suppliers will be positively related to its intent to use Web-based IOISs to share inventory information with those key suppliers.	Confirmed
6	The pressure a manufacturing firm experiences from technology experts will be positively related to its intent to use Web-based IOISs to share inventory information with its key suppliers.	Confirmed
7	The size of a manufacturing firm will be positively related to its intent to use Web-based IOISs to share inventory information with its key suppliers.	Confirmed

ogy experts) are significant (positive values) in both groups whereas organizational readiness and dependency on key suppliers are not significant in either group. The comments in section 5.1 may also apply here to explain why dependency on key suppliers does not influence the dependent variable

Table 5. Relative influence of the determinants according to firm size (Tobit)

Variables	Bottom 1/3 ($n_1 = 173$)		Top 1/3 ($n_2 = 168$)		t-test[b]
	Estimate/ Standard error	p[a]	Estimate/ Standard error	p[a]	
Determinant related to technology					
Organizational readiness	0.2319	0.4083	0.6894	0.2453	0.3783
Determinant related to the present use of e-commerce					
Use of e-commerce to support B-to-B transactions with suppliers[c]	3.0151	0.0013***	0.4042	0.3431	0.0324**
Determinants related to business relationships					
dependency on key suppliers	1.0464	0.1477	0.6591	0.2549	0.1328
Level of collaboration with key suppliers	2.6356	0.0042***	2.1736	0.0149**	0.2566
Pressure exerted by key suppliers	2.5954	0.0047***	3.4333	0.0003****	0.3604
Pressure exerted by experts	2.6018	0.0047***	3.6788	0.0001****	0.3799
Pseudo R² [d]	40.51%		42.98%		
Level of significance	0.0000		0.0000		

[a] p = level of one-tailed significance based on a chi-square distribution

* $p < .10$, ** $p < .05$, *** $p < .01$, **** $p < .001$

[b] p = level of two-tailed significance based on a chi-square distribution

* $p < .10$, ** $p < .05$, *** $p < .01$, **** $p < .001$

[c] Expressed as a natural logarithm in order to normalize the variables

[d] Pseudo $R^2 = 1 + (L_\omega/L_\Omega)^{2/n}$ where L_ω is the maximum likelihood function with all of the parameters (β_0, β_1, ..., β_p), L_Ω is the maximum likelihood function with only the parameter β_0, and *n* is the size of the sample

in both groups. The insignificant relationship between organizational readiness and the dependent variable in both groups can partially be explained by the fact that smaller companies' flexibility and open-mindedness towards new ideas and larger firms' wealth and slack resources may have a stronger influence on the adoption of innovations than technical and financial resources.

One variable was significant only in the bottom group: present use of e-commerce to support B-to-B transactions with suppliers. This result was expected, as large firms are less subject to knowledge barriers than smaller firms (Julien, 1995; Thong, 2001).

The results presented in this section provide supporting evidence that firm size does moderate the impact of the present use of e-commerce to support B-to-B transactions with suppliers on

manufacturing firms' intent to use **Web-based IOISs** with their key suppliers.

COMPARING THE SUPPLIER AND CUSTOMER PERSPECTIVES

To reach our second research objectives, subsequent analyses were conducted to assess whether the **determinants** of manufacturing firms' intent to use **Web-based IOISs** to exchange inventory information with key partners will vary whether the intended **e-collaboration** is to support relationships with key suppliers or key customers. Data collected from the same study sample was thus used to assess the contribution and relative influence of the various determinants on manufacturing firms' intent to use Web-based IOISs to share

Table 6. Construct reliability (subsequent analyses)

	Number of items	Cronbach's α (α)
Level of collaboration with key suppliers	2	0.71

Table 7. Pearson correlation matrix (subsequent analyses)

Variables	(1)	(2)	(3)	(4)	(5)	(6)	(7)	(8)
(1) Firm size	1.000							
(2) Organizational readiness	−0.195****	1.000						
(3) Use of e-commerce to support B-to-B transactions with customers	0.066	-0.069	1.000					
(4) Dependency on key customers	-0.095**	0.029	-0.121***	1.000				
(5) Level of collaboration with key customers	0.077*	-0.159****	0.104**	0.103**	1.000			
(6) Pressure exerted by key customers	0.082*	-0.314****	0.239****	0.052	0.261****	1.000		
(7) Pressure exerted by technology experts	0.163****	−0.456****	0.146****	0.000	0.288****	0.342****	1.000	
(8) Intended use of Web-based IOISs to share inventory information with key customers	0.134***	-0.277****	0.233****	-0.013	0.262****	0.291****	0.413****	1.000

[a] p = level of two-tailed significance based on a chi-square distribution
* $p < .10$, ** $p < .05$, *** $p < .01$, **** $p < .001$

inventory information with key customers. Tables 6, 7, 8 and 9 summarize research findings.

Results of the Tobit regressions (Table 3 and Table 7) demonstrate that the **determinants** of manufacturing firms' intent to use Web-based IOISs to exchange inventory information with key customers are the same as the determinants of manufacturing firms' intent to use Web-based IOISs to exchange inventory information with key suppliers. Nonetheless, findings also show that: (1) the impact of *firm size*, *level of collaboration* and *pressure exerted by key partners* is higher in the supplier perspective than the customer perspective; (2) the positive influence of *organizational readiness* is stronger on the customer side, and (3) the impact of the *use of B-to-B transactions* and *pressure exerted by technology experts* is the same in both perspectives.

Results of the Tobit regressions to assess the relative influence of the **determinants** according to firm size (Table 5 and Table 8) also show that firm size moderates the impact of the present use of e-commerce to support B-to-B transactions with the criterion variable in both the supplier and customer perspective even though this moderation is a little stronger on the supplier side.

Overall, these results indicate that manufacturing firms evolving in tightly coupled supply

Table 8. Determinants of the intended use of IOISs to exchange inventory information with key customer (subsequent analyses)

Variables	Estimate/ Standard error	p^a
Control variables		
Firm size (number of employees)[b]	2.0337	00210**
Determinant related to technology		
Organizational readiness	1.8217	00343**
Determinant related to the present use of e-commerce		
Use of e-commerce to support B-to-B transactions with customers[b]	3.2615	00006****
Determinants related to business relationships		
Dependency on key customers	0.1246	04505
Level of collaboration with key customers	2.6139	00045***
Pressure exerted by key customers	2.9375	00017***
Pressure exerted by technology experts	5.2452	00001****
Pseudo $R^{2\,c}$	46.62%	
Level of significance	0.0000***	

[a] p = level of one-tailed significance based on a chi-square distribution

* p < .10, ** p < .05, *** p < .01, **** p < .001

[b] Expressed as a natural logarithm in order to normalize the variables

[c] Pseudo $R^2 = 1 + (L_\omega/L_\Omega)^{2/n}$ where L_ω is the maximum likelihood function with all of the parameters ($\beta_0, \beta_1, ..., \beta_p$), L_Ω is the maximum likelihood function with only the parameter β_0, and n is the size of the sample

chains from customers to suppliers will be prime candidates to use **Web-based IOISs** to share inventory information with their key partners both upstream and downstream the supply chain. It thus seems that manufacturing firms will approach the adoption of **Web-based IOISs** to share inventory information with key partners from a single business network **perspective**, and not from a disconnected supply and demand approach. These findings corroborate previous studies that have demonstrated that when firms use **e-collaboration** with particular suppliers or customers, it appears natural for them to extend this initiative to other partners in their value network (Léger et al., 2006).

CONCLUSION

This research makes four theoretical contributions to the field. First of all, this study is the first to measure the influence of various **determinants** on manufacturing firms' intent to use **Web-based IOISs** to share inventory information with their key suppliers. Second, it seems to indicate that 7 out of the 8 determinants of the proposed research model are highly influential in manufacturing firms' adoption of Web-based IOISs for this purpose. Third, since hypothesis 4 was confirmed and hypothesis 3 not supported, this study seems to show that **IOIS**-based methods adopted by neighboring partners to share inventory information are not promoted or enforced by a few large suppliers but rather by manufacturing firms' own desire to pool their resources with their upstream supply chain partners. Finally, this research is the first to demonstrate that manufacturing firms will

Table 9. Relative influence of the determinants according to firm size (subsequent analyses)

Variables	Bottom 1/3 (n_1 = 173)		Top 1/3 (n_2 = 168)		t-test[b]
	Estimate/ Standard error	p[a]	Estimate/ Standard error	p[a]	
Determinant related to technology					
Organizational readiness	1.2684	01024	0.5876	0.2784	0.6011
Determinant related to the present use of e-commerce					
Use of e-commerce to support B-to-B transactions with customers[c]	2.4576	0.0070***	0.3896	0.3486	0.0933*
Determinants related to business relationships					
dependency on key customers	0.0149	0.4941	1.1901	0.1170	0.3935
Level of collaboration with key customers	1.7646	0.0388**	1.7709	0.0384**	0.7320
Pressure exerted by key customers	1.5513	0.0605*	2.489	0.0016***	0.6281
Pressure exerted by experts	1.8091	0.0352**	3.9599	0.0001****	0.3249
Pseudo R²[d]	40.44%		43.32%		
Level of significance	0.0000		0.0000		

[a] p = level of one-tailed significance based on a chi-square distribution

* p < .10, ** p < .05, *** p < .01, **** p < .001

[b] p = level of two-tailed significance based on a chi-square distribution

* p < .10, ** p < .05, *** p < .01, **** p < .001

[c] Expressed as a natural logarithm in order to normalize the variables

[d] Pseudo $R^2 = 1 + (L_\omega/L_\Omega)^{2/n}$ where L_ω is the maximum likelihood function with all of the parameters ($\beta_0, \beta_1, ..., \beta_p$), L_Ω is the maximum likelihood function with only the parameter β_0, and n is the size of the sample

approach the adoption of Web-based IOISs to share inventory information with key partners from a single business network perspective, and not from a disconnected supply and demand approach.

Our findings also reveal to practitioners the circumstances in which manufacturing firms should adopt Web-based IOISs to share inventory information with their key suppliers/customers. Second, this study emphasizes the need for managers to consider the characteristics of their supply chain relationships, and not only technological factors, before they decide to adopt an interorganizational innovation such as a Web-based IOIS to support their collaborative processes with partners. Demonstrating the importance of technology experts in the assimilation of **Web-based IOISs** is another practical contribution this study makes, since we hope this finding will encourage firms

to call on technology experts while developing in-house competencies in order to avoid becoming dependent on external resources. Informing governments about the "trigger mechanisms" for innovative **e-collaboration** is an additional practical contribution of this study since these stimuli can guide public institutions in the development of public policies to encourage firms, particularly SMEs, not only to adopt Web-based IOISs but also to ensure that this innovation is smoothly integrated into their organizational processes and individual behaviors.

There are six main limitations on this study. The first is conceptual. We studied the intended (within the next 12 months) rather than current use of **Web-based IOISs** by manufacturing firms to share inventory information with their key suppliers. Nevertheless, as mentioned above, previous studies had used this approach to study radical technological innovations (Lefebvre et al., 1996). The second and third limitations are both conceptual and methodological. We did not consider the full set of possible **determinants** of manufacturing firms' intent to use Web-based IOISs to exchange inventory information with their key suppliers. And, after the pre-test, some items of the survey instrument were eliminated to shorten the questionnaire. These two limitations, nonetheless, allowed us to reach a larger number of firms, and thus to increase the external validity of our findings. The dilemma of choosing between internal validity and external validity is omnipresent in every research process. The fourth limitation is methodological. The research model was tested with data collected from a sample of firms derived from an up-to-date list of manufacturing firms obtained from a business that specializes in Internet-based direct marketing. Evidently, this limits the reach and the generalizability of our results to all Canadian manufacturing firms, let alone manufacturing firms in other countries. The fifth limitation is methodological. As we explained, the use of an electronic questionnaire biases the study. However, our sample size compares favorably with previous surveys carried out in the field of e-commerce. The last limitation is conceptual. As is quite common in the diffusion literature, this study makes the assumption that adopting Web-based IOISs to share inventory information with key suppliers is good for manufacturing firms. However, as we do not measure the costs and risks related to the adoption of Web-based IOISs by manufacturing firms to share inventory information with their key suppliers, we do not really evaluate the "goodness" of that decision. Some researchers have already demonstrated that **e-collaboration** offers would-be deceivers advantages that do not exist with more traditional means of collaboration (George & Marett, 2005).

Future research avenues are numerous. As a first step, the research model proposed in this study could be extended and further tested. For example, researchers could attempt to measure the influence of various **determinants** on manufacturing firms' current use of Web-based IOISs to share inventory information with their suppliers/customers. Researchers could also measure the influence of various determinants on manufacturing firms' use of Web-based IOISs to share other types of information (e.g., product and customer information) with their supply chain partners. Investigating the influence of the use of Web-based IOISs to share inventory information with business partners on various outcome variables (e.g., firm performance, supply chain performance, joint decision making) could also be interesting. Finally, researchers could examine whether the determinants of firms' use of Web-based IOISs to exchange information with their supply chain partners varies from one country to another and from one manufacturing sector to another.

In a second step, more research could be undertaken to further our knowledge of **IOISs**. For example, field studies could be performed to identify the critical capabilities and associated benefits of the various types of IOISs used to support the sharing of different types of information between collaborative partners. Case studies could also help researchers identify the critical success factors of various types of IOIS initiatives to support interorganizational collaboration. Finally, by drawing on contingency research in Organization Theory literature, and Venkatraman's (1989) perspectives of fit, researchers could demonstrate whether or not there is only one way for firms to manage their collaborative **IOIS** strategies.

REFERENCES

Anthony, T. (2000). Supply chain collaboration: Success in the new Internet economy . In Anthony, T. (Ed.), *Achieving supply chain excellence through technology* (*Vol. 2*). San Francisco, CA: Montgomery Research Inc.

Applegate, L. M., McFarlan, F. W., & McKenney, J. L. (1996). *Corporate information systems management: Text and cases* (4th ed.). Boston: Irwin McGraw-Hill.

Bagchi, P. K., & Skjoett-Larsen, T. (2002). Organizational integration in supply chains: a contingency approach. *Global Journal of Flexible Systems Management*, *3*, 1–10.

Barratt, M. (2003). Positioning the role of collaborative planning in grocery supply chains. *The International Journal of Logistics Management*, *14*, 53–66. doi:10.1108/09574090310806594

Barratt, M. (2004). Understanding the meaning of collaboration in the supply chain. *Supply Chain Management: An International Journal*, *9*, 30–42. doi:10.1108/13598540410517566

Batenburg, R., & Rutten, R. (2003). Managing innovation in regional supply networks: A Dutch case of knowledge industry clustering. *Supply Chain Management*, *8*, 263–270. doi:10.1108/13598540310484654

Becerra-Fernandez, I., Del Alto, M., & Stewart, H. (2005). A case study of web-based collaborative decision support at NASA. *International Journal of e-Collaboration*, *2*, 50–64.

Bensaou, M., & Venkatraman, N. (1996). Inter-organizational relationship and information technology: A conceptual synthesis and a research framework. *European Journal of Information Systems*, *5*, 84–91. doi:10.1057/ejis.1996.15

Boone, C. A., Craighead, C. W., & Hanna, J. B. (2007). Postponement: An evolving supply chain concept. *International Journal of Physical Distribution and Logistics Management*, *37*, 594–611. doi:10.1108/09600030710825676

Brynjolfsson, E., Renshaw, A. A., & van Alstyne, M. (1997). The matrix of change. *Sloan Management Review*, *38*, 22–40.

Burgelman, R. A., & Rosenbloom, R. S. (1989). Technology strategy: An evolutionary process perspective. *Research on Technological Innovation . Management and Policy*, *4*, 1–23.

Cash, J. I. Jr, & Konsynski, B. (1985). IS redraws competitive boundaries. *Harvard Business Review*, (March/April): 134–142.

Cassivi, L. (2006). Collaboration planning in a supply chain. *Supply Chain Management: An International Journal*, *11*, 249–258. doi:10.1108/13598540610662158

Cassivi, L., Lefebvre, E., Lefebvre, L. A., & Léger, P.-M. (2004). Supply chain planning and execution tools: E-collaboration and organizational performance. *International Journal of Logistics Management*, *15*, 91–110. doi:10.1108/09574090410700257

Cetinkaya, S., & Lee, C. Y. (2000). Stock replenishment and shipment scheduling for Vendor-Managed Inventory systems. *Management Science*, *46*, 217–232. doi:10.1287/mnsc.46.2.217.11923

Chang, H., & Chen, S. (2005). Assessing the readiness of Internet-based IOS and evaluating its impact on adoption. In *Proceedings of the 38th International Conference of Systems Sciences, Hawaii.*

Charles, S., Ivis, M., & Leduc, A. (2002). *Embracing e-business: Does size matter?* Ottawa, ON: Statistics Canada.

Chen, F. (1999). Decentralized supply chains subject to information delays. *Management Science*, *45*, 1076–1090. doi:10.1287/mnsc.45.8.1076

Chen, X. D., & Fu, L. S. (2001). IT adoption in manufacturing industries: Differences by company size and industrial sectors – The case of Chinese mechanical industries. *Technovation*, *21*, 649–660. doi:10.1016/S0166-4972(00)00078-X

Christensen, C. M., & Bower, J. L. (1996). Customer power, strategic investment, and the failure of leading firms. *Strategic Management Journal, 17*, 197–218. doi:10.1002/(SICI)1097-0266(199603)17:3<197::AID-SMJ804>3.0.CO;2-U

Christy, D. P., & Grout, J. R. (1994). Safeguarding supply chain relationships. *International Journal of Production Economics, 36*, 233–242. doi:10.1016/0925-5273(94)00024-7

Cross, R., Borgatti, S. P., & Parker, A. (2002). Making invisible work visible. *California Management Review, 44*, 25–46.

Crum, C., & Palmatier, G. E. (2004). Demand collaboration: What's holding us back? *Supply Chain Management Review, 8*, 54–61.

Damsgaard, J., & Lyytinen, K. (1996). Government strategies to promote the diffusion of electronic data interchange (EDI): What we know and what we don't know. *Information Infrastructure and Policy, 5*, 169–190.

Dillman, D. A. (2000). *Mail and Internet surveys: The tailored design method.* New York: John Wiley.

Disney, S. M., & Towill, D. R. (2003). Bullwhip reduction in supply chains: The impact of VMI. *International Journal of Operations & Production Management, 23*, 625–651. doi:10.1108/01443570310476654

Downs, G. W., & Mohr, L. B. (1976). Conceptual issues in the study of innovation. *Administrative Science Quarterly, 21*, 700–714. doi:10.2307/2391725

Elgarah, W., Falaleeva, N., Saunders, C. S., Ilie, V., Shim, J. T., & Courtney, J. F. (2005). Data exchange in interorganizational relationships: Review through multiple conceptual lenses. *The Data Base for Advances in Information Systems, 36*, 8–29.

Fawcett, S. E., & Magnan, G. M. (2004). Ten guiding principles for high-impact SCM. *Business Horizons, 47*, 67–74. doi:10.1016/j.bushor.2004.07.011

Fichman, R. G. (2000). The diffusion and assimilation of information technology innovations. In Zmud, R. W. (Ed.), *Framing the domains of IT management: Projecting the future… through the past.* Cincinnati, OH: Pinnaflex Educational Resources Inc.

Fichman, R. G., & Kemerer, C. F. (1993). Adoption of software engineering process innovations: The case of object orientation. *Sloan Management Review, 30*, 47–59.

Fisher, M. L. (1997). What is the right supply chain for your product? *Harvard Business Review, 75*, 105–116.

Foster, R. (1986). *Innovation: The attacker's advantage.* New York: Summit Books.

Frazier, G. L., & Rody, R. C. (1991). The use of influence strategies in interfirm relationships in industrial product channels. *Journal of Marketing, 55*, 52–69. doi:10.2307/1252203

Gadde, L.-E., Huemer, L., & Håkansson, H. (2003). Strategizing in industrial networks. *Industrial Marketing Management, 32*, 357–364. doi:10.1016/S0019-8501(03)00009-9

Ganesan, S. (1994). Determinants of long-term orientation in buyer-seller relationships. *Journal of Marketing, 58*, 1–19. doi:10.2307/1252265

Gatignon, H., & Robertson, T. S. (1989). Technology diffusion: An empirical test of competitive effects. *Journal of Marketing, 53*, 35–49. doi:10.2307/1251523

George, J. F., & Marett, K. (2005). The dark side of e-collaboration. *International Journal of e-Collaboration, 1*, 24–37.

Grandon, E. E., & Pearson, J. M. (2004). Electronic commerce adoption: An empirical study of small and medium US businesses. *Information & Management*, *42*, 197–216.

Greene, W. H. (1997). *Econometric analysis* (3rd ed.). Upper Saddle River, NJ: Prentice-Hall.

Grover, V. (1993). An empirical derived model for the adoption of customer-based interorganizational systems. *Decision Sciences*, *24*, 603–640. doi:10.1111/j.1540-5915.1993.tb01295.x

Hair, J. F., Anderson, R. E., Tatham, R. L., & Black, W. C. (1998). *Multivariate data analysis* (5th ed.). Englewood Cliffs, NJ: Prentice Hall.

Hart, P. J., & Saunders, C. S. (1997). Power and trust: Critical factors in the adoption and use of electronic data interchange. *Organization Science*, *8*, 23–42. doi:10.1287/orsc.8.1.23

Holmström, J., Framling, K., Kaipia, R., & Saranen, J. (2002). Collaborative planning, forecasting and replenishment: New solutions needed for mass collaboration. *Supply Chain Management: An International Journal*, *7*, 136–145. doi:10.1108/13598540210436595

Holweg, M., Disney, S., Holmström, J., & Smaros, J. (2005). Supply chain collaboration: Making sense of the strategy continuum. *European Management Journal*, *23*, 170–181. doi:10.1016/j.emj.2005.02.008

Iacovou, C. L., Benbasat, I., & Dexter, A. S. (1995). Electronic data interchange and small organizations: Adoption and impact of technology. *Management Information Systems Quarterly*, *19*, 465–486. doi:10.2307/249629

Jap, S., & Mohr, J. J. (2002). Leveraging Internet technologies in B2B relationships. *California Management Review*, *44*, 24–38.

Jap, S. D. (2001). "Pie sharing" in complex collaboration contexts. *JMR, Journal of Marketing Research*, *38*, 86–99. doi:10.1509/jmkr.38.1.86.18827

Johnson, E., & Whang, S. (2002). E-business and supply chain management: An overview and framework. *Production and Operations Management*, *11*, 413–423.

Johnson, F. P., Klassen, R. D., Leenders, M. R., & Fearon, H. E. (2002). Determinants of purchasing team usage in the supply chain. *Journal of Operations Management*, *20*, 77–89. doi:10.1016/S0272-6963(01)00078-X

Julien, P. A. (1995). New technologies and technological information in small businesses. *Journal of Business Venturing*, *10*, 459–475. doi:10.1016/0883-9026(95)00084-L

Kemppainen, K., & Vepsäläinen, A. (2003). Trends in industrial supply chains and networks. *International Journal of Physical Distribution & Logistics Management*, *33*, 709–719. doi:10.1108/09600030310502885

Kersten, W., Schroeder, K. A., & Schulte-Bisping, A. (2004). Internet-supported sourcing of complex materials. *Business Process Management Journal*, *10*, 101–114. doi:10.1108/14637150410518356

Kock, N. (2005). What is e-collaboration? *International Journal of e-Collaboration*, *1*, i–vii.

Konczak, L. J. (2001). The process of business/environmental collaborations: Partnering for sustainability. *Personnel Psychology*, *54*, 515–518.

Kumar, K., & van Dissel, H. G. (1996). Sustainable collaboration: Managing conflict and cooperation in inter-organizational systems. *Management Information Systems Quarterly*, *20*, 279–300. doi:10.2307/249657

Lambe, C. J., Spekman, R. E., & Hunt, S. D. (2002). Alliance competence, resources, and alliance success: Conceptualization, measurement, and initial test. *Academy of Marketing Science Journal*, *30*, 141–158. doi:10.1177/03079459994399

Lambert, D. M., Emmelhainz, M. A., & Gardner, J. T. (1999). Building successful partnerships. *Journal of Business Logistics*, *20*, 165–181.

Lee, H. L., Padmanabhan, V., & Whang, S. (1997). The bullwhip effect in supply chains. *Sloan Management Review*, *38*, 93–102.

Lefebvre, L., Lefebvre, E., Elia, E., & Boeck, H. (2005). Exploring B-to-B e-commerce adoption trajectories in manufacturing SMEs. *Technovation*, *25*, 1443–1456. doi:10.1016/j.technovation.2005.06.011

Lefebvre, L. A., Harvey, J., & Lefebvre, E. (1991). Technological experience and the technology adoption decisions in small manufacturing firms. *R & D Management*, *21*, 241–249. doi:10.1111/j.1467-9310.1991.tb00761.x

Lefebvre, L. A., & Lefebvre, E. (2002). E-commerce and virtual enterprises: Issues and challenges for transition economies. *Technovation*, *22*, 313–323. doi:10.1016/S0166-4972(01)00010-4

Lefebvre, L. A., Lefebvre, E., & Harvey, J. (1996). Intangible assets as determinants of advanced manufacturing technology adoption in SMEs. *IEEE Transactions on Engineering Management*, *43*, 307–322. doi:10.1109/17.511841

Léger, P.-M., Cassivi, L., Hadaya, P., & Caya, O. (2006). Safeguarding mechanisms in a supply chain network. *Industrial Management & Data Systems*, *106*, 759–777. doi:10.1108/02635570610671461

Lehman, J. A. (1985). Organizational size and information system sophistication. *Journal of Management Information Systems*, *2*, 78–86.

Lonsdale, C. (2001). Locked-in to supplier dominance: On the danger of asset specificity for the outsourcing decision. *Journal of Supply Chain Management*, *37*, 22–27. doi:10.1111/j.1745-493X.2001.tb00096.x

Malone, T. W., & Crowston, K. (1994). The interdisciplinary study of coordination. *ACM Computing Surveys*, *26*, 87–119. doi:10.1145/174666.174668

Mann, C., & Stewart, F. (2000). *Internet communication and qualitative research: A handbook for researching online*. London: Sage Publications.

Manrodt, K. B., & Fitzgerald, M. (2001). Seven propositions for successful collaboration. *Supply Chain Management Review*, *5*, 66–72.

Markus, M. L. (2005). Technology-shaping effects of e-collaboration technologies: Bugs and features. *International Journal of e-Collaboration*, *1*, 1–23.

Marquez, A. C., Bianchi, C., & Gupta, J. N. D. (2004). Operational and financial effectiveness of e-collaboration tools in supply chain integration. *European Journal of Operational Research*, *159*, 348–363. doi:10.1016/j.ejor.2003.08.020

McCarthy, T. M., & Golicic, S. L. (2002). Implementing collaborative forecasting to improve supply chain performance. *International Journal of Physical Distribution & Logistics Management*, *32*, 431–454. doi:10.1108/09600030210437960

McDonald, J. F., & Moffitt, R. A. (1980). The uses of Tobit analysis. *The Review of Economics and Statistics*, *62*, 318–321. doi:10.2307/1924766

Mehrtens, J., Cragg, P. B., & Mills, A. M. (2001). A model of Internet adoption by SMEs. *Information & Management*, *39*, 165–176. doi:10.1016/S0378-7206(01)00086-6

Min, S., Roath, A., Daugherty, P. J., Genchev, S. E., Chen, H., & Arndt, A. D. (2005). Supply chain collaboration: What's happening? *The International Journal of Logistic Management, 16*, 237–256. doi:10.1108/09574090510634539

Munkvold, B. E., & Zigurs, I. (2005). Integration of e-collaboration technologies: Research opportunities and challenges. *International Journal of e-Collaboration, 1*, 1–24.

Ovalle, O. R., & Marquez, A. C. (2003). The effectiveness of using e-collaboration tools in the supply chain: An assessment study with system dynamics. *Journal of Purchasing and Supply Management, 9*, 151–163. doi:10.1016/S1478-4092(03)00005-0

Palvia, P., Means, D., & Jackson, W. (1994). Determinants of computing in very small business. *Information & Management, 27*, 161–174. doi:10.1016/0378-7206(94)90044-2

Pant, S., Sethi, R., & Bhandari, M. (2003). Making sense of the e-supply chain landscape: An implementation framework. *International Journal of Information Management, 23*, 201–221.

Perks, H. (2000). Marketing information exchange mechanisms in collaborative new product development. *Industrial Marketing Management, 29*, 179–189. doi:10.1016/S0019-8501(99)00074-7

Pfeffer, J., & Salancik, G. (1978). *The external control of organizations: A resource dependence approach.* New York: Harper and Row Publishers.

Pinsonneault, A., & Caya, O. (2005). Virtual teams: What we know, what we don't know. *International Journal of e-Collaboration, 1*, 1–16.

Powell, W. W., White, D. R., Koput, K. W., & Owen-Smith, J. (2005). Network dynamics and field evolution: The growth of interorganizational collaboration in the life sciences. *American Journal of Sociology, 110*, 1132–1206. doi:10.1086/421508

Premkumar, G., & Ramamurthy, K. (1995). The role of interorganizational and organizational factors on the decision mode for adoption of interorganizational systems. *Decision Sciences, 26*, 303–336. doi:10.1111/j.1540-5915.1995.tb01431.x

Premkumar, G., Ramamurthy, K., & Crum, M. (1997). Determinants of EDI adoption in the transportation industry. *European Journal of Information Systems, 6*, 107–121. doi:10.1057/palgrave.ejis.3000260

Premkumar, G., & Roberts, M. (1999). Adoption of new information technologies in rural small businesses. *Omega: The International Journal of Management Science, 27*, 467–484. doi:10.1016/S0305-0483(98)00071-1

Prescott, M. B., & Conger, S. A. (1995). Information technology innovations: A classification by IT focus of impact and research approach. *Data Base Advanced, 36*, 20–41.

Raghunathan, S., & Yeh, A. B. (2001). Beyond EDI: Impact of continuous replenishment program (CRP) between a manufacturer and its retailers. *Information Systems Research, 12*, 406–419. doi:10.1287/isre.12.4.406.9701

Rao, S. S., Metts, G., & Mora Monge, C. A. (2003). Electronic commerce development in small and medium sized enterprises. *Business Process Management Journal, 9*, 11–32. doi:10.1108/14637150310461378

Raymond, L. (1985). Organizational characteristics and MIS success in the context of small business. *Management Information Systems Quarterly, 9*, 37–52. doi:10.2307/249272

Reekers, N., & Smithson, S. (1994). EDI in Germany and UK. *European Journal of Information Systems*, 3, 169–178. doi:10.1057/ejis.1994.18

Riggins, F. J., & Mukhopadyay, T. (1994). Interdependent benefits from interorganizational systems: Opportunities for business partner reengineering. *Journal of Management Information Systems*, 11, 37–57.

Rogers, E. M. (1995). *Diffusion of innovation* (4th ed.). New York: The Free Press.

Sabath, R. E., & Fontanella, J. (2002). The unfulfilled promise of supply chain collaboration. *Supply Chain Management Review*, 6, 24–29.

Saeed, K., Malhotra, M. K., & Grover, V. (2005). Examining the impact of inter-organizational systems on process efficiency and sourcing leverage in buyer-supplier dyads. *Decision Sciences*, 36, 365–396. doi:10.1111/j.1540-5414.2005.00077.x

Saunders, C. S., & Clark, S. (1992). EDI adoption and implementation: A focus on interorganizational linkages. *Information Resources Management Journal*, 5, 9–19.

Sawhney, M. (2002). Don't just relate – collaborate. *MIT Sloan Management Review*, 43, 96.

Sebastian, J. G.-D., & Lambert, D. M. (2003). Internet-enabled coordination in the supply chain. *Industrial Marketing Management*, 32, 251–263. doi:10.1016/S0019-8501(02)00269-9

Sheppard, B. H., & Sherman, D. M. (1998). The grammars of trust: A model and general implications. *Academy of Management Review*, 23, 422–437. doi:10.2307/259287

Simatupang, T. M., & Sridharan, R. (2004). A benchmarking scheme for supply chain collaboration. *Benchmarking: An International Journal*, 11, 9–30. doi:10.1108/14635770410520285

Simatupang, T. M., & Sridharan, R. (2005). The collaboration index: A measure for supply chain collaboration. *International Journal of Physical Distribution & Logistics Management*, 35, 44–62. doi:10.1108/09600030510577421

Singh, K., & Mitchell, W. (2005). Growth dynamics: The bidirectional relationship between inter-firm collaboration and business sales in entrant and incumbent alliances. *Strategic Management Journal*, 26, 497–522. doi:10.1002/smj.462

Stank, T. P., Daugherty, P. J., & Autry, C. W. (1999). Collaborative planning: Supporting automatic replenishment programs. *Supply Chain Management: An International Journal*, 4, 75–85. doi:10.1108/13598549910264752

Steermann, H. (2003). A practical look at CPFR: The Sears-Michelin experience. *Supply Chain Management Review*, 7, 46–53.

Stern, A. J., & Hicks, T. (2000). *The process of business/environmental collaborations: Partnering for sustainability*. Westport, CT: Quorum.

Swatman, P. M. C., & Swatman, P. A. (1991). Electronic data interchange: Organizational opportunity, not technical problem. In *Proceedings of the Second Australian Conference on Database and Information Systems, Australia*.

Thong, J. Y. L. (2001). Resource constraints and information system implementation in Singaporean small business. *Omega: The International Journal of Management Science*, 29, 143–156. doi:10.1016/S0305-0483(00)00035-9

Tobin, J. (1958). Estimation of relationships for limited dependent variables. *Econometrica*, 26, 26–36. doi:10.2307/1907382

Tornatzky, L. G., & Klein, R. J. (1982). Innovation characteristics and innovation adoption implementation: A meta-analysis of findings. *IEEE Transactions on Engineering Management*, 29, 28–45.

Towill, D. R., Naim, N. M., & Wikner, J. (1992). Industrial dynamics simulation models in the design of supply chains. *International Journal of Physical Distribution and Logistics Management, 22*, 3–13. doi:10.1108/09600039210016995

Tuominen, M. (2004). Channel collaboration and firm value proposition. *International Journal of Retail & Distribution Management, 32*, 178–189. doi:10.1108/09590550410528953

Venkatraman, N. (1989). The concept of fit in strategy research: Toward verbal and statistical correspondence. *Academy of Management: The Academy of Management Review, 14*, 423–444. doi:10.2307/258177

Verespej, M. (2005). Supply chain collaboration. Frontline Solutions. Retrieved August 2005 from http://www. frontlinetoday.com

Voluntary Interindustry Commerce Standards Association (VICS). (1998). *Collaborative, planning, forecasting and replenishment voluntary guidelines*. Lawrenceville, NJ: Uniform Code Council.

Wade, M., & Hulland, J. (2004). The resource-based view and information systems research: Review, extension, and suggestions for future research. *Management Information Systems Quarterly, 28*, 107–142.

Waller, M., Johnson, E., & Davis, T. (1999). Vendor-Managed Inventory in the supply chain. *Journal of Business Logistics, 20*, 183–203.

Weible, R., & Wallace, J. (1998). Cyber research: The impact of the Internet on data collection. *Marketing Research, 10*, 19–31.

Wikner, J., Towill, D. R., & Naim, M. (1991). Smoothing supply chain dynamics. *International Journal of Production Economics, 22*, 231–248. doi:10.1016/0925-5273(91)90099-F

Williamson, O. E. (1975). *Markets and hierarchies: Analysis and antitrust implications*. New York: The Free Press.

Zhu, K., & Kraemer, K. L. (2005). Post-adoption variation in usage and value of e-business by organizations: Cross-country evidence from the retail industry. *Information Systems Research, 16*, 61–84. doi:10.1287/isre.1050.0045

Zmud, R. W. (1982). Diffusion of modern software practices: Influence of centralization and formalization. *Management Science, 28*, 1421–1431. doi:10.1287/mnsc.28.12.1421

Zogut, B., & Zander, U. (1992). Knowledge of the firm, combinative capabilities and the replication of technology. *Organization Science, 3*, 383–397. doi:10.1287/orsc.3.3.383

APPENDIX A: SURVEY INSTRUMENT

Intent to use Web-Based IOISs	
	Not at all To a great extent
Within the next 12 months, to what extent will your organization use Web-based IOISs to share inventory information with key suppliers?	1 2 3 4 5 6 7

Organizational Readiness	
	Completely disagree Completely agree
Your organization has the necessary management support for the implementation and support of Web-based IOISs	1 2 3 4 5 6 7
Your organization has the necessary financial resources to implement and support Web-based IOISs	1 2 3 4 5 6 7
Staff members within your organization are willing to change the way they work to use Web-based IOISs	1 2 3 4 5 6 7
The IT staff within your organization is knowledgeable enough to implement and support Web-based IOISs	1 2 3 4 5 6 7
The non-IT staff within your organization is knowledgeable enough to use Web-based IOISs	1 2 3 4 5 6 7
Your organization has an adequate IT infrastructure to implement Web-based IOISs	1 2 3 4 5 6 7
There is an adequate level of integration between your existing information systems to benefit from the use of Web-based IOISs	1 2 3 4 5 6 7

Present use of E-Commerce	
What percentage of your procurement is carried out through e-commerce?	_____ %

Level of Dependency on Key Suppliers	
Do you have a limited number of key suppliers?	Yes ☐ No ☐
If yes, what percentage of your total purchases do they represent?	_____ %

Level of Collaboration with KEY SUPPLIERS	
	Not at all To a great extent
To what extent does your organization engage in collaborative planning with key suppliers?	1 2 3 4 5 6 7
To what extent does your organization take joint actions with key suppliers?	1 2 3 4 5 6 7

Pressure Exerted by Key Suppliers	
	Not at all To a great extent
To what extent do your key suppliers influence your organization's adoption of IOISs	1 2 3 4 5 6 7

Pressure Exerted by Technology Experts	
	Not at all To a great extent
To what extent do the following groups influence your organization's adoption of IOISs?	
Electronic intermediaries	1 2 3 4 5 6 7
Consultants and integrators	1 2 3 4 5 6 7
Technology vendors	1 2 3 4 5 6 7

Firm Size	
Number of full-time employees in your organization	_____

Chapter 11
The Influence of Supply Chain Collaboration on Process, Relational and Product Innovations

Luc Cassivi
Université du Québec à Montréal, Canada

Pierre Hadaya
Université du Québec à Montréal, Canada

Elisabeth Lefebvre
École Polytechnique de Montréal, Canada

Louis A. Lefebvre
École Polytechnique de Montréal, Canada

ABSTRACT

This chapter focuses on the impact of strategic and tactical collaborative actions as well as e-collaboration tools efficiency on process and relational innovations which in turn should influence product innovations. The results of this study show that tactical collaborative actions are more geared to lead firms to innovate rather than strategic actions. Findings also suggest that relational innovation has an effect on product innovation for the upstream perspective, whilst process innovation influences product innovation for the downstream perspective.

INTRODUCTION

In order to gain a competitive advantage and to ensure long term resilience for firms, many industries now rely on innovativeness. Thus, managers have to regularly make strategic decisions pertaining to

the identification of adequate resources and competencies (external partners or internal department/divisions) that can incite innovation. In such contexts, collaboration, which is carried out at different levels (strategic, tactical or operational activities), is inevitable and rapidly becomes a means to address cross-functional activities (De Luca and Atuahene-

DOI: 10.4018/978-1-61520-676-6.ch011

Gima, 2007). The impact of collaboration on product innovation (i.e. new product development) is relatively well covered in the literature (Nieto and Santamaria, 2007). It highlights some of the main challenges of carrying out real-time synchronous interactions between partners (Loch and Terwiesch., 2005) and emphasizes the changes in the relationships and in the inter-organizational processes that dictate the collaboration (Swink, 2006). The pressure to perform in a supply chain has also pushed firms to change management approaches and use information technologies and/ or electronic tools to support product innovation (Swink, 2006; Auramo et al., 2005).

In a supply chain context, process and relational innovations are also essentials parts of the innovation cycle. Indeed, without building a set of strong relationships and gearing processes to their respective partners, it would be difficult for a network of collaborative firms to create new products/services. Unfortunately, to date, literature on the subject is very scarce. In order to partially address this gap in the literature, the objective of this chapter is thus to analyze, from both the upstream and downstream perspectives, the impact of strategic and tactical collaborative actions as well as e-collaboration tools efficiency on process and relational innovations and determine if these two types of innovations generate product innovation. *Strategic collaborative actions* are defined here as actions that enable supply chain partners to gain a global understanding of the supply chain strategies to be undertaken by all parties involved in the chain, while *tactical collaborative actions* are oriented towards supporting supply chain activities (i.e. planning, forecasting, production, etc.) tied to specific products or families of products. *E-collaboration tools efficiency* measures how well e-collaboration tools are used to support a set a supply chain collaboration activities. Finally, *process*, *relational* and *product* innovations are defined here as changes, which require a significant degree of novelty for the firm, that can improve respectively the firm's products, its

business processes (or work methods) and its relationships with business partners.

The remainder of this chapter is structured as follows. The next section presents the relevant theoretical background related to collaboration, e-collaboration and innovation in a supply chain context. Section 3 presents the research model and hypotheses and section 4 describes the research methodology. Findings are then presented in section 5 and discussed in section 6.

THEORETICAL BACKGROUND

Supply Chain Collaboration

Collaboration in a supply chain context is defined by Anthony (2000) as two or more companies sharing the responsibility for exchanging common planning, management, execution, and performance measurement information. The fundamental rationale behind the concept is that by pooling their resources, collaborative supply chain partners can perform better than they could if each of the firms operated individually (Bowersox et al., 2005). Better demand planning, increased operational flexibility to cope with high demand uncertainties, inventory and cost and the development of new skills and competencies are just some of the expected benefits tied to SCM collaboration (Fisher, 1997; McCarthy and Golicic, 2002; Sabath and Fontanella, 2002).

The goal of collaboration is quite precise but the means to attain the objectives are sometimes not as clear. Some studies focus on the strategic activities required to ensure supply chain collaboration (Ogden et al., 2005) while others focus on more pragmatic or tactical actions undertaken by collaborating partners (Simatupang and Sridharan, 2005). Integration and information sharing between members, joint investments and outsourcing are some of the strategic collaborative actions identified (Sezen, 2008; Cassivi, 2006; Ogden et al., 2005). Kotabe et al. (2003) also recognizes the promising role of strategic actions and higher-level technology transfer in establishing strong collaboration within a supply chain.

Tactical supply chain actions have a direct impact on the product, service, or its underlying documents/information (e.g.: sales plan, inventory level). Simatupang and Sridharan (2005) identified a number of supply chain tactical actions relative to information sharing, decision synchronisation and incentive alignment. Daugherty et al. (2006) also pointed to several tactical supply chain actions used to formalize the structure of supply chain relationships.

Several strategic and tactical initiatives have emerged over the last few years to help structure the supply chain. For example, collaborative planning, forecasting and replenishment (CPFR), one of the more popular collaboration initiatives, proposes a sequential approach that proposes a set of key actions to be undertaken during the collaboration initiatives. An initiative of the Voluntary Interindustry Commerce Standards Association (VICS), CPFR defines both strategic (planning) and tactical (replenishment) activities that enable partners to build collaborative mechanisms to facilitate information exchange in supply chains. Another example is the Supply Chain Operations Reference (SCOR) model, initiated by the Supply Chain Council. This model, offering tactical solutions to supply chain challenges, is used by firms to help them describe their actual supply chain processes and design new optimized ones. It encompasses several concepts: standard supply chain process description, dependency networks, standard process performance indicators, supply chain management practices, and finally, supply chain software characteristics and functionalities.

Supply chain actions, whether they be strategic or tactical, should always be aligned with the business strategy of the firm and include upstream (i.e. order processing) and downstream (i.e. demand management, customer service) partnership directives (Sahay and Mohan, 2003) in order to

facilitate the integration of the supply chain and have a global view of supply chain needs (Lummus and Demarie, 2006).

Supply Chain E-Collaboration

Broadly, e-collaboration is defined as collaboration among a group of allies parties through the use of information and communication technologies (ICTs) to initiate and facilitate the sharing of resources especially across national boundaries in order to improve partners' profitability (Lee-Kelley et al., 2004). E-collaboration practices have significantly evolved over the last decade to improve joint collaborative processes and to increase information exchanges through workflows or other mechanisms (Meroño-Cerdán et al., 2008).

More precisely, in a supply chain context, e-collaboration facilitates coordination of various decisions and activities beyond transactions among supply chain partners, both suppliers and customers over the Internet (Lee and Whang, 2002) or other interorganizational information systems (IOISs) (Saeed et al., 2005; Byrne and Heavey, 2006). IOISs are computer networks that support information exchanges across organizational boundaries (Choudhury, 1997) and enable the electronic integration of business transactions and processes carried out by two or more organizations. Electronic data interchange (EDI) is probably the most commonly used technology allowing the exchange of information between business partners. However, in today's digital economy, more and more firms are turning to Web-based approaches to support their interorganizational activities.

E-collaboration encompasses activities such as information sharing and integration, decision sharing, process sharing, and resource sharing (Johnson and Whang, 2002). Some firms will focus on supplier relationships using more traditional (short-term execution) e-collaboration tools, while others will follow demand-driven strategies with their clients and use supply chain planning e-collaboration tools (Cassivi et al., 2004). According to Crespo Marquez et al. (2004), e-collaboration tools can be categorized into five groups: (1) Tools to "wire" the company, offering real time information about the material flow; (2) Tools to share documents in real time; (3) Tools to do collaborative forecasting; Tools to do collaborative planning; and (5) Tools to implement automated payments. These e-collaboration tools enable the trading partners to exchange business information related to supply chain operations in a structured, agile (in real time), stable and leveraged way (Bauknight, 2000; Rubiano Ovalle et al., 2003; Raghunathan, 1999).

E-collaboration can also be analyzed from different perspectives. Amongst those, the two favourites of e-collaboration researchers are task quality (customer perception) and task efficiency (time and cost) (Kock, 2005). Also, with the use of several complementary tools (e.g. forecasting, procurement, design) to exchange information, quality (of information exchanged) and efficiency (accuracy of information and ease of information exchange) are often merged to assess inter-organizational supply chain activities.

E-collaboration has been identified as a key enabler to supply chain integration (Crespo Marquez et al., 2004) and essential to facilitate the flow of information from any one source in the supply chain to all supply chain partners (Mentzer, 2001). Nonetheless, empirical research on the use and impact of information technologies (IT) in the supply chain are not always conclusive. Indeed, IT is often perceived as an important contributor to supply chain collaboration (Carr and Smeltzer, 2002; Grover et al., 2002), even though a handful of research initiatives have come to the opposite conclusion, that, in fact, IT does not improve supply chain activities (Jayaram and Vickery, 1998). This discrepancy in research findings might be explained by the state of the technology. That is, some studies do not analyze the efficiency of IT but rather focus on the presence (or not) of IT to support supply chain relationships. Chae

et al. (2005) push this thought further as they posit that "the effect of IT is not predetermined by its technological capabilities" but rather that supply chain collaboration is influenced by the interplay between IT and some characteristics of the relationship.

Innovation in a Supply Chain Context

In order to compete in global markets, partners collaborating in a supply chain environment are often urged to innovate (Mason-Jones and Towill, 1999). Such innovations, defined as "changes, which require a significant degree of novelty for the firm" (OECD/Eurostat, 1997: 9), can take different forms, namely, process, product and relational innovations. These innovations are, more often than not, driven by a member of the supply chain (customer or supplier). This section presents an overview of the characteristics of each of the three types of innovation.

Product Innovations

Product innovation, in terms of improved product quality and new product development, is often the main objective of collaborating in a supply chain (Kim and Oh, 2005). Being a popular research topic, numerous definitions of product innovation are found in the literature and each product innovation-related disciplines (e.g. engineering, marketing, management) has a different reading of the term (Garcia and Calantone, 2002). Product innovations can take different forms, from completely new innovative products, to upgrades, variations and extensions of existing products (Li and Atuahene-Gima, 2001).

Process Innovations

Lambert and Cooper (2000: 76) define a process as "a structure of activities designed for action with a focus on end customers and on the dynamic management of flows involving products, information, cash, knowledge, and ideas." A process innovation is a new or significantly improved process (method) that may require changes in equipment, personnel and sometimes resulting from the use or availability of new knowledge (OECD/Eurostat, 1997). Process innovation relates to the way products and services are developed, produced and distributed. In a supply chain, processes are often extended to external members and thus affect the business partners' involvement in supply chain activities.

Relational Innovations

Partnering in a supply chain requires opening up some boundaries of the firm. It also changes organizational dynamics. Relational improvements such as improved trust, loyalty and quality of a relationship are, therefore, often required for partners to carry out business in a network as if it was limited to a single firm. Relational innovations are critical elements in supply chain relationships and alliances (Moore, 1998; Zaheer et al., 1998) and are influenced by the way partners interact with each other (i.e. IT systems and structured collaboration methods adopted and implemented).

In practice, relational innovations, intangible in nature, are not always perceived in the same way by all supply chain partners. Some firms will pay little attention to it by developing tangible means of collaboration (e.g. contracts, IT infrastructure), while others will rely mainly on soft characteristics (e.g. trust, loyalty) for the development of supply chain relationships.

RESEARCH FRAMEWORK

The research model (see figure 1) proposes, for both the upstream and downstream perspectives of the supply chain, a set of specific relationships between strategic and tactical collaborative actions as well as e-collaboration tools efficiency and three types of innovations, namely process, relational and product innovation. This framework is aligned with Chae et al.'s (2005) results, which suggest that formative contexts and collaborative actions are tightly linked to IT-based inter-organizational linkage efforts, and that inter-organizational relationships (trust, commitment, etc.) are essential in the performance of supply chain collaboration.

Figure 1. Research framework

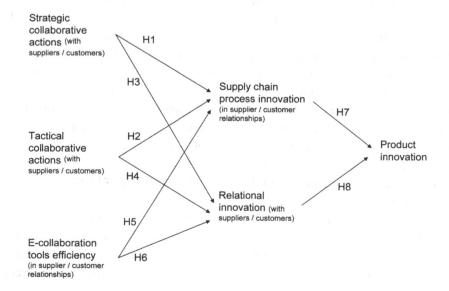

Strategic and Tactical Collaborative Actions, Supply Chain Process Innovation and Relational Innovation

The literature on the role of collaboration in a supply chain relationship is abundant (Gulati, 1998; Spekman et al., 1998). Corbett et al. (1999) state that supply chain cooperation and the adoption of collaborative planning actions agreed upon by the partners should improve the strength of the relationship. Indeed, strategic and tactical collaborative actions (i.e., the sharing of business objectives and values, joint planning) should have a positive impact on trust (Zaheer et al., 1998) and increase the loyalty towards one another (Zineldin, 1998). Strategic and tactical collaborative actions should also encourage the supply partners to improve the inter-organizational processes supporting the relationship (Subramani, 2004; VICS-CPFR, 1998).

Consequently, it is hypothesized that:

H1: Strategic collaborative actions with suppliers/customers will positively influence a firm's supply chain process innovation.

H2: Tactical collaborative actions with suppliers/customers will positively influence a firm's supply chain process innovation.

H3: Strategic collaborative actions with suppliers/customers will positively influence a firm's relational innovation.

H4: Tactical collaborative actions with suppliers/customers will positively influence a firm's relational innovation.

E-Collaboration Tools Efficiency, Supply Chain Process Innovation and Relational Innovation

The effective use of IT is evidently important for the realization of supply chain activities (information, material and monetary exchanges) between partners (Chae et al., 2005; Byrne and Heavey, 2006). Nonetheless, the use of e-collaboration tools and other interorganizational information systems often transforms the way firms do business with their partners (Weston, 2001). Key to enable interorganizational integration (Crespo Marquez et al., 2004), the adoption and implementation of e-collaboration tools will strengthen the relationship between the partners involved (Cagliano et al., 2005) and often necessitates the elaboration of new or revised inter-organisational processes (Auramo et al., 2002; Cagliano et al., 2005; Kock, 2002).

Hence, we can posit the next two hypotheses:

H5: The efficient use of e-collaboration tools with suppliers/customers will positively influence a firm's supply chain process innovation.

H6: The efficient use of e-collaboration tools with suppliers/customers will positively influence a firm's relational innovation with its suppliers/customers.

Supply Chain Process Innovation and Product Innovation

Brown and Eisenhardt (1995) are amongst the many to have observed the impact of organizational structures, processes, and relationships on the development of products and services. More specifically, Utterback and Abernathy (1975) are amid the firsts to have examined the role of process innovations in the adoption of new technologies. Process innovation's tight link with product innovation makes it more difficult to define, as it may also be tricky to differentiate between the two types of innovations (Bhoovaraghavan et al., 1996). The literature is however very clear on the positive impact of product and process innovation on each other. In this research, we are interested on the impact of supply chain processes on product innovation; hence, we focus on analyzing if supply chain partners that decide to work together in an innovative way will lead to the development of new products. Consequently, it is hypothesized that:

H7: A firm's supply chain process innovation when dealing with its suppliers/customers will positively influence its product innovation.

Relational Innovation and Product Innovation

Much work has been done on the inter-organizational relationships during product development (Dyer, 1997; Sobrero and Roberts, 2001). In a supply chain, the strength of the relationship between partners is key to the success of the network. Any variation in the trust and loyalty towards a partner should affect the other elements of the supply chain relationship, one of them being the development of new products. For instance, a firm that continues to have positive experiences with a partner will, on the long run, understand the other's business objectives and distinct competencies, which may lead to joint development projects. These arguments lead to the eight and final hypothesis:

H8: A firm's relational innovation when dealing with its suppliers/customers will positively influence its product innovation.

METHODOLOGY

This section presents the supply chain network analyzed during this research initiative along with the data collection and analysis methods. The variables used in the research model are also presented.

The Selected Network

For this research, the telecommunications equipment industry was targeted due to its important level of supply chain collaboration. This industry includes all the companies involved in the manufacturing of the equipment and software that perform the functions of information processing and communication, including transmission and display.

The supply network selected was that of a large Canadian OEM (system integrator). This supply network has several layers. The upper layer comprises the network operators (i.e. the final users of the optical products) while the lower layers comprise the OEM, the first-tier suppliers, the second-tier suppliers and other upstream suppliers. Most first-tier suppliers are assemblers while second-tier suppliers are generally sub-assemblers. The OEM relies on assemblers (also called electronic manufacturing specialists) because of their ability to produce more flexibly and at a low cost. Sub-assemblers, which are sometimes subsidiaries of large multinationals, focus on component manufacturing and subsystem assembly.

Data Collection Strategy

In order to get a thorough understanding of the supply chain activities carried out in the telecommunications equipment industry, interviews were first conducted with supply chain managers from first-tier and second-tier suppliers in the selected supply chain network of firms within the industry (i.e., integrators, assemblers, sub-assemblers). The information gathered during these interviews along with the findings of a literature review in the fields of operations, information systems and buyer-seller relationships, allowed us to develop or adapt the research constructs.

Once completed, the questionnaire was validated by members of the OEM's Supply Management, Supplier Collaboration, as well as three of the OEM's strategic first-tier suppliers. Based on subjects' remarks and suggestions, some minor adjustments were then made to the questionnaire.

Finally, the electronic questionnaire was distributed via e-mail to supply chain managers at 130 first-tier suppliers identified by the OEM; 76% of the companies are based in the United States, 12% in Canada and 12% in the rest of the world. The request to answer the electronic questionnaire was sent out twice over a two-month period. A total of 53 companies participated in the Web survey, for a 40.8% response rate. This high response rate can be explained by the fact that this study was a joint initiative between the OEM and academia and thus one of the objectives of the research was to improve the OEM's supply chain. Hence, to maximize the participation of its suppliers to the Web survey, the request to answer the questionnaire was sent directly by the OEM, while the university had the responsibility to gather and analyse the data, guaranteeing the anonymity of the respondents.

The possibility of nonresponse bias was also investigated through a series of t-tests comparing the responses from the first and second electronic mailing. The t-tests yielded no statistically significant differences between the two groups, suggesting that nonresponse bias was not an area of concern in this study (Armstrong and Overton, 1977).

Table 1. Items for research constructs

Constructs	Items	Sources
Strategic collaborative actions	Develop an agreed-on partnership strategy	VICS-CPFR (1998)
	Share information about periodic business goals and objectives	
	Compare business plans and agree on a joint business plan	
Tactical collaborative actions	Discuss roles, objectives, and goals for specific categories of items	VICS-CPFR (1998)
	Identify and develop the appropriate pricing actions	
	Develop individual plans based on previously shared information between partners	
E-collaboration tools efficiency	*Efficiency of IS for:*	Field research observations
	direct procurement	
	Replenishment	
	Shortages	
	delivery and tracking	
	design (CAD)	
	Forecasting	
	capacity planning	
	business strategy	
Supply chain process innovation	Generate new design processes	Hawkins and Verhoest (2002), OECD (2000)
	Gear processes to partner requirements	
Relational innovation	Build or improve trust with customers and suppliers	Hawkins and Verhoest (2002), OECD (2000), Moore, (1998), Zaheer et al. (1998)
	Enrich quality of relations	
	Improve loyalty	
Product innovation	Product quality	Beamon (1999), Shin et al. (2000), Hawkins and Verhoest (2002)
	Product variety and product mix	
	New product introductions	

Research Variables

Conceptual definitions and different sources were used to develop the constructs of the research model and the questionnaire items (see table 1). A seven-point Likert scale (where 1 = disagree and 7 = agree, or 1 = significant decrease and 7 = significant increase) was used to measure each item.

The theoretical justifications of *Strategic* and *Tactical collaborative actions* are mainly based on the Voluntary Interindustry Commerce Standards (VICS-CPFR, 1998). When compared to other collaboration methods or frameworks, the CPFR method is very detailed in terms of actions to be taken in planning collaboration.

The first construct, *Strategic collaborative actions*, is comprised of three items: 1) develop an agreed-upon partnership strategy, 2) facilitate strategic information sharing, and 3) compare business plans for the creation of a joint supply chain plan. These three joint collaborative actions are a first step toward more tactical collaborative actions, which make up the second construct.

The second construct, Tactical collaborative actions, also is oriented towards products or families of products rather than the whole business (as is the case for strategic collaborative actions). It is comprised of the following three items: 1) the roles and objectives of specific categories of products, 2) the planning of appropriate pricing,

and 3) the development of individual plans based on previously shared information.

For the third construct, *E-collaboration tools efficiency*, visits at the OEM's and three suppliers' manufacturing sites enabled us to identify how e-collaboration tools were used to support supply chain collaboration between the partners. Overall, e-collaboration tools were used to support eight supply chain activities: direct procurement, replenishment, shortages, delivery and tracking, design, forecasting, capacity planning and business strategy.

The fourth construct, *Supply chain process innovation*, regroups two items: 1) generation of new processes, and 2) adjustment of processes to customer requirements. The fifth and sixth constructs are also each comprised of three items. 1) Trust, 2) quality of relations and 3) loyalty make up *Relational innovation*, while *Product innovation* is comprised of 1) product quality, 2) product variety & mix, and 3) new product introductions.

As presented in Table 2, the reliability of the constructs is satisfactory with Cronbach alpha coefficients ranging from 0.67 to 0.97 (Van de Ven and Ferry, 1980).

Descriptive Statistics

Table 3 shows that first-tier suppliers were very active in conducting strategic and collaborative

Table 2. Cronbach alphas for research constructs

Constructs	Number of items	Cronbach alpha *When dealing with suppliers*	Cronbach alpha *When dealing with customers*
Strategic collaborative actions	3	.885	.798
Tactical collaborative actions	3	.719	.700
E-collaboration tools efficiency	8	.918	.900
Supply chain process innovation	2	.905	.668
Relational innovation	3	.972	.916
Product innovation	3	.760	

actions with their suppliers. They also seemed to efficiently use e-collaboration tools when dealing with their upstream partners. Table 3 also shows that first-tier suppliers are very innovative at the process, relational and product levels.

Descriptive statistics also show that first-tier suppliers are also active in conducting strategic and collaborative actions with their customers. They also seem to properly use e-collaboration tools with the latter. However, the mean of these 3 variables is lower on the downstream side. Also, the mean of the supply chain process innovation

construct is higher on the downstream side, were as the means of the relational innovation and product innovation are very similar on the downstream side than on the upstream side.

Finally, the correlation matrix shows that all but two correlations are at acceptable levels (see Table 3). The high correlation between strategic collaborative actions and tactical collaborative actions on both the upstream and downstream side of the network was expected since strategic actions often lead to specific actions on critical products/services for a company or supply chain

Table 3. Means, standard deviation and the Pearson correlation matrix

Constructs	Mean	Standard deviation	Pearson correlation matrix					
			Strategic collaborative actions	Tactical collaborative actions	E-collaboration tools efficiency	Supply chain process innovation	Relational innovation	Product innovation
Supplier perspective								
Strategic collaborative actions	5,14	1,26	1.00					
Tactical collaborative actions	5,46	0,95	0,86	1.00				
E-collaboration tools efficiency	5,12	1,14	0,58	0,60	1.00			
Supply chain process innovation	5,24	1,27	0,42	0,62	0,48	1.00		
Relational innovation	5,63	1,07	0,63	0,71	0,64	0,57	1.00	
Product innovation	4,97	0,87	0,39	0,44	0,50	0,41	0,40	1.00
Customer perspective								
Strategic collaborative actions	4,83	1,29	1.00					
Tactical collaborative actions	5,40	1,03	0,77	1.00				
E-collaboration tools efficiency	4,85	1,26	0,37	0,41	1.00			
Supply chain process innovation	5,43	1,21	0,18	0,41	0,41	1.00		
Relational innovation	5,61	1,07	0,61	0,64	0,40	0,44	1.00	
Product innovation	4,97	0,87	0,28	0,32	0,22	0,48	0,26	1.00

partners. However, multiple regressions indicated that multicollinearity between the three independent variables was not a concern as the highest Variance Inflation Factor (VIF) was lower than Hair et al.'s (1998) acceptable threshold.

Analysis Method

In order to reach our research objective, structural equation modeling (using the LISREL program) was used to test our research model on both the upstream and downstream sides of the network.

Due to our small sample size, LISREL's (version 8.12a) path analysis model for directly observed variables (i.e. submodel 2) was used to test the research hypotheses. This multivariate regression technique considers the model as a system of equations and estimates all the structural coefficients directly (Jöreskog and Sorbom, 2001). Thus, each variable comprised in the LISREL model was equal to the mean of the construct's items.

RESULTS

The structural model is presented for both upstream and downstream perspectives in which the main results are displayed and the hypotheses tested.

The Supplier's Perspective: Upstream Collaboration

Figure 2 presents the research findings for the upstream perspective (supplier relationships) of supply chain collaboration. Results indicate that the structural model provides a reasonable fit with the observed data. The normed chi-square (the ratio of chi-square to the degrees of freedom) is within the acceptable range of 1 and 3 (Gefen et al., 2000). The other global fit index, RMSEA (Root Mean Square Error of Approximation), was below Mc-Cloy et al.'s (1994) proposed threshold of 0.1. The Comparative Fit Index (CFI) and Tucker-Lewis Index (TLI) were also above their criterion levels of 0.9 (Bentler, 1990; Timothy et al., 1994). As

Figure 2. Impact of upstream collaboration on process, relational and product innovations

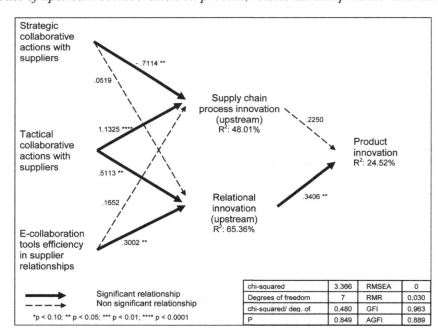

for the Root Mean Square Residual (RMR), it is near the zero mark (Hair et al., 1998).

Results shows that upstream strategic and tactical collaborative actions, along with e-collaboration tools efficiency, explain respectively 48% and 65% of the variance in supply chain process innovation and relational innovation. It is no surprise to see that tactical collaborative actions have a more significant impact on process (1.1325 ****) and relational innovation (0.5113**). These collaborative actions are precise and may guide future operational activities. Hypotheses 2 and 4 for the upstream perspective are hence supported. At a higher level, strategic collaborative actions do not have any impact on relational innovation with the supplier, and moreover, have a negative impact on supply chain process innovation (-0.7114 **). This last result seems to suggest that improving processes in a supplier relationship should be based on a bottom-up approach (from the shop floor up) rather than top-down (from upper management down to the operations). Consequently, hypotheses 1 and 3 (upstream) are not supported. Hypothesis 6 is also supported as the efficiency of e-collaboration tool also seems to positively impact relational innovation (0.3002 **), which highlights the positive influence of having useful and efficient tools to support supply chain activities. However, the influence of the efficient use of collaboration tools on product innovation is not significant (H5 is rejected). The upstream perspective might explain the results of the hypotheses 5 and 6. E-collaboration tools will certainly help your suppliers in their supply chain activities, by first giving them more information on the firm's needs and therefore having them develop and suggest new products to its partners (H5). On the other hand, the (client) firm will benefit from the e-collaboration tools and new innovative products developed by its suppliers, but not necessarily by creating its own product innovation, but rather from having better relationships with this supplier (H6).

Process and relational innovations explain 24.5% of the variance in product innovation, which is an important result. From the suppliers perspective, relational innovation has a significant impact on product innovation (.3406 **) but surprisingly process innovation does not. Hence, these findings (H7 supported, and H8 rejected for the upstream perspective) suggest that it is more important to develop trust and loyalty with suppliers than to develop means or processes that enable supply chain collaboration (It may be all about knowing who you're going to do business with rather than knowing how you are going to do it!)

The Customer's Perspective: Downstream Collaboration

Turning to the customer's perspective, the same model in figure 2 is now tested in figure 3 for the downstream perspective. Results also indicate that from the customer perspective the structural model provides a reasonable fit with the observed data.

Results show that strategic and tactical collaborative actions, along with e-collaboration tools efficiency, explain respectively 30% and 49% of the variance in supply chain process and relational innovation. Tactical collaborative actions and the efficiency of e-collaboration tools positively impact both types of innovations (hypotheses H2, H4, H5 and H6 all supported) while strategic collaborative actions negatively impact process innovation (H1 and H3 rejected). These results are aligned to those obtained for the upstream perspective, but most of the relationships tested in figure 3 are slightly weaker. The field study shed some light on the relationships between the OEM and the suppliers. One of the suppliers explained that the collaborative actions applied with the OEM were mainly strategic and not specific enough to help them in day-to-day supply chain activities. Another supplier, who also had collaborated in the development of the supply chain e-collaboration

Figure 3. Impact of downstream collaboration on process, relational and product innovations

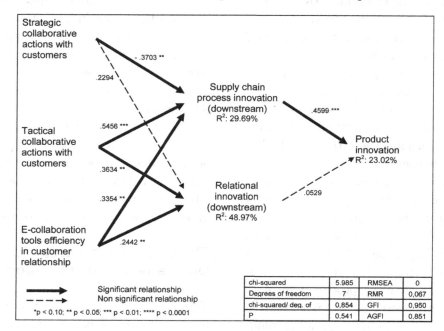

tools and established a strong relationship with the same OEM, had nailed down several joint tactical actions with the OEM that helped them streamline the supply chain.

In an industry that strives on demand-driven strategies (a pull approach in operations management), it was surprising to see that the variance of product innovation was less for the demand side (23%) than the supply side (24.5%). The literature in this field indicates that collaboration with customers increases the information exchanged and improves market knowledge (Samaddar et al., 2006), which leads to better results in satisfying the market with new and improved products and services. Contrary to the supplier relationship model, relational innovation (when dealing with a customer) does not positively impact on product innovation (H8 is rejected for the downstream perspective). This result may be explained by the fact that a customer may never be trusted as he might switch to a competitor at any point in time. However, as predicted (H7 supported), the supply chain process (how you collaborate) seems

to be positively impacting product innovation with customers (0.4599 ***). This can be explained by the significantly positive impact of e-collaboration efficiency on process innovation (0.3354 **) which was not present in the supplier relationship model (figure 2). This is in line with Auramo et al.'s (2005) research findings, which state that to gain strategic benefits in supply chain activities, IT has to be coupled with process redesign.

CONCLUSION

The strengths of this research mainly arise from the research design and two conceptual aspects. The research design is original as it allows for any of the 53 firms to assess some characteristics of both their downstream and upstream collaboration. This study also differs from previous works by introducing the concept of relational innovation in addition to the well investigated concepts of process and product innovations. Furthermore, contrary to past research in the field, our model involves the level of the efficiency of e-collaboration tools rather than to simply measure the level of use of these tools. The research presents some limitations. Indeed, the results should be interpreted with some caution as the sample size is rather small (n=53 firms) and the industry context is specific to the telecommunications equipment sector.

Results of this study strongly suggest that a firm involved in a supply chain must "take care" of both its upstream and downstream relationships in order to build a seamless chain that aims to provide information visibility to all partners. Innovation is always an important factor in the strategies and management activities of firms, and its development increasingly involves partners outside of the firm. Product innovativeness is usually one of the main objectives of firms, but its reach is clearly linked to process innovation and also relationship improvements. In a supply chain, these innovations are being developed by a network of firms, which requires collaboration between partners. The results of this study show that pragmatic and tactical collaborative actions are more geared to lead firms to innovate, both with its suppliers and its customers. A strategic approach to collaboration does not seem to improve innovations; it even reduces them, from both supplier and customer perspectives. This result is in line with previous research in the strategy literature, which emphasises how difficult it is for firms to perform after an alliance/joint venture was undertaken by top management. Innovation often stems from the interactions of partners' operations (e.g., R&D, manufacturing), sometimes without even an agreement being signed.

A noteworthy result when comparing the upstream and downstream perspectives concerns the influence of process innovation and relational innovation on product innovativeness. Performance, in terms of product innovation, is mainly enhanced by an improved supplier relationship. This might be explained by the suppliers' relatively small size within the industry. Assemblers and sub-assemblers are often smaller than their

customers and will rely on good relationships rather than on formal procedures that could impede their flexibility to adapt and respond quickly to demands. In that sense, informal information is much more important than formal procedures to conduct supply chain collaboration. On the other hand, customers, usually large telecommunication firms, are looking for standard formal procedures in order to manage their supply chain. Hence, process innovation is usually well documented in such firms and becomes an integral part of product innovation.

The study points to the fact that supply chain collaboration needs "down to earth" tactical actions in order to foster innovations in a coherent and coercive manner.

REFERENCES

Armstrong, J. S., & Overton, T. S. (1997). Estimating nonresponse bias in mail surveys. *JMR, Journal of Marketing Research, 14*, 396–402. doi:10.2307/3150783

Auramo, J., Aminoff, A., & Punakivi, M. (2002). Research agenda for e-business logistics based on professional opinions. *International Journal of Physical Distribution and Logistics Management, 32*(7), 513–531. doi:10.1108/09600030210442568

Auramo, J., Kauremaa, J., & Tanskanen, K. (2005). Benefits of IT in supply chain management: an explorative study of progressive companies. *International Journal of Physical Distribution & Logistics Management, 35*(2), 82–100. doi:10.1108/09600030510590282

Bauknight, D. N. (2000). The supply chain future in the e-economy. *Supply Chain Management Review, 4*(1), 28–35.

Bentler, P. M. (1990). Comparative fit indexes in structural models. *Psychological Bulletin, 107*(3), 238–246. doi:10.1037/0033-2909.107.2.238

Bhoovaraghavan, S., Vasudevan, A., & Chandran, R. (1996). Resolving the process vs. product innovation dilemma: A consumer choice theoretic approach. *Management Science, 42*(2), 232–246. doi:10.1287/mnsc.42.2.232

Bowersox, D. J., Closs, D. J., & Drayer, R. W. (2005). The digital transformation: Technology and beyond. *Supply Chain Management Review, 9*(1), 22–29.

Brown, S. L., & Eisenhardt, K. M. (1995). Product development: Past research, present findings, and future directions. *Academy of Management Review, 20*(2), 343–378. doi:10.2307/258850

Byrne, P. J., & Heavey, C. (2006). The impact of information sharing and forecasting in capacitated industrial supply chains: A case study. *International Journal of Production Economics, 103*, 420–437. doi:10.1016/j.ijpe.2005.10.007

Cagliano, R., Caniato, F., & Spina, G. (2003). E-business strategy, how companies are shaping their supply chain through the Internet. *International Journal of Operations & Production Management, 23*(10), 1142–1162. doi:10.1108/01443570310496607

Carr, A. S., & Smeltzer, L. R. (2002). The relationship between information technology use and buyer-supplier relationships: An exploratory analysis of the buying firm's perspective. *IEEE Transactions on Engineering Management, 49*(3), 293–304. doi:10.1109/TEM.2002.803389

Cassivi, L. (2006). Collaboration planning in an electronic supply chain . *International Journal of Supply Chain Management, 11*(3), 249–258. doi:10.1108/13598540610662158

Cassivi, L., Lefebvre, E., Lefebvre, L. A., & Leger, P. M. (2004). The impact of e-collaboration tools on firms' performance. *International Journal of Logistics Management, 15*(1), 91–110. doi:10.1108/09574090410700257

Chae, B., Yen, H. R., & Sheu, C. (2005). Information technology and supply chain collaboration: Moderating effects of existing relationships between partners. *IEEE Transactions on Engineering Management, 52*(4), 440–448. doi:10.1109/TEM.2005.856570

Choudhury, V. (1997). Strategic choices in the development of interorganizational information systems. *Information Systems Research, 8*(1), 1–24. doi:10.1287/isre.8.1.1

Corbett, C. J., Blackburn, J. D., & Van Wassenhove, L. N. (1999). Partnerships to improve supply chains. *Sloan Management Review, 40*(4), 71–82.

Crespo Marquez, A., Bianchi, C., & Gupta, J. D. D. (2004). Operational and financial effectiveness of e-collaboration tools in supply chain integration. *European Journal of Operational Research, 159*, 348–363. doi:10.1016/j.ejor.2003.08.020

Daugherty, P. J., Richey, R. G., Roath, A. S., Min, S., Chen, H., Arndt, A. D., & Genchev, S. E. (2006). Is collaboration paying off for firms? *Business Horizons, 49*(1), 61–70. doi:10.1016/j.bushor.2005.06.002

De Luca, L., & Atuahene-Gima, K. (2007). Market knowledge dimensions and cross-functional collaboration: Examining the different routes to product innovation performance. *Journal of Marketing, 71*, 95–112. doi:10.1509/jmkg.71.1.95

Dyer, J. H. (1997). Effective interfirm collaboration: How firms minimize transaction costs and maximize transaction value. *Strategic Management Journal, 18*(7), 535–556. doi:10.1002/(SICI)1097-0266(199708)18:7<535::AID-SMJ885>3.0.CO;2-Z

Fisher, M. L. (1997). What is the right supply chain for your product? *Harvard Business Review, 75*, 105–116.

Garcia, R., & Calantone, R. (2002). A critical look at technological innovation typology and innovativeness terminology: A literature review. *Journal of Product Innovation Management*, *19*(2), 110–132. doi:10.1016/S0737-6782(01)00132-1

Gefen, D., Straub, D., & Boudreau, M. (2000). Structural equation modeling and regression guidelines for research practice. *Communications of the AIS*, *4*(7), 41–79.

Grover, V., Teng, J., & Fiedler, K. (2002). Investigating the role of information technology in building buyer-supplier relationships. *Journal of the Association for Information Systems*, *3*, 217–245.

Gulati, R. (1998). Alliances and networks. *Strategic Management Journal*, *19*(4), 293–317. doi:10.1002/(SICI)1097-0266(199804)19:4<293::AID-SMJ982>3.0.CO;2-M

Hair, J. F., Anderson, R. E., Tatham, R. L., & Black, W. C. (1998). *Multivariate Data Analysis* (5th ed.). NJ: Prentice Hall.

Hawkins, R., & Verhoest, P. (2002). A transaction structure approach to assessing the dynamics and impacts of business-to-business electronic commerce. *Journal of Computer-Mediated Communication*, *7*(3).

Jayaram, J., & Vickery, S. K. (1998). Supply-based strategies, human resource initiatives, procurement leadtime, and firm performance. *International Journal of Purchasing and Material Management*, *34*(1), 12–23.

Johnson, M. E., & Whang, S. (2002). E-business and supply chain management: An overview and framework. *Production and Operations Management*, *11*(4), 412–423.

Jöreskog, K. G., & Sorbom, D. (2001). *LISREL 8: User's Reference Guide*. Lincolnwood, IL: Scientific Software Inc.

Kim, B., & Oh, H. (2005). The impact of decision-making sharing between supplier and manufacturer on their collaboration performance. *Supply Chain Management*, *10*(3/4), 223–237.

Kock, N. (2002). Managing with web-based IT in mind. *Communications of the ACM*, *45*(5), 102–106. doi:10.1145/506218.506223

Kock, N. (2005). What is E-Collaboration? *International Journal of e-Collaboration*, *1*(1), i–vii.

Kotabe, M., Martin, X., & Domoto, H. (2003). Gaining from vertical partnerships: Knowledge transfer, relationship duration, and supplier performance improvement in the US and Japanese automotive industries . *Strategic Management Journal*, *24*(4), 293–316. doi:10.1002/smj.297

Lambert, D. M., & Cooper, M. (2000). Issues in supply chain management. *Industrial Marketing Management*, *29*(1), 65–83. doi:10.1016/S0019-8501(99)00113-3

Lee, H. L., & Whang, S. (2002). Supply Chain Integration over the Internet . In Geunes, P., Pardalos, M., & Romeijn, H. E. (Eds.), *Supply Chain Management: Models*. Applications, and Research Directions.

Lee-Kelley, L., Crossman, A., & Cannings, A. (2004). A social interaction approach to managing the 'invisibles' of virtual teams. *Industrial Management & Data Systems*, *104*(8), 650–657. doi:10.1108/02635570410561636

Li, H., & Atuahene-Gima, K. (2001). Product innovation strategy and the performance of new technology ventures in China. *Academy of Management Journal*, *44*(6), 1123–1134. doi:10.2307/3069392

Loch, C. H., & Terwiesch, C. (2005). Rush and be wrong or wait and be late? A model of information in collaborative processes. *Production and Operations Management*, *14*(3), 331–344.

Lummus, R. R., & Demarie, S. M. (2006). Evolutionary chain. *Industrial Engineer*, *38*(6), 38–42.

Mason-Jones, R., & Towill, D. R. (1999). Using the information decoupling point to improve supply chain performance. *International Journal of Logistics Management*, *10*(2), 13–26. doi:10.1108/09574099910805969

McCarthy, T. M., & Golicic, S. L. (2002). Implementing collaborative forecasting to improve supply chain performance. *International Journal of Physical Distribution & Logistics Management*, *32*, 431–454. doi:10.1108/09600030210437960

McCloy, R. A., Campbell, J. B., & Cudeck, R. (1994). A Confirmatory Test of a Model of Performance Determinants. *The Journal of Applied Psychology*, *79*(4), 493–505. doi:10.1037/0021-9010.79.4.493

Mentzer, J. T. (2001). *Supply Chain Management*. Thousand Oaks, CA: Sage Publications.

Meroño-Cerdán, A. L., Soto-Acosta, P., & López-Nicolás, C. (2008). How do collaborative technologies affect innovation in SMEs? *International Journal of e-Collaboration*, *4*(4), 33–51.

Moore, K. R. (1998). Trust and relationship commitment in logistics alliances: A buyer perspective. *International Journal of Purchasing and Materials Management*, *34*(1), 24–37.

Nieto, M. J., & Santamaria, L. (2007). The Importance of diverse collaborative networks for the novelty of product innovation . *Technovation*, *27*(6/7), 367–377. doi:10.1016/j.technovation.2006.10.001

OECD/Eurostat. (1997). *The measurement of scientific and technological activities: Proposed guidelines for collecting and interpreting technological innovation data*. Paris: OSLO Manual.

Ogden, J. A., Petersen, K. J., Carter, J. R., & Monczka, R. M. (2005). Supply management strategies for the future: A delphi study. *Journal of Supply Chain Management*, *41*(3), 29–48. doi:10.1111/j.1055-6001.2005.04103004.x

Raghunathan, S. (1999). Interorganizational collaborative forecasting and replenishment systems and supply chain implications. *Decision Sciences*, *30*(4), 1053–1071. doi:10.1111/j.1540-5915.1999.tb00918.x

Rubiano Ovalle, O., & Crespo Marquez, A. (2003). The effectiveness of using e-collaboration tools in the supply chain: an assessment study with system dynamics. *Journal of Purchasing and Supply Management*, *9*, 151–163. doi:10.1016/S1478-4092(03)00005-0

Sabath, R. E., & Fontanella, J. (2002). The unfulfilled promise of supply chain collaboration. *Supply Chain Management Review*, *6*, 24–29.

Saeed, K. A., Malhotra, M. K., & Grover, V. (2005). Examining the impact of interorganizational systems on process efficiency and sourcing leverage in buyer-supplier dyads. *Decision Sciences*, *36*(3), 365–397. doi:10.1111/j.1540-5414.2005.00077.x

Sahay, B. S., & Mohan, R. (2003). Supply chain management practices in Indian industry. *International Journal of Physical Distribution & Logistics Management*, *33*(7), 582–606. doi:10.1108/09600030310499277

Samaddar, S., Nargundkar, S., & Daley, M. (2006). Inter-organizational information sharing: the role of supply network configuration and partner characteristics. *European Journal of Operational Research*, *174*(2), 744–765. doi:10.1016/j.ejor.2005.01.059

Sezen, B. (2008). Relative effects of design, integration and information sharing. *Supply Chain Management: An International Journal*, *13*(3), 233–240. doi:10.1108/13598540810871271

Simatupang, T. M., & Sridharan, R. (2005). The collaboration index: a measure for supply chain collaboration. *International Journal of Physical Distribution & Logistics Management*, *35*(1), 44–53. doi:10.1108/09600030510577421

Sobrero, M., & Roberts, E. B. (2001). The trade-off between efficiency and learning in interorganizational relationships for product development. *Management Science*, *47*(4), 493–511. doi:10.1287/mnsc.47.4.493.9828

Spekman, R. E., Kamauff, J. W. Jr, & Myhr, N. (1998). An empirical investigation into supply chain management: a perspective on partnerships. *International Journal of Physical Distribution & Logistics Management*, *28*(8), 630–650. doi:10.1108/09600039810247542

Subramani, M. (2004). How Do Suppliers Benefit from IT Use in Supply Chain Relationships. *Management Information Systems Quarterly*, *28*(1), 45–74.

Swink, M. (2006). Building collaborative innovation capabilitiy. *Research Technology Management*, *49*(2), 37–47.

Timothy, A. J., Boudreau, J. W., & Bretz, R. D. (1994). Job and life attitudes of male executives. *The Journal of Applied Psychology*, *79*(5), 767–782. doi:10.1037/0021-9010.79.5.767

Utterback, J. M., & Abernathy, W. J. (1975). A dynamic model of product and process innovation. *Omega*, *3*(6), 639–656. doi:10.1016/0305-0483(75)90068-7

Van de Ven, A., & Ferry, D. (1980). *Measuring and Assessing Organizations*. New York: Wiley Interscience.

Weston, F. C. (2001). ERP implementation and project management. *Production & Inventory Management Journal*, *42*(3-4), 75–80.

Zaheer, A., McEvily, B., & Perrone, V. (1998). The strategic value of buyer-supplier relationships. *International Journal of Purchasing and Materials Management*, *34*(3), 20–26.

Zineldin, M. A. (1998). Towards an ecological collaborative relationship management: a 'co-operative' perspective. *European Journal of Marketing*, *32*(11-12), 1138–1164. doi:10.1108/03090569810243767

Chapter 12
Collaborative Technologies and Innovation in SMEs:
An Empirical Study

Angel L. Meroño-Cerdan
University of Murcia, Spain

Pedro Soto-Acosta
University of Murcia, Spain

Carolina Lopez-Nicolas
University of Murcia, Spain

ABSTRACT

This study seeks to assess the impact of collaborative technologies on innovation at the firm level. Collaborative technologies' influence on innovation is considered here as a multi-stage process that starts at adoption and extends to use. Thus, the effect of collaborative technologies on innovation is examined not only directly, the simple presence of collaborative technologies, but also based on actual collaborative technologies' use. Given the fact that firms can use this technology for different purposes, collaborative technologies' use is measured according to three orientations: e-information, e-communication and e-workflow. To achieve these objectives, a research model is developed for assessing, on the one hand, the impact of the adoption and use of collaborative technologies on innovation and, on the other hand, the relationship between adoption and use of collaborative technologies. The research model is tested using a dataset of 310 Spanish SMEs. The results showed that collaborative technologies' adoption is positively related to innovation. Also, as hypothesized, distinct collaborative technologies were found to be associated to different uses. In addition, the study found that while e-information had a positive and significant impact on innovation, e-communication and e-workflow did not.

INTRODUCTION

Emerging powerful Information technologies (ITs), such as the Intranet, allow people to collaborate

and share their complementary knowledge (Bhatt et al., 2005). These technologies are responsible for e-Collaboration, which can be defined as the collaboration among individuals engaged in a common task using electronic technologies (Dasgupta

DOI: 10.4018/978-1-61520-676-6.ch012

et al., 2002). As an Intranet evolves, it increases in sophistication and complexity and can be used for advanced applications such as collaborative design, concurrent engineering and workflow support (Duane and Finnegan, 2003). Thus, Intranets are diverse and can integrate different collaborative technologies (CTs).

CTs can be oriented to different, but compatible, uses. These are related to the offering of information online, communications and exchange of information and the automation of internal business processes. Hamel (2002) emphasizes the role of IT as an enabler of product and process innovation. Innovation process requires the support of CTs since they help in the efficient storage and retrieval of codified knowledge (Adamides and Karacapilidis, 2006), get different people together to innovate (Bafoutzsou and Mentzas, 2002), enable the formation of virtual teams to execute the innovation process (Kessler, 2003; Adamides and Karacapilidis, 2006) and create an organizational climate favourable to product innovation. Thus, e-Collaboration is expected to have a positive impact on firm innovation. The reverse direction of causality could exist as well, that is, causality may flow also from innovation to CTs' adoption. However, this paper focuses on analyzing the impact of CTs on innovation.

Computer systems cannot improve organizational performance if they are not used (Davis et al., 1989). Recently, Devaraj and Kholi (2003) showed that actual use may be an important link to IT value. Thus, we need to view CTs' impact on innovation as a multi-stage process that starts at adoption and extends to use. Since knowledge will not necessarily circulate freely firm-wide just because accurate IT to support such circulation is available (Brown and Duguid, 2000), actual CTs' utilization may be a critical phase. In an attempt to address this issue, this research examines the effect of CTs on innovation not only directly, the simple presence of CTs, but also based on actual CTs' use. In this regard, this study will explore the direct relationship between CTs' adoption and innovation, as well as the indirect relationship from CTs' adoption, through CTs' use, to innovation.

The paper consists of six sections and is structured as follows. The next section offers a classification of CTs and a framework differentiating three CTs' uses. In section 3, the theoretical model is proposed and hypotheses are stated. Following that, the methodology used for sample selection and data collection are discussed. Then, data analysis and results are examined. Finally, the paper ends with a discussion of research findings and concluding remarks.

LITERATURE REVIEW

Collaborative Technologies

Collaborative Technologies are applications where ITs are used to help people co-ordinate their work with others by sharing information or knowledge (Doll and Deng, 2001). They are critical in KM programs (Alavi and Leidner, 2001; Marwick, 2001; Skyrme, 1998). Different technologies are used in e-collaborations (Dasgupta et al., 2002). A review of the literature reveals several CTs' classifications. DeSanctis and Gallupe (1987) discuss a taxonomy based on group size (smaller, larger) and task type (planning, creativity, intellective, preference, cognitive, conflict, mixed motive). According to Pinsonneault and Kraemer (1990), there are two categories of group support systems: group decision support systems and group communication support systems. Ellis et al. (1991) describe a taxonomy based on application-functionality and Coleman (1995) also provides twelve categories of CTs in the same domain. Mentzas (1993) classifies CTs' software based on four major criteria: co-ordination model characteristics, type of processing, decision support issues and organizational environment.

This study focuses on a classification of CTs based on the work of Nunamaker et al. (1997), DeSanctis and Gallupe (1987) and Pinsonneault

Table 1. Collaborative technologies classification

	Electronic communication systems (ECS)	**Teamwork systems (TS)**
Concept	They support the exchange of information, documents, and opinions.	Work is done through them.
Aim	Relationship	Integration
Tools	Email; Discussion forums; Repositories; Yellow pages (experts directories)	Workflows/ Document management systems; Project management; Shared databases; Group decision support systems

and Kraemer (1990). In this sense, table 1 shows CTs may be grouped into two: (1) electronic communication systems (ECS), whose purpose is to facilitate information exchange and (2) teamwork systems (TS), where teamwork (processes and decision making) is structured and done. ECS aim at enabling relationships among individuals or institutions, employees or customers, while TS' objective is to integrate information and predefined work processes, as is the case with workflow tools. According to the expected frequency of use, the present study considers four CTs (two for each category), namely, discussion forums, repositories, shared databases and document management systems/workflows.

Discussion forums. Due to their simplicity, discussion forums have been one of the earliest technologies for collaborative knowledge creation and knowledge sharing (Wagner and Bolloju, 2005). The subject is set and the discussion is carried on, either with all participants online, or over time, where anyone can share his or her opinion at any time (Bafoutsou and Mentzas, 2002).

Repositories. Valuable knowledge can be collected and placed into repositories for use by others (Gunnlaugsdottir, 2003). Document repositories are a collection of relevant documents that list tacit and articulated knowledge from the experts about the project using textual, picture and diagrammatic forms (Fernandes et al., 2005).

Shared databases. They are databases whose data may be consulted and modified by different authorised users within a company or a team. Shared databases are necessary to reduce or pre-

vent the repeated typing of data, but in addition they supplement the system with a wealth of update information, thus building the organizational memory (Gunnlaugsdottir, 2003).

Document management systems/Workflows. Document management systems handle documents, storing them in a central server where users can access and work on them. Occasionally, there is a possibility for version control, search, electronic signing and access control (Bafoutsou and Mentzas, 2002). Workflows may be defined as the automation of a business process, in whole or part, during which documents, information or tasks are passed from one participant to another for action, according to a set of procedural rules (WFMC, 2004). Thus, regarding process automation, workflows seem to be more advanced than document management Systems.

Collaborative Technologies' Use

Firms can use CTs for different purposes. Soto-Acosta and Meroño-Cerdan (2006) identified three Website orientations: e-information, e-communication and e-transaction. Based on this classification, three CTs' use orientations have been identified: e-information, e-communication and e-workflow.

E-information. CTs can be used as a corporate channel for information dissemination and data access across functional boundaries and organizational levels. As a result, CTs may reduce the cost and effort associated with corporate information searches. Thus, e-information is considered

Figure 1. Research Model

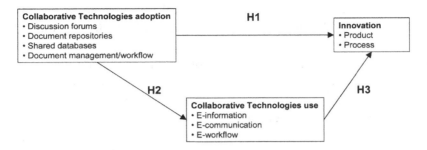

as the use of CTs to provide one-way company electronic information.

E-communication. CTs, besides allowing cost reduction in comparison to traditional communication tools, offer a unique and integrated opportunity for interacting with several business agents (both internal and external to the organization). In this way, these technologies facilitate the exchange of information, collaboration and the possibility of establishing close relationships based on trust and mutual commitment. Thus, e-communication is considered as the use of CTs for two-way information exchange.

E-workflow. In the new economy, work has shifted from the creation of tangible goods to the flow of information through the value chain (Basu and Kumar, 2002). The establishment and development of workflow processes has played a fundamental role in this transition. CTs provide great opportunity for automation of processes and workgroup. Thus, e-workflow is considered as the use of CTs for the establishment of predefined electronic processes through CTs.

MODEL

As mentioned in the introduction, the present study focuses on analyzing the impact of CTs on firm innovation. This effect is evaluated directly from the simple presence of IT, but also according to CTs' actual use. In addition, the relationship

between adoption and use of CTs is examined in order to specify the indirect relationship of CTs' adoption and innovation through CTs' use.

Collaborative Technologies' Adoption and Innovation

Innovation can be defined as the search for, the discovery and development of new technologies, new products and/or services, new processes and new organizational structures (Carneiro, 2000). It is the implementation of new ideas generated within the organization (Gurteen, 1998; Borghini, 2005). IT is considered a key facilitator of innovation. Many researchers are focused on analysis of how the web will change innovation within and between companies (Sawhney and Prandelli, 2000). CTs are web-based tools that allow information and knowledge exchange (electronic communication systems), as well as work execution by integrating information, documents and employees (Teamwork systems). Thus, intranets and other CTs can be used to distribute and share individual experience and innovation throughout the organization (Bhatt et al, 2005) and offer the chance of applying knowledge for the creation of new products. Also, users and partners from remote places may need to participate in the innovation process. This further emphasize the instrumental role of IT as enabler for the formation of virtual teams to execute the innovation process (Adamides and Karacapilidis, 2006; Kessler, 2003). In summary, the benefits from web collaboration, which include efficient information and knowledge sharing as well as working with no distance limitations, are expected to be positively related to the introduction of process and product innovations. Thus, the following hypothesis is proposed:

Hypothesis 1: CTs' adoption is positively related to innovation

H_{1a}: The adoption of discussion forums is positively related to innovation

H_{1b}: The adoption of repositories is positively related to innovation

H_{1c}: The adoption of shared databases is positively related to innovation

H_{1d}: The adoption of document management systems is positively related to innovation

Collaborative Technologies' Adoption and Collaborative Technologies' Use

Distinct CTs are expected to be more suitable for different purpose. However, all those technologies provide information that can be accessed by employees. Discussion forums, although intended to be convenient for e-communication (Hayes and Walsham, 2001; Rubenstein-Montano et al., 2001), can be also used as an information tool, since online forums afford a larger and more diverse set of information resources, and also offer an enhanced opportunity for information exchange and communication (DeSanctis et al., 2003; Walsham, 2001). Repositories store documents (Kwan and Balasubramanian, 2003) and information (Ackerman, 1998), facilitating access to stored knowledge from experts (Fernandes et al., 2005). In the case of CTs labelled as TS, both shared databases and document management systems/workflows are expected to support information and workflow roles. Shared databases include any data and information stored in the business, and make it available to third parties so that they could make decisions and process their transactions (Shah

and Murtaza, 20005). Workflow technologies are natural repositories for organizational memory (Zhao et al., 2000) and allow the inspection of information about the current status of the process of innovation (Chung et al., 2003), as well as the automation of processes and transactions. Thus, the following hypothesis is formulated:

Hypothesis 2: Distinct CTs are expected to be associated to different uses.

H_{2a}: ECS are positively associated with e-information and e-communication uses

H_{2b}: TS are positively associated with e-information and e-workflow uses

Collaborative Technologies' Use and Innovation

The presence of ITs does not guarantee any effect on performance if they are not used (Davis et al., 1989; Forgionee and Kohli, 1996). Since knowledge will not necessarily circulate freely firm-wide just because accurate information technology to support such circulation is available (Brown and Duguid, 2000), actual CTs' utilization may be a critical phase. Thus, this research considers CTs' impact on innovation as a multistage process that starts at adoption and extends to use. That is, this study besides testing the direct relationship between CTs' presence and innovation, also examines the influence of actual CTs' use on innovation. Actual CTs' use is expected to have a positive impact on innovation. CTs' use is measured according to three orientations: e-information, e-communication and e-workflow.

Hypothesis 3: There is a positive relationship between CTs' use and innovation

H_{3a}: There is a positive relationship between e-information and innovation

H_{3b}: There is a positive relationship between e-communication and innovation

H_{3c}: There is a positive relationship between e-workflow and innovation

Table 2. Sample characteristics (N = 310)

Business Industry	%	#	Respondent title	%	#
Textile	12.6	39	Managing director, CEO	58.4	181
Food & Agriculture	40.0	124	Human resources manager	8.7	27
ICTs	1.6	5	Business operations manager	5.2	16
Services to businesses	15.2	47	Administration/Finance manager	23.5	73
Retail	17.7	55	Others	4.2	13
Others	12.9	40			
No. of employees	%	#			
10-49	71.3	221			
50-249	24.5	76			
More than 249	4.2	13			

METHODOLOGY

The organizations selected for this study are SMEs (small and medium size enterprises) from Spain. SMEs were considered because of their importance for economic growth, employment and wealth creation in economies both large and small. Currently, SMEs represent around 99% of the total number of firms in Spain (INE, 2005). SMEs are characterized by having fewer financial, technological and personnel resources than their higher-level counterparts (large firms). Nonetheless, to ensure a minimum firm complexity in which CTs may be relevant, only firms with at least 10 employees were used.

Sample and Data Collection

The target population consisted of SMEs from the Region of Murcia (Spain), with at least 10 employees. 310 valid responses were obtained from different industries. The study assumed an error of 5.4% for p=q=50 and a confidence level of 95.5%. A structured questionnaire consisting of close-ended questions was developed. Face-to-face surveys with the key informant person in each company were conducted in May 2005. Studied companies are mainly SMEs and most of interviewees were CEOs. Table 2 shows the characteristics of the sample.

Measures of Variables

This section describes the variables used for measuring the presence of CTs, CTs' use and innovation. The formulation and criteria for answering the questionnaire is defined in the Appendix.

Collaborative technologies: Using a dichotomous scale, CEOs assessed the presence of 4 tools in their firms: discussion forums, shared databases, repositories and document management systems/workflows.

Collaborative technologies' use: one item (five-point Likert-type scale) was used for measuring each collaborative technology use. Firms were requested to value their CTs' degree of use in order to inform their employees (e-information), to debate or receive employees' suggestions (e-communication) and to support the automation of internal business processes (e-workflow).

Innovation: two items based on Choi and Lee's (2003) research were developed, distinguishing the firm's situation re new products and new processes with respect to the industry average. That distinction is based on previous literature, such as Damanpour and Gopalakrishnan (2001) who

Table 3. Presence of collaborative technologies

Collaborative technology	Total % (n=310)	At least one CT% (n=115)
Discussion forums	9.4%	25.2%
Repositories	21.9%	59.1%
Shared databases	34.2%	92.2%
Document management systems/Workflows	21.3%	57.4%

Table 4. Descriptive statistics and bivariate correlation coefficients

Variables	Mean	S.D.	Correlation							
			1	2	3	4	5	6	7	8
1. Discussion forums	0.09	0.29	1							
2. Shared databases	0.34	0.47	0.39***	1						
3. Document repositories	0.22	0.41	0.44***	0.65***	1					
4. Document Management systems/Workflows	0.21	0.41	0.42***	0.63***	0.69***	1				
5. E-information	2.96	1.57	0.30***	0.18*	0.26**	0.34***	1			
6. E-communication	2.47	1.41	0.36***	0.13	0.18*	0.23**	0.79***	1		
7. E-workflow	4.07	1.14	0.04	0.37***	0.15	0.19*	0.13	0.04	1	
8. Product innovation	3.24	1.01	0.05	0.14**	0.13**	0.13**	0.24**	0.15	0.08	1
9. Process innovation	3.34	0.98	0.04	0.16***	0.13**	0.16***	0.28***	0.19*	0.05	0.68***

p<0.1*; p<0.05**; p<0.01***

found differences in companies when adopting product vs. process innovations.

ANALYSES AND RESULTS

With regard to CTs, 37.1% out of all analyzed firms (310) had at least one type of CT within their intranet. Table 3 shows detailed results. Shared databases were the most frequently found technology, with 34.2% of the total number of firms containing it. This technology was also found in almost all firms that had at least one type of CT (92.2%). The second and third technologies in importance were document repositories and document management systems/workflows, respectively. Less than 10% of all analyzed companies presented discussion forums, while 25.2% of firms containing at least one CT had them. Descriptive statistics and bivariate correlation coefficients are presented in table 4. Although significant correlations among many of the variables were found, to test casual relationships, regression analysis was used.

Collaborative Technologies' Adoption and Innovation

Analysed firms claimed to innovate slightly above the industry average. Also, the degree of product innovation and process innovation were very similar with 3.2 and 3.3, respectively. As presented in table 4, all CTs, except for the discussion forums, had significant correlations with both types of innovation. Regression results (see table 5) showed that, although statistically significant coefficients were not found for any CT, CTs' adoption was associated with innovation. When doing the analysis by the stepwise procedure, it was found that shared databases were positively associated with product innovation (supporting H1c) and document management systems/workflows were positively related to process innovation (supporting H1d). Thus, H1 is partially supported, only TS (shared databases and document management systems/workflows) were found to be associated with innovation.

Collaborative Technologies' Adoption and Collaborative Technologies' Use

As shown in table 6, the most predominant collaborative technology used was e-workflow (mean= 4.21), while the least was e-communication (mean= 2.54). Only a few companies allow electronic employee participation through suggestions or debates. Regression results reveal different CTs were associated to different CTs' uses, thus, supporting Hypothesis 2. More specifically, discussion forums and document management systems/workflows were positively associated with e-information, while discussion forums were positively related to e-communication and shared databases were positively related to e-workflow. This confirms that ECS are more e-information and e-communication oriented, as posited in H2a, particularly when considering discussion forums, whereas TS are used for e-information, in the case

of document management systems/workflows, and for e-workflow when considering shared databases, as posited in H2b.

Collaborative Technologies' Use and Innovation

The relationship between actual CTs' use and organizational innovation was tested through regression analysis. As shown in table 7, CTs' e-information use was statistically significant with a positive impact on innovation (support for hypothesis 3a was provided). The only differences between product and process innovation were that e-information had a grater positive impact on product innovation and, while the influence on product innovation was statistically significant at 5% level, for process innovation it was significant at 10% level. These results indicate that companies which use CTs as informative mediums achieve higher innovation levels. Conversely, e-communication and e-workflow coefficients were not found to be statistically significant. (hypotheses 3b and 3c were rejected). Through this analysis, support for hypothesis H3a was provided, whereas support for hypotheses H3b and H3c was not found.

DISCUSSION AND CONCLUSIONS

The present research examines the impact of CTs on innovation. This effect is evaluated directly

Table 5. Collaborative technologies adoption and innovation

	All variables		Stepwise method	
Independent variables	**New products**	**New processes**	**New products**	**New processes**
Discussion forums	-0.028	-0.049		
Repositories	0.048	-0.002		
Shared databases	0.076	0.099	0.139**	
Document Management systems/Workflows	0.068	0.128		0.169***
F	1.933*	2.768**	6.091**	9.025***
R²	0.012	0.022	0.016	0.025

p<0.1*; p<0.05**; p<0.01***

Table 6. Collaborative technologies adoption and use

Independent variables	Collaborative technologies use (dependent variables)		
	E-information (Mean=3.06)	E-communication (Mean=2.54)	E-workflow (Mean=4.21)
Discussion forums	0.215**	0.323***	-0.078
Repositories	0.061	0.013	0.017
Shared databases	0.069	0.049	0.348***
Document Management systems/Workflows	0.233*	0.120	0.112
F	4.481***	3.866	3.857
R2	0.137	0.115	0.115
$p<0.1$*; $p<0.05$**; $p<0.01$***			

from the mere presence of those technologies, but also indirectly through CTs' use. Given the fact that firms can use this technology for different purposes, CTs' use is measured according to three orientations: e-information, e-communication and e-workflow. In this regard, this research tests three relationships: CTs' adoption and CTs' use, the influence of CTs' adoption on innovation, and, finally, the effect of CTs' use on innovation.

The results indicate that CTs are not widespread among SMEs, since only 37.1% out of all analyzed firms (310) had at least one type of CT within their intranet. The most frequently found CT was shared databases. Specifically, 34.2% of the sample had shared databases. Also, this technology was found in almost all firms that have at least one type of CT (92.2%). These results confirm previous research studies. For instance, Bafoutsou and Mentzas (2002) found that shared

databases are clearly the most common and needed collaboration tools for sharing information. Recently, Meroño-Cerdan (2005) also found that shared databases were the most adopted CT at the firm level. On the contrary, results showed discussion forums were the least presented CT. Although discussion forums have been one of the earliest technologies for collaborative knowledge creation and knowledge sharing (Wagner and Bolloju, 2005), firms seem to relegate this technology to an anecdotal use.

The empirical results demonstrate that CTs classified as Teamwork Systems (TS), shared databases and document management systems/workflow, are directly related to process and product innovation, respectively, since work is done through them. On the contrary, Electronic Communication Systems (ECS), discussion forums and repositories, characterized by supporting

Table 7. Collaborative technologies use and innovation

Independent variables	New products	New processes
E-information	0.331*	0.374**
E-communication	-0.090	-0.112
E-workflow	0.100	0.073
F	2.575*	2.877**
R²	0.091	0.101
$p<0.1$*; $p<0.05$**; $p<0.01$***		

individual and group work, are not associated with innovation. Thus, apparently, ECS' adoption per se has no effect on innovation.

The results showed, as hypothesized, that distinct CTs are associated with different CTs' uses. Specifically, it was found that ECS are more e-information and e-communication oriented (particularly when considering forums), whereas TS are used for e-information (document management/workflow) and e-workflow (shared databases). The lack of relationship between document management/workflow and e-workflow leads us to believe that this technology has been considered, mainly, as a document management system, which does not necessarily include the automation of internal processes.

With regard to the contribution of CTs' use to innovation, only e-information has a significant impact on innovation. Initially, it might be logical to think of a possible influence from e-communication as well. As this is not the case, it could be interpreted that participation and discussion processes, fundamental to innovation, are done outside the intranet. A possible explanation of this can be found in the characteristics of the firms analyzed (SMEs).

In sum, results show that TS are the only CTs that directly influence innovation. The adoption of these technologies involves changing organizational practices, since work is done through them. Research findings also suggest that indirect effects on innovation exist through the influence of e-information. Considering that e-information is significantly influenced by discussion forums and document management systems/workflows, here it is possible to make several recommendations. Document management systems/workflows are found to be the CT that most contributes to innovation. The adoption of this technology influences process innovation, but also product innovation when used with an informative orientation (e-information). The case of discussion forums is particularly interesting. It is the least presented CT and, as an ECS which supports work realization,

the simple presence of this technology does not guarantee effects on innovation. However, when they are employed with an informative orientation, influences on innovation are found. Therefore, this study demonstrates that, when considering TS, CTs have a direct influence on innovation. Also, a mediating effect of e-information exists between document management systems/ workflow and process innovation, although this effect is not stronger than the direct effect. Thus, the presence of that technology is important, and, in addition, process innovation is improved when related to e-information. Finally, it is worthy of note that the size of analyzed firms may influence CTs' use. The use of CTs as informative mediums (e-information) in SMEs is possible and was found to contribute to innovation. However, the limited size of firms may imply that collaboration and debate among employees is done outside the intranet. This argument could explain why significant influences on innovation were not found from e-communication.

While this study presents some interesting findings, it has some obvious limitations which can be addressed in future research. First, the sample was obtained from the Region of Murcia (Spain). In this sense, findings may be extrapolated to other Spanish areas and other countries, since economic and technological development in Murcia and Spain is similar to other OECD Member countries. However, in future research, a sampling frame that combines firms from different countries could be used in order to provide a more international perspective on the subject. Second, the sample consisted of SMEs and according to Spanish Statistics National Institute, large companies are more used to implementing Intranets (INE, 2006). This segment merits a special analysis. Third, the key informant method was used for data collection. This method, while having its advantages, also suffers from the limitation that the data reflects the opinions of one person (not necessarily the user). Future studies could consider research designs that allow data collection from multiple respondents within an organization. Fourth, the variables used for measuring innovation may be too general. However, basing on literature, they reflect the two main outcomes of innovating efforts: new products and new processes. Finally, it could be interesting to complete this research about the influence of CTs on innovation by studying the relationship between innovation and CTs' adoption. That is, analyzing to what extent innovative firms adopt more CTs.

REFERENCES

Ackerman, M. (1998). Augmenting Organizational Memory: A Field Study of Answer Garden. *ACM Transactions on Information Systems, 16*(3), 203–224. doi:10.1145/290159.290160

Adamides, E. D., & Karacapilidis, N. (2006). Information technology support for the knowledge and social processes of innovation management. *Technovation, 26*, 50–59. doi:10.1016/j.technovation.2004.07.019

Alavi, M., & Leidner, D. (2001). Knowledge management and knowledge management systems: conceptual foundations and research issues. *Management Information Systems Quarterly, 23*(1), 107–125. doi:10.2307/3250961

Bafoutsou, G., & Mentzas, G. (2002). Review and functional classification of collaborative systems. *International Journal of Information Management, 22*(4), 281–305. doi:10.1016/S0268-4012(02)00013-0

Basu, A., & Kumar, A. (2002). Research commentary: workflow management issues in e-business. *Information Systems Research, 13*(1), 1–14. doi:10.1287/isre.13.1.1.94

Bhatt, G. D., Gupta, J. N. D., & Kitchens, F. (2005). An exploratory study of groupware use in the knowledge management process. *Journal of Enterprise Information Management, 8*(1), 28–46. doi:10.1108/17410390510571475

Borghini, S. (2005). Organizational creativity: breaking equilibrium and order to innovate. *Journal of Knowledge Management, 9*(4), 19–33. doi:10.1108/13673270510610305

Brown, J. S., & Duguid, P. (2000). Balancing Act: How to Capture Knowledge Without Killing It. *Harvard Business Review, 78*(3), 73–80.

Carneiro, A. (2000). How does knowledge management influence innovation and competitiveness? *Journal of Knowledge Management, 4*(2), 87–98. doi:10.1108/13673270010372242

Carvalho, R., & Ferreira, M. (2001). Using information technology to support knowledge conversion processes. *Information Research, 7*(1). Retrieved from http://InformationR.net/ir/7-1/paper118.html

Choi, B., & Lee, H. (2003). An empirical investigation of KM styles and their effect on corporate performance. *Information & Management, 40*(5), 403–417. doi:10.1016/S0378-7206(02)00060-5

Chung, P., Cheung, L., Stader, J., Jarvis, P., Moore, J., & Macintosh, A. (2003). Knowledge-based process management—an approach to handling adaptive workflow. *Knowledge-Based Systems, 16*(2), 149–160. doi:10.1016/S0950-7051(02)00080-1

Coleman, D. (1995). *Groupware; technology and applications*. Englewood Cliffs, NJ: Prentice Hall.

Damanpour, F., & Gopalakrishnan, S. (2001). The dynamics of the adoption of product and process innovations in organizations. *Journal of Management Studies, 38*(1), 45–65. doi:10.1111/1467-6486.00227

Dasgupta, S., Granger, M., & McGarry, N. (2002). User acceptance of e-collaboration technology an extension of the technology acceptance model. *Group Decision and Negotiation, 11*(2), 87–100. doi:10.1023/A:1015221710638

Davis, F. D., Bagozzi, R. P., & Warshaw, P. R. (1989). User acceptance of computer technology: a comparison of two theoretical models. *Management Science, 35*(8), 982–1003. doi:10.1287/mnsc.35.8.982

DeSanctis, G., Fayard, A. L., Roach, M., & Jiang, L. (2003). Learning in online forums. *European Management Journal, 21*(5), 565–577. doi:10.1016/S0263-2373(03)00106-3

DeSanctis, G., & Gallupe, R. B. (1987). A Foundation for the study of Group Decision Support System. *Management Science, 33*(5), 589–609. doi:10.1287/mnsc.33.5.589

Devaraj, S., & Kohli, R. (2003). Performance impacts of information technology: is actual usage the missing link? *Management Science, 49*(3), 273–289. doi:10.1287/mnsc.49.3.273.12736

Doll, W. J., & Deng, X. (2001). The collaborative use of information technology: End-user participation and systems success. *Information Resources Management Journal, 14*(2), 6–16.

Duane, A., & Finnegan, P. (2003). Managing empowerment and control in an intranet environment. *Information Systems Journal, 13*(2), 133–158. doi:10.1046/j.1365-2575.2003.00148.x

Ellis, L., Gibbs, S. J., & Rein, G. L. (1991). Groupware: some issues and experiences. *Communications of the ACM, 34*(1), 38–58. doi:10.1145/99977.99987

Fernandes, K., Raja, V., & Austin, S. (2005). Portals as a knowledge repository and transfer tool—VIZCon case study. *Technovation, 25*(11), 1281–1289. doi:10.1016/j.technovation.2004.01.005

Forgionne, G., & Kholi, R. (1996). HMSS: a management support system for concurrent hospital decision-making. *Decision Support Systems, 16*(3), 209–229. doi:10.1016/0167-9236(95)00011-9

Gunnlaugsdottir, J. (2003). Seek and you will find, share and you will benefit: organising knowledge using groupware systems. *International Journal of Information Management, 23*(5), 363–380. doi:10.1016/S0268-4012(03)00064-1

Gurteen, D. (1998). Knowledge, creativity and innovation. *Journal of Knowledge Management, 12*(1), 5–13. doi:10.1108/13673279810800744

Hamel, G. (2002). *Leading the Revolution*. New York: Plume.

Hayes, N., & Walsham, G. (2001). Participation in groupware-mediated communities of practice: a socio-political analysis of knowledge working. *Information and Organization, 11*(4), 263–288. doi:10.1016/S1471-7727(01)00005-7

INE. (2005). Estructura y demografía empresarial. Directorio Central de Empresas (DIRCE). Retrieved April 2006 from http://www.ine.es/inebase

Kessler, E. H. (2003). Leveraging e-R&D processes: a knowledge-based view. *Technovation, 23*, 905–915. doi:10.1016/S0166-4972(03)00108-1

Marwick, A. (2001). Knowledge management technology. *IBM Systems Journal, 40*(4), 814–830.

Mentzas, G. (1993). Coordination of joint tasks in organizational processes. *Journal of Information Technology, 8*, 139–150. doi:10.1057/jit.1993.20

Meroño-Cerdan, A. (2005). Uso de tecnologías de grupo en pymes e influencia sobre el desempeño. *4th International Conference of the Iberoamerican Academy of Management*. Lisbon, December.

Nunamaker, J., Briggs, R., Mittleman, D., Vogel, D., & Balthazard, P. (1997). Lessons from a dozen years of group support systems research: a discussion of lab and field findings. *Journal of Management Information Systems, 13*(3), 63–207.

Pinsonneault, A., & Kraemer, K. L. (1990). The effects of electronic meetings on group processes and outcomes: An assessment of the empirical research. *European Journal of Operational Research, 46*(2), 143–161. doi:10.1016/0377-2217(90)90128-X

Rubenstein-Montano, B., Liebowitz, J., Buchwalter, J., McCaw, D., Newman, B., & Rebeck, K.The Knowledge Management Methodology Team. (2001). A system thinking framework for knowledge management. *Decision Support Systems, 31*(1), 5–16. doi:10.1016/S0167-9236(00)00116-0

Sawhney, M., & Prandelli, E. (2000). Communities of creation: managing distributed innovation in turbulent markets. *California Management Review, 42*(4), 24–54.

Shah, J., & Murtaza, M. (2005). Effective customer relationship management through web services. *Journal of Computer Information Systems, 46*(1), 98–109.

Skyrme, D. (1998). *Knowledge Management Solutions - The IT Contribution*. Retrieved May 2006 from http://www.skyrme.com/pubs/acm0398.doc.

Soto-Acosta, P., & Meroño-Cerdan, A. (2006). An analysis and comparison of web development between local governments and SMEs in Spain. *International Journal of Electronic Business, 4*(2), 191–203.

Wagner, C., & Bolloju, N. (2005). Supporting knowledge management in organizations with conversational technologies: discussion forums, weblogs, and wikis. *Journal of Database Management, 16*(2), 1–8.

Walsham, G. (2001). Knowledge Management: The Benefits and Limitations of Computer Systems. *European Management Journal, 19*(6), 599–608. doi:10.1016/S0263-2373(01)00085-8

WFMC. (2004). *Workflow Management Coalition*. Retrieved from http://wfmc.org

Zhao, J. L., Kumar, A., & Stohr, E. A. (2000). Workflow-Centric Information Distribution Through E-Mail. *Journal of Management Information Systems, 17*(3), 45–72.

APPENDIX. MEASURES

Indicators	Description
CTs Adoption Discussion forums Shared databases Repositories Document Management Systems/ Workflows	Does your company have discussion forums within the Intranet? (Y/N) Does your company have share databases within the Intranet? (Y/N) Does your company have document repositories within the Intranet? (Y/N) Does your company have document management systems/workflows within the Intranet? (Y/N)
CTs use E-information E-communication E-workflow	Use of CTs within the Intranet to inform employees (1-5) Use of CTs within the Intranet to receive/debate suggestions from employees (1-5) Use of CTs within the Intranet to support internal processes automation (1-5)
Product innovation	The number of new or improved products and/or services, launched by your company, is greater than the sector's average (1-5)
Process innovation	The number of new or improved internal processes is greater than the sector's average (1-5)
Note. Y/N, dummy variable; 1-5, five-point Likert-type scale.	

Chapter 13
The Launch of Web–Based Collaborative Decision Support at NASA

Irma Becerra-Fernandez
Florida International University, USA

Matha Del Alto
NASA Ames Research Center, USA

Helen Stewart
NASA Ames Research Center, USA

ABSTRACT

Today, organizations rely on decision makers to make mission-critical decisions that are based on input from multiple domains. The ideal decision maker has a profound understanding of specific domains coupled with the experience that allows him or her to act quickly and decisively on the information. Daily, decision makers face problems and failures that are too difficult for any individual person to solve; therefore, teams are now required who share their knowledge in spontaneous collaborations. Since requisite expertise may not all reside in the same organization, nor be geographically colocated, virtual networked teams are needed. This chapter presents a case study describing the development and use of Postdoc, the first Web-based collaborative and knowledge management platform deployed at NASA.

INTRODUCTION

Knowledge-intensive organizations rely on decision makers to make mission-critical decisions based on input from multiple domains (Nonaka & Takeuchi, 1995). The ideal decision maker has

a profound understanding of specific domains that influence the decision-making process coupled with the experience that allows quick and decisive action based on such information (Becerra-Fernandez, Gonzalez, & Sabherwal, 2004; Davenport & Prusak, 1998). The ideal decision maker is usually someone who has lengthy experience and implicit knowledge gained from years of observation (Leonard & Swap, 2004, 2005; Senge, 1990).

While the profile of today's ideal decision maker does not mark a significant departure from past practices, the following four underlying trends are raising the stakes in the decision-making scenario (Becerra-Fernandez et al., 2004).

1. **Increasing complexity:** The complexity of the underlying domains (internal, external, competitive, process, technology, etc.) is increasing.
2. **Accelerating volatility:** The pace of change (volatility) within each domain is increasing.
3. **Speed of responsiveness:** The time required to take action based upon subtle changes within and across domains is decreasing.
4. **Less experience:** Individuals with decision-making authority potentially have less tenure with the organization than ever before due to such factors as high employee turnover rates.

Today's technological environment is complex and changes at an ever-increasing pace. Many problems and failures are too difficult for any individual person or organization to solve. Teams are now required to share their knowledge in spontaneous collaborations. Since requisite expertise may not reside in the same organization, nor be geographically colocated, virtual networked teams are needed. Collaborative decision support technologies enable knowledge sharing and provide access to explicit organizational knowledge, so it is easy to learn from previous experiences. The use of adequate collaboration technology platforms results in the minimization of costly mistakes while reducing time to market in research and development projects (Majchrzak, Cooper, & Neece, 2004). Collaboration tools also help the organization make better decisions by capturing the knowledge from groups of experts and providing the means to mine this knowledge and experience (Malhotra & Majchrzak, 2005; Malone, Crowston, Lee, & Pentland, 1999).

In this chapter, we describe the characteristics of decision making in knowledge-intensive organizations (Becerra-Fernandez et al., 2004). This chapter is based largely on the case study published by Becerra-Fernandez, Del Alto, & Stewart (2006). Given the fact that increasingly complex decisions require the collaboration of individuals who many times are dispersed geographically and across organizations, Web-based collaboration technology platforms can effectively support decision making at such organizations. The balance of the chapter is organized as follows. The second section provides a description of one of the best-known knowledge-intensive organizations, the National Aeronautics and Space Administration (NASA). Given the characteristics of decision making at NASA, it provides for an excellent environment to study how this organization has been able to successfully coordinate complex projects through the use of Postdoc, a Web-based collaboration system. The third section describes the design, development, and implementation of Postdoc. The fourth section describes the use of Postdoc to manage complex projects such as Remote Agent, and the fifth section demonstrates the value of this application as a platform for collaboration in complex decision-making environments. Finally, the last section presents conclusions and lessons that could prove valuable to organizations considering the implementation of such systems, as well as a vision for the future of Web-based collaboration systems in general.

HISTORY OF COLLABORATIVE DECISION MAKING AT NASA

A recent NASA workforce study (*NASA Workforce Analysis Report*, 2003) reveals that the average number of years of service for all occupation groups at NASA has been increasing since 1995. The NASA workforce has in fact been aging since most recent science and engineering graduates are taking jobs outside of government, partly due to the lure of dot-coms and private industry in general, coupled with years of government downsizing and hiring freezes. Most of NASA's employees today are between the ages of 40 and 60 years, and less than 5% of NASA's scientists and engineers are younger than 30 years old. The aforementioned trends provide a backdrop for the decision-making scenario at NASA.

1. **Increasing complexity:** NASA is no exception to increasing complexity as it is being forced to diminish support for personnel devoted to safety assurance due to congressional pressures to downsize while fulfilling increasingly complex safety requirements associated with the launch of the space shuttle. A recent article reports that NASA's safety office manpower at its headquarters in 2003 is at 55% of its peak level in 1994 (Smith, 2003).

2. **Accelerating volatility:** This is certainly the case at NASA, where the rapid changes in technology continue to impact the design of new space vehicles. The volatility in technology development counteracts NASA's safety requirements, resulting in the preference for proven leading technologies over "bleeding," albeit unproven, technologies.

3. **Speed of responsiveness:** During the launch of the Space Shuttle Columbia, one of the aircraft wings' leading edges was hit by falling foam debris, which previously covered the liquid fuel booster.[1] Safety experts who evaluated this particular incident had to make a quick decision as to the impact of this event, which in the case of the Columbia, unfortunately resulted in an incorrect assessment. The required speed of responsiveness contributes an additional dimension to the complexity of making an accurate assessment.

4. **Less experience:** At NASA, there is growing concern that the scarcity of younger scientists and engineers provides few opportunities for mentorship and knowledge transfer to the organization's future decision makers.

NASA is a knowledge-intensive organization, dedicated to the mission of human space flight, space science, Earth observation, and aeronautics research. NASA, like many U.S. government agencies, is a heavily matrixed organization with many entities involved in its mission: NASA field centers, NASA programs carried out at these centers, and industrial and academic contractors. Effective collaboration among these entities is critical for NASA to effectively carry out its mission.

For example, the pioneering research to develop Remote Agent,[2] the innovative software that operated the Deep Space 1 (DS-1) spacecraft and its futuristic ion engine, involved three teams of artificial intelligence experts from Carnegie Mellon University in Pittsburgh, the Jet Propulsion Lab (JPL) in Pasadena, California, and the NASA Ames Research Center (ARC) in Silicon Valley, which jointly developed the system. Together, the scientists developed the intelligent software that operated the DS-1 spacecraft more than 60 million miles away from Earth.

When Remote Agent was designed, it required innovations in highly risky intelligent technologies for systems execution, fault tolerance and recovery, and autonomous planning systems. Due to budget constraints, the Remote Agent design team could not work at the same location. Given that e-mail would not provide an adequate infrastructure, the Postdoc Web-based collaborative document management system was developed to support the need for distributed collaboration. The first version of Postdoc supported the collaboration and project management needs of the 25-researcher team. In the words of computer scientist Kanna Rajan, who participated in the Remote Agent research project:

Postdoc enabled the team to develop a common language that we used to share our design ideas and start talking about them. We created a token dictionary that enabled the defined team to establish clear semantics that were used to exchange comments among the team members.

Although the evidence of Postdoc's success presented in this case is limited to usage statistics and anecdotal comments from users, this case is valuable because it demonstrates that virtual teams can effectively improve their collaboration know-how when doing development work (vs. routine work) if the information technology provides the necessary support for contextualizaton (Malhotra & Majchrzak, 2005). In fact, Postdoc's success can be explained by the finding that information technology support for contextualization may be of particular benefit to distributed teams that are structurally diverse, primarily virtual, and composed of members performing what they perceive as nonroutine tasks (Malhotra & Majchrzak, 2004). In other words, Postdoc enabled virtual teams to share not only their content, but also their context.

THE DESIGN, DEVELOPMENT, AND IMPLEMENTATION OF POSTDOC AT NASA

The need for collaboration tools at NASA dates back to 1995, when the New Millennium Program was tasked with dramatically improving the process by which spacecraft are designed, built, and operated. The vision to develop a collaborative system resulted from the need to support a geographically dispersed team. The New Millennium Program had impressive goals that had to be met using constrained resources due to then NASA administrator Daniel Goldin's[3]

mandate for "faster, better, cheaper, smarter" interplanetary missions. Already, the program was beginning to experience budget cuts and desperately required the use of collaborative tools to ensure meeting mission objectives and schedules. The initial attempt at building such a system, the New Millennium Documentation System, demonstrated shortcomings, specifically (a) a lack of portability, (b) lack of integration flexibility with other systems within NASA, and (c) the inability for users to manage and control access to directories and files.

A team comprised of employees at NASA ARC and JPL, as well as partners from Stanford University's Center for Design Research and private industry, was tasked with the development of a new collaborative system. At that time, most NASA teams involved in software development across the agency were only using the file transfer protocol (FTP) for transferring, sharing, and integrating software code, which did not provide good visual representation or programmatic organization. Also at that time, there were no other commercial off-the-shelf software applications that used the Web for collaborative document sharing and archiving.[4] The team quickly recognized that an adequate collaborative structure would require the development of an application that (a) used the emerging Web infrastructure for document uploading, archiving, visualization, and integration, (b) could easily be implemented agency-wide with access controls and authentication capabilities, (c) had a more portable application source, and (d) had features that allowed users full control of their information anytime and anywhere. It was decided to build these functionalities into Postdoc. Postdoc, which required a development effort of 5 person-years of software coding and testing, is a live system that is currently being used to support teams throughout NASA in their collaborations with other NASA facilities, private industry, and academia.

The first step in designing technology that supports collaborative decision making is to understand the role of collaborative environments in science and engineering. This requires the users to partake in the proactive design and development of the system that will support this new way of doing research (Kumar & van Dissel, 1996; Majchrzak et al., 2004). In order to identify this initial set of user requirements, the user-interface work group worked directly with the New Millennium Program users to understand their needs for information sharing across the mission. The user-interface work group was integrated with the DS-1 mission software development group, with whom they first identified the requirements for effectively collaborating across NASA centers, but later continued work with other mission development teams such as the spacecraft instrumentation team and the communication team. From this study, it was defined that the system needed to provide a specific set of capabilities, which are described in Table 1.

Postdoc was designed to meet these foundation requirements for knowledge management and collaboration by enabling data capture, analysis, and fusion capabilities. Furthermore, the software architecture also allows other virtual collaborative interfaces to be easily integrated

into the structure. Figure 1 represents Postdoc's software architecture.

Postdoc is a multiuser, Web-based collaborative document management system that is used primarily for document storage and retrieval, in-

Figure 1. Postdoc architecture

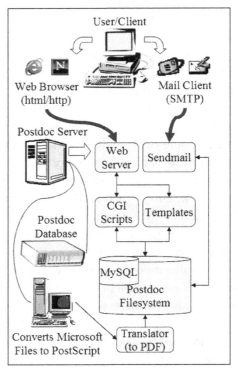

Table 1. Postdoc required capabilities

Name	Description
Access Control	Allow users to define and control access to their information. Inter-organizational users should be able to invite, and grant access to potential team members to collaborate as part of a geographically dispersed group. Postdoc would allow users to define the types of access to the information and manage their own information spaces.
Revision Control	Provide a platform for collaboration and a virtual document file system that supports versioning, document checkout, and revision control.
Audit Trail	Provide an audit trail for interactions with documents that the users can review. When users share documents, its important to know who has read or modified the documents and when they did so.
File-type Transparency	Be equipped with auto-conversion of file-type to portable document format (PDF), and on-demand document conversion to a broader option of document types (i.e., postscript, HTML, text, and digital assistant file types). Image files would need to be converted across different formats (e.g. JPEG, GIF, etc.).
Related Utilities	Have utilities such as fax capabilities, a fully featured email list manager, and an integrated online help.
System Administration	Provide administration features for system administrators monitoring the translations of the documents, maintaining statistics of events, and maintaining the software system.

cluding word processing documents, spreadsheets, slides, illustrations, images, video, audio, software archives, and others. The majority of Postdoc was written in the language Perl; the Web pages for the user interface are dynamically generated using ePerl. The HTML (hypertext markup language) generated conforms to Versions 3.2 and 4.0. Postdoc runs on a Unix operating system with a Web server (Apache), a relational database engine (MySQL), a full-text search engine (SWISH++), a document format conversion software (either Adobe Acrobat® Distiller® or Aladdin Ghostscript), and a facsimile software (HylaFax); most of these components are based on open-source standards. The conversion of Microsoft® Office, Adobe® Illustrator®, and other Macintosh or Windows documents to PostScript (and ultimately to PDF, Portable Document Format) uses a dedicated Windows system with custom software written in Python to perform the document conversions. Postdoc also allows converting image files among a choice of different formats, and it's this file conversion capability that allows Postdoc to stand out among many other similar systems. The Windows system communicates with the Unix system using Samba, an open-source environment that enables Linux and Unix servers to interoperate with Microsoft Windows clients.

In terms of the system's architecture, the Postdoc software uses a template-driven design, with HTML presentation code intermingled with macros and Perl instructions to provide interactivity and customizability with minimum effort. Preprocessor macros allow for the inclusion of common Web elements such as navigation. Libraries of common Perl code elements also reduce the maintenance overhead. Configuration of the software for unique installations is accomplished by redefining configuration parameters in a centralized file. Postdoc's dynamic data are stored both in the file system (for documents and e-mail messages) and in the MySQL relational database. Currently the system runs at NASA ARC on a Sun Solaris 2.6 server. As the system

is written completely in Perl code, porting it to other modern Unix or Linux operating systems is a matter of installing the various off-the-shelf support components and ensuring that Perl is properly installed. The client interaction performance of Postdoc has maintained a high level of usability without the need for more complex Web application server architectures. Off-the-shelf components, such as Adobe Acrobat for PDF conversions, can be integrated into the system to take advantage of technology improvements. System reliability and availability of the Postdoc environment is key in supporting the adoption of the software nationally and internationally. The simplicity of the Apache Web server architecture and CGI interface, coupled with a variety of system monitors, helps to keep the system continuously available for months at a time without interruptions or outages.

POSTDOC IS LAUNCHED

With the initial development of Postdoc, NASA's first efforts toward the implementation of an innovative collaborative computing platform were initiated. The Postdoc team at ARC's Computational Science Division pioneered Web-based collaboration at NASA. Since its launch in 1997, Postdoc has proven to be an effective tool for organizing, storing, and retrieving data and information of all types. This multiuser, Web-based application has dramatically improved the communication of technical, managerial, administrative, and scientific information between members of widely dispersed teams, nationally and internationally. One of the first collaboration tools of its kind, Postdoc allowed NASA scientists and engineers to share mission-critical information in real time, across different organizations, geographies, and computing platforms, regardless of format. One of the unique features of Postdoc is that it can support the needs for secure interorganizational collaboration since the system provides built-in security and may reside outside of the organization's firewall. Given NASA's requirements for knowledge sharing across organizations, which include the agency and collaborating universities and private companies, this specific capability is included among its unique features.

The development of Postdoc focused on effectively supporting knowledge creation by directly enabling collaboration via the sharing of information resources among users. Users are allowed to add structure to those resources that are consistent with their own work practices. Soon after the software was launched, it was viewed as an enabler for sharing meaningful processes, information, and documents between the many geographically distributed programs and enterprise activities at NASA. Bob Kanefsky, staff scientist and lead of the Postdoc development team, recalls the following:

The prototype system that was used during the Remote Agent development itself was…developed rapidly, in the heat of the Remote Agent prototyping effort, and was further refined in parallel with the flight software development for the DS-1 mission. The original model was for the system to be a distributed editing system that would allow multiple authors to create living documents by adding paragraphs of text, links, images, and so on. It quickly became clear, though, that users preferred to use conventional editing tools such as Microsoft Office to create documents, and saw value in Postdoc as a means to pass these documents around for review and editing. We therefore switched to the model that it should act much like a distributed file system: "section headers" became "folders," "paragraphs" became "sticky notes," and documents became the most common type of item to add to a folder.

We experimented with specialized types of folder contents. We briefly used an Action Item object for tracking DS-1 workflow and deadlines, but it proved not to be the most convenient way to do this. We made more extensive use of a

DS-1-specific "Message Dictionary" that automatically cross-linked DS-1 documentation by inter-process message names. For example, the EXECUTE_TURN message was documented by the Attitude Control, Remote Agent Executive, and Remote Agent Planner subsystem documentation, and also appeared in logs of test runs. Hyperlinks were automatically added to these documents, wherever the term EXECUTE_TURN appeared, to cross-link them whenever a new document was posted.

The most popular capabilities of Postdoc, though, were the ability to create and manage "folders," post documents to them, and automatically translate PC/Mac documents to Portable Document Format for use on Unix. Those capabilities, along with new ones [enabled] Postdoc to remain in continuous use into the 21st century.

The DS-1 Remote Agent team quickly became one of Postdoc's most active groups of users, using the system as a repository of source code, design parameters, and software models for the DS-1 Remote Agent. Successful early adoptions of Postdoc by the DS-1 developers demonstrated its ability to support aerospace designers to shorten and enhance the efficiency of the management and design-cycle processes. One of the program milestones was to demonstrate an increase by a factor of 10 times the number of geographically distributed participants using Web-based collaboration in support of science and engineering design, development, and management activities. User participation in Postdoc increased extensively (refer to Table 2) due to its ease of use and wide availability. The teams using Postdoc experienced significant reduction in cross-enterprise project management costs, both by enhancing the communication among various distributed programs, and by enabling project members to share the required information resources. The success of the DS-1 Remote Agent captured the whole New Millennium Program's attention, and Postdoc would become the infrastructure of choice

Table 2. Usage statistics for Postdoc (Summary by Month)

Summary by Month										
Month	Daily Avg				Monthly Totals					
	Hits	Files	Pages	Visits	Sites	KBytes	Visits	Pages	Files	Hits
Sep 2004	4623	2716	917	177	3820	9499477	5143	26607	78789	134084
Aug 2004	4411	2714	764	168	4031	10009662	5235	23712	84143	136742
Jul 2004	4450	2617	803	164	3864	12662925	5086	24893	81156	137965
Jun 2004	6189	3861	837	176	8689	10898199	5297	25115	115835	185698
May 2004	4625	2888	828	176	4155	7584753	5463	25677	89545	143397
Apr 2004	5274	3308	970	207	4296	11154085	6221	29116	99266	158227
Mar 2004	6380	3586	1536	199	4171	10784534	6177	47646	111183	197804
Feb 2004	6252	3864	808	159	3057	12523316	4630	23450	112056	181317
Jan 2004	6177	3816	798	163	3259	18779325	5053	24747	118299	191491
Dec 2003	5042	2681	594	143	2836	11606001	4447	18435	83141	156324
Nov 2003	6666	4549	1056	179	3060	13189635	5384	31696	136482	199998
Oct 2003	11265	4840	1522	200	3787	9502325	6220	47200	150068	349220
Totals						138194237	64356	348294	1259963	2172267

to support this program of six missions and six technology teams. It is estimated that Postdoc resulted in $1 million dollars in savings due to streamlined documentation and reduced travel costs for software development and integration.

Another group of Postdoc's early users was the Combined Federal Campaign (CFC), an annual fundraising drive conducted by federal employees each fall. The CFC pools together millions of dollars from private contributions by federal and military employees to benefit thousands of nonprofit charities. At NASA ARC, approximately 50 federal employee volunteers, working in over 50 divisions, carry out the CFC. Prior to the deployment of Postdoc, the required information flow for decision making between the volunteers was primarily supported by e-mail. The debut of Postdoc at NASA ARC enabled government volunteers to share required documentation via this tool. Deepak Kulkani, a computer scientist in the Collaborative Assistant Systems group, describes the experience:

Bob Lopez and I decided to use Postdoc for sharing documents that were revised continuously over time. This had tremendous benefits in making sure that we had access to the latest information while running the campaign. It saved us significant amount of time.

Postdoc's success as an infrastructure to support collaboration continued to grow within the agency. The Postdoc team quickly recognized that user support would be key to its continued growth, therefore it set up an appropriate human- as well as computer-based infrastructure to ensure that users would have access to an effective and efficient user support system.

Once Postdoc demonstrated its usefulness as a collaborative information-sharing application for cross-agency management and design, there was one remaining issue: Who would take over the operations of this innovative system, considered to be one of the first agency-wide systems? The developers of Postdoc would need to assume this role for the agency. Postdoc had started out as a research project used to define how a Web-based collaboration system could be used to manage research and development projects and programs that need to continually share information with partners across the agency, as well across other organizations. However, gaining acceptance as the Web-based collaboration system of choice meant that Postdoc still had to be put through a last test: the capability maturity model (CMM) process. Since NASA requires software assurance of mission applications, the ARC operations branch performed an operational capability review to ensure the software was ready for operation, and Postdoc successfully achieved CMM status. Postdoc was also certified and accredited in meeting the federal IT security requirements using the National Institute of Standards and Technology's guidance in securing the confidentiality, integrity, and availability of information maintained in the system. Postdoc provided users with guidance on the type of information the system was accredited for, providing prompts within the system to remind users of their information-handling responsibilities in the use of the application.

THE IMPACT OF POSTDOC IN NASA

Postdoc provided a foundation of many key lessons learned for some of NASA's newer technologies that came in to enhance NASA's sharing of information. Perhaps the biggest barrier to the pervasive adoption and utilization of collaboration technologies is changing the way people work (Groth, 1999), even with respect to the notion of time (Saunders, Van Slyke, & Vogel, 2004). Although some barriers may exist to Web-based collaboration, primarily because

of its availability and simplicity to use, as well as its flexibility, elegance, and sophistication in design, the use of Postdoc grew organically across the different NASA centers to more than 6,000 users by 2004. Elegance in design came from utilizing diverse resources in an integrated way to provide functionality. Postdoc was built on top of existing sophisticated server applications and capitalized on all the development efforts that have preceded its code, and its sophistication derived from using system resources in a combined fashion. Resource components were recruited from the system environment when they were required to accomplish specific tasks. Postdoc's simple and intuitive graphic interface was the result of creative ingenuity. Finally, Postdoc achieved simplicity of operation while driving powerful collaborations.

One of the most important lessons learned from this implementation is that users prefer simplicity and ease of use in the application, in particular when uploading and downloading documents for sharing on any platform and in any format. In addition, having a help desk with a live person on the line provided users with the necessary insight for adequate implementation of the collaborative functionality. This combination created the necessary user trust in the application as a platform for sharing data securely with colleagues in a team. Finally, the users as the primary customers contributed to the design requirements of system upgrades, and therefore felt ownership of the application via their ability to contribute to its design.

Collaboration technologies develop a perspective on how each person's work relies on the work of others. Users across NASA centers used Postdoc to conduct document sharing and decision support of all types, such as the following:

1. Programmatic functions including the review of proposals responding to NASA research announcements, program reporting and tracking, and scientific reporting

2. Calls for papers involving large conferences (i.e., American Association for Artificial Intelligence, International Joint Conference on Artificial Intelligence) and many other professional society activities

3. Program initiatives across several centers, supporting collaboration on technology and mission plans and proposals, and enabling the distribution of information throughout the centers

Some of the uses of Postdoc across NASA include the following:

1. **Scientific research:** The Astrobiology Institute. Postdoc supported around 500 users who use the system for sharing publications, data, and scientific results, and for conferencing support. The NASA Astrobiology Virtual Institute Experiment has used the system extensively. Program IT manager William Likens stated, "*An Institute with geographically dispersed staff can use [this] technology to operate effectively as if it was located within a single campus.*"

2. **Business process support:** Ames ISO (International Organization for Standardization) Certification Directorate. Ames used the software as a documentation system for storage of ISO documentation, correction action requests, and revisions.

3. **Field experiments:** The Marsokhod project, for example, used the system to share results in real time with geographically dispersed teams. The Marsokhod, a joint U.S. and Russian effort, is a tele-operated robotic vehicle. In the early part of 1993, a prototype of the rover was brought to NASA ARC from Russia to be interfaced with a virtual environment control system. The rover has since made several missions around the world at locations that exhibit Mars-like terrain, including the Kamchatka Peninsula in Siberia in 1993, the Mojave Desert in the United States in 1994, and in the Kilauea volcano in the United States in 1995. Postdoc provided a platform for automated capture of the data collected by the rover, and supported the creation of higher level data products. Postdoc allowed Marsokhod mission scientists to easily share and collaborate on scientific results internationally.

4. **Scientific proposal review:** Several programs, including the Earth Sciences Enterprise Advanced Information System Technology program, the Space Sciences Enterprise Cross Enterprise Technology Development program, and the Aviation Safety and Security Program at Langley Research Center used the system to review the proposals received as a response to the NASA research announcements. These programs continued to report that the software allowed them to communicate smoothly across platforms, software versions, and the country. George B. Finelli, director of the Aviation Safety and Security Program, made the following comment.

Postdoc has been invaluable to successfully managing the NASA Aviation Safety and Security Program. The system allows us to quickly and easily share information among the Program management team, to report accomplishments, and to prepare for technical meetings and reviews. Postdoc has also enabled the Program to completely demonstrate official record keeping and tracking as required by NASA procedures and guidelines. Because the application accepts virtually all file types and is so simple to use—anytime anywhere—we use it on a daily basis. Our independent reviewers even use it to assess the Program's financial and schedule archives, and it has become a "service" that NASA provides to groups like the Commercial Aviation Safety Team that includes many Government and industry organizations. No formal training required!

5. **Cooperation and collaboration across programs:** Postdoc fostered cooperation and synergy within NASA's Information Technology Base Program and the new Intelligent Synthesis Environments Initiative, which was aimed toward improving NASA's engineering, science culture, and creative process. According to Yuri Gawdiak, Level I program manager for Engineering for Complex Systems (ECS) at NASA Headquarters, Postdoc has been a key collaboration tool for coordination of the Aviation Safety Program design, Non Advocate Review (NAR), Internal Audit Review (IAR), initial implementation and general programmatic operations. The system is used extensively by all the NASA flight centers as well as for our national and international customer base for global aviation safety issues. It has been a great tool in facilitating teleconferences, workshops, and conferences. The Postdoc repository, with its sophisticated user interface, has become an indispensable corporate knowledge database for the entire Aviation Safety Program.

NASA's use of the Postdoc software sparked an awareness in the agency about how large programs can create virtual work spaces to be shared among geographically distributed teams.

It was estimated that during the period of 1995 to 2004, the use of Postdoc as a collaboration infrastructure resulted in savings to the agency of over $4 million a year. Many NASA programs across the NASA organization estimated savings of at least $100,000 and up to $200,000 in travel expenditures due to the use of Web-based collaboration. These savings do not consider the intangible efficiency gains achieved through this Web-based collaboration platform, such as eliminating the hardships associated with attaching large documents to e-mails, as well as increased document security and integrity. The agency continued to save as the user base on the current system continues to grow primarily due to the many benefits that Postdoc provides. Postdoc's use reached across the agency in supporting approximately 30 NASA programs. This even included partnerships across the federal government including programs at the Department of Defense, National Institutes of Standards and Technology, Naval Research Laboratories, and the National Imagery and Mapping Agency. Today Postdoc has been successfully migrated into NX, a new knowledge-management-based technology that leveraged Postdoc's foundation of lessons learned and user requirements. NX is the result of a partnership between NASA Ames Research Center's Computational Sciences Division (the same division that developed Postdoc) and Xerox Corporation. In this partnership, Ames Research is transferring the research and development in collaboration technologies to Xerox, who in turn is implementing this research into Xerox's DocuShare product to create the NX product specifically for NASA. NX incorporates critical collaboration functionality that was not available in the DocuShare product. The NX product will then be available as a commercial off-the-shelf product for use within NASA and other organizations with similar needs.

VISIONS FOR THE FUTURE OF WEB-BASED DECISION SUPPORT

Several projects under way at NASA seek to develop automated interfaces for data collection and analysis, Web-based collaborative and knowledge capture systems, and intelligent systems for autonomous reasoning. Postdoc demonstrated the ability to serve as the foundation to build NASA's collaborative information management capability by strengthening functionalities for knowledge sharing, and serving as the infrastructure for integration of other virtual collaborative interfaces.

Postdoc allowed users to tailor their documentation systems to their processes and work habits, within their time constraints. Providing NASA engineers and scientists with a platform for Web-based collaborative decision support is of high importance. The future of this technology, yet to be determined, is defined by how we apply our own humanity. People are expanding their awareness of space and time in unprecedented ways. The farther our machines and minds explore leading-edge Internet content and tools for communication, collaboration, and visualization, the more we must look within ourselves.

Today the requirements from technologies providing information and knowledge sharing across federal agencies have increased, due in part to the increased information security threat that the Internet poses today. The new Federal Information Security Management Act of 2002 specifies that any technology development for the federal sector must adhere to strict design requirements that focus on the protection of information confidentiality, integrity, and availability. Thus, the federal government requires specific security criteria for technologies used for the sharing of information across agencies and their partners. Most these requirements are found in the National Institute of Standards 800 series.

Improvements in cost-to-performance ratios of IT have caused the cost of digitizing information to approach zero, and the cost of coordinating across individuals, organizational subunits, and organizations to approach zero as well (Grover & Segars, 1996). We envision the future of Web-based collaboration to include technologies that are spawned off by collaboration technologies similar to Postdoc in the exploration and building of virtual worlds on the Internet (Malone et al., 1999). For example, integrating three-dimensional (3-D) avatars[5] and intelligent agents within the system could provide researchers the opportunity to have their body doubles interacting and collaborating in virtual communities inside 3-D collaborative virtual worlds. Considerable progress is expected in the way in which the agents will evolve (i.e., change, develop, and act). Such evolutionary agents may be dramatically different in their abilities to (a) build theories and create a world of their own, (b) assume any virtual identity they wish, (c) possess free will, and (d) develop a moral code and value system of their own. Thus, the future of Web-based collaboration will be dramatically different due to the inevitable, unpredictable over any long period of time, and quantum changes in IT.

REFERENCES

Becerra-Fernandez, I., Del Alto, M., & Stewart, H. (2006). Postdoc: A model for Web-based collaborative decision support at NASA. *International Journal of e-Collaboration, 2*(3), 49-63.

Becerra-Fernandez, I., Gonzalez, A., & Sabherwal, R. (2004). *Knowledge management: Challenges, solutions, and technologies.* Upper Saddle River, NJ: Prentice Hall.

Davenport, T., & Prusak, L. (1998). *Working knowledge: How organizations manage what they know.* Boston: Harvard Business School Press.

Groth, L. (1999). *Future organizational design.* West Sussex, UK: John Wiley & Sons.

Grover, V., & Segars, A. H. (1996). IT: The next 1100102 years. *Database, 27*(4), 45-57.

Kumar, K., & van Dissel, H. G. (1996). Sustainable collaboration: Managing conflict and cooperation in inter-organizational systems. *MIS Quarterly, 20*(3), 279-290.

Leonard, D., & Swap, W. (2004). Deep smarts. *Harvard Business Review, 82*(9), 88-97.

Leonard, D., & Swap, W. (2005). *Deep smarts: How to cultivate and transfer enduring business wisdom.* Boston: Harvard Business School.

Majchrzak, A., Cooper, L., & Neece, O. (2004). Knowledge reuse for Innovation. *Management Science, 50*(2), 174-188.

Malhotra, A., & Majchrzak, A. (2004). Enabling knowledge creation in far-flung teams: Best practices for IT support and knowledge sharing. *Journal of Knowledge Management, 8*(4), 75-86.

Malhotra, A., & Majchrzak, A. (2005). Virtual workspace technologies. *MIT Sloan Management Review, 46*(2), 11-14.

Malone, T. W, Crowston, K., Lee, J., & Pentland, B. (1999). Tools for inventing organizations: Towards a handbook of organizational processes. *Management Science, 45*(11), 65-78.

NASA workforce analysis report. (2003). Retrieved August 14, 2003, from http://nasapeople. nasa.gov/workforce/

Nonaka, I., & Takeuchi, H. (1995). *The knowledge creating company.* New York: Oxford University Press.

Saunders, C. S., Van Slyke, C., & Vogel, D. (2004). My time or yours? Managing time visions in global virtual teams. *Academy of Management Executive, 18*(1), 19-31.

Senge, P. M. (1990). *The fifth discipline: The art and practice of the learning organization.* New York: Currency Doubleday.

Smith, J. (2003, July 13). *Mistakes of NASA touted up.* Washington Post.

ENDNOTES

[1] Space Shuttle Columbia broke during reentry into the atmosphere on February 1, 2003, due to damage at lift-off to its protective tiles.

[2] Remote Agent was a complex software system for controlling and monitoring autonomous spacecraft.

[3] Dan Goldin was the NASA administrator during the period of 1992 until 2001.

[4] The first Web-based document management systems would not appear on the market until late 1996, with the offerings of Livelink by Open Text (http://www.opentext.com) and DocuShare 2.0 by Xerox (http://www.xerox. com).

[5] An avatar is a graphical icon that represents a real person in a cyberspace system. When you enter the system, you can choose from a number of fanciful avatars. Sophisticated 3-D avatars even change shape depending on what they are doing (e.g., walking, sitting, etc.; http://www.webopedia.com).

This work was previously published in E-Collaboration in Modern Organizations: Initiating and Managing Distributed Projects, edited by N. Kock, pp. 113-125, copyright 2008 by Information Science Reference (an imprint of IGI Global).

Chapter 14
Information Technology Adoption by Groups Across Time

Vicki L. Sauter
University of Missouri - St. Louis, USA

ABSTRACT

Today's technologies can support joint, but physically disparate work efforts. Some groups of professionals that could benefit from using these technologies do not adopt them, while others use the technologies frequently. This study provides an in-depth examination of how and when one organization accepted technology in their decision-making efforts. The research examines actual usage of the technology rather than the less strong, but more common measure, intention to use technology. As a result, the paper has helped bridge the gap between what people intend to do and what they actually do, thereby providing both a stronger theoretical basis for the TAM model and some insights into the evolution of the TAM model. It examines an emerging extension to the TAM and provides evidence of the behavior of users when they must act as a group.

INTRODUCTION

Today's technology environment has introduced a productivity paradox, in that despite substantial investments in information technology, it has not been possible to demonstrate improved white collar productivity. Some researchers believe that the solution to technology's productivity paradox is to reduce the number of installed systems that are *under*utilized. [Sichel, 1997] In other words, the issue is not whether there is not enough or too much technology *available* in organizations today, but rather, the issue is that end-users are not embracing the technology that is available. Research from the last 15 years, completed by more than a hundred researchers, has considered how to improve user acceptance through the application of the Technology Acceptance Model (TAM). (See, for example, Brown, Massey, Montoya-Weiss, and Burkman, 2002; Chau and Hu, 2002; Gefen, 2003; Gefen, Karahanna and Straub, 2003; Gefen and Straub, 2000; Karahanna, *et al.*, 1999; Karahanna and Straub, 1998; Keil *et al*, 1995; Lederer, Maupin, Sena and Zhuang, 2000; Ma and Liu, 2004; Morris and Dillon, 1997; Sussman, 2003; Szajna, 1986; Thompson, *et al.*, 1994; Venkatesh, 1999; Venkatesh, 2000; Venkatesh and Davis, 1994; Venkatesh and Davis, 2000) Based on the Theory of Reasoned Action, TAM suggests that one's acceptance of technology is driven by one's beliefs about the consequences of that usage. (Fischbein and Azjen, 1975) In particular, TAM predicts that users embrace a new technology when their perceptions of the ease of use, *and* the usefulness of the technology are positive. (Davis, 1989; Davis, *et al.*, 1989)

The first factor, *perceived ease of use*, represents the level of difficulty the user expects to have in integrating the tool into his or her routine. The second factor, *usefulness*, represents whether the technology will enhance his or her performance in completing a job. "Usefulness" then assumes not only that the system *will* enhance performance, but also that the user can perceive both the enhancement and its impact. (Davis, 1989) TAM suggests the user must be able to perceive *both* ease-of-use (PEOU) *and* usefulness (PU) before he or she will adopt new technology. (Davis, *et al.*, 1989)

While TAM has been validated by its creator and other researchers and applied studying a variety of technologies, there continues to be ambiguity about how to use the theory to improve user acceptance behavior. For example, it is not clear how the first factor, PEOU, plays a role in the decision. Several studies, such as Hendrickson and Collins (1996), Subramanian (1994), and Venkatesh and Davis (1996), suggest PEOU is a critical antecedent to user acceptance. However, other studies, such as those by Szajna (1996) and Venkatesh (1999), suggest PEOU has no effect on adoption decisions, and still others show the impact is indirect through an intermediary impact of PU. (Davis, 1992; Keil, *et al.*, 1995; Morris and Dillon, 1997; Venkatesh and Davis, 1994) The contradictions from these various studies seem difficult to resolve as IT has experienced rapid growth in businesses as programs have become easier to master, and more consistent. Figure 1 illustrates the variety of ways PEOU has been shown to affect the intention to adopt technology.

However, Gefen and Straub's (2000) study shows that PEOU only affects the decision to use technology if the primary task of the system is directly associated with intrinsic IT characteristics. That is, PEOU only affects usage when the task for which the technology is being used is the same as the purpose of the technology (such as e-mail being used to inform, and the purpose of e-mail is to inform). Further, Venkatesh (2000) notes that individuals may be driven by their general beliefs about system usability (regardless of their experience with a particular system), computer anxiety, and perceptions of external control and that these factors might obscure the impact of PEOU. These roles are illustrated in Figure 2.

There is, however, no disagreement in the literature that the second factor, PU influences tool adoption and usage. The impact of this factor has been demonstrated in numerous studies and has not been questioned seriously by any study. Researchers now struggle to isolate the factors contributing to users' perceptions that a tool is useful. For example, Chau and Hu (2002) provide evidence that compatibility of the technology with users' routine operations of completing tasks will impact their perceptions of PU. In that study, the authors looked at physicians in Hong Kong (as examples of independent professionals) and their intentions to use telemedicine in their individual practices. They note that any independent professional becomes accustomed to a particular style of work and will evaluate usefulness of technology in light of its compatibility with that style of work.

Figure 1. Unclear role of PEOU in the decision to adopt

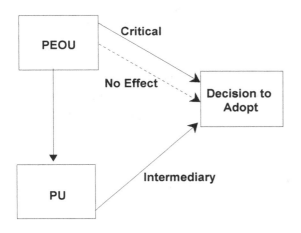

Figure 2. Alternative view of the role of PEOU

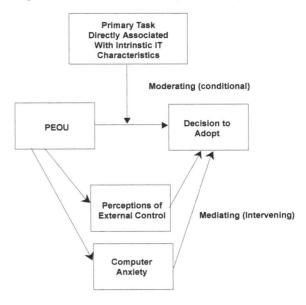

In fact, the authors noted that this compatibility appeared to be a "*critical* antecedent to perceived usefulness." However, the authors noted that while compatibility is a *necessary* factor, it may not be *sufficient* to convince professionals to adopt technology. Similarly, Venkatesh and Davis (2000) note that it is critical to design systems both to meet the needs of the job, and to provide a high quality of output. This behavior might be linked to what Gefen [2003] observed when he investigated the role of "habit" in explaining *continued* use of a technology. He examined online shoppers' intention to continue to use a specific Web site based upon where they purchased before, and found the variable "habit" to contribute, along with both PEOU and PU, to intention to use the technology. That is, that people may not change their behavior regarding technology simply because they are in a particular habit of doing things a particular way.

The literature also questions which factors impact PU in the continued usage of the technology. (Davis, *et al.*, 1989, Karahanna, *et al.*, 1999; Thompson, *et al.*, 1994) For example, a study by Karahanna, *et al.* (1999) demonstrated that attitudes and adoption decisions are not static. Rather, the adoption process is complex and dy-

namic, with relevant factors changing over time. Venkatesh and Davis (2000) found that mandatory or compliance-based introduction of systems tend to be less effective over the long term. In particular, they noted that mandatory introduction of systems caused the systems to be adopted, but did not guarantee that the systems' use would be maintained over time. Further, they found that the subjective norm had positive effects to impact usage when the usage was mandatory, but not when it was voluntary. In addition, studies, such as the one by Karahanna and Straub (1998), in which the quality of media richness was examined, illustrate that technology use must not only be useful, but of high quality. for it to be adopted and maintained. Similarly, Venkatesh and Davis (2003) suggest that a decision maker's beliefs about usefulness are impacted by an interaction between the relevance of the system to their job and the quality of the output from the system. The relationship between perceived usefulness and continued use of the system is shown in Figure 3.

This study examines the behavior of users representing a range of technology experience

Figure 3. Perceived usefulness role in prediction continued system usage

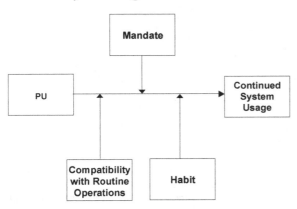

in light of the TAM model, with an emphasis on their behavior over time. In particular, it examines technology usage when adoption is a joint or team decision, such as when the usage is by a virtual organization or team.

The purpose of this paper is to present results from an in-depth case analysis which explores the question: *What underlies the phenomenon to accept technology when the entire group must adopt the tool for it to be useful?* The data will chronicle the experience of an actual organization in adopting and using a tool over a four-year period. There are three distinct time periods examined: (a) the introduction and early use of the product for a fixed period of time; (b) an intervention mandating the use of the tool for a short period; and (c) the post-intervention use, when the use was no longer mandated. Unlike most studies, the analyses in this paper are based on an objective measurement of the *actual use* of the technology, not on the intentions to use the technology. In addition to analysis of actual use, the researchers examined users' reflections (obtained via questionnaire) on their levels of usage during the study.

Hence, based on the literature, we expected to observe the following phenomena:

- Products that are easy to use, but do not enhance the *group task* substantially, will not

be adopted by the group to replace existing tools;

- A mandate requiring tool use can affect the short term usage and the dynamics that drive it; but

- Once the mandate has been relaxed, usage will return to no more than the level that would have been experienced without the mandate and the factors influencing that usage will change.

METHODOLOGY

This research was conducted as a single site case study in which researchers conducted an ex-post evaluation of usage logs and administered a questionnaire. This study involved no external (researcher-induced) manipulation of the subjects, but was, instead, simply an examination of the record of subjects' behavior during the regular operations of an organization. Further, the study did not involve self-reported measures of usage, but, rather, had an objective measure of actual usage of the tool. There was, however, no evaluation of the "quality" of the usage or coding of the specific use.

The Subjects

Study subjects were volunteer decision-makers associated with a not-for-profit organization.[1] At the core of the decision making is a Board of Directors (referred to hereafter as "the Board"); positions on the Board included the standard ones of president, past president, president-elect, secretary and treasurer, as well as vice-presidents, with specific domains of influence, representatives of topical units and representatives elected at large. In addition to the Board, the "community" being examined included support staff and committee chairs, all of whom had access to use the tool. The Board was composed of volunteers who were elected for terms of 2-3 years. Most committee chairs[2] were appointed, generally, for a three-year term. Committee chairs and Board members worked closely with staff "partners" to achieve the goals of the organization. The volunteers were quite "hands-on" and actively involved with the work and decision making of the organization.

Subjects were well versed in the use of various technologies to support their work for the not-for-profit organization. For example, on any given day, the Board, especially the executive committee, exchanged a number of e-mails about the business of the organization.

Before any use of the tool (which will be described shortly), there was appropriate training in the use of the product. At the beginning of the project, training was held during Board meetings so that all volunteers were able to participate. The IT staff, using overhead display equipment, and live Internet access, provided step-by-step instruction in a classroom-like setting. Users did not have hands-on access during the training, but were able to experiment with the system during breaks if they desired. These training sessions included not only information about how to use the system, but also why to use it and how operations would be improved if volunteers took advantage of the opportunity. All volunteers involved with the group during the introduction of the tool received this training. As with any set of volunteers, however, there was turnover during the period examined. When a new volunteer (either as a Board member or as a committee chair) joined, the IT staff provided training on the tool. In addition, online instructions were provided for all volunteers. There was, however, no specific training provided to the group prior to the mandated period of use.

The Tool

This study examined the Board's (and its associated community) use of the Ultimate Bulletin Board (UBB), an online discussion tool available commercially since 1998,[3] to support decision-making. UBB supports discussion through asynchronous postings either of basic text, or of linking to and/or embedding html documents. The system supports a threaded, scrolling interface which allows postings on a particular topic or thread to be grouped (and therefore, read) together and responded to directly, or collapse the tree to view responses on multiple topics.

UBB was chosen jointly by the (volunteer) president-elect and the (staff) executive director of the site organization, in consultation with the IT staff, to achieve greater efficiencies at quarterly meetings. Prior to the adoption of the tool, volunteers were sent written reports to read before the meeting. Often those same reports were repeated (orally) at the meeting prior to discussion, and the volume of matters requiring discussion had outgrown the time available at the meetings. The organization adopted the tool to provide a mechanism for sharing information and for discussing that information *prior* to actual (physical) meetings. The goal of adopting the tool was to reduce the amount of time spent in meetings, and to allocate meeting time better so as to focus on more serious, more sensitive, or more controversial issues that required face-to-face deliberation. This specific tool, UBB, was chosen for two reasons. First, the president-elect had used the tool in another organization and found it worthwhile. Second, at the time of the initial adoption, UBB was by far the most used tool of this kind and had the most features.

THE DATA COLLECTION

Researchers examined data logs of access by users which contained the number of times the tool was used during each of the three of periods of time: pre-intervention, intervention, and post-intervention. The access logs identified the number of times users accessed the information provided with the tool, while the "postings" reported the number of times the users elected to use the tool to communicate. Said differently, the first measure was of the subjects' unobserved usage or "lurking behavior," while the second measure was of the subjects' observed use of the tool. There was no evaluation of the content of the posts during any of the three time periods.

The ex-post evaluation of usage logs was broken into three distinct periods for evaluation. This allowed us to view trends in usage patterns and the factors contributing to them distinctly. Phase I of this study includes subjects' early tool usage, beginning when subjects first used the tool, which we will call Year 1. During this time period, training was provided and tool use was advised. Phase II of the study considered tool usage during a period for which usage was *required* for a short time (late in the fourth quarter of Year 2). A specific major issue needed to be discussed by the organization's board and agreed upon quickly during a time when no face-to-face meeting could be held. Hence, senior decision makers mandated that discussion and resolution of the issue would done using UBB. The exact nature of that issue will be discussed shortly. Phase III of the study considered subjects' tool use after the mandated usage period was finished. This included all usage beginning in the first quarter of Year 3 through the first quarter of Year 5.

The tool was used as a supplement to quarterly face-to-face meetings in both Phase I and Phase III of this analysis. However, tool use became mandatory during Phase II due to difficulties in budget planning during Year 3. The preparation of the budget was delayed because of a combination of staffing changes and budgetary process changes that had occurred and caused the entire process to be off cycle (and not available to be presented at the regular meeting). In addition, preliminary budgets were showing a projected deficit that required budget tightening. In light of the need to approve the budget quickly and the desire not to incur any non-critical additional expenses,

senior decision-makers mandated using the tool for presentation and deliberation, and to take any necessary ballots via e-mail. The follow-up questionnaire provided a mechanism for obtaining qualitative, subjective data about the experience to guide this analysis.

To clarify, the various conditions during the observational periods are illustrated in Figure 4. In all cases, reports were available before meetings using UBB and were archived after the meeting using UBB, and one-on-one training was always available upon request.

THE RESULTS

Pre-Intervention Usage

Figure 5 represents the pre-intervention usage of the tool by the community. If one looks at the raw number of postings, it appears as though early acceptance was significant but tapered off from that initial success, as measured by the number of postings. However, these first two periods (labeled "Summer Year 1" and "Fall Year 1") had a substantial number of postings by a user identified as "administrator" who appeared to post reports for some other individuals.[4] These administrator postings are separated from the general usage in Figure 5. Without the postings by "administrator," there were only 70 and 72 postings in Summer and Fall, respectively.

Similarly, lurking behavior was very low during this period. With the exception of the administrator, the model behavior was to log on twice before each face-to-face meeting. Typically one of these logins was for the purposes of posting a report, and the other was to check for changes or comments just prior to the meeting.

In other words, the technology did not play a significant role in the decision making during this period. While some reports were posted, there was little, if any, discussion about those reports using the technology. When the group met

Figure 4. Conditions for each meeting during the study period

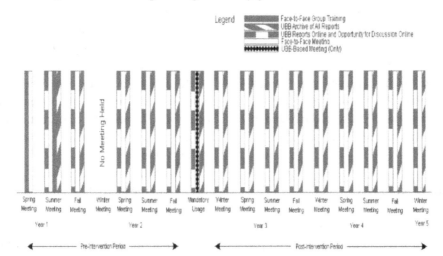

Figure 5. Pre-intervention usage

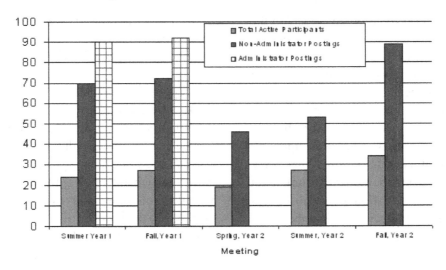

face-to-face, reports were presented and evaluated (generally) without regard to any discussion posted on the UBB.

Interviews with Board members indicated that they just did not find this new tool useful. First and foremost, few people actually read the material posted very far in advance of the meeting, and there was little discussion of it on the UBB. Hence, any discussion that had appeared on the UBB needed to be repeated for the sake of the majority of Board members who had not participated. This, in turn, provided further disincentive to use the system because those who did use it would be doing twice the work (discussion online and discussion at a meeting).

Furthermore, prior to the intervention, Board members did not find the UBB a useful tool for problem solving. While it gave Board members access to information prior to the meeting, users found the UBB to be a less desirable medium for discussion than face-to-face meetings. Instead, users actively used e-mail and telephone contact to discuss issues as needed. Users found these media sufficient to meet their needs.

Thus, given these two problems, without the champion (i.e., the "administrator" who posted reports and comments for others) pushing the use of the technology, the UBB would have been abandoned during this time period.

INTERVENTION USAGE

The intervention represented a mandatory use of the technology for a fixed period of time while the Board discussed a proposed budget. As stated previously, a set of unforeseen circumstances, including an unanticipated change of personnel and computer systems, resulted in a delay in the preparation of financial statements for the fourth quarter meeting of the Board. These financial statements were critical because they constituted the foundation of the discussion of the annual budget (also not completed), which was to have been approved at that meeting. Further, changes in operations and regular pressures upon all not-for-profit organizations required that some priority-setting decisions be made with the budget to ensure deficit-free operation in the subsequent year. Hence, the Board decided to use the available technology of the UBB to host a "discussion" after the budget was available, rather than voting pre-maturely or needing another group face-to-face meeting.

In consideration of the budget, the Board was required to consider a number of ancillary motions to adjust funding for some activities as well as the motion of accepting the budget as presented. In all, ten motions were presented by the treasurer. By the end of the discussion period, one motion had been withdrawn, and the intent of another had been integrated with remaining motions. The budget and all motions passed by a comfortable margin.

The Board used the technology aggressively during the two weeks of discussion and voting on the motions. Board members, committee members and staff were encouraged to discuss the budget during the "discussion weeks". Since the budget would dictate activities in the various departments during the subsequent year, and since this forum was the primary opportunity to discuss the budget, this was *de facto* a "mandatory" usage of the system.

During the "discussion week," there were 4053 accesses of the UBB. Not surprisingly, individual access data were varied significantly. Although on average, participating individuals accessed the system 90 times each (standard deviation of 118.4), the median number of accesses was 42, and the model number of accesses was seven. As the descriptive statistics suggest, the distribution of the usage was quite skewed. Subjects reported that participation required more of their attention than they had expected, and more than they would generally have allocated during this generally "busy period" at their regular employment during the two weeks of Phase II.

When comparing the intervention results with the pre-intervention results, as shown in Figure 6, one can see some slow growth in the number of active participants during the three experiences with the tool immediately prior to the mandatory period, but the number of postings was modest. However, the "budget discussions" period with the UBB brought explosive growth in the usage of the medium. This growth is especially notable considering the fact that a typical UBB experience lasted for up to six weeks before the face-to-face meetings), while the *total period* for the budget discussion and deliberation was *14 days*. In each of the previous discussions, the model of the number of postings was one per individual; during the two weeks of mandatory usage, the model of the number of postings was seven.

Analyses were conducted to determine the factors that could help explain why people were or were not using the technology. As one can see from Table 1 and Figure 6, 72% of the accesses during the intervention period were from Board members, especially Executive Committee members. Committee chairs and staff used the tool to a smaller degree. Board members as a whole accessed the UBB an average of 131.2 times each (standard deviation of 150.7), with a median of 105. If we separate the Executive Committee from the remainder of the Board, it becomes clear that a substantial amount of the traffic was due to Executive Committee participation. EC members accessed the tool an average of 327 times (standard deviation of 157.05), with a median of 345; non

EC-Board members accessed the tool an average of 61 times (standard deviation of 52.8), with a median of 56 times. In fact, the difference in participation between EC and non-EC members was statistically significant, both measured as accesses (t=2.84, p ≤ .05 | unequal variances, df_1=13, df_2=4, one-tail) or postings (t=6.582, p ≤ .05 | unequal variances, df_1=13, df_2=4, one-tail); this one factor represented the greatest individual predictor of participation on the UBB. Subjects reported that usage paralleled normal face-to-face meetings with committee chairs and staff having little or no participation, and the executive com-

Figure 6. Pre-intervention, intervention, and post-intervention usage

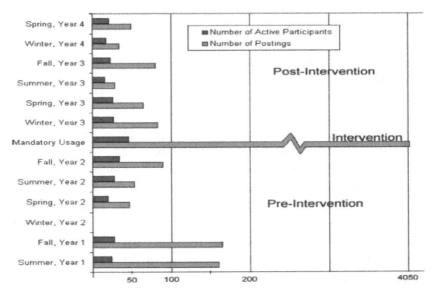

Table 1. Board accesses to UBB during the intervention

	Executive Committee	*Board -- excluding the EC*	*Total Board*
Total Possible No. Of Individuals	5	14	19
Total Accesses	1635	857	2492
Mean Number (Standard Deviation) of Accesses	327 (157.05)	61.2 (52.84)	131.2 (150.68)
Median Number of Accesses	345	56	105

mittee being very active in the discussion. It is impossible to determine, however, whether this participation was because these were the people most involved in the decision, the people with the most information to share, those with the most responsibility for ensuring that the process came to a successful completion, or whether there was another reason these were the most active.

The remaining accesses were by committee chairs, specific program coordinators, incoming Board members, staff, and Finance Committee members, as shown in Table 2. Of those who participated, committee chairs accessed the UBB an average of 44 times (standard deviation of 60.23 and a median of 9); incoming Board members accessed the UBB an average of 90 times (standard deviation of 82.6 and a median of 90) and all eight staff members participated in the UBB.

Although in most categories participation fell short of universal participation, it was substantial. The second row of Table 2, labeled "proportion of the category" represents the proportion of all possible participants in a given category who participated. These data illustrate that about a quarter of all committee chairs accessed the UBB during the discussion, most incoming Board members participated, and all staff members participated. This should be gauged in light of the negligible use by non-Board members prior to the intervention. In this way, use of the UBB *increased* participation by stakeholders. One staff member commented he had never before seen the budget

being discussed, and was glad to have insights into its meaning.

The researchers turned to the survey of participants to help explain why there were differences in participation. Neither comfort and experience with e-mail, nor perceived sophistication of Web experience, provided a significant explanation of either the number of accesses or the number of posts. Similarly, previous use of the UBB (prior to the intervention) did not explain variations in either accesses or posts.

However, experience with the Web environment did help explain some of the variability of behavior. People who reported using the Web for work and/or using the Web for pleasure accessed the UBB more often than those who did not (t= 2.084, $p \leq .05$ | unequal variances, df_1=14, df_2=20, one-tail). That is, those who were experienced with the technology and the concept of getting information from the Web were more likely to read postings on the UBB more often. Further, subjects' use of the Web to share information with others, either on the Internet or an intranet, helped explain their participation. Those individuals who did use the Web to share information posted significantly more items on the UBB than those who did not (t=1.82, $p \leq .05$ | unequal variances, df_1=10, df_2=24, one-tail).

When users were asked *why* they did or did not use the UBB during this time, people expressed simply the desire to get their comments on the record (to support use), or the lack of desire to

Table 2. Non-board accesses to UBB during the intervention

	Chairs[5]	Incoming Board	staff
Number of Individuals Participating	11 *of the 48 possible*	4 *of the 5 possible*	8 *of the 8 possible*
Proportion of the Category	23%	80%	100%
Total Accesses	333	359	655
Mean Number (Standard Deviation) of Accesses	44.75 (60.23)	89.75 (82.59)	81.88 (84.59)
Median Number of Accesses	13	90	61

comment publicly on the document (in support of non-use). Those who did post comments said that they wanted to "get [their] thoughts heard," "to express opinions," or to "respond to comments." One person added that he posted because that's what he was told to do, but also took advantage of the opportunity to learn to use new technology. Those who did not post comments said either they had "nothing to add," "preferred to have someone else post the comment," or "found the technology uncomfortable." In fact, one person added, "[t]he UBB was awkward and difficult to use (for me). If this had been my only way to deal with the budget, I would have felt completely cut off.".

Satisfaction with the use of technology was evaluated after the intervention. Immediately after the budget vote, participants were asked whether the group should use this medium for consideration of other issues, and more than 90% of respondents voiced a resounding "no." However, that may have been an emotional response associated with the intensity of the experience and with the effort of bringing to closure uncertain financial times, rather than a statement about the technology.

Two weeks after completion of the mandated voting period, users were given a questionnaire to evaluate the process more formally. The results of that questionnaire highlighted some issues with the technology and the process. Board members were asked regarding their relative levels of comfort using the UBB (compared to face-to-face meetings) in voting on the budget and in voting on the associated motions.

From a positive side, members perceived that there was more input into the budget using the UBB. When asked whether they had thought more or less about the budget, several members said "more," "too much," "infinitely more," "easily [more]," and "more ... I had more time to sift through details and consider opposing views." In addition, non-Board members who were included in the UBB discussions saw their input being considered directly. Some commented on the inclusiveness of the process with, "I don't get

to attend the meetings to ponder the budgets. In fact, this is the first time I got to see it before it was approved. ... I would probably not have had a direct opportunity to help review the budget for the activity in a meeting. This forum gave me the opportunity to help review our budget." The greater focus on the topic and the increased participation would suggest that a better decision process was followed using the UBB than in a normal Board meeting.

However, when asked about the ease of use of the product, the responses were not as positive. Most individuals found using the UBB difficult. One person summarized the feelings of many in the group with, "[I]t was difficult, but not impossible." Others expressed specific difficulty that was more structural, such as "I had a very difficult time following the discussion and often had to go back and re-read what was posted so that I could understand the response," "non-standardized icon use made it confusing," or "some instructions/clarity may be in order to make the thread of conversation more easy [sic] to follow." On the other hand, using the technology made it easier for one person, "[A]ctually, I subscribed to the entire Treasurer's Report, and received any posting and responded to the ones that I felt needed answers." Finally, one person noted that unforeseen absences can cause problems, especially with a short time horizon such as this, "[T]hroughout the early part of the week before the vote, I was following things fine. I was ill on Friday, Monday and Tuesday (the time of the vote). This did cause problems."

The range of opinions about the UBB discussion and vote when compared to a conventional face-to-face meeting was substantial. While some felt "considerably less comfortable" voting on the budget using the UBB (compared to face-to-face meetings), another felt "considerably more comfortable" voting on the budget, and about a quarter of the participants felt "about the same" level of comfort that they have when meeting face-to-face. Interestingly, the average comfort level for voting on the operating principles was more negative than that for voting on the budget. While about the same number felt "considerably less comfortable" and "less comfortable" in voting on the operating principles represented in the associated motions using the UBB (compared to face-to-face meetings), fewer individuals indicated they felt "more comfortable," and no one felt "much more comfortable" using the UBB. In other words, on average, the sentiment was slightly negative regarding using the UBB for voting.

Among those expressing negative feelings about the process, most commented on the difficulty of using the system. Comments such as "[n]o, I think that the whole process was very confusing. It was not even clear to me what exactly we were voting on (in terms of numbers in the budget) when all was said and done" or "[s]ome instructions/clarity may be in order to make the thread of conversation more easy [sic] to follow," and "the EBB was awkward and difficult to use [for me]" demonstrate the users' frustration with the tool. None of the individuals who expressed those concerns were active users of the Web or the UBB prior to the intervention. This may simply demonstrate the difficulty that major changes in technology can bring.

Those who were positive, however, all focused on the improvement in the decision process. The comments about whether their concerns and issues were addressed is shown in Table 3.

When asked specifically about the medium and its contribution to participants' confidence in the process, about half of the comments were positive and half were negative. Many comments reflected that participants thought the financial documents were too complex, too long, and, often, too confusing. These comments reflected dissatisfaction with the enormous complexity of the budget documents, independent of medium. As such, they do not contribute to our understanding of the impact of the UBB on the understandability of the documents.

Among the comments of those less comfortable were issues such as: "I felt it to be so inadequate (you cannot hear the tone of voice or see body language or get the back and forth in real time) ... I almost didn't vote," or "I felt frustrated that certain items were not discussed as fully as possible and I do not believe that it was necessary for these items to be dealt with in this way." Others who felt negative expressed concern with the time pressure rather than the tool: "it's still a huge load of information to try to sort out under intense time pressure," and "I did not have the time to read all the stuff." One interesting response from a person who felt less comfortable was: "I felt much less confident to vote although I was struck by how prepared the EC was. In the end, and with some regret, I decided to yield to the majority rather than vote." This suggests that perhaps the information was conveyed well, but this person just did not like the medium. Those who were moderate or positive in their comfort level said, "The parallel discussions on the EBB forced me to concentrate on more parts," and "always some questions unanswered (both live and electronic). Less certain

Table 3. Positive comments about the process

• The discussion was very helpful
• It was better to a certain degree
• Yes, it was a remarkably thoughtful and considerate discussion given the time constraints and the severity of the problem
• I think so
• Yes, it worked great – speedy, concise and relevant

of views of some of the primary stakeholders, but clearer on articulated views."

Questionnaires revealed that the UBB represented only part of the discussion about the budget, however. In their questionnaires, most individuals noted they had e-mail and/or telephone discussions about the budget separate from the UBB discussion. On average, Board Members had two phone conversations during the two-week time period. The maximum number of calls reported was five. For example, the Executive Committee spent about two and a half hours on a conference call discussing the budget during the UBB discussion period. Respondents were also asked if they exchanged e-mail with Board members, committee chairs and/or staff. About half of the members reported using e-mail 0-1 times, and the other half reported using it two or more times during the two-week period.

Both the number of sources of e-mail used and the number of telephone conversations did seem to have a positive impact on the confidence that individuals felt with the process, although neither result was statistically significant. That is, those individuals who supplemented the UBB with calls and/or e-mail seemed to feel more comfortable with the outcome of the decision than did the other users. In each case, the greater number of contacts resulted in higher satisfaction scores; however, these were not statistically significant. It does suggest that no one medium is sufficient for communication; that multiple channels, especially those with which we are most comfortable, are necessary to come to consensus. Perhaps this was due to the fact that the UBB did not have a "private" communication section, or, perhaps, as Gerfen [2004] suggested, it is simply a matter of habit.

The use of e-mails as an alternative form of communication was not, interestingly, associated with any significant differences in the number of accesses or postings of individuals. In other words, those who used e-mail did not access the UBB less, nor post less than those who did not rely on e-mails for communication about the budget. Likewise, there was no statistical difference in the number of accesses between those who made more than two phone calls during the intervention period and those who did not. On the other hand, those who made more than two phone calls were more likely to post to the UBB ($t=1.831$, $p \leq .05$ | unequal variances, $df_1=16$, $df_2=18$, one-tail) during the intervention period. It appears as though the number of telephone calls was highly associated with membership in the executive committee and probably also shows the relative interest in the solution of the problem.

When asked why these other discussion vehicles were used, individuals cited: (a) the need for privacy; (b) the need to maintain partnerships (between staff and volunteers); and (c) the improved quality of discussion that could happen via the telephone or private e-mail as the reasons for using e-mail and/or telephone exchanges during the discussion period. The concept of private, off-line discussions has been pervasive in the culture of the Board meetings for years, and so it is not surprising that members wanted to be able to maintain that same option when using the electronic tool. Similarly, the organization had worked hard to develop and promote partnerships between volunteers and staff, and that, too, is something worth preserving. Finally, the comments magnify suggestions in the research literature that media richness can impact choice of technology.

Participants on average believed the UBB provided an adequate forum in which to discuss the budget and understand the ramifications of the possible decisions. Of those who responded to this question, 11 (65%) indicated their concerns regarding specific budget issues were addressed, four (24%) indicated their concerns were not addressed, and two (12%) were unsure. In fact, most thought the UBB provided adequate opportunity to raise issues and facilitate resolution of those issues.

Participants also believed the medium contributed to their greater concentration on the budget than through the standard process. Of those who expressed an opinion, nine participants thought they pondered the budget more than in the standard process, six participants (67%) thought they pondered the budget less than in the standard process, and two participants (22%) were not sure. In terms of the strength of the responses, those who expressed the opinion that they pondered the budget more when using the UBB used comments such as "much more," "easily more," "too much" to show the strength of their feelings, whereas, people who pondered the budget less, simply used the term "less." Their reasons included that they had more time to sift through details and consider opposing views that they might not have seen the budget otherwise, and that they appreciated being able to express concerns before the budget was passed.

Finally, when asked if individuals wanted to use this medium again, participants were surprisingly positive about the experience. Of the 17 who responded, 12 (71%) thought the Board should use the UBB again and five (29%) thought the Board should not use the UBB again. This contrasts sharply with the 90% who immediately after the intervention responded negatively to the question. However, even those who expressed support for further use of the UBB had some level of reservation, generally citing the amount of time the process took when using UBB. Specific comments are shown in Table 4.

Some members of the Board believed there were positive benefits from the technology use. Questionnaires showed that some officers felt Board members and committee chairs were more engaged in the budgeting process than they are in a normal meeting, spending more time reviewing the documents and thinking about the discus-

Table 4. Specific comments about the process

• Yes, but cautiously. I think it is fine for discussion of a specific item. And, it is useful for getting the input of a wide range of individuals. Somehow, though, we need to make it easier to follow through the limiting of icons, the segregation of discussions, or something. Further, the default option should be to e-mail everyone with information about a new posting... let folks turn it off if they don't want to read it.
• For information exchange, but not for true debate
• Find -- contrive if necessary -- a way to get Committee chairs and editors to post reports to the UBB and to read at least portions of it. The reporting frequency of many of these volunteers is still a scandal low. One simple idea would be to post a tabulation of who posted how many messages as an UBB closes, including all the zeros. The board can then be asked to encourage the zero-people to participate in the next UBB. Second, try to reduce the difficulties of accessing the UBB.
• Yes, it saved the necessity for an emergency meeting or a premature decision.
• It was a learning process. This particular situation was critical and everyone had a vested interest. I don't know if we can train everyone to stay attached to the UBB for a typical Board meeting. I invested a fair amount of time out of my workday reading the UBB daily. I am not sure how this would affect my workload if I were responsible for this investment four times per year. Just the same I am looking forward to the next UBB.
• Quoth the raven, "NEVERMORE!"
• Only when necessary
• Since I am going off the Board, I shouldn't bias the results, but if I were not, I would answer a resounding NO!
• I found it much less effective for me
• Yes. I hope we'll have more pleasant topics, though.
• Never ever! Took too much time.
• No, but I don't like Board meetings either.

sion. The officers reported believing the process resulted in a better than average budget.

In summary, the intervention of the mandatory usage resulted in a substantial use of the technology. The data show that those individuals who believed the UBB was difficult to use were also the people who lacked confidence with Web applications generally. These individuals did not surf the Web regularly and did not use the Web to post information. This suggests that the training for the UBB should have been broader to include greater confidence with the Web in general prior to introducing the UBB training.

The surprising part of the analysis was the absence of any measurable outcome differences between the group that was positive about future use of the technology in Board deliberations and that which was negative about future use of the technology in Board deliberations. Those who were negative about future use were no less satisfied with the success of the intervention, and had no more concerns about the ease of use of the technology than were respondents who were positive about the future use of the technology. This may suggest that the complexity and uncertainty of the budget, as well as individual participants' relative exposure to, and understanding of, the budget are better predictors of the relative comfort level with the process.

POST-INTERVENTION RESULTS

From the perspective of the organization, the results of the intervention were mixed. The final decision after this intensive use was that the Board should continue to use the technology to facilitate greater discussion of matters between meetings. This meant the Board continued to post reports, and comment about the reports to the system. While the type of usage was similar to that prior to the intervention, the question remained as to whether the in-depth use and at least some acceptance would cause the Board and associated

individuals to be more likely to use the tool in the future.

The usage of the system for the full period of evaluation is shown in Table 5. It is significant to compare the usage after the intervention compared to that before the intervention. Although reports continued to be posted to the UBB, discussion dropped off significantly using this medium once its usage was no longer mandated. Further, the Board declined to use the technology to support its Summer, Year 4 or Fall, Year 4 meetings, stating that the added value to the decision process did not warrant the effort.

DISCUSSION

Before discussing the contributions of these findings, it is important to note the limitations of this research. First, this research examined data from only one organization, and hence, it is possible the results are not generalizable beyond the organization, or even these specific individuals acting collectively. The subjects were volunteers on the Board, and participation or non-participation had no actual impact on the subjects' jobs or productivity apart from the Board. In fact, all subjects were involved in more activities and other uses of technology than just the Board or the UBB, and hence, may not even reflect their attitudes toward using technology for this particular organization. This may also limit the generalizability of the results. In addition, there was no control group, no experimental manipulations of the data, and no measurements of attitudes prior to the intervention. All of these factors limit the certainty from which it is possible to project these results to other groups.

However, the study is important. It provides a unique contribution for the literature: the analysis of *actual usage* of technology rather than the less strong, but more common measure, *intention* to use technology. This allows us to understand the gap between what people might intend to do and

Table 5. All postings data

	Number of Postings				Number of Active Participants*
	Administrator	EC	All Else	Total	
Summer, Year 1	90	18	52	160	24
Fall, Year 1	92	16	56	164	27
Spring, Year 2		14	32	46	19
Summer, Year 2		8	45	53	27
Fall, Year 2		32	57	89	34
Mandatory Usage		1635	2418	4053	45
Winter, Year 3		35	48	83	26
Spring, Year 3		13	51	64	25
Summer, Year 3		7	21	28	15
Fall, Year 3		28	52	80	23
Winter, Year 4		11	23	34	17
Spring, Year 4		16	33	49	21

Five(5) of the participants are always executive committee members.

what they actually do, thereby providing a stronger theoretical basis for the TAM model. Not only do the results confirm that perceived ease of use and perceived usefulness impact usage of technology, the data provide insight regarding the role played by other factors influencing these variables. A model of technology adoption, which combines variables identified in the literature with factors suggested by this study, is shown in Figure 7.

The results show that perceived ease of use is an important, but not absolute precursor to use of technology. Individuals who were generally uncomfortable with Web-based tools were uncomfortable with the UBB as well. They noted that discomfort in their questionnaires and used the technology less than the average user. They *did* use it, however, because the cost of not using it, that is, not having sufficient budget for programs, was higher than the anxiety they experienced. During the mandatory period, even these inex-

perienced users used the technology successfully (as measured by accomplishing their goals), and there was no evidence they substituted other technologies. This may suggest that perceived usefulness has a stronger influence on usage than perceived ease of use.

People who were regular Web users were more likely to participate—even "lurking" more than those who did not feel comfortable with Web-based applications. Those individuals who had used the Web to disseminate information (because they had personal or professional, or corporate Web pages to which they communicated) were more likely to use the UBB for communication as measured by more posted items.

This is an interesting result. Specifically, it suggests that training needs to go beyond the mechanics of the specific product (the UBB in this case), to include applications of a family of technology products (in this case, the Web). It

Figure 7. Revised technology acceptance model

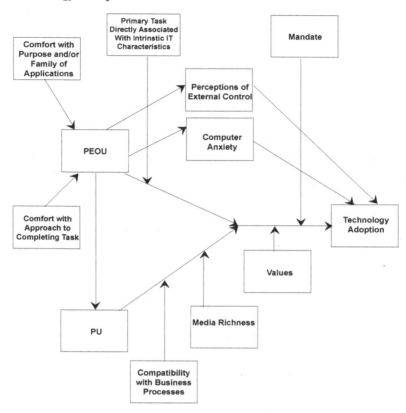

suggests that users must find the software use "comfortable" and "buy into" the *kind* of application *and the reasonableness of that kind of application* prior to their being willing to find it easy to use. Clearly, prior surfing of the Web and/or creation of Web pages did not make it easier to understand how to read the UBB, or how to post items to the UBB, since Web pages generally navigate differently than do discussion boards, and programming is different from both. Instead, it suggests that there is a precursor to PEOU in technology acceptance: comfort with doing things in a particular way (in this case, sharing information on the Web). This new factor, "comfort with a family of applications," is identified in Figure 7. Upon reflection, there are other examples of exactly the same phenomenon. For example, many individuals who were quite comfortable with a

text-based, mainframe environment were often more uncomfortable with GUI interfaces than users without any computer experience. Before they could find comfort in the GUI interface, they needed to gain acceptance of the new way to access computer tools and appreciate why that might make their work easier. Each substantial advancement in the technology brings a need for new acceptance and comfort. Since these advancements occur more quickly now than ever before, addressing this comfort factor may be among the most important issues associated with ease of use of the technology.

"Comfort with a family of applications," is different than what the literature suggests as computer anxiety. The latter, identified as a mediator variable, represents a user's comfort with the specific operations of a program. It is associated with a fear of not being able to finish something, doing something wrong, or not knowing what to do with a program. The new factor, on the other hand, represents a concern about whether or not it is *appropriate* to use technology with specific features. As described above it is not associated with a general computer anxiety, but, rather, with a change in the use of technology.

Related to the question about comfort with changing families of applications is a comfort with significant changes to the approaches to solving problems, in this case to making decisions. These individuals were accustomed to a longer process, and one that was dependent upon face-to-face discussions. Perhaps the reluctance to adopting the UBB was really reluctance to change that process. It is impossible to judge from these data whether it was comfort with the type (family) of applications or if it was a new way of approaching the task (sharing a discussion online) that was the inhibitor. This intertwining of factors often occur in the implementation of technology. It is common for technology to be introduced at the same time business procedures are re-engineered. Either factor, or an interaction of the two, may impact adoption of technology. Hence both factors are identified in Figure 7 as precursors to PEOU.

Insights about perceived usefulness were also suggested by these results, especially when examined in light of earlier research. DoI research clearly identifies a need for early acceptance of technology by some group for it to diffuse through an organization. In this case, the primary early adopter was the sitting president of the organization whose term lasted only one year. According to Rogers (1995), diffusion is maximized when this person must be popular or a social leader. Unfortunately, while the person held the authority position, he was neither popular nor a social leader in his role. That may, in addition to the discussion below, explain why the UBB was not accepted as a useful tool.

However, Moore and Benbasat (1991) suggest that the ability to demonstrate the usefulness of a tool in achieving a particular result is critical to adoption of innovation. Clearly, the budget and associated motions were passed successfully. Although immediate response was negative, when questionnaires were distributed, most individuals thought it was a reasonably good experience. The fact that such a positive demonstration did not encourage the group to adopt the product more fully may suggest that other factors, such as those discussed below, may be more important for the long term adoption of technology.

When the use of the technology was compatible with the temporary procedures of the Board (during the mandatory period), individuals used the product extensively and successfully (as measured by the success in passing the motions, and by the post-use interviews). However, when the procedures were not compatible with the use of the technology—either before the mandatory period, or after it—the subjects did not use the technology extensively. This result seems to agree with the research by Chau and Hu (2002) which notes that compatibility of the technology with the routine operations, or (as labeled in Figure 7) business operations, will impact a user's evaluation of usefulness of the product. The Board did not re-engineer its operations when the UBB became available, and hence, using the tool provided little additional benefit to the users.

This is consistent with the DoI literature which identifies compatibility of the technology in completing one's task as a precursor to adoption of technology. Non-use would have been expected because the relative advantage of using the UBB and, thereby, making the meetings either shorter or more productive, was not present because the meeting process had not been re-engineered. This might be related to what the DoI literature identifies as "complexity of technology," which acts as a barrier to acceptance of technology (Agarwal and Prasad, 1996; Cooper and Zmud 1990; Rogers, 1995). The literature has treated that factor to mean complexity of the commands and actions to interact with the program. These results expand the possible definition of complexity, by suggesting that how the technology increases the overall complexity of completing the task, especially as it increases the amount of effort it takes to complete the task, would also be a barrier to acceptance. The contribution to the model is shown in Figure 7.

However, the DoI literature suggests that compatibility also captures the compatibility of the technology with the *values* of the users. One item noted by the Board was the significant increase in participation by non-Board committee members in the consideration of issues during the mandatory period. Some members even suggested it would be useful to "contrive" operations to continue to get this participation by these stake-holders after the mandatory period. This is similar to the results found in other studies (DeLuca, Gasson and Kock, 2006). Understanding of, and increasing participation in, the budgeting process had been goals to the Board during this period. It is surprising that some additional usage did not begin after the mandatory period. The fact that no re-engineering to continue the openness and participation occurred after the mandatory process may mean that the value was not shared among a large enough group on the Board, or it may mean that consistency with existing procedures was the more significant factor. It is impossible to tell from these data. "Values" as a mediating variable is shown in Figure 7.

Even during the mandatory period there were regular uses of other technologies, including e-mail and telephone conversations. One might think of these as "more traditional" technologies. Interestingly, most of these uses were not substituted for use of the UBB, nor were they by individuals who perceived the tool difficult to use. Further, the use of alternative technologies required additional effort (whatever was discussed needed to be summarized and put on the UBB). There were multiple reasons suggested by the users. Some

decision makers reported that telephone conversations facilitated their understanding of the issues, data, and/or implications of the decisions, while others noted the need to have a faster answer to a question. This suggests that the factor media richness, already identified in the literature (see, for example, Straub, *et al.*, 1997), may impact the perceived usefulness of a particular technology, and is so identified in Figure 7.

Other subjects noted they wanted to have "private" conversations via the telephone or e-mail so they could provide a "united front" when the discussion was "public" on the UBB. This is consistent with both the values factor and the compatibility of process and technology factor discussed previously. That is, people wanted to maintain publicly viewed coalitions and used the appropriate technology to achieve that goal. Or, it may be another example of media richness and its impact on perceived usefulness of technology.

These subjects might also be "creatures of habit" in that they solve problems the way they always have. They used e-mail, telephone conferences, and face-to-face meetings in managing this organization, and did not even think about an alternative approach. Actions by some subjects, such as infrequent checking of the UBB during the mandatory period, suggested subjects were reluctant to change their behaviors. This could be similar to the concept of habit Gerfen (2004) found in his study. Or, it could be that the UBB did not pass the "relative advantage" test of the DoI literature. (Bradford and Florin, 2003; Moore and Benbasat, 1991) The UBB might have been useful, but not useful enough to convince users to adopt it.

These issues of compatibility become increasingly important as technology becomes more pervasive. Often the question is not whether or not to adopt technology, but, rather, the question is *which* technology to adopt. While one tool may appear easier to use or more powerful to some, others may stay with more limited, and sometimes more kludgy, software because it more closely parallels their business processes and, thus, makes it easier to use. The technology must not only be "better" or "easier" to ensure adoption, but also must be "sufficiently better" or "sufficiently easier" to overcome the need to re-engineer processes. That is, both the need for adaption of work processes (because of inconsistency with business processes), and sometimes just habit, provide an additional hurdle that must be overcome to encourage users to select the newer software. These results do not provide evidence that changing the work processes would have increased the adoption of the tool. Conversations with the subjects, however, lead this researcher to hypothesize that such changes would have increased the adoption of the software in the non-mandatory periods.

There were three hypotheses posed at the beginning of the article.

- Products that are easy to use, but do not enhance the *group task* substantially will not be adopted by the group to replace existing tools;
- A mandate requiring tool use can affect the short term usage and the dynamics that drive it; but
- Once the mandate has been relaxed, usage will return to no more than the level that would have been experienced without the mandate and the factors influencing that usage will change.

The obvious question is whether there was evidence of any or all of the hypotheses found in this research. Clearly, the research was an action research study which did not have sufficient controls to prove or disprove *any* hypothesis. In spite of that limitation, the literature suggests one can generate knowledge from such research (Kock, 2005), and it warrants discussion. Both hypothesis one and three were supported by the limited use of the UBB during the non-mandatory period. Since the business process was not re-engineered to

reflect the *explicit need* for the technology, people chose not to use it, or only use it to the extent that was critical for Board operations. Some of that non-use can be associated with some members believing the tool was kludgy. However, the data suggest that *any* Web-based tool, regardless of its features, might have been viewed that way by a subset of the Board. Anything other than face-to-face meetings was unacceptable. Although, face-to-face meetings provide a rich and powerful environment for decision making, often economic needs, such as the expense of bringing people together, or the unavailability of people to have such a meeting at a particular time, require the need for a communication tool (Fink, 2007). If alternative decision tools are to become more pervasive in the workplace, it is critical that IS professionals not only help users become more comfortable with its use, but also be able to identify when the discomfort level might be sufficiently high to prevent the tools from being used effectively. We need to understand more about how to get people to use it, and when not to use it. The evidence seems to support Hypothesis 2: during the mandated period, the group found the tool was helpful and that it could support operations. After all, they demonstrated the usability of the tool by negotiating one of the most critical and sensitive topics—a budget.

Additional research is needed, especially that including controlled experiments, where actual usage is documented. Researchers need to understand better *specific* factors, such as comfort with a family of applications, that affect PEOU of the technology. Similarly, researchers need greater evidence of specific factors that impact PEOU. In turn, these factors need to be operationalized so that designers can use them more effectively in their work. Many practitioners now have a view of what makes something "easy to use" or "useful" and design their products accordingly. Yet, we continue to find that products are either not being used or not being used to their full potential. This tells us that we need more specific parameters, ones that are not subject to individualistic interpretation, that will help systems be more productive and more likely to be used.

REFERENCES

Agarwal, R. & Prasad, J. (1998). Conceptual and Operational Definition of Personal Innovativeness in the Domain of Information Technology. *Information Systems Research*, 9(2), 204-215.

Bradford, M. & Florian, J. (2003). Examining the Role of Innovation Diffusion Factors on the Implementation Success of Enterprise Resource Planning Systems. *International Journal of Accounting Information Systems*, 4(3), 205-225.

Brown, S.A., Massey, A.P. Montoya-Weiss, M.M. & Burkman, J.R. (2002). Do I Really Have to User Acceptance of Mandated Technology. *European Journal of Information Systems*, 11(4), 283-295.

Chau, P.Y.K. & Hu, P.J. (2002). Examining a Model of Information Technology Acceptance by Individual Professionals. *Journal of Management Information Systems*, 18(4), 191-230.

Cooper, R.B. & Zmud, R.W. (1990). Information Technology Implementation Research: A Technological Diffusion Approach. *Management Science*, 36(2), 123-139.

Davis, F.D. (1989). Perceived Usefulness, Perceived Ease of Use and User Acceptance of Information Technology. *MIS Quarterly*, 13(3), 319-340.

Davis, F.D., Bagozzi, R.P. & Warshaw, P.R. (1989). User Acceptance of Computer Technology A Comparison of Two Theoretical Models. *Management Science,* 35(8), 982-1002.

Davis, F.D., Bagozzi, R.P. & Warshaw, P.R. (1992). Extrinsic and Intrinsic Motivation to Use Computers in the Workplace. *Journal of Applied Social Psychology*, 22(14), 1111-1132.

DeLuca, D., Gasson, S., & Kock, N. (2006). Adaptations That Virtual Teams Make So That Complex Tasks Can Be Performed Using Simple e-Collaboration Technologies. *International J. of e-Collaboration*, 2(3), 65-91.

Fink, L. (2007), Coordination, Learning, and Innovation: The Organizational Roles of e-Collaboration and Their Impacts. *International Journal of e-Collaboration,* 3(3), 53-70.

Fischbein, M., & Ajzen, I. (1975). *Belief, Attitude, Intention, Behavior: An Introduction to Theory and Research*, Reading, MA : Addison-Wesley, 1975.

Gefen, D. (2003). TAM or Just Plain Habit: A Look at Experienced Online Shoppers. *Journal of End User Computing,* 15(3), 1-13.

Gefen, D., Karahanna, E. & Straub, D. (2003). Inexperience and Experience with Online Stores: The Importance of Trust. *IEEE Transactions on Engineering Management,* 50(3), 307-321.

Gefen, D., & Straub, D. (2000). The Relative Importance of Ease of Use in IS Adoption: A Study of e-Commerce Adoption. *Journal of the Association for Information Systems*, 1(8), October, 2000, http://jais.isworld.org/articles/1-8/article.htm.

Hendrickson, A.R. and Collins, M.R. (1996). An Assessment of the Structure and Causation of IS Usage. *The DATABASE for Advances in Information Systems,* 27(2), 61-67.

Hu, P.J., Chau, P.Y.K., Sheng, O.R.L. & Tan, K.Y. (1999). Examining Technology Adoption Model Using Physician Acceptance of Telemedicine Technology. *Journal of Management Information Systems*, 16(2), 91-112.

Karahanna, E. & Limayem, M. (2000). Electronic Mail and Voice Mail Usage: Generalizing Across Technologies. *Journal of Organizational Computing and Electronic Commerce*, 10(1), 49-66.

Karahanna, E., Straub, D.W. & Chervany, N.L. (1999). Information Technology Adoption Across Time: A Cross Sectional Comparison of Pre-Adoption and Post-Adoption Beliefs. *MIS Quarterly,* 23(2), 183-213.

Karahanna, E. & Straub, D.W. (1998). The Psychological Origins of Perceived Usefulness and Ease of Use. *Information and Management*, 35, 237-250.

Keil, M., Beranek, P.M. & Konsynski, B.R. (1995). Usefulness and Ease of Use: Field Study Evidence Regarding Task Considerations. *Decision Support Systems,* 13, 75-91.

Kock, N. (2005), Using Action Research to Study E-Collaboration. *International J. of e-Collaboration*, 1(4), i-vii.

Ma, Q. & Liu, L. (2004). The Technology Acceptance Model: A Meta-Analysis of Empirical Findings. *Journal of Organizational and End User Computing*, 16(1), 59-72.

Moore, G.C. & Benbasat, I. (1991). Development of an Instrument to Measure the Perceptions of Adopting an Information Technology Innovation. *Information Systems Research,* 2(3), 1992-222.

Morris, M. & Dillon, A. (1997). How User Perceptions Influence Software Use. *IEEE Software*, 14(4), 58-65.

Rogers, E.M. (1995). *Diffusion of Innovations, Fourth Edition*, New York: Free Press.

Sichel, D.E. (1997). *The Computer Revolution: An Economic Perspective*, Washington D.C.: The Brookings Institute.

Straub, D., Keil, M. & Brenner, W. (1997). Testing the Technology Acceptance Model Across Cultures: A Three Country Study. *Information and Management,* 33(1), 1-11.

Subramanian, G.H. (1994). A Replication of Perceived Usefulness and Perceived Ease of Use Measurement. *Decision Sciences*, 25(5-6), 863-872.

Sussman, S.W. & Siegal, W.S. (2003). Informational Influence in Organizations: An Integrated Approach to Knowledge Adoption. *Information Systems Research*, 14(1), 47-65.

Szajna, B. (1996). Empirical Evaluation of the Revised Technology Acceptance Model. *Management Science*, 42(1), 85-92.

Thompson, R.L., Higgines, C.A. & Howell, J.M. (1994). Personal Computing: Toward a Conceptual Model of Utilization. *MIS Quarterly*, 15(1), 125-142.

Ultimate Bulletin Board™, a product of *INFOPOP*, http://www.infopop.com/aboutus/index.html, no date, site visited on March 15, 2002.

Venkatesh, V. (1999). Creation of Favorable User Perceptions: Exploring the Rule of Intrinsic Motivation. *MIS Quarterly,* 23(2), 239-260.

Venkatesh, V. (2000). Determinants of Perceived Ease of Use Integrating Control, Intrinsic Motivation and Emotion into the Technology Acceptance Model. *Information Systems Research,* 11(4), 342-365.

Venkatesh, V. & Davis, F.D. (1994). Modeling the Determinants of Perceived Ease of Use in *Proceedings of the Fifteenth International Conference on Information Systems*, DeGross, J.I., Huff, S.L. & Munro, M.C. (eds.), Vancouver, British Columbia, 212-227.

Venkatesh, V. & Davis, F.D. (1996). A Model of the Antecedents of Perceived Ease of Use: Development and Test. *Decision Sciences*, 27(3), 451-480.

Venkatesh, V. & Davis, F.D. (2000). A Theoretical Extension of the Technology Acceptance Model: Four Longitudinal Field Studies. *Management Science,* 46(2), 186-204.

ENDNOTES

[1] More information about the Board of Directors, Committees and the exact nature of the not-for-profit organization are being withheld to protect the organization's anonymity as promised.

[2] As with most not-for-profit organizations, volunteers typically began with committee positions and as they gained increasing interest, commitment, and understanding of the organization, ran for offices within the organization. Hence, there is variance in the amount of knowledge about, and commitment to, the organization among these members of the community.

[3] According to its web page, UBB had been installed on 100,000 sites, had over 7,000,000 registered users, and serves over 1 billion pages each month. (UBB, 2002)

[4] The decision to exclude the "administrator" postings was done on the basis of feedback from the subjects. While one might think these postings represented ideas shared through other media, they were, in fact, really just the administrator's attempt to get people using the system. They did not necessarily reflect actual communication between that administrator and other subjects.

[5] Of the 45 standing committees, 36 are not automatically chaired by a Board Member. Only these 36 are considered when the category "committee chairs" is used.

Chapter 15
A Comparison of Audio-Conferencing and Computer Conferencing in a Dispersed Negotiation Setting:
Efficiency Matters!

Abbas Foroughi
University of Southern Indiana, USA

William C. Perkins
Indiana University, USA

Leonard M. Jessup
Washington State University, USA

ABSTRACT

The growing globalization of business is making face-to-face communications, decision-making, and negotiations more the exception than the rule. Internet communication in text-only, audio, and video form are all becoming feasible methods of communication between distantly located parties. However, in order for these new technologies to be used most effectively, more investigation is needed into the impact of various media on decision-making, such as that in negotiation. In particular, negotiators need to have a means of choosing the most appropriate communication medium, based on the amount of richness inherent in the medium, for the particular task at hand. This paper presents the results of an empirical study to examine the effectiveness of a computerized negotiation support system (NSS) in supporting bargaining carried out in a dispersed, but synchronous setting. In the study, pairs of college students, using the NSS, participated in a simulated industrial bargaining scenario that tested the impact of communication media employed and level of conflict on contract outcomes and negotiator attitudes.

The subjects, located in separate rooms, played the roles of buyer and seller engaged in negotiations either by telephone (audio-conferencing) or Lotus Notes (computer conferencing). In both low and high conflict, the efficiency aspects of audio-conferencing — a richer medium in which more communication can take place more quickly — overshadowed any negative social cues transmitted.

INTRODUCTION

Business collaboration is now possible anywhere in real-time, making it location independent. This trend has brought the management of dispersed decision-making activities to the forefront as a crucial managerial function (Chidambaram & Jones, 1993). Dispersed meetings can now be facilitated by a variety of electronic communication media, such as audio-conferencing, video-conferencing, computer conferencing, and electronic mail. What is the impact of various types of electronic communication in different task environments? Previous communication research has already shown the dramatic effects that electronic media can have on communication in general (Bazerman & Carroll, 1987) and on mixed-motive tasks such as negotiation in particular (McGrath, 1984). Furthermore, the amount of richness inherent in a communication medium is also crucial to understanding its impact on negotiation outcomes (Daft & Lengel, 1986).

PURPOSE

This paper presents the results of an experiment that examined the effectiveness of a computerized negotiation support system (NSS) in supporting bargaining carried out in a dispersed, but synchronous setting. The focus of the study was to determine the relative effectiveness of computer conferencing and audio-conferencing—two communication media varying significantly in media richness — when using an NSS in a dispersed setting. The results of the study shed light on the following questions:

1. Which type of communication medium is more effective when using an NSS in a dispersed setting — computer conferencing or audio-conferencing?
2. How does the amount of conflict involved in a negotiation impact the effectiveness of a communication medium when using an NSS in a dispersed setting?

The paper is organized as follows. The review of the literature related to this study is divided into three sections, with the first focusing on negotiation support systems, the second on the role of conflict level in negotiations, and the third on the role of media richness in negotiations. The research model that serves as a foundation for the present research is presented, followed by the hypotheses tested in the study, the research methodology, the statistical analysis and results, a discussion of the results, and finally the conclusions reached from the results of the study.

NEGOTIATION SUPPORT SYSTEMS

Since first being used in the 1960s, computer support for negotiations has been employed in the form of stand-alone decision support systems, used to support either individual negotiators or both sides in a negotiation, and by various forms of electronic communication. NSSs are a category of group support systems (GSSs) designed especially to support decision-makers in non-cooperative, mixed-motive tasks. At a minimum, an NSS includes an individual decision support system (DSS) for each party in the negotiation plus an electronic communication channel between the parties (Lim & Benbasat, 1992-1993). Also suggested is the idea of a full-featured session-oriented NSS (Anson & Jelassi, 1990; Carmel et al., 1993; DeSanctis & Gallupe, 1987; Jelassi & Foroughi, 1989), which offers a structured negotiation process, DSS support, electronic communication, group process structuring techniques, support for a mediator, and documentation of the negotiation. Web-based NSSs are now under development that integrate negotiation software agents with elements of negotiation support systems to facilitate and enhance electronic negotiations (Kersten, 2003; Kersten, Law, & Strecker, 2004).

While DSSs enhance negotiators' information processing, analysis, and decision-making during a negotiation, the communication component of an NSS is meant to enhance communication between negotiators. This communication between negotiators can take many forms. In addition to traditional face-to-face settings (audio and visual), negotiations may be conducted using computer conferencing (text only), a decision room (text and visual), and telephone (audio only). The number of possible negotiation scenarios is growing as technology develops, with an increasing proportion of negotiations today being conducted by audio-conferencing, video-conferencing, or computer conferencing over the Internet.

THE ROLE OF CONFLICT LEVEL IN NEGOTIATIONS

By definition, negotiation and bargaining are characterized by conflict. The intensity of the conflict, however, varies with each negotiation situation. Conflict has been discussed in terms of "level," "size," "degree," "amount," and "intensity." Bargaining research has revealed the importance of conflict intensity in determining the behavior of negotiators and the outcomes they achieve. The amount of conflict in a bargaining situation has been described as an extremely

important, if not the most important, factor affecting both negotiator behavior and negotiation outcomes (Hiltrop & Rubin, 1981). For instance, bargainers in high conflict tend to engage in more competitive behavior, perform less effectively, and achieve poorer joint outcomes than those in low conflict (Deutsch, 1969; Rubin & Brown, 1975). Communication between bargainers, including holistic consideration of issues, idea identification, and role reversal, for example, is quite effective under conditions of low conflict, but these approaches have sometimes been found ineffective in a high conflict situation, decreasing the chances of successful conflict resolution (Rubin & Brown, 1975). More recent research, however, has indicated that communication and information exchange in bargaining situations increases the likelihood that bargainers will move from distributive outcomes to integrative, mutually beneficial outcomes (Clopton, 1984; Lindskold & Hans, 1988; Olekalns, Smith, & Walsh, 1996).

Several NSS empirical research studies have used level of conflict as an independent variable. Jones (1988) found that DSS support in the form of joint outcome-maximizing contract suggestions was beneficial for subjects in low conflict of interest treatments, but not for those in high conflict of interest treatments.

Sheffield (1995) manipulated conflict level by instructing some subjects to assume an individualistic bargaining orientation, in which they maximized their own outcome, while others were instructed to assume a cooperative bargaining orientation, in which they maximized joint outcome. The results of Sheffield's study showed that dyads who had been instructed to assume a cooperative bargaining orientation achieved greater joint outcomes than those instructed to assume an individualistic orientation. Cooperative dyads attained more insight into each other's profit tables, perceived the outcome of the negotiation as more profitable for both parties, and perceived the bargaining partner as having a less difficult disposition and as being a more credible source of information than themselves. Bargaining orientation also impacted the effectiveness of communication media. In the absence of visual communication, individualistic and cooperative bargainers achieved similar negotiation outcomes. When visual communication was present, cooperative bargainers maximized joint outcomes. However, for individualistic bargainers, the additional social cues inherent in visual communication increased bargainers' perception that their partner intended to dominate the negotiation, which reduced their motivation and their ability to pay attention to the negotiation process, and led to lower joint outcomes.

Two laboratory studies by Foroughi, Perkins, and Jelassi (1995) and Perkins, Hershauer, Foroughi, and Delaney (1996) operationalized conflict of interest by assigning weights to the issues in a four-issue engine subcomponent contract to create a low conflict of interest treatment, in which mutually beneficial trade-offs were possible, and a high conflict of interest treatment, in which issues for both parties were weighted similarly, creating a zero-sum situation. Both studies found strong evidence for the benefit of DSS support for alternative generation evaluation in both levels of conflict. The Foroughi, Perkins, and Jelassi study (1995) compared NSS-supported dyads to non-NSS dyads, crossed with low conflict of interest vs. high conflict of interest scenarios. They found that NSS-supported dyads achieved higher joint outcomes, greater contract balance, and greater satisfaction, but required longer negotiation time. No differences were found for number of contract proposals and perception of the collaborative climate, but NSS support led to less negative climate in the low conflict scenario. A second similar study by Perkins, Hershauer, Foroughi, and Delaney (1996) reduced the NSS to a stand-alone DSS and employed managers as subjects. As in the first study, the DSS users achieved significantly higher joint outcomes and contract balance in both levels of conflict. Surprisingly,

DSS-supported managers took less time to reach agreement than non-supported managers.

THE ROLE OF MEDIA RICHNESS IN NEGOTIATIONS

The increasing frequency of negotiations in dispersed settings has created an urgent need to determine which type of communication medium is appropriate for a given situation. Insight into the impact of various types of media is provided by media richness theory, which argues that the various communication media differ in richness. "Rich" communication media allow the transmission of a multiplicity of cues, provide immediate feedback, allow communication with both natural language and numbers, and facilitate the personal focus of messages (Daft & Lengel, 1986). Existing communication media can be viewed on a continuum of rich to lean, with face-to-face communication being the richest, followed by electronic meeting systems, video-conferencing, and audio-conferencing, with electronic mail, voice mail, and computer conferencing being the leanest (Kydd & Ferry, 1991).

In face-to-face communication, the richest communication medium, close physical proximity enables the communication of many different types of information — visual, aural, and nonverbal (Daft, Lengel, & Trevino, 1987). Negotiators are aware of each other's physical appearance, and they communicate through gestures, facial expressions, eye contact, and body movement. Negotiators communicate information aurally, through pitch, volume and quality of voice, speed of talking, and use of pauses, filler words, and laughter (Baird & Wieting, 1979). Video-conferencing, which links negotiators with televised images of each other's head and shoulders, enables fewer information cues to pass between them. The impact of physical proximity is lost, gestures and postures are not communicated (Drolet & Morris, 1995), real eye contact is not possible (Rose & Clark, 1995), and aural cues are often not communicated. The audio-conferencing mode is often used for negotiations in dispersed settings. Telephone communication is less rich than face-to-face or video-conferencing, because visual clues such as facial expressions, movement, body language, and the impact of physical proximity are not conveyed between negotiators. Aural cues from verbal and nonverbal vocal sounds, such as those possible in face-to-face communication, are available, however. Further down still on the media richness continuum is computer-mediated communication (computer conferencing), which conveys text messages between negotiators, synchronously or asynchronously. Richness is limited to text communication alone, and aural and visual cues are nonexistent.

Daft & Lengel (1986) suggest that organizational decision-making could be improved by matching the decision-making task at hand with the communication medium that best fits the needs and purpose of the task. Equivocality resolution, the basic task in a negotiation, involves the complex task of arriving at a shared meaning of, or agreement on, information. Because a communication medium's richness determines the amount of information it conveys (Poole, Shannon, & DeSanctis, 1992), richness or leanness can impact significantly on the process and outcome of a negotiation (Purdy, Nye, & Balakrishnan, 2000). Because facial and vocal cues may account for more than 90 percent of a message's meaning, negotiators using leaner media may experience a lack of commonality of meaning necessary for successful negotiation (Mehrabian, 1971). The more limited amount and type of information communicated by leaner media can result in a depersonalized, anonymous negotiation environment (Straus & McGrath, 1994) that impacts the rapport between negotiators (Drolet & Morris, 1995), the frequency of impasses experienced (Moore, Kurtzberg, Thompson, & Morris, 1999), and the negotiators' perceptions of power and influence (Hollingshead, 1996).

Communication medium has been used as an independent variable in several NSS laboratory studies. Sheffield (1995) compared the impact of four different communication media—computer conferencing (text only), decision room (text and visual), telephone (audio only), and face-to-face (audio and visual) on negotiator behavior in a bilateral monopoly task, in integrative as well as in distributive bargaining scenarios. This research concentrated on the efficiency (speed of processing information to reach a solution) and the richness (social and emotional information) of the various types of communication media. A cooperative bargaining orientation and/or audio mode of communication led to higher joint outcomes. The results indicated that, for bilateral negotiations, the audio mode was more efficient than the text mode. Richer media helped bargainers reach higher joint outcomes in integrative bargaining settings. However, in distributive situations when trade-offs are not so obvious, the socio-emotional content of the communication that is possible with richer media increased tension and distracted bargainers from their task. Sheffield concluded that decision room settings are more appropriate for more cooperative bargaining, while computer conferencing may be more useful for more distributive negotiation situations.

In an extension of the Foroughi, Perkins, and Jelassi study (1995) described earlier, Delaney, Foroughi, and Perkins (1997) compared the effects of a DSS used in combination with electronic communication with those of DSS support alone. An interactive DSS was used for alternative generation and evaluation. Face-to-face communication was compared to electronic communication between bargainers for inputting their comments and proposals and viewing each other's inputs on a public screen. In both conditions the NSS featured a structured integrative bargaining process, guided by a facilitator, which included a statement of interests, role reversal, searching for common ground, generation and analysis of alternative solutions, and reaching an agreement.

The DSS alone brought higher joint outcomes and more balanced contracts, but satisfaction was higher in both low and high levels of conflict with electronic communication.

In a study by Rangaswamy and Shell (1997), pairs of bargainers used NEGOTIATION ASSISTANT, which employs an Internet connection to link the two parties electronically and provides a DSS which incorporates conjoint analysis to help negotiators prepare for the negotiation by determining their preferences for different settlement options. The study compared four types of communication — face-to-face, e-mail only, DSS used only for preparation, and DSS plus electronic exchange of contract offers and messages during the negotiation (i.e., an NSS). Results showed that the negotiation process was perceived as friendlier for dyads in face-to-face treatments. In a few cases, dyads that communicated electronically failed to reach an agreement, whereas all face-to-face dyads did reach agreements. The researchers concluded that when there is little room for making an integrative agreement, the impersonal quality of electronic communication has the potential to increase tensions, sometimes so much that negotiators reach an impasse and never reach agreement. They found no advantages in electronic communication (e-mail treatment) by itself over simple face-to-face bargaining. The edge for bargainers came, instead, from the structured negotiation preparation process in the DSS and NSS conditions.

Purdy, Nye, and Balakrishnan (2000) compared the impact of four different communication media — face-to-face, video-conferencing, telephone, and computer-mediated communication (computer conferencing) — on objective negotiation outcomes (negotiation time, joint outcomes, and profit inequality) and subjective negotiation outcomes (outcome satisfaction and desire for future negotiation interaction). Subjects, assuming the role of retail store buyer or manufacturer's representative, negotiated a three-attribute sales contract for a men's clothing line. Dyads who

bargained integratively could achieve a maximum payoff of $52 million each, and those who bargained distributively could achieve a payoff of $40 million each. Results showed that, although face-to-face negotiators did not achieve higher joint outcomes, they collaborated more, achieved more time efficiency than those using leaner media, and expressed greater desire for future negotiation interaction. Subjects who used richer media achieved greater profit equality in less time. Greater media richness increased satisfaction indirectly by increasing the intent to collaborate and by reducing time to achieve a given profit. The impact of video-conferencing was found to be similar to that of face-to-face communication, in contrast to that of the leaner media — telephone and computer-mediated communication.

As the previous discussion shows, NSS research findings about the role of media richness on negotiation outcomes are somewhat inconsistent. However, in most of the studies, joint outcomes and contract balance were better with richer media. Richer media improved negotiation time and, except for one study, also increased perceptions of satisfaction and positive atmosphere in the negotiation. Interestingly, in one study (Sheffield, 1995), face-to-face communication increased tension in a distributive (high conflict) setting, while Rangaswamy and Shell (1997) found the leanness of computer-mediated communication to be too impersonal in a high-conflict negotiation situation.

Considering the growing frequency of negotiation in dispersed settings, NSS research focused on the use of various communication media is very sparse. The present research will shed more light on the role of media richness in negotiations. It will build on the Delaney, Foroughi, and Perkins study (1997), using the same task, setting, and decision support system, but providing communication in the form of audio-conferencing and computer conferencing. The present study will provide a more comprehensive comparison of these two modes of communication than prior studies, considering two levels of conflict and employing a more complex and more realistic negotiation scenario than prior studies.

RESEARCH FRAMEWORK

The framework for NSS research that serves as the foundation for the present study (see Figure 1) has been adapted from an integrated research framework developed by Dennis et al. (1988). The Dennis et al. framework integrates other causal models that have been used for the study of group processes and outcomes (i.e., McGrath, 1984; Kraemer & King, 1986; DeSanctis & Gallupe, 1987). The framework for NSS research identifies six classes of variables that should be considered in empirical NSS studies. How these variables were operationalized in the present study is described in the discussion to follow (see Figure 1).

Figure 1. Framework for NSS research

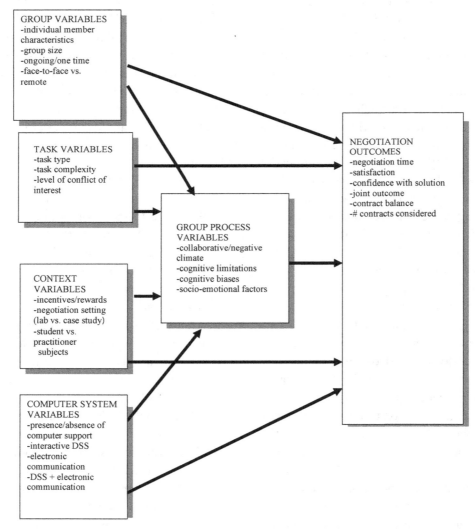

[Adapted from Dennis et al., 1988]

Group Variables

Characteristics of the groups and individuals were all controlled. The study used only dyads with zero history of previous negotiating together, and the negotiations were one-time only. All dyads negotiated in a dispersed situation. Subjects were assigned randomly to pairs and to roles within pairs, and pairs were assigned randomly to experimental conditions; gender differences were controlled by assigning subjects to bargain with members of the same sex.

Task Variables

The study used a mixed-motive task (McGrath, 1984), in which group members must resolve conflicts of interest. Pairs of bargainers resolved a manufacturing bargaining problem involving negotiation of four issues of a three-year purchase agreement for an engine subcomponent. The amount of conflict of interest between the bargainers was manipulated to create high and low conflict situations. Equal weights were assigned to the negotiation issues in the high conflict condition to create a win-lose, conflict-laden situation. Different weights were assigned to the issues in the low conflict condition, so that there was room for trade-offs and a win-win solution beneficial for both sides was easier to achieve.

Context Variables

Context variables were controlled. All subjects were chosen from the multiple sections of the same School of Business course, with experimentation taking place in the same three small rooms in the same behavioral laboratory. All subjects were given the incentive of earning class credit for participation in the study; they were also given a chance to win a monetary reward presented to the dyads with the highest joint outcomes in each condition at the end of the study.

Computer System Variables

Communication medium was used as an independent variable. Computer conferencing treatments featured communication using Lotus Notes on personal computers connected via a local area network. Audio-conferencing treatments featured communication via telephone lines. All other computer system variables were controlled, with subjects using the same type of decision support software for alternative generation and evaluation.

Group Process Variables

Several group process variables were controlled. All experimental bargaining conditions were supported by a human mediator and were one-time sessions, and all used the same structured, integrative bargaining process.

Negotiation Outcome Variables

Outcome measures of several dependent variables were collected. Objective outcomes included joint outcome, contract balance, negotiation time, and number of alternative contracts proposed. Subjective outcomes included post-bargaining measures of negotiator satisfaction, the amount of negative climate (suspiciousness, inflexibility, difficulty of resolution), and the amount of collaborative climate (cooperativeness and consideration) perceived by the negotiators.

HYPOTHESES

The hypotheses examined in the present study are listed next. After each grouping of hypotheses is presented, the rationale for the hypotheses, including the relevant literature, is provided.

Joint Outcomes

H1: In the low conflict treatments, there will be no significant difference between the joint outcomes achieved by dyads using audio-conferencing and dyads using computer conferencing.

H2: In the high conflict treatments, dyads using audio-conferencing will achieve higher joint outcomes than dyads using computer conferencing.

In the low conflict treatments, mutually beneficial trade-offs are relatively easy for the bargainers to achieve. The benefits of the additional information exchange possible with audio-conferencing as compared to the leaner computer conferencing mode should not make a significant difference on joint outcomes. In contrast, the high conflict treatments presented a negotiation task that was more difficult for the bargainers, in which one party's gain was essentially equal to the other's loss. The richer medium of audio-conferencing should enable bargainers to engage in the "give and take" that is necessary for reaching a negotiation solution. The support for collaborative problem-solving behaviors should enhance the bargainers' discovery of a mutually acceptable negotiation solution that matches their expectations and maximizes high joint outcomes (Pruitt & Carnevale, 1993). Thus, for high conflict treatments, audio-conferencing dyads should achieve higher joint outcomes than dyads using computing conferencing.

Several empirical studies have provided evidence of the positive relationship between media richness and integrativeness in a negotiation (Drolet & Morris, 1995; Morley & Stephenson, 1997; Williams, 1977). Compared to audio-conferencing, computer conferencing lacks social context cues that would help convey the meaning of messages (Rice & Love, 1987; Sproull & Kiesler, 1986). The leaner computer conferencing would tend to make negotiators in high conflict feel frustrated and alone in their task, a type of social anonymity that can encourage uninhibited behavior (Kiesler, Siegel, & McGuire, 1984) and less cooperation, and often leads to impasses in contexts with little integrative potential (Rangaswamy & Shell, 1997). With computer conferencing, bargainers show less accuracy in judging bargaining partners' interests, often obtaining lower, more unequally distributed joint outcomes (Arunachalam & Dilla, 1995; Eliashberg, Rangaswamy, & Balakrishnan, 1987).

Contract Balance

H3: In the low conflict treatments, there will be no significant difference between the contract balance achieved by dyads using audio-conferencing and dyads using computer conferencing.

H4: In the high conflict treatments, dyads using audio-conferencing will achieve more balanced contracts than dyads using computer conferencing.

In the low conflict treatments, as described earlier, mutually beneficial trade-offs are relatively easy for the bargainers to achieve. Therefore, just as for joint outcomes, the richer audio-conferencing mode should not make a significant difference on contract balance. However, because the high conflict treatments presented a zero-sum situation, the richer medium of audio-conferencing should better facilitate the bargainers' engagement in the "give and take" integrative behavior that is necessary for reaching a mutually agreeable result with balance in the joint outcomes achieved. The social cues conveyed through audio-conferencing should tend to motivate negotiators away from trying to divide the pie to their own advantage (Kiesler, Kiesler, & Pallak, 1967). Previous studies have shown that the lack of social cues and the social isolation of bargainers in computer conferencing often result in less contract balance, in addition to lower joint outcomes (Arunachalam & Dilla,

1995; Eliashberg, Rangaswamy, & Balakrishnan, 1987).

Negotiation Time

H5: In both low and high conflict treatments, dyads using audio-conferencing will have shorter negotiation times than those using computer conferencing.

Less information can be conveyed in a given amount of time with the text-based exchanges of computer conferencing as compared to the aural exchanges of audio-conferencing (Heid, 1997). Negotiators who use computer conferencing tend to use fewer words, but inputting them into text form takes a longer time than aural communication (Sheffield, 1995). Computer conferencing also increases the amount of time needed to understand the structure of a negotiation task (Sheffield, 1995). The inefficiency of computer-mediated communication compared to aural communication is thus expected to yield increased negotiation times for both low and high levels of conflict.

Number of Contracts Proposed

H6: In both low and high conflict treatments, dyads using audio-conferencing will propose more contracts than those using computer conferencing.

As argued previously, the spoken word is faster than typing and aural communication enables negotiators to understand the negotiation task faster and interact more efficiently. For these reasons, audio-conferencing is expected to facilitate the conveyance of more proposed contracts than computer conferencing.

Collaborative Climate

H7: In the low conflict treatments, there will be no significant difference between perceived collaborative climate for dyads using audio-conferencing and dyads using computer conferencing.

H8: In the high conflict treatments, perceived collaborative climate will be higher for dyads using audio-conferencing than for those using computer conferencing.

Negative Climate

H9: In the low conflict treatments, there will be no significant difference between perceived negative climate for dyads using audio-conferencing and dyads using computer conferencing.

H10: In the high conflict treatments, perceived negative climate will be less for dyads using audio-conferencing than for those using computer conferencing.

Satisfaction

H11: In the low conflict treatments, there will be no significant difference in satisfaction for dyads using audio-conferencing and dyads using computer conferencing.

H12: In the high conflict treatments, satisfaction will be greater for dyads using audio-conferencing than for those using computer conferencing.

Because low conflict dyads will encounter a minimal amount of conflict in their task, the wider range of information conveyed through the richer audio-conferencing medium, compared to the leaner computer conferencing medium, should not make a significant difference on collaborative climate, negative climate, and satisfaction in low conflict treatments.

In high conflict, however, audio-conferencing is expected to be more beneficial to the negotiation process by enabling bargainers to interact more fully and engage in fruitful problem solving (Kydd & Ferry, 1991). In turn, the outcome measures are expected to be more favorable for audio-conferencing, which also impacts the attitude measures. Thus, in high conflict, audio-conferencing is expected to result in greater collaborative climate, less negative climate, and more satisfaction than in the computer conferencing mode.

RESEARCH METHODOLOGY

Research Design

The research design included two independent variables (level of conflict and type of communication media), each with two treatments (high or low conflict, computer conferencing or audio-conferencing), thus necessitating a two-by-two random factorial design (CRF-22) with fixed-effects.

Independent Variables

Level of Conflict of Interest

Bargaining research has revealed the importance of the amount of conflict of interest inherent in a negotiation situation as a determinant of negotiator behavior as well as of the outcomes achieved (Rubin & Brown, 1975). Level of conflict of interest was chosen as an independent variable for this study in order to examine the effectiveness of an NSS in two different bargaining situations (low and high conflict of interest). These two treatments represent two extremes of conflict of interest that are encountered in real-world negotiation situations.

The bargaining task chosen for this research involved negotiation between a buyer and a seller over four issues of a three-year purchase agreement for an engine subcomponent (Jones, 1988). The issues were unit price, purchase quantity, time of first delivery, and warranty period. Low conflict treatments were simulated by assigning

different weights to the issues, creating a bargaining situation in which mutually beneficial trade-offs were possible between the buyer and the seller. In the high conflict treatments, issues for both parties were weighted similarly, creating a zero-sum situation in which one party's gain was equal to the other one's loss. For both low and high conflict levels, point sheets of outcomes were constructed for buyer and seller using these weights (see Appendices A and B).

Communication Medium

Two types of communication media were used in the study — computer conferencing and audio-conferencing (see Figure 2). In the computer conferencing treatments, bargainers were located in two different rooms, so that visual and verbal communications were not possible. They communicated by using personal computers (PCs) connected via a local area network (LAN) using Lotus Notes. A three-PC computer conferencing system was designed on a LAN so that the negotiators could communicate with each other in real-time from their own PCs and the experimenter (acting as a mediator) could monitor the communication and intervene when necessary from the experimenter's PC[1]. Lotus Notes was used as the vehicle for computer conferencing. During the computer conferencing, the negotiators identified themselves as the buyer (Roberts) or seller (Simo) before giving input so that the experimenter could follow the online conversation.

In the audio-conferencing treatments, subjects were also in different rooms, but these bargainers communicated via telephone lines, and the experimenter could also monitor and intervene when necessary from a third telephone instrument on the same line. During the telephone-mediated communication, negotiators also identified themselves as buyer (Roberts) or seller (Simo) before giving input so that the experimenter could follow the conversation. The experimenter always identified himself (orally in audio-conferencing,

Figure 2. Audio-Conferencing and Computer Conferencing

Audio-Conferencing: Bargainers communicated via telephone connections. Each had an individual decision support system to use for alternative generation and evaluation.

Computer Conferencing: Bargainers communicated on personal computers via Lotus Notes. Each had an individual decision support system to use for alternative generation and evaluation.

in text in computer conferencing) before giving any instructions to the bargainers.

In both computer conferencing and audio-conferencing treatments, each bargainer was provided with a Negotiation Decision Support Tool (NDST), the DSS that was developed for use in this series of NSS studies to support alternative generation and evaluation. The NDST consisted of a spreadsheet with two windows, running on a stand-alone microcomputer. Window #1, the Decision Tool, was used by negotiators to input their own priorities for the issues as well as their perception of the other party's priorities based on what they learned about the other party during the statement-of-interests stage of negotiation. Based on the priorities input by the subjects, the Decision Tool estimated the point structure of the other party, generated all the possible contract alternatives (748 altogether), and ranked them in descending order according to the joint outcome they would give. The Decision Tool then displayed — for the user only — the three contract alternatives that would give the highest joint outcome. The Decision Tool was designed to display only

these three contract alternatives in order to avoid the possibility of information overload that might result from displaying too many contract options. Window #2 contained a Contract Point Evaluator, which was used for alternative evaluation. It incorporated the complete point structure of the negotiator. The negotiator plugged in alternative contracts, and the algorithm determined the total score (for the user only) that could be achieved with each one.

Dependent Variables

Joint outcome was measured by adding buyer and seller points on the final agreement. *Contract balance* was the absolute value of the difference between the outcomes of the two bargainers in each negotiating pair. *Negotiation time* was measured as the time needed to reach an agreement or deadlock, with no time limit placed on negotiators for reaching an agreement. The *number of contracts proposed* was determined from the computer records in the computer conferencing treatments; in the audio treatments, the experimenter used a third telephone instrument on the same line to listen to and record the number of contracts offered.

Post-bargaining negotiator attitudes (perceived collaborative climate, perceived negative climate, and satisfaction) were measured by a questionnaire administered at the end of the bargaining session. The subjects responded to each item in the questionnaire by circling a number from 1 to 7 on a 7-point Likert scale. Based on factor analysis on the questionnaire data collected in the initial study in this program of research (Foroughi, Perkins, & Jelassi, 1995), the items were condensed into a set of three factors that we have named perceived collaborative climate, perceived negative climate, and satisfaction. Davis' Technology Acceptance Model questionnaire (1985) was also administered to measure overall evaluation, perceived ease of use, and perceived usefulness of computer conferencing or audio-conferencing and the DSS.

Control Variables

Group structure was controlled, with each negotiating side consisting of one person, and with each person in the dyad having zero history in negotiating with the other. Subjects were randomly assigned to the role of buyer or seller and to dyads, and dyads were randomly assigned to experimental treatments. The same task type was performed by all treatment dyads, with the only difference being the assigned weights to the issues. The physical environment was essentially the same for all treatment dyads, with each bargainer located in a separate room and supplied with an individual DSS. The only difference was in the communication medium, computer conferencing or audio-conferencing, that was used.

Experimental Procedures

This experiment was conducted during the spring semester, using three small adjacent rooms in a behavioral laboratory in a School of Business building, with communication provided via telephone lines or a data communications network (LAN). During the experiment, the experimenter was in the middle room directing and monitoring the negotiators, who were junior or senior students majoring in information systems or accounting. The two negotiators were located in the rooms on either side of the experimenter, entering their individual rooms before the beginning of the experiment and leaving the rooms only after completing the post-bargaining questionnaires.

The experiment was conducted in three phases. During Phase 1, subjects filled out a consent form and were given a printed outline of the procedures for the entire experiment and a listing of the rules to be observed. Next, subjects were assigned randomly to the role of buyer or seller, to an experimental treatment, and to a room from which they would negotiate. They were given a 10-minute training session on the use of the communication medium to which they had been assigned. Then they were given the case materials and a page of confidential information about their company. After these materials had been read by the subjects, they were given point sheets for their respective companies. Next, subjects completed a Point Sheet Exercise in which they were asked to add up the points for each issue of the alternative ("third party") contract and verify that the score given at the bottom of the point sheet was correct. This was done to make sure that the subjects understood the task. At this time, ten minutes of software training on the NDST was given to all dyads. Subjects then filled out a pre-negotiation questionnaire that provided demographic information about themselves as well as information about their typing ability, experience with Lotus Notes, and experience with computers.

During Phase 2, subjects were given a final instructions sheet with an outline of the negotiation process. They then proceeded to negotiate, beginning with a statement-of-interests phase to share what factors were important to each party.

Each negotiator stated which of the four issues — unit price, purchase quantity, time of first delivery, and warranty period — were most important to the company that he or she represented. When an agreement was reached, they signed a final agreement form.

During Phase 3, all subjects answered a post-bargaining attitude questionnaire, as well as Davis' Technology Acceptance Model questionnaire.

Subjects

One hundred and twenty eight student volunteers from an undergraduate information systems course (all information systems and accounting majors) at a large Midwestern university served as subjects for this experiment. All of the subjects had used e-mail before, making it easy for them to master the use of the computer conferencing software in the 10-minute training session. In addition, all these students had used Microsoft Excel in their classes, making it easy for them to learn how to use the NDST, which was itself an easy-to-use Microsoft Excel-based tool, in the ten-minute training session. Furthermore, the NDST had been successfully used in three previous studies (Foroughi, Perkins, & Jelassi, 1995; Perkins, Hershauer, Foroughi, & Delaney, 1996; Delaney, Foroughi, & Perkins, 1997) and had received a favorable technology evaluation in each of these studies. To provide an incentive for subjects to participate and to perform well, course credit was offered to all participants and a monetary reward ($100) was given to the top pair of bargainers (in terms of joint outcome) in each of the four experimental cells.

Task

The bargaining task used in this study involved negotiation between a buyer and seller over four issues of a three-year purchase agreement for an engine subcomponent. The issues were unit price, purchase quantity, time of first delivery, and warranty period. Low conflict treatments were simulated by assigning different weights to the issues, creating a bargaining situation in which mutually beneficial trade-offs were possible. High conflict treatments featured issues for both parties being weighted similarly, creating a distributive bargaining, zero-sum situation in which one party's gain was essentially equal to the other one's loss.

STATISTICAL ANALYSIS AND RESULTS

The SPSS statistical package was used to perform statistical analysis of the experimental results, using a fixed-effects two-way analysis of variance (2-way ANOVA) model for *joint outcome*, *contract balance*, *negotiation time*, *number of alternatives*, and *post-bargaining negotiator attitudes*. See Table 1 for a summary of these results. t-tests were used to analyze the results of the technology evaluation questionnaire; these results are reported in the text but not in tabular form.

Joint Outcomes

No significant difference was found between joint outcomes for audio-conferencing and computer conferencing in low conflict, but joint outcomes for audio-conferencing were significantly higher in high conflict. Both hypothesis H1 and hypothesis H2 were supported.

Contract Balance

No significant difference was found between contract balance for audio-conferencing and computer conferencing in low conflict, thus supporting hypothesis H3. No significant difference was found between contract balance for audio-conferencing and computer conferencing in high conflict, and thus hypothesis H4 was not

Table 1. Hypotheses and results (sample size: four cells, 16 dyads per cell, total of 64 dyads, total of 128 subjects)

Hypothesis	Mean Audio-conferencing	Mean Computer Conferencing	Level of Significance (p)	Hypothesis Supported
Joint outcome				
H1: low audio = low computer	128.75	129.00	N.S.	YES
H2: high audio > high computer	101.50	99.88	p<.005	YES
Contract balance				
H3: low audio = low computer	8.00	10.63	N.S.	YES
H4: high audio > high computer	4.38	4.88	N.S.	NO
Negotiation time				
H5.1: low audio < low computer	20.31	43.75	p<.005	YES
H5.2: high audio < high computer	30.31	57.13	p<.005	YES
Number of contracts proposed				
H6.1: low audio > low computer	3.81	6.00	p<.02	NO
H6.2: high audio > high computer	13.13	9.81	N.S.	NO
Perceived collaborative climate				
H7: low audio = low computer	6.02	5.64	p<.05	NO
H8: high audio > high computer	5.69	5.57	N.S.	NO
Perceived negative climate				
H9: low audio = low computer	2.51	3.13	p<.10	NO
H10: high audio <high computer	3.04	3.19	N.S.	NO
Satisfaction				
H11: low audio = low computer	5.83	5.50	p<.07	NO
H12: high audio >high computer	5.06	5.16	N.S.	NO

supported. However, although not statistically significant, the results do indicate better contract balance for audio-conferencing dyads than for computer conferencing dyads.

Negotiation Time

Negotiation time was significantly greater for computer conferencing dyads at both low and high conflict levels. Hypothesis H5 was supported.

Number of Alternatives

In low conflict dyads, significantly more alternatives were generated with computer conferencing than with audio-conferencing. In high conflict dyads, there was no difference in the number of alternatives generated with audio-conferencing and with computer conferencing. Hypothesis H6 was not supported.

Collaborative Climate

Perceived collaborative climate was significantly lower for computer conferencing dyads than for audio-conferencing dyads in low conflict, and there was no difference in collaborative climate for the two communication media in high conflict. Neither hypothesis H7 nor hypothesis H8 was supported.

Negative Climate

In low conflict dyads, there was a significantly greater amount of negative climate for computer conferencing dyads than for audio-conferencing dyads, whereas in high conflict dyads there was no significant difference in the amount of negative climate for the two communication media. Again, neither hypothesis H9 nor hypothesis H10 was supported.

Satisfaction

In low conflict dyads, satisfaction was significantly lower for computer conferencing dyads than for audio-conferencing dyads, whereas in high conflict there was no difference in the amount of satisfaction for the two communication media. Again, neither hypothesis H11 nor hypothesis H12 was supported.

DSS Evaluation

In terms of evaluating the DSS using the Technology Acceptance Model, the means for both low and high conflict treatments in both computer conferencing and audio-conferencing were all above the midpoint (4.0) on the Likert scale (in fact, all means were above 5.0), indicating a favorable evaluation of the DSS under all conditions. In both low and high conflict treatments, the DSS was rated as having higher perceived usefulness by the audio-conferencing dyads than by the computer conferencing dyads ($p < 0.005$ for low conflict, $p < 0.03$ for high conflict). There was no difference across communication media in terms of overall evaluation and ease of use of the DSS.

Communication Media

In terms of evaluating the communication media using the Technology Acceptance Model, the means for both low and high conflict treatments in both computer conferencing and audio-confer-encing were all above the midpoint (4.0) on the Likert scale, indicating a favorable evaluation of the communication media under all conditions. In low conflict dyads, audio-conferencing was rated as having higher perceived usefulness than computer conferencing ($p < 0.05$), whereas in high conflict dyads there was no difference in perceived usefulness ratings for the two communication media. There was no difference across communication media in terms of overall evaluation and ease of use of the media.

DISCUSSION

The hypotheses had predicted that audio-conferencing would enhance negotiation outcomes and attitudes in high conflict treatments, and this was partially substantiated by the results. Audio-conferencing was shown to help high conflict dyads achieve *greater* joint outcomes than did computer conferencing. While contract balance in high conflict was better with audio-conferencing than with computer conferencing, the difference was not statistically significant. Surprisingly, audio-conferencing did not increase the number of alternative contracts proposed in high conflict. There were no differences between the two communication media in terms of perceived collaborative climate, perceived negative climate, and satisfaction. In summary, audio-conferencing *did* enhance negotiation results and *did not* negatively impact attitudes in high conflict. The key result is that joint outcomes were higher with audio-conferencing. As expected, negotiation time was greater with computer conferencing than with audio-conferencing.

In the low conflict treatments, it was expected that there would be no differences between the two communication modes except for the negotiation time (expected to be greater for computer conferencing) and the number of contracts proposed (expected to be greater for audio-conferencing). These expectations held true for joint outcome, contract balance, and negotiation time, but not for number of contracts proposed or for the attitude measures (collaborative climate, negative climate, satisfaction). These are very interesting results; when there is little conflict, it appears as though computer conferencing (e.g., the mechanics of using the system and the impersonality of communicating via the computer) just got in the way, while the audio-conferencing let the bargainers get the job done quickly and easily. Or, to phrase this conclusion another way, *efficiency matters* to the bargainers! They were able to achieve outcomes that were just as good, with less time and fewer proposed contracts, with audio-conferencing, and thus their attitudes towards audio-conferencing were more favorable than towards computer conferencing.

This same "efficiency matters" argument also applies to the high conflict results. Here the bargaining task was much more difficult, and it was possible that the transmission of negative social cues via audio-conferencing might result in less favorable outcomes and attitudes. But it appears as though the efficiency aspects of audio-conferencing—a richer medium in which more communication can take place more quickly (people can speak faster than they can type) — overshadowed any negative social cues transmitted. The result was improved joint outcomes, using less negotiation time, with audio-conferencing, and no significant differences in the attitude measures.

Of course, there is more than one possible explanation for the poor showing of computer conferencing. For example, the results may be explained by the novelty of the communications software and the fact that this was a "one-shot" performance. Subjects in computer conferencing dyads used two types of software (the DSS and Lotus Notes) for the first time. The novelty of both may have combined to hamper their potential performance in the negotiation as opposed to the audio-conferencing dyads, which also used the unfamiliar DSS but communicated over the telephone, a familiar means of commu-

nication. The implication of these results is that longitudinal testing of computer conferencing versus audio-conferencing might provide a more accurate comparison of the two communication media. Such testing would overcome the "novelty effect," if any, of both the DSS and computer conferencing.

CONCLUSION

The results of this study — as well as earlier studies by Sheffield (1995), Rangaswamy and Shell (1997), and Purdy, Nye, and Balakrishnan (2000) — tend to provide support for media richness theory. High conflict dyads, whose task was more equivocal than that of low conflict dyads, achieved higher joint outcomes with the richer audio-conferencing mode of communication than with the leaner computer communications mode. Whereas audio-conferencing provided two types of cues (voice and voice inflection), computer communication provided only one type of cue (text). The leaner mode of communication appears to have hindered successful problem resolution rather than facilitating it. The implication is that in certain task settings where cooperation between parties is essential for conflict resolution, the impersonal, rational atmosphere created by computer communication may not create a beneficial atmosphere.

Computer conferencing might prove to be more advantageous in dispersed bargaining involving multiple members on each bargaining side. Whereas several bargainers speaking in an audio-conference might have difficulty in distinguishing each other's voices, the written text of computer conferencing, which identifies the inputs of bargainers, might help to keep bargainers' inputs straight. The written text would also provide bargainers with an ongoing log of what had transpired thus far in the negotiation.

The implications of the results of this research project are, of course, limited by the use of student subjects in a simulated bargaining situation, where real-life bargaining conflict was not possible. Future research in the area of communication media for computerized negotiation support systems should include longitudinal testing, the use of real-life bargaining situations containing actual conflict of interest (but this will be very difficult to do except in a case study setting), and the use of multiple members on each bargaining team. Further experimentation into the value of a DSS for dispersed negotiators should also be conducted. Do dispersed negotiators really achieve better results with a DSS? What difference does it make if only the buyer, or only the seller, has access to a DSS?

REFERENCES

Anson, R., & Jelassi, M.T. (1990). A developmental framework for computer-supported conflict resolution. *European Journal of Operational Research*, *46*(2), 181-199.

Arunachalam, V., & Dilla, W.N. (1995). Judgment accuracy and outcomes in negotiations: A causal modeling analysis of decision-aiding effects. *Organizational Behavior and Human Decision Processes*, *61*(3), 289-304.

Baird, J., & Wieting, G. (1979). Nonverbal communication can be a motivational tool. *Personnel Journal*, *19*, 637-654.

Bazerman, M.H., & Carroll, J.S. (1987). Negotiator cognition. In L.L. Cummings & B.M. Staw (eds.), *Research in Organizational Behavior* (Vol. 9), (pp. 247-288). Greenwich, CT: JAI Press.

Carmel, E., Herniter, B.C., & Nunamaker, Jr., J.F. (1993). Labor-management contract negotiations in an electronic meeting room: A case study. *Group Decision and Negotiation*, *2*, 27-60.

Chidambaram, L., & Jones, B. (1993). Impact of communication medium and computer support on group perceptions and performance: A comparison of face-to-face and dispersed meetings. *MIS Quarterly*, *17*(4), 465-491.

Clopton, S.W. (1984, February). Seller and buying firm factors affecting industrial buyers' negotiation behavior and outcomes. *Journal of Marketing Research*, *21*, 39-53.

Daft, R.L., & Lengel, R.H. (1986). Organizational information requirements, media richness and structural design. *Management Science*, *32*(5), 554-571.

Daft, R.L., Lengel, R.H., & Trevino, L.K. (1987). Message equivocality, media selection, and manager performance: Implications for information systems. *MIS Quarterly*, *11*(3), 354-367.

Davis, F. (1985). *A technology assessment model for empirically testing new end-user information systems: Theory and results*. Unpublished doctoral dissertation. Cambridge, MA: Massachusetts Institute of Technology.

Delaney, M.M., Foroughi, A., & Perkins, W.C. (1997). An empirical study of the efficacy of a computerized negotiation support system. *Decision Support Systems*, *20*(3), 185-197.

Dennis, A.R., George, J.F., Jessup, L.M., Nunamaker, Jr., J.F., & Vogel, D.R. (1988). Information technology to support electronic meetings. *MIS Quarterly*, *12*(4), 591-624.

DeSanctis, G., & Gallupe, B. (1987). A foundation for the study of group decision support systems. *Management Science*, *33*(2), 589-609.

Deutsch, M. (1969). Conflicts: Productive and destructive. *Journal of Social Issues*, *25*, 7-41.

Drolet, A.L., & Morris, M.W. (1995). *Communication media and interpersonal trust in conflicts: The role of rapport and synchrony of nonverbal behavior*. Paper presented at the Academy of Management meeting, Vancouver, Canada.

Eliashberg, J., Rangaswamy, A., & Balakrishnan, P.V. (1987). *Two party negotiations: A theoretical and empirical analysis.* Paper presented at ORSA/TIMS Marketing Science conference, June, Jouy-en-Josas, France.

Foroughi, A., & Jelassi, M.T. (1990). NSS solutions to major negotiation stumbling blocks. In *Proceedings of the 23rd Annual Hawaii International Conference on System Sciences* (Vol. IV), Kailua-Kona, Hawaii, (pp. 2-11).

Foroughi, A., Perkins, W.C., & Jelassi, M.T. (1995). An empirical study of an interactive, session-oriented computerized negotiation support system (NSS). *Group Decision and Negotiation, 4,* 485-512.

Heid, J. (1997). Face-to-face online. *Macworld, 14*(1), 146-151.

Hiltrop, J.M., & Rubin, J.Z. (1981). Position loss and image loss in bargaining. *Journal of Conflict Resolution, 25*(3), 521-534.

Hollingshead, A.B. (1996). Information suppression and status persistence in group decision making: The effects of communication media. *Human Communication Research, 23,* 193-220.

Jelassi, M.T., & Foroughi, A. (1989). Negotiation support systems: An overview of design issues and existing software. *Decision Support Systems, 5*(2), 167-181.

Jones, B.H. (1988). *Analytical negotiation: An empirical examination of the effects of computer support for different levels of conflict in two-party bargaining.* Unpublished doctoral dissertation. Bloomington, Indiana: Indiana University.

Kersten, G. (2003). *E-negotiations: Towards engineering of technology-based social processes.* InterNet Working Paper, Concordia University, University of Ottawa, and Carleton University.

Kersten, G., Law, K.P., & Strecker, S. (2004). *A software platform for multiprotocol e-negotiations.* InterNet Working Paper, Concordia University, University of Ottawa, and Carleton University.

Kydd, C.T., & Ferry, D.L. (1991). Computer supported cooperative work tools and media richness: An integration of the literature. In *Proceedings of the 24th Annual Hawaii International Conference on Systems Sciences* (Vol. III), (pp. 324-332). Los Alamitos, CA: IEEE Society Press.

Lim, L.H., & Benbasat, I. (1992-1993). A theoretical perspective of negotiation support systems. *Journal of Management Information Systems, 9*(3), 27-44.

Lindskold, S., & Hans, G. (1988). GRIT as a foundation for integrative bargaining. *Personality and Social Psychology Bulletin, 14*(2), 335-345.

McGrath, J.E. (1984). *Groups, interaction and performance.* Englewood Cliffs, NJ: Prentice Hall.

Mehrabian, A. (1971). *Silent messages.* Belmont, CA: Wadsworth.

Moore, D.A., Kutzberg, T.R., Thompson, L.L., & Morris, M.W. (1999). Long and short routes to success in electronically mediated negotiations: Group affiliations and good vibrations. *Organizational Behavior and Human Decision Processes, 77*(1), 22-43.

Morley, I.E., & Stephenson, G.M. (1997). *The social psychology of bargaining.* London, UK: Allen & Unwin.

Olekalns, M., Smith, P.L., & Walsh, T. (1996). The process of negotiating: Strategy and timing as predictors of outcomes. *Organizational Behavior and Human Decision Processes, 68*(1), 68-77.

Perkins, W.C., Hershauer, J.C., Foroughi, A., & Delaney, M.M. (1996, Spring). Can a negotiation support system help a purchasing manager? *International Journal of Purchasing and Materials Management, 32,* 37-45.

Poole, M.S., Shannon, D.L., & DeSanctis, G. (1992). Communication media and negotiation processes. In L. Putnam & S. Rolloff (eds.), *Communication and Negotiation: Sage Annual Reviews of Communication Research* (Vol. 20), (pp. 46-66). Newbury Park, CA: Sage Publications.

Pruitt, D.G., & Carnevale, P. (1993). *Negotiation in social conflict*. Pacific Grove, CA: Brooks/Cole.

Purdy, J.M., Nye, P., & Balakrishnan, P.V. (2000). The impact of communication media on negotiation outcomes. *International Journal of Conflict Management, 11*(2), 162-187.

Rangaswamy, A., & Shell, G.R. (1997). Using computers to realize joint gains in negotiations: Toward an electronic bargaining table. *Management Science, 43*(8), 1147-1163.

Rice, R.E., & Love, G. (1987). Electronic emotion. *Communication Research, 14*, 85-108.

Rose, D.A.D., & Clark, P.M. (1995). A review of eye-to-eye videoconferencing techniques. *BT Technology Journal, 13* (4), 127.

Rubin, J.Z., & Brown, B.R. (1975). *The social psychology of bargaining and negotiation*. New York: Academic Press.

Sheffield, J. (1995). The effect of communication medium on negotiation performance. *Group Decision and Negotiation, 4*, 159-179.

Sproull, L., & Kiesler, S. (1986). Reducing social context cues: Electronic mail in organizational communication. *Management Science, 32*(11), 1492-1512.

Straus, S.G., & McGrath, J.E. (1994). Does the medium matter? The interaction of task type and technology on group performance and member reactions. *Journal of Applied Psychology, 79*(1), 87-97.

Williams, E. (1977). Experimental comparisons of face-to-face and mediated communication: A review. *Psychological Bulletin, 84*, 963-976.

ENDNOTE

[1] Interventions by the experimenter were rare in both the computer conferencing and audio-conferencing modes. Interventions were employed only when the bargainers did not appear to know what step to take next (no more than four instances) or when one of the bargainers raised a procedural question (approximately 20 times).

APPENDIX A

Point Sheets for Low Conflict Treatments

ROBERTS' POINT SHEETS (BUYER/LC) possible terms for the contract

Possible terms for the three-year contract

QUANTITY UNITS=POINTS	WARRANTY PERIOD YEARS=POINTS	$PRICE $ = POINTS	DELIVERY TIME MONTHS=POINTS
5000=39 5500=33 6000=27 6500=20 7000=13 7500=7 8000=0	4-years=16 3-years=10 2-years=5 1-years=0	$200=16 $204=13 $208=11 $212=8 $216=5 $220=3 $224=0	5-months=29 6-months=16 7-months=10 8-months=0

The total points on your alternative contract is 44.

SIMO'S POINT SHEETS (SELLER/LC) possible terms for the contract

Possible terms for the three-year contract

QUANTITY UNITS=POINTS	WARRANTY PERIOD YEARS=POINTS	$PRICE $ = POINTS	DELIVERY TIME MONTHS=POINTS
8000=15 7500=13 7000=10 6500=8 6000=5 5500=3 5000=0	1-year=28 2-years=19 3-years=9 4-years=0	$224=37 $220=31 $216=24 $212=18 $208=12 $204=6 $200=0	8-months=20 7-months=13 6-months=7 5-months=0

APPENDIX B

Point Sheets for High Conflict Treatments

ROBERTS' POINT SHEET(BUYER/HC) possible terms for the contract

Possible terms for the three years contract

QUANTITY UNITS=POINTS	WARRANTY PERIOD YEARS=POINTS	$PRICE $ = POINTS	DELIVERY TIME MONTHS=POINTS
5000=29 5500=25 6000=20 6500=15 7000=10 7500=5 8000=0	4-years=15 3-years=10 2-years=5 1-years=0	$200=39 $204=32 $208=26 $212=19 $216=13 $220=6 $224=0	5-months=17 6-months=11 7-months=6 8-months=0

The total points on your alternative contract is 44.

SIMO'S POINT SHEET(SELLER/HC) possible terms for the contract

Possible terms for the three year contract

QUANTITY UNITS=POINTS	WARRANTY PERIOD YEARS=POINTS	$PRICE $ = POINTS	DELIVERY TIME MONTHS=POINTS
8000=29 7500=24 7000=19 6500=14 6000=10 5500=5 5000=0	1-year=19 2-years=13 3-years=7 4-years=0	$224=35 $220=29 $216=23 $212=17 $208=12 $204=6 $200=0	8-months=17 7-months=11 6-months=6 5-months=0

The total points on your alternative contract is 46.

APPENDIX C

Screen Shot of Negotiation Decision Support Tool (NDST): NDST Software for Simo

	A	B	C	D	E	F	G	H	I	J	K	L	M	N	O	P	Q	R	S	V	W	X	Z	AA	AB
1																									
2	|	************************ SIMO'S(SELLER) DECISION TOOL (LC)														****************************									
3	| Input Your Priorities & Estimated					|			-------------------- SUGGESTED OFFERS ---- |															
4	| Priorities for Your Opponent					|								BEST	SECOND	THIRD		|						
5	| PRIORITY 1 is highest					| QUANTITY								5000	5000	5000		|						
6	| PRIORITY 4 is lowest			Your		| WARRANTY								1	1	1		|						
7	|	YOURS		Opponent's		| PRICE								224	224	220		|						
8	| QUANTITY	4		1		| DELIVERY								5	6	5		|						
9	| WARRANTY	2		4		| YOUR POINTS								65	72	59		|						
10	| PRICE	1		3		| Your Opponent's Points								65	56	69		|						
11	| DELIVERY	3		2		| JOINT POINTS								130	128	128		|						
12	*After you enter your priorities & estimates*					**PUSH**																			
13	*of your opponent's priorities click on push*																								
14	****************************					CONTRACT POINT CALCULATOR								**************************** |										
15	| QUANTITY : PTS		| WARRA. : PTS		| PRICE : PTS		| DELIV.: PTS		TOTAL								|						
16	| --------- : ------ |		--------- : ------ |		------- : -------- |		------ : ------ |: ---------		:::::::::::::: |										
17	| 7000 : 10 |		2 : 19 |		216 : 24 |		7 : 13 |: 66		:::::::::::::: |										
18	| 5000 : 0 |		1 : 28 |		224 : 37 |		5 : 0 |: 65		:::::::::::::: |										
19	| 6000 : 5 |		1 : 28 |		220 : 31 |		6 : 7 |: 71		:::::::::::::: |										
20	| 0 : #### |		0 : #### |		0 : ##### |		0 : #### |: #####		:::::::::::::: |										
21	| 0 : #### |		0 : #### |		0 : ##### |		0 : #### |: #####		:::::::::::::: |										
22	| 0 : #### |		0 : #### |		0 : ##### |		0 : #### |: #####		:::::::::::::: |										

This screen shot shows the NDST for Simo (the seller) after it has been used in a negotiation. Window #1, the DECISION TOOL, is the top half of the screen (down to the CONTRACT POINT CALCULATOR heading). The negotiator playing the role of Simo enters his/her priorities under the YOURS column (originally containing four zeros); these priorities would be known from the confidential information sheet distributed to Simo at the beginning of the negotiation. For instance, price might be most important (a "1" has been entered under YOURS next to PRICE), warranty might be second most important (2), delivery third most important (3), and quantity least important (4). In the Your Opponent's column, the negotiator playing the role of Simo enters his/her best estimates of the opponent's priorities, as identified during the statement-of-interests stage of negotiation. Simo will not know these priorities for certain, but he/she should have a reasonably good idea of them after the statement-of-interests. For instance, quantity might be most important for the opponent (a "1" has been entered under Your Opponent's next to QUANTITY), delivery second most important (2), price third most important (3), and warranty least important (4). Then the negotiator presses the PUSH button, and the NDST computes the three contract alternatives that provide the highest joint outcome (130 points, 128 points, and 128 points in our example) and places them in the columns on the right-hand side of Window #1. Please note that if the priorities for both parties are accurate, these three contract alternatives are the best available from the standpoint of maximizing joint outcome.

Window #2, the CONTRACT POINT CALCULATOR, occupies the bottom half of the screen. This is a very simple tool designed to make the calculation of Simo's contract points from any alternative contract very easy. The negotiator replaces the zeros in any line (we will start at the first line, as is usual) with the values of a possible contract — for example, 7000 for quantity, two years for warranty, 216 dollars for price, and seven months for delivery. The spreadsheet translates these values to points (see Appendices A and B) and then provides the total number of points to Simo in the right-most column — in this case, 66 points in the low conflict situation. The second and third lines show alternative contracts worth 65 and 71 contract points, respectively.

This work was previously published in the Journal of Organizational and End User Computing, Vol. 17, Issue 3, edited by M. Mahmood, pp. 1-26, copyright 2005 by IGI Publishing (an imprint of IGI Global).

Chapter 16
The Role of Culture in Knowledge Management:
A Case Study of Two Global Firms

Dorothy Leidner
Baylor University, USA

Maryam Alavi
Emory Univeristy, USA

Timothy Kayworth
Baylor University, USA

ABSTRACT

Knowledge management approaches have been broadly considered to entail either a focus on organizing communities or a focus on the process of knowledge creation, sharing, and distribution. While these two approaches are not mutually exclusive and organizations may adopt aspects of both, the two approaches entail different challenges. Some organizational cultures might be more receptive to the community approach whereas others are more receptive to the process approach. Although culture has been widely cited as a challenge in knowledge management initiatives and many studies have considered the implications of organizational culture on knowledge sharing, few empirical studies address the influence of culture on the approach taken to knowledge management. Using a case-study approach to compare and contrast the cultures and knowledge management approaches of two organizations, the study suggests the ways in which organizational culture influences knowledge management initiatives as well as the evolution of knowledge management in organizations. Whereas in one organization the KM effort became little more than an information repository, in the second organization, the KM effort evolved into a highly collaborative system fostering the formation of electronic communities.

INTRODUCTION

Knowledge management (KM) efforts are often seen to encounter difficulties from corporate culture and, as a result, have limited impact (DeLong & Fahey, 2000; O'Dell & Grayson, 1998). An Ernst and Young study identified culture as the biggest impediment to knowledge transfer, citing the inability to change people's behaviors as the biggest hindrance to managing knowledge (Watson, 1998). In another study of 453 firms, over half indicated that organizational culture was a major barrier to success in their knowledge management initiatives (Ruggles, 1998). The importance of culture is also evident from consulting firms such as KPMG, who report that a major aspect of knowledge management initiatives involves working to shape organizational cultures that hinder their knowledge management programs (KPMG Management Consulting, 1998). These findings and others (Hasan & Gould, 2001; Schultze & Boland, 2000) help demonstrate the profound impact that culture may have on knowledge management practice and the crucial role of senior management in fostering cultures conducive to these practices (Brown & Duguid, 2000; Davenport, DeLong, & Beers, 1998; DeLong & Fahey, 2000; KPMG Management Consulting; Gupta & Govindarajan, 2000; Hargadon, 1998; von Krogh, 1998).

While studies have shown that culture influences knowledge management and, in particular, knowledge sharing (DeLong &Fahey, 2000; Jarvenpaa & Staples, 2001), there is little research on the broader aspects of the nature and means through which organizational culture influences the overall approach taken to knowledge management in a firm. The purpose of this research is to examine how organizational culture influences knowledge management initiatives. We use a case-study methodology to help ascertain the relationship of the organizational culture to the knowledge management approaches within two companies. The following section discusses knowledge management approaches and organiza-

tional culture. The third presents the methodology. The fourth section presents the two cases, and the fifth discusses the case findings, the implications, and the conclusion.

LITERATURE REVIEW

Knowledge Management

Knowledge can be defined as a form of high-value information (either explicit or tacit) combined with experience, context, interpretation, and reflection that is ready to be applied to decisions and actions (Davenport et al., 1998). While all firms may have a given pool of knowledge resources distributed throughout their respective organization, they may be unaware of the existence of these resources as well as how to effectively leverage them for competitive advantage. Therefore, firms must engage in activities that seek to build, sustain, and leverage these intellectual resources. These types of activities, generally characterized as knowledge management, can be defined as the conscious practice or process of systematically identifying, capturing, and leveraging knowledge resources to help firms compete more effectively (Hansen, Nohria, & Tierney, 1999; O'Dell & Grayson, 1998).

Approaches and strategies for managing knowledge have been conceptualized in various ways. One early conceptualization of KM approaches distinguished between the process and practice approaches (Hansen et al., 1999). The process approach attempts to codify organizational knowledge through formalized controls, processes, and technologies (Hansen et al.). Organizations adopting the process approach may implement explicit policies governing how knowledge is to be collected, stored, and disseminated throughout the organization. The process approach frequently involves the use of information technologies, such as intranets, data warehousing, knowledge repositories, decision support tools, and groupware (Ruggles, 1998), to enhance the quality and speed of knowledge creation and distribution in the organizations. The main criticisms of this process approach are that it fails to capture much of the tacit knowledge embedded in firms and that it forces individuals into fixed patterns of thinking (Brown & Duguid, 2000; DeLong & Fahey, 2000; Hargadon, 1998; von Krogh, 2000).

In contrast, the practice approach to knowledge management assumes that a great deal of organizational knowledge is tacit in nature and that formal controls, processes, and technologies are not suitable for transmitting this type of understanding. Rather than building formal systems to manage knowledge, the focus of this approach is to build the social environments or communities of practice necessary to facilitate the sharing of tacit understanding (Brown & Duguid, 2000; DeLong & Fahey, 2000; Gupta & Govindarajan, 2000; Hansen et al, 1999; Wenger & Snyder, 2000). These communities are informal social groups that meet regularly to share ideas, insights, and best practices.

More recent work on approaches to KM has suggested three KM strategies: knowledge hierarchies, knowledge markets, and knowledge

communities (Dennis & Vessey, 2004). These three strategies reflect differing approaches to handling the three primary knowledge processes: knowledge creation, knowledge development, and knowledge reuse (Dennis & Vessey). Knowledge hierarchies are a strategy in which knowledge is treated as a formal, organizational resource in which one person's knowledge is substituted for another. As such, this strategy suggests knowledge repositories (or expert systems or templates) that are directed toward a specific subset of users rather than to the organization as a whole (Dennis & Vessey). The structural requirements for a knowledge hierarchy are significant: A staff must be available to isolate appropriate knowledge, prepare it for consumption by others, and identify the others who might benefit from such knowledge. Knowledge markets represent another extreme in which organizational efforts are focused more on capturing and storing knowledge than in systematically creating and developing it for consumption by specific others (Dennis & Vessey). Use of a knowledge market is unlikely to be required, and depending upon the enthusiasm of potential contributors, may be overpopulated, or underpopulated, with knowledge. The knowledge market is a laissez-faire approach in which

Table 1. The process vs. practice approaches to knowledge management

	Process Approach	**Practice Approach**
Type of Knowledge Supported	Explicit knowledge codified in rules, tools, and processes	Mostly tacit knowledge unarticulated and not easily captured or codified
Means of Transmission	Formal controls, procedures, and standard operating procedures with heavy emphasis on information technologies to support knowledge creation, codification, and transfer	Informal social groups that engage in storytelling and improvisation
Benefits	Provides structure to harness generated ideas and knowledge Achieves scale in knowledge reuse	Provides an environment to generate and transfer high-value tacit knowledge Provides spark for fresh ideas and responsiveness to changing environment
Disadvantages	Fails to tap into tacit knowledge; may limit innovation and forces participants into fixed patterns of thinking	Can result in inefficiency; abundance of ideas with no structure to implement them
Role of Information Technology	Heavy investment in IT to connect people with reusable codified knowledge	Moderate investment in IT to facilitate conversations and transfer of tacit knowledge

the supply and demand of knowledge are left to reach some equilibrium with little pressure from managers. The knowledge-community strategy lies somewhere in between the focused, specific knowledge-hierarchy approach and the unstructured, unfocused knowledge-market approach. Knowledge communities organize knowledge around communities in which norms of participation, contribution, and reuse are established by each community. An organization might have several such communities. Less controls exist in the development of the knowledge, and hence the quality is lower than in a hierarchy, but more flexibility exists in reuse, with attention focused on augmenting users' knowledge rather than replacing it (Dennis & Vessey). This latter strategy recognizes the time dependence of knowledge and that complete substitution of knowledge across time and contexts might be unwise, even while learning from the previous knowledge and context might be quite valuable.

Organizational Culture

Schein (1985) defines organizational culture as a set of implicit assumptions held by members of a group that determines how the group behaves and responds to its environment. At its deepest level, culture consists of core values and beliefs that are embedded tacit preferences about what the organization should strive to attain and how it should do it (DeLong & Fahey, 2000). These tacit values and beliefs determine the more observable organizational norms and practices that consist of rules, expectations, rituals and routines, stories and myths, symbols, power structures, organizational structures, and control systems (Bloor & Dawson, 1994; Johnson, 1992). In turn, these norms and practices drive subsequent behaviors through providing the social context through which people communicate and act (DeLong & Fahey). Putting this into the context of knowledge management, organizational culture determines the social context (consisting of norms and practices) that determines "who is expected to control what knowledge, as well as who must share it, and who can hoard it" (Delong & Fahey, p. 118). Figure 1 illustrates this conceptual linkage between culture and knowledge management behavior.

As Figure 1 depicts, the social context (consisting of norms and practices) is the medium for transmission of underlying values and beliefs into specific knowledge management behaviors. While Figure 1 is useful to explain the conceptual linkage between culture and knowledge management behavior, further explanation is needed to inform

Figure 1. The impact of organizational culture on knowledge management behaviors

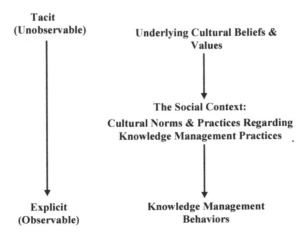

our understanding of the types of cultures that exist within organizations.

A number of theories have attempted to define culture at the organizational level. Wallach (1983) conceptualizes organizational culture as a composite of three distinctive cultural types: bureaucratic, innovative, and supportive. In bureaucratic cultures, there are clear lines of authority and work is highly regulated and systematized. Innovative cultures are characterized as being creative, risk-taking environments where burnout, stress, and pressure are commonplace. In contrast, supportive cultures are those that provide a friendly, warm environment and where workers tend to be fair, open, and honest. From Wallach's standpoint, any given firm will have all three types of culture, each to varying levels of degree. Wallach's cultural dimensions were developed based upon a synthesis of other major organizational culture indices. Wallach's cultural dimensions were applied by Kanungo, Sadavarti, and Srinivas (2001) to study the relationship between IT strategy and organizational culture. Part of the attractiveness of Wallach's dimensions, in comparison with other commonly used cultural indices, such as the organizational culture profile scale (O'Reilly, Chatman, & Caldwell, 1991), the competing values framework (Quinn & Rohrbaugh, 1983), or the organizational value congruence scale (Enz, 1986), is that it is highly intuitive. Managers can readily identify with the descriptions of the three general culture types. Consistent with Kanungo et al., we will employ Wallach's approach to describe organizational cultures.

Organizational Culture and KM

While not extensive, there is an early stream of work developing in the area of culture and KM. One focus has been on the effect of culture on knowledge-sharing practices (Barrett, Capplemann, Shoib, & Walsham, 2004; Davenport et al., 1998; DeTiene & Jackson, 2001; Janz & Prasarnphanich, 2003; Knapp & Yu, 1999; Levinthal

& March, 1993; Miles, Snow, Matthews, Miles, & Coleman, 1997). In general, the studies show an important connection between the openness and collectiveness of a culture and the extent of sharing. For example, Delong and Fahey (2000) identified specific value orientations believed to facilitate or hinder knowledge sharing. They found that value orientations such as trust and collaboration led to greater willingness among firm members to share insights and expertise with each other. In contrast, value systems that emphasized individual power and competition among firm members led to knowledge-hoarding behaviors. Consequently, they argue that firms should seek to reinforce and mold those cultural values most consistent with knowledge-sharing behaviors. In another study, Jarvenpaa and Staples (2001) draws from Goffee and Jones' (1996) dimensions of culture to define the relationship between organizational culture and perception of organizational ownership of information and knowledge and the resulting relationship of this construct with knowledge-sharing practices. Their results suggest that organizations with values emphasizing the pursuit of shared objectives (solidarity) will tend to have a higher perception of organizational ownership of information and knowledge produced by its individual members. As a result, this perception should presumably lead to greater levels of organizational knowledge sharing.

Another focus of KM-culture research has been on the concept of knowledge creation. This area is less concerned with whether, and how, knowledge is shared as it is with how new knowledge emerges, particularly in groups. For example, Lee and Choi (2003) found that the culture of the extended Linux community was important in regulating the norm of open sharing, in addition to providing a quality-control mechanism. They discovered that culture acted as a social control mechanism to manage community members and to sanction those who deviated from norms. The freedom to express criticism was found to be a significant underpinning of the development process that enabled knowledge to expand. Likewise, Styhre, Roth, and Ingelgard's (2002) study of a major pharmaceutical company found that values emphasizing caring relationships facilitated a greater level of knowledge creation within the organization.

In a broader attempt to isolate specific values that affect knowledge creation, Lee and Choi (2003) examined the organizational values of collaboration, trust, and learning. They found support for their hypothesis of a positive relationship of organizational culture (defined by collaboration, trust, and learning) and knowledge-creation processes and conclude that shaping an organization's cultural factors are key to a firm's ability to manage knowledge effectively.

A third area of KM-culture research has been that of the effect of culture on the effectiveness of KM. Organizations with more open and supportive value orientations have been found to have more constructive knowledge behaviors such as firm members sharing insights with others (Gold, Malhotra, & Segars, 2001). Another study reveals that constructive-type values (achievement, self-actualization, encouragement, and affiliation) have a positive impact on certain organizational factors (role clarity, communication quality, organizational fit, creativity, and job satisfaction) believed to promote KM effectiveness (Baltahazard & Cooke, 2003).

Drawing from the literature review, some key questions emerge. We know that culture influences KM approaches, behaviors, and effectiveness, but little is known about how this influence occurs and how lasting its effect is. We are thus interested in understanding the process through which culture affects organizations' knowledge management strategy as well as the process through which culture influences the primary KM activities of knowledge creation, sharing, and use. To address these questions, we employ a case study of two organizations.

METHODOLOGY

A case-study method involving multiple (two) cases was used. The approach of the study is depicted in Figure 2. The figure, based on the work of Yin (1994), displays the replication approach to multiple-case studies. As illustrated in Figure 2, the initial step in the study involved the development of a theoretical framework on the relationship between organizational culture and organizational KM strategies. This step was then followed by the selection of the two specific cases (the data collection sites) and the design of the data collection protocol. Following the case selection and data collection steps, the individual case reports were developed. A cross-case analysis of the findings was then undertaken. This analysis

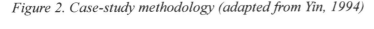

Figure 2. Case-study methodology (adapted from Yin, 1994)

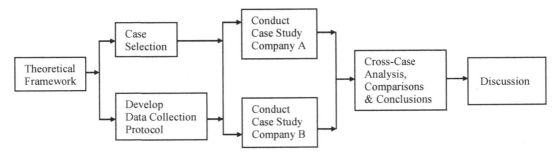

provided the basis for the theoretical and normative discussions and implications presented in the final section of the chapter.

The two case studies involve two very large and global corporations: Company A and Company B. Company A is a global consumer goods company with 369,000 employees worldwide. The company is headquartered in the United States and operates in four other regions: Europe, Middle East and Africa, Central and South America, and Asia. The company revenues consistently exceed $20 billion. In Company A, large-scale knowledge management projects were initiated at the North American region in 1996. Company B is a high-tech global company with multiple product lines and services. Similar to Company A, Company B is headquartered in the United States and operates globally in other regions of the world. With approximately 316,000 employees, its revenues exceed $80 billion. Large-scale knowledge management projects were initiated in Company B in 1995.

These two particular companies were selected for the purpose of this study for the following reasons. First, significant opportunities and challenges are associated with knowledge management activities in large and geographically dispersed companies. Thus, the identification of factors such as organizational culture that may influence KM outcomes in this type of organizations can potentially lead to high payoffs. Second, considering the high levels of organizational resources required for the implementation of large-scale knowledge management initiatives, these initiatives are most likely encountered in very large firms. Thus, the phenomenon of interest to these researchers could be best investigated in the context of very large firms with an established track record in KM projects. Lastly, past contacts that one of the researchers had with these two firms facilitated their recruitment as case-study sites.

Data Collection

Data for this study were collected through semistructured interviews with a small group of managers and professional employees at the two company locations in the United States. Identical approaches to data collection were used at Company A and Company B.[1] Six individuals at each of the two companies were interviewed. In each of the two companies, three of the interviewees were the current or the potential users of the KM systems. The remaining three interviewees in each company were the KM system sponsors or supporters. The interviews took between 45 to 85 minutes and were conducted between October 2001 and January 2002. All the interviews were tape-recorded and then transcribed for data analysis. The interviews all followed the same protocol. The informants were first asked to characterize their organization's culture in their own words. The three cultures described by Wallach (1983) were then portrayed and the informants were requested to identify which one best described their organization. The interviewees were next asked to describe and characterize the KM practices in their company. A set of specific questions guided the discussions of these practices. For example, each informant was asked to describe the specific KM activities that he or she engaged in and to discuss the effects of these activities on the self and/or on peers. Each informant was also asked to describe any resistance and impediments to KM that he or she might have noticed in the organization. The same interviewer, using identical data collection protocols, conducted all the interviews in Company A and Company B. The interviewer carefully read the transcripts to ensure accuracy.

Data Analysis

An author not involved in the interviews, and hence having no predisposed interpretation of the transcripts, conducted the data analysis. Based upon the transcribed interviews, 12 profiles were written, each one based upon the perspective of a single informant. These profiles described the informants' perspective of culture and their perspective of KM. The profiles of informants for Company A were compared and contrasted with each other, as were those of Company B. Cases for each company, reported in the next section, were then written based upon the within-case analysis. The cases for each company were then interpreted from the perspective of how the culture appeared to be influencing the organizational KM initiative. This is also reported in the next section. After the two cases and their within-case analysis were complete, a cross-case comparison and contrast was undertaken, leading to the formulation of the discussion section.

CASE DESCRIPTIONS AND ANALYSES

Knowledge Management at Company A

Knowledge management at Company A began as a top-down idea, courted by senior management "as a way of helping the company become more leading edge," according to one informant. A small group of eight or nine individuals at the headquarters was charged with driving knowledge management and facilitating knowledge sharing. As a result of larger issues surfacing, most notably the economic downturn that rocked U.S.-based businesses in early 2000, the top-level initiative "fell into the background" and the small dedicated group was disbanded. Thus, at the organizational level, KM was an idea that received neither funding nor action. However, at the business-unit level, successful KM initiatives have been built around intranet or around Lotus Notes team rooms.

Intranet-Based KM Projects

One initiative in the marketing area of the corporate headquarters is called MIC (Marketing Information Center). MIC serves the global marketing community of several thousand individuals around the world. It is an intranet-based library containing links to agencies, compensations, human resource (HR) information, and contracts, among other things. MIC is opportunity oriented rather than problem oriented. The members did not use the community to post problem inquiries and await responses, but rather to look for ideas performed in other parts of the company and think about adopting the ideas for their local groups.

MIC is intended to be a catalyst for collaboration and to "propel a universal worldwide marketing community." Because the chief marketing officer no longer allowed the budgeting of glossy manuals or brochures, MIC was widely accepted as the primary means of obtaining such static information. In fact, as attempts were made to include best practices in MIC, the initiative encountered resistance. Explains one informant, "we could never nudge the culture enough to have people understand and be motivated to enter their information." Another informant felt that there were challenges in overcoming "people's fear of being judged for their ideas and their indifference to yet another information site."

CM Connection (CMC) is another KM initiative within the North America marketing unit. This is a Web-based marketing repository used to disseminate information such that wholesalers that are responsible for store-level execution can have access to the most recent information on how to merchandise the latest promotions. As with MIC, the major impact of CMC has been the reduction of the number of printed catalogs, in this case by 80%. Among the challenges experienced with CMC has been convincing content providers to own the information in the sense of both providing it and keeping it up to date. Another issue has been that CMC is seen by some as distracting them from their relationships with clients. Even while CMC may reduce the amount of time spent traveling, this is not necessarily welcome in "a sales and marketing oriented relationship company because you are taking away relationship points."

The human resources unit with the corporate functions unit also has an intranet-based KM initiative, referred to as My Career. My Career is designed for managers and employees to help provide information about what tools, classes, and coaching is available for development. One of the goals of My Career has been to merge all of the training information into one place.

Many such intranet-based KM projects have been developed throughout Company A, so many that a portal project was initiated to alleviate the problem of "too much information in too many places, different IDs and passwords for each database, having to remember what is in the database to even go to get the information." However, despite some initial receptiveness to the idea from the head of the new-business ventures unit, IT budgets were frozen and the project never got under way.

The common thread running through the intranet-based KM projects at Company A is that they all are geared toward housing static information with the most major of impacts being the reduction in printed catalogs. Among the greatest resistances, according to informants, is that these KM projects appear to try to standardize work practices in a company comprised of "creative assertive people who want to do it their way and make their own individual mark."

Lotus-Notes-Based KM

Lotus Notes forms the basis of other KM initiatives within Company A. What distinguishes the Lotus-Notes-based KM projects from the intranet-based KM projects is the added focus on facilitating teamwork. The Lotus-Notes-based initiatives developed independently from the intranet-based

initiatives. The North American marketing group developed a Lotus-Notes-based community of interest. The system contains examples of briefs, shared research, shared examples of different sites, and information on internal research. This micro KM initiative has 50 to 60 regular users. An important feature of the system is that whenever new information is added, community members receive an e-mail. In this way, members visit the community when new information that is relevant to them has been posted. This KM project has served as a means of sharing best practices. For example, a marketing manager from the United Kingdom posted information concerning a successful auction initiative that was then emulated by five other countries. On an individual level, the KM project has helped to increase the frequency of communication among members of the community. Similarly, human resources developed HR Source, a Lotus-Notes-based general bulletin board where meeting notes, follow-up action items, strategy documents, and work plans are placed. It is shared by the HR community on a global basis.

Lotus Notes is also the platform used to develop team rooms. The individual responsible for managing team rooms for North America has what he calls the "6-month rule": If a team room is not getting regular utilization over 6 months, it is deleted so that they can save money on the server expense. He says that he deletes about 70 to 80% of team rooms. He thinks the lack of reward is the biggest barrier toward KM system usage: "People who don't have technology in their title don't take it upon themselves and are not generally rewarded for exploiting technology." Also, content management is a barrier: "This is the responsibility of the end user but it is perceived as the responsibility of the technology group." However, a marketing manager had another opinion, attributing lack of use of the team rooms to self-preservation:

"Even if someone took the time to put something out there, even if I knew it was there, went and got it, had the time to review it, and understand it, I am going to create this other thing by myself. I might look at that as input, but then it is the new XYZ program and I created it."

Analysis of Company A's Knowledge Management: The Impact of Culture on KM Behaviors and Outcomes

The Perceptions of Culture

While each individual interviewed gave their own perception of the culture at Company A and the perceptions naturally contain some variance, there is a marked theme running through the individuals' views. Informants describe Company A as "risk averse" and bureaucratic. They speak of an environment where people "don't want to be noticed," where direction is "unclear," and where "individual survival" trumps teamwork. Moreover, informants state that people "work in silos," "feel isolated," and "are afraid of being criticized for their ideas." The "slow, bureaucratic, hierarchical" culture at Company A has resulted in "silos of information." As a consequence, managers indicate that even though they have "great consumer and customer information," they "end up reinventing the wheel 1,000 times." However, our informants also maintained that although they

characterize the culture as bureaucratic, they also sense that Company A is "striving" to become more innovative and supportive.

The Possible Impacts of Culture on KM

The statements and observations of our informants point to two largely shared perspectives: (a) that the culture emphasizes the individual and (b) that the culture is in a state of transition. In understanding the impacts of KM, one can see the influence of individuality within Company A. Table 2 lists the characteristics of the culture, KM initiatives, and KM behaviors as expressed by the informants.

At work within Company A seems to be a tension between a culture that demands individuality and the communal aspects of KM. The informants talk about a culture that is one of "individual survival" where individuals "fear being judged for their ideas," where there is individual isolation, and where individuals try to go unnoticed. The overall feeling is that of individuals trying to avoid being noticed. Such a culture does little to foster the sense of community that may be necessary to enable KM to move beyond static repositories of information into the kind of dynamic system envisioned by developers where ideas flow freely

Table 2. Characteristics of culture, KM initiatives, and KM behaviors

Culture Characteristics	KM Characteristics	KM Behaviors
Dominant culture is bureaucratic	Intranet-based static repositories of information	Individuals access information on as-needed basis
Emphasis on individual:		Individuals reluctant to contribute information
*individuals are risk averse	Failed top-down effort	
*individuals fear being criticized for ideas		Individuals reluctant to own and maintain content
*individuals are uneasy and prefer to go unnoticed	Bottom-up initiatives largely targeted creation of repositories	Individuals uncomfortable using ideas from the systems since they do not own the ideas
*relationships externally, particularly within the marketing unit, are perceived as critical to their success	Some use of Lotus Notes to create team rooms	Individuals use a repository when rules prohibit printing brochures
	Team rooms have high failure rate	Individuals reluctant to use tools that would result in a loss of touch points with customers

and where KM provides a catalyst for collaborative engagement. Not only are individuals reluctant to share their information for fear of being criticized for their ideas, they are also reluctant to use information posted in a KM project for lack of credit for the idea. Such behaviors can spring from a culture that emphasizes individual ideas and contribution.

The individual aspects of the culture go well beyond individuals behaving a certain way because of a reward system, but reflects an underpinning notion that to succeed in a marketing-oriented organization, one must be creative and that creativity is, perforce, of an individual nature so that to survive as an individual, one must capture ideas and only share them if they are going to be favorably judged. One must not look to others for learning or for problem solving, but might look to reuse creative ideas in some circumstances (like the auction site example from the United Kingdom) where one may tailor the idea to one's environment. It is telling that the informants speak of using outsiders (e.g., consultants) to assist with problem solving and learning instead of attempting to use any of the existing KM initiatives to post queries, and this in spite of the fact that it is recognized that the company "reinvents the wheel 1,000 times."

Another tension within Company A seems to stem from the expectations of what should occur in a bureaucratic culture and what was occurring. The top-down approach to KM, an approach that would be consistent with a bureaucratic organization, had failed at Company A. Yet, despite the failure of the top-down approach to KM and the seeming success of several bottom-up approaches such as MIC and the marketing team room for the community of 50, one informant still proffered the need for top-management leadership to be the key to success with KM. He considered the bottom-up approaches as "band-aid approaches." In his opinion, power within Company A comes "from knowledge hoarding not knowledge sharing." In order for KM to be assimilated in this

environment, "behavior really has to come from the top. Leadership needs to walk the walk." In a bureaucratic culture, individuals become accustomed to clear guidance from senior management. The absence of clearly stated support from senior management may be sufficient to deter many from experimenting with the KM tools available to help them.

Summary: Company A has many KM initiatives that have largely been developed as bottom-up initiatives. The KM tools seem well designed and housed with valuable information. The informants are able to use the tools to facilitate the retrieval of information they need in the performance of their jobs. However, the tools have not, as yet, progressed to the level of fostering collaboration. While there are some successful communities from the standpoint of providing a place to share meeting notes and plans, the majority of team rooms remains unused and, if used, become as much a library of information as a communication tool. In some ways, the culture of Company A appears to foster the types of KM behaviors observed in that the individual is seen as the primary source of innovation and ideas as opposed to the community being the ultimate source of success. Thus, individuals will use the systems as needed, but are mostly occupied with their individual roles and work and do not attribute value to the collaborative features of technology.

The Case of Company B

Company B is organized into seven major units. Our interviews were concentrated within the innovations services group of the consulting wing (referred to as worldwide services group, or WSG).

Knowledge management at Company B began in 1996 with the view that KM was about "codifying and sharing information," leading to the creation of "huge repositories of procedures and process approaches." It was assumed that people would go to a central site, called the intellectual capital management system (ICM), pull information, and "would all be more knowledgeable." ICM is under the protection of Company B. There is a process one must undertake to have information submitted and approved. The process is complicated by legalities and formalities. As a result, ICM is not used as widely as it could be. What was discovered from the initial foray into knowledge management was that the information was not being refreshed and that the approach was not complimenting the way people really learned, which was through communities. Consequently, the KM initiative began to shift toward providing tools to communities that would help foster collaboration "both within teams and within locations and across the globe." Among the tools are team rooms and communities.

Team Rooms

Lotus-Notes-based team rooms are widely used at Company B to coordinate virtual teams and to share important documents. Access to the databases of a team is limited to the members because of the confidential nature of a lot of the issues. The project manager or someone delegated by the project manager takes the responsibility of sanitizing the material and posting the most relevant parts to a community system such as OC-zone (to be discussed below) and/or to ICM after the team's project has been completed.

The team rooms are valuable tools to help members keep track of occurrences as well as to help newly assigned members get quickly up to speed. Because of the itinerant nature of the Company B consultant's job, it is invaluable to have the documents he or she needs stored in an easily accessible manner that does not require sending and receiving files over a network. Team-room databases are also used for managing the consulting practices. It is important in helping new people with administrative tasks: how to order a piece of computer equipment, or how to

order business cards, for example. The team rooms keep track of such metrics as utilization so that members of the team know "who's on the bench and who's not." One informant gave the example of a recent project she was put on at the last minute involving a selling project to a government department in another country. She was able to access all the documentation from the team room and was able to become a productive member of a new team very quickly: "I can go in and start getting information about a particular topic and work with colleagues almost immediately. It allows me to work more easily with colleagues across disciplines."

Although the team rooms are invaluable in organizing and coordinating project teams, there are also some potential drawbacks. Some view the team rooms as engendering "a false sense of intimacy and connectedness." This sense of intimacy can be productive for the team as long as things are going well. However, "if things go south," says an informant, "you don't have the history or skill set to really deal with difficult situations." As a result, instead of "dealing with the conflict," the group is more likely to "just take someone off the team" and replace the person with another. In this sense, problems are not solved so much as they are avoided, and team members take on an expendable quality.

Communities

Communities serve members based not upon project or organizational position, but based upon interest. By 2000, a group referred to as the organizational change (OC) group had established a successful community of 1,500 members cutting across all lines of business and was beginning to act as consultants to the other groups trying to set up communities. The OC community has gone so far as to quantify the business return of such a community in terms of cycle-time reductions and sophistication of responses to clients. The

OC community is comprised of tools, events, and organization.

1. **Tools:** The technology tools at the disposal of the OC community are databases of information submitted by team rooms, including such things as white papers, projects, and deliverables, as well as client information. The databases also contain pictures of community members with personal information about the members.

2. **Events:** An important aspect of the OC community is the events that are organized for community members. These include monthly conference-call meetings, which generally get attendance of between 40 and 90 members, and replay meetings, which draw another 40 t0 70 members. In the past, the community had sponsored a face-to-face conference for members. Members often meet others for the first time, yet they already feel they know each other.

3. **Organization:** The organization of the community is managed by two community leaders. When someone requests information or has a query to post to members, he or she sends a message to one of the community leaders. The leader first tries to forward the message directly to a subject-matter expert (SME). If the leader does not know offhand of an appropriate SME, he or she will post the question to the entire group. In this event, the group members respond to the leader rather than to the community in order to avoid an inundation of messages. The leader normally receives responses within an hour. The leader then forwards the responses to the individual with the query. He or she later sends an e-mail to the person who made the inquiry, asking how the response was, and how many days-time it saved. The leader says that as many as 28 responses will be made to a particular inquiry. The leader has manually loaded a portion of what they've

developed in the past 7 months: There are 114 pieces of intellectual capital that was loaded, and it is just a portion of what was received.

The community has a structure that consists of a senior global board of 30 members representative of different parts of the business. There is a subject-matter council that constantly scans the intellectual capital as well as an expert council and the health-check team.

The health-check team examines such things as how well members communicate with each other. It conducted an organizational network analysis to help better understand the communication networks. The team has a series of questions to help assess how the group is doing in terms of high-performance teaming. It uses a survey that measures perceptions from the community members about what they see is happening and does a gap analysis on what is actually happening. Finally, the team does a self-assessment of where they are compared with the community maturity model developed by the OC community leaders. There is a community mission, vision, and goals, and it is working on capturing data to support the metrics to demonstrate value to the company and community members.

The goal is to attain Level 5 maturity, when a group is considered "an adaptive organization." There are 13 areas of focus that the community leaders look at in building a sustained community. While communities are felt to be organic, there is also a community developers' kit with an assessment tool to determine at what level of maturity a community is and what steps need to be taken to move the community forward. One community leader says that the purpose of the development kit "is not to confine, but to provide a road map in which to navigate and build." For this leader, the essence of community is "continuous learning." Of the initial KM efforts focused on information repositories, the leader says, "I could see the technology coming that was going to enslave people, like an intellectual sweat shop." By contrast, the primary tools for a community are "passion and environment."

Impact of OC

Among the major impacts of the OC-zone is that having a community helps people "not feel isolated. People feel they are affiliated, that they are part of the company." Thirty percent of Company B employees do not have offices and work instead from home or from client sites. Such a work environment can easily be associated with isolation. However, the community is claimed by some to provide a clarity of purpose: "I see it as a conduit for both developing thought leadership and enabling thought leadership to get into the hearts and minds of the workers so that they all have a common vision, goals, and objectives."

Community members view the purpose of the community as a knowledge-sharing forum and as a means to creating a sense of belonging. One member went so far as to suggest that she would "not be at Company B any longer if it wasn't for this community." The reason is that most of her connections at Company B have been made through the community. Also, being in the community helps her get assigned to projects. For example, the leader of a new project will call someone in the community and say that they are looking for a person with a certain profile. She finds that she gets asked to work on projects this way.

Other members refer to the community as a "supportive family" and state that within the community is someone who has already encountered any issue they will encounter on a project, so that the community keeps them from reinventing the wheel. The norms of operation exist to help OC-zone be as effective as possible. No one is under obligation to contribute, but individuals contribute in order to help other members. One member credits the success of the community to the two leaders, whom she feels "in their hearts, care about the members of the community." She

feels that the community is more than a community of people who like the topic of organizational change, but it is a community of people who support one another.

The primary resistance to the OC community has been the practice managers. Most of the community members report to practice managers. The practice managers are used to thinking in terms of billable hours. Indeed, the performance evaluation system requires that an individual's goals support those of his or her boss. The community leaders hope that one day, participating in a community will be included as a standard part of this evaluation system.

Analysis of Company B Knowledge Management: The Impact of Culture on KM Behaviors and Outcomes

The Perceptions of Culture

All of the respondents from Company B work within the same business unit. The respondents describe the culture of Company B as a blend of hierarchical and innovative. The hierarchical aspects are evident in that little innovation is undertaken until senior management has officially supported the innovation, but once senior management does give the green light to an idea, "everybody jumps on it."

One aspect of culture that is highlighted by the informants is the importance of collaboration. Informants characterize the "street values" within Company B as "win, team, and execute." The informants recognize a duality of culture that on the one hand gives individuals control over their work and at the same time is highly supportive of the individual. The culture is autonomous in the sense of "not having someone looking over your shoulder and telling you what to do." And while there is certainly competition as everyone has objectives they are trying to meet, things "are always done in a collaborative, helpful spirit."

The other dominant aspect of culture as related by the informants is that of hierarchy. The hierarchy is as much a hierarchy of experience as of structure. Community members, for example, proffered that becoming a subject-matter expert is more about length of service to the company than one's inherent knowledge. Another aspect of the bureaucratic culture is that "there is very much a correct way to do things."

Table 3 lists the characteristics of culture, KM initiatives, and KM behaviors expressed by the Company B informants.

Company B's emphasis on collaboration seems to have enabled the progression of KM from a static information repository system to an active, vital community of interest wherein individuals feel a sense of belonging to the extent that they identify themselves first with the community, and only second, if at all, with the actual formal business unit. One informant claimed to not identify herself at all with the innovation services unit. Of course, one could ponder whether such identity transfer from the business unit to the community serves the best interest of the unit.

At the same time, the bureaucratic and innovative aspects of the culture have also helped.

Having senior management show interest in KM was a catalyst to individual groups undertaking KM initiatives with great enthusiasm. In addition, rather than ad hoc communities that are entirely organic, the community model emerging at Company B is a relatively structured one.

While one can make the argument that Company B's culture influences KM development and use, one can also argue that KM at Company B is itself influencing the culture. OC members claim that without a sense of connection provided by the OC community, the company would be nothing but a "big and scary" company in which individuals "get lost." The community, though, allows and enables a culture of connection. In effect, one informant believes that the OC community attempts to shift a very technical, phone-oriented, work-product-oriented way of communicating with each other into a more personal work-in-process movement toward what Company B refers to as "thought leadership." When asked why members take the time to participate in the community when there is no formal reward for doing so, one informant said simply, "it's just how we do business." Thus, the community has infused the culture of the members.

Table 3. Characteristics of Company B culture, KM initiatives, and KM behaviors

Culture Characteristics	KM Characteristics	KM Behaviors
Hierarchical, yet collaborative and innovative	Company-wide information repository consisting of hundreds of information databases	Team members actively coordinate via the team rooms
Individuals largely responsible for their own careers, yet competition is undertaken in a cooperative manner	Team rooms used by project teams	Community members obtain a sense of belonging to the community
The team is the unit of success, more so than the individual	Communities of practice emerging; these communities include tools, events, and structures	Community members post information from completed team projects to the community out of a sense of commitment, not coercion
Absence of extreme supervision of individuals' work; individuals have a sense of control	OC community used as an example of a successful community and as a consultant to other emerging communities	Community members are more loyal to the company (less likely to depart) because of their belonging to the community
		Assignments to projects made through community references

Yet this does not suggest that an organizational utopia has been, or will be, achieved. While the culture is becoming more connected, there is another angle. One informant believes that when you have widespread access to knowledge management, you can also have a culture where people that know very little about something have access to enough information to be dangerous. People get too comfortable with having access to knowledge and then they feel free to share it. This informant remained unconvinced that the knowledge one acquires through the network is as solid a foundation as the knowledge one has acquired through experience and traditional learning. Moreover, she feels that the notion of dialogue can get redefined in a way that you lose the quality of participation that one might be looking for.

Summary: Company B has many KM databases, collectively referred to as ICM. While these databases serve an important role of housing and organizing information in a huge organization, they do not go so far as to foster collaboration. Instead, team rooms and communities of interest, largely left to the discretion of team members and community members, have proven to be vital tools to achieving collaboration, community, and belonging. And as the culture of Company B has been receptive to individual group setting and pursuing community agendas, the culture is also being subtly altered by the communities as members feel more belonging to the community than to their business units.

DISCUSSION

The two cases offer insights into the role that organizational culture plays in the inception and maturation of knowledge management. This section summarizes the key findings that help us answer the question, how does organizational culture influence KM approaches? We suggest four responses to this question.

1. Organizational culture influences knowledge management through its influence on the values organizational members attribute to individual vs. cooperative behavior.
    The two companies we examined share several similarities: Both are huge multinational organizations widely regarded by organizational members as being predominantly bureaucratic in culture, both organizations had initial KM approaches that were strongly supported by senior management, and both had initial KM approaches focused on the creation of a large centralized repository of organizational knowledge to be shared across the organization. These two large bureaucratic organizations began their KM quests with the process approach. The most striking difference between the organizational cultures of these two companies was the emphasis at Company A on the individual and the emphasis at Company B on the collectivity: the team or the community. This evinces itself even in the interpretation of innovation. While individuals at both companies spoke of the need for innovation in their organizations and of the striving of their organizations to develop an innovative culture, in the case of Company A, innovation was perceived as an individual attribute whereas at Company B, innovation was perceived as a team-level attribute.
    The individualistic view of innovation at Company A seemed to militate against the requisite sharing and cooperation that makes the evolution of KM from the process approach to a community-of-practice approach possible. In both companies, microlevel experimentation of the various possibilities of KM was undertaken within teams or business units. The value placed on individualism vs. cooperation seems to have

played a significant role in the nature and form of the KM approach. The microlevel experimentations by teams or business units were carried out with their own assumptions about the usefulness of repositories of knowledge and the usefulness of communities of practice. We suggest that it is not organizational culture at the organizational level or even the subunit level that has the most significant influence on KM approach, but organizational culture as embodied in the individualistic vs. cooperative tendencies of organizational members. Thus, organizational culture influences KM approaches through its influence on individualism vs. cooperation. From a theoretical view, it seems that Wallach's (1983) cultural dimensions and those of Earley (1994) were both valuable at explaining organizational-level culture. However, Earley's cultural dimensions at the organizational level seem best able to explain why a KM approach tended to become more process or more practice based.

2. Organizational culture influences the evolution of knowledge management initiatives. Our findings suggest that firms do not decide in advance to adopt a process or practice approach to KM, but that this evolves. The most natural starting point is one of process, perhaps because the benefits seem more evident and because it can more closely align with the existing organizational structure. Moreover, the practice approach may not only fail to align with existing structure, but it may engender a virtual structure and identity. It is interesting that at Company B, having a culture dominantly viewed as bureaucratic, once the initial organizational change community was established, the evolution of the community then became a highly structured process of maturation. The community leaders developed a tool kit to help other communities develop, and

developed a maturation model to help them determine how mature a community was and a plan to move the community forward. What some might see as an organic process—that of establishing and developing a community of practice—became in a bureaucratic organization a structured process. Even if the idea for the community emerged from interested potential members, the evolution took on a structured form with tools, kits, assessments, and plans. The cooperative aspect of culture at the individual level made the community possible; the bureaucratic elements of culture at the organizational level enabled the community to mature. Hence, the evolution of the community was highly dependent on the individual willingness of organizational members to sustain and nurture their community. This appeared tied to the importance they placed on cooperation with their community members, most of whom they had never met.

3. Organizational culture influences the migration of knowledge. In the case of Company A, where as mentioned the informants seemed to identify the individual as the ultimate unit of responsibility in the organization, the individuals were also viewed as the owners of knowledge and had the responsibility to share their knowledge. This in fact created a major challenge since the individuals rejected this new responsibility. At Company B, where the team seemed to be the focus of responsibility, knowledge migrated from the team to the community to the organizational-level system and back down to the team. The leader of the team would take responsibility for cleaning the team's data and submitting them to the community and to the central information repository. Thus, knowledge migrated upward from the team to the central repository. Interestingly, the most useful knowledge was claimed to be that at the team and community level. Once the

knowledge had completed its migration to the central repository, it was seen primarily as an item of insurance: for use in case of need. Knowledge sharing and transfer occurred primarily at the team and community level whereas knowledge storage was the function of the central repository.

The migration of knowledge is also influenced by the structural processes put in place to ensure that knowledge finds its way to the appropriate persons. Of key importance seems to be the way the queries are handled. The marketing group at Company A adopted the approach of notifying individuals when new information had been added to the KM system. However, little interference was put in place to either guide people to the appropriate knowledge or encourage people to contribute knowledge. Contrarily, believing that the community should not become a bulletin board of problems and solutions, the leaders of the organizational change community at Company B worked arduously to find the subject-matter experts so that queries would be submitted to the community leader who would serve as an intermediary between the individual with the query and the expert.

It has been widely reported that the use of knowledge directories is a primary application of KM in organizations. Our study suggests that the facilitated access to experts rather than direct access via the location of an individual through a directory or via a problem posted to a forum may lead to a more favorable community atmosphere.

4. Knowledge management can become embedded in the organizational culture. Over time, as KM evolves and begins to reflect the values of the organization, the KM itself can become a part of the organizational culture. At Company B, individuals spoke of their community involvement and their team rooms as simply the "way we work."

In fact, the communities became so much part of the culture that even though they were not part of the organizational structure, they were part of individuals' implicit structure. The sense of belonging that the individuals reported feeling toward their community suggests that the community had become an essential aspect of their value system, and hence, had become part of organizational culture. That the organizational change community members at Company B identified themselves first and foremost with their community, in spite of receiving neither reward nor recognition within their formal reporting unit for participating in the community, indicates the extent to which community participation had become a value and an aspect of the individual culture.

IMPLICATIONS AND CONCLUSION

The findings of our study suggest that a dominantly bureaucratic culture seems to tend toward an initial process-based KM approach. Furthermore, a bureaucratic culture seems to create the expectation among organizational members that senior management needs to provide a vision of purpose for KM before the organizational members should embark on KM activities. As well, the members view senior management support as validating any KM activities that they undertake. Innovative cultures, even if not the dominant culture at the organizational level, seem to enable subgroups to experiment with KM or create micro KM initiatives. In essence, in organizations having dominant bureaucratic cultures with traces of innovativeness, senior management support legitimizes KM, but the innovativeness of the culture enables it to expand far beyond an organization-wide repository. Specific KM behaviors such as the ownership and maintenance of knowledge, knowledge sharing, and knowledge reuse seem largely influenced by the individualistic or co-

Table 4. Summary of organizational culture's influence on KM

Cultural Perspective	Influence of Culture on Knowledge Management
Bureaucratic (Wallach, 1983)	Favors an initial process approach to KM Creates expectation among members that senior-management vision is essential to effective KM
Innovative (Wallach, 1983)	Enables subgroups in organizations to experiment with KM and develop KM useful to their groups
Individualistic (Earley, 1994)	Inhibits sharing, ownership, and reuse of knowledge
Cooperative (Earley, 1994)	Enables the evolution of process-oriented KM to practice-oriented KM Enables the creation of virtual communities

operative nature of the culture. Individualistic cultures inhibit sharing, ownership, and reuse, while cooperative cultures enable the creation of virtual communities. Earley's (1994) work on organizational culture emphasized the individualistic and collectivistic aspects of culture. Organizations encouraging individuals to pursue and maximize individual goals and rewarding performance based on individual achievement would be considered as having an individualistic culture whereas organizations placing priority on collective goals and joint contributions and rewards for organizational accomplishments would be considered collectivist (Chatman & Barsade, 1995; Earley). This dimension of organizational culture emerged as critical in our examination of the influence of culture on KM initiatives. These findings are summarized in Table 4.

This research set out to examine the influence of organizational culture on knowledge management approaches. Using a case study approach, we have gathered the perspectives of individuals in two firms that share some cultural similarities yet differ in other aspects. The findings suggest that organizational culture influences the KM approach initially chosen by an organization, the evolution of the KM approach, and the migration of knowledge. Moreover, the findings suggest that KM can eventually become an integral aspect of

the organizational culture. Much remains to be discovered about how organizational cultures evolve and what role information technology takes in this evolution. This case study is an initial effort into a potentially vast array of research on the issue of the relationship of information technology and organizational culture.

REFERENCES

Alavi, M., Kayworth, T., & Leidner, D. (2005). An empirical examination of the influence of organizational culture on knowledge management practices. *Journal of Managment Information Systems, 22*(3), 191-224.

Baltahazard, P. A., & Cooke, R. A. (2003). *Organizational culture and knowledge management success: Assessing the behavior-performance continuum.* AZ: Arizona State University West.

Barrett, M., Capplemann, S., Shoib, G., & Walsham, G. (2004). Learning in knowledge communities: Managing technology and context. *European Management Journal, 22*(1), 1-11.

Bloor, G., & Dawson, P. (1994). Understanding professional culture in organizational context. *Organization Studies, 15*(2), 275-295.

Brown, S. J., & Duguid, P. (2000). Balancing act: How to capture knowledge without killing it. *Harvard Business Review*, 73-80.

Chatman, J. A., & Barsade, S. G. (1995). Personality, organizational culture, and cooperation: Evidence from a business simulation. *Administrative Science Quarterly, 40*(3), 423-443.

Davenport, T. H., DeLong, D. W., & Beers, M. C. (1998). Successful knowledge management. *Sloan Management Review, 39*(2), 43-57.

DeLong, D. W., & Fahey, L. (2000). Diagnosing cultural barriers to knowledge management. *Academy of Management Executive, 14*(4), 113-127.

Dennis, A., & Vessey, I. (2004). Three knowledge management strategies: Knowledge hierarchies, knowledge markets, and knowledge communities. *MIS Quarterly Executive, 3*(4), 399-412.

DeTiene, K. B., & Jackson, L. A. (2001). Knowledge management: Understanding theory and developing strategy. *Competitiveness Review, 11*(1), 1-11.

Earley. (1994). Self or group? Cultural effects of training on self-efficacy and performance. *Administrative Science Quarterly, 39*, 89-117.

Enz, C. (1986). *Power and shared values in the corporate culture.* Ann Arbor, MI: The University of Michigan Press.

Goffee, R., & Jones, G. (1996). What holds the modern company together? *Harvard Business Review, 74*(6), 133-148.

Gold, A. H., Malhotra, A., & Segars, A. H. (2001). Knowledge management: An organizational capabilities perspective. *Journal of Management Information Systems, 18*(1), 185-214.

Gupta, A. K., & Govindarajan, V. (2000). Knowledge management's social dimension: Lessons from Nucor Steel. *Sloan Management Review, 42*(1), 71-80.

Hansen, M. T., Nohria, N., & Tierney, T. (1999). What's your strategy for managing knowledge? *Harvard Business Review*, 106-115.

Hargadon, A. B. (1998). Firms as knowledge brokers: Lessons in pursuing continuous innovation. *California Management Review, 40*(3), 209-227.

Hasan, H., & Gould, E. (2001). Support for the sense-making activity of managers. *Decision Support Systems, 31*(1), 71-86.

Janz, B. D., & Prasarnphanich, P. (2003). Understanding the antecedents of effective knowledge management: The importance of knowledge-centered culture. *Decision Sciences, 34*(2), 351-384.

Jarvenpaa, S. L., & Staples, S. D. (2001). Exploring perceptions of organizational ownership of information and expertise. *Journal of Management Information Systems, 18*(1), 151-183.

Johnson, G. (1992). Managing strategic change: Strategy, culture and action. *Long Range Planning, 25*(1), 28-36.

Kanungo, S., Sadavarti, S., & Srinivas, Y. (2001). Relating IT strategy and organizational culture: An empirical study of public sector units in India. *Journal of Strategic Information Systems, 10*, 29-57.

Knapp, E., & Yu, D. (1999). How culture helps or hinders the flow of knowledge. *Knowledge Management Review, 2*(1), 16-21.

KPMG Management Consulting. (1998). *Knowledge management: Research report.*

Lee, H., & Choi, B. (2003). Knowledge management enablers, processes, and organizational performance: An integrative view and empirical examination. *Journal of Management Information Systems, 20*(1), 179-228.

Levinthal, D., & March, J. (1993). The myopia of learning. *Strategic Management Journal, 14*(8), 95-112.

Miles, R., Snow, C., Matthews, J., Miles, G., & Coleman, H. (1997). Organizing in the knowledge age: Anticipating the cellular form. *Academy of Management Executive, 11*(4), 7-24.

O'Dell, C., & Grayson, C. J. (1998). If only we know what we know: Identification and transfer of best practices. *California Management Review, 40*(3), 154-174.

O'Reilly, C. A., Chatman, J., & Caldwell, D. F. (1996). Culture as social control: Corporations, cults, and commitment. *Research in Organizational Behavior, 18*, 157-200.

Quinn, R. E., & Rohrbaugh, I. (1983). A spatial model of effectiveness criteria: Towards a competing values approach to organizational analysis. *Management Science, 29*, 363-377.

Ruggles, R. (1998). The state of the notion: Knowledge management in practice. *California Management Review, 40*(3), 80-89.

Schein, E. H. (1985). *Organizational culture and leadership.* San Francisco: Jossey-Bass.

Schultze, U., & Boland, R. (2000). Knowledge management technology and the reproduction of knowledge work practices. *Journal of Strategic Information Systems, 9*(2-3), 193-213.

Styhre, A., Roth, J., & Ingelgard, A. (2002). Care of the other: Knowledge-creation through care in professional teams. *Scandinavian Journal of Management, 18*(4), 503-522.

Von Krogh, G. (1998). Care in knowledge creation. *California Management Review, 40*(3), 133-153.

Wallach, E. J. (1983). Individuals and organizations: The cultural match. *Training and Development Journal.*

Watson, S. (1998, January 26). Getting to "aha!" companies use intranets to turn information and experience into knowledge: And gain a competitive edge. *Computer World.*

Wenger, E. C., & Snyder, W. M. (2000). Communities of practice: The organizational frontier. *Harvard Business Review*, 139-145.

ENDNOTE

[1] After this initial data collection, we returned to Company B a year later and conducted more widespread interviews across different business units. This data collection and analysis is discussed in Alavi, Kayworth, and Leidner (2005).

This work was previously published in E-Collaboration in Modern Organizations: Initiating and Managing Distributed Projects, edited by N. Kock, pp. 8199-219, copyright 2008 by Information Science Reference (an imprint of IGI Global).

Section 3
Advanced Conceptual and Theoretical Issues

Chapter 17
Can Virtual Worlds Support E-Collaboration and E-Commerce?
A Look at Second Life and World of Warcraft

Ned Kock
Texas A&M International University, USA

ABSTRACT

Recent years have seen the growing use of virtual worlds such as Second Life and World of Warcraft for entertainment and business purposes, and a rising interest from researchers in the impact that virtual worlds can have on patterns of e-collaboration behavior and collaborative task outcomes. This chapter looks into whether actual work can be accomplished in virtual worlds, whether virtual worlds can provide the basis for trade (B2C and C2C e-commerce), and whether they can serve as a platform for credible studies of e-collaboration behavior and related outcomes. The conclusion reached at is that virtual worlds hold great potential in each of these three areas, even though there are certainly pitfalls ahead.

INTRODUCTION

Virtual worlds can be defined as environments created by technologies that incorporate virtual representations of various elements found in the real world. Among those elements are virtual human beings with whom one can interact, virtual physical environments that include land and oceans, and virtual objects like chairs and tables. Recent years have seen a growing use of virtual worlds for entertainment and business purposes, and a

corresponding growing interest from researchers in the impact of virtual worlds on e-collaboration behavior and outcomes (Bessière et al., 2007; Bonsu & Darmody, 2008; Kock, 2008; Mennecke et al., 2008; Pinckard, 2006; Traum, 2007).

Some virtual worlds, like Second Life attempt to replicate elements of the real world with practical applications in mind (Bonsu & Darmody, 2008; Mennecke et al., 2008). Others, like World of Warcraft, are designed with the goal of making people forget about the real world and become immersed in multiplayer games (Bessière et al., 2007; Pinckard, 2006). Users of virtual worlds, sometimes referred

DOI: 10.4018/978-1-61520-676-6.ch017

to as players or characters, appear to each other as avatars, which are virtual world representations of individuals. Most but not all of the avatars have either human or humanoid form; e.g., a wolf-like creature that walks upright and has hands with opposable thumbs.

The emergence and growing use of virtual worlds begs some interesting questions. Can actual work be accomplished in virtual worlds? Can they provide the basis for trade? Can they serve as a platform for the study of human behavior? This chapter tries to answer these questions. User interface problems are discussed through a retrospective look at the emergence of online learning courseware several years ago and the discussion of analogies between that and the more recent emergence of virtual worlds. Human evolutionary arguments are put forth for the qualification of the potential of virtual worlds to support modern trade. A discussion of pros and cons to conducting behavioral research in virtual worlds is also presented.

VIRTUAL WORLDS

Virtual reality technologies (Briggs, 2002; Pimentel & Teixeira, 1993; Sherman & Craig, 2003) and artificial worlds created by such technologies may seem now radically new and cutting-edge to many e-collaboration technology users. Yet, virtual reality pioneer Morton Heilig developed an immersive virtual reality technology in the 1960s called Sensorama (see Figure 1), one of the earliest examples of this type of technology (Packer & Jordan, 2002; Ryan, 2001). Among other unexpected features for its time, Sensorama simulated odors.

Also, several virtual environments have been conceptualized, designed and used since the 1960s and 1970s for a variety of purposes, notably for online learning. Those early virtual environments were definitely low-tech when compared with more modern ones, and even modern ones pres-

Figure 1. Sensorama virtual reality system

ent a great degree of variability in terms of their technology sophistication and features offered. Strictly speaking, the courseware suites that emerged in the 1990s to support online learning are in fact virtual environments, but fall short of the features that characterize virtual worlds.

Virtual worlds are defined here as virtual environments that incorporate most of the elements of the real world, even if those elements are presented in a stylized and somewhat unrealistic manner. Thus a virtual world would have a terrain, animated things, gravity, and would impose some laws of physics. For example, users could be allowed to fly in the virtual world without the constraints of gravity; but they could also walk, which requires gravity. Two objects would not be allowed to occupy the same physical space at the same time, which is a common requirement for virtual interaction. And so on.

Many virtual worlds exist that can be used through the Internet, each offering different forms of interaction. The underlying technologies are still evolving. Therefore it is difficult to place virtual worlds into clearly defined categories, and most classifications likely would not be useful

Figure 2. Park scene from Second Life

for a long time. Still, there seem to be some clear differences between virtual worlds that attempt to replicate elements of the real world to enable concrete applications and those that are designed with the goal of making people forget about the real world. The former seem to be designed with more practical purposes in mind, such as to facilitate commercial transactions, while the latter are designed to serve as multiplayer computer gaming platforms.

Second Life, developed by Linden Research (also known as Linden Lab), is a good example of a virtual world that attempts to replicate elements of the real world with practical applications in mind. World of Warcraft, developed by Blizzard Entertainment (a division of Vivendi Games), is a good example of virtual world designed with the goal of making people forget about the real world and become immersed in multiplayer games.

The type of virtual world that is exemplified by Second Life usually contains more human-made elements found in the real world, such as chairs, rooms, buildings, and parks (see Figure 2). Arguably this type of virtual world is less of a departure from the real world than the type of virtual world represented by World of Warcraft. Also, the ele-

ments in the Second Life type of virtual world seem to be easier to reproduce without advanced graphics, which may be one of the reasons why this type of virtual world contains less stunning graphics than the virtual worlds of the World of Warcraft type. (Another reason may be simply that video game users expect stunning graphics, because they are associated with perceived video game quality.) Users in Second Life-type virtual worlds appear to each other as avatars, which are virtual world representations of individuals, and most of the avatars have human form. Since users choose the appearance of their avatars, most of the avatars have physical characteristics that many people would consider attractive.

As one can imagine, not everything is possible in Second Life. For example, there are some limits to the size and appearance of avatars, even though users are given many choices. Also, characters in Second Life cannot give themselves just any type of superpowers, even though they can do some supernatural things like flying.

The type of virtual world that is exemplified by World of Warcraft normally contains fewer human-made elements found in the real world, and a great deal more natural elements such as forests, canyons, rivers, mountains, and waterfalls (see Figure 3). The graphics used are generally of higher quality than in the Second Life type of virtual world, and often evoke fantastic and/or mystic themes. Players interact with each other and with artificial intelligence characters, such as monsters, which they often have to fight for the good of a community in the virtual world or simply to remain alive (in the virtual world).

Other examples of virtual worlds that could be loosely placed in the same category as Second Life are Active Worlds, There, and ViOS. Other virtual worlds that could be loosely placed in the same category of World of Warcraft are Ever-Quest, Guild Wars, and Ultima Online. Still other virtual worlds that do not fit either category, but lean more toward the World of Warcraft type, are Entropia Universe, Red Light Center (modeled after Amsterdam's Red Light District), and The Sims Online.

USER INTERFACE PROBLEMS

The virtual worlds theme received quite a lot of attention in the 2007 installment of the International Conference on Information Systems, held in December 2007 in Montreal, Canada. This is the most prestigious conference in the discipline of information systems, which is primarily concerned with the impact of technology on individuals, groups and organizations. Two panels in that conference focused on the discussion of technological aspects and user perceptions of Second Life and World of Warcraft, as well as one or two lesser known multi-user virtual reality environments.

There was a significant contrast between the perceptions of technology designers and users about virtual worlds. Technology designers, including representatives from IBM and Linden Labs, were quite enthusiastic and positive in their discussions of the technologies that enabled the existence of the virtual worlds. That enthusiasm about technological aspects is arguably well founded, since virtual worlds are indeed major technological achievements.

Figure 3. Dark forest scene from World of Warcraft

The views from users were quite different, especially when presented by information systems researchers who had conducted apparently disinterested analyses of samples of user perceptions. A constant complaint heard from new users of Second Life is that the interface is rudimentary and the graphics are worse than those found in World of Warcraft and other video games. Users of World of Warcraft, which is much more video game-like than Second Life, also tended to display stronger signs of addiction to their virtual life experiences. Nevertheless Second Life seems to have many more registered users than World of Warcraft, and concerns about user addiction exist in Second Life as well. Perhaps Second Life has more users because use of World of Warcraft requires purchase of the computer game, while individual use of Second Life is generally free.

It seems from the discussions at the 2007 International Conference on Information Systems that users were much less enthusiastic about the virtual worlds than the technology designers, and that the majority of users had serious problems with the user interfaces. Possibly the users would have preferred a 1960s Sensorama-like interface updated with today's technology, but it is doubtful that they would be willing to pay what that type of technology would cost now. Other consistent complaints were related to the CPU-intensive nature of the computer programs and the time delays associated with multiple users accessing the systems at the same time over the Internet. Those problems arguably make virtual worlds much less realistic than their designers intended them to be.

Judging from these initial views of Second Life, World of Warcraft and other virtual worlds it appears that there is a great deal of room for progress in the design of the interfaces. It is likely that much progress will happen in the context of video game design, and then be transferred to virtual world technologies that are not inspired in video games. As the huge success of the Nintendo Wii has taught us, one possible direction for progress is improvement in interactivity support through interface devices whose use are more natural than mice and keyboards. The Wii's remote wireless controller, for example, is a handheld pointing device that detects three-dimensional motion and translates that into game actions.

CAN ACTUAL WORK BE ACCOMPLISHED IN VIRTUAL WORLDS?

Several organizations have set up shop in Second Life, and even allow users to buy products and services there using Linden Dollars, the local currency used by Second Life users that is exchangeable by US Dollars. In fact, the designers of Second Life seem to have had support for e-collaboration and e-commerce in the back of their minds when they developed the initial set of features and rules that regulate user interaction. This begs the question as to whether actual work, which would also include commerce-related work, can be accomplished in virtual worlds like Second Life.

Gary Anthes wrote a very interesting article for Computerworld, and information technology industry magazine, on his experiences in Second Life (Anthes, 2007). What makes the article unique and particularly useful for the discussion presented here is that it is written from the perspective of someone who was looking at the potential of Second Life to serve as an actual e-collaboration and e-business tool. That is, the article looked into whether actual work and commerce could in fact be accomplished in Second Life, and the possible implications for real organizations.

The main conclusion that one can infer from that article is that Second Life is still far from reaching the point at which it will serve as an effective e-collaboration tool for organizations, if it ever reaches that point. Several problems are raised, some of which are related to the design of the virtual environment and many to the way in which organizations use the environment. For example, new users have some obstacles that they need to overcome in order to experience the full interactivity features of Second Life: "Newbies are required to start out doing four simple exercises in a place called Orientation Island. Well three were simple and one was impossible." (Anthes, 2007, p. 31)

After new users overcome the initial obstacles faced at the orientation stage, if they go through the full orientation stage at all (they can skip the full orientation), there are other difficulties related to the use of certain interaction features. As anybody who has participated in Web-based text chat rooms can attest, new users often have a hard time sending their comments to the right people. Often comments are sent to the whole group when they are intended to only one individual or two. The same problem occurs in Second Life: "Many in the audience [of a presentation] apparently didn't realize that the [Second Life] text-chat function allows a user to chat with just one person or with everybody at once. As a result, there were frequent interruptions … as well as all kinds of random comments." (Anthes, 2007, p. 32)

And organizations have apparently made mistakes in the establishment of their virtual presence in Second Life, some of which are very basic mistakes. For example, Second Life allows users to jump out of it and into plain Web sites, as long as hyperlinks are properly inserted into it. After all, Second Life runs on an operating system window that can be minimized while its user shifts his or her attention to programs running on other windows or does other things. This is a feature that can be used by companies to turn an interesting experience in Second Life into a business transaction enabled by a plain e-commerce Web site whose hyperlink is strategically inserted in Second Life. However, that is not always done properly: "I walked into a huge, round auditorium called IBM Theatre I. The seats were all empty, and the stage was bare save for a big whiteboard with some semi-interesting techno-items written on it, each followed by an ordinary Web address.

Problem was, the addresses were grayed out, and when I clicked on them, nothing happened." (Anthes, 2007, p. 34)

There are many gems in Anthes's article, which is a relatively long one for an industry magazine. The article also contains inserted in it a rebuttal by Ian Lamont, who agrees with the problems yet is much more enthusiastic about Second Life's future potential. Toward the end of the article, Anthes makes a suggestion that goes to the heart of the problems that many users likely experience in their interactions with companies with a Second Life presence. Following that suggestion could potentially go a long way toward improving their customers' experience: "Each major company location in SL should be staffed by a real person, at least during business hours." (Anthes, 2007, p. 37)

What about World of Warcraft and related virtual worlds? Since they were designed as computer games their potential in their original form to support e-collaboration and e-commerce is much more limited, with some exceptions such as brand development and other selected marketing applications. Nevertheless, a recent event in World of Warcraft points at its potential as a simulation environment that could have real world benefits. The event was the accidental spread of a virtual plague, called the Corrupted Blood plague, which very closely resembled a real-world epidemic. Characters affected by the virtual disease, which was contagious, had their abilities impaired in a way that mimicked what would happen if they contracted a disease in the real world. After Blizzard Entertainment contained the disease and confined it to a specific virtual region, researchers started looking at the potential of World of Warcraft for the study of human behavior in response to epidemics. The interest comes in part from recent real world epidemics, such as the severe acute respiratory syndrome (SARS) outbreak in 2002 and 2003, and the apparent lack of preparedness by governments and other organizations in dealing with those epidemics (Ho & Su, 2004).

The prominent emergence of virtual worlds such as Second Life and their rapidly growing user base does not necessarily imply that they have an immediately practical e-collaboration appeal. For a virtual world to have a practical e-collaboration appeal, meaning that actual work can be done in the virtual world, the benefits of e-collaborating through the virtual world must outweigh the costs. Possible benefits are time and dollar savings due to the reduced need for physical transportation to meeting sites; possible costs are reduced communication fluency and increased communication ambiguity due to cumbersome interfaces and interaction delays.

Past experience tells us that if a virtual community of users is created around a technology and grows beyond a critical mass, then practical e-collaboration applications will follow. One example is the Internet and e-mail, which were initially difficult to use and had little business appeal. Their use is now ubiquitous in business. Any virtual world that attracts a large number of users on a global scale will eventually have a business impact, even if for no other reason than its marketing appeal. This will in turn lead to technological improvements that will eventually make e-collaboration through virtual worlds attractive as the benefits of e-collaboration outweigh the costs.

THE FUTURE OF VIRTUAL TRADE: B2C OR C2C?

One of the interesting characteristics of virtual worlds is that they enable interaction between individuals who may physically far apart from one another (e.g., individuals located in different countries) in a common virtual environment. Those individuals interact as if they were in the same place at the same time, which is sometimes referred to as real-time interaction. Whenever individuals can freely interact in this fashion, one can reasonably expect something to happen.

That something is not necessarily falling in love or getting into conflict, although those things may happen as well. That something is a human universal called trade.

A propensity to engage in trade is a human universal in the sense that it is observed in human groups in a wide variety of cultural and physical contexts. In fact, some anthropologists believe that trade is a key element of all human cultures. This means that trade is observed even among non-urban human groups that can individually produce all that they need for their survival. There are many examples of non-urban groups that specialize in the production of items that are consumed by other groups, and that are exchanged by other items produced by the other groups. (The technical term used to refer to this type of exchange is bartering; this term is used to indicate any form of trade where money is not used). In non-urban cultures, the reason for this phenomenon seems to be alliance formation rather than the utilitarian need for the items that are traded (the Ricardian model of trade), which in turn reduces the chances of violent conflict among the trading groups (see, e.g., Chagnon, 1977).

In our evolutionary past, this would have increased the reproductive success of the individuals of the groups that engaged in trade compared to groups that did not engage in trade. Violent conflict among any two groups could lead to multiple deaths in both groups. Any environmental element that creates a differential impact on reproductive success also creates the opportunity for genes coding for a related trait to evolve; the trait in this case would be a trading instinct, or a propensity to engage in trade. The idea here is that all human beings may share genes that induce them to engage in trade. This would explain why, for example, often people buy things that they do not need. Meg Whitman, the long term senior management leader of eBay, has said that trade is in the human DNA. She might not have meant it in the way just discussed here, but that statement is certainly consistent with the notion that trade may well be an evolved mechanism that increased the reproductive fitness of those human ancestors that possessed it.

Trade in virtual worlds is essentially a more sophisticated version of e-commerce, which can be roughly categorized into two main types: business-to-consumer (B2C) and consumer-to-consumer (C2C). There is a growing trend for both B2C and C2C trade to take place on the Web, and many companies have emerged and done quite well in terms of revenues and profits by providing the infrastructure on which e-commerce can take place. Good examples are Amazon, Craigslist and eBay.

Virtual worlds have the potential to be the new infrastructure providers for B2C and, particularly, C2C. Virtual worlds are likely to be particularly effective at promoting C2C trade because they are exceptionally effective at putting individuals who are geographically dispersed into virtual contact with each other. That, in turn, has the potential to support the growth of virtual worlds, by bringing in users interested in trade who would not otherwise join them, in a closed feedback loop process. Processes that benefit from self-reinforcing feedback loops often experience exponential growth. In this respect Second Life and similar virtual worlds are perhaps better positioned than their World of Warcraft type counterparts, since the former have apparently been designed to support virtual trade and work involving geographically dispersed individuals.

One of the reasons why virtual worlds may be particularly appealing as enablers of trade is that they offer a more natural environment than existing Web sites for C2C trade, which is a mode of e-commerce that has been experiencing significant growth recently. If human beings posses a trading instinct, as discussed earlier, then the genes that evolved to code for that instinct did so in what is referred to by evolutionary psychologists as the environment of our evolutionary adaptation (Barkow et al, 1992; Buss, 1999). In that environment our ancestors interacted face-to-face,

since there was no e-mail, instant messaging or videoconferencing in the Pleistocene or before that. Therefore one could reasonably expect that the trading instinct will operate more effectively in a face-to-face-like environment today. Second Life provides a more face-to-face-like environment for interaction than Amazon, Craigslist or eBay. Of course, those companies can set up shop in Second Life and get ready for the opportunity that will face them as the self-reinforcing feedback loop process gets started. If the line of reasoning presented here is correct, that would be a wise line of action.

Another interesting conclusion that one can infer from the discussion presented here is that trade growth in virtual worlds is likely to be moderated by human intervention in the form of virtual sales representatives. As pointed out in Gary Anthes's article, discussed earlier, it may be quite frustrating for a potential buyer to visit a company-sponsored area in Second Life and not find a sales representative avatar there to help the potential buyer.

The reason is probably analogous to the reason why people generally dislike emoticons when they are used in e-mails to express emotions. Emoticons are a poor approximation of facial expressions, often perceived as idiotic and/or mocking little faces. Analogously, a company branch in Second Life without helpful sales representatives is a poor approximation of a real company branch.

Our species evolved a very complex web of facial muscles, probably more complex than that of any other species (Bates & Cleese, 2001; McNeill, 1998). Nearly all of the evidence available suggests that that complex web of muscles has been evolved almost exclusively for communication through facial expressions in various situations. Given this, poor approximations of faces (e.g., emoticons) are likely to be particularly frustrating, because of the significant amount of information given off by and likely sought from real faces. If the hypothesis that our species also evolved a trading instinct is correct, then one would expect trade in virtual worlds to depend not only on the existence of an environment that is similar to the real world, but on human interactions that are also similar to those found in the real world where our human ancestors lived. In that ancient world one would not exchange spears for bananas by following instructions on a cave painting. One would likely interact with another ancestral human who would extol the qualities of his or her bananas, sort of like a virtual sales representative would do in a virtual world, and ask pointed questions about the quality of the spears.

Hence the need for virtual sales representatives that act like real human beings; that is, that have real human beings behind them. This would be necessary at least initially, as users become familiar with the virtual world, after which experienced users would likely be willing to engage in trade without virtual human intervention, much like users do today through Web sites designed for e-commerce transactions. Virtual sales representatives entirely created by artificial intelligence software are not likely to do very well in that respect. The famous Turing Test suggests that human beings are exceptionally good at recognizing artificial systems trying to pass as real human beings. Another implication of this discussion is that, at least initially, C2C trade may become a stronger driver than B2C trade in the establishment of virtual worlds as mainstream trading environments.

STUDYING HUMAN BEHAVIOR IN VIRTUAL WORLDS

As mentioned earlier, the 2007 International Conference on Information Systems had several presentations and panel discussions that focused on virtual worlds and their impact on various aspects of human behavior. Several researchers hailed virtual worlds as new and promising tools for research on human behavior in those presentations and discussions. However, in the questions-and-answers period that followed those presentations and discussions, virtual world users in the audience noted that, particularly in Second Life, all avatars look like beautiful people in their 20s and 30s. It was pointed out in follow-up discussions that quite a lot of deception may be going on in virtual worlds. That creates a problem for researchers, who often want to find out if there are correlations between certain types of behavioral patterns and demographic variables such as age, gender, income and country of origin. Even if virtual world users were willing to disclose demographic information about them, probably many would be inclined to lie a bit about that information.

Another difficulty of using virtual worlds to conduct behavioral research is that the multitude of possible effects on individual behavior may make isolation of specific effects difficult. Much of human-technology interaction research is conducted through controlled experiments for exactly that reason. In controlled experiments the investigators focus on one or a few particular independent variables, such as communication media naturalness (Kock, 2004; 2005; 2007; 2009), and then randomly group the subjects they are studying (i.e., the human participants in the experiment) into conditions associated with those variables. The goal is usually to isolate the effect of the independent variable (or variables) on an important dependent variable. One example of important dependent variable would be an individual's satisfaction with a trade interaction conducted in the virtual world. By employing this procedure the investigators can study in a focused manner the effect of the independent on the dependent variable, much in the same way that pharmaceutical drug researchers do. Drug researchers often isolate the effect of certain drugs by randomly assigning their study subjects to control (placebo) and treatment (drug) groups.

On the other hand, virtual worlds can be quite useful tools for research that requires more realistic scenarios than those normally used in controlled experiments. One example is the study of large-scale human behavior in response to a disease outbreak or an environmental disaster. What differentiates this type of investigation from the controlled experiment form discussed above is that the researchers are interested primarily in large-scale group responses. In these types of responses the characteristics and behavior of one individual or of small groups are not of major importance. One useful analogy is the modern study of the behavior of investors in certain markets in response to macroeconomic changes, such as changes in a country's government-regulated interest rates. In many cases these types of studies can be credibly done even if the researchers disregard individual differences.

This is not to say that controlled experiments cannot be done in virtual worlds. They can, as long as certain precautions are taken. For example, a researcher can assemble a group of human subjects prior to them creating their avatars, and collect reliable demographic information from each of them. Then each subject would create a unique avatar in a controlled manner (e.g., no major changes in appearance compared to the real world), and have his or her behavior studied over a period of time in particular circumstances in the virtual world that also contain controlled elements (e.g., virtual crowding or information overload levels). The researcher could create sub-environments where different subjects' avatars would interact, randomly assigning different individuals to sub-environments, and then comparing behavior patterns observed in each sub-environment.

CONCLUSION

As we look at the user interface problems of emergent virtual worlds it is instructive to also look back at the early versions of online courseware like Blackboard and WebCT. Many of the problems with early online courseware suites were interface-related, and some of those problems led to dire predictions about the demise of

online instruction and of the companies behind it. Those predictions were made by those at one end of a spectrum of enthusiasm regarding online learning, the very negative end of the spectrum. At the other positive end of the spectrum there were those who felt that online learning tools were going to revolutionize education, changing it dramatically and forever. That in turn led some successful enterprises to be established and flourish over the years, such as for-profit educational institutions like the University of Phoenix. It also led to some miserable failures in similar areas, such as various fully online branches of traditional not-for-profit universities.

And where are we today with online learning? Well, after all the hype in the 1990s, the main trend seems to be to use it to deliver selected courses online and to augment more traditional forms of instruction in other courses. Most university classes are still taking place face-to-face, with a slowly growing proportion of them taking place online. There are clear tradeoffs for students and instructors, and more growth is seen in contexts where the cost-benefit ratio is low; for instance, among working students in areas where high-bandwidth Internet access is available.

Several empirical studies suggest that it is more cognitively demanding to interact online, for both instructors and students. That is, interacting online requires more mental effort, and can often lead to mental fatigue faster than face-to-face interaction. Nevertheless online instruction also gives students who work full time, who live in rural areas, or who suffer from physical disabilities the opportunity to obtain the education that they need to improve their professional and personal lives. Also, in spite of cognitive demands, there is evidence that learning performance is not significantly affected, either positively or negatively. This no-significant-difference effect probably is a result of compensatory adaptation to the less natural online learning media (Kock et al, 2007).

It is difficult to predict the impact that virtual worlds will have on individuals, groups and the society as a whole in the future. One possibility is particularly enticing though, and is related to the potential of virtual worlds to contribute to world peace. As mentioned earlier, a propensity to engage in trade appears to be a human universal, a social instinct evolved in part to reduce the chances of violent conflict among the trading parties. Trade also often has a utilitarian purpose, which is to enable the economic production and consumption of goods and services at cost and quality levels that would not otherwise be possible.

From an international trade perspective, this can lead to two main benefits: a reduction in the likelihood that individuals from different trading nations will be willing engage one another in violent conflict, and possibly better and cheaper products and services. Yet the trading instinct evolved in our evolutionary past, when our ancestors communicated primarily through natural face-to-face interactions. Thus one would expect that its social catalyst effect will be realized if modern humans: (a) trade on a one-on-one basis (i.e., in a C2C mode) or in small groups; and (b) interact through communication media that have levels of naturalness that are similar to face-to-face interaction. As user interface problems are gradually resolved, virtual worlds will provide those natural communication media, and may in turn help promote world peace through C2C trade.

ACKNOWLEDGMENT

This chapter is adapted from an article previously published in the *International Journal of e-Collaboration*. The author would like to thank Arthur Kock and Monica Kock, who know a great deal about computer games, for their comments and suggestions on an earlier version of this chapter. Various publicly available definitions, descriptions, and multimedia materials related to virtual reality and virtual worlds have been used as a basis for this chapter. Particularly useful sources were the Web sites maintained by Google and Wikipedia.

REFERENCES

Anthes, G. (2007). Second Life: Is there any there there? *Computerworld, 41*(49), 30–38.

Barkow, J. H., Cosmides, L., & Tooby, J. (Eds.). (1992). *The adapted mind: Evolutionary psychology and the generation of culture*. New York: Oxford University Press.

Bates, B., & Cleese, J. (2001). *The human face*. New York: DK Publishing.

Bessière, K., Seay, A. F., & Kiesler, S. (2007). The ideal elf: Identity exploration in World of Warcraft. *Cyberpsychology & Behavior, 10*(4), 530–535. doi:10.1089/cpb.2007.9994

Bonsu, S. K., & Darmody, A. (2008). Co-creating Second Life: Market-consumer co-operation in contemporary economy. *Journal of Macromarketing, 28*(4), 355–368. doi:10.1177/0276146708325396

Briggs, J. C. (2002). Virtual reality is getting real: Prepare to meet your clone. *The Futurist, 36*(3), 34–42.

Burdea, G., & Coiffet, P. (2003). *Virtual reality technology*. Hoboken, N.J.: J. Wiley-Interscience.

Buss, D. M. (1999). *Evolutionary psychology: The new science of the mind*. Needham Heights, MA: Allyn & Bacon.

Chagnon, N. A. (1977). *Yanomamo: The fierce people*. New York: Holt, Rinehart and Winston.

Ho, M.-S., & Su, I.-J. (2004). Preparing to prevent severe acute respiratory syndrome and other respiratory infections. *The Lancet Infectious Diseases, 4*(11), 684–689. doi:10.1016/S1473-3099(04)01174-0

Kock, N. (2004). The psychobiological model: Towards a new theory of computer-mediated communication based on Darwinian evolution. *Organization Science*, *15*(3), 327–348. doi:10.1287/orsc.1040.0071

Kock, N. (2005). Media richness or media naturalness? The evolution of our biological communication apparatus and its influence on our behavior toward e-communication tools. *IEEE Transactions on Professional Communication*, *48*(2), 117–130. doi:10.1109/TPC.2005.849649

Kock, N. (2007). Media naturalness and compensatory encoding: The burden of electronic media obstacles is on senders. *Decision Support Systems*, *44*(1), 175–187. doi:10.1016/j.dss.2007.03.011

Kock, N. (Ed.). (2008). *Encyclopedia of e-collaboration*. Hershey, PA: Information Science Reference.

Kock, N. (2009). Information systems theorizing based on evolutionary psychology: An interdisciplinary review and theory integration framework. *MIS Quarterly*. (Article in press at the time of writing.)

Kock, N., Verville, J., & Garza, V. (2007). Media naturalness and online learning: Findings supporting both the significant- and no-significant-difference perspectives. *Decision Sciences Journal of Innovative Education*, *5*(2), 333–356. doi:10.1111/j.1540-4609.2007.00144.x

McNeill, D. (1998). *The face: A natural history*. Boston, MA: Little, Brown and Company.

Mennecke, B. E., McNeill, D., Ganis, M., Roche, E. M., Bray, D. A., & Konsynski, B. (2008). Second Life and other virtual worlds: A roadmap for research. *Communications of AIS*, *22*(1), 371–388.

Packer, R., & Jordan, K. (2002). *Multimedia: From Wagner to virtual reality*. New York: Norton.

Pimentel, K., & Teixeira, K. (1993). *Virtual reality*. New York: McGraw-Hill.

Pinckard, J. (2006). World of Warcraft is the new golf. *PC Magazine*, *25*(7), 108–109.

Ryan, M.-L. (2001). *Narrative as virtual reality: Immersion and interactivity in literature and electronic media*. Baltimore, MD: Johns Hopkins University Press.

Sherman, W. R., & Craig, A. B. (2003). *Understanding virtual reality: Interface, application, and design*. Boston, MA: Morgan Kaufmann Publishers.

Traum, M. J. (2007). Second Life: A virtual universe for real engineering. *Design News*, *62*(15), 75–78.

Chapter 18

Electronic Deception:
How Proximity, Computer–Mediation, and the Truth Bias May Influence Deceptive Messages

Randall J. Boyle
University of Utah, USA

Charles J. Kacmar
The University of Alabama, USA

Joey F. George
Florida State University, USA

ABSTRACT

This research examines the impact of computer-mediated communication, distributed communication, and knowledge of prior baseline behavior on an individual's propensity to make veracity judgments. Subjects were motivated to detect deception by participating in a Prisoner's Dilemma game with monetary rewards. Methodologies of other deception detection studies are compared and existing theoretical models are extended. This study found that more detection confidence can come from knowledge of a person's prior baseline behavior, being proximally located, the type of communication media used, and perceived relational closeness. These factors indirectly lead to less deception detection through more detection confidence and reliance on the truth bias, a fundamental belief in the truthfulness of others, even in a computer mediated environment.

INTRODUCTION

Today's firms are relying more on non-traditional communication media such as email, voice mail, and virtual meetings (Burke and Chidambaram, 1999; Guicking, Tandler and Grasse, 2008; Hoffman and Novak, 1996). In a globalized work environ-

ment, these types of communication media are important to quality decision-making (Fjermstad, 2005). However, a question arises as to whether the use of these communication media, together with distributed information sources, may mitigate an individual's ability to detect deception (Kahai, Avolio, and Sosik, 1998; Kahai and Cooper, 1999). Deception is a regular part of daily communicative

DOI: 10.4018/978-1-61520-676-6.ch018

interaction (DePaulo and Kashy, 1998), accounting for 26-33% of daily social interactions (DePaulo, Kashy, Kirkendol, Wyer and Epstein, 1996; Hancock, Thom-Santelli and Ritchie, 2004). As computer-mediated communication (CMC) use continues to spread, the ability to detect deception using lean communication media will be increasingly important in the workplace (Zhou, Burgoon, Twitchell, Qin, and Nunamaker, 2004).

Research in the area of deception detection over distributed media has not been widespread. While individual research streams such as media richness, computer-mediated communication, and deception detection have extensive bodies of literature, the intersection of these streams has scarcely been examined (George and Marett, 2005; Giordano, Stoner, Brouer, and George, 2007). For example, **deception detection** research has focused on techniques such as training to recognize deceptive cues (Feeley and Young, 1998; Ekman and O'Sullivan, 1991), and suspicion arousal (Stiff and Miller, 1986; George, Marett, and Tilley, 2008) to increase face-to-face deception detection rates. Face-to-face deceptive cues such as greater pupil dilation, more blinking, decreased response length, more speech errors and hesitations, greater voice pitch, more negative statements, and more irrelevant information (Feeley and Young, 1998) are of limited applicability to deception detection in computer-mediated or distributed environments.

Similarly, the ability to detect deception between communication partners is widely believed to be related to the type and strength of the personal relationship that exists between the communicating parties (Feeley and Young, 1998). Past research in the area of deception detection has mainly focused on individuals who are either strangers or intimate partners (Anderson, Ansfield, and DePaulo, 1997). However, working relationships typified by high levels of familiarity but low levels of intimacy, have been largely ignored. The relationship between partners impacts deception detection rates because of a fundamental

assumption that their partner is being truthful. This fundamental assumption of truthfulness is often referred to as the **truth bias** (McCornack and Parks, 1986).

The purpose of this study is to investigate the effects of differing contextual factors on deception detection confidence and the relationship between confidence and truth bias. More specifically, this study will contribute to existing IS literature by examining the effects of working relationships, computer-mediated, and distributed environments within the context of deception detection. The next section of the paper presents the theoretical background for the study, including a research model and hypotheses. This is followed by a discussion of the research method, findings, and implications for research and practice.

THEORETICAL BACKGROUND

Research surrounding **deception detection** has focused on detection skills of observers (Brandt, Miller, and Hocking, 1982), conversational task demands (Burgoon and Newton, 1991), honesty judgments (Fiedler and Walka, 1993), the influence of relational closeness (Anderson et al., 1997), environmental influence (Storms, 1973), observer ability to detect deception (Buller, Strzyzewski, and Hunsaker, 1991), and the impact of suspicion on detection accuracy (Buller, Strzyzewski, and Comstock, 1991). Findings have shown that individuals have significant difficulty discerning truth from deception. Deception detection rates have been shown to range from 54% to 60% (Feeley and Young, 1998; Bond and DePaulo, 2006). However, other studies have found that deception detection rates may be as low as 35-40%, while truth detection rates have ranged from 70-80% (Levine, McCornack, and Park, 1998). It is important to note that deception detection and truth detection, correctly identifying lies as lies and truths as truths respectively, vary in overall task difficulty.

Table 1. Concept definitions

Term	Definition
Truth Bias	The inherent belief that people are telling the truth (Stiff, Kim, and Ramesh, 1992)
Relational Closeness	The degree of interdependence that exists between relationship partners as evidenced by their day to day activities (Berscheid, Snyder, and Omoto, 1989)
Baseline Knowledge	Knowledge of a person's nominal/truthful behavior (Feeley, deTurck, and Young, 1995)
Proximity	The physical presence or absence of individuals in the same room
Deception Detection	The ability of an individual to recognize deviations from nominal, or truthful, behavior (Miller, Mongeau, and Sleight, 1986)
Detection Confidence	Belief that a truth or lie is correctly identified
Detection Accuracy	Correctly identifying truths as truths, and lies as lies (Feeley and Young, 1998)
Deception	A message knowingly transmitted by a sender to foster a false belief or conclusion by the receiver (Knapp and Comadena, 1979)
Deception Accuracy	Correctly identifying lies as lies (Feeley and Young, 1998)
False Accusation	Incorrectly identifying a truthful statement as a lie.
Information Cue	Acts that give away information the sender wishes to conceal (Zuckerman and Driver, 1985)

Deception Models

In order to identify the factors influencing differences in deception detection, several theoretical models have been developed and empirically tested by different research groups. One of the most influential theories originates with the work of McCornack and Parks (1986) in which the antecedents of the truth bias were investigated. Specifically, they looked at the impact of relational closeness on deception detection. They found that as relationships develop and people become closer, they tend to be more confident of their ability to detect truths/lies. This increased confidence causes participants to subsequently rely more on their basic assumption of truthfulness (i.e., the truth bias).

The theoretical model developed by McCornack and Parks (1986), shown in Figure 1, has received additional support in a meta-analysis indicating a strong linkage between relational closeness and detection confidence (DePaulo, Charlton, Cooper, Lindsay, and Muhlenbruck, 1997). As detection confidence increases, individuals will reduce the amount of effort they put forth in detecting deceptive behavior by relying increasingly on truth bias and reducing detection accuracy. Some scholars have operationalized truth bias as the percentage of truthful judgments during lie detection; others as the number of truthful judgments (McCornack and Parks, 1986); and yet others have operationalized it using self-report measures (Stiff, Kim, and Ramesh, 1992).

Stiff et al. (1992) similarly showed that there is a significant relationship between relational development and truth bias. They note that there is substantial support for the claim that more developed relationships, typified by intimacy, reduced

Figure 1. Conceptual model from McCornack and Parks (1986)

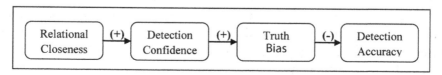

Figure 2. Research model

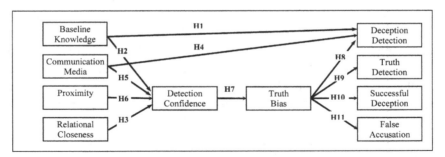

uncertainty, satisfaction, and commitment, tend to be much more subject to truth bias. They also note that participants in those relationships are only marginally less able to detect deception. In turn, participants who rely more on the truth bias in making veracity judgments also tend to view their partner's statements as truthful. Stiff et al. (1992) found that aroused suspicion had significant negative correlations with both truth bias and judgments of truthfulness. However, the study procedures used to induce heightened suspicion may produce findings that are only generalizable to situations where individuals already anticipate deception (Miller and Stiff, 1993). In sum, both theoretical models suggest that an increase in relational closeness will increase the level of truth bias and reduce deception detection.

Research Model

The research model put forth and tested in this research, shown in Figure 2, extends prior work with new constructs and relationships. The model hypothesizes associations from baseline knowledge, detection confidence, and truth bias to deception detection. The model extends the work of McCornack and Parks (1986) with constructs for baseline knowledge, media richness, and proximity. Unlike prior studies, the research model distinguishes baseline knowledge from relational closeness in order to separately test the influences of relational intimacy and knowl-

edge of prior baseline behavior on detection confidence. Prior research has also focused on deception detection within nominal groups. This study adds to existing theory by examining the impact of computer-mediation and distributed communication on deception detection. These new constructs will allow us to investigate the impact of new methods of communication on deception detection.

In deception detection research it is important to note the distinction between deception detection and detection accuracy (Biros, George, and Zmud, 2002). Deception detection refers to the correct identification of a deceptive statement, while detection accuracy refers to the correct identification of a truthful statement, a deceptive statement, or both. In order to distinguish deception detection from a broader definition of detection accuracy, this study measures deception detection, truth detection, successful deception, and false accusations separately. Figure 2 shows the decomposition of the construct detection accuracy into four separate dependent variables. Decomposing detection accuracy into four separate variables provides a more rigorous methodology and greater clarity when interpreting outcomes.

Relational Closeness and Baseline Behavior

As previously mentioned, baseline behavior is a key factor in predicting deception detection. In order for an individual to recognize deviations from nominal or truthful behavior he/she must first acquire a "baseline" of truthful behavior. This **baseline knowledge** is important because an individual may naturally exhibit cues typically associated with deceptive behavior (Brandt et al., 1982). Feeley and Young (1998) note that the majority of deception detection studies are based on the premise that there is a set of identifiable cues that are specifically related to deceptive behavior. However, other researchers argue that identifying changes in individual-specific behaviors during deception greatly reduces the possibility of misinterpretation (Anderson et al., 1997; Walters, 2000). Brandt, Miller, and Hocking (1980) found that observers with truthful baseline knowledge were three times as accurate in detecting deceptive behavior as individuals without truthful baseline knowledge. Similar studies have shown that observers with a small amount of baseline knowledge had better detection rates (72%) than observers without baseline knowledge (56%) (Feeley, deTurck, and Young, 1995). The fact that many previous studies have used zero-history dyads may well explain the low detection rates. Constructs such as suspicion (Stiff and Miller, 1986), anonymity (Kahai and Avolio, 2006), and trust (McKnight, Cummings, and Chervany, 1998) have also been shown to influence group interactions. However, the addition of these constructs to the research model is beyond the scope of this paper.

While baseline knowledge is vital in making veracity judgments, more relational closeness, which often comes in obtaining baseline knowledge, can severely mitigate any advantage. Miller and Stiff (1993) demonstrated that individuals in intimate relationships may not want to view their partners as deceptive due to emotional attachments. In fact, studies have shown that relational intimacy may not influence detection accuracy (Comadena, 1982). McCornack and Parks (1986) examined the relationship between relational closeness, truth bias, and detection confidence and found that increased **relational closeness** decreases the ability to detect deceptive behaviors. This leads to the conclusion that, while knowing truthful baseline behaviors and cues are essential to deception detection, relational closeness is detrimental to veracity judgments and significantly increases an individual's level of truth bias.

Knowledge of the other person's baseline behavior is predicted to have a positive influence on detection confidence and detection accuracy. In other words, as individuals become more able to "read" their communication partner, their ability to detect deceptive behavior will increase. Detection accuracy can be broken down into deception detection accuracy and truth detection accuracy. Knowledge of baseline behavior is predicted to have a positive influence on truth detection and deception detection. Individuals will be able to detect truthful cues, deceptive cues, and deviations from nominal behavior. With regards to social interaction, the model predicts that optimal deception detection is obtained by minimizing relational closeness, not being proximally located, and maximizing the amount of baseline behavior knowledge. By minimizing intimacy and maintaining familiarity in a relationship, an individual should theoretically be able to detect deception. Thus the following hypotheses are put forth:

Hypothesis 1: Knowledge of baseline behaviors will be positively associated with deception detection.

Hypothesis 2: Knowledge of baseline behaviors will be positively associated with detection confidence.

Hypothesis 3: Relational closeness will be positively associated with detection confidence.

Communication Media

As previously noted, media richness theory (MRT) suggests that as media become richer the amount of information cues conveyed increases (Daft and Lengel, 1986). Within the context of truth bias and deception detection, the ability to detect information cues is critical in evaluating the truthfulness of a message (Zuckerman and Driver, 1985). Information cues can consist of verbal, visual, paralingual, and textual cues (Williams, 1977; Zuckerman, DePaulo, and Rosenthal, 1981). Cues provide receivers with the evidence necessary to make veracity judgments. It has been shown that individuals assume a person is telling the truth until additional cues indicate otherwise (McCornack and Parks, 1986). For this study, deception will be defined as a message knowingly transmitted by a sender to foster a false belief or conclusion by the receiver (Knapp and Comadena, 1979).

Zuckerman and Driver's (1985) meta-analysis of 24 possible deceptive behaviors yielded 14 specific behaviors that were related to deception. An analysis by Feeley and Young (1998) shows that eight cues are significantly correlated with deception: greater pupil dilation, more blinking, decreased response length, more speech errors and hesitations, greater voice pitch, more negative statements, and more irrelevant information.

Recent studies have explored the ability to detect deception using linguistic based cues (Zhou, Burgoon, Nunamaker, and Twitchell, 2004). One study found deception detection rates as high as 74% (Fuller, Biros, and Wilson, 2009). These studies have focused on feature-based classification schemes to correctly identify deception. More recent studies have tried to detect deception based on word dependency relationships that may have been overlooked by feature-based systems. (Zhou, Yongmei, and Dongsong, 2008). Despite using only text-based cues to detect deception, automated deception detection systems may ultimately help improve the ability of decision makers to correctly identify deceptive statements if appropriate features and relationships can be identified.

The ability for decision makers to make correct veracity judgments may be dependent on the quantity, quality, and variety of information cues (McCornack, 1997). The quantity, quality, and variety of information cues is dependent upon the type of media used (Burgoon, Blair, and Strom, 2008). Media selection may be, as suggested by Media Richness Theory, dictated by the need to make veracity judgments. Media Richness Theory (Daft and Lengel, 1986) has been used to explain the effects and choice of communication media in a variety of tasks such as planning, creativity, intellectual tasks, decision making, and brainstorming (Hollingshead, McGrath, and O'Connor, 1993). Prior research has also shown that partners with a history of working together communicate differently across varying types of media (Yoon and Alavi, 2001; Carlson and Zmud, 1999).

Media richness can be defined as the ability of information to change understanding within a given time interval (Daft and Lengel, 1986; Dennis and Kinney, 1998). Depending on the degree of equivocality and task uncertainty, an individual will choose a richer medium in order to provide better feedback, draw upon a wider variety of cues, use a variety of language, and convey a more personally focused message (Daft, Lengel, and Trevino, 1987). With respect to the current study, the focus is *not* on what type of media is best for deception detection, but rather, how different levels of media richness affect an individual's ability to make veracity judgments and mitigate the truth bias.

Communication media, or the richness of the communication media (Ngwenyama and Lee, 1997), is predicted to have a positive influence on detection confidence, and detection accuracy. Increased media richness increases the number of information cues individuals can use to make veracity judgments. More cues should lead to higher levels of confidence in deception detection because of reduced equivocality. Thus the following hypotheses will be tested in this study:

Hypothesis 4: The richness of the communication medium will be positively associated with deception detection.

Hypothesis 5: The richness of the communication medium will be positively associated with detection confidence.

Proximity

Social facilitation, as conceptualized by Zajonc (1965), focuses on changes in behavior due to the physical presence of others. In a review of 287 studies examining the effects of social facilitation, Guerin (1986) notes that the presence of another person may cause behavioral changes in four ways. First, the physical presence of another individual may cause more apprehension due to the expectation that he/she will be evaluated. Second, the physical presence of someone else may cause "cognitive or physical conflict" between task focus and having to attend to the other person. Third, the presence of another person may enhance task performance in order to make a good impression on the other person. Fourth, another's physical presence may cause an increase in "conforming to public and private norms" because of greater self-focus and comparison of behavioral standards (Guerin, 1986).

Distributed communication has been shown to have an impact on the final outcome of a process (Maznevski and Chudoba, 2000), communication act itself (Rice, 1984), and the effort an individual puts into maintaining social networks (Miranda and Carter, 2005). Research has also shown that distributed teams can experience escalation in conflict (Armstrong and Cole, 1995) and the formation of hostile coalitions (Cramton, 2001). Whitty (2002) showed that there was a propensity for anti-social behaviors in chat rooms where individuals were relatively new. However, more intimate relationships did develop over time. Despite the significant effects of presence on behavior, the influence of proximity and computer mediation has typically been difficult to separate due to methodological inconsistencies (Hedlund, Ilgen, and Hollenbeck, 1998).

In sum, distributed communication decreases the level of social influence, thereby changing individual behavior and expectations (Pena, Walther, and Hancock, 2007). The presence of another person encourages an individual to conform to social norms and to restrain from engaging in anti-social behaviors (Berger, Hampton, Carli, Grandmaison, Sadow, and Donath, 1981). Proximally located subjects may be more confident of their ability to detect deception due to their belief that their communication partner is more likely to conform to social norms (i.e. be truthful).

The **proximal** influence of another person has not only been shown to cause a change in behavior but also a change in the level of cognitive effort put forth (Geen and Gange, 1977; Zajonc, 1965). Individuals will put forth more effort toward task performance in the presence of others. Subjects may put forth more effort in detecting deception when proximally located to their communication partner. As a result, subjects may be more confident in their ability to detect a deceptive decision. In this study it is predicted that physical proximity will influence individuals to be more confident in detecting deception. Therefore, the following hypothesis is put forth:

Hypothesis 6: Proximally located subjects will have higher detection confidence than subjects that are distributed.

Truth Bias and Deception Detection

Truth bias is the inherent belief that people are telling the truth (Stiff, Kim, and Ramesh, 1992). While this fundamental assumption of truthfulness simplifies decision making by reducing the quantity and quality of veracity judgments, it may also inhibit deception detection. Research on truth bias has been aimed at trying to reduce an individual's reliance on this fundamental assumption of truthfulness. Studies have explored reduction techniques such as training (Ekman and O'Sullivan, 1991) and suspicion arousal (Stiff and Miller, 1986). In these studies, subjects were trained to recognize cues (e.g., eye twitching, specific words) thought to be specifically associated with deception, or were told that their communication partner may be lying. Efforts have also been made to reduce truth bias by lowering the level of cognitive demand through passively observing dialogue (Buller et al., 1991). This was accomplished by allowing subjects to watch video recordings, or read the dialogue between two other subjects. In general, research has focused on enabling individuals to better detect deception (Masip, Garrido, and Herrero, 2006).

As hypothesized and reported by McCornack and Parks (1986), the level of confidence an individual has in his/her assessment of truthfulness should positively affect his/her reliance on the truth bias as a simplifying heuristic. In turn, greater dependence on the truth bias should negatively affect his/her ability to detect deception and lead to fewer false accusations due to the general belief that his/her communication partner is telling the truth. Conversely the truth bias should have a positive affect on an individual's ability to detect truthful statements and the individual's susceptibility to being successfully deceived. The authors argue that as individuals become more certain of their evaluation, they devote fewer cognitive resources toward determining truthfulness. Subsequently, they will rely more on cognitive heuristics to make veracity judgments and therefore will be less able to distinguish between truthful and deceptive statements. Thus:

Hypothesis 7: Detection confidence will be positively associated with truth bias.

Hypothesis 8: Truth bias will be negatively associated with deception detection.

Hypothesis 9: Truth bias will be positively associated with truth detection.

Hypothesis 10: Truth bias will be positively associated with being successful deception.

Hypothesis 11: Truth bias will be negatively associated with false accusation.

METHOD

This study utilized a controlled laboratory experiment employing a 2x2x2 factorial design (computer-mediated/non-computer-mediated, proximal/distributed, familiar/unfamiliar with communication partner). A total of 97 dyads were randomly assigned to one of eight possible treatment conditions (N=194). Dyads comprised of subjects familiar with each other were recruited from groups in the preceding semester taught by the first author. Proximal dyads completed the task in the same room, while distributed dyads completed the task in separate rooms (even though the rooms were adjacent to each other subjects could not see each other or communicate directly). Computer-mediated dyads exchanged messages using the Microsoft NetMeeting© chat software; non-computer-mediated groups communicated using either face-to-face or cellular telephone.

Task

The **prisoner's dilemma** task, developed by Albert Tucker (c.f., Axelrod, 1984), was chosen because of its characteristics in studying deception detection. Studies involving deception detection are difficult to conduct because incorrect procedures can often lead to internal and external validity problems (Miller and Stiff, 1993). To overcome such problems, Miller and Stiff (1993) specified eight factors that would result in an "ideal procedure" to study deception detection (Miller and Stiff, 1993:39). Figure 3 shows a comparison of procedures used in the past, and the procedure to be used in the current study. Studies utilizing all

Figure 3. Description detection research procedures adapted from Miller and Stiff (1993)

Ideal Research Procedure	Motivated to Deceive	Motivated to Detect	Anticipate Deception	Deception Sanctioned	Relational Deception	Verbal & Nonverbal	Deception Detection	Transactive Process	Ethical
	Yes	Yes	No	No	Yes	Yes	Yes	Yes	Yes
Message Presentations (Knapp et al. 1974)						X	X		X
Reaction Assessment (Ekman & Friesen, 1974)	X					X	X		X
Exline Procedure (Exline et al. 1970)	X			X		X	X		
Relational Interviews (Comadena, 1982)	?	?			X	X	X	X	X
Simulated Interviews (Stiff et al. 1989)	N/A			N/A		X			X
Survey Interviews (Miller et al. 1984)	X	X	X	X	X	?	X	?	X
Interaction Analysis (Stiff et al. 1992)	X	X	?	X		X	X	X	X
Prisoner's Dilemma (current study)	X	X	X	X	X	X	X	X	X

of the factors listed below are better able to reduce internal and external validity issues.

The classic version of the prisoner's dilemma task does not allow for communication between subjects. However, this study used a derivative of the prisoner's dilemma task that allowed for real-time interpersonal interactions where subjects were motivated to deceive and detect deception. Anticipation of deception was not heightened by the researchers, nor was deception sanctioned in the experiment. Scoring allowed for measurement of deception, deception detection, and truth bias. Matching of participants with prior experience allowed individuals to use their prior knowledge to detect deception. Lastly, playing the prisoner's dilemma game does not raise any serious ethical or human subjects concerns.

In the classical prisoner's dilemma game, there are two players. Players can choose to either "defect" or "collude." Each player makes his/her decision without the knowledge of what the other person will do. Defection always yields a higher payoff than collusion. The dilemma is that if both players defect, they will lose more than if they had both colluded. In other words, the greatest positive and negative payoffs are achieved when one player defects and his/her partner colludes, respectively. Since both players are trying to obtain this optimal solution, it is in their best interests to convince each other that they are going to collude, and then defect.

Within the context of the game subjects were given the options to either "confess" (defect) or "stay quiet" (collude). Possible decision outcomes have the following reward structure $T > C > 0 > D > S$ (Dawes and Orbell, 1995). The "temptation" payoff (T) of +$5 was rewarded for unilateral defection of one player, while the other remains silent. The "cooperative" payoff (C) of +$1 was rewarded for joint cooperation between individuals (i.e., both remain silent). The "defect" payoff (D) of -$1 was rewarded for joint defection of both individuals (i.e., both confess). The (more negative) "sucker" payoff (S) of -$3 was rewarded for unilateral cooperation. Negative dollar payoffs were given for mutual defection, and even greater negative dollar payoffs for unilateral cooperation. Figure 4 shows how each combination of decisions form the final dependent variables in the purposed research model.

Consistent with prior research, participants were able to lose all of their money, or more than double the amount they possessed before the game began. Subjects were told that they were to be given $3 for participating in the experiment and would gain or lose money according to their decisions. Researchers paid each subject in cash a week after the conclusion of the experiment. Subjects were

Figure 4. Detection Matrix

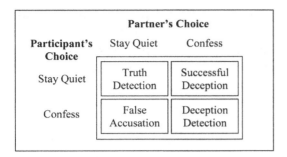

paid at a later time to avoid any possible reprisal from another subject due to defection during the experiment.

Measures

The constructs in the research model were operationalized as described below. *Relational closeness* was operationalized using a 14-item short form of the relational closeness inventory (RCI) 27-item measure from Berscheid, Snyder, and Omoto (1989) (Polimeni, Hardie, and Buzwell, 2002). These items assess the strength of the relationship and frequency of contact between conversational partners. Items are measured using seven-point Likert scales with higher scores indicating a higher level of relational closeness. The RCI scale has been shown to be highly consistent, with a coefficient alpha of .90 (short form Cronbach alpha=.87) (Polimeni et al., 2002).

Baseline knowledge was operationalized by pre-assigning subjects to the baseline knowledge condition if they had worked together on a large group project for 3 months during the semester prior to the experiment. Subjects who had never met before were assigned to the no baseline knowledge condition. Subjects were coded 2=baseline knowledge and 1=no baseline knowledge depending on their respective experiment condition. To ensure that subjects were correctly identified as having sufficient baseline knowledge a manipulation check consisting of three previously

validated measures (Cronbach alpha=.90) was implemented. These measures indicated a subject's general knowledge about their communication partner, nature of their relationship, and length of time they have known each other (Berscheid et al., 1989).

Proximity, an individual's awareness that another person is proximally located, was indicated as a factor of the treatment condition. Proximal subjects were seated such that they faced each other at a distance of no greater than 3 feet, while subjects in the distributed condition were seated in separate rooms, and could not see or communicate visually or verbally with each other. Responses were coded 2=proximal and 1=distributed depending on their respective condition.

Richness of the communication media was operationalized using eight seven-point items (Cronbach alpha=.85) (Daft and Lengel, 1986; Dennis and Kinney, 1998). In the CMC group, subjects communicated with their partner through a chat program. In the non-CMC group subjects communicated face-to-face or by cellular telephone.

Detection confidence was operationalized using a single item that asked subjects their level of confidence in predicting their communication partner's choice (confess, stay quiet). This self-report measure ranged from 0 (not sure) to 100 (very sure) with a mean of 86.13 (S.E.=18.512).

Truth bias was operationalized using four seven-point Likert measures of perceived truth bias (Stiff, Kim, and Ramesh, 1992). Truth bias was computed as an average with scores ranging from 1 to 7 and a mean of 5.6 (S.E.=1.18).

The four constructs truth detection, deception detection, successful deception, and false accusation were calculated based on subjects' decisions to either "stay quiet" or to "confess". Deception detection was operationalized as a correct estimation of a communication partner's choice to confess. Truth detection was operationalized as a correct estimation of a communication partner's choice to stay quiet. Successful deception and false accusation were operationalized as incorrect estimations of a communication partner's choice to confess or stay quiet.

SAMPLE

Subjects (N=194) were juniors and seniors majoring in management information systems (MIS) at a large southeastern university in the U.S. Subjects' mean age was 23.4 years (S.E.=4.3) with 58.8% of the subjects being male. To ensure that subjects were correctly identified as having prior baseline knowledge of their partner's behavior, subjects were asked how long they had known their partner. Subjects in the baseline group indicated that they had known their partner for an average of 9.18 months (S.E.=8.5) and had a mean relational closeness measure of 1.72 (S.E.=0.094). Individuals in the no-baseline condition indicated that they had known their partner for an average of 0.85 months and had a mean relational closeness measure of 1.29 months (S.E.=0.074). The mean difference in the time subjects had known their partner in the baseline and no-baseline groups was statistically significant (F=13.172; p<0.001).

A manipulation check asking subjects if they could see their partner indicated that the proximal/distributed manipulation was successful and statistically significant (F=45.335; p<0.001). To address a possible concern of information leakage in proximal groups, subjects were asked if they were able to gain information from overhearing other conversations during the experiment. Responses across all conditions indicated that subjects were not able to gain information from other groups (Mean=1.28; S.E.=0.737).

ANALYSIS AND RESULTS

Scatter-plots and histograms indicated that some measures experienced minor departures from normality. The distribution of detection confidence scores was somewhat peaked (Kurtosis=2.06). The distribution for relational closeness was also peaked (Kurtosis=4.02) and somewhat skewed (Skewness=2.09). Despite minor departures from normality, the F statistics reported in this study were robust. Kirk (1995) notes that the F statistic remains robust when "populations are symmetrical, but not normal, and the sample sizes are equal or greater than 12 (Kirk, 1995:99; Clinch and Keselman, 1982)." Analysis of histograms across experiment conditions indicated that populations were homogeneous in form (positively skewed), and sample sizes were approximately equal. Therefore, minor departures from normality were not a threat to the validity of the statistical procedures used in this study.

Factor Analysis

Three of the seven constructs (Relational Closeness, Truth Bias, and Communication Media) were measured using multiple items to identify specific underlying latent constructs in the measurement model. The remaining independent, intermediate, and dependent variables were operationalized using single measures. Factor analysis was used to condense information gathered from multiple variables into a minimal number of factors representing the theoretically proposed latent constructs. The dimensionality of relational closeness (RC), truth bias (TB), and communication media (CM) were determined using principal components analysis (PCA) (Kaiser-Meyer-Olkin=0.796).

A series of initial unconstrained principal component analyses were done to determine the amount of variance explained by the latent factors. Initial analyses indicated that several items did not explain a significant amount of variance. Factors with loadings below .50 or cross-loadings above .30 were dropped (Hair, Anderson, Tatham, and Black, 1998). Factors having loadings of .50 or greater are considered practically significant and a factor will account for 50% of the variance if the factor loading exceeds .70 (Hair et al., 1998).

Based on these criteria, seven of the items in the relational closeness factor and two items from the media richness factor were eliminated. All other constructs yielded acceptable statistics and, therefore, no other items were dropped. The follow-up factor analysis revealed that all factors had loadings of .70 or greater except for RC2 (.681) when using a constrained three-factor solution. There were no cross loadings greater than .25. Table 2 shows the variance explained by each item and respective factor loadings. Varimax rotation was used throughout the factor analysis to give a better interpretation of the underlying factors by reducing the ambiguities that often accompany initial unrotated factor solutions (Hair et al., 1998).

All factors exhibited reliabilities consistent with prior research scoring above .70. Constructs exhibited convergent and discriminant validity by having Cronbach's alpha values greater than 0.70 (Nunnally, 1978) and by each indicator loading more highly on its associated construct than any other construct. Means, Standard Errors, Cronbach's alphas and intercorrelations for all constructs can be seen in Table 3.

Research Model and Hypothesis Results

Partial Least Squares (PLS) was used to test the research model because it accommodates limited sample sizes, a large number of constructs, and restrictions on measurement scales (Chin, Marcolin, and Newsted, 2003). PLS has also been shown to be robust when dealing with discrete single-indicator variables (Pavlou and Fygenson, 2006). While PLS is typically used in exploratory research it can also

Table 2. Factor loadings and variance explained[abcd]

	Variance Explained	CM	RC	TB
CM1	57.4%	**0.737**	-0.012	0.176
CM2	65.5%	**0.802**	-0.062	0.089
CM3	55.8%	**0.740**	0.051	0.091
CM4	64.1%	**0.786**	0.109	0.106
CM5	52.5%	**0.716**	-0.033	0.105
CM6	66.2%	**0.800**	-0.054	0.139
RC1	58.0%	0.050	**0.756**	-0.077
RC2	48.5%	-0.038	**0.681**	-0.140
RC3	65.9%	0.029	**0.809**	0.061
RC4	68.6%	-0.011	**0.828**	0.025
RC5	50.4%	0.002	**0.707**	0.063
RC6	64.2%	-0.033	**0.795**	0.092
TB1	62.6%	0.124	-0.044	**0.780**
TB2	63.4%	0.145	-0.049	**0.782**
TB3	86.5%	0.229	0.057	**0.900**
TB4	73.4%	0.119	0.069	**0.845**
[a]RC=Relational Closeness; TB=Truth Bias; CM=Communication Media				
[b]Extraction Method: Principal Component Analysis.				
[c]Rotation Method: Varimax with Kaiser Normalization.				
[d]Rotation converged in 4 iterations.				

be used in confirmatory research if sample size is an issue (Gefen, Straub, and Boudreau, 2000). Path coefficients and R^2 values for the purposed research model are shown in Figure 5.

Hypothesis 1 (H1) stated that knowledge of baseline behaviors will be positively associated with deception detection. Surprisingly, individuals with baseline knowledge about their partner had a significantly *lower* deception detection accuracy rate (b=.063, t=2.06, p=0.020) than those without. Overall, deception detection rates were (31.6%) for baseline groups and (68.4%) for groups with no baseline knowledge. A "hit" included successful

detection of deceptive decisions. Thus, we reject H1. However, we did find a significant relationship in the opposite direction.

Hypothesis 2 (H2) stated that knowledge of baseline behaviors will be positively associated with detection confidence. Detection confidence was scored on a scale from 1 (very unconfident) to 100 (very confident). Subjects in the baseline condition (N=92) had a mean detection confidence level of 91.54 (S.E.=15.9), while subjects in the no baseline condition (N=102) had a mean detection confidence level of 81.31 (S.E.=19.2). Individuals with baseline knowledge were significantly

Table 3. Intercorrelations and reliabilities

	Mean	S.E.	RC	BK	P	MR	DC	TB	DD	TD	SD	FA
Relational Closeness (RC)	1.50	0.860	0.86									
Baseline Knowledge (BK)	1.53	0.501	0.27	*								
Proximity (P)	1.47	0.501	-0.10	0.01	*							
Communication Media (CM)	4.89	1.31	0.00	0.14	0.12	0.86						
Detection Confidence (DC)	86.1	18.4	0.13	0.28	0.13	0.19	**					
Truth Bias (TB)	5.61	1.17	0.02	0.30	0.10	0.33	0.52	0.85				
Deception Detection (DD)	0.979	0.214	-0.12	-0.10	0.00	-0.05	-0.04	-0.15	**			
Truth Detection (TD)	0.717	0.324	0.08	0.19	0.11	0.07	0.17	0.36	-0.52	**		
Successful Deception (SD)	0.119	0.023	-0.02	-0.09	-0.07	0.04	-0.01	0.00	-0.12	-0.58	**	
False Accusation (FA)	0.067	0.018	0.01	-0.09	-0.12	-0.12	-0.24	-0.49	-0.09	-0.43	-0.09	**

Reliabilities are shown on the diagonal.
* Factors of treatment condition, ** Single item measure

Figure 5. Model results

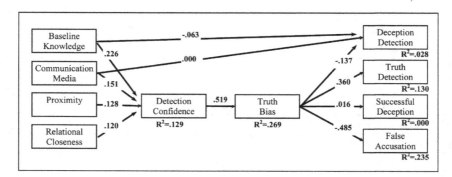

more confident (b=.226, t=3.32, p<0.001) than those without baseline knowledge. Thus, there is evidence to support H2.

Hypothesis 3 (H3) stated that more relational closeness will be positively associated with detection confidence. Consistent with prior research, results confirmed that relational closeness had a positive relationship on detection confidence (b=.120, t=2.56, p=0.006). Therefore, there is sufficient evidence to support H3.

Hypothesis 4 (H4) stated that the richness of the communication medium will be positively associated with deception detection. Table 4 shows deception detection rates, attempts at deception, successful deception rates, and deception detection confidence rates. Subjects in the non-CMC condition did not have significantly higher detection accuracy rate than subjects in the CMC condition (b=0.00, t=0.685, p<0.247). Overall, deception detection rates were low for both manual (42.9%) and computer (47.6%) groups where subjects were deceived. Thus, we find that there is insufficient support for H4.

Hypothesis 5 (H5) stated that the richness of the communication medium will be positively associated with detection confidence. Subjects in the non-CMC condition communicated with their partner either face-to-face or by cellular telephone, while subjects in the CMC condition communicated with their partner using NetMeeting©. Subjects in the manual condition (N=94) had a mean detection confidence level of 89.61

(S.E.=16.8), while subjects in the computer condition (N=100) had a mean detection confidence level of 82.92 (S.E.=19.4). Results indicate that the means were significantly different (b=.151, t=3.17, p<0.001). Thus, H5 was supported.

Hypothesis 6 (H6) stated that proximally located subjects will have higher detection confidence than subjects that are distributed. Subjects in the proximal condition (N=102) had a mean detection confidence level of 88.45 (S.E.=16.8), while subjects in the distributed condition (N=92) had a mean detection confidence level of 83.62 (S.E.=19.8). Results showed that proximally located subjects did have significantly higher detection confidence than subjects that were distributed (b=.128, t=2.19, p=.015). Overall, baseline knowledge, communication media, proximity, and relational closeness accounted for 12.9% of the variance in detection confidence (R^2=.129). Thus, there is sufficient evidence to support H6.

Hypothesis 7 (H7) stated that detection confidence will be positively associated with truth bias. Results showed that detection confidence had a positive effect on truth bias (b=.519, t=8.75, p<0.001). Detection confidence accounted for 26.9% of the variance in truth bias (R^2=.269). Therefore, there is sufficient evidence to support H7.

Hypotheses 8 (H8) and 11 (H11) stated that truth bias will be negatively associated with deception detection and false accusation respectively. Truth bias had a negative effect on detection

Table 4. Subject decisions

Detection Accuracy	Baseline Proximal Computer	Baseline Proximal Manual	Baseline Distributed Computer	Baseline Distributed Manual	NoBase Proximal Computer	NoBase Proximal Manual	NoBase Distributed Computer	NoBase Distributed Manual	Total
Accurate Prediction	23	21	17	19	23	21	16	18	158
Inaccurate Prediction	1	3	7	1	3	7	10	4	36
Deception Attempt	3	2	6	3	6	9	6	7	42
Successful Deception	1	2	4	1	1	4	5	3	21
Detection Confidence	95%	96%	84%	92%	79%	86%	75%	85%	
Total	24	24	24	20	26	28	26	22	194

Table 5. Hypothesis results

Hypothesis		t	p	Outcome
H1	Knowledge of baseline behaviors will be positively associated with deception detection.	2.0670	0.0200	Reject†
H2	Knowledge of baseline behaviors will be positively associated with detection confidence.	3.3222	0.0005	**Accept***
H3	Relational closeness will be positively associated with detection confidence.	2.5614	0.0056	**Accept***
H4	The richness of the communication medium will be positively associated with deception detection.	0.6849	0.2471	Reject
H5	The richness of the communication medium will be positively associated with detection confidence.	3.1669	0.0009	**Accept***
H6	Proximally located subjects will have higher detection confidence than subjects that are distributed	2.1990	0.0145	**Accept***
H7	Detection confidence will be positively associated with truth bias.	8.7516	0.0001	**Accept***
H8	Truth bias will be negatively associated with deception detection.	1.9730	0.0250	**Accept***
H9	Truth bias will be positively associated with truth detection.	4.4594	0.0001	**Accept***
H10	Truth bias will be positively associated with successful deception.	1.3724	0.0858	**Accept****
H11	Truth bias will be negatively associated with false accusation.	6.3836	0.0001	**Accept***
* Significant at p< 0.05, ** Significant at p< 0.10, † Significant at p< 0.05 but in reverse direction				

(b=-.137, t=1.97, p=.025) and a negative effect on false accusations (b=-.485, t=6.38, p<0.001). Truth bias and baseline knowledge accounted for 2.8% of the variance in deception detection (R^2=.028), and truth bias alone accounted for 23.5% of the variation in false accusations (R^2=.235). Therefore, H8 and H11 were supported.

Hypotheses 9 (H9) and 10 (H10) stated that truth bias will be positively associated with truth detection and successful deception respectively. Truth bias had a positive effect on truth detection (b=.360, t=4.46, p<0.001) and a positive effect on successful deceptions (b=.016, t=1.37, p<0.086). Truth bias accounted for 13.0% of the variance in truth detection (R^2=.130), and truth bias accounted for less than 0.1% of the variation in false accusations (R^2=.001). Therefore, H8 and H11 were supported.

DISCUSSION

This study investigated the direct and indirect effects of differing contextual factors on deception detection and the relationship between detection confidence and truth bias. The contextual factors studied were the closeness of the relationship between the communicating partners, their baseline knowledge of each other, whether the partners were co-located or dispersed, and the particular media used for communication. All four hypotheses dealing with detection confidence were supported. Subjects who were familiar with their communication partners, who had baseline information about them, were co-located, and who used richer communication media had higher levels of confidence in their abilities to detect deception in their partners, compared to subjects in the opposite conditions. The positive effects of baseline knowledge, richer communication media, and proximity on deception detection confidence are significant contributions of this study to existing research. High levels of detection confidence also were found associated with high levels of truth bias, supporting another hypothesis and confirming that existing deception theories are robust within computer-mediated environments.

Of the two factors thought to directly affect **deception detection** (baseline knowledge, communicate media), only the link from baseline knowledge to deception detection was supported. Further, this relationship was negative. This finding indicates that in some work situations, there will be little or no relationship between communication media and deception detection. Results confirm the existence and potency of the truth bias within computer-mediated environments by negatively influencing deception detection, and false accusations. Conversely the truth bias was shown to positively influence truth detection and successful deception. Each of these findings is explored in more depth below.

Knowledge of Baseline Behavior

As noted earlier, a surprising finding of this study is that subjects with prior knowledge of their partner's **baseline behavior** were less accurate in detecting deceptive decisions made by their communication partners. Past research has indicated that individuals who have known their partner, even for a short period of time should be more accurate in detecting deceptive behavior (Brandt, Miller, and Hocking, 1980). Past studies looking at deceptive behavior examined the ability of individuals to detect deception in intimate relationships, between friends, and among strangers (Anderson et al., 1997). The proposed model theorized that familiarity with an individual's baseline behaviors would aid in detecting deception cues. Results, however, indicate that a small amount of familiarity reduces an individual's ability to detect deception. This may be due to increased levels of trust and/or individuals' inability to correctly recognize deceptive behaviors. Thus, by separating baseline knowledge from relational closeness this study adds to existing theory by showing that both

familiarity and intimacy (Feeley and Young, 1998; Comadena, 1982) are separate factors contributing to decreased deception detection.

Results indicate that more knowledge of baseline behaviors was significantly associated with more detection confidence. This suggests that individuals draw upon past experience when making veracity judgments and feel more confident about those judgments. Overall the effect of having knowledge of a partner's prior behavior caused individuals to be more confident in their veracity judgments yet were significantly less accurate in those judgments.

Communication Media

This study extends existing deception detection theory by showing that individuals who communicate with their communication partner via face-to-face interaction or telephone are significantly more confident of their ability to detect deceptive behaviors, yet are not any better at actually detecting deception. In fact, they were indirectly less able to detect deception due to more detection confidence and subsequently more truth bias. Changes in behavior and decision making due to richer communication is supported by prior research (Barkhi, Jacob, and Pirkul, 1999).

In the context of deception detection, a **richer communication media** provides more information cues that might be used to detect deception (Ngwenyama and Lee, 1997). More truthful/deceptive cues in a richer communication medium can lead to more confidence in veracity judgments by providing more evidence and reducing equivocality. While cues may cause individuals to be more confident, it is the inherent uncertainty in discerning between truthful and deceptive statements that makes deception detection so difficult. In fact, most successful deceptions consist of many truthful statements and contain only a small, albeit critical, number of deceitful statements (Zhou, Burgoon, Nunamaker, and Twitchell, 2004; Zhou, Burgoon, Twitchell, Qin, and Nunamaker, 2004). By providing more informational cues that might indicate deceptive/truthful behavior, an individual may have greater justification for making a veracity judgment. Of course the results presented here are not meant to imply that information cues are not important. Rather, a minimal amount of information cues may be necessary to make a simple veracity judgment within the context of this study.

Proximity

In this study the physical presence of another individual led to more detection confidence due to the fact that individuals most likely felt compelled to conform to public and private norms (Hofstede, 1997). In this study the public norm would be to tell the truth. Individuals in the proximal condition may have assumed that their communication partner would tell the truth to make a good impression and to avoid possible confrontation (Guerin, 1986) thus leading to more confidence in their decision. The converse would also be true in the distributed condition. As noted earlier, distributed communication decreases the level of social influence, thereby changing individual behavior and expectations. This study adds to existing theory by showing how **proximity** affects deception confidence, and ultimately deception detection, in computer-mediated environments. It should be noted that more detection confidence does not necessarily imply more deception detection.

Relational Closeness

As noted earlier, prior research co-mingled the constructs familiarity and relational closeness (Anderson et al., 1997). This study has expanded existing research by showing that **relational closeness** itself is a contributing factor to detection confidence separate from baseline knowledge. This finding was significant (p=0.045) and consistent with prior research (DePaulo et al., 1997).

Relational closeness has a positive influence on detection confidence because, as feelings of closeness to another person grow, an individual will feel more confident of his/her ability to detect deception/truthfulness. Prior research indicates that this confidence may stem from the fact that individuals in intimate relationships may want to view their partners as truthful because of emotional attachments (Miller and Stiff, 1993). The results from this study imply that even minor levels of relational closeness developed over the course of a few months in work related relationships might lead to significantly more detection confidence.

Detection Confidence

As predicted, the relationship between detection confidence and truth bias was positive and significant (p=0.001). Consistent with prior research, the level of confidence subjects had in their assessments of truthfulness positively affected their reliance on the truth bias as a simplifying heuristic (McCornack and Parks, 1986). Subjects who were more certain of what they believed their partners were going to do devoted less cognitive resources toward making veracity judgments. In this study, more detection confidence was shown to come from levels of perceived relational closeness (H3), knowledge of a person's prior baseline behavior (H2), being proximally located (H6), and the type of communication media used (H5). Consistent with cognitive bias research, subjects inherently proscribed to the "cognitive miser" paradigm and attempted to reduce mental effort by using simplifying heuristics when possible. Subjects felt comfortable relying on the truth bias as a way of making veracity judgments about their communication partners because of their confidence in their decision.

Truth Bias

Consistent with prior research, **truth bias** had negative relationships with deception detection and false accusations. Using the assumption of truthfulness, individuals systematically mislabeled deceptive statements as truthful statements. Conversely, truth bias also had positive relationships with truth detection and successful deception. Individuals who relied more on the truth bias to make veracity judgments were more likely to identify deceptive statements as truthful.

This study adds to existing deception detection research by showing that the truth bias is robust in computer mediated environments, across varying types of studies, and differing operationalizations of the truth bias construct. In fact, this study matched all nine of Miller and Stiff's (1993) criteria for an ideal deception detection study. This study also showed that Prisoner Dilemma scenarios are an acceptable method of studying deception detection and the truth bias without the negative side effects mentioned by Miller and Stiff. It is also interesting to note that there were almost twice as many truth bias errors (N=21) as there were lie bias errors (N=13).

LIMITATIONS AND IMPLICATIONS

This study is limited in that subjects were offered monetary rewards from $0 to $8. Subjects indicated that they viewed these rewards as nominal, and consequently may not have been motivated enough to exert significant amounts of motivational effort to affect changes in cognitive bias. However, even with small financial incentives subjects did attempt to deceive their assigned partner and detect deception from that partner. In fact, in transcribed recordings and chat logs subjects indicated that they would willingly deceive even close friends for $25.

This study may also have limited generalizability due to differences between student subjects and workers. However, given the general nature of the deception detection process it is unlikely that there will be significant variation between students and workers.

Implications for Researchers

This study has three main implications for researchers. First, the study furthers our understanding of new communication media because it shows that richer media may provide more confidence in predicting behavior. However, richer media do not necessarily improve predictive accuracy. In the context of deception, researchers must account for the fact that computer-mediated communication may lead to comparable deception detection rates, compared to face-to-face communication, without additional detection confidence.

Second, researchers gain an understanding of how distributed communication can lead to low levels of detection confidence. The widespread use of new communication media has allowed real-time communication across vast distances, yet the impact of proximity on deception detection has not been investigated. Researchers must recognize that the presence of another individual is a vital factor in studying deception.

Third, researchers must recognize that familiarity and intimacy are separate constructs that both contribute to detection confidence. Researchers also need to be aware that individuals who have known each other for even a relatively short period of time are less accurate at detecting deception than complete strangers. Future studies using subjects that know each other must account for the familiarity and intimacy between subjects.

Implications for Practitioners

This study has three main implications for practitioners. First, practitioners need to understand that richer communication, such as face-to-face meetings, can actually lead to less deception detection compared to traditional face-to-face interactions. While richer communications may not directly affect an individual's ability to detect deception, the findings indicate that they may *reduce* the individual's ability indirectly by mistakenly relying on the truth bias. Conversely, using less rich media may comparatively increase deception detection compared to face-to-face communication. This means that corporations could use non-traditional communication media such as email, voice mail, and virtual meetings to boost performance, and actually be less susceptible to deception. Improved deception detection within corporations would valuable for both employers and stakeholders (Shih, Chiang, and Yen, 2005).

Second, individuals can expect higher detection confidence and decreased veracity judgments when proximally located to the person with whom they are communicating, regardless of the communication medium. Managers can be confident that increasing utilization of distributed teams for productivity enhancements will not increase susceptibility to deception. In fact, it will lead to relatively higher deception detection rates compared to proximally located teams. However, it may also lead to more false accusations.

Third, practitioners need to understand the impact of working relationships and relational closeness on deception detection. While it may not be possible to eliminate familiarity (baseline knowledge) from the workplace, it would be beneficial if businesses limited the amount of relational closeness among co-workers. By limiting relational closeness and, to the extent possible, familiarity practitioners will indirectly increase their ability to detect deception.

FUTURE RESEARCH

Results from this study have generated several new research questions and directions for future research. First, further research exploring the impact of suspicion, trust, and deception detection in computer-mediated environments, is clearly warranted. The inclusion of these closely related constructs in a larger model is likely to lead to a clearer picture of how they affect deception detection rates. Examinations of workplace deception within a small group context would also yield valuable clues relative to the impact of deception detection beyond dyadic communication.

Second, future research would benefit from iterated prisoner dilemma sessions with different partners at both the group and individual level. Iterated prisoner dilemma games played in both computer and manual conditions would yield valuable insights into the effect of media richness on negotiation, deception, and strategic decision making. Future research could also include a comparison of different monetary rewards on deception attempts and an individual's ability to detect deception.

Third, future research should focus on measuring the influence of both situational veracity judgments and past experience. Past research has been driven by the assumption that there is a set of identifiable cues that are specifically related to deceptive behavior (Feeley and Young, 1998). However, the relationship between deceptive cues and pre-established valuations of personal truthfulness has not been investigated. Current knowledge would benefit from additional research aimed at determining the relative predictive powers and interaction of these two factors.

CONCLUSION

This study has yielded several valuable insights into the effects of computer mediation, distributed communication, and knowledge of baseline behavior on deception detection and the truth bias. This study showed that more detection confidence can come from knowledge of a person's baseline behavior, being proximally located, the type of communication media used, and perceived relational closeness. These factors lead to less deception detection through more detection confidence and reliance on the truth bias. Knowledge of an individual's baseline behavior also had a direct negative relationship with deception detection. This study found that subjects with a high level of confidence in their ability to detect truthful/deceptive behavior were more reliant on the truth bias to make veracity judgments even in a computer mediated environment.

REFERENCES

Anderson, D. E., Ansfield, M. E., & Depaulo, B. M. (1997). Love's best habit: Deception in the context of relationships. In Philippot, P., Feldman, R. S., & Coats, E. J. (Eds.), *The social context of nonverbal behavior* (pp. 1–46). Cambridge: Cambridge University Press.

Armstrong, D., & Cole, P. (1995). Managing distances and differences in geographically distributed work groups. In Jackson, S., & Ruderman, M. (Eds.), *Diversity in Work Teams* (pp. 187–216). Washington, DC: American Psychological Association. doi:10.1037/10189-007

Axelrod, R. (1984). *The evolution of cooperation.* New York: Basic Books.

Barkhi, R., Jacob, V. S., & Pirkul, H. (1999). An experimental analysis of face-to-face versus computer mediated communication channels. *Group Decision and Negotiation, 8*(4), 325–347. doi:10.1023/A:1008621423120

Berger, S., Hampton, K. L., Carli, L. L., Grandmaison, P. S., Sadow, J. S., & Donath, C. H. (1981). Audience-induced inhibition of overt practice during learning. *Journal of Personality and Social Psychology, 40,* 479–491. doi:10.1037/0022-3514.40.3.479

Berscheid, E., Snyder, M., & Omoto, A. M. (1989). The relationship closeness inventory: Assessing the closeness of interpersonal relationships. *Journal of Personality and Social Psychology, 57,* 792–807. doi:10.1037/0022-3514.57.5.792

Biros, D. P., George, J. F., & Zmud, R. W. (2002). Inducing sensitivity to deception in order to improve decision making performance: A field study. *Management Information Systems Quarterly, 26*(2), 119–144. doi:10.2307/4132323

Bond, C. F., & DePaulo, B. M. (2006). Accuracy of deception judgments. *Personality and Social Psychology Review, 10*(3), 214–234. doi:10.1207/s15327957pspr1003_2

Brandt, D. R., Miller, G. R., & Hocking, J. E. (1980). The truth deception attribution: Effects of familiarity on the ability of observers to detect deception. *Human Communication Research, 6,* 99–110. doi:10.1111/j.1468-2958.1980.tb00130.x

Brandt, D. R., Miller, G. R., & Hocking, J. E. (1982). Familiarity and lie detection: A replication and extension. *Western Journal of Speech Communication, 46,* 276–290.

Buller, D. B., Strzyzewski, K. D., & Comstock, J. (1991). Interpersonal deception: I. deceivers' reactions to receivers' suspicions and probing. *Communication Monographs, 58,* 1–24. doi:10.1080/03637759109376211

Buller, D. B., Strzyzewski, K. D., & Hunsaker, F. (1991). Interpersonal deception: II. The inferiority of conversational participants as deception detectors. *Communication Monographs, 58,* 25–40. doi:10.1080/03637759109376212

Burgoon, J. K., Blair, P. J., & Strom, R. E. (2008). Cognitive biases and nonverbal cue availability in detecting deception. *Human Communication Research, 34*(4), 572–599. doi:10.1111/j.1468-2958.2008.00333.x

Burgoon, J. K., & Newton, D. A. (1991). Applying a social meaning model to relational messages of conversational involvement: Comparing participant and observer perspectives. *The Southern Communication Journal, 56,* 96–113.

Burke, K., & Chidambaram, L. (1999). How much bandwidth is enough? A longitudinal examination of media characteristics and group outcomes. *Management Information Systems Quarterly, 23*(4), 557–580. doi:10.2307/249489

Carlson, J. R., & Zmud, R. W. (1999). Channel expansion theory and the experiential nature of media richness perceptions. *Academy of Management Journal, 42*(2), 153–171. doi:10.2307/257090

Chin, W. W., Marcolin, B. L., & Newsted, P. R. (2003). A partial least squares latent variable modeling approach for measuring interaction effects: Results from a Monte Carlo simulation study and an electronic-mail emotion/adoption study. *Information Systems Research, 14*(2), 189–217. doi:10.1287/isre.14.2.189.16018

Clinch, J. J., & Keselman, H. J. (1982). Parametric alternatives to the analysis of variance. *Journal of Educational Statistics, 7*, 207–214. doi:10.2307/1164645

Comadena, M. E. (1982). Accuracy in detecting deception: Intimate and friendship relationships. In Burgoon, M. (Ed.), *Communication Yearbook, 6* (pp. 446–472). Beverly Hills, CA: Sage.

Cramton, C. D. (2001). The mutual knowledge problem and its consequences for dispersed collaboration. *Organization Science, 12*(3), 346–371. doi:10.1287/orsc.12.3.346.10098

Daft, R. L., & Lengel, R. H. (1986). Organizational information requirements: media richness and structural design. *Management Science, 32*(5), 554–571. doi:10.1287/mnsc.32.5.554

Daft, R. L., Lengel, R. H., & Trevino, L. K. (1987). Message equivocality, media selection, and manager performance: Implications for information systems. *Management Information Systems Quarterly, 11*(3), 355–366. doi:10.2307/248682

Dawes, R. M., & Orbell, J. M. (1995). The benefit of optional play in anonymous one-shot prisoner's dilemma games. In Arrow, K. J., Mnookin, R. H., Ross, L., Tversky, A., & Wilson, R. B. (Eds.), *Barriers to conflict resolution* (pp. 62–85). New York: W.W. Norton & Company.

Dennis, A. R., & Kinney, S. T. (1998). Testing media richness theory in the new media: The effects of cues, feedback, and task equivocality. *Information Systems Research, 9*(3), 256–275. doi:10.1287/isre.9.3.256

DePaulo, B. M., Charlton, K., Cooper, H., Lindsay, J. J., & Muhlenbruck, L. (1997). The accuracy-confidence correlation in the detection of deception. *Personality and Social Psychology Review, 1*, 346–357. doi:10.1207/s15327957pspr0104_5

DePaulo, B. M., & Kashy, D. A. (1998). Everyday lies in close and casual relationships. *Journal of Personality and Social Psychology, 74*, 63–79. doi:10.1037/0022-3514.74.1.63

DePaulo, B. M., Kashy, D. A., Kirkendol, S. E., Wyer, M. M., & Epstein, J. E. (1996). Lying in everyday life. *Journal of Personality and Social Psychology, 70*, 979–995. doi:10.1037/0022-3514.70.5.979

Ekman, P., & Friesen, W. V. (1974). Detecting deception from the body or face. *Journal of Personality and Social Psychology, 20*, 288–298. doi:10.1037/h0036006

Ekman, P., & O'Sullivan, M. (1991). Who can catch a liar? *The American Psychologist, 46*, 913–920. doi:10.1037/0003-066X.46.9.913

Exline, R. E., Thibaut, J., Hickey, C. B., & Gumpert, P. (1970). Visual interaction in relation to Machiavellianism and an unethical act. In Christie, R., & Geis, F. L. (Eds.), *Studies in Machiavellianism* (pp. 53–75). New York: Academic Press.

Feeley, T. H., deTurck, M. A., & Young, M. J. (1995). Baseline familiarity in lie detection. *Communication Research, 12*(2), 160–169.

Feeley, T. H., & Young, M. J. (1998). Humans as lie detectors: Some more second thoughts. *Communication Quarterly, 46*(2), 109–126.

Fiedler, K., & Walka, I. (1993). Training lie detectors to use nonverbal cues instead of global heuristics. *Human Communication Research, 20*, 199–223. doi:10.1111/j.1468-2958.1993.tb00321.x

Fjermestad, J. (2005). Virtual group strategic decision making using structured conflict and consensus approaches. *International Journal of e-Collaboration, 1*(1), 43–46.

Fuller, C. M., Biros, D. P., & Wilson, R. L. (2009). Decision support for determining veracity via linguistic-based cues. *Decision Support Systems, 46*(3), 695–703. doi:10.1016/j.dss.2008.11.001

Geen, R. G., & Gange, J. J. (1977). Drive theory of social facilitation: Twelve years of theory and research. *Psychological Bulletin, 84*, 1267–1288. doi:10.1037/0033-2909.84.6.1267

Gefen, D., Straub, D. W., & Boudreau, M.-C. (2000). Structural equation modeling and regression: Guidelines for research practice. *Communications of AIS, 1*(7), 1–78.

George, J. F., & Marett, K. (2005). Deception: The dark side of e-collaboration. *International Journal of e-Collaboration, 1*(4), 24–37.

George, J. F., Marett, K., & Tilley, P. A. (2008). The effects of warnings, computer-based media and probing activity on successful lie detection. *IEEE Transactions on Professional Communication, 51*(1), 1–17. doi:10.1109/TPC.2007.2000052

Giordano, G. A., Stoner, J. S., Brouer, R. L., & George, J. F. (2007). The influences of deception and computer-mediation on dyadic negotiations. *Journal of Computer-Mediated Communication, 12*(2), 362–383. doi:10.1111/j.1083-6101.2007.00329.x

Guerin, B. (1986). Mere presence effects in humans: A review. *Journal of Experimental Social Psychology, 22*, 38–77. doi:10.1016/0022-1031(86)90040-5

Guicking, A., Tandler, P., & Grasse, T. (2008). Supporting synchronous collaboration with heterogeneous devices. *International Journal of e-Collaboration, 4*(1), 1–19.

Hair, J. F., Anderson, R. E., Tatham, R. L., & Black, W. C. (1998). *Multivariate Analysis* (5th ed.). Upper Saddle River, NJ: Simon & Schuster Co.

Hancock, J. T., Thom-Santelli, J., & Ritchie, T. (2004). *Deception and design: The impact of communication technologies on lying behavior.* Paper presented at the Conference on Computer Human Interaction, New York.

Hedlund, J., Ilgen, D. R., & Hollenbeck, J. R. (1998). Decision accuracy in computer-mediated versus face-to-face decision-making teams. *Organizational Behavior and Human Decision Processes, 76*(1), 30–47. doi:10.1006/obhd.1998.2796

Hoffman, D. L., & Novak, T. P. (1996). Marketing in hypermedia computer-mediated environments: Conceptual foundations. *Journal of Marketing, 60*(July), 50–68. doi:10.2307/1251841

Hofstede, G. (1997). *Cultures and organizations: Software of the mind.* New York: McGraw Hill.

Hollingshead, A. B., McGrath, J. E., & O'Connor, K. M. (1993). Group task performance and communication technology: A longitudinal study of computer-mediated versus face-to-face work groups. *Small Group Research, 24*(3), 307–333. doi:10.1177/1046496493243003

Kahai, S. S., & Avolio, B. J. (2006). Leadership style, anonymity, and the discussion of an ethical issue in an electronic context. *International Journal of e-Collaboration, 2*(2), 1–26.

Kahai, S. S., Avolio, B. J., & Sosik, J. J. (1998). Effects of source and participant anonymity and initial difference in opinions in an EMS context. *Decision Sciences, 29*(2), 427–460. doi:10.1111/j.1540-5915.1998.tb01583.x

Kahai, S. S., & Cooper, R. B. (1999). The effect of computer-mediated communication on agreement and acceptance. *Journal of Management Information Systems, 16*(1), 165–188.

Kirk, R. E. (1995). *Experimental design: Procedures for the behavioral sciences*. Pacific Grove, CA: Brooks/Cole.

Knapp, M. L., & Comadena, M. E. (1979). Telling it like it isn't: A review of theory and research on deceptive communications. *Human Communication Research, 1*, 15–29. doi:10.1111/j.1468-2958.1974.tb00250.x

Knapp, M. L., Hart, R. P., & Dennis, H. S. (1974). An exploration of deception as a communication construct. *Human Communication Research, 1*, 15–29. doi:10.1111/j.1468-2958.1974.tb00250.x

Levine, T. R., McCornack, S. A., & Park, H. S. (1998, March). *Accuracy in detecting truths and lies: Three studies documenting the "veracity effect"*. Paper presented at the annual meeting of the Western States Communication Association, Denver, CO.

Locke, E. A. (1986). Generalizing from laboratory to field: Ecological validity or abstraction of essential elements? In Lock, E. A. (Ed.), *Generalizing from laboratory to field settings* (pp. 5–9). Lexington, MA: Lexington Books.

Masip, J., Garrido, E., & Herrero, C. (2006). Observers' decision moment in deception detection experiments: Its impact on judgment, accuracy, and confidence. *International Journal of Psychology, 41*(4), 304–319. doi:10.1080/00207590500343612

Maznevski, M. L., & Chudoba, K. M. (2000). Bridging space over time: Global virtual team dynamics and effectiveness. *Organization Science, 11*(5), 473–492. doi:10.1287/orsc.11.5.473.15200

McCornack, S. A. (1997). The generation of deceptive messages: Laying the groundwork for a viable theory of interpersonal deception. In Greene, J. O. (Ed.), *Message Production: Advances of communication theory* (pp. 91–126). Mahwah, NJ: Erlbaum.

McCornack, S. A., & Parks, M. R. (1986). Deception detection and relational development: the other side of trust. In McLaughlin, M. L. (Ed.), *Communication yearbook, 9* (pp. 377–389). Beverly Hills, CA: Sage.

McKnight, D. H., Cummings, L. L., & Chervany, N. L. (1998). Initial trust formation in new organizational relationships. *Academy of Management Review, 23*(3), 473–490. doi:10.2307/259290

Miller, G. R., Mongeau, P. A., & Sleight, C. (1984, June). *Fudging with friends and lying to lovers: Deceptive communication in interpersonal relationships*. Paper presented at the Second International Conference on Personal Relationships, Madison, WI.

Miller, G. R., Mongeau, P. A., & Sleight, C. (1986). Fudging with friends and lying to lovers: Deceptive communication in personal relationships. *Journal of Social and Personal Relationships, 3*, 495–512. doi:10.1177/0265407586034006

Miller, G. R., & Stiff, J. B. (1993). *Deceptive communication*. Newbury Park, CA: Sage.

Miranda, S. M., & Carter, P. E. (2005). Innovation diffusion and e-collaboration: The effects of social proximity on social information processing. *International Journal of e-Collaboration, 1*(3), 35–57.

Ngwenyama, O. K., & Allen, L. (1997). Communication richness in electronic mail: Critical social theory and the contextuality of meaning. *Management Information Systems Quarterly, 21*(2), 145–167. doi:10.2307/249417

Nunnally, J. C. (1978). *Psychometric Theory* (2nd ed.). New York: McGraw-Hill.

Pavlou, P. A., & Fygenson, M. (2006). Understanding and predicting electronic commerce adoption: An extension of the theory of planned behavior. *Management Information Systems Quarterly, 30*(1), 115–143.

Pena, J., Walther, J. B., & Hancock, J. T. (2007). Effects of Geographic Distribution on Dominance Perceptions in Computer-Mediated Groups. *Communication Research, 34*, 313–331. doi:10.1177/0093650207300431

Polimeni, A. M., Hardie, E., & Buzwell, S. (2002). Friendship closeness inventory: Development and psychometric evaluation. *Psychological Reports, 91*(1), 142–152. doi:10.2466/PR0.91.5.142-152

Rice, R. (1984). *The new media: Communication, research, and technology*. Beverly Hills, CA: Sage.

Shih, D. H., Chiang, H. S., & Yen, C. D. (2005). Classification methods in the detection of new malicious emails. *Information Sciences, 172*(1-2), 241–261. doi:10.1016/j.ins.2004.06.003

Stiff, J. B., Kim, H. J., & Ramesh, C. (1992). Truth biases and aroused suspicion in relational communication. *Communication Research, 19*, 326–345. doi:10.1177/009365092019003002

Stiff, J. B., & Miller, G. R. (1986). "Come to think of it...'"" Interactive probes, deceptive communication, and deception detection. *Human Communication Research, 12*, 339–357. doi:10.1111/j.1468-2958.1986.tb00081.x

Stiff, J. B., Miller, G. R., Sleight, C., Mongeau, P. A., Garlick, R., & Rogan, R. (1989). Explanations for visual cue primacy in judgments of honesty and deceit. *Journal of Personality and Social Psychology, 56*, 555–564. doi:10.1037/0022-3514.56.4.555

Storms, M. D. (1973). Videotape and the attribution process: Reversing actors' and observers' points of view. *Journal of Personality and Social Psychology, 27*, 165–175. doi:10.1037/h0034782

Walters, S. B. (2000). *The truth about lying: How to spot a lie and protect yourself from deception*. Naperville, IL: Sourcebooks Inc.

Whitty, M. T. (2002). Liar, liar! An examination of how open, supportive and honest people are in chat rooms. *Computers in Human Behavior, 18*, 343–352. doi:10.1016/S0747-5632(01)00059-0

Williams, E. (1977). Experimental comparisons of face-to-face and mediated communication. *Psychological Bulletin, 84*(5), 963–976. doi:10.1037/0033-2909.84.5.963

Yoo, Y., & Alavi, M. (2001). Media and Group Cohesion: Relative Influences on Social Pretense. *Management Information Systems Quarterly, 25*(3), 371–390. doi:10.2307/3250922

Zajonc, R. B. (1965). Social facilitation. *Science, 149*, 269–274. doi:10.1126/science.149.3681.269

Zhou, L., Burgoon, J. K., Nunamaker, J. F., & Twitchell, D. (2004). Automated linguistics based cues for detecting deception in text-based asynchronous computer-mediated communication: An empirical investigation. *Group Decision and Negotiation, 13*(1), 81–106. doi:10.1023/B:GRUP.0000011944.62889.6f

Zhou, L., Burgoon, J. K., Twitchell, D. P., Qin, T., & Nunamaker, J. F. (2004). A comparison of classification methods for predicting deception in computer-mediated communication. *Journal of Management Information Systems, 20*(4), 139–166.

Zhou, L., Shi, Y., & Zang, D. (2008). A statistical language modeling approach to online deception detection. *IEEE Transactions on Knowledge and Data Engineering, 20*(8), 1077–1081. doi:10.1109/TKDE.2007.190624

Zhou, L., Yongmei, S., & Dongsong, Z. (2008). A statistical language modeling approach to online deception detection. *IEEE Transactions on Knowledge and Data Engineering, 20*(8), 1077–1081. doi:10.1109/TKDE.2007.190624

Zuckerman, M., DePaulo, B. M., & Rosenthal, R. (1981). Verbal and nonverbal communication of deception. In Berkowitz, L. (Ed.), *Advances in experimental social psychology* (*Vol. 14*, pp. 1–59). New York: Academic Press.

Zuckerman, M., & Driver, R. (1985). Telling lies: Verbal and nonverbal correlates of deception. In Siegman, A. W., & Feldstien, S. (Eds.), *Nonverbal communication: An integrated perspective* (pp. 129–147). Hillsdale, NJ: Lawrence Erlbaum.

APPENDIX

Relational Closeness Scale (RC)

1. X does *not* influence everyday things in my life. *†
2. X affects my romantic relationships.*
3. X influences my plans to join a club, social organization, church, etc.*
4. X affects my school related plans.
5. X influences my plans for achieving a particular standard of living.*
6. X does *not* influence how I choose to spend my money. †
7. X influences the way I feel about myself.
8. X does *not* influence the opinions that I have of other important people in my life. †
9. X does *not* influence when I see, and the amount of time I spend with, my family. †
10. X influences when I see, and the amount of time I spend with, my friends.*
11. X does *not* influence which of my friends I see. †
12. X influences how I spend my free time.*
13. X influences when I see X and the amount of time the two of us spend together.
14. X influences what I watch on TV.

Communication Media (CM)

1. When we disagreed, the communication conditions made it more difficult for us to come to an agreement.
2. The conditions under which we communicated helped us to better understand each other.* †
3. The conditions under which we communicated slowed down our communications.*
4. When we disagreed, our communication environment helped us come to a common position. †
5. I could easily explain things in this environment.* †
6. The communication conditions helped us exchange communications quickly.* †
7. There were ideas I couldn't relate to the other party because of the communication conditions.*
8. The conditions under which we communicated got in the way of our sharing of opinions.*

Truth Bias (TB)

1. I believe what my partner says with little doubt.
2. I think my partner is generally honest.
3. Overall, my partner was truthful.
4. Overall, my partner was very deceptive. †

Chapter 19
Advertised Waist–to–Hip Ratios of Online Female Escorts:
An Evolutionary Perspective

Gad Saad
Concordia University, Canada

ABSTRACT

The Web's global reach provides evolutionary behavioral scientists unique opportunities to investigate human universals steeped in a common and evolved human nature. In the current article, it is argued that many forms of online sexual communication are indicative of our evolved mating minds, including the manner by which female escorts are "advertised" online. It is demonstrated that online advertisers provide a restricted set of morphological cues whilst advertising female escorts, these being congruent with men's evolved aesthetic preferences. Specifically, it is shown that irrespective of cultural setting, online escorts advertise waist-to-hip ratios (WHR) that are in line with the near-universal male preference for women that possess WHRs of 0.70.

INTRODUCTION

The Internet's ubiquitous and global reach provides scholars with countless new opportunities to study evolutionary-based human universals. Perhaps the most obvious of these is the study of human sexuality in the online setting. The importance of sex within the Web manifests itself in a myriad of ways. Cooper (2004) reported that the most searched subject matter on the Internet was sex, and added that online dating constituted

the most profitable instantiation of paid content on the Internet. Cronin and Davenport (2001) discussed the importance of pornography within the greater phenomenon of e-commerce. They stated (p. 41), "Certainly, it is universally acknowledged by information technology experts that the adult entertainment industry has been at the leading edge in terms of building high-performance Web sites with state-of-the-art features and functionality." Stern and Handel (2001) raised the same point in their historical analysis of sexual content in various forms of mass media. Spink, Jansen, Wolfram, and Saracevic (2002) used *Excite* query data from 1997, 1999, and 2001 to determine the general topics that were most often searched on the Internet. "Sex and pornography" was ranked in the top five categories in each of the latter three data sets. Using an *Excite* query data set from 1999, Spink, Ozmutlu, and Lorence (2004) found that 15.9% of all queries were sex-related. Li (2000) divulged that online revenues originating from adult websites for the years 1998 to 2001 represented more than two-thirds of the aggregate online revenues. In light of all of these disparate facts, it is not surprising that Peter and Valkenburg (2006, p. 178) concluded, "More than any other medium, the Internet is a sexual medium."

Of relevance to the current article are forms of online sexual communication that are demonstrative of the Darwinian forces that shape human sexuality. Loosely speaking, online sexual communication can take place either between groups of Internet users (e.g., via online personal ads, in chat rooms, or at www.myspace.com) or between companies and prospective online customers (e.g., spam, Internet pornographic sites, or online escort services). In the current article, I explore a ubiquitous instantiation of online business-to-consumer communication, namely, the manner by which online advertisers and related professional communicators (e.g., pornographers) advertise female escorts. Not surprisingly from an evolutionary perspective, men constitute the majority of consumers that are targeted by such ads. More generally, there exists a strong male effect across a wide range of online sexual activities. Using longitudinal data from the General Social Survey, Buzzell (2005) found that irrespective of the technology (movie theaters in 1973, movie theaters or VCRs in 1994, and Internet in 2000), men outnumbered women by significant amounts as the consumers of pornography. In the online setting, men were more than six times as likely

to have visited a pornographic Web site. Cooper, Delmonico, and Burg (2000) found that men constituted the overwhelming proportion of sexually compulsive (88%) and cybersex individuals (79%). Additionally, they propose that men are more likely to use visual images in their online sexual pursuits while women make greater use of chat rooms in their attempt to form and develop relationships. Cooper, Delmonico, Griffin-Shelley, and Mathy (2004) replicated the general pattern of findings, albeit they proposed that differential socialization of the two sexes is the explanatory mechanism (i.e., innate biological forces that shape sex-specific sexual phenomena were not recognized). Using a college sample, Goodson, McCormick, and Evans (2001) concluded that men are more likely to search for sexual images on the Internet while Philaretou, Mahfouz, and Allen (2005) recognized that men constitute the substantial majority of Internet sex users. Finally, Vartti (2001) investigated various types of German matchmaking Web sites and concluded that women constituted well over 99% of the "advertised" individuals. In other words, it is seldom the case that women are seeking men via these online mediums. This universal and robust male effect is demonstrative of evolutionary-based sex differences in human sexuality.

In the remainder of the article, I report the results of a content analytic study that was conducted to explore the manner by which female escorts are "advertised" online. I demonstrate that male customers seek universal cues of beauty whilst foraging online for prospective escorts (see DiClemente & Hantula, 2003; Rajala & Hantula, 2000; and Smith & Hantula, 2003, for evolutionary approaches to online foraging albeit in non-pornographic contexts). Prior to doing so, I provide a brief discussion of three theoretical ideas relevant to the content analysis namely media richness/media naturalness, ecological rationality, and the Savanna Principle.

MEDIA RICHNESS / NATURALNESS, ECOLOGICAL RATIONALITY, AND THE SAVANNA PRINCIPLE

The notion of media richness is pivotal to many computer-mediated communication (CMC) research streams. One of the central tenets of media richness theory is that various media can be mapped onto a "rich to poor" continuum as a function of the amount of information and the meaning that they transmit. For example, face-to-face interactions are generally richer than phone conversations as they contain greater amount of information (e.g., nonverbal cues). Of relevance to the current context, Cronin and Davenport (2001, see Figure 1, p. 40) mapped various pornographic services along a two-dimensional space of interactivity versus media richness. When it comes to online pornography, I propose that the two sexes experience the "richness" of the medium differentially because of their sex-specific evolved sensorial preferences. That said studies that have explored sex differences in the media richness literature have been typically void of Darwinian-based theorizing. For instance, Dennis, Kinney, and Hung (1999) found that women's performance (but not men's) improved with richer media. Guadagno and Cialdini (2007) investigated sex differences in the extent to which online persuasion (via e-mail) was effective. Sussman and Tyson (2000) explored sex differences in cybertalk including the length of an entry and how opinionated the entry was. Finally, Hess, Fuller, and Mathew (2003) studied sex differences in user involvement with a computerized interface. While all of the latter studies are valuable, they do not provide an ultimate account as to why and when sex differences should manifest themselves in CMC settings.

Ned Kock is one of the few scholars to have incorporated Darwinian notions within the media richness literature. For example, Kock (2001, 2005a) relied on Darwinian principles in arguing that when interacting in lean mediums, individuals oftentimes adapt their behaviors by compensating for the poorer environments (e.g., they rise to the occasion by engaging in greater effort). This compensatory adaptation (a term used by Kock) explains why poorer mediums might, at times, yield superior performance. See also Spink and Cole (2006) for a recent attempt to "Darwinize" human information behavior (e.g., in the library sciences). I take a somewhat different perspective in the current work, namely, I propose that the Internet is perceived as a rich medium by men when seeking short-term mates as it provides the necessary cues when judging the attractiveness of prospective mates (especially for short-term mating). In other words, in the current context the Internet's media naturalness (see Kock, 2005b) makes it particularly enticing as a sexual medium for men, an empirical fact that has been repeatedly found as mentioned earlier (see Costa, Braun, & Birbaumer, 2003 for sex differences in physiological responses when viewing nude images). Hence, men need not engage in compensatory adaptation when foraging online for prospective mates, as the informational structure of this medium is "natural" to them in this particular domain-specific pursuit.

Gigerenzer, Todd, and the ABC Research Group (1999) have proposed that human decision-making adheres to ecological rationality, an evolutionarily grounded definition of rationality. Specifically, they posit that the human mind has evolved domain-specific fast and frugal heuristics that, in most instances, yield accurate results whilst requiring a "bearable" level of cognitive effort (i.e., no explicit tradeoff is assumed between the cognitive costs and associated benefits/accuracy of particular decisional strategies). How is ecological rationality relevant to the current online context? Within the mating domain, individuals have evolved fast and frugal heuristics for gauging the physical attractiveness of prospective suitors (cf. Maner, et al., 2003; Olson & Marshuetz, 2005). In the online context, men are faced with a computationally difficult problem, namely, to identify a desirable short-term mate amongst a very large set of available options. Given the intractable nature of the task at hand (i.e., choosing an escort amongst hundreds, if not thousands, of available prospects) and, in light of the male-based penchant to engage in rapid visual evaluations of key physical attributes, it is, perhaps, not surprising that the main attributes advertised by female escorts adhere to men's evolved visual aesthetic preferences.

Kanazawa (2004) proposed the Savanna Principle as means for determining the veracity of a proposed theory. Specifically, he argued that a theory that is incongruent with the phylogenetic history and evolutionarily relevant ancestral realities of *Homo sapiens* would eventually be falsified. A concrete example might clarify the epistemological value of the Savanna Principle. The sex makeup of a dyad within the Ultimatum Game yields differential results as a function of the experimental setup in which the game is played (Saad, 2007, chapter 7). Specifically, sex differences in the Ultimatum Game are profoundly altered as a function of whether the game is played face-to-face (experimental setup that is congruent with the Savanna Principle) or via the use of computers wherein the players are anonymous to one another (experimental setup that is incongruent with the Savanna Principle). Humans have evolved in small bands wherein daily repeat interactions were the norm. As such, individuals have evolved both emotional and social intelligence as a means of managing their reputations. Clearly, a behavioral economic game that is played face-to-face mimics the evolutionarily-relevant environment that we have evolved in whilst the anonymity afforded by computer-based interactions does not. In a sense, the Savanna Principle is congruent with media naturalness in that it recognizes that novel technological settings vary in terms of their congruence with evolved sensorial preferences. To the extent that the Internet is a visual medium, and given that men's foraging behaviors when seeking short-term mates are largely driven by attributes that are visually gauged (e.g., physical attributes, and not personality), the Savanna Principle would propose that the Internet provides a "natural" medium for this particular pursuit.

In the next section, the near-universal male preference for women possessing a waist-to-hip ratio (WHR) of 0.70 is briefly discussed. This is followed by the results of a content analysis wherein it is shown that where as little information is provided when advertising the profiles of online female escorts, their WHRs are almost always listed with these being congruent with the latter near-universal preference of 0.70.

EVOLUTIONARY-BASED MATING PREFERENCES

Evolutionary psychologists have amassed substantial evidence that numerous mating preferences are universal because they correspond to adaptive solutions to mating problems of evolutionary import (for reviews, see Buss, 1994; Gangestad & Scheyd, 2005; Sugiyama, 2005; Symons, 1979). For example, facial symmetry, skin condition, height (in men), and WHR are some of the key morphological traits used in evaluating prospective suitors. As mentioned earlier, I wish to demonstrate that online escort services use the near-universal male preference WHR of 0.70 when "advertising" their female escorts. I restrict my analysis to female escorts, as these constitute the overwhelming majority of escorts "advertised" on the Internet (recall Vartti, 2001). The evolutionary psychologist Devendra Singh has been at the forefront of the WHR literature. He has firmly established the evolutionary reasons that drive men to hold a near-universal preference for women possessing a WHR of 0.70 (the preference typically varies between 0.68 to 0.72), these being linked to cues of health and fertility (see Singh, 1993, 2002a, 2002b). Not surprisingly, cultural products (e.g., statues, fashion shows, advertisements) that are meant to serve as realistic representations of the ideal female form adhere to this near-universal 0.70 WHR preference (see Saad, 2004 for a discussion of WHR in the advertising context, and Singh, Frohlich, & Haywood, 1999 for a WHR analysis of sculptures). Note that the near-universal preference of 0.70 recognizes the fact that the preference can be adjusted as a function of idiosyncratic ecological niches. For example, in environments that might be defined by greater caloric scarcity and/or caloric uncertainty, males might prefer slightly higher female WHRs (cf. Sugiyama, 2004; Westman & Marlowe, 1999; see also several chapters in Swami & Furnham, in press, for a discussion of the universality versus cultural specificity of the WHR, as well as discussions of the differential importance of WHR versus a woman's body mass index in judgments of attractiveness).

CONTENT ANALYSIS: WHRS OF ONLINE FEMALE ESCORTS

A research assistant surfed the Internet and identified Web sites/portals from around the world wherein female escorts were being advertised (note that the sampling procedure used varied across the Web sites[1]. The overriding sampling objective was to obtain a manageable data set from a heterogeneous set of countries). Subsequently, the research assistant transcribed various advertised metrics including waist, hip, and bust

sizes, height, weight, and age. Data was obtained from Europe (25 countries; n = 491), Asia (13 countries; n = 160), Latin America (6 countries; n = 100), North America (Canada and the United States; n = 214), and Oceania (Australia and New Zealand; n = 103). Hence, in total, the sample size was 1,068 (including a very few transsexuals) and covered 48 countries from around the world. The mean WHRs were 0.70, 0.75, 0.71, 0.76, and 0.69 for Europe, Oceania, Asia, North America, and Latin America, respectively. The global mean (i.e., across all 48 countries) was 0.72, which is slightly higher but, nonetheless, very close to the near-universal preference of 0.70. Given that the data is comprised of WHRs, the standard assumption of normality is tenuous and, hence, required explicit testing. A visual inspection of the data (via histograms) along with an investigation of the skewness and kurtosis measures did confirm that the data was right-skewed and hence required a transformation. Typical transformations for right-skewed data include $1/x$, $\sqrt{x}$, and $\log(x)$, all of which were attempted in the current analysis. One-sample t-tests were conducted, using both the original data as well as the transformed data, on each of the five regions as well as on the total sample, using 0.70 as the test mean. The pattern of findings for the transformed data was almost identical to that of the untransformed data[2]. As such, the findings of the untransformed data are solely reported for expository clarity (see Table 1).

Table 1. Summary of Findings

Region	n	Mean WHR	s.d.	p-value	95% Confidence Interval
Europe	491	.703	.080	> 0.10	.696, .710
Asia	160	.712	.065	< 0.02	.702, .722
Oceania	103	.750	.094	0.00	.731, .768
Lat. America	100	.691	.067	> 0.10	.678, .705
Nor. America	214	.763	.100	0.00	.749, .776
TOTAL	1,068	.720	.086	0.00	.714, .725

The mean WHRs for Europe and Latin America were equal to 0.70 with the remaining four means being statistically different from the test mean. The latter one-sample t-tests are perhaps too stringent given that evolutionary psychologists recognize the near-universal and, hence, malleable nature of the WHR preference (e.g., it typically varies between 0.68 to 0.72). In other words, it is undoubtedly too conservative to expect that the sample WHRs will adhere to an exact value (i.e., 0.70) rather than falling within 0.68 to 0.72. With that in mind, Table 1 reports the 95% confidence interval for each of the six WHR means. The mean for the total sample as well as those of three of the sampled regions, namely, Europe, Asia, and Latin America, overlapped with the prescribed range. On the other hand, the mean WHRs for North America and Oceania fell outside the expected WHR range.

DISCUSSION

Much of the academic research that has explored pornography has done so with a near-complete paucity of Darwinian-based theorizing (but, see Malamuth, 1996; Pound, 2002; Saad, 2007, chapter 6; Shepher & Reisman, 1985; and Symons, 1979, for evolutionary approaches). Within the growing research streams investigating online pornography and/or online sexuality, evolutionary-based work is equally rare. For example, Fisher and Barak (2001) discussed Internet pornography from a social psychological perspective without ever recognizing that Darwinian forces shape the consumption of online pornography. In the current article, I have argued that one form of online sexual communication, namely, the manner by which pornographers advertise online female escorts, cannot be fully explained without the explicit recognition of the Darwinian mating forces that shape the male mind. Specifically,

the advertised WHRs of online female escorts (spanning 48 countries in the content analysis) adhere to men's near-universal evolved sensorial preference of a WHR of 0.70. As discussed earlier, commercial sexual content has driven a substantial share of online revenues since the advent of the Internet. Hence, the individuals mandated to create online advertisements within the sex industry constitute some of the most powerful professional communicators to be found on the Internet. Not surprisingly, online pornographers are fully aware of the advertising copy that is required to yield maximally efficacious results in reaching their largely male target market.

One of the longest standing, and yet unresolved, debates in international advertising has been to determine which of two approaches, namely, standardization or adaptation, is optimal within a given context (see Agrawal, 1995; Ryans, Griffith, & White, 2003; Theodosiou & Leonidou, 2003, for reviews). In other words, should an advertising campaign be universally the same in its execution or should it be tailored to idiosyncratic cultural settings? Saad (2007, chapter 4) has argued that evolutionary psychology can inform the latter debate given its ability to catalogue human universals versus culture-specific phenomena. In the current context, where as many aspects of Web design are shaped by cultural settings (cf. Singh, Fassott, Zhao, & Boughton, 2006), I have argued here that the online advertising of sexuality contains universal elements that transcend cultures (but see Moss, Gunn, & Heller, 2006, for an exploration of sex differences in the preferences for specific Web design albeit from a non-evolutionary perspective). Hence, whereas online professional communicators navigating within an international sphere need to address a myriad of culture-specific issues in designing efficacious Web sites, these concerns are of lesser importance when selling sexuality, as shown in the current article.

ACKNOWLEDGMENT

Many thanks to Assaad Bassil for having collected and transcribed the data on online escorts, to Drs. Ali Hadi, Mikhail Bernshteyn, Mark Tomiuk, and Yoshio Takane for having suggested various data transformations, and to my graduate student, Eric Stenstrom, for having conducted many of the statistical analyses. Finally, I am grateful to Dr. Ned Kock for his editorial guidance.

REFERENCES

Agrawal, M. (1995). Review of a 40-year debate in international advertising: Practitioner and academician perspectives to the standardization/ adaptation issue. *International Marketing Review*, 12(1), 26-48.

Buss, D. M. (1994). *The evolution of desire: Strategies of human mating*. New York: BasicBooks.

Buzzell, T. (2005). Demographic characteristics of persons using pornography in three technological contexts. *Sexuality & Culture*, 9(1), 28-48.

Cooper, A. (2004). Online sexual activity in the new millennium. *Contemporary Sexuality*, 38(3), i-vii.

Cooper, A., Delmonico, D. L. & Burg, R. (2000). Cybersex users, abusers, and compulsives: New findings and implications. *Sexual Addiction & Compulsivity*, 7(1/2), 5-29.

Cooper, A., Delmonico, D. L., Griffin-Shelley, E. & Mathy, R. M. (2004). Online sexual activity: An examination of potentially problematic behaviors. *Sexual Addiction & Compulsivity*, 11(3), 129-143.

Costa, M., Braun, C. & Birbaumer, N. (2003). Gender differences in response to pictures of nudes: A magnetoencephalographic study. *Biological Psychology*, 63(2), 129-147.

Cronin, B. & Davenport, E. (2001). E-rogenous zones: Positioning pornography in the digital economy. *The Information Society*, 17(1), 33-48.

Dennis, A. R., Kinney, S. T. & Hung, Y. T. C. (1999). Gender differences in the effects of media richness. *Small Group Research*, 30(4), 405-437.

DiClemente, D. F. & Hantula, D. A. (2003). Optimal foraging online: Increasing sensitivity to delay. *Psychology & Marketing*, 20(9), 785-809.

Fisher, W. A. & Barak, A. (2001). Internet pornography: A social psychological perspective on Internet sexuality. *Journal of Sex Research*, 38(4), 312-323.

Gangestad, S. W. & Scheyd, G. J. (2005). The evolution of human physical attractiveness. *Annual Review of Anthropology*, 34, 523-548.

Gigerenzer, G., Todd, P. M. & the ABC Research Group (1999). *Simple heuristics that make us smart*. New York: Oxford University Press.

Goodson, P., McCormick, D. & Evans, A. (2001). Searching for sexually explicit materials on the Internet: an exploratory study of college students' behavior and attitudes. *Archives of Sexual Behavior*, 30(2), 101-118.

Guadagno, R. E. & Cialdini, R. B. (2007). Persuade him by e-mail, but see her in person: Online persuasion revisited. *Computers in Human Behavior*, 23(2), 999-1015.

Hess, T. J., Fuller, M. A. & Mathew, J. (2003). Gender and personality in media rich interfaces: Do birds of a feather flock together? P. Zhang, F. Nah, J. Lazar & S. McCoy (Eds.), *Proceedings of the second pre-ICIS annual workshop on HCI research in MIS* (pp. 22-26). Atlanta, GA: Association for Information Systems.

Kanazawa, S. (2004). The Savanna Principle. *Managerial and Decision Economics*, 25(1), 41-54.

Kock, N. (2001). Compensatory adaptation to a lean medium: An action research investigation of electronic communication in process improvement groups. *IEEE Transactions on Professional Communication*, 44(4), 267-285.

Kock, N. (2005a). Compensatory adaptation to media obstacles: An experimental study of process redesign dyads. *Information Resources Management Journal*, 18(2), 41-67.

Kock, N. (2005b). Media richness or media naturalness? The evolution of our biological communication apparatus and its influence on our behavior toward E-communication tools. *IEEE Transactions on Professional Communication*, 48(2), 117-130.

Li, K. (2000). Porn goes public. *Industry Standard*, 3 (45), 94.

Malamuth, N. M. (1996). Sexually explicit media, gender differences, and evolutionary theory. *Journal of Communication*, 46(3), 8-31.

Maner, J. K., Kenrick, D. T., Becker, D. V., Delton, A. W., Hofer, B., Wilbur, C. J. & Neuberg, S. L. (2003). Sexually selective cognition: Beauty captures the mind of the beholder. *Journal of Personality and Social Psychology*, 85(6), 1107-1120.

Moss, G., Gunn, R. & Heller, J. (2006). Some men like it black, some women like it pink: Consumer implications of differences in male and female website design. *Journal of Consumer Behaviour*, 5(4), 328-341.

Olson, I. R. & Marshuetz, C. (2005). Facial attractiveness is appraised in a glance. *Emotion*, 5(4), 498-502.

Peter, J. & Valkenburg, P. M. (2006). Adolescents' exposure to sexually explicit material on the Internet. *Communication Research*, 33(2), 178-204.

Philaretou, A. G., Mahfouz, A. Y. & Allen, K. R. (2005). Use of Internet pornography and men's well-being. *International Journal of Men's Health*, 4(2), 149-169.

Pound, N. (2002). Male interest in visual cues of sperm competition risk. *Evolution and Human Behavior*, 23(6), 443-466.

Rajala, A. K. & Hantula, D. A. (2000). Towards a behavioral ecology of consumption: Delay-reduction effects on foraging in a simulated Internet mall. *Managerial and Decision Economics*, 21(3-4), 145-158.

Ryans, Jr., J. K., Griffith, D. A. & White, D. S. (2003). Standardization/adaptation of international marketing strategy: Necessary conditions for the advancement of knowledge. *International Marketing Review*, 20(6), 588-603.

Saad, G. (2004). Applying Evolutionary Psychology in Understanding the Representation of Women in Advertisements. *Psychology & Marketing*, 21(8), 593-612.

Saad, G. (2007). *The evolutionary bases of consumption*. Mahwah, NJ: Lawrence Erlbaum.

Shepher, J. & Reisman, J. (1985). Pornography: A sociobiological attempt at understanding. *Ethology and Sociobiology*, 6(2), 103-114.

Singh, D. (1993). Adaptive significance of female physical attractiveness: Role of waist-to-hip ratio. *Journal of Personality and Social Psychology*, 65(2), 293-307

Singh, D. (2002a). Female mate value at a glance: Relationship of waist-to-hip ratio to health, fecundity and attractiveness. *Neuroendocrinology Letters*, 23(suppl. 4), 81-91.

Singh, D. (2002b). Waist-to-hip ratio: An indicator of female mate value. K. Aoki & T. Akazawa (Eds.), *Proceedings of human mate choice and prehistoric marital networks international symposium* (Vol. 16, pp. 79-99). Kyoto, Japan: International Research Center for Japanese Studies.

Singh, D., Frohlich, T. & Haywood, M. (1999). *Waist-to-hip ratio representation in ardent sculptures from four cultures*. Paper presented at the meeting of the Human Behavior and Evolution Society, Salt Lake City, Utah, 2-6 June 1999.

Singh, N., Fassott, G., Zhao, H. & Boughton, P. D. (2006). A cross-cultural analysis of German, Chinese and Indian consumers' perception of web site adaptation. *Journal of Consumer Behaviour*, 5(1), 56-68.

Smith, C. L. & Hantula, D. A. (2003). Pricing effects on foraging in a simulated Internet shopping mall. *Journal of Economic Psychology*, 24(5), 653-674.

Spink, A. & Cole, C. (2006). Human information behavior: Integrating diverse approaches and information use. *Journal of the American Society for Information Science and Technology*, 57(1), 25-35.

Spink, A., Jansen, B. J., Wolfram, D. & Saracevic, T. (2002). From E-sex to E-commerce: Web search changes. *Computer*, 35(3), 107-109.

Spink, A., Ozmutlu, H. C. & Lorence, D. P. (2004). Web searching for sexual information: An exploratory study. *Information Processing & Management*, 40(1), 113-123.

Stern, S. E. & Handel, A. D. (2001). Sexuality and mass media: The historical context of psychology's reaction to sexuality on the Internet. *Journal of Sex Research*, 38(4), 283-291.

Sussman, N. M. & Tyson, D. H. (2000). Sex and power: Gender differences in computer-mediated interactions. *Computers in Human Behavior*, 16(4), 381-394.

Sugiyama, L. S. (2004). Is beauty in the context-sensitive adaptations of the beholder? Shiwiar use of waist-to-hip ratio in assessments of female mate value. *Evolution and Human Behavior*, 25(1), 51-62.

Sugiyama, L. S. (2005). Physical attractiveness in adaptationist perspective. D. M. Buss (Ed.), *The handbook of evolutionary psychology* (pp. 292-343). New York: John Wiley.

Swami, V. & Furnham, A. (Eds.) (in press). *The body beautiful: Evolutionary and sociocultural perspectives*. Basingstoke, UK: Palgrave Macmillan.

Symons, D. (1979). *The evolution of human sexuality*. New York: Oxford University Press.

Theodosiou, M. & Leonidou, L. C. (2003). Standardization versus adaptation of international marketing strategy: An integrative assessment of the empirical research. *International Business Review*, 12(2), 141-171.

Vartti, R. (2001). German matchmaking websites: Online trafficking in women? *Sexuality & Culture*, 5(3), 49-76.

Westman, A. & Marlowe, F. (1999). How universal are preferences for female waist-to-hip ratios? Evidence from the Hadza of Tanzania. *Evolution and Human Behavior*, 20(4), 219-228.

ENDNOTES

[1] The Web site portal www.escorttown.com was used for Europe, Asia, Oceania, and North America, with specific country and region links chosen from within. For Latin America, the following sites/portals were used: http://www.openadultdirectory.com/, http://www.tangoescorts.com, http://www.vicesisters.com, http://www.sexoplexo.com, http://www.pimp.com.br, http://www.dreamsmaster.tk/, http://www.vipmodelscr.com, http://www.exoticretreat.net, www.cancunfemaleescorts.com and http://www.chicasindependientes.com/. Additional portals used for Oceania (Australia) include www.openadultdirectory.com, www.

mensguide.com.au, and the Web sites www.femaleescorts.com.au, www.ntynikki.com, www.taraportman.com.

2   The inverse transformation yielded two different findings from those obtained for the untransformed data namely the mean WHR for AsiaInv became equal to 0.70 while that for LatinInv was no longer equal to 0.70. There was only one change between the results of the log transformation and the untransformed findings namely the mean WHR for AsiaLog was equal to 0.70 (p = 0.056). Finally, the pattern of findings for the square transformation did not yield any results that were different from those of the untransformed data.

This work was previously published in the International Journal of e-Collaboration, Vol. 4, Issue 3, edited by N. Kock, pp. 40-50, copyright 2008 by IGI Publishing (an imprint of IGI Global).

Chapter 20
When Technology Does Not Support Learning:
Conflicts Between Epistemological Beliefs and Technology Support in Virtual Learning Environments

Steven Hornik
University of Central Florida, USA

Richard D. Johnson
University of South Florida, USA

Yu Wu
University of Central Florida, USA

ABSTRACT

Central to the design of successful virtual learning initiatives is the matching of technology to the needs of the training environment. The difficulty is that while the technology may be designed to complement and support the learning process, not all users of these systems find the technology supportive. Instead, some users' conceptions of learning, or epistemological beliefs may be in conflict with their perceptions of what the technology supports. Using data from 307 individuals, this research study investigated the process and outcome losses that occur when friction exists between individuals' epistemological beliefs and their perceptions of how the technology supports learning. Specifically, the results indicated that when there was friction between the technology support of learning and an individual's epistemological beliefs, course communication, course satisfaction, and course performance were reduced. Implications for design of virtual learning environments and future research are discussed.

INTRODUCTION

Advances in information technology have enabled organizations and educational institutions to deliver training and learning initiatives free from time and/or place constraints, creating virtual learning environments (VLEs).[1] These environments are becoming central to the design and development of both corporate training programs and university curricula. While there are multiple ways to design these environments, common characteristics of virtual learning environments include the mediation of course interactions and materials through information and communication technologies (Alavi & Leidner, 2001) and greater control over the learning environment (Piccoli, Ahmad, & Ives, 2001).

The market for this type of training is substantial, with recent estimates suggesting that the industry will generate nearly $25 billion by 2006 (IDC, 2003) and grow annually at approximately 37% (Mayor, 2001). Universities are also undertaking distance initiatives, with estimates suggesting that nearly 90% of public universities offer distance education courses, over three million students participate in these courses, and these numbers are projected to grow (Wirt & Livingston, 2004). The major push behind these initiatives has been both convenience and cost. These initiatives have both potential and pitfalls as can be seen through the findings of two recent studies. Although the potential for cost savings is large, with some large companies finding cost savings of between $30-$400 million dollars per year and reductions in training costs of nearly 50% (Salas, DeRouin & Littrell, 2005), another study has suggested that as many as 80% of employees drop out of these programs before they are complete (Flood, 2000).

Thus, it is important to understand the factors that affect the successful implementation of VLE initiatives. Previous research has suggested that instructor characteristics, pedagogical approach or learning models, learner/user characteristics, and the technology each play a key role in creating successful outcomes (Alavi & Leidner, 2001; Piccoli et al., 2001; Webster & Hackley, 1997). Recently it has also been argued that a key to the successful implementation of these environments is the convergence between the technology used in the learning environment and the implemented learning model (cf. Benbunan-Fich, 2002; Leidner & Jarvenpaa, 1995; Robson, 2000).

However, when the technology used to support learning is designed to support a specific learning model, this can often lead to a compulsory learning process that users must follow to reach the course objectives (Vermunt, 1998). For some users, the learning approach supported by the technology can be in direct conflict with their beliefs about how learning should occur (i.e., their epistemological beliefs) (Bakx, Vermetten, & Van der Sanden, 2003; Schommer-Aikins, 2004). Relatively little is known regarding the implications of the conflict between an individual's epistemological beliefs (EBs) and the learning environment supported by the technology, but given the centrality of technology to the learning process in VLEs and the central role of EBs in how individuals approach learning and how they learn (Marton, Dall'Alba, & Beaty, 1993; Marton & Säljö, 1976; Perry, 1968; Vermunt, 1996), the relationship between the two is likely to be important. Thus this research represents the beginning of a systematic examination of the role of EBs in VLEs.

Drawing from research on EB, evidence suggests that when users do not perceive that the technology supports their optimal learning approach (i.e., there is friction between the individual's EBs and the learning approach supported by the technology), there will be both process and outcome losses. If negative expectations regarding the ability of the technology to adequately support a learning environment consistent with the user's EB emerge it can be difficult for the user to accept this novel way of course delivery (Vermunt & Verloop, 1999, 2000). We argue that when users perceive a mismatch between their EBs and the learning model that the technology supports, learning processes and outcomes will be impacted. Thus, the following research question was investigated:

Are learning processes and outcomes negatively affected when there is friction between a user's perceptions of what learning model the technology supports and his or her personal epistemological beliefs?

The remainder of this article is organized as follows. First, the paper briefly introduces the virtual learning environment context. Second the paper discusses EBs and how these beliefs influence individual learning processes and outcomes. Next, the paper further builds the argument that friction between individual EBs and beliefs about the technological support of learning models can affect learning processes and outcomes. Fourth, the research context and methods are then discussed. Finally, the results are presented, along with a discussion of the findings, implications, and directions for future research.

VIRTUAL LEARNING ENVIRONMENTS

While training has traditionally taken place in a face-to-face setting, technology has enabled new forms of learning, unconstrained by time or place. In these virtual learning environments, learning processes, communications, shared social context and learning community are mediated through information technology, creating a novel learning environment for users. Specifically, VLEs are characterized by high levels of learner control, computer mediation of communication, and the flexibility for learners to restructure learning in nontraditional ways (Piccoli et al., 2001). As with traditional environments, researchers have focused on how effective VLEs are at producing effective outcomes such as learning, performance, and affective reactions to the training setting.

Previous research has found that VLEs can be as effective as face-to-face environments in supporting both learning and affective reactions to the learning environment (cf. Hiltz & Wellman, 1997; Piccoli et al., 2001).

In the development of these environments, the design will reflect some pedagogical approach, or learning model (Leidner & Jarvenpaa, 1995). As such, the learning environment will reflect the instructor's beliefs about what the best way to transfer knowledge is and how the technology will be designed to support this pedagogical approach. However, it is important to note that it is not the methods implemented, but rather student *perceptions* of these methods that most strongly affect student learning most directly (Entwistle, 1998 a, b; Entwistle, McCune, & Hounsell, 2002). Although, there are many learning models that an instructor can choose from this study focuses on three that are among the more widely accepted and which have been of interest to information technology researchers – the objectivist model, constructivist model and collaborative model (cf. Alavi, 1994; Alavi, Marakas, & Yoo, 2002; Liedner & Jarvenpaa, 1995). In the objectivist model, learning is seen as a process of transferring objective knowledge of an expert to the novice. To facilitate this transfer, VLEs will typically provide capabilities such as online presentation of syllabi, lectures, lecture notes, and so forth, in a non-interactive format. In constructivist models, learning is seen as a process where individuals discover knowledge through active participation in the learning process. Constructivist learning best occurs as individuals actively pursue new knowledge. The collaborative model extends the constructivist model by suggesting that learning occurs as individuals work together to create a shared understanding based upon the contributions of multiple individuals. Typically, these latter learning models employ interactive capabilities designed into the VLE including asynchronous communication capabilities such as e-mail, discussion, or chat. Whatever underlying pedagogical approach is desired, we argue that it will be most effective when there is a fit between the technology design and the learning model implemented by the instructor.

Research has also begun investigating the processes through which effective VLEs are developed, finding that effective VLEs are not simply created by the technologies used, but instead are enabled through information and communication technologies (ICTs) as students create a shared social context and feel part of a learning community (Rovai, 2002). It has been argued that for this to occur, learners must communicate and perceive the social presence of others, or "the degree of salience of the other person in the interaction and the consequent salience of the interpersonal relationships" (Short, Williams, & Christie, 1976, p. 65). While communication can facilitate the exchange and sharing of information, social presence enables the connections between learners that create course community and improve learning and satisfaction (Tu & McIsaac, 2002; Tu, 2000).

With ICTs mediating VLE processes, it is also important to understand the influence of user's perceptions about whether or not the technology supports the learning environment and if this perception affects their learning processes and outcomes. To do this, we first focus on an individual's beliefs about learning, or their EBs.

Epistemological Beliefs

Beyond the technical and pedagogical considerations that go into the design of effective VLEs, instructors and designers should also consider student perceptions of how learning best occurs. Just as instructors design the environment around a particular learning model, the users of the system will also have specific beliefs about how learning best occurs. Van der Sanden, Terwel and Vosniadou (2000) describe these beliefs as Individual Learning Theories or internalized frameworks of instruction and learning, which influence the approach individuals take when encountering new learning situations. These EBs are beliefs individuals have regarding knowledge and knowing, including their beliefs about what knowledge is and how one acquires knowledge (Schommer-Aikins, 2004; Schommer, 1994). Schommer also states that individual's EBs affect learning outcomes and suggests that these beliefs are a system of independent dimensions with the following anchors: (1) Certainty—knowledge ranges from absolute to tentative; (2) Structure— knowledge is considered to be either organized as distinct bits or as highly interwoven concepts; (3) Source—knowledge is handed down by authority or derived by reason; (4) Control—An individuals cognitive ability is fixed at birth or their ability can be changed; and (5) Speed —knowledge is either acquired quickly or gradually.[2]

Elen and Lowyck (2000) also identify another aspect of EBs, learning conceptions. Learning conceptions are learner perceptions about what is the most effective way of learning. In this study, we chose to focus on an individual's learning conceptions for two reasons. First, learning conceptions have been shown to affect the learning process and outcomes (Entwistle, 1991; Marton et al., 1993; Vermunt, 1996) including the extent to which learners utilize the capabilities of the environment (Elen & Lowyck, 1998). Second, learning conceptions should be thought of as the mirror of the pedagogical approaches implemented by the instructors. Just as instructors have a specific learning pedagogy in mind when implementing the course, so also learners have specific EBs about the best approach to learning.

These EBs are triggered as individuals engage in the learning process (Hofer, 2004) and are thought to affect how individuals approach learning (cf. Marton et al., 1993; Vermunt, 1996), how individuals learn (Entwistle, 1991), how they devise learning plans and strategies, their self-assessment and monitoring of comprehension (Schommer, Crouse, & Rhodes, 1992), their preferred learning situations (Bakx et al.,

2003), and the extent to which they leverage the environment to their advantage (Elen & Lowyck, 1998, 1999).

EBs are argued to be even more important to learning than the learning model chosen by the instructor because these beliefs filter the learning models implemented by the instructor (Bakx et al., 2003). For example, Bakx et al. (2003) examined the relationship between self-perceived competence, EBs and preferred learning situations, finding that an individual's EBs about learning were related to their preferred learning situations. When individuals believed that learning best occurred as part of an interactive, constructive process they were more inclined to prefer situations that encouraged interaction and more active shared learning. Thus, differences in learning outcomes can be attributed to individual differences in beliefs about the process of learning (Marton & Säljö, 1976). One manner in which users' EBs can act as a filter is through the congruence or friction that is created between the users' EBs and the technological support of learning in the VLE.

Technology and Beliefs: Congruence or Friction

Discrepancy theory states that individuals hold a set of expectations about their environment and also perceptions about how well their expectations of the environment are met (Locke & Latham, 1990). In turn these expectations affect how individuals interpret and interact in their environment. When expectations are met, individuals are positively disposed to the environment, and are more satisfied with the environment than when they are not met. The findings of this stream are also consistent with research on expectation-confirmation theory (ECT), which suggests that when individuals expectations about a product or technology are not met (i.e., they are disconfirmed) they are less satisfied and less likely to continue to use the product or technology (Anderson & Sullivan, 1993; Bhattacherjee, 2001; Oliver, 1980).

In VLEs, although the instructor may design the technological support around a particular pedagogical approach (learning model), users will have their own expectations regarding the effectiveness of the chosen learning approach (Vermunt & Verloop, 1999) and how technology can best be leveraged. As suggested by discrepancy theory, when a match exists between an individual's EBs and the technologically supported learning model, the two are considered to be in congruence. When there is a discrepancy between these beliefs and the technologically supported learning model, friction occurs. In turn, perceptions of congruence or friction affect the learner's expectations of how positive or negative their learning outcomes will be. These expectations often become self-fulfilling, especially in novel learning settings (O'Mara, Allen, Long, & Judd, 1996). As such, congruence and friction are expected to have an impact on both course processes such as course communication, and perceptions of social presence, as well as course outcomes such as performance and satisfaction (Figure 1).

Friction can affect both the user's approach to learning within the environment as well as causing an underutilization of the tools available to them (Lowyck & Elen, 1994). This can occur because individuals do not see the value of the technology in the setting for supporting their learning. The technology can be seen as a barrier to learning, something placed between the user and the learning outcomes that obfuscate the necessary conditions for learning to occur (Fiore, Salas, Cuevas, & Bowers, 2003). In other words, for these users, cognitive focus moves away from learning processes and towards use of the technology; making communication and participation in the environment more difficult, as well as decreasing the value the technology brings to the course. The effect of focusing on the technology as opposed to the training material

Figure 1. Epistemological beliefs, technology support and VLE outcomes

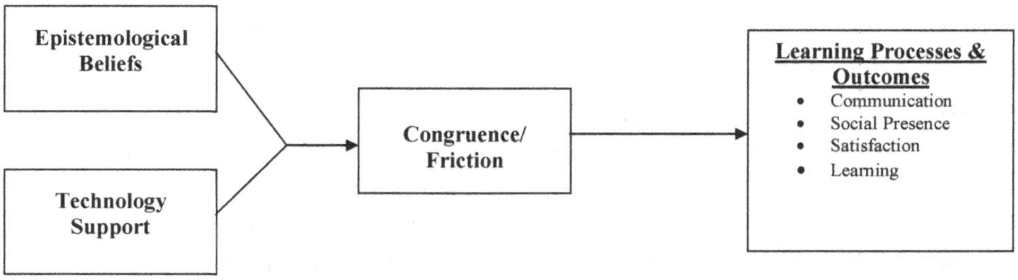

may lead users to disengage from the course, or to not engage it at all. As individuals disengage, they will interact and communicate less. Conversely, those who perceive congruence will perceive the technology as an important tool in support of learning and be more likely to use the technology capabilities, thus communicating and interacting within the VLE.

In the case of friction, as communication is reduced, individuals will find fewer opportunities to ease isolation and develop perceptions of social presence (Burke & Chidambaram, 1999; Gunawardena, 1995; Walther, 1995). Conversely, those whose EBs are congruent with the technology supporting the learning process, will have greater opportunities to create connections using the technology and therefore, be more likely to feel the connections of the other learners in the environment and feel like they are part of a learning community with increased perceptions of social presence. Thus the following hypotheses were investigated:

H1a:

When there is congruence between a user's epistemological beliefs and beliefs about the learning model supported by the technology, the user will communicate to a greater extent than when there is friction.

H1b:

When there is congruence between a user's epistemological beliefs and beliefs about the

learning model supported by the technology, the user will perceive greater social presence than when there is friction.

We also expect friction to have an impact on learners' affective reactions to the VLE. As learning in VLEs can still be novel experiences for learners, users are utilizing technology to communicate in ways in which they are potentially unfamiliar and uncomfortable. Evidence has shown that when faced with a conflict between technology functionality and the way the users wish to use the system, users will attempt to match their approach to the approach designed into the system (cf. Todd & Benbasat, 1991). Vermetten, Vermunt, and Lodewijks (2002) also suggest that learners tend to make best use of the elements in the learning environment that fit their preferred way of learning and ignore or underutilize those that do not. In VLEs, this suggests that while users may feel compelled to adopt a learning strategy supported by the technology, they may not effectively utilize the tool. Friction between the user's EBs and the learning model supported by the technology can exacerbate negative feelings about the environment, because of the user's need to adapt their learning conceptions even though they may not see it as appropriate. As discussed above, the technology can be seen as a barrier to the learning process, increasing the user's frustration with learning in the VLE. Together, these outcomes would be expected to lead to lower levels of satisfaction with the VLE.

353

Finally, we believe that friction will also lead to a reduction in learning outcomes (Vermunt & Verloop, 1999). An individual's prior educational experiences are reflected in their EBs, which in turn play a role in forming the learner's perceptions of the instructional measures. The match between those perceptions and the types of teaching-learning environment affects the quality of learning achieved (Entwistle et al., 2002). Among other things, for learning to be most successful, connections between individuals are needed (Vygotsky, 1978; Feuerstein, Rand, Hoffman, & Miller, 1980). When friction occurs, learners are more likely to disengage from both the learning process and from their peers, engaging in fewer behaviors that can lead to successful learning outcomes. With other studies also arguing for the importance of ongoing observational learning process (Bandura, 1986; Yi, & Davis, 2003) where individuals learn new behavior and skills through attending and processing the behavior of others, any reduction in connections can lead to reduced attention to the behaviors, ideas and contributions of others. When this occurs, system users are likely to be exposed to less information, process less information, and therefore have reduced learning. In turn, the likelihood of successful learning outcomes will be reduced (Geiger & Cooper, 1996; Harrell, Caldwell, & Doty, 1985). Thus, the following hypotheses were investigated:

H2a:

When there is congruence between a user's epistemological beliefs and beliefs about the learning model supported by the technology, the user will be more satisfied than when there is friction.

H2b:

When there is congruence between a user's epistemological beliefs and beliefs about the learning model supported by the technology, the user will perform better than when there is friction.

METHOD

Research Setting

The study was conducted in an MIS fundamentals course at a large university in the United States. This course was a required course for all business majors and was taught exclusively online using WebCT. The course was taught over 15 weeks and was divided into 6 modules. Each module focused on different topical areas, such as the strategic use of information and technology, e-commerce, decision support, and so forth, with each module lasting approximately two weeks. Students were assigned to groups of approximately 30 and were asked to both post comments to case questions and respond to the comments of others in their group. Student assessment occurred at the end of each module through the use of individual multiple-choice tests. The course was managed by one instructor and two graduate assistants (GAs), who communicated exclusively online (all were not physically on campus during the semester), and one GA held office hours both online and in person.[3] At the end of the fifth module of the course, the survey was made available for one week using WebCT.

The course was designed based on principles from the constructivist and collaborative learning models. To encourage active discovery and knowledge construction (i.e., constructivist learning), students were required to gather information from a variety of sources including text, video, and cases and to integrate these into their understanding of the topic. In support of the collaborative model of learning students wrote, read and posted responses to case questions associated with each module.

Research Participants

A total of 332 students participated in the study, of which usable data was obtained from 324. The sample consisted of 156 males and 152 females.[4] The average age was 25.9 (SD = 6.5), with a range of 19-54. All of those participating in the course indicated that they were currently employed and had previous computer and Internet experience with over 50% indicating that they had high levels of experience in both.

Measures

Satisfaction

Satisfaction was measured with an 8-item Likert-type scale developed by Biner (1993). The scale used a 7-point strongly disagree to strongly agree response format. The coefficient alpha reliability estimate for this scale was 0.87.

Learning

Two types of learning outcomes, considered to be important by training researchers, were assessed in this study: cognitive/knowledge based outcomes and skill based outcomes (Kraiger, Ford, & Salas, 1993). Each of these outcomes was measured in this study. The form of cognitive knowledge assessed in this study was declarative knowledge. Declarative knowledge was assessed using a 50-point end of module exam score from the next to last course module (Module 5). This exam was chosen because, by the time the participants got to the end of this module, they had enough exposure to and interaction with WebCT for the effect of technology mediation to be manifest. The correlation between Module 5 exam score and participants' overall course grade is 0.41 (p < .001). Thus, it is indicative of the participants' overall performance of declarative knowledge. Skill development was measured using the 6-item perceived skill development scale developed by Alavi (1994). This scale used a 7-point strongly disagree to strongly agree response format. The coefficient alpha reliability estimate for this scale was 0.86.

Social Presence

Social presence was measured with a 5-item scale developed by Short et al. (1976). For each question, respondents evaluated the characteristics of the environment using a 5-point, Likert-type scale with anchors such as "unsociable-sociable" and "impersonal-personal." The coefficient alpha reliability estimate for this scale was 0.80. A complete list of all scale items used in the study is found in Appendix A.

Communication

Communication was measured using three types of course communication: the number of discussion postings read, the number of original discussion postings, and the number of follow-up discussion posts. Each of these was standardized and then an aggregate measure was created to represent communication.

Friction

Friction was measured as a gap between what the system users believed was the best way to learn and what they felt the technology supported. Participants were first given descriptions of objectivist, constructivist, and collaborative approaches to learning that an instructor might use. These are shown below:

1. In the objectivist model, learning takes place as the student absorbs the knowledge of the instructor. Therefore, it is the efficiency by which the instructor can transmit his knowledge that will improve a student's ability to learn.

2. In the constructivist model, learning only takes place as the students construct knowledge for themselves. The learners do this through active discovery supported by the instructor.

3. In the collaborative model, students create learning by interacting (discussing and sharing information) with other students.

Next, participants selected the learning approach that would be the most effective way for them to learn. Following this, participants selected the learning approach that they felt WebCT supported. Each scale was scored as follows: 1-objectivist, 2-constructivist, 3-collaborative. Using these two scales, if there was no difference between the learning method they learn best in and the one they feel that WebCT supports, it was coded as a 0. If there was a difference in the approach selected, it was coded as a 1. Overall, 142 people felt that that there was congruence between the technology support of learning and their EBs, while 182 perceived friction to exist. Thus, over 55% of the individuals felt friction between the technology support of learning and their EBs.

Preliminary Analysis

As a manipulation check, we assessed whether or not individuals correctly identified the learning model supported by the technology. Recall that the instructor designed the course to include elements of both constructivist and collaborative learning models. Of those participating, 95% identified WebCT as supporting either the constructivist or collaborative learning models (Table 1). Those

Table 1. Learning model identified as desired by learner or supported by WebCT

Learning Model	Frequency	
	Desired	Technology Supported
Objectivist	80	17
Constructivist	98	118
Collaborativist	146	189

who were unable to identify the supported environment were dropped from further analysis, leaving a sample of 307. Of these, 140 individuals felt that there was congruence (45.6%) and 167 individuals perceived friction (54.4%).

To confirm no significant demographic differences between the groups, the groups were compared on a number of variables, including age, gender, GPA, computer experience, Internet experience, confidence in using computers, and previous VLE course experience. Evidence from this analysis suggested that the groups were not different.

Results

Table 2 shows the means and standard deviations of the learning process and outcomes based upon whether the learner perceived congruence or friction and Table 3 shows the correlations among the dependent variables. Learning, communication, social presence, and course satisfaction were all correlated ($p < .001$). An initial multivariate analysis of variance (MANOVA) was run. The overall test was significant (Wilks' lambda $F_{(4,301)} = 4.01$, $p < .01$), which allowed for an individual ANOVA to be performed for each process and outcome variable.

As shown in Table 4, the results of the ANOVA on communication were significant, providing support for H1. Users who perceived congruence between technological support and EBs communicated more ($M = .12$) than when friction was perceived ($M = -.08$), $F_{(1,305)} = 4.98$, $p < 0.05$. H2 predicted that when users perceived congruence, they would experience enhanced social presence ($M = 3.15$) than when they perceived friction ($M = 2.97$); support was not found for this hypothesis ($F_{(1,305)} = 3.08$, $p = .08$). Supporting H3, users who perceived congruence between their EBs and technology support of learning were more satisfied ($M = 5.25$) with the learning environment than those who perceived friction ($M = 4.76$) $F_{(1,305)} = 11.97$, $p < 0.001$. Finally, support was

Table 2. Means and standard deviations of processes and outcomes

						Variable					
		Comm.[a]		Social Presence		Satisfaction		Declarative Knowledge		Skill Development	
Group	n	M	SD	M	SD	M	SD	M	SD	M	SD
Congruence	140	0.12	.76	3.15	0.86	5.25	1.10	41.66	8.22	5.52	0.97
Friction	167	-0.08	.77	2.97	0.85	4.76	1.31	38.83	13.43	5.13	1.15
Total	307	0.01	.77	3.05	0.86	4.99	1.24	40.12	11.42	5.31	1.09

[a] *The values listed represent standardized scores.*

Table 3. Correlation of study dependent variables

	Construct	1.	2.	3.	4.	5.
1.	Communication	—				
2.	Social Presence	.22***	—			
3.	Satisfaction	.24***	.50***	—		
4.	Declarative Knowledge	.24***	.06	.17**	—	
5.	Skill Development	.09	.26***	.35***	.16**	—

* p < .05, **, p < .01, *** p < .001

found for H4, with users who perceived congruence between EBs and technology learned more than when friction was perceived. This was true both for declarative knowledge (i.e., score on the skills test) (M = 41.66 vs. 38.83, F (1,305) = 4.76, p < .05) and for skill development (M = 5.52 vs. 5.13, F (1,305) = 10.06, p < .01).

DISCUSSION

Summary of Findings

The results of this study provide evidence that congruence between the technology support of learning and an individual's conceptions of the best way to learn can create more effective VLE processes and outcomes than when friction occurs. Specifically, when users feel congruence, they communicate more, learn more, and are more satisfied with the learning experience than when

there is friction. While previous research was justified in calling for a fit between the technology used to support learning and the learning model implemented by the instructor, these calls may not go far enough. The shortcoming is that they do not take into account the relationship between an individual's EBs and the technology support of learning. When friction occurs, it becomes difficult for individuals to leverage and appropriate the technology to support their optimal learning strategy or to adapt their learning to match the model supported by the technology. Instead, the findings suggest that the learners will disengage from the course by communicating less, perform less effectively, and become less satisfied with the learning environment.

Implications

One of the greatest advantages from using VLE's is the inherent flexibility of VLEs. Thus, the

Table 4. Results of analysis of variance on course process and outcomes

Source of Variation	SS	df	MS	F
Communication				
Group	2.91	1	2.91	4.98*
Residual	178.44	305	0.59	
Total	181.35	306		
Social Presence				
Group	2.26	1	2.26	3.08[a]
Residual	223.78	305	.73	
Total	226.04	306		
Satisfaction				
Group	17.88	1	17.88	11.97***
Residual	455.57	305	1.49	
Total	473.45	306		
Declarative Knowledge				
Group	613.36	1	613.36	4.76*
Residual	39309.19	305	128.88	
Total	39922.55	306		
Skill Development				
Group	11.61	1	11.61	10.06**
Residual	351.74	305		
Total	363.35	306		

[a] $p < .10$, * $p < .05$, ** $p < .01$, *** $p < .001$

primary implication of this research is the need to flexibly design VLEs such that the technology support of learning is flexible and adaptable to match users' learning conceptions.

Beyond matching the technological support of an instructor's chosen learning model to the instructional design of the technology, the technology should be flexible enough to adjust to multiple user's beliefs, as some users may not be able to adapt their preferred learning model to the one supported by the technology (Vermunt & Verloop, 2000).

Associated with this, while the technology exists to deliver training via multiple methods, doing so does not currently seem to be the predominant model for delivering VLE initiatives. It is our

experience that the vast majority of VLE training and educational settings use the same model despite the realization that people have different preferred learning environments. One reason for the simplification of design is that organizations and instructors choose a specific learning model to implement and then design the technology to support that environment. Various constraints, such as time, technical expertise, and effort to leverage technology for ways in which it was not designed, can make it difficult for the designers of VLEs to take into account these multiple approaches to learning pursued by those using the system. Using a development system based on the convergence of instructional design and Web design, Janicki and Steinberg (2003) found that increased learning occurred when flexible learning content was delivered via multiple methods such as narratives, examples and hands-on exercises. The same type of system could be developed for delivery of learning content based on various learning conceptions and matched with a user's preferred learning approach.

The problem is that when static approaches to technological support occur, some learners are put at a learning disadvantage over their peers. Unlike face-to-face settings, where the instructor can better gauge a persons' learning conceptions, in a VLE they can remain hidden. Thus, these findings suggest that a process for discovering the EBs of those in VLEs needs to be developed. If a learner's beliefs are found to be in conflict with the model used in the VLE, adaptive VLE's can provide the learning content in a manner best suited for the user.

Alternatively in situations where users' will be engaging in multiple VLE experiences over time, those experiencing friction could be provided with training or social behavior modification to change there EBs, as these beliefs have been found to be malleable as one proceeds through various levels of education (Perry, 1968). Echoing the developmental nature of learning conceptions, Vermunt and Verloop (1999) suggest that friction can have positive consequences by catalyzing users to develop new learning strategies. Future research needs to investigate the effectiveness of the various approaches for aligning a VLE technological support of learning with users' learning conceptions. Finally, although this research has focused on the negative consequences of friction, more needs to be done to investigate the potential positive effects that friction might create by changing a user's learning conceptions, specifically what circumstances are needed within the VLE context for this to occur.

Managerial Implications

This research also has implications for managers seeking to maximize returns on their investments of VLEs. This study reinforces the importance of matching user beliefs about learning to the technological support of learning. When this congruence occurs, learning processes and outcomes are enhanced. This benefits managers in two ways. First, congruence leads to better learning, which should translate to improved employee performance. Second, less satisfied individuals are less likely to choose to engage in behaviors that they view negatively, such as enrolling or participating in future VLE initiatives (Ajzen, 1988; Bhattacherjee, 2001). The importance of this cannot be underestimated in environments such as the current one, where over 55% of those participating felt that the technology did not support the way they learned best and because one of the biggest threats to VLEs is the large discontinuance rate (Flood, 2000).

Finally, managers should consider developing their VLE architectures so that they can be flexible enough to tailor course offerings to the preferences of the users. By adopting flexible approaches, managers can provide learning environments that provide the greatest potential for learning. As an example of flexibility in training approaches, Hewlett Packard has developed their corporate training initiatives to allow regional managers to tailor a mix of traditional, blended, and Web-based initiatives to meet the preferences of the region (O'Leonard, 2004). Given these options, users have been able to self-choose the learning approach that they are most comfortable with. This flexibility has led to improved employee performance and improved customer service (O'Leonard, 2004). Future research should investigate how this flexibility translates to improved learning and transfer.

Limitations

As with any study, there are several potential limitations that pertain to the generalizability of these findings. First, the results from this study represent a specific technology implementation in a single course. While there was no evidence to suggest that the results found in this study would be different in different settings, we cannot generalize to other settings. Future research should replicate and extend the findings of this study with different technologies and different contexts. Additionally, participants were required to choose a single learning model between objectivist, constructivist, and collaborative learning models, which did not allow us to investigate the blending of multiple learning models as part of this study. Finally, EBs are more than an individual's learning conceptions but rather a system of interconnected beliefs about knowledge and how knowledge is accumulated (Hofer, 2004; Schommer-Aikins, 2004; Schommer, 1994); as such a more systematic investigation of the aspects of a user's EBs would allow for a deeper understanding of the beliefs on VLE outcomes.

CONCLUSION

This study was motivated by the desire to better understand the implications of friction between the technology support of learning and the EBs of those engaged in the learning process. Results indicated that friction between a user's belief about their learning approach and that provided by a VLE can lead to reduced participation, peer connections, performance and satisfaction. With technology central to the learning processes and outcomes in a VLE, it is important for those designing VLE initiatives to understand that successful VLEs depend not only on the matching of instructor learning models with technology support, but also allowing the technology to be flexible enough for those with differing EBs to have the opportunity to leverage the technology to support their desired learning approach. Without considering the fit between EBs and technology support of learning, the potential exists for organizations to waste large amounts of resources in their investments in their distributed initiatives

and for employees participating in these initiatives to learn less, participate less, and ultimately have reduced skills and knowledge than if fit were considered.

REFERENCES

Ajzen, I. (1988). *Attitudes, personality, and behavior.* Chicago: Dorsey.

Alavi, M. (1994). Computer-mediated collaborative learning: An empirical evaluation. *MIS Quarterly, 18*(2), 159-174.

Alavi, M., Marakas, G.M., & Yoo, Y. (2002) A comparative study of distributed learning environments on learning outcomes. *Information Systems Research, 13*(4), 404-415.

Alavi, M., & Leidner, D.E. (2001). Technology mediated learning: A call for greater depth and breadth of research. *Information Systems Research, 12*(1), 1-10.

Anderson, E.W., & Sullivan, M.W. (1993). The antecedents and consequences of customer satisfaction for firms. *Marketing Science, 12*(2), 125-143.

Bakx, A.W.E.A., Vermetten, Y.J.M., & Van der Sanden, J.M.M. (2003). Self-perceived competence, learning conceptions and preferred learning situations in the domain of communication. *British Journal of Educational Psychology, 73*(2), 223-245.

Bandura, A. (1986). *Social foundations of thought and action: A social cognitive theory.* Englewood Cliffs, NJ: Prentice Hall.

Benbunan-Fich, R. (2002). Improving education and training with IT. *Communications of the ACM, 45*(6), 94-99.

Bhattacherjee, A. (2001). Understanding information systems continuance: An expectation-confirmation model. *MIS Quarterly, 25*(3), 351-370.

Biner, P.M. (1993). The development of an instrument to measure student attitudes toward televised courses. *The American Journal of Distance Education, 7*(1), 63-73.

Burke, K., & Chidambaram, L. (1999). How much bandwidth is enough? A longitudinal examination of media characteristics and group outcomes. *MIS Quarterly, 23*(4), 557-579.

Elen, J., & Lowyck, J. (1998). Students' views on the efficiency of instruction: An exploratory survey of the instructional metacognitive knowledge of university freshmen. *Higher Education, 36*(2), 231-252.

Elen, J., & Lowyck, J. (1999). Metacognitive instructional knowledge: Cognitive mediation and instructional design. *Journal of Structural Learning & Intelligent Systems, 13*(3-4), 145-169.

Elen, J., & Lowyck, J. (2000). Instructional metacognitive knowledge: A qualitative study on conceptions of freshmen about instruction. *Journal of Curriculum Studies, 32*(3), 421-444.

Entwistle, N. J. (1991). Approaches to learning and perceptions of the learning environment. *Higher Education, 22*, 201-204.

Entwistle, N.J. (1998a). Approaches to learning and forms of understanding. In B. Dart & G. Boulton-Lewis (Eds.), *Teaching and learning in higher education* (pp. 72–101). Melbourne: Australian Council for Educational Research.

Entwistle, N.J. (1998b). Improving teaching through research on student learning. In J.J.F. Forest (Ed.), *University teaching: International perspectives* (pp. 73–112). New York: Garland.

Entwistle, N., McCune, V., & Hounsell, J. (2002). *Approaches to studying and perceptions of university teaching-learning environments: Concepts, measures and preliminary findings.* ETL Project Occasional Report.

Feurestein, R., Rand, Y., Hoffman, M., & Miller, R. (1980). *Instrumental enrichment.* Baltimore, MD: University Park Press.

Fiore, S.M., Salas, E., Cuevas, H.M., & Bowers, C.A. (2003). Distributed coordination space: Toward a theory of distributed team process and performance. *Theoretical Issues in Ergonomics Science, 4*(3-4), 340-364.

Flood, J. (2000). Read all about it: Online learning facing 80% attrition rates. *Turkish Online Journal of Distance Education, 3.*

Geiger, M.A., & Cooper, E.A. (1996). Using expectancy to address student motivation. *Issues in Accounting Education, 11*(1), 113-129.

Gunawardena, C.N. (1995). Social presence theory and implications for interaction and collaborative learning in computer conferences. *International Journal of Educational Telecommunications, 1*(2/3), 147-166.

Harrell, A., Caldwell, C., & Doty, E. (1985, October). Expectancy theory predictions of accounting students' academic success motivation. *The Accounting Review*, pp. 724-735.

Hiltz, S.R., & Wellman, B. (1997). Asynchronous learning networks as a virtual classroom. *Communications of the ACM, 40*(9), 44-49.

Hofer, B.K. (2004). Epistemological understanding as a metacognitive process: Thinking aloud during online searching. *Educational Psychologist, 39*(1), 43-55.

IDC. (2003). Press release. Retrieved November 30, 2006, from *http://www.idc.com/getdoc.jhtml ?containerId=pr2003_01_14_145111*

Janicki, T., & Steinberg, G. (2003). Evaluation of a computer-supported learning system. *Decision Sciences Journal of Innovative Education, 1*(2), 203-223.

Kraiger, K., Ford, J.K., & Salas, E. (1993). Application of cognitive, skill-based, and affective theories of learning outcomes to new methods of training evaluation. *Journal of Applied Psychology, 78*(2), 311-328.

Leidner, D.E., & Jarvenpaa, S. L. (1995). The use of information technology to enhance management school education: A theoretical view. *MIS Quarterly, 19*(3), 265-291.

Locke, E., & Latham, G. (1990). *A theory of goal setting and task performance.* Englewood Cliffs, NJ: Prentice Hall.

Lowyck, J., & Elen, J. (1994). *Student's instructional metacognition in learning environments (SIMILE).* Paper presented at the Leuven: K.U. Leuven, C.I.P. & T.

Marton, F., Dall'Alba, G. & Beaty, E. (1993). Conceptions of learning. *International Journal of Educational Research, 19*, 277-300.

Marton, F. & Säljö, R. (1976). On qualitative differences in learning: 1 - Outcome and process. *British Journal of Educational Psychology, 46*, 4-11.

Mayor, T. (2001). E-learning: Does it make the grade. *CIO Magazine. 14*(7), 132-144.

O'Leonard, K. (2004). *HP case study: Flexible solutions for multi-cultural learners.* Oakland, CA: Bersin & Associates.

O'Mara, J., Allen, J.L., Long, K.M. & Judd, B. (1996). Communication apprehension, nonverbal immediacy, and negative expectations for learning. *Communication Research Reports, 13*, 109-128.

Oliver, R.L. (1980). A cognitive model for the antecedents and consequences of satisfaction. *Journal of Marketing Research, 17*, 460-469.

Perry, W. (1968). *Patterns of development in thought and values of students in a liberal arts college: A validation of a scheme* (No. 5-0825, Contract No. SAE-8973). Washington, DC: Department of Health, Education and Welfare.

Piccoli, G., Ahmad, R. & Ives, B. (2001). Web-based virtual learning environments: A research framework and a preliminary assessment of effectiveness in basic IT skills training. *MIS Quarterly, 25*(4), 401-426.

Robson, J. (2000). Evaluating on-line teaching. *Open Learning, 15*(2), 151-172.

Rovai, A.P. (2002). A preliminary look at the structural differences of higher education classroom communities in traditional and ALN courses. *Journal of Asynchronous Learning Networks, 6*(1), 41-56.

Salas, E., DeRouin, R., & Littrell, L. (2005). Research-based guidelines for designing distance learning: What we know so far. In H.G. Geutal & D.L. Stone (Eds.), *The brave new world of e-HR: human resources management in the digital age.* San Francisco: Jossey-Bass.

Schommer-Aikins, M. (2004). Explaining the epistemological belief system: Introducing the embedded systemic model and coordinated research approach. *Educational Psychologist, 39*(1), 19-29.

Schommer, M. (1994). An emerging conceptualization of epistemological beliefs and their role in learning. In R. Garner & P.A. Alexander (Eds.), *Beliefs about text and instruction with text* (pp. 25-40). Hillsdale, NJ: Lawrence Erlbaum.

Schommer, M., Crouse, A. & Rhodes, N. (1992). Epistemological beliefs and mathematical text comprehension: Believing it is simple does not make it so. *Journal of Educational Psychology, 84*(4), 435-443.

Short, J., Williams, E., & Christie, B. (1976). *The social psychology of telecommunciations.* New York: John Wiley & Sons.

Todd, P. & I. Benbasat (1991). An experimental investigation of the impact of computer based decision aids on decision making strategies. *Information Systems Research, 2*(2), 87-115.

Tu, C.-H. & McIsaac, M. (2002). The relationship of social presence and interaction in online classes. *American Journal of Distance Education, 16*(3), 131-150.

Tu, C.H. (2000). On-line learning migration: From social learning theory to social presence theory in a CMC environment. *Journal of Network and Computer Applications, 23*(1), 27-37.

Van der Sanden, J.M.M., Terwel, J. & Vosniadou, S. (2000). New learning in science and technology: A competency perspective. In P.R.J. Simons, S.J.L. van der Linden & T.M. Duffy (Eds.), *New learning.* Dordrecht, The Netherlands: Kluwer Academic Publishers.

Vermetten, Y.J., Vermunt, J.D., & Lodewijks, H.G. (2002). Powerful learning environments? How university students differ in their response to instructional measures. *Learning & Instruction, 12*(3), 263-284.

Vermunt, J.D. (1996). Metacognitive, cognitive and affective aspects of learning styles and strategies: A phenomenographic analysis. *Higher Education, 31*, 25-50.

Vermunt, J.D. (1998). The regulation of constructive learning processes. *British Journal of Educational Psychology, 68*, 149-171.

Vermunt, J.D. & Verloop, N. (1999). Congruence and friction between learning and teaching. *Learning & Instruction, 9*, 257-280.

Vermunt, J.D. & Verloop, N. (2000). Dissonance in students' regulation of learning processes. *European Journal of Psychology of Education, 15*(1), 75-89.

Vygotsky, L.S. (1978). *Mind in society.* Cambridge, MA: Harvard University Press.

Walther, J.B. (1995). Relational aspects of computer-mediated communication: Experimental observations over time. *Organization Science, 6*(2), 186-203.

Webster, J. & Hackley, P. (1997). Teaching effectiveness in technology-mediated distance learning. *Academy of Management Journal, 40*(6), 1282-1309.

Wirt, J. & Livingston, A. (2004). *Condition of education 2002 in brief* (No. NCES 2002011): National Center for Education Statistics.

Yi, M.Y. & Davis, F.D. (2003). Developing and validating an observational learning model of computer software training and skill acquisition. *Information Systems Research, 14*(2), 146-149.

ENDNOTES

[1] While multiple terms have been used to describe these environments, such as virtual learning environments (VLE), distributed training, distance learning, e-learning, and technology-mediated learning (TML), we use the term Virtual Learning Environment in this study.

[2] Individual differences in learning styles have also been suggested as an important criterion in understanding individual learning. Unlike EB, however, learning styles —which vary in their measurement —pertain more to personality traits often having to deal with how an individual views the world and how that view impacts their learning processes. In contrast EB, as defined and measured in this study, are an individual's conceptions about the best way in which learning material are best delivered as either an objectivist, constructivist, or collaborative approach.

3   Discussions with the last GA found that other than first week assistance in setting up WebCT by a few students (<20), students chose to communicate via course e-mail for assistance.

4   Sixteen individuals did not indicate their gender.

APPENDIX A. SCALE ITEMS

Social Presence

Higher numbers represent more presence and lower numbers represent less presence.

Impersonal...Personal
Unsociable...Sociable
Insensitive...Sensitive
Cold...Warm
Passive...Active

Satisfaction

I am satisfied with the clarity with which the class assignments were communicated

I am satisfied with the timeliness with which papers, tests, and written assignments were graded and returned.

I am satisfied with the degree to which the types of instructional techniques that were used to teach the class helped me gain a better understanding of the class material.

I am satisfied with the extent to which the instructor made the students feel that they were part of the class and "belonged".

I am satisfied with the instructor's communication skills.

I am satisfied with the accessibility of the instructor outside of class.

I am satisfied with the present means of material exchange between myself and the course instructor.

I am satisfied with the accessibility of the graduate assistants.

Perceived Skill Development

I feel more confident in expressing ideas related to Information Technology.

I improved my ability to critically think about Information Technology.

I improved my ability to integrate facts and develop generalizations from the course material.

I increased my ability to critically analyze issues.

I learned to interrelate the important issues in the course material.

I learned to value other points of view

This work was previously published in the Journal of Organizational and End User Computing, Vol. 19, Issue 2, edited by M. Mahmood, pp. 23-46, copyright 2007 by IGI Publishing (an imprint of IGI Global).

Chapter 21
Interdepartmental Knowledge Transfer Success During Information Technology Projects

Kevin Laframboise
Concordia University, Canada

Anne-Marie Croteau
Concordia University, Canada

Anne Beaudry
Concordia University, Canada

Mantas Manovas
Concordia University, Canada

ABSTRACT

This article reports on a study that investigates the knowledge transfer between an information systems/ technology (IS/IT) department and non-IT departments during IT projects. More specifically, we look into the link between the knowledge management capabilities of the IT department and the effectiveness and efficiency of the knowledge transfer to a client department. Knowledge management (KM) capabilities are defined by Gold, Malhotra, and Segars (2001) as the combination of knowledge infrastructure capabilities (structural, technical, and cultural) and knowledge processes capabilities (acquisition, conversion, application, and protection). Data collected through a Web-based survey result in 127 usable questionnaires completed by managers in large Canadian organizations. Data analysis performed using partial least squares (PLS) indicates that knowledge infrastructure capabilities are related to the knowledge transfer success, and more specifically to its effectiveness whereas knowledge processes capabilities are only related to the efficiency of such transfer. Implications of our results for research and practice are also discussed.

INTRODUCTION

Knowledge transfer (k-transfer) is a process through which one entity is affected by the knowledge of another (Argote, Ingram, Levine, & Moreland, 2000). k-transfer, a key element of KM research, has been shown to play a critical role in increasing a company's productivity and helping it gain a competitive advantage (Argote & Ingram, 2000; Szulanski, 2000). From a market perspective, the transfer of knowledge between two groups establishes a provider-receiver relationship. As might be inferred from Lin, Geng, and Whinston (2005) interdepartmental transfer of knowledge allows for mutual benefits and represents the knowledge market within a firm.

Although the issue of intra-firm k-transfer has been addressed already (Gruenfeld, Martorana, & Fan, 2000; Gupta & Govindarajan, 2000; Hansen, 1999; O'Dell, 1998), there is a lack of research in interdepartmental k-transfer, in particular during IT projects. This research gap is especially significant since most IT projects are cross functional and interdepartmental (Hoopes, 2001, Sharda, Franckwick, Deosthali & Delahoussaye, 1998). The present research attempts to narrow this gap by empirically investigating interdepartmental k-transfer success during IT projects. The most obvious knowledge asset of the IT department lies in the conception, development, and exploitation of IT applications that support the business processes, characteristically examples of tacit knowledge (Edvinsson & Malone, 1997). However, the IT-related managerial skills constitute knowledge that must be transferred to the client department (as explicit knowledge) during any project if IT is to contribute to creating and sustaining a competitive advantage (Mata, Fuerst, & Barney, 1995). This emphasizes the importance of investigating further how KM capabilities can be fostered to successfully conduct an IT project that suits the needs of another business unit.

A capability is the "firm's capacity to deploy its assets" (Maritan, 2001, p. 514). KM capabili-

ties characterize a firm's ability to build upon its current knowledge to scan for and recognize the value of new information, assimilate it, and apply it in order to create new knowledge (Gold et al., 2001). More specifically, KM capabilities are developed through the processes of combining and exchanging knowledge to foster the creation of new ideas and resources. They are enabled by the presence of the knowledge infrastructure capabilities, which are leveraged by the critical knowledge processes capabilities (Gold et al., 2001).

The present research aims at answering the following research question: *Are KM capabilities of an IT department related to the success of knowledge transfer to non-IT department during an IT project?* Although different authors point out that various aspects of such capabilities are essential to achieving k-transfer success (Nonaka & Takeuchi, 1995; O'Dell, 1998), none of them have actually empirically tested interdepartmental knowledge transfer. Given that IT projects are knowledge intensive, it seems appropriate to assume that some form of deliberate management of knowledge should be present in both the development and the implementation processes of such projects.

This paper is structured as follows: first, the theoretical background is reviewed. Next, the research objectives, variables, hypotheses, and model are presented. The third section describes the methodology used for this research project. The data analysis is followed by a discussion of the results. The last section addresses the limitations and contributions of this study for practice and research and identifies future research avenues.

THEORETICAL BACKGROUND

Resource-Based View

Organizations can gain a sustained competitive advantage when they are capable of exploiting their valuable, rare, difficult to transfer, and not easily replicated internal resources and capabilities (Barney, 1995; Grant, 1991; Von Krogh & Grand, 2002). A resource corresponds to the input used during a production process (e.g., employee, skill, equipment), whereas a capability is the capacity for a set of resources to perform some task or activity that will be the main source of the competitive advantage (Grant, 1991). A key organizational capability is the ability to effectively manage the firm's resources. For example, when an organization uses its technology to distinguish itself from its competitors, such technology is much more than just a set of IT functionalities; it becomes the firm's IT capability (Henderson & Venkatraman, 1999).

It is recognized that a critical element for organizations to stay competitive lies in their ability to successfully manage and internally transfer their resources and capabilities, and more particularly their knowledge, which constitutes organizations' most fundamental resource (Grant, 1996). New knowledge is valuable when it can be successfully leveraged in existing operations (Spanos & Prastacos, 2004). The resource-base view is therefore quite useful in investigating the link between KM capabilities and the success of knowledge transfer during an IT project.

Knowledge

There is no universal definition of knowledge management (KM) since there is no agreement as to what constitutes knowledge in the first place. For this reason, it's best to think of KM in the broadest context. Succinctly put, KM is the process through which organizations generate value from their intellectual and knowledge-based assets. (Levinson, 2005, p. 20)

Furthermore, there are many types of knowledge and these may be defined from specific perspectives. For example, from an epistemological perspective we would classify knowledge as logical, semantic, systemic, or empirical. In the field of education, Frick (2004) identifies six types of knowledge of education where knowledge is scientific, praxiological, or philosophical under either situational or theoretical circumstances. From an organizational perspective, knowledge may be tacit or explicit.

As per Edvinsson and Malone (1997) tacit knowledge is the implicit knowledge used by workers to perform their work. It is personal, often difficult to articulate and is embedded in a person's actions or experiences. These authors include within tacit knowledge both technical level know-how (skills and crafts) as well as a cultural/cognitive level dimension (beliefs, ideals, perceptions, or values.)

Explicit knowledge is knowledge that has been formally codified using a system of symbols (words and numbers) for diffusion in the form of data for example, product specifications, computer applications, or manuals. Further, it is considered to be objective and unambiguously expressed (Chua, 2001).

This article uses the tacit-explicit framework of knowledge. We assume that one member of the firm has articulated a need that the IT department would respond to. Our work examines how the provider (IT department) using its expertise (tacit knowledge) responds to the need from the customer department (tacit knowledge converted into explicit knowledge). Specifically, the IT department represents tacit knowledge that must become explicit for the customer department.

Knowledge, particularly tacit knowledge, is one resource that is difficult to replicate and hence is key in achieving advantage over other firms (Lubit, 2001, Spanos and Prastacos, 2004). Zack (1999) defines knowledge as "that which we come to believe and value on the basis of information (messages) through experience, communication, or inference" (p. 278). This definition reflects two components of knowledge, that is, an object and a process (Alavi & Leider, 2001). Knowledge as an object corresponds to what is known whereas knowledge as a process implies applying expertise or simply using it.

As per Zack (1999), three types of knowledge exist and are present in IT projects: (1) declarative (know-what), (2) procedural (know-how), and (3) causal (know-why). Specifically, declarative knowledge facilitates effective communication whereby, for example, the customer department describes concepts and elements required. Procedural knowledge, embedded in organizational routines and processes, represents knowing and using the interaction of elements in the system to produce results where, for example, different methodologies and processes convert customer requirements into end-products. Finally, causal knowledge represents an understanding of fundamental principles and is used to formulate goals and strategies. The latter implies that even though the actors in a request for a product or service do not have sufficient knowledge of each other, particularly awareness of the other's tacit knowledge, or do not share a common technical language, they may still need to effectuate a knowledge transfer, that is, make the knowledge explicit.

Knowledge Capabilities

Although Gold et al. (2001) do not explicitly define KM capabilities, we view the construct as a department's ability to manage knowledge in order to improve performance or gain competitive advantage. This definition is similar to one provided by Croteau and Li (2003) who describe KM capabilities as "the ability of an organization to capture, manage, and deliver time-authenticated customer, product, and service information in order to improve customer response and provide faster decision-making based on reliable information" (p. 23). However, the context of their study was customer relationship management (CRM) and is reflected in their definition.

Gold et al. (2001) investigated KM capabilities from an infrastructure capabilities perspective and a process capabilities perspective. First, *k-infra-structure capabilities* refer to the support made available to maximize the social capital that can be found through the network relationships within a social unit. This concept can be broken further into three main components: technological, structural, and cultural capabilities. The *technological* k-infrastructure refers to technology-enabled ties that exist within a firm. These ties consist of the existence of common representation schemes for capturing knowledge, as well as collaboration, knowledge discovery, knowledge mapping, knowledge application, and opportunity generation technologies. The *structural* k-infrastructure refers to the presence of norms and trust mechanisms. Furthermore, the presence of a flexible structure that encourages interactions among departments and incentive systems that reward k-sharing are the major elements of this construct. IT groups and line groups (customer departments) should be provided with opportunities to socially interact and communicate about their work, thus fostering trust and influence as determinants of shared knowledge (Nelson & Cooprider, 1996). *Cultural* k-infrastructure refers to shared contexts. It pertains to the value attributed to knowledge sharing in the corporate vision and practice as well as the support given by senior management to knowledge practices. Effectively managing knowledge across boundaries requires that the actors not only share their knowledge, but that they also assess each other's knowledge (Carlile, 2004).

Second, Gold et al. (2001) define the organization's *knowledge process capabilities* in terms of the capacity to perform four fundamental k-processes: acquisition, conversion, application, and protection. The term *acquisition* refers to the process of seeking and acquiring new knowledge, or creating new knowledge out of existing knowledge in the course of cooperation between individuals or business partners. *Conversion* processes consist of converting knowledge into a useful form. To achieve this, the following key processes must be present: knowledge organization and structure, knowledge integration, and tacit-to-explicit knowledge conversion. They define *application* processes as those oriented toward the use of knowledge. For knowledge to be used, it must be accessible. Knowledge from past mistakes and experiences must be stored for later retrieval and use. Processes for the *protection* of knowledge from inappropriate use or theft must exist in any company that wishes to preserve or generate its competitive advantage. These must include procedures that limit the access to critical knowledge as well as protection policies that are openly communicated to all employees.

Knowledge Transfer

KM deals with many knowledge processes including k-transfer. According to Wiig (1997), k-transfer had been studied for many years before KM was even termed as a concept (for example, technology and cognitive skills transfer). He indicates that within the past 20 years, an extensive interest has appeared on the topic. Yet, tacit knowledge transfer, content and process, is poorly understood (Foos, Schum, & Rothenberg, 2006). Goh (2005) points out, "it is much harder to grasp what is in peoples' heads and the real difficulty is figure out how to document, share, and manage it correctly" (p. 11). Conversely, the resource-based view of the firm underlines the importance of transferability of the company's resources and capabilities as vital in gaining a competitive advantage (Barney, 1986). The transferability is especially important within the firm (Grant, 1996) and organizations that capitalize on knowledge-based assets and drive the most value from them will be the industry winners (Goh, 2005).

The process of k-transfer goes beyond the simple communication process through which knowledge is transmitted. Communication by itself is not sufficient for knowledge sharing; mutual trust and influence must be present for knowledge-sharing success (Nelson & Cooprider, 1996). Trust, early involvement, and due diligence

influence the extent of meeting technology transfer expectations (Foos et al., 2006). Moreover, shared knowledge must be successfully absorbed by the receiver (Lane & Lubatkin, 1998). Stated otherwise, it implies the creation of the capabilities of using the knowledge in the client department and hence create value (Argote & Ingram, 2000).

While some would classify absorption as a firm-level mechanism (Rivera, Dussauge, & Mitchell, 2001), it is an integral part of any transfer process (Szulanski, 2000) and involves knowledge utilization (Verkasolo & Lappalainen, 1998). This includes dyadic transfer within a firm whereby "the value of knowledge provided by the sender is realized when the receiver has assimilated the product and put the information to use" (Lin et al., 2005, p. 199) (see also, Darr & Kurtzberg, 2000). This reflects Davenport and Prusak's (1998) definition: "the transfer of knowledge then involves both the transmission of information to a recipient and absorption and transformation by that person or group" (p. 110). This definition also captures the fact that a k-transfer is a two-way process. It can be broken down into two subprocesses: knowledge distribution from the sender's point of view and knowledge acquisition from the receiver's point of view (Bolino, 2002; Huber, 1991; Schulz, 2000). Consequently, a critical success factor to IT projects success lies in the ability to enhance the knowledge base of the recipient (Ayas, 1996). This implies that the ability to affect a k-transfer, where the IT department transfers its knowledge to its client, is vital (Karlsen & Gottschalk, 2003). Specifically, the use of protocols to convert tacit to explicit knowledge may assure an efficient and effective transfer (Herschel, Nemati, & Steiger, 2001). Accordingly, based on the aforementioned and particularly Argote and Ingram (2000) and Ko, Kirsch, and King (2005), we define interdepartmental k-transfer as the process by which a source department within an organization communicates knowledge to a recipient department which absorbs and applies the knowledge.

Knowledge Transfer Success

A lack of appropriate k-infrastructure can seriously affect a department's ability to successfully transfer knowledge, as well as receive and absorb outside knowledge for its own use (O'Dell & Grayson, 1999). Using proper technology as a transfer medium facilitates the transfer process and its effectiveness (Goh, 2002; Rasmus, 2001). The appropriate technological infrastructure plays an especially critical role in managing codified knowledge by supporting key enabling processes: knowledge search, capture, storage, and presentation (Zack, 1999). A departmental structure that inhibits cross-functional interaction impedes knowledge transfer success (O'Dell, 1998), rendering the implementation of technology solutions problematic (Barki & Hartwick, 2001). K-transfer success also depends in part on the type of organizational culture that the recipient unit possesses (Kostova, 1999). Indeed, the social aspect of KM cannot be overemphasized (Thomas, Kellogg, & Erickson, 2001). A departmental culture that values high participation, interaction, and involvement within the group as well as with other groups will positively influence k-transfer success (DeLong & Fahey, 2000; McDermott & O'Dell, 2001).

Certain key processes allow an entity to successfully absorb knowledge. Without such absorption, a transfer cannot be called successful (Bresman, Birkinshaw, & Nobel, 1999). Part of the acquisition process is the ability to obtain knowledge from an external source. If this process is not present, the transfer will hardly be successful (Byrd, Cossick, & Zmud, 1992). Within the system development context, the customer requirements have to be translated into design specifications. For this task, appropriate knowledge conversion processes must be present. Processes are needed for making the knowledge accessible for effective team member collaboration (Calabrese, 1999) as well as for keeping knowledge up-to-date.

Verkasolo and Lappalainen (1998) point out that the efficiency of the k-transfer process depends on the presence and efficiency of subprocesses such as k-acquisition, documentation, transmission, reception, and perception. Thus, the lack of appropriate processes to manage knowledge will impede k-transfer success.

Borrowing from Faraj and Sproull (2000) who assessed the knowledge team performance by its effectiveness and efficiency, we believe that the success of the k-transfer from the IT department toward a non-IT department should also be investigated using the dimensions of effectiveness and efficiency. K-transfer success is defined as the achievement of a desired or intended goal in a process where knowledge is transmitted by one department and is absorbed and applied by a second one (Argote & Ingram, 2000; Darr & Kurtzberg, 2000; Kostova, 1999; Szulanski, 2000). When the knowledge transferred relates to organizational practices, the effectiveness of k-transfer can be judged based on the value attached to the knowledge by the recipient unit. A successful knowledge transfer process is one that is both effective (Argote et al., 2000; Goh, 2002) and efficient (Verkasolo & Lappalainen, 1998), that is, the knowledge is properly transmitted and used (effectiveness), using minimal resources (efficiency).

RESEARCH MODEL

This research investigates the relationship between an IT department's KM capabilities and the success of knowledge transfer during an IT project. More specifically, our study aims at answering the following question as shown in Figures 1a and 1b:

Are KM capabilities of an IT department related to the success of knowledge transfer to non-IT department during an IT project?

Our unit of measure is the IT department that, using its members' expertise, prepares a response to a customer department need. Thus, we measure the IT department manager's perception of its KM capabilities and the success of k-transfer to client departments. We also measure the perception of the customer department regarding k-transfer success. We hypothesize that an IT department that is KM-capable that is, has technological, structural, and cultural capabilities as described in this research, will be successful in k-transfers.

Our models are an adaptation of the Gold et al. (2001) model. Based on past literature, positive relationships between the independent and dependent variables are expected. The general research model (Figure 1a) addresses the link between the two types of knowledge capabilities and the knowledge transfer success, whereas the detailed research model (Figure 1b) addresses the four possible links between the two types of knowledge capabilities and both the effectiveness and the efficiency of the knowledge transfer success.

Knowledge Infrastructure and Knowledge Transfer Success

Our first hypothesis implies that without the proper technological, cultural, and structural infrastructures, k-transfer will not be successful.

H1: K-infrastructure capabilities are positively related to the k-transfer success.

This hypothesis can be further broken down into two parts. Technology, structure, and culture are all enablers of effective and efficient k-transfer (Goh, 2002). First, with regards to effectiveness, the use of appropriate technologies will facilitate k-transfer. A structure that encourages horizontal communication and cross-functional teams, while providing a reward system that recognizes knowledge sharing, will further enhance the effectiveness of k-transfer. Culture is one of the most

important elements for effective k-transfer in IT projects (Karlsen & Gottschalk, 2004). A strong, cooperative and collaborative culture will create the necessary trust for k-transfer to take place. Second, the efficiency of k-transfer can be greatly affected by the cultural values of the recipient unit. If the recipient is resistant to change or lacks motivation to collaborate, the transfer process is likely to be problematic. The term "fertile" organizational context can be used to describe one that has the appropriate values, incentive systems, and support for efficient k-transfer (Szulanski, 2000). Standardized IT infrastructure has already been successfully linked to efficiency of operations and processes (Ross, 2003), whereas technology and culture were positively related to both efficiency and effectiveness of k-transfer (Syed-Ikhsan & Rowland, 2004).

H1a: K-infrastructure capabilities are positively related to the effectiveness of k-transfer.

H1b: K-infrastructure capabilities are positively related to the efficiency of k-transfer.

Knowledge Processes and Knowledge Transfer Success

Just as k-transfer cannot be successful without a proper infrastructure, neither can it be successful without certain basic KM processes. k-transfer is but one of many essential business processes which are closely interlinked. It is not enough to transfer knowledge; its active management will ensure its effective use. It must be kept up-to-date, converted into appropriate formats, distributed to those concerned, protected, applied to related problems, and organized for efficient retrieval. These processes support K-transfer and without them we cannot expect the transfer to be successful. Thus, our second hypothesis:

H2: K-process capabilities are positively related to the k-transfer success.

Figure 1.

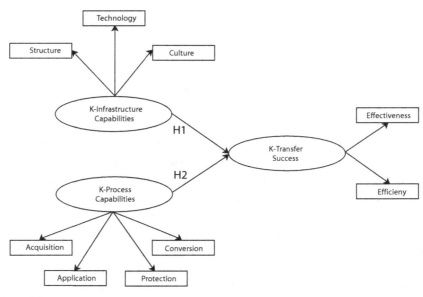

a. General research model

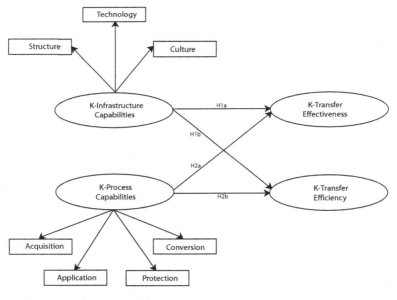

b. Detailed research model

An organization cannot accomplish certain critical processes if it does not possess the necessary capabilities. The success of k-transfer should increase if the transfer is strongly supported by k-process capabilities. Processes have direct bearing on operational efficiency and organizational effectiveness (Kallio, Saarinen, & Tinnila, 2002). Knowledge is an important organizational resource and a company can utilize it only with the presence of proper knowledge processes

(Davenport, Jarvenpaa, & Beers, 1996). Thus, we posit:

H2a: K-process capabilities are positively related to the effectiveness of k-transfer.
H2b: K-process capabilities are positively related to the efficiency of k-transfer.

Measurement

The k-infrastructure capabilities and k-process capabilities constructs replicate the Gold et al. (2001) model but in a different context, that is in IT projects. The authors originally tested organizational KM capabilities with relation to organizational effectiveness. This research will test KM capabilities on a departmental level of analysis and in a context of knowledge transfer success. K-transfer success is to be tested as a new construct in this research. In our model, the k-infrastructure capabilities construct is a second order factor (latent construct) composed of three first-order factors: technological, structural, and cultural infrastructures. The k-process capabilities construct is also a second-order factor composed of four first order factors: acquisition, conversion, application, and protection processes.

The purpose of k-transfer is to allow the receiver to generate value with the new knowledge that it was not able to generate before (Bozeman & Rogers, 2001). The dependent variable, k-transfer success is a second-order factor defined by effectiveness and efficiency. First, a k-transfer process is effective if knowledge sent corresponds to knowledge received. An effective process is one that considers customer requirements and whose end product corresponds to original expectations and satisfies the user. User satisfaction with the system is one of the criteria by which the success of k-transfer is judged (Garrity & Sanders, 1998) because it allows an evaluation of whether the receiver of knowledge (1) received the right knowledge, (2) correctly interpreted it, and (3) correctly applied it (DeLone & McLean, 1992). Second, the k-transfer process is efficient if it is timely and does not create problems in the client department. An efficient process is one that respects its schedule (Verkasolo & Lappalainen, 1998) and involves a minimal number of problems in its duration (Szulanski, 2000). A first proxy to measure the efficiency of k-transfer is the time requirements of the process (Jacob & Ebrahimpur, 2001). A second proxy for the efficiency of k-transfer is its stickiness (Szulanski, 2000). Stickiness refers to the difficulties experienced during the transfer process and is often communication related.

In this research, the k-infrastructure capabilities and k-process capabilities constructs are operationalized based on Gold et al. (2001) whereas the k-transfer efficiency is operationalized based on Franz and Robey (1986); Doll and Torkzadeh (1988), and Kostova (1999). For k-transfer effectiveness, the items from by Szulanski (2000) and Verkasolo and Lappalainen (1998) are used.

Data Collection

Interdepartmental IT projects were selected because they present an opportunity to study a cross-functional k-transfer process. Since effective communication and understanding may be relatively difficult to achieve in such contexts, there is a need to establish what elements of KM capabilities will increase k-transfer success. IT projects are also transactional, that is, projects requiring two parties—one acting as supplier, the other as customer of the end product. As discussed earlier, such a view is appropriate for the study of k-transfer.

A pre-test was conducted with four IT practitioners and resulted mainly in editorial corrections to the instrument. An introductory message providing the links to the online survey was sent by e-mails to the 2,425 IT managers in our sample. To identify them, we relied on the list of 3,281 companies in the Canadian Capabilities Directory. Although not all firms in the directory listed e-mail addresses, 2,425 firms met our criteria, that is, to ensure (sizeable) IT departments, we used medium-sized firms or larger (50 employees or more). Our survey contained two Web links: one with questions appropriate to providers, that is, IT managers, the other for the customer department managers, that is, those department managers who received an IT solution within the last year from the IT department. We requested the firm contact, the IT manager, to forward the link to part of the questionnaire (the items for the dependent variable and satisfaction) to at least one customer department for which the project had been completed. Both IT and non-IT managers were asked to base their answers on a "typical" project that was implemented during the last year. To this end, the IT managers were asked to complete the full questionnaire, which allows us to measure their departments' capabilities and their perception of k-transfer success. Respondents from the customer department were asked to complete only the part of the questionnaire pertaining to their perception of k-transfer success. Two weeks after the initial mailing, 51 usable responses had been received. A reminder was sent which was followed by 76 complete surveys.

ANALYSIS AND RESULTS

A total of 127 usable questionnaires, representing a good cross-section of the population, were received. Although the majority of the respondents came from the heavily populated province of Ontario, there were respondents from 8 out of the 10 Canadian provinces. While 30% of the respondents were from the manufacturing industry, the balance was spread evenly among service industries, such as communications and media, finance, insurance and real estate, construction, and wholesale. Regarding firm size, 19% of the sample had less than 100 employees, 37% between 101 and 500 employees, and 44% were large enterprises.

As suggested by Armstrong and Overton (1977), nonresponse bias was assessed by performing t-tests between the initial and the latest waves of respondents. More specifically, the 21 IT managers and 30 customer department managers who had completed the survey in the first week were considered early respondents. The 30 IT managers and 46 customer department managers who completed the survey after the reminder was sent were considered late respondents. The t-tests between early and late respondents were not significant on any variable under study.

Table 1. K-Infrastructure capabilities discriminant validity (CFA)

	Technological	Cultural	Structural
Technological (ρ=0.88)	0.46		
Cultural (ρ=0.91)	0.44	0.45	
Structural (ρ=0.85)	0.35	0.46	0.45

Table 2. K-Process capabilities discriminant validity (CFA)

	Acquisition	Conversion	Application	Protection
Acquisition (ρ=0.94)	0.62			
Conversion (ρ=0.96)	0.53	0.67		
Application (ρ=0.90)	0.54	0.38	0.52	
Protection (ρ=0.94)	0.27	0.26	0.16	0.66

The research model was analyzed using PLS, a second-generation multivariate technique permitting the validation of the psychometric properties of the scales used, as well as the strength and direction of the relationships among variables (Cassel, Hackl, & Westlund, 1999). Performing structural equation modeling with PLS requires two major steps: (1) assessment of the measurement model by investigating both convergent and discriminant validity and (2) assessment of the structural model, which reveals the item loadings and path coefficients measures (Hulland, 1999; Thompson, Higgins, & Howell, 1991). The computer program used for this analysis was PLS Graph 2.91 developed by Chin and Frye (1995).

The measurement model assessment began by using confirmatory factor analysis (CFA). It is first achieved by keeping constructs with reliability values higher than 0.70 (Hulland, 1999; Nunnally, 1967). The ρ coefficient (rho[1]) is used to verify this criterion. All k-process, k-infrastructure, and k-transfer success rho values were above 0.70, ranging from 0.79 to 0.96 (see Tables 1, 2, and 8). Convergent validity is then evaluated by calculat-

ing the average variance extracted (AVE[2]), which should be higher than 0.50 (Fornell & Larcker, 1981). Results as indicated in Table 1 shows that this threshold was not met for the k-infrastructure capabilities construct. The last assessment step to be conducted is the discriminant validity used to verify if each construct is unique. AVE should have a higher value than the shared variance between each construct (Compeau, Higgins, & Huff, 1999). This criterion was not met for both the k-process capabilities and the k-infrastructure capabilities constructs (see Table 1 and Table 2).

Because the discriminant validity of certain constructs was not confirmed, an exploratory factorial analysis (EFA) was conducted for k-infrastructure and k-process constructs respectively. Using SPSS, the factorial analysis produced seven factors with a total of 21 items for k-infrastructure capabilities and four factors with 25 items for the k-process capabilities. All the necessary steps to assess the new model were followed and produced satisfactory results. Loadings and shared loadings are indicated in Tables 3 to 5. Note that both ρ values and AVE values are now above minimum thresholds as indicated in Tables 6 to 8.

Table 3. Loadings and shared loadings for k-infrastructure capabilities[3]

	Scanning	Facilitate	Sharing	Standard	Learning	Collaborate	Rewards
TI11	0.83	0.33	0.27	0.44	0.33	0.35	0.19
TI12	0.87	0.35	0.34	0.46	0.33	0.56	0.32
SI09	0.80	0.13	0.10	0.32	0.28	0.09	0.23
SI10	0.88	0.40	0.37	0.36	0.44	0.46	0.31
SI2	0.37	0.72	0.09	0.24	0.15	0.45	0.18
SI3	0.32	0.84	0.43	0.34	0.51	0.42	0.45
SI4	0.25	0.82	0.36	0.15	0.47	0.40	0.34
SI7	0.22	0.72	0.32	0.08	0.19	0.27	0.28
SI11	0.19	0.67	0.34	0.11	0.24	0.40	0.04
CI7	0.14	0.33	0.76	-0.09	0.41	0.25	0.18
CI8	0.30	0.29	0.84	0.07	0.35	0.37	0.01
CI11	0.25	0.36	0.83	0.07	0.31	0.50	0.29

continued on the following page

Table 3. continued

CI12	0.33	0.32	0.70	0.31	0.27	0.38	0.26
TI1	0.49	0.32	0.16	0.90	0.30	0.32	0.40
TI2	0.20	0.13	0.03	0.84	0.09	0.30	0.20
TI3	0.50	0.16	0.07	0.79	0.04	0.10	0.21
CI4	0.47	0.34	0.30	0.35	0.88	0.31	0.29
CI5	0.16	0.46	0.46	-0.03	0.72	0.19	0.34
CI6	0.36	0.28	0.32	0.09	0.87	0.23	0.26
TI4	0.34	0.40	0.32	0.26	0.27	0.88	0.18
TI5	0.49	0.34	0.39	0.34	0.39	0.86	0.16
TI6	0.27	0.57	0.52	0.12	0.08	0.78	0.20
SI5	0.33	0.29	0.27	0.26	0.35	0.19	0.95
SI6	0.26	0.38	0.18	0.36	0.32	0.22	0.95

Table 4. Loadings and shared loadings for k-process capabilities [4]

	Acquisition	Conversion	Protection	Application
ACP2	0.81	0.62	0.50	0.62
ACP3	0.80	0.39	0.31	0.52
ACP5	0.83	0.62	0.37	0.52
ACP6	0.77	0.52	0.17	0.54
ACP8	0.85	0.53	0.45	0.63
ACP9	0.77	0.44	0.45	0.59
CP1	0.50	0.83	0.53	0.26
CP4	0.58	0.84	0.31	0.48
CP5	0.61	0.91	0.54	0.46
CP9	0.62	0.76	0.27	0.58
AP1	0.50	0.88	0.49	0.28
AP2	0.53	0.86	0.38	0.48
AP3	0.44	0.76	0.41	0.29
AP4	0.61	0.82	0.35	0.50
ACP1	0.43	0.81	0.51	0.21
PP1	0.33	0.38	0.89	0.26
PP2	0.42	0.42	0.83	0.34
PP3	0.41	0.44	0.96	0.29
PP4	0.45	0.45	0.92	0.26
PP5	0.41	0.52	0.88	0.19
PP7	0.46	0.51	0.83	0.29
AP7	0.55	0.29	0.22	0.91
AP8	0.57	0.35	0.22	0.89
AP11	0.65	0.41	0.39	0.86
CP7	0.68	0.61	0.22	0.78

Table 5. Loadings and shared loadings for k-transfer success [5]

	Effectiveness	Efficiency
KS1	0.77	0.56
KS2	0.86	0.58
KS3	0.76	0.50
KS4	0.61	0.85
KS5	0.32	0.57
KS6	0.53	0.80
KS7	0.48	0.65

Table 6. K-Infrastructure capabilities discriminant validity (EFA)

	Scanning (ρ=0.91)	Facilitate (ρ=0.87)	Sharing (ρ=0.86)	Standard (ρ=0.88)	Learning (ρ=0.87)	Collaborate (ρ=0.88)	Rewards (ρ=0.95)
Scanning	0.72						
Facilitate	0.13	0.57					
Sharing	0.11	0.17	0.62				
Standard	0.22	0.06	0.01	0.71			
Learning	0.17	0.18	0.18	0.03	0.68		
Collaborate	0.19	0.26	0.23	0.08	0.09	0.71	
Rewards	0.10	0.13	0.05	0.11	0.12	0.05	0.90

Table 7. K-Process capabilities discriminant validity (EFA)

	Acquisition (ρ=0.92)	Conversion (ρ=0.95)	Application (ρ=0.92)	Protection (ρ=0.96)
Acquisition	0.65			
Conversion	0.42	0.69		
Application	0.50	0.22	0.74	
Protection	0.22	0.26	0.10	0.79

Table 8. K-Transfer success discriminant validity (CFA)

	Effectiveness (ρ=0.79)	Efficiency (ρ=0.71)
Effectiveness	0.66	
Efficiency	0.45	0.53

Table 9. Descriptive data of the final model assessment

	Min	Max	Median	Mean	Std. Dev.
Technological Scanning	1	7	5.00	4.82	1.22
Facilitation Mechanism	4	7	5.40	5.33	0.79
Culture of Sharing	4	7	6.00	5.84	0.81
Establishment of Standards	1	7	4.67	4.70	1.16
Culture of Learning	3	7	6.33	6.13	0.78
Collaboration Technology	2	7	5.00	4.96	1.20
Systems of Rewards	1	7	3.50	3.65	1.82
Acquisition	2	7	5.17	4.94	1.19
Conversion	2	7	5.78	5.52	0.96
Application	1	7	5.33	5.02	1.23
Protection	2	7	6.00	5.55	1.38
Effectiveness	4	7	6.00	5.73	0.80
Efficiency	3	7	5.50	5.46	0.76

Following the model assessment, the final descriptive data for each construct are provided in Table 9.

PLS graph was used to assess the structural model (Figures 2a and 2b). The analysis was two-fold. First, the general model was assessed to test for Hypotheses 1 and 2. Then, a separate model was analyzed in order to test Hypotheses 1a, 1b, 2a, and 2b. The path coefficients were calculated using the PLS Jack-Knife procedure (Wildt, Lambert, & Durand, 1982). All the independent and dependent variables were assessed as second-order factors in the general model.

As depicted in Figure 2a, hypothesis 1 tested for a positive relationship between k-infrastructure capabilities and k-transfer success. This relationship was confirmed (path Coefficient = 0.572, p<0.001). Hypothesis 2 tested for a positive relationship between k-process capabilities and k-transfer success. This relationship was not confirmed (path Coefficient = 0.160). Almost 50% of the k-transfer success is explained by the contribution of the k-infrastructure capabilities (R^2 = 0.491).

The second analysis was performed to test the sub-hypotheses (Figure 2b). K-infrastructure and k-process constructs were tested in a direct relationship with k-transfer efficiency and effectiveness. Efficiency and effectiveness were assessed as first-order factors while k-infrastructure and k-process capabilities were tested as second-order factors.

Hypothesis 1a tested for a positive relationship between k-infrastructure capabilities and k-transfer effectiveness. This relationship was confirmed (path coefficient = 0.600, p<0.001). Hypothesis 1b tested for a positive relationship between k-infrastructure capabilities and k-transfer efficiency. This relationship was not confirmed. Hypotheses 2a tested for a positive relationship between k-process capabilities and k-transfer effectiveness. This relationship was not confirmed. The last subhypothesis (2b) was confirmed with a positive relationship between k-process capabilities and k-transfer efficiency (path coefficient = 0.415, p<0.01).

Figure 2.

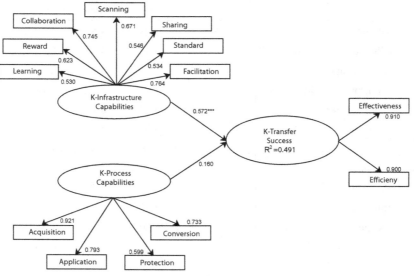

a. Tested general model

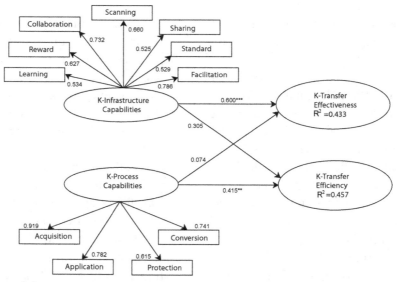

b. Tested detailed model

DISCUSSION

The overall results indicate that even if only the k-infrastructure capabilities lead to k-transfer success, it still explains close to 50% of variance of the dependent variable. This reflects the posi-tion of Sambarmuthy, Bharadway, and Grover (2003) and Ross (2003) who indicate that firms need proper, well integrated, and standardized technological infrastructure to grow and reach some organizational flexibility and agility. With-out the necessary technological resources, it is therefore difficult for firms to help employees to successfully exchange some of their knowledge about a specific project.

Our results also suggest that both aspects of KM capabilities play an important role in ensuring the success of k-transfer, namely its efficiency and effectiveness. The tests for our subhypotheses have shown that KM capabilities have a significant impact on the particular aspects of k-transfer. Specifically, k-process capabilities contribute to k-transfer efficiency and k-infrastructure capabilities contributes to k-transfer effectiveness. A k-transfer is said to be efficient if it is timely and involves a minimal number of problems. This can only be achieved if the processes, upon which k-transfer depends, function smoothly. We can say that if an IT department has such processes in place, it is in a better position to efficiently deliver IT solutions to its clients. Whether these solutions will correspond to the original client demands (effectiveness), will be largely determined by the presence of k-infrastructure elements within the IT department. Namely, whether its culture and structure promote sharing and collaboration, and whether it has technology that enables collaboration and new opportunity generation.

Interestingly, k-infrastructure capabilities did not prove to significantly contribute to k-transfer efficiency. Infrastructure elements can be viewed as a set of tools and enablers for k-transfer (Goh, 2002). They do not however guarantee its efficiency. Our survey verified the presence of infrastructure elements, but not the extent and modes of their application. Similarly, k-process capabilities did not prove significant with respect to k-transfer effectiveness. This was an unexpected result. Certainly, processes have an important bearing on improving efficiency (Kallio et al., 2002). We can speculate that in cases where firms did have k-processes capabilities in place and were not able to achieve k-transfer effectiveness, these processes may have been either improperly implemented or badly managed.

In interpreting our results, some limitations have to be kept in mind. For one, the response rate is low due to the following reasons. First, because we used an online survey, concern for spam and e-mail security may have contributed to the low response rate. Second, Canadian law restricts corporate lists from public provision and therefore we used the *Canadian Capabilities Directory,* a registry of voluntary association. This informal structure behind the directory may also have contributed to the low response rate. Third, the questionnaire and the Canadian Capabilities Directory existed solely in English, a fact that surely limited response from Canada's second largest province, French-speaking Quebec. Moreover, we asked the respondents to consider an inter-departmental project that had been completed within the last year. This obviously limits the number of eligible respondents.

Fifty-four IT managers and managers from 73 of their customer departments provided the 127 usable responses. Because the IT department respondent was asked to direct the appropriate part of the questionnaire to the customer departments, there is the possibility of a bias in favor of satisfied customer departments. If this is the case, the "selected" customer departments would however have been perceived as "satisfied" by the IT respondent. Our survey did not include a control check in this regard.

Contributions and Research Avenues

The main academic contribution of this research is that it is one of the few that has empirically measured the success of k-transfer. Although several models were proposed for measuring k-transfer success, to our knowledge we are the first to design an instrument that combines proposed measurements of efficiency and effectiveness into one construct, *interdepartmental* k-transfer success. The statistical results have shown it to be both valid and reliable. We also have learned that measuring k-transfer success only would not have provided us with enough information on the impact of k-process capabilities. Indeed, the general research model showed a nonsignificant link between these two constructs whereas the detailed research model indicated that the k-process capabilities are positively related to the efficiency aspect of k-transfer success but not to its effectiveness.

The model assessment of KM capabilities showed that each construct had to be revisited, more specifically the k-infrastructure capabilities construct. Because the technology, culture, and structure subconstructs were redistributed as seven new subconstructs, our results suggest that these new components are more precise and better indicators of a department's k-infrastructure capabilities than the original components (e.g. technology, culture, and structure) (See Table 3). Each of the new subconstructs, except technological scanning, was related to only one of the original scales. This is another contribution of this research since our revised k-infrastructure capabilities construct is more detailed and provides practitioners with even more specific guidelines than did the original construct. As such, IT managers' attention is directed at specific technological, cultural, and structural components of their k-infrastructure capabilities. Focussing on each of them instead of on the whole picture should help them to identify weaknesses and problems much more easily and quickly. This identification will enable them to rely on the appropriate actions and mechanisms to improve their capabilities which will, in turn, lead to more effective k-transfer during their IT projects.

In addition, our results show that both aspects of KM capabilities are needed to make k-transfer effective and efficient. More specifically, managers should keep in mind that k-infrastructure capabilities must be put in place and used properly if they want to increase the effectiveness of k-transfer. On the other hand, if the main objective is to en-hance the efficiency of k-transfer, managers must put more efforts on developing strong k-process capabilities related to the acquisition, conversion, application, and protection of knowledge.

Replications of our study are needed to further our understanding of the mechanisms and key factors involved in successful k-transfer within organizations. Larger samples would allow for more flexible analyses and further assessment of the reliability and validity of our model. They would also allow for the examination of the effect of departmental subcultures within organizations, which potentially play a role in success of k-transfers. It would be interesting to investigate whether different processes and infrastructure elements would play a more or less critical role in k-transfer success.

REFERENCES

Alavi, M., & Leider, D. (2001). Knowledge management and knowledge management systems: Conceptual foundations and research issues. MIS Quarterly, 25(1), 107-136.

Argote, L., & Ingram, P. (2000). Knowledge transfer: A basis for competitive advantage in firms. Organizational Behavior and Human Decision Processes, 82(1), 150-169.

Argote, L., Ingram, P., Levine, J., & Moreland, R. (2000) Knowledge transfer in organizations: Learning from the experience of others. Organizational Behavior and Human Decision Processes, 82(1), 1-8.

Armstrong, J. S., & Overton, T. S. (1977). Estimating non-response bias in mail surveys. Journal of Marketing Research, 14(8), 396-402.

Ayas, K. (1996). Professional project management: A shift toward learning and knowledge creating structure. International Journal of Project Management, 14(3), 131-136.

Barki, H., & Hartwick, J. (2001). Interpersonal conflict and its management in information system development. MIS Quarterly, 25(2), 195-228.

Barney, J. (1986). Strategic factor markets: Expectations, luck and business strategy. Management Science, 31(10), 1231-1241.

Barney, J. B. (1995). Looking inside for competitive advantage. The Academy of Management Executive, 9(4), 49-61.

Bolino, A. V. (2002). A model of intersubsidiary knowledge transfer effectiveness. South Bend, IN: University of South Carolina.

Bozeman, B., & Rogers, J. D. (2001). Use-and-transformation: A theory of knowledge value for research evaluation. Retrieved from http://rvm.pp.gatech.edu/papers/

Bresman, H., Birkinshaw, J., & Nobel, R. (1999). Knowledge transfer in international acquisitions. Journal of International Business Studies, 30(3), 439-462.

Byrd, T. A., Cossick, K. L., & Zmud, R. W. (1992). A synthesis of research on requirements analysis and knowledge acquisition techniques. MIS Quarterly, 16(1), 117-138.

Calabrese, G. (1999). Managing information in product development. Logistics Information Management, 12(6), 128-152.

Carlile, P. R. (2004). Transferring, translating, and transforming: An integrative framework for managing knowledge across boundaries. Organization Science, 15(5), 555-568.

Cassel, C., Hackl, P., & Westlund, A. H. (1999). Robustness of partial least-squares method for estimating latent variable quality structures. Journal of Applied Statistics, 26(4), 435-446.

Chua, A. (2001, October). Relationship between the types of knowledge shared and types of communication channels used. Journal of Knowledge Management Practice. Retrieved from http://www.tlainc.com/articl26.htm

Compeau, D. R., Higgins, C. A., & Huff, S. (1999). Social cognitive theory and individual reactions to computing technology: A longitudinal study. MIS Quarterly, 23(2), 145-158.

Croteau, A.-M., & Li, P. (2003). Critical success factors of CRM initiatives. Canadian Journal of Administrative Sciences, 20(1), 21-34.

Darr, E. D., & Kurtzberg, T. R. (2000). An investigation of partner similarity dimensions on knowledge transfer. Organizational Behavior and Human Decision Processes, 82(1), 22-44.

Davenport, H. T., Jarvenpaa, S. L., & Beers, M. C. (1996). Improving knowledge work processes. Sloan Management Review, 37(4), 53-66.

Davenport, T. H., & Prusak, L. (1998). Working knowledge: How organizations manage what they know. Boston: Harvard Business School Pressxz.

DeLone, W. H., & McLean, E. R. (1992). Information systems success: The quest for the dependent variable. Information Systems Research, 3(1), 60-95.

DeLong, D. W., & Fahey, L. (2000). Diagnosing cultural barriers to knowledge management. Academy of Management Executive, 14(4), 113-127.

Doll, W. J., & Torkzadeh, G. (1988). The measurement of end-user computing satisfaction. MIS Quarterly, 12(2), 259-274.

Edvinsson, L., & Malone, M. (1997). Intellectual capital: Realizing your company's true value by finding its hidden brainpower. New York: Harper Business.

Faraj, S., & Sproull, L. (2000). Coordinating expertise in software development teams. Management Science, 46(12), 1554-1568.

Foos, T., Schum, G., & Rothenberg, S. (2006). Tacit knowledge transfer and the knowledge disconnect. Journal of Knowledge Management, 10(1), 6-18.

Fornell, C. R., & Larcker, D. F. (1981). Two structural equation models with unobservable variables and measurement error: Algebra and statistics. Journal of Marketing Research, 18(3), 382-389.

Franz, C. R., & Robey, D. (1986). Organizational context, user involvement, and the usefulness of information systems. Decision Sciences, 17(3), 329-356.

Frick, T. (2004). Types of knowledge of education created through disciplined inquiry. Bloomington: Indiana University, School of Education. Retrieved from www.indiana.edu/~tedfrick/typesofknowledgesept1.pdf

Garrity, E. J., & Sanders, G. L. (1998). Dimensions of information systems success. Hershey, PA: Idea Group Publishing.

Goh, A. L. S. (2005). Harnessing knowledge for innovation: An integrated management framework. Journal of Knowledge Management, 9(4), 6-18.

Goh, S. C. (2002). Managing effective knowledge transfer: An integrative framework and some practical implications. Journal of Knowledge Management, 6(1), 23-30.

Gold, A. H., Malhotra, A., & Segars, A. H. (2001). Knowledge management: An organizational capabilities perspective. Journal of Management Information Systems, 18(1), 185-214.

Grant, R.M. (1991). The resource-based theory of competitive advantage: Implications for strategy formulation. California Management Review, 33(3), 114-135.

Grant, R. (1996). Towards a knowledge-based theory of the firm [Winter special issue]. Strategic Management Journal, 17, 102-122.

Gruenfeld, D. H., Martorana, P. V., & Fan, E. T. (2000). What do groups learn from their worldliest members? Direct and indirect influence in dynamic teams. Organizational Behavior and Human Decision Processes, 82(1), 45-59.

Gupta, A. K., & Govindarajan, V. (2000). Knowledge management's social dimension: Lessons from Nucor steel. Sloan Management Review, 42(1), 77-80.

Hansen, T. M. (1999). The search-transfer problem: The role of weak ties in sharing knowledge across organization subunits. Administrative Science Quarterly, 44(1), 82-111.

Henderson, J. C., & Venkatraman, N. (1999). Strategic alignment: Leveraging information technology for transforming organizations. IBM Systems Journal, 38(2&3), 472-484.

Herschel, R. T., Nemati, H., & Steiger, D. (2001). Tacit to explicit knowledge conversation: Knowledge exchange protocols. Journal of Knowledge Management, 5(5), 107-116.

Hoopes, D. G. (2001). Why are there glitches in product development? R&D Management, 31(4), 381-390.

Huber, G. P. (1991). Organizational learning: The contributing processes and the literatures. In M. D. Cohen & L. S. Sproull (Eds.), Organization learning (pp. 124-162). Thousand Oaks, CA: Sage.

Hulland, J. (1999). Use of partial least squares (PLS) in strategic management research: A review of four recent studies. Strategic Management Journal, 20(2), 195-204.

Jacob, M., & Ebrahimpur, G. (2001). Experience vs. expertise: The role of implicit understandings of knowledge in determining the nature of knowledge transfer in two companies. Journal of Intellectual Capital, 2(1), 74-88.

Kallio, J., Saarinen, T., & Tinnila, M. (2002). Efficient change strategies: Matching drivers and chasers in change products. Business Process Management Journal, 8(1), 80-93.

Karlsen, J., & Gottschalk, P. (2004). Factors affecting knowledge transfer in it projects. Engineering Management Journal, 16(1), 3-11.

Karlsen, J. T., & Gottschalk, P. (2003). An empirical evaluation of knowledge transfer mechanisms for IT projects. The Journal of Computer Information Systems, 44(1), 112-119.

Ko, D.-G., Kirsch, L. J., & King, W. R. (2005). Antecedents of knowledge transfer from consultants to clients in enterprise system implementations. MIS Quarterly, 29(1), 58-87.

Kostova, T. (1999). Transnational transfer of organizational practices: A contextual perspective. Academy of Management Review, 24(2), 308-324.

Lane, P. J., & Lubatkin, M. (1998). Relative absorptive capacity and interorganizational learning. Strategic Management Journal, 19(5), 461-477.

Levinson, M. (2005, December 27). The ABCs of KM. CIO Magazine. Retrieved from http://www.cio.com/research/knowledge/edit/kmabcs.html

Lin, L., Geng, X., & Whinston, A. B. (2005). A sender- receiver framework for knowledge transfer. MIS Quarterly, 29(2), 197-219.

Lubit, R. (2001). Tacit knowledge and knowledge management: The keys to sustainable management. Organizational Dynamics, 29(3), 164-178.

Madu, C. N., Kuei, C. H., & Chen, J. H. (1995). A decision support systems approach to adjust maintenance float system availability levels. Computers & Industrial Engineering, 28(4), 773-786.

Maritan, C. A. (2001). Capital investment as investing in organizational capabilities: An empirically grounded process model. Academy of Management Journal, 44(3), 513-531.

Mata, F. J., Fuerst, W. L., & Barney, J. B. (1995). Information technology and sustained competitive advantage: A resource-based analysis. MIS Quarterly, 19(4), 487-505.

McDermott, R., & O'Dell, C. (2001). Overcoming cultural barriers to sharing knowledge. Journal of Knowledge Management, 5(1), 76-85.

Nelson, K., & Cooprider, J. G. (1996). The contribution of shared knowledge to IS group performance. MIS Quarterly, 20(4), 409-430.

Nonaka, I., & Takeuchi, H. (1995). The knowledge creating company—How Japanese companies create the dynamics of innovation. Oxford University Press.

Nunnally, J. (1967). Psychometric theory. New York: McGraw-Hill.

O'Dell, C. (1998). If only we knew what we know: Identification and transfer of internal best practices. California Management Review, 40(3), 144-174.

O'Dell, C., & Grayson, C. J., Jr. (1999). Knowledge transfer: Discover your value proposition. Strategy & Leadership, 27(2), 10-17.

Rasmus, D. W. (2001). Transferring knowledge with technology. Giga Information Group.

Rivera, M., Dussauge, P., & Mitchell, W. (2001). Coordination, creation and protection: Micromechanisms for learning from an alliance. Jouy-en-Josas, France: HEC Graduate School of Management.

Ross, J. W. (2003). Creating a strategic it architecture competency: Learning in stages. MIS Quarterly Executive, 2(1), 31-43.

Sambamurthy, V., Bharadway, A., & Grover, V. (2003). Shaping agility through digital options: Reconceptualizing the role of information technology in contemporary firms. MIS Quarterly, 27(2), 237-263.

Schulz, M. (2000). Pathways of relevance: Exploring inflows of knowledge into subunits of mncs. Retrieved from http://iis.stanford.edu/docs/knexus/MartinSchulz.pdf

Sharda, R., Franckwick, G. L., Deosthali, A., & Delahoussaye, R. (1998). Information support for new product development teams. Cambridge, MA: Marketing Science Institute.

Spanos, Y. E., & Prastacos, G. (2004). Understanding organizational capabilities: Towards a conceptual framework. Journal of Knowledge Management, 8(3), 31-43.

Syed-Ikhsan, S., & Rowland, F. (2004). Knowledge management in a public organization: A study on the relationship between organizational elements and the performance of knowledge transfer. Journal of Knowledge Management, 8(2), 95-111.

Szulanski, G. (2000). The process of knowledge transfer: A diachronic analysis of stickiness. Organizational Behavior and Human Decision Processes, 82(1), 9-27.

Thomas, J. C., Kellogg, W. A., & Erickson, T. (2001). The knowledge management puzzle: Human and social factors in knowledge management. IBM Systems Journal, 40(4), 863-884.

Thompson, R. L., Higgins, C. A., & Howell, J. M. (1991). Personal computing: Toward a conceptual model of utilization. MIS Quarterly, 15(1), 125-143.

Verkasolo, M., & Lappalainen, P. (1998). A method of measuring the efficiency of the knowledge utilization process. IEEE Transactions on Engineering Management, 45(4), 414-423.

Von Krogh, G., & Grand, S. (2002). From economic theory toward a knowledge-based theory of the firm. In N. Bontis & C. W. Choo (Eds.), The strategic management of intellectual capital and organizational knowledge (pp. 163-184). New York: Oxford University Press.

Wiig, K. (1997). Knowledge management: An introduction and perspective. Journal of Knowledge Management, 1(1), 6-14.

Wildt, A. R., Lambert, Z. V., Durand, R. M. (1982). Applying the jackknife statistics in testing and interpreting canonical weights, loadings, and cross-loadings. Journal of Marketing Research, 19(1), 99-107.

Zack, M. (1999). Managing codified knowledge. Sloan Management Review, 40(4), 45-58.

ENDNOTES

[1] $\rho = (\Sigma|\lambda_i|)^2 / (\Sigma|\lambda_i|)^2 + \Sigma(1-\lambda_i^2)$ where λ_i is the loading for factor i.

[2] $AVE = \Sigma\lambda i2 / (\Sigma\lambda_i^2 + \Sigma(1-\lambda_i^2))$ where λ_i is the loading for factor i.

[3]   Note that each indicator was labelled as follows: TI—technological infrastructure, SI—Structural infrastructure, and CI—Cultural infrastructure. The legend for the new constructs of k-infrastructure capabilities is the following:

Scanning	Technological Scanning
Facilitate	Facilitation Mechanism
Sharing	Culture of Sharing
Standard	Establishment of Standards
Learning	Culture of Learning
Collaborate	Collaboration Technology
Rewards	Systems of Rewards

[4]   Note that each indicator was labelled as follows: CP—Conversion process, PP—Protection process, AP—Application process, and ACP—Acquisition process.

[5]   Note that each indicator was labelled as follows: KS – Knowledge success.

Compilation of References

Ackerman, M. (1998). Augmenting Organizational Memory: A Field Study of Answer Garden. *ACM Transactions on Information Systems, 16*(3), 203–224. doi:10.1145/290159.290160

Ackerman, M. (2000). The intellectual challenge of CSCW: The gap between social requirements and technical feasibility. *Human-Computer Interaction, 15*(2-3), 181-205.

Adamides, E. D., & Karacapilidis, N. (2006). Information technology support for the knowledge and social processes of innovation management. *Technovation, 26*, 50–59. doi:10.1016/j.technovation.2004.07.019

Agarwal, R. & Prasad, J. (1998). Conceptual and Operational Definition of Personal Innovativeness in the Domain of Information Technology. *Information Systems Research, 9*(2), 204-215.

Agrawal, M. (1995). Review of a 40-year debate in international advertising: Practitioner and academician perspectives to the standardization/adaptation issue. *International Marketing Review, 12*(1), 26-48.

Ajzen, I. (1985). From Intentions to Action: A Theory of Planned Behavior . In Kuhl, J., & Beckmann, J. (Eds.), *Action Control From Cognition to Behavior* (pp. 11–39). New York: Springer-Verlag.

Ajzen, I. (1988). *Attitudes, personality, and behavior*. Chicago: Dorsey.

Ajzen, I., & Fishbein, M. (1980). *Understanding Attitudes and Predicting Behavior*. Englewood Cliffs, NJ: Prentice-Hall.

Alavi, M. (1994). Computer-mediated collaborative learning: An empirical evaluation. *MIS Quarterly, 18*(2), 159-174.

Alavi, M., & Leidner, D. (2001). Knowledge management and knowledge management systems: conceptual foundations and research issues. *Management Information Systems Quarterly, 23*(1), 107–125. doi:10.2307/3250961

Alavi, M., & Leidner, D.E. (2001). Technology mediated learning: A call for greater depth and breadth of research. *Information Systems Research, 12*(1), 1-10.

Alavi, M., Kayworth, T., & Leidner, D. (2005). An empirical examination of the influence of organizational culture on knowledge management practices. *Journal of Managment Information Systems, 22*(3), 191-224.

Alavi, M., Marakas, G.M., & Yoo, Y. (2002) A comparative study of distributed learning environments on learning outcomes. *Information Systems Research, 13*(4), 404-415.

Amabile, T. (1996). *Creativity in context: Update to the social psychology of creativity*. Westview Press.

Amabile, T. M. (1982). *The Social Psychology of Creativity*. New York: Springer.

Ancona, D. G. (1990). Outward Bound: Strategies for Team Survival in an Organisation. *Academy of Management Journal, 33*, 334–365. doi:10.2307/256328

Anderson, D. E., Ansfield, M. E., & Depaulo, B. M. (1997). Love's best habit: Deception in the context of relationships . In Philippot, P., Feldman, R. S., & Coats, E. J. (Eds.), *The social context of nonverbal behavior* (pp. 1–46). Cambridge: Cambridge University Press.

Anderson, E.W., & Sullivan, M.W. (1993). The antecedents and consequences of customer satisfaction for firms. *Marketing Science, 12*(2), 125-143.

Anson, R., & Jelassi, M.T. (1990). A developmental framework for computer-supported conflict resolution. *European Journal of Operational Research, 46*(2), 181-199.

Anthes, G. (2007). Second Life: Is there any there there? *Computerworld, 41*(49), 30–38.

Anthony, T. (2000). Supply chain collaboration: Success in the new Internet economy . In Anthony, T. (Ed.), *Achieving supply chain excellence through technology* (*Vol. 2*). San Francisco, CA: Montgomery Research Inc.

Applegate, L. M., McFarlan, F. W., & McKenney, J. L. (1996). *Corporate information systems management: Text and cases* (4th ed.). Boston: Irwin McGraw-Hill.

Argote, L., & Ingram, P. (2000). Knowledge transfer: A basis for competitive advantage in firms. Organizational Behavior and Human Decision Processes, 82(1), 150-169.

Argote, L., Ingram, P., Levine, J., & Moreland, R. (2000) Knowledge transfer in organizations: Learning from the experience of others. Organizational Behavior and Human Decision Processes, 82(1), 1-8.

Arias, E. G., Eden, H., Fischer, G., Gorman, A., & Scharff, E. (2000). Transcending the individual human mind - Creating shared understanding through collaborative design. *ACM Transactions on Computer-Human Interaction, 7*(1), 84-113.

Armstrong, D., & Cole, P. (1995). Managing distances and differences in geographically distributed work groups . In Jackson, S., & Ruderman, M. (Eds.), *Diversity in Work Teams* (pp. 187–216). Washington, DC: American Psychological Association. doi:10.1037/10189-007

Armstrong, J. S., & Overton, T. S. (1977). Estimating non-response bias in mail surveys. *Journal of Marketing Research*, 14(8), 396-402.

Armstrong, S., J., & Priola, V. (2001). Individual differences in cognitive style and their effects in task and social orientations of self-managed work teams. *Small Group Research, 32*(3), 283–312. doi:10.1177/104649640103200302

Arrow, H., McGrath, J. E., & Berdahl, J. (2000). *Small groups as complex systems: Formation, coordination, development, and adaptation.* Thousand Oaks, CA: Sage.

Arunachalam, V., & Dilla, W.N. (1995). Judgment accuracy and outcomes in negotiations: A causal modeling analysis of decision-aiding effects. *Organizational Behavior and Human Decision Processes, 61*(3), 289-304.

Auramo, J., Aminoff, A., & Punakivi, M. (2002). Research agenda for e-business logistics based on professional opinions. *International Journal of Physical Distribution and Logistics Management, 32*(7), 513–531. doi:10.1108/09600030210442568

Auramo, J., Kauremaa, J., & Tanskanen, K. (2005). Benefits of IT in supply chain management: an explorative study of progressive companies. *International Journal of Physical Distribution & Logistics Management, 35*(2), 82–100. doi:10.1108/09600030510590282

Axelrod, R. (1984). *The evolution of cooperation.* New York: Basic Books.

Ayas, K. (1996). Professional project management: A shift toward learning and knowledge creating structure. International Journal of Project Management, 14(3), 131-136.

Baeza-Yates, R., & Ribeiro-Neto, B. (1999). *Modern information retrieval.* Addison-Wesley.

Bafoutsou, G., & Mentzas, G. (2002). Review and functional classification of collaborative systems. *International Journal of Information Management, 22*(4), 281–305. doi:10.1016/S0268-4012(02)00013-0

Bagchi, P. K., & Skjoett-Larsen, T. (2002). Organizational integration in supply chains: a contingency approach. *Global Journal of Flexible Systems Management, 3,* 1–10.

Baird, J., & Wieting, G. (1979). Nonverbal communication can be a motivational tool. *Personnel Journal, 19,* 637-654.

Bakx, A.W.E.A., Vermetten, Y.J.M., & Van der Sanden, J.M.M. (2003). Self-perceived competence, learning conceptions and preferred learning situations in the domain of communication. *British Journal of Educational Psychology, 73*(2), 223-245.

Baltahazard, P. A., & Cooke, R. A. (2003). *Organizational culture and knowledge management success: Assessing the behavior-performance continuum.* AZ: Arizona State University West.

Bandura, A. (1986). *Social foundations of thought and action: A social cognitive theory.* Englewood Cliffs, NJ: Prentice Hall.

Bardram, J.E., & Bossen, C. (2003). Moving to get aHead: Local mobility and collaborative work. In *Proceedings of the European Conference on Computer-Supported Cooperative Work (ECSCW)*, Helsinki, Finland (pp. 355-374). ACM Press.

Barkhi, R., Jacob, V. S., & Pirkul, H. (1999). An experimental analysis of face-to-face versus computer mediated communication channels. *Group Decision and Negotiation, 8*(4), 325–347. doi:10.1023/A:1008621423120

Barki, H., & Hartwick, J. (2001). Interpersonal conflict and its management in information system development. MIS Quarterly, 25(2), 195-228.

Barkow, J. H., Cosmides, L., & Tooby, J. (Eds.). (1992). *The adapted mind: Evolutionary psychology and the generation of culture.* New York: Oxford University Press.

Barley, S. R. (1986). Technology as an Occasion for Structuring: Evidence from Observations of CT Scanners and the Social Order of Radiology Departments. *Administrative Science Quarterly, 31,* 78–108. doi:10.2307/2392767

Barney, J. (1986). Strategic factor markets: Expectations, luck and business strategy. Management Science, 31(10), 1231-1241.

Barney, J. B. (1995). Looking inside for competitive advantage. The Academy of Management Executive, 9(4), 49-61.

Barratt, M. (2003). Positioning the role of collaborative planning in grocery supply chains. *The International Journal of Logistics Management, 14,* 53–66. doi:10.1108/09574090310806594

Barratt, M. (2004). Understanding the meaning of collaboration in the supply chain. *Supply Chain Management: An International Journal, 9,* 30–42. doi:10.1108/13598540410517566

Barrett, M., Capplemann, S., Shoib, G., & Walsham, G. (2004). Learning in knowledge communities: Managing technology and context. *European Management Journal, 22*(1), 1-11.

Barros, B., & Verdejo, F. (2000). Analyzing student interaction processes in order to improve collaboration. The DEGREE approach. *International Journal of AIED, 11,* 221–241.

Basu, A., & Kumar, A. (2002). Research commentary: workflow management issues in e-business. *Information Systems Research, 13*(1), 1–14. doi:10.1287/isre.13.1.1.94

Batenburg, R., & Rutten, R. (2003). Managing innovation in regional supply networks: A Dutch case of knowledge industry clustering. *Supply Chain Management, 8,* 263–270. doi:10.1108/13598540310484654

Bates, B., & Cleese, J. (2001). *The human face.* New York: DK Publishing.

Bauknight, D. N. (2000). The supply chain future in the e-economy. *Supply Chain Management Review, 4*(1), 28–35.

Bazerman, M.H., & Carroll, J.S. (1987). Negotiator cognition. In L.L. Cummings & B.M. Staw (eds.), *Research in Organizational Behavior* (Vol. 9), (pp. 247-288). Greenwich, CT: JAI Press.

Becerra-Fernandez, I., Del Alto, M., & Stewart, H. (2005). A case study of web-based collaborative decision support at NASA. *International Journal of e-Collaboration, 2*, 50–64.

Becerra-Fernandez, I., Del Alto, M., & Stewart, H. (2006). Postdoc: A model for Web-based collaborative decision support at NASA. *International Journal of e-Collaboration, 2*(3), 49-63.

Becerra-Fernandez, I., Gonzalez, A., & Sabherwal, R. (2004). *Knowledge management: Challenges, solutions, and technologies.* Upper Saddle River, NJ: Prentice Hall.

Belloti, V., & Bly, S. (1996). Walking away from the desktop computer: Distributed collaboration and mobility in a product design team. In *Proceedings of the Conference on Computer-Supported Cooperative Work (CSCW)*, Boston, Massachusetts (pp. 209-218). ACM Press.

Benbunan-Fich, R. (2002). Improving education and training with IT. *Communications of the ACM, 45*(6), 94-99.

Benbunan-Fich, R., & Hiltz, R. (1999). Impacts of asynchronous learning networks on individual and group problem solving: A field experiment. *Group Decision and Negotiation, 8*(5), 409–426. doi:10.1023/A:1008669710763

Bensaou, M., & Venkatraman, N. (1996). Inter-organizational relationship and information technology: A conceptual synthesis and a research framework. *European Journal of Information Systems, 5*, 84–91. doi:10.1057/ejis.1996.15

Bentler, P. M. (1990). Comparative fit indexes in structural models . *Psychological Bulletin, 107*(3), 238–246. doi:10.1037/0033-2909.107.2.238

Berger, S., Hampton, K. L., Carli, L. L., Grandmaison, P. S., Sadow, J. S., & Donath, C. H. (1981). Audience-induced inhibition of overt practice during learning. *Journal of Personality and Social Psychology, 40*, 479–491. doi:10.1037/0022-3514.40.3.479

Bernoux, P. (1999). *La sociologie des entreprises.* Paris: Éditions du Seuil.

Berscheid, E., Snyder, M., & Omoto, A. M. (1989). The relationship closeness inventory: Assessing the closeness of interpersonal relationships. *Journal of Personality and Social Psychology, 57*, 792–807. doi:10.1037/0022-3514.57.5.792

Bessière, K., Seay, A. F., & Kiesler, S. (2007). The ideal elf: Identity exploration in World of Warcraft. *Cyberpsychology & Behavior, 10*(4), 530–535. doi:10.1089/cpb.2007.9994

Bhatt, G. D., Gupta, J. N. D., & Kitchens, F. (2005). An exploratory study of groupware use in the knowledge management process. *Journal of Enterprise Information Management, 8*(1), 28–46. doi:10.1108/17410390510571475

Bhattacherjee, A. (2001). Understanding information systems continuance: An expectation-confirmation model. *MIS Quarterly, 25*(3), 351-370.

Bhoovaraghavan, S., Vasudevan, A., & Chandran, R. (1996). Resolving the process vs. product innovation dilemma: A consumer choice theoretic approach. *Management Science, 42*(2), 232–246. doi:10.1287/mnsc.42.2.232

Biner, P.M. (1993). The development of an instrument to measure student attitudes toward televised courses. *The American Journal of Distance Education, 7*(1), 63-73.

Biros, D. P., George, J. F., & Zmud, R. W. (2002). Inducing sensitivity to deception in order to improve decision making performance: A field study. *Management Information Systems Quarterly, 26*(2), 119–144. doi:10.2307/4132323

Bloor, G., & Dawson, P. (1994). Understanding professional culture in organizational context. *Organization Studies, 15*(2), 275-295.

Bly, S. (1998). Special section on collaboratories. *ACM Interactions, 5*(3), 31.

Boaz, N. T., & Almquist, A. J. (2001). *Biological anthropology: A synthetic approach to human evolution.* Upper Saddle River, NJ: Prentice Hall.

Boden, M. A. (2004). *The creative mind: Myths and mechanisms.* London: Routledge.

Bolino, A. V. (2002). A model of intersubsidiary knowledge transfer effectiveness. South Bend, IN: University of South Carolina.

Bond, C. F., & DePaulo, B. M. (2006). Accuracy of deception judgments. *Personality and Social Psychology Review, 10*(3), 214–234. doi:10.1207/s15327957pspr1003_2

Bonsu, S. K., & Darmody, A. (2008). Co-creating Second Life: Market-consumer cooperation in contemporary economy. *Journal of Macromarketing, 28*(4), 355–368. doi:10.1177/0276146708325396

Boone, C. A., Craighead, C. W., & Hanna, J. B. (2007). Postponement: An evolving supply chain concept. *International Journal of Physical Distribution and Logistics Management, 37*, 594–611. doi:10.1108/09600030710825676

Borghini, S. (2005). Organizational creativity: breaking equilibrium and order to innovate. *Journal of Knowledge Management, 9*(4), 19–33. doi:10.1108/13673270510610305

Bostrom, R., Anson, R., & Clawson, R. (1993). Group facilitation and group support systems. In L.M. Jessup & J.S. Valacich (Eds.), *Group support systems: New perspectives* (pp. 146-168). New York: Macmillan Publishing Company.

Bouwen, R., & Fry, R. (1996). Facilitating group development: Interventions for a relational and contextual construction. In M. A. West (Ed.), *The handbook of work group psychology* (pp. 531-552). Chichester, UK: Wiley.

Bowersox, D. J., Closs, D. J., & Drayer, R. W. (2005). The digital transformation: Technology and beyond. *Supply Chain Management Review, 9*(1), 22–29.

Bozeman, B., & Rogers, J. D. (2001). Use-and-transformation: A theory of knowledge value for research evaluation. Retrieved from http://rvm.pp.gatech.edu/papers/

Brace-Govan, J. (2003). A method to track discussion forum activity: The Moderators' Assessment Matrix. *The Internet and Higher Education, 6*, 303–325. doi:10.1016/j.iheduc.2003.08.003

Bradford, M. & Florian, J. (2003). Examining the Role of Innovation Diffusion Factors on the Implementation Success of Enterprise Resource Planning Systems. *International Journal of Accounting Information Systems, 4*(3), 205-225.

Brandt, D. R., Miller, G. R., & Hocking, J. E. (1980). The truth deception attribution: Effects of familiarity on the ability of observers to detect deception. *Human Communication Research, 6*, 99–110. doi:10.1111/j.1468-2958.1980.tb00130.x

Brandt, D. R., Miller, G. R., & Hocking, J. E. (1982). Familiarity and lie detection: A replication and extension. *Western Journal of Speech Communication, 46*, 276–290.

Bratitsis, T. (2007). *Development of flexible supporting tools for asynchronous discussions, by analyzing interactions among participants, for technology supported learning.* Unpublished doctoral thesis, School of Humanities, University of the Aegean, Rhodes, Greece.

Bratitsis, T., & Dimitracopoulou, A. (2005). Data Recording and Usage Interaction Analysis in Asynchronous Discussions: The D.I.A.S. System. In C. Choquet, V. Luengo, & K. Yacef (organizers), *Workshop on Usage Analysis in Learning Systems, The 12th International Conference on Artificial Intelligence in Education AIED 2005*, Amsterdam.

Bratitsis, T., & Dimitracopoulou, A. (2006). Monitoring and Analyzing Group Interactions in Asynchronous Discussions with the DIAS system. *The 12th Int. Workshop on Groupware, CRIWG 2006, Spain* (pp. 54-61). Springer Verlag.

Bratitsis, T., & Dimitracopoulou, A. (2006). Indicators for measuring quality in asynchronous discussion forae. *International Conference, Cognition and Exploratory Learning in the Digital Age*, CELDA 2006, 8-10 December 2006, Barcelona, Spain.

Bratitsis, T., & Dimitracopoulou, A. (2007). Interaction Analysis n Asynchronous Discussions: Lessons learned on the learners' perspective, using the DIAS system. *Int. Conference CSCL 2007*, New Jersey, USA

Bratitsis, T., & Dimitracopoulou, A. (2007). Collecting and analyzing interaction data in computer-based group learning discussions: An overview. *Workshop on Personalization in E-Learning Environments at Individual and Group Level, 11ᵗʰ International conference on User Modeling,* Corfu, Greece, 25-29 June 2007

Bratitsis, T., & Dimitracopoulou, A. (2008). Monitoring and Analysing Group Interactions in Asynchronous Discussions with DIAS system. *International Journal of e-Collaboration, 4*(1), 20–40.

Bratitsis, T., & Dimitracopoulou, A. (2009). Studying the effect of Interaction Analysis indicators on students' Selfregulation during asynchronous discussion learning activities. In A. Dimitracopoulou, C., O'Malley, D. Suthers, P. Reimann (eds) Computer Supported Collaborative Learning Practices - CSCL 2009 Community Events Proceedings, ISLS, Volume I, pp 601-605

Bresman, H., Birkinshaw, J., & Nobel, R. (1999). Knowledge transfer in international acquisitions. Journal of International Business Studies, 30(3), 439-462.

Briggs, J. C. (2002). Virtual reality is getting real: Prepare to meet your clone. *The Futurist, 36*(3), 34–42.

Brown, J. S., & Duguid, P. (2000). Balancing Act: How to Capture Knowledge Without Killing It. *Harvard Business Review, 78*(3), 73–80.

Brown, S. L., & Eisenhardt, K. M. (1995). Product development: Past research, present findings, and future directions. *Academy of Management Review, 20*(2), 343–378. doi:10.2307/258850

Brown, S.A., Massey, A.P. Montoya-Weiss, M.M. & Burkman, J.R. (2002). Do I Really Have to User Acceptance of Mandated Technology. *European Journal of Information Systems*, 11(4), 283-295.

Brynjolfsson, E., Renshaw, A. A., & van Alstyne, M. (1997). The matrix of change. *Sloan Management Review, 38*, 22–40.

Buller, D. B., Strzyzewski, K. D., & Comstock, J. (1991). Interpersonal deception: I. deceivers' reactions to receivers' suspicions and probing. *Communication Monographs, 58*, 1–24. doi:10.1080/03637759109376211

Buller, D. B., Strzyzewski, K. D., & Hunsaker, F. (1991). Interpersonal deception: II. The inferiority of conversational participants as deception detectors. *Communication Monographs, 58*, 25–40. doi:10.1080/03637759109376212

Burdea, G., & Coiffet, P. (2003). *Virtual reality technology.* Hoboken, N.J.: J. Wiley-Interscience.

Burgelman, R. A., & Rosenbloom, R. S. (1989). Technology strategy: An evolutionary process perspective. *Research on Technological Innovation . Management and Policy, 4*, 1–23.

Burgoon, J. K., & Newton, D. A. (1991). Applying a social meaning model to relational messages of conversational involvement: Comparing participant and observer perspectives. *The Southern Communication Journal, 56*, 96–113.

Burgoon, J. K., Blair, P. J., & Strom, R. E. (2008). Cognitive biases and nonverbal cue availability in detecting deception. *Human Communication Research, 34*(4), 572–599. doi:10.1111/j.1468-2958.2008.00333.x

Burke, K., & Chidambaram, L. (1999). How much bandwidth is enough? A longitudinal examination of media characteristics and group outcomes. *Management Information Systems Quarterly, 23*(4), 557–580. doi:10.2307/249489

Burleson, W., & Selker, T. (2002). Creativity and interface. *Communications of the ACM, 45*(10), 89-90.

Burns, T., & Stalker, G. M. (1961). *The Management of Innovation.* London: Tavistock.

Buss, D. M. (1994). *The evolution of desire: Strategies of human mating.* New York: BasicBooks.

Buss, D. M. (1999). *Evolutionary psychology: The new science of the mind.* Needham Heights, MA: Allyn & Bacon.

Buzzell, T. (2005). Demographic characteristics of persons using pornography in three technological contexts. *Sexuality & Culture*, 9(1), 28-48.

Byrd, T. A., Cossick, K. L., & Zmud, R. W. (1992). A synthesis of research on requirements analysis and knowledge acquisition techniques. *MIS Quarterly*, 16(1), 117-138.

Byrne, P. J., & Heavey, C. (2006). The impact of information sharing and forecasting in capacitated industrial supply chains: A case study. *International Journal of Production Economics*, 103, 420–437. doi:10.1016/j.ijpe.2005.10.007

Cagliano, R., Caniato, F., & Spina, G. (2003). E-business strategy, how companies are shaping their supply chain through the Internet. *International Journal of Operations & Production Management*, 23(10), 1142–1162. doi:10.1108/01443570310496607

Calabrese, G. (1999). Managing information in product development. Logistics Information Management, 12(6), 128-152.

Candy, L. (1997). Computers and creativity support: Knowledge, visualization, and collaboration. *Knowledge-Based Systems*, 9(6), 3-13.

Candy, L., & Hori, K. (2003). The digital muse: HCI in support of creativity: "Creativity and cognition" come of age: Towards a new discipline. *ACM Interactions*, 10(4), 44-54.

Card, S., Mackinlay, D., & Shneiderman, B. (1999). *Readings in Information Visualization, using vision to think*. Morgan Kaufmann.

Carlile, P. R. (2004). Transferring, translating, and transforming: An integrative framework for managing knowledge across boundaries. Organization Science, 15(5), 555-568.

Carlson, J. R., & Zmud, R. W. (1999). Channel expansion theory and the experiential nature of media richness perceptions. *Academy of Management Journal*, 42(2), 153–171. doi:10.2307/257090

Carmel, E., Herniter, B.C., & Nunamaker, Jr., J.F. (1993). Labor-management contract negotiations in an electronic meeting room: A case study. *Group Decision and Negotiation*, 2, 27-60.

Carneiro, A. (2000). How does knowledge management influence innovation and competitiveness? *Journal of Knowledge Management*, 4(2), 87–98. doi:10.1108/13673270010372242

Carr, A. S., & Smeltzer, L. R. (2002). The relationship between information technology use and buyer-supplier relationships: An exploratory analysis of the buying firm's perspective. *IEEE Transactions on Engineering Management*, 49(3), 293–304. doi:10.1109/TEM.2002.803389

Carroll, J. M. (1995). How to avoid designing digital libraries: A scenario-based approach. *SIGOIS Bulletin*, 16(2), 5-7.

Carroll, J. M., & Farooq, U. (2006). Enhancing digital libraries to support creativity in distributed scientific communities: Making CiteSeer collaborative. *Designing for Usability in e-Science: An International Workshop on Interrogating Usability Issues in New Scientific Practice, within the Lab and within Society, Edinburgh, Scotland, January 26-27, 2006*.

Carroll, J. M., Neale, D. C., Isenhour, P. L., Rosson, M. B., & McCrickard, D. S. (2003). Notification and awareness: Synchronizing task-oriented collaborative activity. *International Journal of Human-Computer Studies*, 58, 605-632.

Carstensen, P., & Schmidt, K. (2002). Self governing production groups: Towards requirements for IT support. In *Proceedings of the 5th IFIP International Conference on Information Technology in Manufacturing and Services (BASYS'02)* (pp. 49-60). Netherlands: Kluwer Academic Publishers.

Carter, S. M., & West, M. A. (1998). Reflexivity, effectiveness, and mental health in BBC-TV production teams. *Small Group Research*, 5, 583-601.

Cartwright, J. (2000). *Evolution and human behavior: Darwinian perspectives on human nature*. Cambridge, MA: The MIT Press.

Carvalho, R., & Ferreira, M. (2001). Using information technology to support knowledge conversion processes. *Information Research, 7*(1). Retrieved from http://InformationR.net/ir/7-1/paper118.html

Cash, J. I. Jr, & Konsynski, B. (1985). IS redraws competitive boundaries. *Harvard Business Review*, (March/April): 134–142.

Casper, T. A., Meyer, W. M., Moller, J. M., Henline, P., Keith, K., McHarg, B., Davis, S., & Greenwood, D. (1998). Collaboratory operations in magnetic fusion scientific research. *ACM Interactions, 5*(3), 56-65.

Cassel, C., Hackl, P., & Westlund, A. H. (1999). Robustness of partial least-squares method for estimating latent variable quality structures. Journal of Applied Statistics, 26(4), 435-446.

Cassivi, L. (2006). Collaboration planning in an electronic supply chain . *International Journal of Supply Chain Management, 11*(3), 249–258. doi:10.1108/13598540610662158

Cassivi, L., Hadaya, P., Lefebvre, E., & Lefebvre, L. A. (2008). The Role of Collaboration on Process, Relational, and Product Innovations in a Supply Chain. *International Journal of e-Collaboration, 4*(4), 11–32.

Cassivi, L., Lefebvre, E., Lefebvre, L. A., & Leger, P. M. (2004). The impact of e-collaboration tools on firms' performance. *International Journal of Logistics Management, 15*(1), 91–110. doi:10.1108/09574090410700257

Cassivi, L., Lefebvre, E., Lefebvre, L. A., & Léger, P.-M. (2004). Supply chain planning and execution tools: E-collaboration and organizational performance. *International Journal of Logistics Management, 15*, 91–110. doi:10.1108/09574090410700257

Castells, M. (1996). *A sociedade em rede* (8th ed.) [portuguese translation of The Rise of the Network Society]. São Paulo, Paz e Terra.

Cetinkaya, S., & Lee, C. Y. (2000). Stock replenishment and shipment scheduling for Vendor-Managed Inventory systems. *Management Science, 46*, 217–232. doi:10.1287/mnsc.46.2.217.11923

Chae, B., Yen, H. R., & Sheu, C. (2005). Information technology and supply chain collaboration: Moderating effects of existing relationships between partners. *IEEE Transactions on Engineering Management, 52*(4), 440–448. doi:10.1109/TEM.2005.856570

Chagnon, N. A. (1977). *Yanomamo: The fierce people.* New York: Holt, Rinehart and Winston.

Chang, H., & Chen, S. (2005). Assessing the readiness of Internet-based IOS and evaluating its impact on adoption. In *Proceedings of the 38th International Conference of Systems Sciences, Hawaii.*

Charles, S., Ivis, M., & Leduc, A. (2002). *Embracing e-business: Does size matter?* Ottawa, ON: Statistics Canada.

Chatman, J. A., & Barsade, S. G. (1995). Personality, organizational culture, and cooperation: Evidence from a business simulation. *Administrative Science Quarterly, 40*(3), 423-443.

Chau, P.Y.K. & Hu, P.J. (2002). Examining a Model of Information Technology Acceptance by Individual Professionals. *Journal of Management Information Systems,* 18(4), 191-230.

Chen, F. (1999). Decentralized supply chains subject to information delays. *Management Science, 45*, 1076–1090. doi:10.1287/mnsc.45.8.1076

Chen, X. D., & Fu, L. S. (2001). IT adoption in manufacturing industries: Differences by company size and industrial sectors – The case of Chinese mechanical industries. *Technovation, 21*, 649–660. doi:10.1016/S0166-4972(00)00078-X

Cheng, R., & Vassileva, J. (2004). Adaptive rewarding mechanism for sustainable online learning community . In Looi, C.-K. (Eds.), *Artificial Intelligence in Education.* IOS Press.

Cherns, A. B., & Bryant, D. T. (1984). Studying the client's role in construction management. *Construction Management and Economics, 2*, 177–184.

Chidambaram, L., & Jones, B. (1993). Impact of communication medium and computer support on group perceptions and performance: A comparison of face-to-face and dispersed meetings. *MIS Quarterly, 17*(4), 465-491.

Chin, G., Jr., & Lansing, C. S. (2004). Capturing and supporting contexts for scientific data sharing via the biological sciences collaboratory. *Proceedings of the ACM Conference on Computer Supported Cooperative Work* (pp. 409-418).

Chin, W. W., Marcolin, B. L., & Newsted, P. R. (2003). A partial least squares latent variable modeling approach for measuring interaction effects: Results from a Monte Carlo simulation study and an electronic-mail emotion/adoption study. *Information Systems Research, 14*(2), 189–217. doi:10.1287/isre.14.2.189.16018

Choi, B., & Lee, H. (2003). An empirical investigation of KM styles and their effect on corporate performance. *Information & Management, 40*(5), 403–417. doi:10.1016/S0378-7206(02)00060-5

Choudhury, V. (1997). Strategic choices in the development of interorganizational information systems. *Information Systems Research, 8*(1), 1–24. doi:10.1287/isre.8.1.1

Christensen, C. M., & Bower, J. L. (1996). Customer power, strategic investment, and the failure of leading firms. *Strategic Management Journal, 17*, 197–218. doi:10.1002/(SICI)1097-0266(199603)17:3<197::AID-SMJ804>3.0.CO;2-U

Christy, D. P., & Grout, J. R. (1994). Safeguarding supply chain relationships. *International Journal of Production Economics, 36*, 233–242. doi:10.1016/0925-5273(94)00024-7

Chua, A. (2001, October). Relationship between the types of knowledge shared and types of communication channels used. Journal of Knowledge Management Practice. Retrieved from http://www.tlainc.com/articl26.htm

Chung, P., Cheung, L., Stader, J., Jarvis, P., Moore, J., & Macintosh, A. (2003). Knowledge-based process management—an approach to handling adaptive workflow. *Knowledge-Based Systems, 16*(2), 149–160. doi:10.1016/S0950-7051(02)00080-1

Clark, K. B., & Wheelwright, S. C. (1997). Organizing and Leading "Heavyweight" Development Teams. In Tushman, M. L., & Anderson, P. (Eds.), *Managing Strategic Innovation and Change* (pp. 419–432). New York: Oxford University Press.

Clinch, J. J., & Keselman, H. J. (1982). Parametric alternatives to the analysis of variance. *Journal of Educational Statistics, 7*, 207–214. doi:10.2307/1164645

Clopton, S.W. (1984, February). Seller and buying firm factors affecting industrial buyers' negotiation behavior and outcomes. *Journal of Marketing Research, 21*, 39-53.

Coch, L., & French, J. R. (1948). Overcoming resistance to change. *Human Relations, 1*, 512-532.

Cohen, W.W., Carvalho, V.R., & Mitchell, T.M. (2004). Learning to classify email into speech acts. In *Proceedings of the 2004 Conference on Empirical Methods in Natural Language Processing*, Barcelona, Spain.

Coleman, D. (1995). *Groupware; technology and applications.* Englewood Cliffs, NJ: Prentice Hall.

Collins, M., & Berge, Z. (2001). *Resources for moderators and facilitators of online discussion.* Retrieved from http://www.emoderators.com/moderators.html

Comadena, M. E. (1982). Accuracy in detecting deception: Intimate and friendship relationships . In Burgoon, M. (Ed.), *Communication Yearbook, 6* (pp. 446–472). Beverly Hills, CA: Sage.

Compeau, D. R., Higgins, C. A., & Huff, S. (1999). Social cognitive theory and individual reactions to computing technology: A longitudinal study. MIS Quarterly, 23(2), 145-158.

Contractor, N., & Eisenberg, E. Communication Networks and New Media in Organizations . In Fulk, J., & Steinfield, C. (Eds.), *Organizations and Communication Technology* (pp. 143–172). Newbury Park, CA: Sage.

Convertino, G., Ganoe, C. H., Schafer, W. A., Yost, B., & Carroll, J. M. (2005). A multiple view approach to support common ground. *Proceedings of the 3rd Inter-*

national Conference on Coordinated and Multiple Views in Exploratory Visualization, London.

Cooper, A. (2004). Online sexual activity in the new millennium. *Contemporary Sexuality*, 38(3), i-vii.

Cooper, A., Delmonico, D. L. & Burg, R. (2000). Cybersex users, abusers, and compulsives: New findings and implications. *Sexual Addiction & Compulsivity*, 7(1/2), 5-29.

Cooper, A., Delmonico, D. L., Griffin-Shelley, E. & Mathy, R. M. (2004). Online sexual activity: An examination of potentially problematic behaviors. *Sexual Addiction & Compulsivity*, 11(3), 129-143.

Cooper, R.B. & Zmud, R.W. (1990). Information Technology Implementation Research: A Technological Diffusion Approach. *Management Science*, 36(2), 123-139.

Corbett, C. J., Blackburn, J. D., & Van Wassenhove, L. N. (1999). Partnerships to improve supply chains. *Sloan Management Review*, 40(4), 71–82.

Corich, S., Kinshuk, Hunt L. (2004). Assessing Discussion Forum Participation: In Search of Quality. *Int. Journal of Instructional Technology and Distance Learning*, 1(12), 3–12.

Costa, M., Braun, C. & Birbaumer, N. (2003). Gender differences in response to pictures of nudes: A magnetoencephalographic study. *Biological Psychology*, 63(2), 129-147.

Crampton, C. D. (2002). Attribution in distributed work groups . In Hinds, P., & Keisler, S. (Eds.), *Distributed work: new ways of working across distance using technology*. Cambridge, MA: The MIT Press.

Cramton, C. D. (2001). The mutual knowledge problem and its consequences for dispersed collaboration. *Organization Science*, 12(3), 346–371. doi:10.1287/orsc.12.3.346.10098

Crane, D. (1972). *Invisible colleges: Diffusion of knowledge in scientific communities*. Chicago: University of Chicago Press.

Crespo Marquez, A., Bianchi, C., & Gupta, J. D. D. (2004). Operational and financial effectiveness of e-collaboration

tools in supply chain integration. *European Journal of Operational Research*, 159, 348–363. doi:10.1016/j.ejor.2003.08.020

Cronin, B. & Davenport, E. (2001). E-rogenous zones: Positioning pornography in the digital economy. *The Information Society*, 17(1), 33-48.

Cross, R., Borgatti, S. P., & Parker, A. (2002). Making invisible work visible. *California Management Review*, 44, 25–46.

Croteau, A.-M., & Li, P. (2003). Critical success factors of CRM initiatives. Canadian Journal of Administrative Sciences, 20(1), 21-34.

Crum, C., & Palmatier, G. E. (2004). Demand collaboration: What's holding us back? *Supply Chain Management Review*, 8, 54–61.

Csikszentmihalyi, M. (1996). *Creativity: Flow and the psychology of discovery and invention*. New York: HarperCollins.

Csikszentmihalyi, M. (1999). Implications of a systems perspective for the study of creativity. In R. Sternberg (Ed.), *Handbook of Creativity* (pp. 313-335). Cambridge University Press.

Czerwinski, M., Horvitz, E., & Wilhite, S. (2004). A diary study of task switching and interruptions. In *Proceeding of the Conference on Human Factors in Computing Systems (CHI)*, Vienna, Austria (pp. 175-182). ACM Press.

Daft, R. L., & Lengel, R. H. (1986). Organizational information requirements: media richness and structural design. *Management Science*, 32(5), 554–571. doi:10.1287/mnsc.32.5.554

Daft, R. L., Lengel, R. H., & Trevino, L. K. (1987). Message equivocality, media selection, and manager performance: Implications for information systems. *Management Information Systems Quarterly*, 11(3), 355–366. doi:10.2307/248682

Damanpour, F. (1995). Is Your Creative Organization innovative? In Ford, C. M., & Gioia, D. A. (Eds.), *Creative Action in Organizations: Ivory Tower Visions and Real World Voices* (pp. 125–130). Thousand Oaks, CA: Sage.

Damanpour, F., & Gopalakrishnan, S. (2001). The dynamics of the adoption of product and process innovations in organizations. *Journal of Management Studies, 38*(1), 45–65. doi:10.1111/1467-6486.00227

Damsgaard, J., & Lyytinen, K. (1996). Government strategies to promote the diffusion of electronic data interchange (EDI): What we know and what we don't know. *Information Infrastructure and Policy, 5*, 169–190.

Danwood, N., Akinsola, A., & Hobbs, B. (2002). Development of automated communication of system for managing site information using internet technology. *Automation in Construction, 11*(5), 557–572. doi:10.1016/S0926-5805(01)00066-8

Darr, E. D., & Kurtzberg, T. R. (2000). An investigation of partner similarity dimensions on knowledge transfer. Organizational Behavior and Human Decision Processes, 82(1), 22-44.

Darwin, C. R. (1859). On the origin of species by means of natural selection. Cambridge, MA: Harvard University Press. (Facsimile of the first edition, reprinted in 1966).

Darwin, C. R. (1871). *The descent of man, and selection in relation to sex.* London, England: John Murray.

Dasgupta, S., Granger, M., & McGarry, N. (2002). User acceptance of e-collaboration technology an extension of the technology acceptance model. *Group Decision and Negotiation, 11*(2), 87–100. doi:10.1023/A:1015221710638

Daugherty, P. J., Richey, R. G., Roath, A. S., Min, S., Chen, H., Arndt, A. D., & Genchev, S. E. (2006). Is collaboration paying off for firms? *Business Horizons, 49*(1), 61–70. doi:10.1016/j.bushor.2005.06.002

Davenport, H. T., Jarvenpaa, S. L., & Beers, M. C. (1996). Improving knowledge work processes. Sloan Management Review, 37(4), 53-66.

Davenport, T. H., & Prusak, L. (1998). Working knowledge: How organizations manage what they know. Boston: Harvard Business School Pressxz.

Davenport, T. H., DeLong, D. W., & Beers, M. C. (1998). Successful knowledge management. *Sloan Management Review, 39*(2), 43-57.

Davenport, T., & Prusak, L. (1998). *Working knowledge: How organizations manage what they know.* Boston: Harvard Business School Press.

Davenport, T.H., & Beck, J.C. (2001). *The attention economy: Understanding the new currency of business.* Boston: Harvard Business School.

Davis, F. (1985). *A technology assessment model for empirically testing new end-user information systems: Theory and results.* Unpublished doctoral dissertation. Cambridge, MA: Massachusetts Institute of Technology.

Davis, F. D., Bagozzi, R. P., & Warshaw, P. R. (1989). User acceptance of computer technology: a comparison of two theoretical models. *Management Science, 35*(8), 982–1003. doi:10.1287/mnsc.35.8.982

Davis, F.D. (1989). Perceived Usefulness, Perceived Ease of Use and User Acceptance of Information Technology. *MIS Quarterly*, 13(3), 319-340.

Davis, F.D., & Venkatesh, V. (1996). A critical assessment of potential measurement biases inthe technology acceptance model: Three experiments. *International Journal of Human Computer Studies, 45*(1), 19-45.

Davis, F.D., Bagozzi, R.P. & Warshaw, P.R. (1992). Extrinsic and Intrinsic Motivation to Use Computers in the Workplace. *Journal of Applied Social Psychology*, 22(14), 1111-1132.

Davis, R. D., Bagozzi, R. R., & Warshaw, P. R. (1989). User Acceptance of Computer Technology: Comparison of Two Theoretical Models. *Management Science, 35*(8), 982–1003. doi:10.1287/mnsc.35.8.982

Dawes, R. M., & Orbell, J. M. (1995). The benefit of optional play in anonymous one-shot prisoner's dilemma games. In Arrow, K. J., Mnookin, R. H., Ross, L., Tversky, A., & Wilson, R. B. (Eds.), *Barriers to conflict resolution* (pp. 62–85). New York: W.W. Norton & Company.

Dawkins, R. (1990). *The selfish gene*. Oxford, UK: Oxford University Press.

De Dreu, C. K. W., & De Vries, N. K. (1993). Numerical support, information processing, and attitude change. *European Journal of Social Psychology, 23*, 647-662.

De Dreu, C. K. W., & West, M. A. (2001). Minority dissent and team innovation: The importance of participation in decision-making. *Journal of Applied Psychology, 86*, 1191-1201.

De Luca, L., & Atuahene-Gima, K. (2007). Market knowledge dimensions and cross-functional collaboration: Examining the different routes to product innovation performance. *Journal of Marketing, 71*, 95–112. doi:10.1509/jmkg.71.1.95

Deerwester, S., Dumais, S., Furnas, G.W., Landauer, T.K., & Harshman, R. (1990). Indexing by latent semantic analysis. *Journal of the Society for Information Science, 41*(6), 391-407. John Wiley & Sons.

Delaney, M.M., Foroughi, A., & Perkins, W.C. (1997). An empirical study of the efficacy of a computerized negotiation support system. *Decision Support Systems, 20*(3), 185-197.

DeLone, W. H., & McLean, E. R. (1992). Information systems success: The quest for the dependent variable. Information Systems Research, 3(1), 60-95.

DeLong, D. W., & Fahey, L. (2000). Diagnosing cultural barriers to knowledge management. *Academy of Management Executive, 14*(4), 113-127.

DeLuca, D., Gasson, S., & Kock, N. (2006). Adaptations That Virtual Teams Make So That Complex Tasks Can Be Performed Using Simple e-Collaboration Technologies. *International J. of e-Collaboration, 2*(3), 65-91.

Dennis, A. R., & Kinney, S. T. (1998). Testing media richness theory in the new media: The effects of cues, feedback, and task equivocality. *Information Systems Research, 9*(3), 256–275. doi:10.1287/isre.9.3.256

Dennis, A. R., Kinney, S. T. & Hung, Y. T. C. (1999). Gender differences in the effects of media richness. *Small Group Research*, 30(4), 405-437.

Dennis, A., & Vessey, I. (2004). Three knowledge management strategies: Knowledge hierarchies, knowledge markets, and knowledge communities. *MIS Quarterly Executive, 3*(4), 399-412.

Dennis, A., & Williams, M. (2005). A meta-analysis of group size effects in electronic brainstorming. *International Journal of e-Collaboration, 1*(1), 24-42.

Dennis, A., Pinsonneault, A., Hilmer, K., Barki, H., Galupe, B., Huber, M., & Bellavance, F. (2005). Pattern in electronic brainstorming. *International Journal of e-Collaboration, 1*(4), 38-57.

Dennis, A.R., George, J.F., Jessup, L.M., Nunamaker, Jr., J.F., & Vogel, D.R. (1988). Information technology to support electronic meetings. *MIS Quarterly, 12*(4), 591-624.

DePaulo, B. M., & Kashy, D. A. (1998). Everyday lies in close and casual relationships. *Journal of Personality and Social Psychology, 74*, 63–79. doi:10.1037/0022-3514.74.1.63

DePaulo, B. M., Charlton, K., Cooper, H., Lindsay, J. J., & Muhlenbruck, L. (1997). The accuracy-confidence correlation in the detection of deception. *Personality and Social Psychology Review, 1*, 346–357. doi:10.1207/s15327957pspr0104_5

DePaulo, B. M., Kashy, D. A., Kirkendol, S. E., Wyer, M. M., & Epstein, J. E. (1996). Lying in everyday life. *Journal of Personality and Social Psychology, 70*, 979–995. doi:10.1037/0022-3514.70.5.979

DeRosa, D. M., Hantula, D. A., Kock, N., & D'Arcy, J. P. (2004). Communication, trust, and leadership in virtual teams: A media naturalness perspective. *Human Resource Management Journal, 34*(2), 219–232.

DeSanctis, G., & Gallupe, R. B. (1987). A Foundation for the study of Group Decision Support System. *Management Science, 33*(5), 589–609. doi:10.1287/mnsc.33.5.589

DeSanctis, G., & Poole, M. (1994). Capturing the Complexity in Advanced Technology Use: Adaptive Structuration Theory. *Organization Science, 5*(2), 121–147. doi:10.1287/orsc.5.2.121

DeSanctis, G., Fayard, A. L., Roach, M., & Jiang, L. (2003). Learning in online forums. *European Management Journal, 21*(5), 565–577. doi:10.1016/S0263-2373(03)00106-3

DeTiene, K. B., & Jackson, L. A. (2001). Knowledge management: Understanding theory and developing strategy. *Competitiveness Review, 11*(1), 1-11.

Deutsch, M. (1969). Conflicts: Productive and destructive. *Journal of Social Issues, 25*, 7-41.

Devaraj, S., & Kohli, R. (2003). Performance impacts of information technology: is actual usage the missing link? *Management Science, 49*(3), 273–289. doi:10.1287/mnsc.49.3.273.12736

DiClemente, D. F. & Hantula, D. A. (2003). Optimal foraging online: Increasing sensitivity to delay. *Psychology & Marketing, 20*(9), 785-809.

Dillenbourg, P. (1999). Introduction: What do you mean by collaborative learning? In Dillenbourg, P. (Ed.), *Collaborative learning: Cognitive and computational approaches* (pp. 1–19). Elsevier.

Dillenbourg, P., Ott, D., Wehrle, T., Bourquin, Y., Jermann, P., Corti, D., & Salo, P. (2002). The socio-cognitive functions of community mirrors. In F. Fluckiger, C. Jutz, P. Schulz & L. Cantoni (Eds.), *Proceedings of the 4th International Conference on New Educational Environments*. Lugano, May 8-11, 2002.

Dillman, D. A. (2000). *Mail and Internet surveys: The tailored design method.* New York: John Wiley.

Dimitracopoulou, A. (2009). Computer based Interaction Analysis Supporting Self-regulation: Achievements and Prospects of an Emerging Research Direction. In M. Spector, D. Sampson, Kinshuk, P. Isaias (Guest Eds.), Special Issue: Cognition and Exploratory Learning in Digital Age, Technology, Instruction, Cognition and Learning (TICL). Vol 6(4), pp 291-314.

Dimitracopoulou, A., & Bruillard, É. (2006). Enrichir les interfaces de forums par la visualisation d'analyses automatiques des interactions et du contenu. *Revue STICEF, 13.*

Dimitracopoulou, A., et al. (2005). State of the art of interaction analysis for Metacognitive Support & Diagnosis. *IA JEIRP Deliverable D. 31.1.1.* Kaleidoscope NoE, December 2005. Retrieved from www.noe-kaleidoscope.org

Disney, S. M., & Towill, D. R. (2003). Bullwhip reduction in supply chains: The impact of VMI. *International Journal of Operations & Production Management, 23*, 625–651. doi:10.1108/01443570310476654

Doll, W. J., & Deng, X. (2001). The collaborative use of information technology: End-user participation and systems success. *Information Resources Management Journal, 14*(2), 6–16.

Doll, W. J., & Torkzadeh, G. (1988). The measurement of end-user computing satisfaction. MIS Quarterly, 12(2), 259-274.

Dougherty, D. (1992). Interpretive Barriers to Successful Product Innovation in Large Firms. *Organization Science, 3*, 179–202. doi:10.1287/orsc.3.2.179

Dourish, P., & Bly, S. (1992). Portholes: Supporting awareness in distributed work group. In P. Bauersfeld, J. Bennett, & G. Lynch (Eds.), *Proceedings of the 1992 ACM Conference on Human Factors in Computing Systems (CHI'92)* (pp. 541-547). New York: ACM Press.

Downs, G. W., & Mohr, L. B. (1976). Conceptual issues in the study of innovation. *Administrative Science Quarterly, 21*, 700–714. doi:10.2307/2391725

Drolet, A.L., & Morris, M.W. (1995). *Communication media and interpersonal trust in conflicts: The role of rapport and synchrony of nonverbal behavior.* Paper presented at the Academy of Management meeting, Vancouver, Canada.

Duane, A., & Finnegan, P. (2003). Managing empowerment and control in an intranet environment. *Information Systems Journal, 13*(2), 133–158. doi:10.1046/j.1365-2575.2003.00148.x

Dudek, S. Z., & Cote, R. (1994). Problem finding revisited. In M.A. Runco (Ed.), *Problem finding, problem solving, and creativity* (pp. 130-150). Norwood, NJ: Ablex.

Dunbar, K. (1995). How scientists really reason: Scientific reasoning in real-world laboratories. In R. J. Sternberg & J. E. Davidson (Eds.), *The nature of insight*. Cambridge, MA: MIT Press.

Dunbar, K. (1997). How scientists think: Online creativity and conceptual change in science. In T. B. Ward, S. M. Smith, & S. Vaid (Eds.), *Conceptual structures and processes: Emergence, discovery, and change*. Washington, DC: APA Press.

Dunbar, R. I. M. (1996). *Grooming, gossip and the evolution of language*. London, England: Faber & Faber.

Dyer, J. H. (1997). Effective interfirm collaboration: How firms minimize transaction costs and maximize transaction value. *Strategic Management Journal, 18*(7), 535–556. doi:10.1002/(SICI)1097-0266(199708)18:7<535::AID-SMJ885>3.0.CO;2-Z

Earley. (1994). Self or group? Cultural effects of training on self-efficacy and performance. *Administrative Science Quarterly, 39*, 89-117.

Edmonds, E. A. (1994). Introduction: Computer-based systems that support creativity. In T. Dartnall (Ed.), *Artificial intelligence and creativity* (pp. 327-334). Dordrecht, Netherlands: Kluwer Academic.

Edvinsson, L., & Malone, M. (1997). Intellectual capital: Realizing your company's true value by finding its hidden brainpower. New York: Harper Business.

Edwards, K., & Mynatt, E. (1997). Timewarp: Techniques for autonomous collaboration. In *Proceedings of the 1997 Conference on Human Factors in Computing Systems (CHI 1997)*. New York: ACM Press. Retrieved July 19, 2007, from http://acm.org/sigchi/chi97/proceedings/paper/wke.htm

Ekman, P., & Friesen, W. V. (1974). Detecting deception from the body or face. *Journal of Personality and Social Psychology, 20*, 288–298. doi:10.1037/h0036006

Ekman, P., & O'Sullivan, M. (1991). Who can catch a liar? *The American Psychologist, 46*, 913–920. doi:10.1037/0003-066X.46.9.913

Ekstedt, E., Lundin, R. A., Söderholm, A., & Wirdenius, H. (1999). *Neo-Industrial Organising, Renewal by action and knowledge formation in a project-intensive economy*. London: Routledge.

Elam, J. J., & Mead, M. (1990). Can Software Influence Creativity? *Information Systems Research, 1*(1), 1–22. doi:10.1287/isre.1.1.1

Elen, J., & Lowyck, J. (1998). Students' views on the efficiency of instruction: An exploratory survey of the instructional metacognitive knowledge of university freshmen. *Higher Education, 36*(2), 231-252.

Elen, J., & Lowyck, J. (1999). Metacognitive instructional knowledge: Cognitive mediation and instructional design. *Journal of Structural Learning & Intelligent Systems, 13*(3-4), 145-169.

Elen, J., & Lowyck, J. (2000). Instructional metacognitive knowledge: A qualitative study on conceptions of freshmen about instruction. *Journal of Curriculum Studies, 32*(3), 421-444.

Elgarah, W., Falaleeva, N., Saunders, C. S., Ilie, V., Shim, J. T., & Courtney, J. F. (2005). Data exchange in interorganizational relationships: Review through multiple conceptual lenses. *The Data Base for Advances in Information Systems, 36*, 8–29.

Eliashberg, J., Rangaswamy, A., & Balakrishnan, P.V. (1987). *Two party negotiations: A theoretical and empirical analysis*. Paper presented at ORSA/TIMS Marketing Science conference, June, Jouy-en-Josas, France.

Ellis, L., Gibbs, S. J., & Rein, G. L. (1991). Groupware: some issues and experiences. *Communications of the ACM, 34*(1), 38–58. doi:10.1145/99977.99987

Entwistle, N. J. (1991). Approaches to learning and perceptions of the learning environment. *Higher Education, 22*, 201-204.

Entwistle, N., McCune, V., & Hounsell, J. (2002). *Approaches to studying and perceptions of university teaching-learning environments: Concepts, measures and preliminary findings*. ETL Project Occasional Report.

Entwistle, N.J. (1998a). Approaches to learning and forms of understanding. In B. Dart & G. Boulton-Lewis (Eds.), *Teaching and learning in higher education* (pp. 72–101). Melbourne: Australian Council for Educational Research.

Entwistle, N.J. (1998b). Improving teaching through research on student learning. In J.J.F. Forest (Ed.), *University teaching: International perspectives* (pp. 73–112). New York: Garland.

Enz, C. (1986). *Power and shared values in the corporate culture.* Ann Arbor, MI: The University of Michigan Press.

Erickson, T., & Kellogg, W. A. (2000). Social translucence: An approach to designing systems that mesh with social processes. *ACM Transactions on Computer Human Interaction, 7*(1), 59-83.

Evaristo, R., & Watson-Manheim, M. (2005). E-collaboration in distributed requirements determination. *International Journal of e-Collaboration, 1*(2), 40-56.

Exline, R. E., Thibaut, J., Hickey, C. B., & Gumpert, P. (1970). Visual interaction in relation to Machiavellianism and an unethical act . In Christie, R., & Geis, F. L. (Eds.), *Studies in Machiavellianism* (pp. 53–75). New York: Academic Press.

Faraj, S., & Sproull, L. (2000). Coordinating expertise in software development teams. Management Science, 46(12), 1554-1568.

Farooq, U., Carroll, J. M., & Canoe, C. H. (2008). Designing for Creativity in Computer-Supported Cooperative Work. *International Journal of e-Collaboration, 4*(4), 51–75.

Farooq, U., Carroll, J. M., & Ganoe, C. H. (2005). Supporting creativity in distributed scientific communities. *Proceedings of the International GROUP Conference on Supporting Group Work, Sanibel Island, Florida, November 6-9, 2005* (pp. 217-226). New York: ACM Press.

Farooq, U., Ganoe, C. H., Carroll, J. M., & Giles, C. L. (2007). Supporting distributed scientific collaboration: Implications for designing the CiteSeer collaboratory.

Proceedings of the Hawaii International Conference on System Sciences, Waikoloa, Hawaii, January 3-6, 2007 (p. 26c). Washington, DC: IEEE Computer Society.

Farooq, U., Rodi, C., Carroll, J. M., & Isenhour, P. L. (2003). Avatar proxies: Configurable informants of collaborative activities. *Proceedings of the ACM Conference on CHI* (pp. 792-793).

Farrell, M. P. (2001). *Collaborative circles: Friendship dynamics and creative work.* Chicago: University of Chicago Press.

Fawcett, S. E., & Magnan, G. M. (2004). Ten guiding principles for high-impact SCM. *Business Horizons, 47,* 67–74. doi:10.1016/j.bushor.2004.07.011

Fayad, M., & Schmidt, D.C. (1997). Object-oriented application frameworks. *Communications of the ACM, 40*(10), 32-38.

Feeley, T. H., & Young, M. J. (1998). Humans as lie detectors: Some more second thoughts. *Communication Quarterly, 46*(2), 109–126.

Feeley, T. H., deTurck, M. A., & Young, M. J. (1995). Baseline familiarity in lie detection. *Communication Research, 12*(2), 160–169.

Feist, G. J. (1999). The influence of personality on artistic and scientific creativity. In R. J. Sternberg (Ed.), *Handbook of creativity* (pp. 273-296). New York: Cambridge University Press.

Feldman, M. S., & March, J. G. (1981). Information in Organisations as Signal and Symbol. *Administrative Science Quarterly, 26*(2), 171–186. doi:10.2307/2392467

Fernandes, K., Raja, V., & Austin, S. (2005). Portals as a knowledge repository and transfer tool—VIZCon case study. *Technovation, 25*(11), 1281–1289. doi:10.1016/j.technovation.2004.01.005

Fesakis, G., Petrou, A., & Dimitracopoulou, A. (2004). Collaboration Activity Function: An interaction analysis tool for Computer Supported Collaborative Learning activities. In *4th IEEE International Conference on Advanced Learning Technologies* (ICALT 2004), August 30-Sept 1, 2004, Joensuu, Finland.

Feurestein, R., Rand, Y., Hoffman, M., & Miller, R. (1980). *Instrumental enrichment.* Baltimore, MD: University Park Press.

Fichman, R. G. (2000). The diffusion and assimilation of information technology innovations . In Zmud, R. W. (Ed.), *Framing the domains of IT management: Projecting the future... through the past.* Cincinnati, OH: Pinnaflex Educational Resources Inc.

Fichman, R. G., & Kemerer, C. F. (1993). Adoption of software engineering process innovations: The case of object orientation. *Sloan Management Review, 30,* 47–59.

Fichman, R. G., & Kemerer, C. F. (1997). The Assimilation of Software Process Innovations: An Organizational Learning Perspective. *Management Science, 43*(10), 1345–1363. doi:10.1287/mnsc.43.10.1345

Fiedler, K., & Walka, I. (1993). Training lie detectors to use nonverbal cues instead of global heuristics. *Human Communication Research, 20,* 199–223. doi:10.1111/j.1468-2958.1993.tb00321.x

Finholt, T. A., & Olson, G. M. (1997). From laboratories to collaboratories: A new organizational form for scientific collaboration. *Psychological Science, 8*(1), 28-36.

Fink, L. (2007), Coordination, Learning, and Innovation: The Organizational Roles of e-Collaboration and Their Impacts. *International Journal of e-Collaboration, 3*(3), 53-70.

Fiore, S.M., Salas, E., Cuevas, H.M., & Bowers, C.A. (2003). Distributed coordination space: Toward a theory of distributed team process and performance. *Theoretical Issues in Ergonomics Science, 4*(3-4), 340-364.

Fischbein, M., & Ajzen, I. (1975). *Belief, Attitude, Intention, Behavior: An Introduction to Theory and Research,* Reading, MA : Addison-Wesley, 1975.

Fischer, G. (1999). Symmetry of ignorance, social creativity, and meta-design. *Proceedings of the 3rd Conference on Creativity and Cognition* (pp. 116-123). New York: ACM Press..

Fischer, G. (2005). Distances and diversity: Sources for social creativity. *Proceedings of the 5th Conference on Creativity and Cognition* (pp. 128-136). New York: ACM Press.

Fischer, G., Nakakoji, K., Ostwald, J., Stahl, G., & Sumner, T. (1998). Embedding critics in design environments. In M. T. Maybury & W. Wahlster (Eds.), *Readings in intelligent user interfaces* (pp. 537-559). San Francisco, CA: Morgan Kaufmann.

Fisher, D., & Dourish, P. (2004). Social and temporal structures in everyday collaboration. In *Proceedings of the 2004 Conference on Human Factors in Computing Systems (CHI 2004)* (pp. 551-558). New York: ACM Press.

Fisher, M. L. (1997). What is the right supply chain for your product? *Harvard Business Review, 75,* 105–116.

Fisher, W. A. & Barak, A. (2001). Internet pornography: A social psychological perspective on Internet sexuality. *Journal of Sex Research, 38*(4), 312-323.

Fitzpatrick, G. (1998). *The locales framework: Understanding and designing for cooperative work.* Unpublished doctoral thesis, University of Queensland, Australia.

Fitzpatrick, G., Kaplan, S., & Mansfield, T. (1998). Applying the locales framework to understanding and designing. In *Proceedings of the 1998 Australasian Computer Human Interaction Conference (OzCHI 1998)* (pp. 122-129). IEEE Computer Society.

Fitzpatrick, G., Kaplan, S., Mansfield, T., David, A., & Segall, B. (2002). Supporting public availability and accessibility with Elvin: Experiences and reflections. *Computer Supported Cooperative Work, 11*(3), 447-474. Norwell, MA: Kluwer Academic Publishers.

Fitzpatrick, G., Tolone, W., & Kaplan, S. (1995). Work, locales and distributed social worlds. In *Proceedings of the 1995 European Conference on Computer Supported Cooperative Work (ECSCW 1995)* (pp. 1-16). Berlin: Springer.

Fjermestad, J. (2005). Virtual group strategic decision making using structured conflict and consensus approaches. *International Journal of e-Collaboration, 1*(1), 43-61.

Flood, J. (2000). Read all about it: Online learning facing 80% attrition rates. *Turkish Online Journal of Distance Education, 3*.

Florida, R. (2002). *The rise of the creative class: And how it's transforming work, leisure, community, and everyday life.* New York: Basic Books.

Florida, R. (2005). *The flight of the creative class: The new global competition talent.* New York: HarperCollins.

Foos, T., Schum, G., & Rothenberg, S. (2006). Tacit knowledge transfer and the knowledge disconnect. Journal of Knowledge Management, 10(1), 6-18.

Ford, C. M. (1995). Creativity is a Mystery: Clues for the Investigators' Notebooks . In Ford, C. M., & Gioia, D. A. (Eds.), *Creative Action in Organizations: Ivory Tower Visions and Real World Voices* (pp. 12–51). Thousand Oaks, CA: Sage.

Ford, C. M., & Gioia, D. A. (1995). Multiple Visions and Multiple Voices: Academic and Practitioner Conceptions of Creativity in Organizations. In *C.M. Ford & D.A. Gioia, Creative Action in Organizations: Ivory Tower Visions and Real World Voices* (pp. 3–11). Thousand Oaks, CA: Sage.

Forgionne, G., & Kholi, R. (1996). HMSS: a management support system for concurrent hospital decision-making. *Decision Support Systems, 16*(3), 209–229. doi:10.1016/0167-9236(95)00011-9

Fornell, C. R., & Larcker, D. F. (1981). Two structural equation models with unobservable variables and measurement error: Algebra and statistics. Journal of Marketing Research, 18(3), 382-389.

Foroughi, A., & Jelassi, M.T. (1990). NSS solutions to major negotiation stumbling blocks. In *Proceedings of the 23rd Annual Hawaii International Conference on System Sciences* (Vol. IV), Kailua-Kona, Hawaii, (pp. 2-11).

Foroughi, A., Perkins, W.C., & Jelassi, M.T. (1995). An empirical study of an interactive, session-oriented computerized negotiation support system (NSS). *Group Decision and Negotiation, 4*, 485-512.

Foster, R. (1986). *Innovation: The attacker's advantage.* New York: Summit Books.

Franz, C. R., & Robey, D. (1986). Organizational context, user involvement, and the usefulness of information systems. Decision Sciences, 17(3), 329-356.

Fraser, C. (1971). Group risk taking and group polarization. *European Journal of Social Psychology, 1*, 493-510.

Frazier, G. L., & Rody, R. C. (1991). The use of influence strategies in interfirm relationships in industrial product channels. *Journal of Marketing, 55*, 52–69. doi:10.2307/1252203

Frese, M., & Zapf, D. (1994). Action as the core of work psychology: A German approach. In H. C. Triandis, M. D. Dunnette, & L. M. Hough (Eds.), *Handbook of industrial and organizational psychology, 2nd ed.: Vol. 4* (pp. 271-340). Palo Alto, CA: Consulting Psychologists Press.

Frick, T. (2004). Types of knowledge of education created through disciplined inquiry. Bloomington: Indiana University, School of Education. Retrieved from www.indiana.edu/~tedfrick/typesofknowledgesept1.pdf

Fruchterman, T., & Rheingold, E. (1991). Graph drawing by force-directed placement. *Software: Practice and Experience, 21*(11), 1129-1164. John Wiley & Sons.

Fuller, C. M., Biros, D. P., & Wilson, R. L. (2009). Decision support for determining veracity via linguistic-based cues. *Decision Support Systems, 46*(3), 695–703. doi:10.1016/j.dss.2008.11.001

Gadde, L.-E., Huemer, L., & Håkansson, H. (2003). Strategizing in industrial networks. *Industrial Marketing Management, 32*, 357–364. doi:10.1016/S0019-8501(03)00009-9

Ganesan, S. (1994). Determinants of long-term orientation in buyer-seller relationships. *Journal of Marketing, 58*, 1–19. doi:10.2307/1252265

Gangestad, S. W. & Scheyd, G. J. (2005). The evolution of human physical attractiveness. *Annual Review of Anthropology*, 34, 523-548.

Ganoe, C. H., Somervell, J. P., Neale, D. C., Isenhour, P. L., Carroll, J. M., Rosson, M. B., & McCrickard, D. S. (2003). Classroom BRIDGE: Using collaborative public and desktop timelines to support activity awareness. *Proceedings of ACM UIST, Vancouver* (pp. 21-30).

Garcia, R., & Calantone, R. (2002). A critical look at technological innovation typology and innovativeness terminology: A literature review. *Journal of Product Innovation Management*, 19(2), 110–132. doi:10.1016/S0737-6782(01)00132-1

Gardner, H. (1993). Seven creators of the modern era. In J. Brockman (Ed.), *Creativity* (pp. 28-47). New York: Simon & Schuster.

Garisson, D. R., Anderson, T., & Archer, W. (2001). Critical thinking, cognitive presence and computer conferencing in distance education. *American Journal of Distance Education*, 15(1), 7–23. doi:10.1080/08923640109527071

Garrity, E. J., & Sanders, G. L. (1998). Dimensions of information systems success. Hershey, PA: Idea Group Publishing.

Gatignon, H., & Robertson, T. S. (1989). Technology diffusion: An empirical test of competitive effects. *Journal of Marketing*, 53, 35–49. doi:10.2307/1251523

Geen, R. G., & Gange, J. J. (1977). Drive theory of social facilitation: Twelve years of theory and research. *Psychological Bulletin*, 84, 1267–1288. doi:10.1037/0033-2909.84.6.1267

Gefen, D. (2003). TAM or Just Plain Habit: A Look at Experienced Online Shoppers. *Journal of End User Computing*, 15(3), 1-13.

Gefen, D., & Straub, D. (2000). The Relative Importance of Ease of Use in IS Adoption: A Study of e-Commerce Adoption. *Journal of the Association for Information Systems*, 1(8), October, 2000, http://jais.isworld.org/articles/1-8/article.htm.

Gefen, D., Karahanna, E. & Straub, D. (2003). Inexperience and Experience with Online Stores: The Importance of Trust. *IEEE Transactions on Engineering Management*, 50(3), 307-321.

Gefen, D., Straub, D. W., & Boudreau, M.-C. (2000). Structural equation modeling and regression: Guidelines for research practice. *Communications of AIS*, 1(7), 1–78.

Geiger, M.A., & Cooper, E.A. (1996). Using expectancy to address student motivation. *Issues in Accounting Education*, 11(1), 113-129.

George, J. F., & Marett, K. (2005). Deception: The dark side of e-collaboration. *International Journal of e-Collaboration*, 1(4), 24–37.

George, J. F., Marett, K., & Tilley, P. A. (2008). The effects of warnings, computer-based media and probing activity on successful lie detection. *IEEE Transactions on Professional Communication*, 51(1), 1–17. doi:10.1109/TPC.2007.2000052

Gerosa, M. A., Pimentel, G. P., Fuks, H., & Lucena, C. (2005). No need to read messages right now: helping mediators to steer educational forums using statistical and visual information. In T. Koschmann, T. Chan, D. Suthers (Eds.), Proceedings of Computer Supported Collaborative Learning 2005: The Next Ten Years! (pp. 160-169). Taipei, May 30-June 4, 2005, Taiwan, ISLS, LEA editions.

Gerosa, M. A., Pimentel, M. G., Fuks, H., & Lucena, C. (2004). Analyzing Discourse Structure to Coordinate Educational Forums. Intelligent Tutoring Systems. *7th International Conference, ITS 2004* (pp. 262-272). Berlin: Springer.

Geyer, W., Richter, H., Fuchs, L., Frauenhofer, T., Daijavad, S., & Poltrock, S. (2001). A team collaboration space supporting capture and access of virtual meetings. In *Proceedings of the 2001 International ACM SIGGROUP Conference on Supporting Group Work (GROUP'01)* (pp. 188-196). New York: ACM Press.

Giaccardi, E. (2004). *Principles of metadesign: Processes and levels of co-creation in the new design space.* Doctoral dissertation, CAiiA-STAR, School of Computing, Plymouth, UK.

Giddens, A. (1979). *Central problems in social theory.* Berkeley, CA: University of California Press.

Giddens, A. (1984). *The Constitution of Society: Outline of the Theory of Structuration.* Berkeley, CA: University of California Press.

Gigerenzer, G., Todd, P. M. & the ABC Research Group (1999). *Simple heuristics that make us smart.* New York: Oxford University Press.

Giles, C. L., Bollacker, K., & Lawrence, S. (1998). CiteSeer: An automatic citation indexing system. *Proceedings of the Conference on Digital Libraries, Pittsburgh, PA, June 23-26, 1998* (pp. 89-98). New York: ACM Press.

Giordano, G. A., Stoner, J. S., Brouer, R. L., & George, J. F. (2007). The influences of deception and computer-mediation on dyadic negotiations. *Journal of Computer-Mediated Communication, 12*(2), 362–383. doi:10.1111/j.1083-6101.2007.00329.x

Goffee, R., & Jones, G. (1996). What holds the modern company together? *Harvard Business Review, 74*(6), 133-148.

Goh, A. L. S. (2005). Harnessing knowledge for innovation: An integrated management framework. Journal of Knowledge Management, 9(4), 6-18.

Goh, S. C. (2002). Managing effective knowledge transfer: An integrative framework and some practical implications. Journal of Knowledge Management, 6(1), 23-30.

Gold, A. H., Malhotra, A., & Segars, A. H. (2001). Knowledge management: An organizational capabilities perspective. *Journal of Management Information Systems, 18*(1), 185-214.

Gollwitzer, P. M. (1996). The volitional benefits of planning. In P. M. Gollwitzer & J. A. Bargh (Eds.), *The psychology of action: Linking cognition and motivation to behaviour* (pp. 287-312). New York: Guilford.

Gonzalés, V.M., & Mark, G. (2005). Managing currents of work: Multi-tasking among multiple collaborations. In H.

Gellersen et al. (Eds.), *ECSCW 2005: Proceedings of the 9th European Conference on Computer-Supported Cooperative Work* (pp. 143-162). Netherlands: Springer.

González, V., & Mark, G. (2004). Constant, constant, multi-tasking craziness: Managing multiple working spheres. In *Proceedings of the Conference on Human Factors in Computing Systems (CHI)*, Vienna, Austria (pp. 113-120). ACM Press.

Goodhue, D. L., & Thompson, R. L. (1995). Task Technology Fit and Individual Performance. *Management Information Systems Quarterly, 19*(2), 213–236. doi:10.2307/249689

Goodson, P., McCormick, D. & Evans, A. (2001). Searching for sexually explicit materials on the Internet: an exploratory study of college students' behavior and attitudes. *Archives of Sexual Behavior,* 30(2), 101-118.

Grandon, E. E., & Pearson, J. M. (2004). Electronic commerce adoption: An empirical study of small and medium US businesses. *Information & Management, 42,* 197–216.

Granovetter, M. (1973). The strength of weak ties. *American Journal of Sociology,* 78(6), 1360-1380.

Granovetter, M. (1983). The strength of weak ties: A network theory revisited. *Sociological Theory, 1,* 201-233. American Sociological Association.

Grant, R. (1996). Towards a knowledge-based theory of the firm [Winter special issue]. Strategic Management Journal, 17, 102-122.

Grant, R.M. (1991). The resource-based theory of competitive advantage: Implications for strategy formulation. *California Management Review, 33*(3), 114-135.

Grasse, T. (2005). *Eine Systemarchitektur zur effizienten Steuerung von mobilen Einsatzkräften* [in German]. Diploma thesis, FernUniversität Hagen, Germany.

Greenberg, S., & Johnson, B. (1997). *Studying awareness in contact facilitation.* Paper presented at the Workshop on Awareness and Collaborative Systems at the 1997 Conference on Human Factors in Computing Systems, Atlanta, Georgia.

Greenberg, S., Boyle, M., & Laberge, J. (1999). PDAs and shared public displays: Making personal information public, and public information personal. *Personal Technologies, 3*(1), 54-64.

Greene, S. L. (2002). Characteristics of applications that support creativity. *Communications of the ACM, 45*(10), 100-104.

Greene, W. H. (1997). *Econometric analysis* (3rd ed.). Upper Saddle River, NJ: Prentice-Hall.

Gross, T. (1999, May 16-17). Supporting awareness and cooperation in digital information environments. In *Proceedings of the Basic Research Symposium at the Conference on Human Factors in Computing Systems (CHI'99)*, Pittsburgh, Pennsylvania.

Groth, K. (2003). *Using social networks for knowledge management.* Paper presented at the Workshop on Moving From Analysis to Design: Social Networks in the CSCW Context at the 2003 European Conference on Computer Supported Cooperative Work (ECSCW 2003), Helsinki, Finland.

Groth, L. (1999). *Future organizational design.* West Sussex, UK: John Wiley & Sons.

Grover, V. (1993). An empirical derived model for the adoption of customer-based interorganizational systems. *Decision Sciences, 24,* 603–640. doi:10.1111/j.1540-5915.1993.tb01295.x

Grover, V., & Segars, A. H. (1996). IT: The next 1100102 years. *Database, 27*(4), 45-57.

Grover, V., Teng, J., & Fiedler, K. (2002). Investigating the role of information technology in building buyer-supplier relationships. *Journal of the Association for Information Systems, 3,* 217–245.

Grudin, J. (1994). Groupware and social Dynamics: Eight Challenges for Developers. *Communications of the ACM, 37*(1), 93–105. doi:10.1145/175222.175230

Gruenfeld, D. H., Martorana, P. V., & Fan, E. T. (2000). What do groups learn from their worldliest members? Direct and indirect influence in dynamic teams. *Organizational Behavior and Human Decision Processes, 82*(1), 45-59.

Guadagno, R. E. & Cialdini, R. B. (2007). Persuade him by e-mail, but see her in person: Online persuasion revisited. *Computers in Human Behavior, 23*(2), 999-1015.

Guerin, B. (1986). Mere presence effects in humans: A review. *Journal of Experimental Social Psychology, 22,* 38–77. doi:10.1016/0022-1031(86)90040-5

Guicking, A., & Grasse, T. (2006). A framework designed for synchronous groupware applications in heterogeneous environments. In Y.A. Dimitriadis, I. Zigurs, & E. Gómez-Sánchez (Eds.), *Proceedings of the 12th International Workshop on Groupware* (pp. 203-218). Berlin: Springer-Verlag.

Guicking, A., Tandler, P., & Avgeriou, P. (2005). Agilo: A highly flexible groupware framework. In H. Fuks, S. Lukosch, & A.C. Salgado (Eds.), *Proceedings of the 11th International Workshop on Groupware* (pp. 49-56). Berlin: Springer-Verlag.

Guicking, A., Tandler, P., & Grasse, T. (2008). Supporting synchronous collaboration with heterogeneous devices. *International Journal of e-Collaboration, 4*(1), 1–19.

Guilford, J. P. (1983). Transformation: Abilities or functions. *Journal of Creative Behavior, 17,* 75-86.

Gulati, R. (1998). Alliances and networks. *Strategic Management Journal, 19*(4), 293–317. doi:10.1002/(SICI)1097-0266(199804)19:4<293::AID-SMJ982>3.0.CO;2-M

Gunawardena, C., Lowe, C., & Anderson, T. (1997). Analysis of global online debate and development of interaction analysis model for examining social construction of knowledge in computer conferencing. *Educational Computing Research, 17*(4), 397–431.

Gunawardena, C.N. (1995). Social presence theory and implications for interaction and collaborative learning in computer conferences. *International Journal of Educational Telecommunications, 1*(2/3), 147-166.

Gunnlaugsdottir, J. (2003). Seek and you will find, share and you will benefit: organising knowledge using groupware systems. *International Journal of Informa-*

tion Management, 23(5), 363–380. doi:10.1016/S0268-4012(03)00064-1

Gupta, A. K., & Govindarajan, V. (2000). Knowledge management's social dimension: Lessons from Nucor Steel. *Sloan Management Review, 42*(1), 71-80.

Gurteen, D. (1998). Knowledge, creativity and innovation. *Journal of Knowledge Management, 12*(1), 5–13. doi:10.1108/13673279810800744

Gutwin, C., & Greenberg, S. (2002). A descriptive framework of workspace awareness for real-time groupware. *Computer Supported Cooperative Work, 11*, 411-446. Kluwer Academic Publishers.

Gutwin, C., & Greenberg, S. (2004). The importance of awareness for team cognition in distributed collaboration. In E. Salas & M. Fiore (Eds.), *Team cognition: Understanding the factors that drive process and performance* (pp. 177-201). APA Press.

Gutwin, C., & Greenberg, S. A. (2002). Descriptive framework for workspace awareness for real-time groupware. *Computer Supported Cooperative Work, 11*(3-4), 411-446.

Gutwin, C., Greenberg, S., Blum, R., & Dyck, J. (2005). *Supporting informal collaboration in shared-workspace groupware* (Interaction Lab Tech. Rep. No. HCI-TR-2005-01). University of Saskatchewan, Canada.

Hackman, J. R., & Morris, C. G. (1975). Group tasks, group interaction processes, and group performance effectiveness: A review and proposed integration. In L. Berkowitz (Ed.), *Advances in experimental social psychology: Vol. 8* (pp. 45-99). New York: Academic Press.

Hagita, N., & Sawaki, M. (1995). Robust recognition of degraded machine-printed characters using complementary similarity measure and error-correction learning. *Proceedings of the SPIE – The International Society for Optical Engineering, 2442*, (pp. 236-244).

Hair, J. F., Anderson, R. E., Tatham, R. L., & Black, W. C. (1998). *Multivariate Data Analysis* (5th ed.). NJ: Prentice Hall.

Hamel, G. (2002). *Leading the Revolution*. New York: Plume.

Hancock, J. T., Thom-Santelli, J., & Ritchie, T. (2004). *Deception and design: The impact of communication technologies on lying behavior.* Paper presented at the Conference on Computer Human Interaction, New York.

Hansen, M. T., Nohria, N., & Tierney, T. (1999). What's your strategy for managing knowledge? *Harvard Business Review*, 106-115.

Hansen, T. M. (1999). The search-transfer problem: The role of weak ties in sharing knowledge across organization subunits. Administrative Science Quarterly, 44(1), 82-111.

Hantula, D. A., Brockman, D. D., & Smith, C. L. (2008). Online shopping as foraging: The effects of increasing delays on purchasing and patch residence. *IEEE Transactions on Professional Communication, 51*(2), 147–154. doi:10.1109/TPC.2008.2000340

Harakawa, J., Nagai, Y., & Taura, T. (2005). Study on Conceptual Synthesis in Design Creation—Role of Thematic Relation in Creativity— *2005 IDC International Design Congress IASDR,* on CD-ROM.

Harasim, L. (1993). *Global Networks: Computers and International Communication.* London, Cambridge: MIT Press.

Hargadon, A. B. (1998). Firms as knowledge brokers: Lessons in pursuing continuous innovation. *California Management Review, 40*(3), 209-227.

Harrell, A., Caldwell, C., & Doty, E. (1985, October). Expectancy theory predictions of accounting students' academic success motivation. *The Accounting Review,* pp. 724-735.

Hart, P. J., & Saunders, C. S. (1997). Power and trust: Critical factors in the adoption and use of electronic data interchange. *Organization Science, 8*, 23–42. doi:10.1287/orsc.8.1.23

Hartl, D. L., & Clark, A. G. (2007). *Principles of population genetics.* Sunderland, MA: Sinauer Associates.

Hasan, H., & Gould, E. (2001). Support for the sense-making activity of managers. *Decision Support Systems, 31*(1), 71-86.

Hawkins, R., & Verhoest, P. (2002). A transaction structure approach to assessing the dynamics and impacts of business-to-business electronic commerce. *Journal of Computer-Mediated Communication, 7*(3).

Hayes, N., & Walsham, G. (2001). Participation in groupware-mediated communities of practice: a socio-political analysis of knowledge working. *Information and Organization, 11*(4), 263–288. doi:10.1016/S1471-7727(01)00005-7

Hayne, S. C., & Smith, C. A. P. (2005). The Relationship Between e-Collaboration and Cognition . *International Journal of e-Collaboration, 1*(3), 17–34.

Hayne, S.C. (1999). The facilitators perspective on meetings and implications for group support systems design. *ACM SIGMIS Database, 30*(3-4), 72-91.

Hedlund, J., Ilgen, D. R., & Hollenbeck, J. R. (1998). Decision accuracy in computer-mediated versus face-to-face decision-making teams. *Organizational Behavior and Human Decision Processes, 76*(1), 30–47. doi:10.1006/obhd.1998.2796

Heid, J. (1997). Face-to-face online. *Macworld, 14*(1), 146-151.

Helander, M. G., & Emami, M. R. (2008). Engineering eLaboratories: Integration of remote access and eCollaboration. *International Journal of Engineering Education, 24*(3), 466–479.

Henderson, J. C., & Venkatraman, N. (1999). Strategic alignment: Leveraging information technology for transforming organizations. IBM Systems Journal, 38(2&3), 472-484.

Hendrickson, A.R. and Collins, M.R. (1996). An Assessment of the Structure and Causation of IS Usage. *The DATABASE for Advances in Information Systems, 27*(2), 61-67.

Henle, M. (1962). The birth and death of ideas. In H. Gruber, G. Terrell, & M. Wertheimer (Eds.), *Contempo-rary approaches to creative thinking* (pp. 31-62). New York: Atherton.

Henri, F. (1992). Computer conferencing and content analysis . In Kaye, A. R. (Ed.), *Collaborative learning through computer conferencing: The Najaden papers* (pp. 117–136). Berlin: Springer-Verlag.

Herschel, R. T., Nemati, H., & Steiger, D. (2001). Tacit to explicit knowledge conversation: Knowledge exchange protocols. Journal of Knowledge Management, 5(5), 107-116.

Hertel, G., Geister, S., & Konradt, U. (2005). Managing virtual teams: A review of current empirical research. *Human Resource Management Review, 15*, 69-95. Elsevier.

Hess, T. J., Fuller, M. A. & Mathew, J. (2003). Gender and personality in media rich interfaces: Do birds of a feather flock together? P. Zhang, F. Nah, J. Lazar & S. McCoy (Eds.), *Proceedings of the second pre-ICIS annual workshop on HCI research in MIS* (pp. 22-26). Atlanta, GA: Association for Information Systems.

Hevner, A. R., March, S. T., & Park, J. (2004). Design Science in Information Systems Research. *Management Information Systems Quarterly, 28*(1), 75–105.

Hewitt, J. (2005). Towards an Understanding of How Threads Die in Asynchronous Computer Conferences. *Journal of the Learning Sciences, 14*(4), 567–589. doi:10.1207/s15327809jls1404_4

Hiltrop, J.M., & Rubin, J.Z. (1981). Position loss and image loss in bargaining. *Journal of Conflict Resolution, 25*(3), 521-534.

Hiltz, S. R. (1997). Impacts of college level courses via asynchronous learning networks: Some preliminary results. *Journal of Asynchronous Learning Networks, 1*(2).

Hiltz, S.R., & Wellman, B. (1997). Asynchronous learning networks as a virtual classroom. *Communications of the ACM, 40*(9), 44-49.

Hinds, P. J., & Bailey, D. E. (2003). Out of sight, out of sync: Understanding conflict in distributed teams.

Organization Science, 14(6), 615–632. doi:10.1287/orsc.14.6.615.24872

Hlapanis, G., & Dimitracopoulou, A. (2007). A School-Teachers' Learning Community: Matters of Communication Analysis . In Kirschner, P., & Lai, K.-W. (Eds.), *Journal of Technology, Pedagogy, and Education, 16(1).*

Ho, M.-S., & Su, I.-J. (2004). Preparing to prevent severe acute respiratory syndrome and other respiratory infections. *The Lancet Infectious Diseases, 4*(11), 684–689. doi:10.1016/S1473-3099(04)01174-0

Hofer, B.K. (2004). Epistemological understanding as a metacognitive process: Thinking aloud during online searching. *Educational Psychologist, 39*(1), 43-55.

Hoffman, D. L., & Novak, T. P. (1996). Marketing in hypermedia computer-mediated environments: Conceptual foundations. *Journal of Marketing, 60*(July), 50–68. doi:10.2307/1251841

Hofstede, G. (1997). *Cultures and organizations: Software of the mind.* New York: McGraw Hill.

Hollingshead, A. B., McGrath, J. E., & O'Connor, K. M. (1993). Group task performance and communication technology: A longitudinal study of computer-mediated versus face-to-face work groups. *Small Group Research, 24*(3), 307–333. doi:10.1177/1046496493243003

Hollingshead, A.B. (1996). Information suppression and status persistence in group decision making: The effects of communication media. *Human Communication Research, 23,* 193-220.

Holmström, J., Framling, K., Kaipia, R., & Saranen, J. (2002). Collaborative planning, forecasting and replenishment: New solutions needed for mass collaboration. *Supply Chain Management: An International Journal, 7,* 136–145. doi:10.1108/13598540210436595

Holweg, M., Disney, S., Holmström, J., & Smaros, J. (2005). Supply chain collaboration: Making sense of the strategy continuum. *European Management Journal, 23,* 170–181. doi:10.1016/j.emj.2005.02.008

Hoopes, D. G. (2001). Why are there glitches in product development? R&D Management, 31(4), 381-390.

Hu, P.J., Chau, P.Y.K., Sheng, O.R.L. & Tan, K.Y. (1999). Examining Technology Adoption Model Using Physician Acceptance of Telemedicine Technology. *Journal of Management Information Systems,* 16(2), 91-112.

Huber, G. P. (1991). Organizational learning: The contributing processes and the literatures. In M. D. Cohen & L. S. Sproull (Eds.), Organization learning (pp. 124-162). Thousand Oaks, CA: Sage.

Hubona, G. S., & Shirah, G. W. (2006). The Paleolithic Stone Age effect? Gender differences performing specific computer-generated spatial tasks. *International Journal of Technology and Human Interaction, 2*(2), 24–46.

Hulland, J. (1999). Use of partial least squares (PLS) in strategic management research: A review of four recent studies. Strategic Management Journal, 20(2), 195-204.

Hutchins, E. (1995). *Cognition in the wild.* Cambridge, MA: MIT.

Iacovou, C. L., Benbasat, I., & Dexter, A. S. (1995). Electronic data interchange and small organizations: Adoption and impact of technology. *Management Information Systems Quarterly, 19,* 465–486. doi:10.2307/249629

IDC. (2003). Press release. Retrieved November 30, 2006, from *http://www.idc.com/getdoc.jhtml?containerId=pr2003_01_14_145111*

INE. (2005). Estructura y demografía empresarial. Directorio Central de Empresas (DIRCE). Retrieved April 2006 from http://www.ine.es/inebase

Isaacs, E.A., Tang, J.C., & Morris, T. (1996). Piazza: A desktop environment supporting impromtu and planned interactions. In M. Ackerman (Ed.), *Proceedings of the 1996 ACM Conference on Computer Supported Cooperative Work (CSCW'96)* (pp. 315-324). New York: ACM Press.

Isaksen, S. G. (1995). CPS: Linking creativity and problem solving. In G. Kaufmann, T. Helstrup, & K. H. Teigen, (Eds.), *Problem solving and cognitive processes:*

A festschrift in honour of Kjell Raaheim (pp. 145-181). Bergen-Sandviken, Norway: Fagbokforlaget Vigmostad & Bjørke AS.

Isaksen, S. G., Murdock, M. C., Firestien, R. L., & Treffinger, D. J. (Eds.). (1993). *Understanding and Recognizing Creativity: The Emergence of a Discipline.* Norwood, NJ: Ablex.

Isenhour, P. L., Rosson, M. B., & Carroll, J. M. (2001). Supporting interactive collaboration on the Web with CORK. *Interacting with Computers, 13*, 655-676.

Jacob, M., & Ebrahimpur, G. (2001). Experience vs. expertise: The role of implicit understandings of knowledge in determining the nature of knowledge transfer in two companies. Journal of Intellectual Capital, 2(1), 74-88.

Janicki, T., & Steinberg, G. (2003). Evaluation of a computer-supported learning system. *Decision Sciences Journal of Innovative Education, 1*(2), 203-223.

Janis, I. L. (1982). *Groupthink: Psychological studies of policy decisions and fiascoes, 2nd ed.* Boston: Houghton Mifflin.

Janz, B. D., & Prasarnphanich, P. (2003). Understanding the antecedents of effective knowledge management: The importance of knowledge-centered culture. *Decision Sciences, 34*(2), 351-384.

Jap, S. D. (2001). "Pie sharing" in complex collaboration contexts. *JMR, Journal of Marketing Research, 38*, 86–99. doi:10.1509/jmkr.38.1.86.18827

Jap, S., & Mohr, J. J. (2002). Leveraging Internet technologies in B2B relationships. *California Management Review, 44*, 24–38.

Jarvenpaa, S. L., & Leidner, D. E. (1998). Communication and Trust in Global Virtual Teams. [online journal]. *Journal of Computer-Mediated Communication, 3*(4).

Jarvenpaa, S. L., & Staples, S. D. (2001). Exploring perceptions of organizational ownership of information and expertise. *Journal of Management Information Systems, 18*(1), 151-183.

Jayaram, J., & Vickery, S. K. (1998). Supply-based strategies, human resource initiatives, procurement leadtime,

and firm performance. *International Journal of Purchasing and Material Management, 34*(1), 12–23.

Jehn, K. A. (1997). Affective and cognitive conflict in work groups: Increasing performance through value-based intragroup conflict. In C. K. W. De Deru & E. Van de Vliert (Eds.), *Using conflict in organizations* (pp. 87-100). Thousand Oaks, CA: Sage.

Jelassi, M.T., & Foroughi, A. (1989). Negotiation support systems: An overview of design issues and existing software. *Decision Support Systems, 5*(2), 167-181.

Jermann, P. (2004). *Computer Support for Interaction Regulation in Collaborative Problem Solving*, PhD Thesis, University of Geneva.

Jermann, P., Soller, A., & Muehlenbrock, M. (2001). From Mirroring to Guiding: A Review of State of the Art Technology for Supporting Collaborative Learning . In Dillenbourg, P., Eurelings, A., & Hakkarainen, K. (Eds.), *Proceedings of EuroCSCL* (pp. 324–331). Maastricht.

Johnson, E., & Whang, S. (2002). E-business and supply chain management: An overview and framework. *Production and Operations Management, 11*, 413–423.

Johnson, F. P., Klassen, R. D., Leenders, M. R., & Fearon, H. E. (2002). Determinants of purchasing team usage in the supply chain. *Journal of Operations Management, 20*, 77–89. doi:10.1016/S0272-6963(01)00078-X

Johnson, G. (1992). Managing strategic change: Strategy, culture and action. *Long Range Planning, 25*(1), 28-36.

Johnson, M. E., & Whang, S. (2002). E-business and supply chain management: An overview and framework. *Production and Operations Management, 11*(4), 412–423.

John-Steiner, V. (2000). *Creative collaboration.* New York: Oxford University Press.

Jones, B.H. (1988). *Analytical negotiation: An empirical examination of the effects of computer support for different levels of conflict in two-party bargaining.* Unpublished doctoral dissertation. Bloomington, Indiana: Indiana University.

Jöreskog, K. G., & Sorbom, D. (2001). *LISREL 8: User's Reference Guide*. Lincolnwood, IL: Scientific Software Inc.

Julien, P. A. (1995). New technologies and technological information in small businesses. *Journal of Business Venturing, 10*, 459–475. doi:10.1016/0883-9026(95)00084-L

Jun-feng, S., Wei-ming, Z., Wei-dong, X., Guo-hui, L., & Zhen-ning, X. (2005). Ontology-based information retrieval model for the semantic Web. In *Proceedings of the 2005 IEEE International Conference on e-Technology, e-Commerce and e-Service (EEE'05)* (pp. 152-155).

Kahai, S. S., & Avolio, B. J. (2006). Leadership style, anonymity, and the discussion of an ethical issue in an electronic context. *International Journal of e-Collaboration, 2*(2), 1–26.

Kahai, S. S., & Cooper, R. B. (1999). The effect of computer-mediated communication on agreement and acceptance. *Journal of Management Information Systems, 16*(1), 165–188.

Kahai, S. S., Avolio, B. J., & Sosik, J. J. (1998). Effects of source and participant anonymity and initial difference in opinions in an EMS context. *Decision Sciences, 29*(2), 427–460. doi:10.1111/j.1540-5915.1998.tb01583.x

Kallio, J., Saarinen, T., & Tinnila, M. (2002). Efficient change strategies: Matching drivers and chasers in change products. Business Process Management Journal, 8(1), 80-93.

Kanazawa, S. (2004). The Savanna Principle. *Managerial and Decision Economics*, 25(1), 41-54.

Kanungo, S., Sadavarti, S., & Srinivas, Y. (2001). Relating IT strategy and organizational culture: An empirical study of public sector units in India. *Journal of Strategic Information Systems, 10*, 29-57.

Kanzaki, K., Yamamoto, E., Ma, Q., & Isahara, H. (2004). Construction of an objective hierarchy of abstract concepts via directional similarity. *Proceedings of the 20th International Conference on Computational Linguistics, 2*, (pp. 1147-1153).

Kaptelinin, V. (2003). UMEA: Translating interaction histories into project context. In *Proceedings of the Conference on Human Factors in Computing Systems (CHI)*, Fort Lauderdale, Florida (pp. 353-360). ACM Press.

Karahanna, E. & Limayem, M. (2000). Electronic Mail and Voice Mail Usage: Generalizing Across Technologies. *Journal of Organizational Computing and Electronic Commerce*, 10(1), 49-66.

Karahanna, E. & Straub, D.W. (1998). The Psychological Origins of Perceived Usefulness and Ease of Use. *Information and Management*, 35, 237-250.

Karahanna, E., Straub, D.W. & Chervany, N.L. (1999). Information Technology Adoption Across Time: A Cross Sectional Comparison of Pre-Adoption and Post-Adoption Beliefs. *MIS Quarterly,* 23(2), 183-213.

Karlsen, J. T., & Gottschalk, P. (2003). An empirical evaluation of knowledge transfer mechanisms for IT projects. The Journal of Computer Information Systems, 44(1), 112-119.

Karlsen, J., & Gottschalk, P. (2004). Factors affecting knowledge transfer in it projects. Engineering Management Journal, 16(1), 3-11.

Kautz, H., Selman, B., & Shah, M. (1997). ReferralWeb: Combining social netwroks and collaborative filtering. *Communications of the ACM, 40*(3), 63-65. New York: ACM Press.

Kawell, L., Jr., Beckhardt, S., Halvorsen, T., Ozzie, R., & Greif, I. (1988). Replicated document management in a group communication system. In *Proceedings of the 1988 ACM Conference on CSCW* (pp. 395-404). New York: ACM Press.

Kay, J., Yacef, K., & Reimann, P. (2007). Visualisations for Team Learning: Small Teams Working on Long-term Projects. In C. Chinn, G. Erkens, S. Puntambekar, (Eds). *Proceedings of the International Congress CSCL 2007: Computer Supported Collaborative Learning, Mice, Minds and Society* (pp. 351-353), July 21-26, 2007, Rutgers, The State University of New Jersey, USA. ISLS Inc.

Keil, M., Beranek, P.M. & Konsynski, B.R. (1995). Usefulness and Ease of Use: Field Study Evidence Regarding Task Considerations. *Decision Support Systems, 13*, 75-91.

Kemppainen, K., & Vepsäläinen, A. (2003). Trends in industrial supply chains and networks. *International Journal of Physical Distribution & Logistics Management, 33*, 709–719. doi:10.1108/09600030310502885

Kersten, G. (2003). *E-negotiations: Towards engineering of technology-based social processes.* InterNet Working Paper, Concordia University, University of Ottawa, and Carleton University.

Kersten, G., Law, K.P., & Strecker, S. (2004). *A software platform for multiprotocol e-negotiations.* InterNet Working Paper, Concordia University, University of Ottawa, and Carleton University.

Kersten, W., Schroeder, K. A., & Schulte-Bisping, A. (2004). Internet-supported sourcing of complex materials. *Business Process Management Journal, 10*, 101–114. doi:10.1108/14637150410518356

Kessler, E. H. (2003). Leveraging e-R&D processes: a knowledge-based view. *Technovation, 23*, 905–915. doi:10.1016/S0166-4972(03)00108-1

Khazanchi, D., & Zigurs, I. (2006). Patterns for Effective Management of Virtual Projects: Theory and Evidence. *International Journal of e-Collaboration, 2*(3), 25–49.

Kibrick, R., Conrad, A., & Perala, A. (1998). Through the far looking glass: Collaborative remote observing with the W. M. Keck Observatory. *ACM Interactions, 5*(3), 32-39.

Kidd, A. (1994). The marks are on the knowledge worker. In *Proceedings of the Conference on Human Factors in Computing Systems (CHI)*, Boston, Massachusetts (pp. 186-191). ACM Press.

Kim, B., & Oh, H. (2005). The impact of decision-making sharing between supplier and manufacturer on their collaboration performance. *Supply Chain Management, 10*(3/4), 223–237.

Kirk, R. E. (1995). *Experimental design: Procedures for the behavioral sciences.* Pacific Grove, CA: Brooks/Cole.

Kirsh, D. (2001). The context of work. In *Proceedings of the Conference on Human Factors in Computing Systems (CHI)* (pp. 305-322). ACM Press.

Knapp, E., & Yu, D. (1999). How culture helps or hinders the flow of knowledge. *Knowledge Management Review, 2*(1), 16-21.

Knapp, M. L., & Comadena, M. E. (1979). Telling it like it isn't: A review of theory and research on deceptive communications. *Human Communication Research, 1*, 15–29. doi:10.1111/j.1468-2958.1974.tb00250.x

Knapp, M. L., Hart, R. P., & Dennis, H. S. (1974). An exploration of deception as a communication construct. *Human Communication Research, 1*, 15–29. doi:10.1111/j.1468-2958.1974.tb00250.x

Ko, D.-G., Kirsch, L. J., & King, W. R. (2005). Antecedents of knowledge transfer from consultants to clients in enterprise system implementations. MIS Quarterly, 29(1), 58-87.

Kock, N. (2001). Compensatory adaptation to a lean medium: An action research investigation of electronic communication in process improvement groups. *IEEE Transactions on Professional Communication, 44*(4), 267-285.

Kock, N. (2002). Managing with web-based IT in mind. *Communications of the ACM, 45*(5), 102–106. doi:10.1145/506218.506223

Kock, N. (2004). The psychobiological model: Towards a new theory of computer-mediated communication based on Darwinian evolution. *Organization Science, 15*(3), 327–348. doi:10.1287/orsc.1040.0071

Kock, N. (2005), Using Action Research to Study E-Collaboration. *International J. of e-Collaboration, 1*(4), i-vii.

Kock, N. (2005). Media richness or media naturalness? The evolution of our biological communication apparatus and its influence on our behavior toward e-communication tools. *IEEE Transactions on Professional Communication, 48*(2), 117–130. doi:10.1109/TPC.2005.849649

Kock, N. (2005). What is e-collaboration? *International Journal of e-Collaboration, 1*(1), i-vii.

Kock, N. (2005). Compensatory adaptation to media obstacles: An experimental study of process redesign dyads. *Information Resources Management Journal, 18*(2), 41-67.

Kock, N. (2005). Media richness or media naturalness? The evolution of our biological communication apparatus and its influence on our behavior toward E-communication tools. *IEEE Transactions on Professional Communication, 48*(2), 117-130.

Kock, N. (2007). Media naturalness and compensatory encoding: The burden of electronic media obstacles is on senders. *Decision Support Systems, 44*(1), 175–187. doi:10.1016/j.dss.2007.03.011

Kock, N. (2009). Information systems theorizing based on evolutionary psychology: An interdisciplinary review and theory integration framework. *MIS Quarterly.* (Article in press at the time of writing.)

Kock, N. (Ed.). (2008). *Encyclopedia of e-collaboration.* Hershey, PA: Information Science Reference.

Kock, N., & D'Arey, J. (2002). Resolving the e-collaboration paradox: The competing influences of media naturalness and compensatory adaptation. *Information Management and Consulting* (Special Issue on Electronic Collaboration), *17*(4), 72-78.

Kock, N., & Hantula, D. A. (2005). Do we have e-collaboration genes? *International Journal of e-Collaboration, 1*(2), i–ix.

Kock, N., Chatelain-Jardón, R., & Carmona, J. (2008). An experimental study of simulated Web-based threats and their impact on knowledge communication effectiveness. *IEEE Transactions on Professional Communication, 51*(2), 183–197. doi:10.1109/TPC.2008.2000345

Kock, N., Verville, J., & Garza, V. (2007). Media naturalness and online learning: Findings supporting both the significant- and no-significant-difference perspectives.

Decision Sciences Journal of Innovative Education, 5(2), 333–356. doi:10.1111/j.1540-4609.2007.00144.x

Kohut, H. (1985). *Self psychology and the humanities.* New York: W. W. Norton.

Konczak, L. J. (2001). The process of business/environmental collaborations: Partnering for sustainability. *Personnel Psychology, 54,* 515–518.

Kostova, T. (1999). Transnational transfer of organizational practices: A contextual perspective. Academy of Management Review, 24(2), 308-324.

Kotabe, M., Martin, X., & Domoto, H. (2003). Gaining from vertical partnerships: Knowledge transfer, relationship duration, and supplier performance improvement in the US and Japanese automotive industries . *Strategic Management Journal, 24*(4), 293–316. doi:10.1002/smj.297

Kouzes, R. T., Myers, J. D., & Wulf, W. A. (1996). Collaboratories: Doing science on the Internet. *IEEE Computer, 29*(8), 40-46.

KPMG Management Consulting. (1998). *Knowledge management: Research report.*

Kraiger, K., Ford, J.K., & Salas, E. (1993). Application of cognitive, skill-based, and affective theories of learning outcomes to new methods of training evaluation. *Journal of Applied Psychology, 78*(2), 311-328.

Krebs, A.M., Ionescu, M., Dorohonceanu, B., & Marsic, I. (2003). The DISCIPLE system for collaboration over the heterogeneous Web. In *Proceedings of the 36th Annual Hawaii International Conference on System Sciences.* Washington, DC: IEEE Computer Society Press.

Kumar, K., & van Dissel, H. G. (1996). Sustainable collaboration: Managing conflict and cooperation in inter-organizational systems. *MIS Quarterly, 20*(3), 279-290.

Kydd, C.T., & Ferry, D.L. (1991). Computer supported cooperative work tools and media richness: An integration of the literature. In *Proceedings of the 24th Annual Hawaii International Conference on Systems Sciences*

(Vol. III), (pp. 324-332). Los Alamitos, CA: IEEE Society Press.

Lambe, C. J., Spekman, R. E., & Hunt, S. D. (2002). Alliance competence, resources, and alliance success: Conceptualization, measurement, and initial test. *Academy of Marketing Science Journal, 30,* 141–158. doi:10.1177/03079459994399

Lambert, D. M., & Cooper, M. (2000). Issues in supply chain management. *Industrial Marketing Management, 29*(1), 65–83. doi:10.1016/S0019-8501(99)00113-3

Lambert, D. M., Emmelhainz, M. A., & Gardner, J. T. (1999). Building successful partnerships. *Journal of Business Logistics, 20,* 165–181.

Lane, P. J., & Lubatkin, M. (1998). Relative absorptive capacity and interorganizational learning. Strategic Management Journal, 19(5), 461-477.

Laudel, G. (2001). Collaboration, creativity and rewards: why and how scientists collaborate. *International Journal of Technology Management, 22*(7-8), 762–781. doi:10.1504/IJTM.2001.002990

Lawler, E. E., III, & Hackman, J. R. (1969). Impact of employee participation in the development of pay incentive plans: A field experiment. *Journal of Applied Psychology, 53,* 467-471.

Lee, H. L., & Whang, S. (2002). Supply Chain Integration over the Internet. In Geunes, P., Pardalos, M., & Romeijn, H. E. (Eds.), *Supply Chain Management: Models.* Applications, and Research Directions.

Lee, H. L., Padmanabhan, V., & Whang, S. (1997). The bullwhip effect in supply chains. *Sloan Management Review, 38,* 93–102.

Lee, H., & Choi, B. (2003). Knowledge management enablers, processes, and organizational performance: An integrative view and empirical examination. *Journal of Management Information Systems, 20*(1), 179-228.

Lee-Kelley, L., Crossman, A., & Cannings, A. (2004). A social interaction approach to managing the 'invisibles' of virtual teams. *Industrial Management & Data Systems, 104*(8), 650–657. doi:10.1108/02635570410561636

Lefebvre, L. A., & Lefebvre, E. (2002). E-commerce and virtual enterprises: Issues and challenges for transition economies. *Technovation, 22,* 313–323. doi:10.1016/S0166-4972(01)00010-4

Lefebvre, L. A., Harvey, J., & Lefebvre, E. (1991). Technological experience and the technology adoption decisions in small manufacturing firms. *R & D Management, 21,* 241–249. doi:10.1111/j.1467-9310.1991.tb00761.x

Lefebvre, L. A., Lefebvre, E., & Harvey, J. (1996). Intangible assets as determinants of advanced manufacturing technology adoption in SMEs. *IEEE Transactions on Engineering Management, 43,* 307–322. doi:10.1109/17.511841

Lefebvre, L., Lefebvre, E., Elia, E., & Boeck, H. (2005). Exploring B-to-B e-commerce adoption trajectories in manufacturing SMEs. *Technovation, 25,* 1443–1456. doi:10.1016/j.technovation.2005.06.011

Léger, P.-M., Cassivi, L., Hadaya, P., & Caya, O. (2006). Safeguarding mechanisms in a supply chain network. *Industrial Management & Data Systems, 106,* 759–777. doi:10.1108/02635570610671461

Lehman, J. A. (1985). Organizational size and information system sophistication. *Journal of Management Information Systems, 2,* 78–86.

Leidner, D.E., & Jarvenpaa, S. L. (1995). The use of information technology to enhance management school education: A theoretical view. *MIS Quarterly, 19*(3), 265-291.

Leonard, D., & Swap, W. (2004). Deep smarts. *Harvard Business Review, 82*(9), 88-97.

Leonard, D., & Swap, W. (2005). *Deep smarts: How to cultivate and transfer enduring business wisdom.* Boston: Harvard Business School.

Leonard-Barton, D. (1988). Implementation as Mutual Adaptation of Technology and Organization. *Research Policy, 17,* 251–267. doi:10.1016/0048-7333(88)90006-6

Levina, N., & Vaast, E. (2008). Innovating or Doing as Told? Status Differences and Overlapping Boundaries in Offshore Collaboration. *Management Information Systems Quarterly, 32*(2), 307–332.

Levine, J. M., & Moreland, R. L. (2004). Collaboration: The social context of theory development. *Personality and Social Psychology Review, 8*(2), 164-172.

Levine, T. R., McCornack, S. A., & Park, H. S. (1998, March). *Accuracy in detecting truths and lies: Three studies documenting the "veracity effect"*. Paper presented at the annual meeting of the Western States Communication Association, Denver, CO.

Levinson, M. (2005, December 27). The ABCs of KM. CIO Magazine. Retrieved from http://www.cio.com/research/knowledge/edit/kmabcs.html

Levinthal, D., & March, J. (1993). The myopia of learning. *Strategic Management Journal, 14*(8), 95-112.

Li, H., & Atuahene-Gima, K. (2001). Product innovation strategy and the performance of new technology ventures in China. *Academy of Management Journal, 44*(6), 1123–1134. doi:10.2307/3069392

Li, K. (2000). Porn goes public. *Industry Standard, 3*(45), 94.

Lim, L.H., & Benbasat, I. (1992-1993). A theoretical perspective of negotiation support systems. *Journal of Management Information Systems, 9*(3), 27-44.

Lin, A., & Silva, L. (2005). The social and political construction of technological frames. *European Journal of Information Systems, 14*, 49–59. doi:10.1057/palgrave.ejis.3000521

Lin, L., Geng, X., & Whinston, A. B. (2005). A sender-receiver framework for knowledge transfer. MIS Quarterly, 29(2), 197-219.

Lindskold, S., & Hans, G. (1988). GRIT as a foundation for integrative bargaining. *Personality and Social Psychology Bulletin, 14*(2), 335-345.

Link, F. (2007). Coordination, Learning, and Innovation: the organizational roles of e-collaboration and their Impacts. *International Journal of e-Collaboration, 33*, 53–70.

Lipnack, J., & Stamps, J. (1997). *Virtual Teams*. New York: Wiley.

Loch, C. H., & Terwiesch, C. (2005). Rush and be wrong or wait and be late? A model of information in collaborative processes. *Production and Operations Management, 14*(3), 331–344.

Locke, E. A. (1986). Generalizing from laboratory to field: Ecological validity or abstraction of essential elements? In Lock, E. A. (Ed.), *Generalizing from laboratory to field settings* (pp. 5–9). Lexington, MA: Lexington Books.

Locke, E., & Latham, G. (1990). *A theory of goal setting and task performance*. Englewood Cliffs, NJ: Prentice Hall.

Lonsdale, C. (2001). Locked-in to supplier dominance: On the danger of asset specificity for the outsourcing decision. *Journal of Supply Chain Management, 37*, 22–27. doi:10.1111/j.1745-493X.2001.tb00096.x

Lowyck, J., & Elen, J. (1994). *Student's instructional metacognition in learning environments (SIMILE)*. Paper presented at the Leuven: K.U. Leuven, C.I.P. & T.

Lubit, R. (2001). Tacit knowledge and knowledge management: The keys to sustainable management. Organizational Dynamics, 29(3), 164-178.

Lummus, R. R., & Demarie, S. M. (2006). Evolutionary chain. *Industrial Engineer, 38*(6), 38–42.

Ma, Q. & Liu, L. (2004). The Technology Acceptance Model: A Meta-Analysis of Empirical Findings. *Journal of Organizational and End User Computing, 16*(1), 59-72.

Madu, C. N., Kuei, C. H., & Chen, J. H. (1995). A decision support systems approach to adjust maintenance float system availability levels. Computers & Industrial Engineering, 28(4), 773-786.

Majchrzak, A. Rice, R. E. Malhotra & King, N. (2000). Technology adaptation: The case of a computer-supported inter-organisational virtual team. *Management Information Systems Quarterly, 24*(4), 569–600. doi:10.2307/3250948

Majchrzak, A., Cooper, L., & Neece, O. (2004). Knowledge reuse for Innovation. *Management Science, 50*(2), 174-188.

Majchrzak, A., Malhotra, A., & John, R. (2005). Perceived Individual Collaboration Know-How Development through Information Technology – Enabled Contextualisation: Evidence from distributed teams. *Information Systems Research, 16*(1), 9–27. doi:10.1287/isre.1050.0044

Malamuth, N. M. (1996). Sexually explicit media, gender differences, and evolutionary theory. *Journal of Communication*, 46(3), 8-31.

Malhotra, A., & Majchrzak, A. (2004). Enabling knowledge creation in far-flung teams: Best practices for IT support and knowledge sharing. *Journal of Knowledge Management, 8*(4), 75-86.

Malhotra, A., & Majchrzak, A. (2005). Virtual workspace technologies. *MIT Sloan Management Review, 46*(2), 11-14.

Malone, T. (1983). How do people organize their desks? Implications for the design of office information systems. *ACM Transactions on Office Information Systems, 1*(1), 99-112.

Malone, T. W, Crowston, K., Lee, J., & Pentland, B. (1999). Tools for inventing organizations: Towards a handbook of organizational processes. *Management Science, 45*(11), 65-78.

Malone, T. W., & Crowston, K. (1994). The interdisciplinary study of coordination. *ACM Computing Surveys, 26*, 87–119. doi:10.1145/174666.174668

Mamykina, L., Candy, L., & Edmonds, E. (2002). Collaborative creativity. *Communications of the ACM, 45*(10), 96-99.

Maner, J. K., Kenrick, D. T., Becker, D. V., Delton, A. W., Hofer, B., Wilbur, C. J. & Neuberg, S. L. (2003). Sexually selective cognition: Beauty captures the mind of the beholder. *Journal of Personality and Social Psychology*, 85(6), 1107-1120.

Mann, C., & Stewart, F. (2000). *Internet communication and qualitative research: A handbook for researching online*. London: Sage Publications.

Manrodt, K. B., & Fitzgerald, M. (2001). Seven propositions for successful collaboration. *Supply Chain Management Review, 5*, 66–72.

Maritan, C. A. (2001). Capital investment as investing in organizational capabilities: An empirically grounded process model. Academy of Management Journal, 44(3), 513-531.

Markus, M. L. (2005). The Technology Shaping Effects of e-Collaboration Technologies: Bugs and Features. *International Journal of e-Collaboration, 1*(1), 1–23.

Marquez, A. C., Bianchi, C., & Gupta, J. N. D. (2004). Operational and financial effectiveness of e-collaboration tools in supply chain integration. *European Journal of Operational Research, 159*, 348–363. doi:10.1016/j.ejor.2003.08.020

Marsic, I. (1999). DISCIPLE: A framework for multimodal collaboration in heterogeneous environments. *ACM Computing Surveys, 31*(2).

Marsic, I. (2001). An architecture for heterogeneous groupware applications. In *Proceedings of the International Conference on Software Engineering* (pp. 475-484). Washington, DC: IEEE Computer Society Press.

Martin, R., & Noyes, C. (1996). Minority influence and argument generation. In C. J. Nemeth (Ed.), *British Journal of Social Psychology: Special Issue on Minority Influence, 35*, 91-103.

Martinez, A., Dimitriadis, Y., Tardajos, J., Velloso, O., & Villacorta, M. (2003). *Integration of SNA in a mixed evaluation approach for the study of participatory aspects of collaboration.* Paper presented at the Workshop on Moving From Analysis to Design: Social Networks in the CSCW Context at the 2003 European Conference on Computer Supported Cooperative Work (ECSCW 2003), Helsinki, Finland.

Marton, F. & Säljö, R. (1976). On qualitative differences in learning: 1 - Outcome and process. *British Journal of Educational Psychology, 46*, 4-11.

Marton, F., Dall'Alba, G. & Beaty, E. (1993). Conceptions of learning. *International Journal of Educational Research, 19,* 277-300.

Marwick, A. (2001). Knowledge management technology. *IBM Systems Journal, 40*(4), 814–830.

Masip, J., Garrido, E., & Herrero, C. (2006). Observers' decision moment in deception detection experiments: Its impact on judgment, accuracy, and confidence. *International Journal of Psychology, 41*(4), 304–319. doi:10.1080/00207590500343612

Mason-Jones, R., & Towill, D. R. (1999). Using the information decoupling point to improve supply chain performance. *International Journal of Logistics Management, 10*(2), 13–26. doi:10.1108/09574099910805969

Mata, F. J., Fuerst, W. L., & Barney, J. B. (1995). Information technology and sustained competitive advantage: A resource-based analysis. MIS Quarterly, 19(4), 487-505.

Maynard Smith, J. (1998). *Evolutionary genetics.* New York: Oxford University Press.

Mayor, T. (2001). E-learning: Does it make the grade. *CIO Magazine. 14*(7), 132-144.

Maznevski, M. L., & Chudoba, K. M. (2000). Bridging space over time: Global virtual team dynamics and effectiveness. *Organization Science, 11*(5), 473–492. doi:10.1287/orsc.11.5.473.15200

Mazza, R., & Milani, C. (2005). Exploring Usage Analysis in Learning Systems: Gaining Insights from Visualizations. In C. Choquet, V. Luengo & K. Yacef (organizers), *Workshop on Usage Analysis in Learning Systems, The 12th International Conference on Artificial Intelligence in Education AIED 2005,* Amsterdam.

McArthur, R., & Bruza, P. (2003). *Discovery of social networks and knowledge in social networks by analysis of email utterances.* Paper presented at the Workshop on Moving From Analysis to Design: Social Networks in the CSCW Context at the 2003 European Conference on Computer Supported Cooperative Work (ECSCW 2003), Helsinki, Finland.

McCarthy, T. M., & Golicic, S. L. (2002). Implementing collaborative forecasting to improve supply chain performance. *International Journal of Physical Distribution & Logistics Management, 32,* 431–454. doi:10.1108/09600030210437960

McCloy, R. A., Campbell, J. B., & Cudeck, R. (1994). A Confirmatory Test of a Model of Performance Determinants. *The Journal of Applied Psychology, 79*(4), 493–505. doi:10.1037/0021-9010.79.4.493

McCornack, S. A. (1997). The generation of deceptive messages: Laying the groundwork for a viable theory of interpersonal deception. In Greene, J. O. (Ed.), *Message Production: Advances of communication theory* (pp. 91–126). Mahwah, NJ: Erlbaum.

McCornack, S. A., & Parks, M. R. (1986). Deception detection and relational development: the other side of trust . In McLaughlin, M. L. (Ed.), *Communication yearbook, 9* (pp. 377–389). Beverly Hills, CA: Sage.

McDaniel, S. E., Olson, G. M., & Olson, J. S. (1994). Methods in search of methodology—Combining HCI and object orientation. *Proceedings of the ACM Conference on CHI* (pp. 145-151).

McDermott, R., & O'Dell, C. (2001). Overcoming cultural barriers to sharing knowledge. Journal of Knowledge Management, 5(1), 76-85.

McDonald, J. F., & Moffitt, R. A. (1980). The uses of Tobit analysis. *The Review of Economics and Statistics, 62,* 318–321. doi:10.2307/1924766

McEwan, G., & Greenberg, S. (2005). *Community bar: Designing for awareness and interaction.* Paper presented at the Workshop on Awareness Systems: Known Results, Theory, Concepts and Future Challenges at the 2005 Conference on Human Factors in Computing Systems (CHI 2005), Portland, Oregon.

McGrath, J. E., & Tschan, F. (2004). *Temporal matters in social psychology: Examining the role of time in the lives of groups and individuals.* Washington, DC: APA.

McGrath, J.E. (1984). *Groups, interaction and performance.* Englewood Cliffs, NJ: Prentice Hall.

417

McKnight, D. H., Cummings, L. L., & Chervany, N. L. (1998). Initial trust formation in new organizational relationships. *Academy of Management Review, 23*(3), 473–490. doi:10.2307/259290

McNamara, K., Dennis, A. R., & Carte, T. A. (2008). It's the Thought that Counts: The Mediating Effect of Information Processing in Virtual Team Decision Making. *Information Systems Management, 25*(1), 20–32. doi:10.1080/10580530701777123

McNeill, D. (1998). *The face: A natural history.* Boston, MA: Little, Brown and Company.

Mehrabian, A. (1971). *Silent messages.* Belmont, CA: Wadsworth.

Mehrabian, A. (1981). *Silent Messages: Implicit Communication of Emotions and Attitudes* (pp. 75–80). Wadsworth Publishing Co.

Mehrtens, J., Cragg, P. B., & Mills, A. M. (2001). A model of Internet adoption by SMEs. *Information & Management, 39*, 165–176. doi:10.1016/S0378-7206(01)00086-6

Mennecke, B. E., McNeill, D., Ganis, M., Roche, E. M., Bray, D. A., & Konsynski, B. (2008). Second Life and other virtual worlds: A roadmap for research. *Communications of AIS, 22*(1), 371–388.

Mentzas, G. (1993). Coordination of joint tasks in organizational processes. *Journal of Information Technology, 8*, 139–150. doi:10.1057/jit.1993.20

Mentzer, J. T. (2001). *Supply Chain Management.* Thousand Oaks, CA: Sage Publications.

Meroño-Cerdan, A. (2005). Uso de tecnologías de grupo en pymes e influencia sobre el desempeño. *4th International Conference of the Iberoamerican Academy of Management.* Lisbon, December.

Meroño-Cerdán, A. L., Soto-Acosta, P., & López-Nicolás, C. (2008). How do collaborative technologies affect innovation in SMEs? *International Journal of e-Collaboration, 4*(4), 33–51.

Miles, R., Snow, C., Matthews, J., Miles, G., & Coleman, H. (1997). Organizing in the knowledge age: Anticipating the cellular form. *Academy of Management Executive, 11*(4), 7-24.

Miller, G. A., Galanter, E., & Pribam, K. (1960). *Plans and the structure of behavior.* New York: Rinehart & Winston/Holt.

Miller, G. F. (2000). *The mating mind: How sexual choice shaped the evolution of human nature.* New York: Doubleday.

Miller, G. R., & Stiff, J. B. (1993). *Deceptive communication.* Newbury Park, CA: Sage.

Miller, G. R., Mongeau, P. A., & Sleight, C. (1986). Fudging with friends and lying to lovers: Deceptive communication in personal relationships. *Journal of Social and Personal Relationships, 3*, 495–512. doi:10.1177/0265407586034006

Min, S., Roath, A., Daugherty, P. J., Genchev, S. E., Chen, H., & Arndt, A. D. (2005). Supply chain collaboration: What's happening? *The International Journal of Logistic Management, 16*, 237–256. doi:10.1108/09574090510634539

Miranda, S. M., & Carter, P. E. (2005). Innovation diffusion and e-collaboration: The effects of social proximity on social information processing. *International Journal of e-Collaboration, 1*(3), 35–57.

Mitchell, K. A. C. (1998). *The effect of break task on performance during a second session of brainstorming.* Unpublished master's thesis, University of Texas, Arlington.

Mochizuki, T., Kato, H., Hisamatsu, S., Yaegashi, K., Fujitani, S., Nagata, T., et al. (2005). Promotion of Self-Assessment for Learners in Online Discussion Using the Visualization Software. In T. Koschmann, T. Chan, & D. Suthers (Eds.), Proceedings of Computer Supported Collaborative Learning 2005: The Next Ten Years! (pp. 440-449). Taipei, May 30-June 4, 2005, Taiwan, ISLS, LEA editions, USA.

Mohrman, S. A., Cohen, S. G., & Mohrman, A. M. Jr. (1995). *Designing Team-Based Organizations: New Forms for Knowledge Work.* San Francisco, CA: Jossey-Bass Publishers.

Monalisa, M., Daim, T., Mirani, F., Dash, P., Khamis, R. & Bhusari, V. (2008). Managing Global Design Teams. *Research Technology Management*, July-August, 48-59.

Moore, D.A., Kutzberg, T.R., Thompson, L.L., & Morris, M.W. (1999). Long and short routes to success in electronically mediated negotiations: Group affiliations and good vibrations. *Organizational Behavior and Human Decision Processes*, 77(1), 22-43.

Moore, G.C. & Benbasat, I. (1991). Development of an Instrument to Measure the Perceptions of Adopting an Information Technology Innovation. *Information Systems Research,* 2(3), 1992-222.

Moore, K. R. (1998). Trust and relationship commitment in logistics alliances: A buyer perspective. *International Journal of Purchasing and Materials Management*, 34(1), 24–37.

Morán, A.L., Favela, J., Martínez-Enríquez, A.M., & Decouchant, D. (2002). Before getting there: Potential and actual collaboration. In *Proceedings of the 2002 International Workshop in Groupware (CRIWG 2002)*. Berlin: Springer-Verlag.

Moran, E.B., Tentori, M., Gonzalez, V., Favela, J., & Martinez, A. (2006). Mobility in hospital work: Towards a pervasive computing hospital environment. *International Journal of Electronic Healthcare, 3*(1), 72-89.

Moran, T. P. (1983). Getting into a system: External-internal task mapping analysis. *Proceedings of the ACM Conference on CHI* (pp. 45-49).

Moran, T. P., & Carroll, J. M. (Eds.). (1996). *Design rationale: Concepts, techniques, and use.* Hillsdale, NJ: Lawrence Erlbaum.

Moran, T.P. (2005). Unified activity management: Explicitly representing activity in work support systems. Paper presented at the Workshop on Activity: From a Theoretical to a Computational Construct at the 2005 European Conference on Computer Supported Cooperative Work (ECSCW 2005), Paris, France.

Morley, I.E., & Stephenson, G.M. (1997). *The social psychology of bargaining*. London, UK: Allen & Unwin.

Morris, M. & Dillon, A. (1997). How User Perceptions Influence Software Use. *IEEE Software*, 14(4), 58-65.

Morteo, R., Gonzalez, V., Favela, J., & Mark, G. (2004). Sphere Juggler: Fast context retrieval in support of working spheres. In *Proceedings of the 5th Mexican International Conference in Computer Science (ENC)*, Colima, Mexico (pp. 361-367). IEEE Press.

Moscovici, S., & Zavalloni, M. (1969). The group as a polarizer of attitudes. *Journal of Personality and Social Psychology, 12*, 124-135.

Moss, G., Gunn, R. & Heller, J. (2006). Some men like it black, some women like it pink: Consumer implications of differences in male and female website design. *Journal of Consumer Behaviour*, 5(4), 328-341.

Muehlenbrock, M., & Hoppe, H. U. (1999). Computer-supported interaction analysis of group problem solving. In C. Hoadley & J. Roschelle (eds.), *Proceedings of the conference on Computer-supported Collaborative Learning, CSCL-99*, (pp. 398-405). Mahwah, NJ: Erlbaum

Mühlpfordt, M., & Stahl, G. (2007). The integration of synchronous communication across dual interaction spaces. In *Proceedings of Computer Supported Collaborative Learning.*

Muller, M.J., Geyer, W., Brownholtz, B., Wilcox, E., & Millen, D.R. (2004). One-hundred days in an activity-centric collaboration environment based on shared objects. In *Proceedings of the SIGCHI Conference on Human Factors in Computing Systems* (pp. 375-382). New York: ACM Press

Mumford, M. D., & Gustafson, S. B. (1988). Creativity syndrome: Integration, application, and innovation. *Psychological Bulletin, 103*, 27-43.

Munkvold, B. E., & Zigurs, I. (2005). Integration of e-collaboration technologies: Research opportunities and challenges. *International Journal of e-Collaboration, 1*, 1–24.

Munoz, M., Rodriguez, M., Favela, J., Gonzalez, V., & Martinez-Garcia, A. (2003). Context-aware mobile communication in hospitals. *IEEE Computer, 36*(8), 60-67.

Murdock, G. P. (1958). Outline of world cultures. New Haven, CN: Human Relations Area Files Press.

Myers, M. D. (1997) Qualitative Research in Information Systems. Retrieved from http://www.misq.org/misqd961/isworld

Nagai, Y., & Taura, T. (2006). Formal Description of Concept-Synthesizing Process for Creative Design. In J. Gero (Ed.), *Design, Computing and Cognition 06* (pp. 443-460). Springer.

Nakahara, J., Kazaru, Y., Shinichi, H., & Yamauchi, Y. (2005). iTree. Does the mobile phone encourage learners to be more involved in collaborative learning? In T. Koschmann, T. Chan, & D. Suthers (Eds.), Proceedings of Computer Supported Collaborative Learning 2005: The Next Ten Years! (pp. 470-478).Taipei, May 30-June 4, 2005, Taiwan, ISLS, LEA editions, USA.

Nakakoji, K., Yamamoto, Y., & Ohira, M. (1999). A framework that supports collective creativity in design using visual images. *Proceedings of the 3rd Conference on Creativity and Cognition* (pp. 166-173). New York: ACM Press.

Nanda, T., & Singh, T. P. (2009). Determinants of creativity and innovation in the workplace: a comprehensive review. *International Journal of Technology . Policy and Management, 9*(1), 84–106.

Nardi, B., Whittaker, S., & Schwarz, H. (2002). Net-WORKers and their activity in intensional networks. *Computer Supported Cooperative Work, 11*, 205-242. Kluwer Academic Publishers.

Narine, T., Leganchuk, A., Mantei, M., & Buxton, W. (1997). Collaboration awareness and its use to consolidate a disperse group. In *Proceedings of TC13 International Conference on Human-Computer Interaction (Interact 1997)*. Chapman & Hall.

NASA workforce analysis report. (2003). Retrieved August 14, 2003, from http://nasapeople.nasa.gov/workforce/

Neale, D. C., Carroll, J. M., & Rosson, M. B. (2004). Evaluating computer-supported cooperative work: Models and frameworks. *Proceedings of the ACM Conference on CSCW*, 112-121.

Nelson, K., & Cooprider, J. G. (1996). The contribution of shared knowledge to IS group performance. MIS Quarterly, 20(4), 409-430.

Nemeth, C. (1995). Dissent as driving cognition, attitudes, and judgments. *Social Cognition, 13*, 273-291.

Nemeth, C., & Nemeth-Brown, B. (2003). Better than individuals? The potential benefits of dissent and diversity. In P. B. Paulus & B. A. Nijstad (Eds.), *Group creativity: Innovation through collaboration* (pp. 63-84). New York: Oxford University Press.

Nemeth, C., & Rogers, J. (1996). Dissent and the search for information. *British Journal of Social Psychology, 35*, 67-76.

Nemeth, C., Rogers, J. D., & Brown, K. S. (2001). Devil's advocate vs. authentic dissent: Stimulating quantity and quality. *European Journal of Social Psychology, 31*, 707-729.

Ngwenyama, O. K., & Allen, L. (1997). Communication richness in electronic mail: Critical social theory and the contextuality of meaning. *Management Information Systems Quarterly, 21*(2), 145–167. doi:10.2307/249417

Nickerson, R. S. (1999). Enhancing creativity. In R. J. Sternberg (Ed.), *Handbook of creativity* (pp. 392-430). New York: Cambridge University Press.

Nieto, M. J., & Santamaria, L. (2007). The Importance of diverse collaborative networks for the novelty of product innovation. *Technovation, 27*(6/7), 367–377. doi:10.1016/j.technovation.2006.10.001

Nonaka, I., & Takeuchi, H. (1995). The knowledge creating company—How Japanese companies create the dynamics of innovation. Oxford University Press.

Nonaka, I., & Takeuchi, H. (1995). *The knowledge creating company.* New York: Oxford University Press.

Nosek, J. (2005). Collaborative sensemaling support: Progressing from portals and tools to collaboration envelopes. *International Journal of e-Collaboration, 1*(2), 25-39.

Nunamaker, J., Briggs, R., Mittleman, D., Vogel, D., & Balthazard, P. (1997). Lessons from a dozen years of group support systems research: a discussion of lab and field findings. *Journal of Management Information Systems, 13*(3), 63–207.

Nunamaker, J.F., Briggs, R.O., Mittleman, D.D., Vogel, D.R., & Balthazard, P.A. (1997). Lessons from a dozen years of group support systems research: A discussion of lab and field findings. *Journal of Management Information Systems, 13*(3), 163-207.

Nunnally, J. (1967). Psychometric theory. New York: McGraw-Hill.

Nunnally, J. C. (1978). *Psychometric Theory* (2nd ed.). New York: McGraw-Hill.

O'Dell, C., & Grayson, C. J. (1998). If only we know what we know: Identification and transfer of best practices. *California Management Review, 40*(3), 154-174.

O'Dell, C., & Grayson, C. J., Jr. (1999). Knowledge transfer: Discover your value proposition. Strategy & Leadership, 27(2), 10-17.

O'Leonard, K. (2004). *HP case study: Flexible solutions for multi-cultural learners.* Oakland, CA: Bersin & Associates.

O'Mara, J., Allen, J.L., Long, K.M. & Judd, B. (1996). Communication apprehension, nonverbal immediacy, and negative expectations for learning. *Communication Research Reports, 13*, 109-128.

O'Reilly, C. A., Chatman, J., & Caldwell, D. F. (1996). Culture as social control: Corporations, cults, and commitment. *Research in Organizational Behavior, 18*, 157-200.

OECD/Eurostat. (1997). *The measurement of scientific and technological activities: Proposed guidelines for collecting and interpreting technological innovation data.* Paris: OSLO Manual.

Ogden, J. A., Petersen, K. J., Carter, J. R., & Monczka, R. M. (2005). Supply management strategies for the future: A delphi study. *Journal of Supply Chain Management, 41*(3), 29–48. doi:10.1111/j.1055-6001.2005.04103004.x

Olekalns, M., Smith, P.L., & Walsh, T. (1996). The process of negotiating: Strategy and timing as predictors of outcomes. *Organizational Behavior and Human Decision Processes, 68*(1), 68-77.

Oliver, R.L. (1980). A cognitive model for the antecedents and consequences of satisfaction. *Journal of Marketing Research, 17*, 460-469.

Ollman, B. (1971). *Alliennation: Marx's Conception of Man in Capitalist society.* Cambridge University Press.

Olson, G. M., Atkins, D. E., Clauer, R., Finholt, T. A., Jahanian, F., Killeen, T. L., Prakash, A., & Weymouth, T. (1998). The upper atmospheric research collaboratory (UARC). *ACM Interactions, 5*(3), 48-55.

Olson, I. R. & Marshuetz, C. (2005). Facial attractiveness is appraised in a glance. *Emotion, 5*(4), 498-502.

Orlikowski, W. J. (1992). The Duality of Technology: Rethinking The Concept of Technology in Organizations. *Organization Science, 3*(3), 398–427. doi:10.1287/orsc.3.3.398

Orlikowski, W. J. (1993). CASE Tools as Organizational Change: Investigating Incremental and Radical Changes in Systems Development. *Management Information Systems Quarterly, 17*(3), 309–340. doi:10.2307/249774

Orlikowski, W. J., & Baroudi, J. J. (1991). Studying Information Technology in Organizations: Research Approaches and Assumptions. *Information Systems Research, 2*, 1–28. doi:10.1287/isre.2.1.1

Orlikowski, W. L. (1996). Improvising Organisational Transformation Over Time: A situated change perspective. *Information Systems Research, 7*(1), 63–92. doi:10.1287/isre.7.1.63

Orlikowski, W. L. (2000). Using technology and constituting structures: A Practice Lens for Studying Technology in Organisations. *Organization Science, 11*(4), 404–428. doi:10.1287/orsc.11.4.404.14600

Ovalle, O. R., & Marquez, A. C. (2003). The effectiveness of using e-collaboration tools in the supply chain: An assessment study with system dynamics. *Journal of Purchasing and Supply Management, 9,* 151–163. doi:10.1016/S1478-4092(03)00005-0

Packer, R., & Jordan, K. (2002). *Multimedia: From Wagner to virtual reality.* New York: Norton.

Palloff, R. M., & Pratt, K. (1999). *Building Learning Communities in Cyberspace: Effective strategies for the online classroom.* San Francisco: Jossey-Bass Publishers.

Palvia, P., Means, D., & Jackson, W. (1994). Determinants of computing in very small business. *Information & Management, 27,* 161–174. doi:10.1016/0378-7206(94)90044-2

Pant, S., Sethi, R., & Bhandari, M. (2003). Making sense of the e-supply chain landscape: An implementation framework. *International Journal of Information Management, 23,* 201–221.

Paralic, J., & Kostial, I. (2003, September). Ontology-based information retrieval. In *Proceedings of the 14th International Conference on Information and Intelligent Systems (IIS 2003),* Varazdin, Croatia (pp. 23-28).

Pavlou, P. A., & Fygenson, M. (2006). Understanding and predicting electronic commerce adoption: An extension of the theory of planned behavior. *Management Information Systems Quarterly, 30*(1), 115–143.

Pearce, J. A., & Ravlin, E. C. (1987). The design and activation of self-regulating work groups. *Human Relations, 40,* 751-782.

Pena, J., Walther, J. B., & Hancock, J. T. (2007). Effects of Geographic Distribution on Dominance Perceptions in Computer-Mediated Groups. *Communication Research, 34,* 313–331. doi:10.1177/0093650207300431

Perer, A., Shneiderman, B., & Oard, D.W. (2005). *Using rhythms of relationships to understand email archives* (Tech. Rep. No. TR 2005-82). Institute for Systems Research, University of Maryland. Retrieved July 19, 2007, from http://techreports.isr.umd.edu/ARCHIVE/dsp_details.php?isrNum=82&year=2005&type=TR&center=ISR

Perkins, D. N. (1981). *The mind's best work.* Cambridge, MA: Harvard University Press.

Perkins, W.C., Hershauer, J.C., Foroughi, A., & Delaney, M.M. (1996, Spring). Can a negotiation support system help a purchasing manager? *International Journal of Purchasing and Materials Management, 32,* 37-45.

Perks, H. (2000). Marketing information exchange mechanisms in collaborative new product development. *Industrial Marketing Management, 29,* 179–189. doi:10.1016/S0019-8501(99)00074-7

Perry, W. (1968). *Patterns of development in thought and values of students in a liberal arts college: A validation of a scheme* (No. 5-0825, Contract No. SAE-8973). Washington, DC: Department of Health, Education and Welfare.

Peter, J. & Valkenburg, P. M. (2006). Adolescents' exposure to sexually explicit material on the Internet. *Communication Research, 33*(2), 178-204.

Petrou, A. (2005). *Teachers' roles and strategies during educational exploitation of collaborative learning, being supported by appropriate computational environments.* PhD Thesis, School of Humanities, University of the Aegean, Greece.

Petrou, A., & Dimitracopoulou, A. (2003). Is synchronous computer mediated collaborative problem solving 'justified' only when by distance? Teachers' point of views and interventions with co-located groups during every day class activities . In Wasson, B., Ludvigsen, S., & Hoppe, U. (Eds.), *Proceedings of Computer Supported Collaborative Learning 2003: Designing for Change in Networked Learning Environments.* Kluwer Academic Publishers.

Pfeffer, J., & Salancik, G. (1978). *The external control of organizations: A resource dependence approach.* New York: Harper and Row Publishers.

Philaretou, A. G., Mahfouz, A. Y. & Allen, K. R. (2005). Use of Internet pornography and men's well-being. *International Journal of Men's Health, 4*(2), 149-169.

Phillips, W.G. (1999). *Architectures for synchronous groupware* (Tech. Rep. No. 1999-425). Kingston, Canada: Queen's University.

Piccoli, G., Ahmad, R. & Ives, B. (2001). Web-based virtual learning environments: A research framework and a preliminary assessment of effectiveness in basic IT skills training. *MIS Quarterly, 25*(4), 401-426.

Pimentel, K., & Teixeira, K. (1993). *Virtual reality.* New York: McGraw-Hill.

Pinckard, J. (2006). World of Warcraft is the new golf. *PC Magazine, 25*(7), 108–109.

Pinelle, D., & Gutwin, C.A. (2005). Groupware design framework for loosely coupled groups. In *Proceedings of the 2005 European Conference on Computer Supported Cooperative Work (ECSCW 2005).* Berlin: Springer.

Pinker, S. (2002). *The blank slate: The modern denial of human nature.* New York: Penguin Putnam.

Pinsonneault, A., & Caya, O. (2005). Virtual Teams: What We Know, What We Don't Know. *International Journal of e-Collaboration, 1*(3), 1–16.

Pinsonneault, A., & Kraemer, K. L. (1990). The effects of electronic meetings on group processes and outcomes: An assessment of the empirical research. *European Journal of Operational Research, 46*(2), 143–161. doi:10.1016/0377-2217(90)90128-X

Pinto, J. K., & Prescott, J. E. (1987). Changes in critical success factor importance over the life of a project. *Academy of Management Proceedings* (pp. 328-332).

Polimeni, A. M., Hardie, E., & Buzwell, S. (2002). Friendship closeness inventory: Development and psychometric evaluation. *Psychological Reports, 91*(1), 142–152. doi:10.2466/PR0.91.5.142-152

Poole, M.S., Shannon, D.L., & DeSanctis, G. (1992). Communication media and negotiation processes. In L. Putnam & S. Rolloff (eds.), *Communication and Negotiation: Sage Annual Reviews of Communication Research* (Vol. 20), (pp. 46-66). Newbury Park, CA: Sage Publications.

Popper, K. R. (1992). *Logic of scientific discovery.* New York: Routledge.

Pound, N. (2002). Male interest in visual cues of sperm competition risk. *Evolution and Human Behavior, 23*(6), 443-466.

Powell, W. W., White, D. R., Koput, K. W., & Owen-Smith, J. (2005). Network dynamics and field evolution: The growth of interorganizational collaboration in the life sciences. *American Journal of Sociology, 110,* 1132–1206. doi:10.1086/421508

Preguiça, N., Martins, J.L., Domingos, H.J.L., & Duarte, S. (2000). Data management support for asynchronous groupware. In *Proceedings of the 2000 ACM Conference on CSCW* (pp. 69-78). New York: ACM Press.

Preguiça, N., Martins, J.L., Domingos, H.J.L., & Duarte, S. (2005). Integrating synchronous and asynchronous interactions in groupware applications. In H. Fuks, S. Lukosch, & A.C. Salgado (Eds.), *Proceedings of the 11th International Workshop on Groupware* (pp. 89-104). Berlin: Springer-Verlag.

Premkumar, G., & Ramamurthy, K. (1995). The role of interorganizational and organizational factors on the decision mode for adoption of interorganizational systems. *Decision Sciences, 26,* 303–336. doi:10.1111/j.1540-5915.1995.tb01431.x

Premkumar, G., & Roberts, M. (1999). Adoption of new information technologies in rural small businesses. *Omega: The International Journal of Management Science, 27,* 467–484. doi:10.1016/S0305-0483(98)00071-1

Premkumar, G., Ramamurthy, K., & Crum, M. (1997). Determinants of EDI adoption in the transportation industry. *European Journal of Information Systems, 6,* 107–121. doi:10.1057/palgrave.ejis.3000260

Prescott, M. B., & Conger, S. A. (1995). Information technology innovations: A classification by IT focus of impact and research approach. *Data Base Advanced, 36,* 20–41.

Prinz, W. (1999). NESSIE: An awareness environment for cooperative settings. In S. Bødker, M. Kyng, & K. Schmidt (Eds.), *Proceedings of the 6th European Conference on Computer Supported Cooperative Work (ECSCW'99)* (pp. 391-410). Kluwer Academic Publishers.

Pruitt, D.G., & Carnevale, P. (1993). *Negotiation in social conflict*. Pacific Grove, CA: Brooks/Cole.

Purdy, J.M., Nye, P., & Balakrishnan, P.V. (2000). The impact of communication media on negotiation outcomes. *International Journal of Conflict Management*, *11*(2), 162-187.

Pycior, H. M., Slack, N. G., & Abir-Am, P. G. (Eds.). (1996). *Creative couples in the sciences*. New Brunswick, NJ: Rutgers Press.

Quinn, R. E., & Rohrbaugh, I. (1983). A spatial model of effectiveness criteria: Towards a competing values approach to organizational analysis. *Management Science, 29*, 363-377.

Raatikainen, K.E., Christensen, H.B., & Nakajima, T. (2002). Application requirements for middleware for mobile and pervasive systems. *ACM Mobile Computing and Communications Review, 6*(4), 16-24.

Raghunathan, S. (1999). Interorganizational collaborative forecasting and replenishment systems and supply chain implications. *Decision Sciences*, *30*(4), 1053–1071. doi:10.1111/j.1540-5915.1999.tb00918.x

Raghunathan, S., & Yeh, A. B. (2001). Beyond EDI: Impact of continuous replenishment program (CRP) between a manufacturer and its retailers. *Information Systems Research*, *12*, 406–419. doi:10.1287/isre.12.4.406.9701

Rajala, A. K., & Hantula, D. A. (2000). Towards a behavioral ecology of consumption: Delay-reduction effects on foraging in a simulated Internet mall. *Managerial and Decision Economics*, *21*(1), 145–158. doi:10.1002/mde.979

Ramduny, D., Dix, A., & Rodden, T. (1998). Exploring the design space for notification servers. In S. Poltrock & J. Grudin (Eds.), *Proceedings of the 2002 ACM Conference on Computer Supported Cooperative Work (CSCW '98)* (pp. 227-235). New York: ACM Press.

Rangaswamy, A., & Shell, G.R. (1997). Using computers to realize joint gains in negotiations: Toward an electronic bargaining table. *Management Science*, *43*(8), 1147-1163.

Rao, S. S., Metts, G., & Mora Monge, C. A. (2003). Electronic commerce development in small and medium sized enterprises. *Business Process Management Journal*, *9*, 11–32. doi:10.1108/14637150310461378

Rasmus, D. W. (2001). Transferring knowledge with technology. Giga Information Group.

Raymond, L. (1985). Organizational characteristics and MIS success in the context of small business. *Management Information Systems Quarterly*, *9*, 37–52. doi:10.2307/249272

Reekers, N., & Smithson, S. (1994). EDI in Germany and UK. *European Journal of Information Systems*, *3*, 169–178. doi:10.1057/ejis.1994.18

Reffay, C., & Chanier, T. (2003). How social network analysis can help to measure cohesion in collaborative distance-learning. In B. Wasson, S. Ludvigsen, & U. Hoppe (Eds.), *Designing for Change in Networked Learning Environments (Proceedings of the CSCL 2003 Conference)* (pp. 343-352). Bergen, Norway: Kluwer AP

Reimann, P. (2003). How to support groups in learning: More than problem solving. In V. Aleven, et al (Eds.), *Artificial Intelligence in Education (AIED 2003)*. Supplementary Proceedings. University of Sydney.

Reyes, P., & Tchounikine, P. (2005). Mining learning groups' activities in Forum-type tools. In T. Koschmann, T. Chan, & D. Suthers (Eds.), Proceedings of Computer Supported Collaborative Learning 2005: The Next Ten Years! (pp. 509-513). Taipei, May 30-June 4, 2005, Taiwan, ISLS, LEA editions, USA.

Rice, R. (1984). *The new media: Communication, research, and technology*. Beverly Hills, CA: Sage.

Rice, R.E., & Love, G. (1987). Electronic emotion. *Communication Research*, *14*, 85-108.

Riggins, F. J., & Mukhopadyay, T. (1994). Interdependent benefits from interorganizational systems: Opportunities for business partner reengineering. *Journal of Management Information Systems*, *11*, 37–57.

Rittel, H., & Webber, M. (1973). Dilemmas in a general theory of planning. *Policy Sciences*, *4*, 155-169.

Rivera, M., Dussauge, P., & Mitchell, W. (2001). Coordination, creation and protection: Micro-mechanisms for learning from an alliance. Jouy-en-Josas, France: HEC Graduate School of Management.

Robinson, W.N., Pawlowski, S.D., & Volkov, V. (2003). Requirements interaction management. *ACM Computing Surveys, 35*(2), 132-190.

Robson, J. (2000). Evaluating on-line teaching. *Open Learning, 15*(2), 151-172.

Rodden, T. (1996). Populating the application: A model of awareness for cooperative applications. In *Proceedings of the 1996 Conference on Computer Supported Cooperative Work (CSCW 1996)* (pp. 87-96). New York: ACM Press.

Rodríguez, M., & Favela, J. (2003). Autonomous agents to support interoperability and physical integration in pervasive environments. In *Proceedings of the International Atlantic Web Intelligence Conference (AWIC)* (pp. 278-287). Springer-Verlag.

Rogers, E. M. (1983). *Diffusion of Innovations* (3rd ed.). New York: The Free Press.

Rogers, E. M. (1995). *Diffusion of innovation* (4th ed.). New York: The Free Press.

Rogoff, B. (1995). Observing sociocultural activity on three planes: Participatory appropriation, guided participation, and apprenticeship. In J. V. Wertsch, P. del Rio, & A. Alvarez (Eds.), *Sociocultural studies of mind* (pp. 139-164). New York: Cambridge University Press.

Romano, N. Jr, Nunamaker, J., Briggs, R., & Vogel, D. (1998). Architecture, Design, and Development of An HTML/Javascript Web-Based Group Support System. *Journal of the American Society for Information Science American Society for Information Science, 49*(7), 649–667. doi:10.1002/(SICI)1097-4571(19980515)49:7<649::AID-ASI6>3.0.CO;2-1

Romero, N., McEwan, G., & Greenberg, S. (2006). A field study of community bar: (mis)-matches between theory and practice (Rep. No. 2006-826-19). Department of Computer Science, University of Calgary, Alberta, Canada. T2N 1N4.

Root, R. (1988). Design of a multi-media vehicle for social browsing. In I. Greif (Ed.), *Proceedings of the 1988 ACM Conference on Computer Supported Cooperative Work (CSCW'88)* (pp. 25-38). New York: ACM Press.

Rose, D.A.D., & Clark, P.M. (1995). A review of eye-to-eye videoconferencing techniques. *BT Technology Journal, 13* (4), 127.

Ross, J. W. (2003). Creating a strategic it architecture competency: Learning in stages. MIS Quarterly Executive, 2(1), 31-43.

Roth, J. (2000). DreamTeam: A platform for synchronous collaborative applications. *AI & Society, 14*(1), 98-119.

Roth, J. (2003). The resource framework for mobile applications: Enabling collaboration between mobile users. In *Proceedings of the 2003 International Conference on Enterprise Information Systems* (pp. 87-94).

Roth, J., & Unger, C. (2000). An extensible classification model for distribution architectures of synchronous groupware. In R. Dieng-Kuntz, A. Giboin, L. Karsenty, & G. De Michelis (Eds.), *Proceedings of the 4th International Conference on the Design of Cooperative Systems* (pp. 113-127). Amsterdam: IOS Press.

Roth, J., & Unger, C. (2001). Using handheld devices in synchronous collaborative scenarios. *Personal and Ubiquitous Computing, 5*(4), 243-252.

Rouncefield, M., Hughes, J.A., Rodden, T., & Viller, S. (1994). Working with constant interruption: CSCW and the small office. In *Proceedings of the Conference on Computer-Supported Cooperative Work (CSCW)*, Chapel Hill, North Carolina (pp. 275-286). ACM Press.

Rovai, A.P. (2002). A preliminary look at the structural differences of higher education classroom communities in traditional and ALN courses. *Journal of Asynchronous Learning Networks, 6*(1), 41-56.

Rubenstein-Montano, B., Liebowitz, J., Buchwalter, J., McCaw, D., Newman, B., & Rebeck, K.The Knowledge Management Methodology Team. (2001). A system thinking framework for knowledge management. *Decision Support Systems, 31*(1), 5–16. doi:10.1016/S0167-9236(00)00116-0

Rubiano Ovalle, O., & Crespo Marquez, A. (2003). The effectiveness of using e-collaboration tools in the supply chain: an assessment study with system dynamics. *Journal of Purchasing and Supply Management, 9,* 151–163. doi:10.1016/S1478-4092(03)00005-0

Rubin, J.Z., & Brown, B.R. (1975). *The social psychology of bargaining and negotiation.* New York: Academic Press.

Ruggles, R. (1998). The state of the notion: Knowledge management in practice. *California Management Review, 40*(3), 80-89.

Runco, M. A., & Chand, I. (1994). Problem finding, evaluative thinking, and creativity. In M. A. Runco (Ed.), *Problem finding, problem solving, and creativity* (pp. 40-76). Norwood, NJ: Ablex.

Ryan, M.-L. (2001). *Narrative as virtual reality: Immersion and interactivity in literature and electronic media.* Baltimore, MD: Johns Hopkins University Press.

Ryans, Jr., J. K., Griffith, D. A. & White, D. S. (2003). Standardization/adaptation of international marketing strategy: Necessary conditions for the advancement of knowledge. *International Marketing Review, 20*(6), 588-603.

Saad, G. (2004). Applying Evolutionary Psychology in Understanding the Representation of Women in Advertisements. *Psychology & Marketing, 21*(8), 593-612.

Saad, G. (2007). *The evolutionary bases of consumption.* Mahwah, NJ: Lawrence Erlbaum.

Saad, G. (2008). Advertised waist-to-hip ratios of online female escorts: An evolutionary perspective. *International Journal of e-Collaboration, 4*(3), 40–50.

Sabath, R. E., & Fontanella, J. (2002). The unfulfilled promise of supply chain collaboration. *Supply Chain Management Review, 6,* 24–29.

Sacerdoti, E. D. (1974). Planning in a hierarchy of abstraction spaces. *Artificial Intelligence, 5,* 115-135.

Saeed, K. A., Malhotra, M. K., & Grover, V. (2005). Examining the impact of interorganizational systems on process efficiency and sourcing leverage in buyer-supplier dyads. *Decision Sciences, 36*(3), 365–397. doi:10.1111/j.1540-5414.2005.00077.x

Sahay, B. S., & Mohan, R. (2003). Supply chain management practices in Indian industry. *International Journal of Physical Distribution & Logistics Management, 33*(7), 582–606. doi:10.1108/09600030310499277

Sahay, S. (1997). Implementation of information technology: A time-space perspective. *Organization Studies, 18*(2), 229–260. doi:10.1177/017084069701800203

Salas, E., DeRouin, R., & Littrell, L. (2005). Research-based guidelines for designing distance learning: What we know so far. In H.G. Geutal & D.L. Stone (Eds.), *The brave new world of e-HR: human resources management in the digital age.* San Francisco: Jossey-Bass.

Salmon, G. (2000). *E-moderating: the key to teaching and learning online.* London: Kogan Page.

Salton, G. (1988). *Automatic text processing: The transformation, analysis and retrieval of information by computer.* Addison-Wesley Publishing.

Samaddar, S., Nargundkar, S., & Daley, M. (2006). Inter-organizational information sharing: the role of supply network configuration and partner characteristics. *European Journal of Operational Research, 174*(2), 744–765. doi:10.1016/j.ejor.2005.01.059

Sambamurthy, V., Bharadway, A., & Grover, V. (2003). Shaping agility through digital options: Reconceptualizing the role of information technology in contemporary firms. MIS Quarterly, 27(2), 237-263.

Sarker, S., & Sahay, S. (2003). Understanding virtual team development: An interpretive study. *Journal of the Association for Information Systems, 4*(1), 1–38.

Saunders, C. S., & Clark, S. (1992). EDI adoption and implementation: A focus on interorganizational linkages. *Information Resources Management Journal, 5,* 9–19.

Saunders, C. S., Van Slyke, C., & Vogel, D. (2004). My time or yours? Managing time visions in global virtual teams. *Academy of Management Executive, 18*(1), 19-31.

Sawhney, M. (2002). Don't just relate – collaborate. *MIT Sloan Management Review, 43*, 96.

Sawhney, M., & Prandelli, E. (2000). Communities of creation: managing distributed innovation in turbulent markets. *California Management Review, 42*(4), 24–54.

Scanlin, J. (1998) The Internet as an enabler of the Bell Atlantic project office. *Project Management Journal*, June 6-7

Schein, E. H. (1985). *Organizational culture and leadership.* San Francisco: Jossey-Bass.

Schellens, T., & Valcke, M. (2005). Collaborative learning in asynchronous discussion groups: What about the impact on cognitive processing? *Computers in Human Behavior, 21*, 957–975. doi:10.1016/j.chb.2004.02.025

Schneiderman, B. (2007). Creativity Support Tools: Accelerating Discovery and Innovation. *Communications of the ACM, 50*(12), 20–32. doi:10.1145/1323688.1323689

Schommer, M. (1994). An emerging conceptualization of epistemological beliefs and their role in learning. In R. Garner & P.A. Alexander (Eds.), *Beliefs about text and instruction with text* (pp. 25-40). Hillsdale, NJ: Lawrence Erlbaum.

Schommer, M., Crouse, A. & Rhodes, N. (1992). Epistemological beliefs and mathematical text comprehension: Believing it is simple does not make it so. *Journal of Educational Psychology, 84*(4), 435-443.

Schommer-Aikins, M. (2004). Explaining the epistemological belief system: Introducing the embedded systemic model and coordinated research approach. *Educational Psychologist, 39*(1), 19-29.

Schuckmann, C., Kirchner, L., Schümmer, J., & Haake, J.M. (1996). Designing object-oriented synchronous groupware with COAST. In M.S. Ackerman (Ed.), *Proceedings of the 1996 ACM Conference on CSCW* (pp. 30-38). New York: ACM Press.

Schultze, U., & Boland, R. (2000). Knowledge management technology and the reproduction of knowledge work practices. *Journal of Strategic Information Systems, 9*(2-3), 193-213.

Schulz, M. (2000). Pathways of relevance: Exploring inflows of knowledge into subunits of mncs. Retrieved from http://iis.stanford.edu/docs/knexus/MartinSchulz.pdf

Schur, A., Keating, K. A., Payne, D. A., Valdez, T., Yates, K. R., & Myers, J. D. (1998). Collaborative suites for experiment-oriented scientific research. *ACM Interactions, 5*(3), 40-47.

Scott, J. (1991). *Social network analysis: A handbook.* London: Sage Publication.

Sebastian, J. G.-D., & Lambert, D. M. (2003). Internet-enabled coordination in the supply chain. *Industrial Marketing Management, 32*, 251–263. doi:10.1016/S0019-8501(02)00269-9

Senge, P. M. (1990). *The fifth discipline: The art and practice of the learning organization.* New York: Currency Doubleday.

Sezen, B. (2008). Relative effects of design, integration and information sharing. *Supply Chain Management: An International Journal, 13*(3), 233–240. doi:10.1108/13598540810871271

Shah, J., & Murtaza, M. (2005). Effective customer relationship management through web services. *Journal of Computer Information Systems, 46*(1), 98–109.

Sharda, R., Franckwick, G. L., Deosthali, A., & Delahoussaye, R. (1998). Information support for new product development teams. Cambridge, MA: Marketing Science Institute.

Sheffield, J. (1995). The effect of communication medium on negotiation performance. *Group Decision and Negotiation, 4*, 159-179.

Shepher, J. & Reisman, J. (1985). Pornography: A sociobiological attempt at understanding. *Ethology and Sociobiology, 6*(2), 103-114.

Sheppard, B. H., & Sherman, D. M. (1998). The grammars of trust: A model and general implications. *Academy of Management Review, 23*, 422–437. doi:10.2307/259287

Sherman, W. R., & Craig, A. B. (2003). *Understanding virtual reality: Interface, application, and design.* Boston, MA: Morgan Kaufmann Publishers.

Shih, D. H., Chiang, H. S., & Yen, C. D. (2005). Classification methods in the detection of new malicious emails. *Information Sciences, 172*(1-2), 241–261. doi:10.1016/j.ins.2004.06.003

Shneiderman, B. (2000). Creating creativity: User interfaces for supporting innovation. *ACM TOCHI, 7*(1), 114-138.

Short, J., Williams, E., & Christie, B. (1976). *The social psychology of telecommunciations.* New York: John Wiley & Sons.

Sichel, D.E. (1997). *The Computer Revolution: An Economic Perspective*, Washington D.C.: The Brookings Institute.

Simatupang, T. M., & Sridharan, R. (2004). A benchmarking scheme for supply chain collaboration. *Benchmarking: An International Journal, 11*, 9–30. doi:10.1108/14635770410520285

Simatupang, T. M., & Sridharan, R. (2005). The collaboration index: a measure for supply chain collaboration. *International Journal of Physical Distribution & Logistics Management, 35*(1), 44–53. doi:10.1108/09600030510577421

Simonton, D. (1988). *Scientific genius: A psychology of science.* Cambridge University Press.

Singh, D. (1993). Adaptive significance of female physical attractiveness: Role of waist-to-hip ratio. *Journal of Personality and Social Psychology, 65*(2), 293-307

Singh, D. (2002). Female mate value at a glance: Relationship of waist-to-hip ratio to health, fecundity and attractiveness. *Neuroendocrinology Letters, 23*(suppl. 4), 81-91.

Singh, D. (2002). Waist-to-hip ratio: An indicator of female mate value. K. Aoki & T. Akazawa (Eds.), *Proceedings of human mate choice and prehistoric marital networks international symposium* (Vol. 16, pp. 79-99).

Kyoto, Japan: International Research Center for Japanese Studies.

Singh, D., Frohlich, T. & Haywood, M. (1999). *Waist-to-hip ratio representation in ardent sculptures from four cultures.* Paper presented at the meeting of the Human Behavior and Evolution Society, Salt Lake City, Utah, 2-6 June 1999.

Singh, K., & Mitchell, W. (2005). Growth dynamics: The bidirectional relationship between interfirm collaboration and business sales in entrant and incumbent alliances. *Strategic Management Journal, 26*, 497–522. doi:10.1002/smj.462

Singh, N., Fassott, G., Zhao, H. & Boughton, P. D. (2006). A cross-cultural analysis of German, Chinese and Indian consumers' perception of web site adaptation. *Journal of Consumer Behaviour, 5*(1), 56-68.

Skyrme, D. (1998). *Knowledge Management Solutions - The IT Contribution.* Retrieved May 2006 from http://www.skyrme.com/pubs/acm0398.doc.

Smith, A. (1776). The wealth of nations. Vols. I and II. J.M. London, England: Dent & Sons.

Smith, C. L., & Hantula, D. A. (2003). Pricing effects on foraging in a simulated Internet shopping mall. *Journal of Economic Psychology, 24*(5), 653–674. doi:10.1016/S0167-4870(03)00007-2

Smith, J. (2003, July 13). *Mistakes of NASA touted up.* Washington Post.

Sobrero, M., & Roberts, E. B. (2001). The trade-off between efficiency and learning in interorganizational relationships for product development. *Management Science, 47*(4), 493–511. doi:10.1287/mnsc.47.4.493.9828

Sohlenkamp, M., & Chwelos, G. (1994). Integrating communication, cooperation, and awareness: The DIVA virtual office environment. In *Proceedings of the 1994 Conference on Computer Supported Cooperative Work (CSCW '94)* (pp. 331-343). New York: ACM Press.

Sonnenwald, D. H., Whitton, M. C., & Maglaughlin, K. L. (2003). Evaluating a scientific collaboratory: Results of a controlled experiment. *ACM TOCHI, 10*(2), 150-176.

Soto-Acosta, P., & Meroño-Cerdan, A. (2006). An analysis and comparison of web development between local governments and SMEs in Spain. *International Journal of Electronic Business, 4*(2), 191–203.

Spanos, Y. E., & Prastacos, G. (2004). Understanding organizational capabilities: Towards a conceptual framework. Journal of Knowledge Management, 8(3), 31-43.

Spekman, R. E., Kamauff, J. W. Jr, & Myhr, N. (1998). An empirical investigation into supply chain management: a perspective on partnerships. *International Journal of Physical Distribution & Logistics Management, 28*(8), 630–650. doi:10.1108/09600039810247542

Spink, A., & Cole, C. (2006). Human information behavior: Integrating diverse approaches and information use. *Journal of the American Society for Information Science and Technology, 57*(1), 25–35. doi:10.1002/asi.20249

Spink, A., Jansen, B. J., Wolfram, D. & Saracevic, T. (2002). From E-sex to E-commerce: Web search changes. *Computer, 35*(3), 107-109.

Spink, A., Ozmutlu, H. C. & Lorence, D. P. (2004). Web searching for sexual information: An exploratory study. *Information Processing & Management, 40*(1), 113-123.

Sproull, L. S., & Goodman, P. S. (1990). Technology and organisation: Integration and opportunities . In Sproull, L. S., & Goodman, P. S. (Eds.), *Technology and Organiations* (pp. 254–265). San Francisco: Jossey-Bass.

Sproull, L., & Kiesler, S. (1986). Reducing social context cues: Electronic mail in organizational communication. *Management Science, 32*(11), 1492-1512.

Sproull, L.S. (1984). The nature of managerial attention. *Advances in Information Processing in Organizations, 1,* 9-27.

Stahl, G. (2006). *Group Cognition: Computer Support for Building Collaborative Knowledge*. Acting with Technology Series. MIT Press.

Stahl, G., & Herrmann, T. (1999). Intertwining perspectives and negotiation. *Proceedings of ACM GROUP* (pp. 316-325).

Stank, T. P., Daugherty, P. J., & Autry, C. W. (1999). Collaborative planning: Supporting automatic replenishment programs. *Supply Chain Management: An International Journal, 4,* 75–85. doi:10.1108/13598549910264752

Stasser, G., & Birchmeier, Z. (2003). Group creativity and collective choice. In P. B. Paulus & B. A. Nijstad (Eds.), *Group creativity: Innovation through collaboration* (pp. 85-109). New York: Oxford University Press.

Steermann, H. (2003). A practical look at CPFR: The Sears-Michelin experience. *Supply Chain Management Review, 7,* 46–53.

Steiner, I. D. (1972). *Group process and productivity.* New York: Academic Press.

Stern, A. J., & Hicks, T. (2000). *The process of business/ environmental collaborations: Partnering for sustainability.* Westport, CT: Quorum.

Stern, S. E. & Handel, A. D. (2001). Sexuality and mass media: The historical context of psychology's reaction to sexuality on the Internet. *Journal of Sex Research, 38*(4), 283-291.

Sternberg, R. J. & Lubart, T. I. (1999). The concept of creativity: Prospects and paradigms. In R. J. Sternberg (Ed.), *Handbook of creativity* (pp. 3-15). New York: Cambridge University Press.

Sternberg, R. J. (Ed.). (1999). *Handbook of creativity.* New York: Cambridge University Press.

Sternberg, R., & Lubart, T. (1991). An investment theory of creativity and its development. *Human Development, 34,* 1-31.

Stiff, J. B., & Miller, G. R. (1986). "Come to think of it..." Interactive probes, deceptive communication, and deception detection. *Human Communication Research, 12,* 339–357. doi:10.1111/j.1468-2958.1986.tb00081.x

Stiff, J. B., Kim, H. J., & Ramesh, C. (1992). Truth biases and aroused suspicion in relational communication. *Communication Research, 19,* 326–345. doi:10.1177/009365092019003002

Stiff, J. B., Miller, G. R., Sleight, C., Mongeau, P. A., Garlick, R., & Rogan, R. (1989). Explanations for visual cue primacy in judgments of honesty and deceit. *Journal of Personality and Social Psychology, 56*, 555–564. doi:10.1037/0022-3514.56.4.555

Storms, M. D. (1973). Videotape and the attribution process: Reversing actors' and observers' points of view. *Journal of Personality and Social Psychology, 27*, 165–175. doi:10.1037/h0034782

Straub, D., Keil, M. & Brenner, W. (1997). Testing the Technology Acceptance Model Across Cultures: A Three Country Study. *Information and Management, 33*(1), 1-11.

Straus, S.G., & McGrath, J.E. (1994). Does the medium matter? The interaction of task type and technology on group performance and member reactions. *Journal of Applied Psychology, 79*(1), 87-97.

Styhre, A., Roth, J., & Ingelgard, A. (2002). Care of the other: Knowledge-creation through care in professional teams. *Scandinavian Journal of Management, 18*(4), 503-522.

Subramani, M. (2004). How Do Suppliers Benefit from IT Use in Supply Chain Relationships. *Management Information Systems Quarterly, 28*(1), 45–74.

Subramanian, G.H. (1994). A Replication of Perceived Usefulness and Perceived Ease of Use Measurement. *Decision Sciences, 25*(5-6), 863-872.

Suchman, L. A. (1986). *Plans and situated actions*. New York: Cambridge University Press.

Suchman, L. A. (1995). Making work visible. *Communications of the ACM, 38*(9), 56-64.

Sugimoto, M., Hosoi, K., & Hashizume, H. (2004). Caretta: A system for supporting face-to-face collaboration by integrating personal and shared spaces. *Proceedings of the ACM Conference on Computer-Human Interaction* (pp. 41-48).

Sugiyama, L. S. (2004). Is beauty in the context-sensitive adaptations of the beholder? Shiwiar use of waist-to-hip ratio in assessments of female mate value. *Evolution and Human Behavior, 25*(1), 51-62.

Sugiyama, L. S. (2005). Physical attractiveness in adaptationist perspective. D. M. Buss (Ed.), *The handbook of evolutionary psychology* (pp. 292-343). New York: John Wiley.

Sun, L., & Vassileva, J. (2006). Social Visualization Encouraging Participation in Online Communities. *The 12th International Workshop on Groupware* (pp. 349-363). CRIWG 2006, Spain: Springer Verlag

Susman, G., Gray, B. L., Perry, J., & Blair, C. E. (2003). Recognition and reconciliation of differences in interpretation of misalignments when collaborative technologies are introduced into new product development teams. *Journal of Engineering and Technology Management, 20*, 141–159. doi:10.1016/S0923-4748(03)00008-0

Sussman, N. M. & Tyson, D. H. (2000). Sex and power: Gender differences in computer-mediated interactions. *Computers in Human Behavior, 16*(4), 381-394.

Sussman, S.W. & Siegal, W.S. (2003). Informational Influence in Organizations: An Integrated Approach to Knowledge Adoption. *Information Systems Research, 14*(1), 47-65.

Swami, V. & Furnham, A. (Eds.) (in press). *The body beautiful: Evolutionary and sociocultural perspectives.* Basingstoke, UK: Palgrave Macmillan.

Swatman, P. M. C., & Swatman, P. A. (1991). Electronic data interchange: Organizational opportunity, not technical problem. In *Proceedings of the Second Australian Conference on Database and Information Systems, Australia.*

Swink, M. (2006). Building collaborative innovation capabilitiy. *Research Technology Management, 49*(2), 37–47.

Syed-Ikhsan, S., & Rowland, F. (2004). Knowledge management in a public organization: A study on the relationship between organizational elements and the performance of knowledge transfer. Journal of Knowledge Management, 8(2), 95-111.

Symons, D. (1979). *The evolution of human sexuality.* New York: Oxford University Press.

Szajna, B. (1996). Empirical Evaluation of the Revised Technology Acceptance Model. *Management Science,* 42(1), 85-92.

Szulanski, G. (2000). The process of knowledge transfer: A diachronic analysis of stickiness. Organizational Behavior and Human Decision Processes, 82(1), 9-27.

Tandler, P. (2004). *Synchronous collaboration in ubiquitous computing environments.* Doctoral thesis, Darmstadt University of Technology, Darmstadt, Germany.

Taura, T., & Nagai, Y. (2005). Primitives and principles of synthetic process for creative design— Taxonomical relation and thematic relation. In J. Gero & M. Maher (Eds.), *Computational and Cognitive Models of Creative Design VI* (pp. 177-194). Key Centre of Design Computing and Cognition University of Sydney.

Taylor, S., & Todd, R. A. (1995). Understanding IT Usage: A Test of Competing Models. *Information Systems Research,* 6(2), 144–176. doi:10.1287/isre.6.2.144

Teplovs, C., Donoahue, Z., Scardamalia, M., & Philip, D. (2007). Tools for Concurrent, Embedded, and Transformative Assessment of Knowledge Building Processes and Progress In C. Chinn, G. Erkens, & S. Puntambekar (Eds.), *Proceedings of the International Congress CSCL 2007: Computer Supported Collaborative Learning, Mice, Minds and Society* (pp. 720-722). July 21-26, 2007, Rutgers, The State University of New Jersey, USA. ISLS Inc.

Thagard, P. (1998). Ulcers and bacteria II: Instruments, experiments, and social interactions. *Studies in History and Philosophy of Biological and Biomedical Sciences,* 29, 317-342.

Theodosiou, M. & Leonidou, L. C. (2003). Standardization versus adaptation of international marketing strategy: An integrative assessment of the empirical research. *International Business Review,* 12(2), 141-171.

Thomas, D., & Bostrom, R. (2008). Building Trust and Cooperation through Technology Adaptation in Virtual Teams: Empirical Field Evidence. *Information Systems Management,* 25(1), 45–56. doi:10.1080/10580530701777149

Thomas, J. C., Kellogg, W. A., & Erickson, T. (2001). The knowledge management puzzle: Human and social factors in knowledge management. IBM Systems Journal, 40(4), 863-884.

Thompson, L., & Choi, H. S. (Eds.). (2006). *Creativity and Innovation in Organizational Teams.* Mahweh, NJ: Erlbaum.

Thompson, R.L., Higgines, C.A. & Howell, J.M. (1994). Personal Computing: Toward a Conceptual Model of Utilization. *MIS Quarterly,* 15(1), 125-142.

Thong, J. Y. L. (2001). Resource constraints and information system implementation in Singaporean small business. *Omega: The International Journal of Management Science,* 29, 143–156. doi:10.1016/S0305-0483(00)00035-9

Tietze, D. (2001). *A framework for developing component-based cooperative applications.* Doctoral thesis, Darmstadt University of Technology, Darmstadt, Germany.

Timothy, A. J., Boudreau, J. W., & Bretz, R. D. (1994). Job and life attitudes of male executives. *The Journal of Applied Psychology,* 79(5), 767–782. doi:10.1037/0021-9010.79.5.767

Tobin, J. (1958). Estimation of relationships for limited dependent variables. *Econometrica,* 26, 26–36. doi:10.2307/1907382

Todd, P. & I. Benbasat (1991). An experimental investigation of the impact of computer based decision aids on decision making strategies. *Information Systems Research,* 2(2), 87-115.

Tornatzky, L. G., & Klein, R. J. (1982). Innovation characteristics and innovation adoption implementation: A meta-analysis of findings. *IEEE Transactions on Engineering Management,* 29, 28–45.

Towill, D. R., Naim, N. M., & Wikner, J. (1992). Industrial dynamics simulation models in the design of supply chains. *International Journal of Physical*

Distribution and Logistics Management, 22, 3–13. doi:10.1108/09600039210016995

Townsend, A., DeMarie, S., & Hendrickson, A. (1998). Virtual Teams: Technology and the Workplace of the Future. *The Academy of Management Executive, 12*(3), 17–29.

Traum, M. J. (2007). Second Life: A virtual universe for real engineering. *Design News, 62*(15), 75–78.

Tu, C.-H. & McIsaac, M. (2002). The relationship of social presence and interaction in online classes. *American Journal of Distance Education, 16*(3), 131-150.

Tu, C.H. (2000). On-line learning migration: From social learning theory to social presence theory in a CMC environment. *Journal of Network and Computer Applications, 23*(1), 27-37.

Tuominen, M. (2004). Channel collaboration and firm value proposition. *International Journal of Retail & Distribution Management, 32*, 178–189. doi:10.1108/09590550410528953

Tyler, J., & Tang, J. (2003). When can I expect an email response? A study of rhythms in email usage. In *Proceedings of the 2003 European Conference on Computer Supported Cooperative Work (ECSCW 2003)*. Berlin: Springer.

Tyre, M. J., & Orlikowski, W. J. (1994). Windows of Opportunity: Temporal Patterns of Technological Adaptation In Organizations. *Organization Science, 5*(1), 98–118. doi:10.1287/orsc.5.1.98

Ultimate Bulletin Board™, a product of *INFOPOP*, http://www.infopop.com/aboutus/index.html, no date, site visited on March 15, 2002.

Utterback, J. M., & Abernathy, W. J. (1975). A dynamic model of product and process innovation. *Omega, 3*(6), 639–656. doi:10.1016/0305-0483(75)90068-7

Vaidyanathan, G. (2006). Networked Knowledge Management Dimensions in Distributed Projects. *International Journal of e-Collaboration, 2*(4), 19–36.

Van de Ven, A., & Ferry, D. (1980). *Measuring and Assessing Organizations*. New York: Wiley Interscience.

Van der Sanden, J.M.M., Terwel, J. & Vosniadou, S. (2000). New learning in science and technology: A competency perspective. In P.R.J. Simons, S.J.L. van der Linden & T.M. Duffy (Eds.), *New learning*. Dordrecht, The Netherlands: Kluwer Academic Publishers.

Van Dyne, L., & Saavedra, R. (1996). A naturalistic minority influence experiment: Effects on divergent thinking, conflict, and originality in work groups. *British Journal of Social Psychology, 35*, 151-168.

Vartti, R. (2001). German matchmaking websites: Online trafficking in women? *Sexuality & Culture, 5*(3), 49-76.

Vassileva, J., Cheng, R., Sun, L., & Han, W. (2004). Designing Mechanisms to Stimulate Contributions in Collaborative Systems for Sharing Course-Related Materials. *ITS 2004, Workshop on Computational Models of Collaborative Learning.* Maceio, Alagoas, Brazil, August 30 - September 3, 2004

Venkatesh, V. & Davis, F.D. (1994). Modeling the Determinants of Perceived Ease of Use in *Proceedings of the Fifteenth International Conference on Information Systems*, DeGross, J.I., Huff, S.L. & Munro, M.C. (eds.), Vancouver, British Columbia, 212-227.

Venkatesh, V. & Davis, F.D. (1996). A Model of the Antecedents of Perceived Ease of Use: Development and Test. *Decision Sciences, 27*(3), 451-480.

Venkatesh, V. & Davis, F.D. (2000). A Theoretical Extension of the Technology Acceptance Model: Four Longitudinal Field Studies. *Management Science, 46*(2), 186-204.

Venkatesh, V. (1999). Creation of Favorable User Perceptions: Exploring the Rule of Intrinsic Motivation. *MIS Quarterly, 23*(2), 239-260.

Venkatesh, V. (2000). Determinants of Perceived Ease of Use Integrating Control, Intrinsic Motivation and Emotion into the Technology Acceptance Model. *Information Systems Research, 11*(4), 342-365.

Venkatraman, N. (1989). The concept of fit in strategy research: Toward verbal and statistical correspondence.

Academy of Management: The Academy of Management Review, 14, 423–444. doi:10.2307/258177

Verespej, M. (2005). Supply chain collaboration. Frontline Solutions. Retrieved August 2005 from http://www.frontlinetoday.com

Verkasolo, M., & Lappalainen, P. (1998). A method of measuring the efficiency of the knowledge utilization process. IEEE Transactions on Engineering Management, 45(4), 414-423.

Vermetten, Y.J., Vermunt, J.D., & Lodewijks, H.G. (2002). Powerful learning environments? How university students differ in their response to instructional measures. *Learning & Instruction, 12*(3), 263-284.

Vermunt, J.D. & Verloop, N. (1999). Congruence and friction between learning and teaching. *Learning & Instruction, 9*, 257-280.

Vermunt, J.D. & Verloop, N. (2000). Dissonance in students'regulation of learning processes. *European Journal of Psychology of Education, 15*(1), 75-89.

Vermunt, J.D. (1996). Metacognitive, cognitive and affective aspects of learning styles and strategies: A phenomenographic analysis. *Higher Education, 31*, 25-50.

Vermunt, J.D. (1998). The regulation of constructive learning processes. *British Journal of Educational Psychology, 68*, 149-171.

Vivacqua, A.S., Barthès, J.P., & Souza, J.M. (2007a). Supporting self governing software design groups. In *Proceedings of the Computer Supporative Work in Design III 10th International Conference (CSCWD 2006)*. Berlin: Springer-Verlag. Lecture Notes in Computer Science, 4402.

Vivacqua, A.S., Mello, C.R., Souza, D.K., Menezes, J.A., Marques, L.C., Ferreira, M.S., & Souza, J.M. (2007b). Time based activity profiles to recommend partnership in a P2P network. In *Proceedings of the 11th Conference on Computer Supported Cooperative Work in Design (CSCWD'07)*, Melbourne, Australia.

Vivacqua, A.S., Moreno, M., & Souza, J.M. (2005). Using agents to detect opportunities for collaboration. In *Proceedings of the Computer Supported Cooperative Work in Design II 9th International Conference (CSCWD 2005)*. Berlin: Springer-Verlag. Lecture Notes in Computer Science, 3865.

Voida, S., Mynatt, E.D., MacIntyre, B., & Corso, G.M. (2002). Integrating virtual and physical context to support knowledge workers. *IEEE Pervasive Computing, 1*(3), 73-79.

Volpato, C., Maass, A., Mucchi-Faina, A., & Vitti, E. (1990). Minority influence and social categorization. *European Journal of Social Psychology, 20*, 119-132.

Voluntary Interindustry Commerce Standards Association (VICS). (1998). *Collaborative, planning, forecasting and replenishment voluntary guidelines*. Lawrenceville, NJ: Uniform Code Council.

Von Krogh, G. (1998). Care in knowledge creation. *California Management Review, 40*(3), 133-153.

Von Krogh, G., & Grand, S. (2002). From economic theory toward a knowledge-based theory of the firm. In N. Bontis & C. W. Choo (Eds.), The strategic management of intellectual capital and organizational knowledge (pp. 163-184). New York: Oxford University Press.

Von Stamm, B. (2003). *Managing Innovation, Design and Creativity*. West Sussex, England: Wiley.

Vygotsky, L.S. (1978). *Mind in society*. Cambridge, MA: Harvard University Press.

Wade, M., & Hulland, J. (2004). The resource-based view and information systems research: Review, extension, and suggestions for future research. *Management Information Systems Quarterly, 28*, 107–142.

Wagner, C., & Bolloju, N. (2005). Supporting knowledge management in organizations with conversational technologies: discussion forums, weblogs, and wikis. *Journal of Database Management, 16*(2), 1–8.

Walker, G. (2005). Critical Thinking in Asynchronous Discussions. *Int. Journal of Instructional Technology & Distance Learning, 2*(6), 15–21.

Wallach, E. J. (1983). Individuals and organizations: The cultural match. *Training and Development Journal*.

Waller, M., Johnson, E., & Davis, T. (1999). Vendor-Managed Inventory in the supply chain. *Journal of Business Logistics, 20*, 183–203.

Walsham, G. (1993). Interpretive Case Studies in IS research: Nature and Method. *European Journal of Information Systems, 4*, 74–81. doi:10.1057/ejis.1995.9

Walsham, G. (2001). Knowledge Management: The Benefits and Limitations of Computer Systems. *European Management Journal, 19*(6), 599–608. doi:10.1016/S0263-2373(01)00085-8

Walters, S. B. (2000). *The truth about lying: How to spot a lie and protect yourself from deception.* Naperville, IL: Sourcebooks Inc.

Walther, J.B. (1995). Relational aspects of computer-mediated communication: Experimental observations over time. *Organization Science, 6*(2), 186-203.

Wasserman, S., & Faust, K. (1994). *Social network analysis: Methods and applications.* Cambridge: Cambridge University Press.

Watson, J. D. (1968). *The double helix.* New York: Signet.

Watson, S. (1998, January 26). Getting to "aha!" companies use intranets to turn information and experience into knowledge: And gain a competitive edge. *Computer World.*

Webster, J. & Hackley, P. (1997). Teaching effectiveness in technology-mediated distance learning. *Academy of Management Journal, 40*(6), 1282-1309.

Weible, R., & Wallace, J. (1998). Cyber research: The impact of the Internet on data collection. *Marketing Research, 10*, 19–31.

Weick, K. (1990) Technology as equivoque. P. S. Goodman, L. S. Sproull and Associates, eds. Technology and Organisation (pp. 1-44). San Francisco: Jossey-Bass.

Weiser, M. (1991, September). The computer for the 21st century. *Scientific American*, pp. 94-104.

Wellman, B., & Gulia, M. (1999). Netsurfers don't ride alone: Virtual communities as communities. In B. Wellman (Ed.), *Networks in the global village* (pp. 331-366). Boulder, CO: Westview Press.

Wellman, B., Salaff, J., Dimitrova,, D., Garton, L., Gulia, M., & Haythornthwaite, C. (1996). Computer networks as social networks: Collaborative work, telework, and virtual community. *Annual Review of Sociology, 22*, 213-238.

Wenger, E. C., & Snyder, W. M. (2000). Communities of practice: The organizational frontier. *Harvard Business Review*, 139-145.

Wenger, E., McDermott, R., & Snyder, W. (2002). *Cultivating communities of practice: A guide to managing knowledge.* Harvard Business School Press.

West, M. A. (1995). Creative Values and Creative Visions in Teams at Work . In *C. M. Ford & D. A. Gioia (1995), Creative Action in Organizations: Ivory Tower Visions and Real World Voices* (pp. 71–77). Thousand Oaks, CA: Sage.

West, M. A. (1996). Reflexivity and work group effectiveness: A conceptual integration. In M. A. West (Ed.), *Handbook of work group psychology* (pp. 555-579). Chichester, UK: Wiley.

West, M. A. (2003). Innovation implementation in work teams. In P. B. Paulus & B. A. Nijstad (Eds.), *Group creativity: Innovation through collaboration* (pp. 245-276). New York: Oxford Press.

West, M. A., Sacramento, C. A., & Fay, D. (2006). Creativity and Innovation Implementation in Work Groups: The Paradoxical Role of Demands . In Thompson, L., & Choi, H. S. (Eds.), *Creativity and Innovation in Organizational Teams* (pp. 137–159). Mahweh, NJ: Erlbaum.

Westman, A. & Marlowe, F. (1999). How universal are preferences for female waist-to-hip ratios? Evidence from the Hadza of Tanzania. *Evolution and Human Behavior, 20*(4), 219-228.

Weston, F. C. (2001). ERP implementation and project management. *Production & Inventory Management Journal, 42*(3-4), 75–80.

WFMC. (2004). *Workflow Management Coalition.* Retrieved from http://wfmc.org

Whitty, M. T. (2002). Liar, liar! An examination of how open, supportive and honest people are in chat rooms. *Computers in Human Behavior, 18*, 343–352. doi:10.1016/S0747-5632(01)00059-0

Whitworth, B., Gallupe, B., & McQueen, R. (2001). Generating agreement in computer-mediated groups . *Small Group Research, 32*(5), 625–665. doi:10.1177/104649640103200506

Wiberg, M. (2001). RoamWare: An integrated architecture for seamless interaction in between mobile meetings. In *Proceedings of the International ACM SIGGROUP Conference on Supporting Group Work* (pp. 288-297). New York: ACM Press.

Wiig, K. (1997). Knowledge management: An introduction and perspective. Journal of Knowledge Management, 1(1), 6-14.

Wikner, J., Towill, D. R., & Naim, M. (1991). Smoothing supply chain dynamics. *International Journal of Production Economics, 22*, 231–248. doi:10.1016/0925-5273(91)90099-F

Wildt, A. R., Lambert, Z. V., Durand, R. M. (1982). Applying the jackknife statistics in testing and interpreting canonical weights, loadings, and cross-loadings. Journal of Marketing Research, 19(1), 99-107.

Williams, E. (1977). Experimental comparisons of face-to-face and mediated communication. *Psychological Bulletin, 84*(5), 963–976. doi:10.1037/0033-2909.84.5.963

Williamson, O. E. (1975). *Markets and hierarchies: Analysis and antitrust implications.* New York: The Free Press.

Wirt, J. & Livingston, A. (2004). *Condition of education 2002 in brief* (No. NCES 2002011): National Center for Education Statistics.

Wisniewski, E., & Bassok. M. (1999). What makes a man similar to a tie? *Cognitive Psychology, 39*, 208-238.

Wulf, W. (1993). The collaboratory opportunity. *Science, 261*, 854-855.

Wynekoop, J. L. (1992). Strategies for Implementation Research: Combining Research Methods. In J.l. DeGross, J.D. Becker & J.J. Elam (Eds.), *Proceedings of the 13th International Conference on Information Systems* (pp. 195-206).

Yamamoto, E., Kanzaki, K., & Isahara, H. (2005). Extraction of hierarchies based on inclusion of co-occurring words with frequency information. In *Proceedings of the 19th International Joint Conference on Artificial Intelligence,* (pp. 1166-1172).

Ye, Y. (2001). *Supporting component-based software development with active component repository systems.* Doctoral dissertation, University of Colorado at Boulder.

Yi, M.Y. & Davis, F.D. (2003). Developing and validating an observational learning model of computer software training and skill acquisition. *Information Systems Research, 14*(2), 146-149.

Yin, R. K. (1994). *Case Study Research, Design and Methods* (2nd ed.). Newbury Park, CA: Sage.

Yoo, Y., & Alavi, M. (2001). Media and Group Cohesion: Relative Influences on Social Pretense. *Management Information Systems Quarterly, 25*(3), 371–390. doi:10.2307/3250922

Yusuf, S. (2009). From Creativity to Innovation. *Technology in Society, 31*(1), 1–8. doi:10.1016/j.techsoc.2008.10.007

Zack, M. (1999). Managing codified knowledge. Sloan Management Review, 40(4), 45-58.

Zaheer, A., McEvily, B., & Perrone, V. (1998). The strategic value of buyer-supplier relationships. *International Journal of Purchasing and Materials Management, 34*(3), 20–26.

Zajonc, R. B. (1965). Social facilitation. *Science, 149*, 269–274. doi:10.1126/science.149.3681.269

Zhang, D., & Lowry, P. B. (2008). Issues, Limitations and Opportunities in Cross-cultural Research on Collaborative Software in Information Systems. *Journal of Global Information Management, 16*(1), 61–84.

Zhao, J. L., Kumar, A., & Stohr, E. A. (2000). Workflow-Centric Information Distribution Through E-Mail. *Journal of Management Information Systems, 17*(3), 45–72.

Zhou, L., Burgoon, J. K., Nunamaker, J. F., & Twitchell, D. (2004). Automated linguistics based cues for detecting deception in text-based asynchronous computer-mediated communication: An empirical investigation. *Group Decision and Negotiation, 13*(1), 81–106. doi:10.1023/B:GRUP.0000011944.62889.6f

Zhou, L., Burgoon, J. K., Twitchell, D. P., Qin, T., & Nunamaker, J. F. (2004). A comparison of classification methods for predicting deception in computer-mediated communication. *Journal of Management Information Systems, 20*(4), 139–166.

Zhou, L., Shi, Y., & Zang, D. (2008). A statistical language modeling approach to online deception detection. *IEEE Transactions on Knowledge and Data Engineering, 20*(8), 1077–1081. doi:10.1109/TKDE.2007.190624

Zhou, L., Yongmei, S., & Dongsong, Z. (2008). A statistical language modeling approach to online deception detection. *IEEE Transactions on Knowledge and Data Engineering, 20*(8), 1077–1081. doi:10.1109/TKDE.2007.190624

Zhu, K., & Kraemer, K. L. (2005). Post-adoption variation in usage and value of e-business by organizations: Cross-country evidence from the retail industry.

Information Systems Research, 16, 61–84. doi:10.1287/isre.1050.0045

Zineldin, M. A. (1998). Towards an ecological collaborative relationship management: a 'co-operative' perspective. *European Journal of Marketing, 32*(11-12), 1138–1164. doi:10.1108/03090569810243767

Zmud, R. W. (1982). Diffusion of modern software practices: Influence of centralization and formalization. *Management Science, 28*, 1421–1431. doi:10.1287/mnsc.28.12.1421

Zogut, B., & Zander, U. (1992). Knowledge of the firm, combinative capabilities and the replication of technology. *Organization Science, 3*, 383–397. doi:10.1287/orsc.3.3.383

Zuckerman, M., & Driver, R. (1985). Telling lies: Verbal and nonverbal correlates of deception . In Siegman, A. W., & Feldstien, S. (Eds.), *Nonverbal communication: An integrated perspective* (pp. 129–147). Hillsdale, NJ: Lawrence Erlbaum.

Zuckerman, M., DePaulo, B. M., & Rosenthal, R. (1981). Verbal and nonverbal communication of deception . In Berkowitz, L. (Ed.), *Advances in experimental social psychology* (*Vol. 14*, pp. 1–59). New York: Academic Press.

Zumbach, J., Schonemann, J., & Reimann, P. (2005). Analyzing and Supporting Collaboration in Cooperative Computer-Mediated Communication . In Koschmann, T., Suthers, D., & Chan, T. W. (Eds.), *Computer Supported Collaborative Learning 2005: The Next 10 Years!* (pp. 758–767). Mahwah, NJ: Lawrence Erlbaum.

About the Contributors

Ned Kock is Professor of Information Systems and Director of the Collaborative for International Technology Studies at Texas A&M International University. He holds degrees in electronics engineering (B.E.E.), computer science (M.S.), and management information systems (Ph.D.). Ned has authored and edited several books, including the bestselling Sage Publications book titled Systems Analysis and Design Fundamentals: A Business Process Redesign Approach. He has published his research in a number of high-impact journals including Communications of the ACM, Decision Support Systems, European Journal of Information Systems, European Journal of Operational Research, IEEE Transactions (various), Information & Management, Journal of the Association for Information Systems, MIS Quarterly, and Organization Science. He is the Founding Editor-in-Chief of the International Journal of e-Collaboration, Associate Editor for Information Systems of the journal IEEE Transactions on Professional Communication, and Associate Editor of the Journal of Systems and Information Technology. His main research interests are biological and cultural influences on human-technology interaction, electronic communication and collaboration, action research, ethical and legal issues in technology research and management, and business process improvement.

* * *

Maryam Alavi, PhD, is the John and Lucy Cook Chair of Information Strategy and the former Senior Associate Dean of Faculty and Research at the Goizueta Business School of Emory University. She also serves as the Director of Knowledge@Emory, a web-based publication of the Goizueta Business School. Dr. Alavi has authored numerous scholarly papers. Her research has been supported by funds and hardware grants from the AT&T Foundation, AT&T Corporation, IBM, and Lucent Technologies. She has served on the editorial boards of several scholarly journals including MIS Quarterly, Information Systems Research, Journal of MIS, and Journal of Strategic Information Systems. Dr. Alavi was awarded the distinguished Marvin Bower Faculty Fellowship at the Harvard Business School. She also was a recipient of the University of Maryland Distinguished Scholar-Teacher Award, and was elected as the recipient of the prestigious AIS (Association of Information Systems) Fellows Award.

Anne Beaudry, Ph.D., is an Associate-Professor of MIS at the John Molson School of Business, Concordia University. She obtained her Ph.D. from HEC-Montreal. Her work has been published in MIS Quarterly, Communications of the AIS, and the International Journal of Information and Operations Management Education as well as in national and international conference proceedings. Her research interests focus on IT-induced behaviors and on individual and organizational impacts of IT implementation and use.

Irma Becerra-Fernandez is Associate Professor at Florida International University College of Business Administration. Her research focuses on knowledge management (KM), KM systems, and enterprise systems. She founded the FIU KM Lab, and has obtained funding as principal investigator for over $1.7 million primarily from NASA to develop innovative KM systems. She has published extensively in leading journals including the Journal of MIS, Decision Sciences, Communications of the ACM, and European Journal of Operational Research, among others. She is an author of the book Knowledge Management: Challenges, Solutions, and Technologies. She has delivered many invited presentations at federal sites, universities around the world, and international conferences. She was selected the 2004 FIU Outstanding Faculty Torch Award, and serves as the faculty director for the Masters in MIS and on the editorial board of the International Journal of Knowledge and Learning. She earned her Ph.D. from FIU in Electrical Engineering, and her Masters and Bachelors in Electrical Engineering from University of Miami.

Randall J. Boyle is in the Department of Operations and Information Systems at the University of Utah. His research areas include deception detection in computer-mediated environments, the effects of IT on cognitive biases, the effects of IT on knowledge workers, and e-commerce. He has published in several academic journals such as Journal of Management Information Systems, International Journal of E-Collaboration and Journal of International Technology and Information Management. He has received the college teaching award at the University of Alabama in Huntsville and the Marvin J. Ashton Teaching Excellence Award at the University of Utah. He is the author of the forthcoming Pearson Prentice Hall book titled Applied Computer Security.

Tharrenos Bratitsis is a Lecturer at the University of Western Macedonia, Department of Early Childhood Education. He holds a degree in Electrical Engineering and Computer Science (University of Patras, 1994) and a PhD in Technology Based Education (University of the Aegean, 2007). His research interests include: (a) the design of technology-based learning environments (modeling systems, collaborative systems, discussion forae and computer based interaction analysis), (b) adult education via communities of learning, (c) ICTs in education, (d) design, implementation and evaluation of Educational Software, and (e) systems' design. During the last years, he works intensively on collaborative learning environments as well as on computer based interaction analysis supporting learning activities participants' selfregulation.

Jesus Camacho received an MSc degree from the computer science department at CICESE research center, a CONACYT research center in Ensenada, México. His research interests include CSCW, Personal Activity Management (PAM), Activity Based Computing and Mobility. Jesus is now involved in the private sector, working with mobile applications.

John M. Carroll is the Edward M. Frymoyer Chair Professor of information sciences and technology at Pennsylvania State University. His research interests include methods and theory in human–computer interaction, particularly as applied to networking tools for collaborative learning and problem solving, and design of interactive information systems. Carroll has a PhD in experimental psychology from Columbia University. He is a fellow of the ACM, the IEEE, and the Human Factors and Ergonomics Society.

Luc Cassivi is an associate professor in the Department of Management and Technology at the Université du Québec à Montréal, Canada. He received his Ph.D from École Polytechnique de Montréal, Canada and École Centrale de Paris, France. His research interests include information systems, innovation management and supply chain management.

Anne-Marie Croteau, Ph.D., is associate professor of MIS at the John Molson School of Business at Concordia University. Professor Croteau's research mainly focuses on the strategic management of information technology and the impact of information technology on business performance. Her research has been published in various journals such as Journal of Strategic Information Systems, Journal of Information Technology, Industrial Management & Data Systems, and Canadian Journal of Administrative Sciences as well as in various national and international conference proceedings.

Jano de Souza holds a PhD from the University of East Anglia, UK (1986), and is an associate professor at the Graduate School of Engineering, at the Federal University of Rio de Janeiro, where he heads the database group. He has extensive experience in the fields of databases, knowledge management and computer supported cooperative work, and has supervised more than 50 students and written more than 200 papers in these areas. His activities include consulting for a number of Brazilian companies and governmental institutions. His current interests are in scientific knowledge management, ontologies and collaborative systems. He is a member of the steering committee of the yearly CSCWD conference and has participated in several program committees for other conferences.

Martha del Alto is currently serving as the Software Release Authority in the Technology Partnerships Division office at NASA Ames Research Center. In this position she is responsible for the release of software, as well as Open Source within the center. Additionally, she contributes to the development of partnerships between researchers in the industrial, academic and governmental sectors for the purpose of advancing the space exploration vision and creating terrestrial benefits. Prior to that she was in the Intelligent Systems Division office, where she co-founded, and helped establish successful research document management systems. The first one was the New Millennium Documentation Project, and the second was the Postdoc Project. Her professional interests include issues of software/open source, proprietary data, knowledge management and the commercialization of space. Her most recent interests lie in contributing to the national vision of space exploration and making it more affordable through partnerships.

Angelique Dimitracopoulou is Professor of the University of the Aegean, School of Humanities and Director of the Learning Technology and Educational Engineering Laboratory (LTEE). She holds a degree in Physics Sciences (Univ Patras, 1986), Master and PhD in Information and Communication Technologies in Education (University of Paris VII, 1995). She is the author of more than 130 scientific publications related to: (a) the design of technology-based learning environments (modelling systems, intelligent tutoring systems, collaborative systems, computer based interaction analysis), most of them concern the field of sciences education; (b) the implementation of ICTs in genuine educational contexts; in a large variety of levels of education (from pre-primary school to vocational education), (c) the Educational Policy concerning ICTs in Education, and (d) teachers education via communities of learning. During the last years, she works intensively on collaborative learning environments as well as on computer based interaction analysis supporting learning activities participants' selfregulation.

Umer Farooq is a final year PhD student in information sciences and technology at Pennsylvania State University. His dissertation research focuses on supporting creativity in computer-supported collaborative systems. Farooq has a BS in computer science from the National University of Computer and Emerging Sciences, Pakistan, and an MS in computer science from Virginia Tech. He is a member of the ACM.

Jesus Favela is a professor of computer science at CICESE, where he leads the Collaborative Systems Laboratory and heads the Department of Computer Science. His research interests include CSCW, ubiquitous computing and medical informatics. He holds a BS from the National Autonomous University of Mexico (UNAM) and MSc and PhD from the Massachusetts Institute of Technology (MIT). He is a member of the ACM and the American Medical Informatics Association (AMIA), and former president of the Sociedad Mexicana de Ciencia de la Computacion (SMCC).

Jane Fedorowicz, the Rae D. Anderson Professor of Accounting and Information Systems, holds a joint appointment in the Accountancy and Information & Process Management departments at Bentley University. Dr. Fedorowicz earned MS and PhD degrees in Systems Sciences from Carnegie Mellon University. She is principal investigator of a National Science Foundation project team studying design issues for police and government agency collaboration using public safety networks. She also served as principal investigator for the Bentley Invision Project, an international research team housed at Bentley examining interorganizational information sharing and the coordination infrastructures supporting these relationships in supply chain, government, and health care. Dr. Fedorowicz has published over 100 articles in refereed journals and conference proceedings. The Association for Information Systems recognized her contributions to the Information Systems field by naming her an AIS Fellow in 2006.

Abbas Foroughi is professor of computer information systems at the University of Southern Indiana, where he also serves as coordinator for the eBusiness program and for the eCenter. He has received the USI School of Business Faculty Service and Research Awards and the Sadelle Berger USI Faculty Community Service Award. He holds a PhD in business administration from the Kelley School of Business, Indiana University. His research interests include negotiation support systems, decision support systems, Internet security, XBRL, e-business, electronic supply chain management, electronic procurement, and online distance education. He has published papers in Decision Support Systems, Group Decision and Negotiation, and other journals. Dr. Foroughi has served as board member and chair of the Education Committee of the Rotary Club of Evansville, Indiana, which named him a Paul Harris Fellow and Rotarian of the Decade.

Leonardo Galicia is a PhD student of computer science department at CICESE, a CONACYT research center in Ensenada, México. He is actually working in the Human Computer Interaction area under the advice of Dr. Victor M. Gonzalez and Dr. Jesus Favela. His research work aims to understand the processes and strategies involved in Personal Activity Management (PAM), focusing on planning, managing and organizing of multiples activities to provide appropriate supportive information technology. Leonardo also received a MSc degree in the networking area from the computer science department at CICESE research center.

Craig H. Ganoe is an instructor in Information Sciences and Technology at Pennsylvania State University. His research interests include multiple-device interactions, computer supported cooperative work and learning, collaboration in community network contexts, and ubiquitous computing. Ganoe has a BS in Computer Science from The Pennsylvania State University, and an MS in Computer Science from Virginia Tech. He is a member of the ACM.

Joey F. George is Professor of Information Systems and the Thomas L. Williams Jr. Eminent Scholar in Information Systems in the MIS Department in the College of Business at Florida State University. His research interests focus on the use of information systems in the workplace, including deceptive computer-mediated communication, computer-based monitoring, and group support systems. He was the Editor-in-Chief of Communications of the Association for Information Systems from 2006-2009, and he currently serves as a Senior Editor for Information Systems Research. He served as Conference Co-Chair for the 2001 International Conference on Information Systems (ICIS) in New Orleans, LA, and he will also be the Conference Co-Chair for the 2012 ICIS to be held in Orlando, FL. In 2008, he was selected as a Fellow of the AIS.

Victor M. Gonzalez is a Lecturer in Human-Computer Interaction and member of the Interactive Systems Group at the University of Manchester, specialized on the study of people's usage, adoption and adaptation of information and communication technologies. He is also a Senior Research Fellow of CRITO (Centre for Research on Information Technology and Organizations) at the University of California at Irvine, USA. He conducts investigations on technology usage in home, office and hospital settings and specializes on the application of ethnographic methods (e.g. interviews, participant observation) and participatory design techniques (e.g. scenario-based design). He received Ph.D. and Master degrees in Information and Computer Science from the University of California at Irvine and a Master degree in Telecommunications and Information Systems from the University of Essex, United Kingdom. He is a member of ACM SIGCHI and vice-president of the ACM SIGCHI Mexican Chapter.

Thomas Grasse is a research engineer at Jeppesen GmbH, Neu-Isenburg, Germany, which is providing aeronautical information services. He studied computer science at the University of Hagen with economics as subsidiary subject. From December 2004 until November 2005 he worked as student assistant at Fraunhofer IPSI (Integrated Publication and Information Systems Institute), Darmstadt, Germany. During this time, he wrote his diploma thesis which was about the design and implementation of a system architecture for the efficient collaboration of emergency units.

Axel Guicking is a research associate at Fraunhofer IPSI (Integrated Publication and Information Systems Institute) located in Darmstadt, Germany, working in the division Collaborative Environments and e-Learning. He joined IPSI in November 2001. He studied computer science at the University of Würzburg (Germany) with chemistry as additional subject and focusing on artificial intelligence. His diploma thesis was about adaptivity of web-based e-learning systems. He currently works on his Ph.D. in the area of electronic meeting systems in heterogeneous environments. His research interests include computer-supported cooperative work, electronic meeting support systems, human-computer interaction, adaptive software systems as well as software architectures, framework design, and reusability aspects of software systems.

Pierre Hadaya is a professor in the Department of Management and Technology at the École des Sciences de la Gestion de l'Université du Québec à Montréal. He holds a Ph.D. in Management of Technology from the École Polytechnique de Montréal. His main research interests lie at the intersection of information technology management, business strategy, and interorganizational design.

Steven Hornik is a faculty member of the Dixon School of Accounting at the University of Central Florida, College of Business Administration. His research interests include the social context of technology mediation in learning, training and other virtual environments, the effectiveness of technology mediated learning for training and higher education and the social implications of technology. He has been involved in the Research Initiative for Teaching Effectiveness, University of Central Florida, to examine the impact of distance learning outcomes and was selected as a 2005 UFC Fellow of the Academy for Teaching, Learning and Leadership. Dr. Hornik has published in several journals include the Journal of Global Information Management, IEEE Transactions on Professional Communication and the Journal for Information Systems.

Hitoshi Isahara received the B.E., M.E., and Ph.D. degrees in electrical engineering from Kyoto University, Kyoto, Japan, in 1978, 1980, and 1995, respectively. His research interests include natural language processing and lexical semantics. He is a Leader of the Computational Linguistics Group and a Director of the Thai Computational Linguistics Laboratory (TCL) at the National Institute of Information and Communications Technology (NICT), Japan. He is a Professor at Kobe University Graduate School of Engineering, Japan. He is a Vice-President of the International Association for Machine Translation (IAMT), a President of the Asia-Pacific Association for Machine Translation (AAMT), a board member of GSK (Gengo Shigen Kyokai, linguistic resource association) and a board member of the Association for Natural Language Processing, Japan. He is a member of the Institute of Electronics, Information and Communication Engineers, Japan, the Association for Natural Language Processing, Japan, the Japanese Society for Artificial Intelligence, and the Information Processing Society of Japan.

Len Jessup is dean of the College of Business and Economics, Washington State University, and the Philip L. Kays distinguished professor in management information systems. While at WSU, he has guided the school through AACSB reaccreditation, developed the Boeing Classroom of the Future, and managed the implementation of a Web-based, online version of the MIS curriculum. Dr. Jessup earned his BA and MBA at California State University, Chico, and his PhD in organization behavior and MIS from the University of Arizona. His research interests include groupware, wireless collaboration, electronic commerce, and technology supported learning and decision-making. He has authored and co-authored numerous scholarly articles, as well as the MIS textbooks Information Systems Foundation and Information Systems Today with his colleague Joe Valacich. With his wife, Joy Egbert, he won Zenith Data Systems' Masters of Innovation Award for Education.

Richard Johnson is as Assistant Professor of Management Information Systems at the University of Central Florida. He received this Ph.D. from the University of Maryland, College Park. His research interests focus on psychological and sociological impacts of computing technology, computer self-efficacy, technology-mediated/distributed learning and training, and issues surrounding digital divide. Dr. Johnson has published in several journals including Information Systems Research and the International Journal of Human Computer Studies, as well as numerous international research conferences.

Charles ("Chuck") Kacmar is in the Information Systems, Statistics, and Management Science Department in the College of Commerce and Business Administration at the University of Alabama. His research projects include perceptions of trust in the use of information systems and individual affectivity and its impact on organizational outcomes. Some of his publications have appeared in MIS Quarterly, Information Systems Research, Communications of the ACM, ACM Transactions on Information Systems, Hypermedia, Academy of Management Journal, Journal of Strategic Information Systems, Journal of Organizational Behavior, Journal of Leadership & Organizational Studies, and Behaviour and Information Technology. He serves on the editorial board for the Journal of Database Management and Communications of the AIS, and is the secretary/treasurer for the Special Interest Group (SIG) on Human-Computer Interaction of the Association for Information Systems.

Tim Kayworth, PhD is an Associate Professor and department chair of Management Information Systems in the Hankamer School of Business at Baylor University. He has prior industry experience in information systems consulting and has also held positions as MIS director and operations manager for private sector firms. Dr. Kayworth's research interests center on the management of IT in organizations. Recent research projects have included such topics as leadership in global virtual teams, the impact of organizational culture on knowledge management practice, and the role of culture in information systems research. His work has been published in the European Management Journal, the Journal of Management Information Systems, The DATABASE for Advances in Information Systems, the Information Resources Management Journal as well as in such international conferences as AMCIS, ICIS, and the Strategic Management Society.

Kevin Laframboise, Ph.D., is an assistant professor of MIS at the John Molson School of Business at Concordia University, from which he obtained his Ph.D. Professor Laframboise's research centers quality management and on enterprise information systems and the impact of these on business performance. His research has been published in Journal of Supply Chain Management, International Journal of Enterprise Information Systems and Leadership Quarterly. As well, his papers appear in international conference proceedings such as ECIS, EUROMA and DEXA.

Isidro Laso-Ballesteros is a Scientific Officer at the Directorate General Information Society and Media of the European Commission where he is in charge of the long term research activities and strategy of the Networked Media unit, and is now dealing with the Future Media Internet initiative. In addition, he teaches as lecturer in several universities and currently keeps permanent teaching slots in several postgraduate courses of the Virtual School of the Universidad Politecnica de Madrid-CEPADE. He holds a degree on civil engineering and postgraduate studies on computational engineering and systems/networking engineering. Isidro has authored various books on the topic of Internet: "Internet y Comercio Electronico", "Internet, Comercio Colaborativo y mComercio". He has also published chapters in Japanese, English and Spanish in reviewed books edited by IOS press and Kluwer Academic publ. He has also authored three publications on Collaborative technologies, innovation, collaborative work environments and innovation published by the Official Publication Office of the European Communities (OPOCE). He is member of scientific boards of several IEEE and international conferences on ICT. He is regularly invited as keynote speaker on research institutions and conferences to talk about long term ICT research.

Elisabeth Lefebvre is professor in the Department of Mathematics and Industrial Engineering at École Polytechnique in Montréal. She received the Ph.D. degree in business administration from the University of Montréal. Her current research interests are in the area of technology management, supply chain management and interorganizational collaboration.

Louis A. Lefebvre is professor in the Department of Mathematics and Industrial Engineering at École Polytechnique in Montréal and invited professor at University of Wageningen (NL). He received the Ph.D. degree in business administration from the University of Montréal. His current research interests are in the area of technology and innovation management, supply chain management and RFID technologies.

Dorothy E. Leidner, PhD is the Randall W. and Sandra Ferguson Professor of Information Systems and Director of the Center for Knowledge Management at Baylor University. Prior to rejoining the Baylor faculty, she was associate professor at INSEAD and at Texas Christian University. She is a regular visiting professor at the University of Mannheim, Germany, and has been a visiting professor at the Instituto Tecnologico y des Estudios Superiores de Monterrey, Mexico, at the Institut d'Administration des Entreprises at the Université de Caen, France, and at Southern Methodist University. Dr. Leidner received her PhD in Information Systems from the University of Texas at Austin. Dr. Leidner's research has been published in a variety of journals, such as MIS Quarterly, Information Systems Research, Journal of Management Information Systems, Decision Sciences, Decision Support Systems, and Organization Science. She has received several prestigious best paper awards, including one in 1993 from the Hawaii International Conference on System Sciences, one in 1995 from MIS Quarterly, and one in 1999 from the Academy of Management. She is currently serving as co-editor of the journal Data Base for Advances in Information Systems, senior editor for MIS Quarterly and associate editor for the Decision Sciences Journal and for the Decision Support Systems Journal. She serves on the editorial boards of MISQ Executive, the International Journal of Knowledge Management, and the International Journal of Information Technology Education.

Carolina López-Nicolás is an assistant professor in the Department of Management and Finance at the University of Murcia, Spain. She has been a visiting professor at Delft University of Technology in The Netherlands and Michigan State University in USA. Her current research relates to knowledge management, information systems, business strategy and mobile communications. She has published on these topics in such journals as the Information & Management, Journal of Knowledge Management, International Journal of Information Management, International Journal of Internet Marketing and Advertising, Journal of Enterprise Information Management, among others.

Mantas Manovas, M.Sc, is a native of Lithuania. After completing his M.Sc. degree from Concordia University, he went on to establish and manage an online marketing firm that successfully serves the U.S. and Canadian market.

Angel L. Meroño-Cerdan is Associate Professor of Management at the University of Murcia in Spain. He holds a Master in Business and Foreign Trade including a three months training at USA-Spanish Chamber of Commerce in New York and a PhD in Business Administration (University of Murcia, Spain). He has published in International Journal of Information Management, European Journal of Information

Systems, Journal of Computer Information Systems, Journal of Enterprise Information Management, Journal of Knowledge Management, International Journal of Electronic Business, among others. His teaching and research are related to information systems, knowledge management and e-business.

Athanasios Nikas holds a PhD degree in Information Systems Management from the Department of Management Science and Technology of the Athens University of Economics & Business (2007), an MSc degree in the Analysis, Design and Management of Information Systems obtained at the London School of Economics and Political Science (2001) and a BSc degree from the Department of Financial and Banking Management of the University of Piraeus (2000). His research interest is focusing on studying the social and organisational dynamics which underlie recent technological and work developments in networked organisations from both social and management perspective. Among others, he participated in many research projects in the field of Information Systems Management and R&D assessment, funded from EU, the Greek General Secretarial for Research & Technology and Greek Ministry of Development. Finally, his PhD research was cofunded from the Hellenic Republic Ministry of Education and the European Union under the HRAKLEITOS scholarships programme. His research work has been published in selected academic international journals, books and scientific conferences.

Antonio Padilla-Meléndez is Associate Professor of Management at the University of Malaga (Spain). He holds degrees in economics and business administration (BA, major in management) and business administration (PhD). He has attended postgraduate courses at Harvard University (USA) and the University of Oxford (UK), and has been Visiting Scholar in Texas A&M International University (Laredo, TX, USA). He is managing director of the research team "E-business: Electronic commerce and teleworking" of the University of Malaga. It is financed by the Andalusian government. He is Technical Manager of innostrategy!, a knowledge and technology based company started initially as spin-off from the University of Malaga and with Novasoft as industrial partner. And he has served as expert and evaluator for the European Commission (2005, 2006, 2007). Antonio has authored various books and published in different journals including Journal of Global Information Management, Computers & Education, International Journal of E-Collaboration, International Journal of Technology Management, International Journal of Information Management, Technovation, Journal of Global Information Technology Management and Internet Research. He has also published chapters in reviewed books edited by Kluwer Academic Publishers and Idea Group Inc., and papers in Spanish reviewed journals such as Economía Industrial, Revista Europea de Dirección y Economía de la Empresa, and Información Comercial Española. Revista de Economía. His research interests include e-Collaboration, technology adoption, and techno and academic entrepreneurship.

Robert Pellerin is Associate Professor in the Department of Mathematics and Industrial engineering at Ecole Polytechnique de Montreal. He holds degrees in engineering management (B.Eng.) and industrial engineering (Ph.D.). He has practiced for more than 12 years in reengineering projects and enterprise resource planning (ERP) systems implementation including 10 years as a project manager. His current research interests include enterprise system adoption, implementation, and integration. He is a member of the CIRRELT research group.

Bill Perkins is professor emeritus of information systems and decision sciences in the Kelley School of Business, Indiana University. He received his BSCE from Rose Polytechnic Institute and his MBA and DBA from Indiana University. Dr. Perkins has received 11 major teaching awards from Indiana University, and he has published papers in Decision Sciences, the Journal of Political Economy, and other journals. He has co-authored seven books, including Managing Information Technology (Fifth Edition, 2005). At Indiana University he has served as chair of the undergraduate program of the School of Business, chair of the Operations and Systems Management Department, and director of the Institute for Research on the Management of Information Systems (IRMIS). He has received Distinguished Service Awards from Indiana University, the Kelley School of Business, and the Decision Sciences Institute.

Angeliki Poulymenakou is Assistant Professor in Information Systems Management. Prior to that she has served as lecturer in Information Systems in the Informatics Department of the Athens School of Economics and Business and in the Information Systems Department of the London School of Economics and Political Science. She holds a first degree in Mathematics (Athens), and MSc and PhD degrees in Information Systems (London School of Economics). More recently she has offered consultancy work to the European Commission, DG Information Society (on the socio-economic impact of electronic commerce, the emergence of new organisational forms, the evaluation of proposals and projects on related issues in FP5), as well as to the Greek Government (Ministries of Development and of Employment on e-Business and the impact of the Information Society respectively). Her several publications in international journals and conferences draw from the full range of activities outlined above. She has served as a member of the scientific committee of four international conferences in information systems (ICIS, ECIS, IFIP) and has acted as a referee in several international journals in the field. In 2003 she chaired the organisation of the IFIP joint WG8.2 and 9.4 Conference on Information Systems and Globalisation, in Athens.

Gad Saad is an Associate Professor of Marketing at Concordia University (Montreal, Canada). He has held Visiting Associate Professorships at Cornell University, Dartmouth College, and the University of California-Irvine. He was listed as one of the "hot" professors of Concordia University in both the 2001 and 2002 Maclean's reports on Canadian universities. He received his Faculty's Distinguished Teaching Award in June 2000. His book titled The Evolutionary Bases of Consumption (Lawrence Erlbaum, 2007) is the first academic book to demonstrate the links between evolutionary theory and consumption. He has published close to 40 scientific papers many of which lie at the intersection of evolutionary psychology and a broad range of disciplines including medicine, behavioral game theory, marketing, advertising, and consumer behavior. He received a B.Sc. in Mathematics and Computer Science (1988) and an M.B.A. (1990) both from McGill University, and his M.S. (1993) and Ph.D. (1994) from Cornell University.

Vicki Sauter is Professor of Information Systems at University of Missouri - St. Louis. She has published extensively in the area of in the area of systems development and design. She has one book, Decision Support Systems: An Applied Managerial Approach, and many publications in scholarly journals, primarily focusing on DSS design. Her primary research interest is how decision makers make choices as it reflects upon the design of decision support systems. She has focused her research on the models and the model management features that would facilitate their use in a DSS, and examined these issues in both the public and private sectors, and in cross-cultural domains. Her current focus involves the design issues for internet-based decision support, especially with a focus on better design of decision-based intranets, and about trends of women in computing careers.

Pedro Soto-Acosta is a Professor of Management at the University of Murcia (Spain). He holds a PhD in Management Information Systems (MISs) and a Master's degree in Technology Management from the University of Murcia. He received his BA in Accounting and Finance in Europe from the Manchester Metropolitan University (UK) and attended Postgraduate Courses in Management at Harvard University (USA). His work has been published in journals such as the European Journal of Information Systems, the International Journal of Information Management, the International Journal of Electronic Business, the Journal of Enterprise Information Management, and the Telematics and Informatics, among others.

Helen Stewart today is the NASA Ames Research Center IT Security Manager, primarily focused on the Federal Information Security Management Act (FISMA), information handling issues dealing with confidentiality, integrity, and availability with federal information and technology. She founded and managed the New Millennium Documentation Project and the Postdoc Project in the Computational Sciences Division of NASA Ames Research Center, where she has worked since 1987. Her research and development efforts are primarily focused on ensuring compliance with National and NASA Policies, IT Security, and Secure Collaborative Assistant Systems and Environments. She has worked in many projects involving secure advanced federated environments, where primary focus was on secure information sharing for risk management, for the Space Shuttle Program and Mission Control Center. Ms Stewart continues today to research, policy, procedures, and contractual influences on Knowledge Management (KM), IT Security, and Risk Management (RM) to determine impacts these may have on National space based assets.

Peter Tandler is a senior research associate at Fraunhofer IGD (Institute for Computer Graphics) located in Darmstadt, Germany. He joined IGD in January 2007. From August 1997 until December 2006, he was senior research associate at Fraunhofer IPSI (Integrated Publication and Information Systems Institute). He studied computer science at the Darmstadt University of Technology (Germany) with education and psychology as additional subjects. His diploma thesis was about the design of object-oriented modeling languages for technical systems. In 2004, he received a Ph.D. in computer science from the Darmstadt University of Technology for his work on application models and software infrastructure for roomware environments. He serves as program committee member and reviewer for international conferences, workshops, and journals in the areas of software architectures for ubiquitous computing environments, collaboration in ubiquitous computing environments, and human-computer interaction. His research interests include computer-supported cooperative work, integration of virtual and physical environments, new forms of human-computer and team-computer interaction for roomware components, electronic meeting support systems, but also software architectures and frameworks, object and component technology, and design of programming languages.

Adriana Vivacqua holds is a last-year PhD student at the Federal University of Rio de Janeiro. She has extensive consulting experience, both in the private sector and working with governmental environments. She is interested in computer support for cooperative work, specifically in system to facilitate work in distributed groups and in supporting self organization in groups; community formation, maintenance and motivation and in adaptation and personalization systems using applied artificial intelligence techniques, topics in which she has written several papers. She has been a member of the committee of the

ISMICK conference since 2005. She holds an MSc from MIT (2000), where she worked as a research assistant in the Software Agents Group at the Media Lab.

Yu "Andy" Wu is a Ph.D. candidate in the MIS Department at the University of Central Florida. He has an MS in MIS from UCF and an MS in Finance from Golden Gate University. Before his academic pursuit, Andy had various experiences in Accounting, management and IT> His experience in supporting organizational users and administering computer networks to a large extent engenders his research interests in computer training and information systems security. Andy has published papers for various Information Systems conferences and in CAIS.

Eiko Yamamoto received the B.E., M.E., and Ph.D. degrees in engineering (information and computer science) from Toyohashi University of Technology, Aichi, Japan in 1996, 1998, and 2002 respectively. Her Research interests include natural language processing, information extraction, and knowledge acquisition. She is working as an expert researcher for Computational Linguistics group at National Institute of Information and Communications Technology (NICT), Japan. She received Best Paper Award for Young Researcher of Information Processing Society in Japan (IPSJ) National Convention in 1999. She is a member of Information Processing Society in Japan, and the Association for Natural Language Processing, Japan.

Index

V

W

Y